The Writings Against the Manichaeans and Against the Donatists
Part I - The Manichaeans
Written by Aurelius Augustine
Edited By Philip Schaff, D.D., LL.D.
This edition edited by Anthony Uyl

Woodstock, Ontario, 2017

The Writings Against the Manichaeans and Against the Donatists: Part I - The Manichaeans

Written by Aurelius Augustine
Edited By Philip Schaff, D.D., LL.D. (1819-1893) (Editor)
Professor in the Union Theological Seminary, New York
This edition edited by Anthony Uyl

Originally Published by:
T&T Clark Edinburgh
WM. B. Eerdmans Publishing Company
Grand Rapids, Michigan

Originally Published in 1887

The text of The Writings Against the Manichaeans and Against the Donatists: Part I - The Manichaeans is all in the Public Domain. The layout, covers, background and Devoted Publishing logo are Copyright ©2017 Devoted Publishing. This edition is published by Devoted Publishing a division of 2165467 Ontario Inc.

What kind of philosophies do you have?
Let us know!

Visit our online store: www.devotedpublishing.com
Contact us at: devotedpub@hotmail.com
Visit us on Facebook: @DevotedPublishing

Published in Woodstock, Ontario, Canada 2017

For bulk educational rates, please contact us at the above email address.

ISBN: 978-1-77356-118-9

Philip Schaff, D.D., LL.D.

Table of Contents

Writings in connection with the Manichæan controversy 11
   Introductory Essay on the Manichæan Heresy, ... 11
      Chapter I - Literature... 11
      Chapter II - Philosophical Basis, and Antecedents of Manichæism 14
      Chapter III - The Manichæan System 15
      Chapter IV - Relation of Manichæism to Zoroastrianism..................................... 24
      Chapter V - The Relation of Manichæism to the Old Babylonian Religion as Seen in Mandæism and Sabeanism.. 26
      Chapter VI - The Relation of Manichæism to Buddhism 27
      Chapter VII - The Relation of Manichæism to Judaism 28
      Footnotes: 35
   Preface to the Anti-Manichæan Writings. 37
      Footnotes: 40
On the Morals of the Catholic Church 43
   Chapter 1 - How the Pretensions of the Manichæans are to Be Refuted. Two Manichæan Falsehoods 43
   Chapter 2 - He Begins with Arguments, in Compliance with the Mistaken Method of the Manichæans 44
   Chapter 3 - Happiness is in the Enjoyment of Man's Chief Good.

   Two Conditions of the Chief Good: 1st, Nothing is Better Than It; 2d, It Cannot Be Lost Against the Will.

   44

   Chapter 4 - Man--What? 45
   Chapter 5 - Man's Chief Good is Not the Chief Good of the Body Only, But the Chief Good of the Soul.. 45
   Chapter 6 - Virtue Gives Perfection to the Soul; The Soul Obtains Virtue by Following God; Following God is the Happy Life 46
   Chapter 7 - The Knowledge of God to Be Obtained from the Scripture. The Plan and Principal Mysteries of the Divine Scheme of Redemption 47
   Chapter 8 - God is the Chief Good, Whom We are to Seek After with Supreme Affection 47
   Chapter 9 - Harmony of the Old and New Testament on the Precepts of Charity. [51] 48
   Chapter 10 - What the Church Teaches About God. The Two Gods of the Manichæans......... 49
   Chapter 11 - God is the One Object of Love; Therefore He is Man's Chief Good. Nothing is Better Than God. God Cannot Be Lost Against Our Will. 50
   Chapter 12 - We are United to God by Love, in Subjection to Him 51
   Chapter 13 - We are Joined Inseparably to God by Christ and His Spirit................ 51
   Chapter 14 - We Cleave to the Trinity, Our Chief Good, by Love 52
   Chapter 15 - The Christian Definition of the Four Virtues 52
   Chapter 16 - Harmony of the Old and New Testaments... 53
   Chapter 17 - Appeal to the Manichæans, Calling on Them to Repent..................... 54
   Chapter 18 - Only in the Catholic Church is Perfect Truth Established on the Harmony of Both Testaments 55

The Writings Against the Manichaeans and Against the Donatists: Part I - The Manichaeans

Chapter 19 - Description of the Duties of Temperance, According to the Sacred Scriptures .. 55

Chapter 20 - We are Required to Despise All Sensible Things, and to Love God Alone 56

Chapter 21 - Popular Renown and Inquisitiveness are Condemned in the Sacred Scriptures .. 57

Chapter 22 - Fortitude Comes from the Love of God.. 57

Chapter 23 - Scripture Precepts and Examples of Fortitude 58

Chapter 24 - Of Justice and Prudence 59

Chapter 25 - Four Moral Duties Regarding the Love of God, of Which Love the Reward is Eternal Life and the Knowledge of the Truth... 59

Chapter 26 - Love of Ourselves and of Our Neighbor... 60

Chapter 27 - On Doing Good to the Body of Our Neighbor... 61

Chapter 28 - On Doing Good to the Soul of Our Neighbor. Two Parts of Discipline, Restraint and Instruction. Through Good Conduct We Arrive at the Knowledge of the Truth................ 61

Chapter 29 - Of the Authority of the Scriptures 63

Chapter 30 - The Church Apostrophised as Teacher of All Wisdom. Doctrine of the Catholic Church 64

Chapter 31 - The Life of the Anachoretes and Coenobites Set Against the Continence of the Manichæans... 65

Chapter 32 - Praise of the Clergy 66

Chapter 33 - Another Kind of Men Living Together in Cities. Fasts of Three Days 67

Chapter 34 - The Church is Not to Be Blamed for the Conduct of Bad Christians, Worshippers of Tombs and Pictures... 68

Chapter 35 - Marriage and Property Allowed to the Baptized by the Apostles 69

Footnotes: 71

On the Morals of the Manichæans 74

Chapter 1 - The Supreme Good is that Which is Possessed of Supreme Existence................. 74

Chapter 2 - What Evil is. That Evil is that Which is Against Nature. In Allowing This, the Manichæans Refute Themselves 74

Chapter 3 - If Evil is Defined as that Which is Hurtful, This Implies Another Refutation of the Manichæans... 75

Chapter 4 - The Difference Between What is Good in Itself and What is Good by Participation 76

Chapter 5 - If Evil is Defined to Be Corruption, This Completely Refutes the Manichæan Heresy... 76

Chapter 6 - What Corruption Affects and What It is 77

Chapter 7 - The Goodness of God Prevents Corruption from Bringing Anything to Non-Existence. The Difference Between Creating and Forming... 77

Chapter 8 - Evil is Not a Substance, But a Disagreement Hostile to Substance 78

Chapter 9 - The Manichæan Fictions About Things Good and Evil are Not Consistent with Themselves 79

Chapter 10 - Three Moral Symbols Devised by the Manichæans for No Good...................... 81

Chapter 11 - The Value of the Symbol of the Mouth Among the Manichæans, Who are Found Guilty of Blaspheming God 81

Chapter 12 - Manichæan Subterfuge... 83

Chapter 13 - Actions to Be Judged of from Their Motive, Not from Externals. Manichæan Abstinence to Be Tried by This Principle 83

Chapter 14 - Three Good Reasons for Abstaining from Certain Kinds of Food 85

Chapter 15 - Why the Manichæans Prohibit the Use of Flesh 87

Chapter 16 - Disclosure of the Monstrous Tenets of the Manichæans 88

Chapter 17 - Description of the Symbol of the Hands Among the Manichæans 93

Chapter 18 - Of the Symbol of the Breast, and of the Shameful Mysteries of the Manichæans 96

Chapter 19 - Crimes of the Manichæans 97

Chapter 20 - Disgraceful Conduct Discovered at Rome 99

Footnotes: 100

On Two Souls, Against the Manichæans 102

One Book 102

Chapter 1 - By What Course of Reasoning the Error of the Manichæans Concerning Two Souls, One of Which is Not from God, is Refuted. Every Soul, Inasmuch as It is a Certain Life, Can Have Its Existence Only from God the Source of Life. 102

Chapter 2 - If the Light that is Perceived by Sense Has God for Its Author, as the Manichæans Acknowledge, Much More The Soul Which is Perceived by Intellect Alone 102

Chapter 3.--How It is Proved that Every Body Also is from God. That the Soul Which is Called Evil by the Manichæans is Better Than Light 103

Chapter 4 - Even the Soul of a Fly is More Excellent Than the Light 104

Chapter 5 - How Vicious Souls, However Worthy of Condemnation They May Be, Excel the Light Which is Praiseworthy in Its Kind 104

Chapter 6 - Whether Even Vices Themselves as Objects of Intellectual Apprehension are to Be Preferred to Light as an Object of Sense Perception, and are to Be Attributed to God as Their Author 105

Chapter 7 - How Evil Men are of God, and Not of God 107

Chapter 8 - The Manichæans Inquire Whence is Evil and by This Question Think They Have Triumphed 108

Chapter 9 - Augustin Deceived by Familiarity with the Manichæans, and by the Succession of Victories Over Ignorant Christians Reported by Them 109

Chapter 10 - Sin is Only from the Will 109

Chapter 11 - What Sin is 111

Chapter 12 - From the Definitions Given of Sin and Will, He Overthrows the Entire Heresy of the Manichæans 111

Chapter 13 - From Deliberation on the Evil and on the Good Part It Results that Two Classes of Souls are Not to Be Held to 113

Chapter 14 - Again It is Shown from the Utility of Repenting that Souls are Not by Nature Evil 114

Chapter 15 - He Prays for His Friends Whom He Has Had as Associates in Error 115

Footnotes: 116

Acts or Disputation Against Fortunatus the Manichæan 119

Disputation of the First Day 119

Disputation of the Second Day 126

Footnotes: 132

Against the Epistle of Manichæus, Called Fundamental 134

Chapter 1 - To Heal Heretics is Better Than to Destroy Them 134

The Writings Against the Manichaeans and Against the Donatists: Part I - The Manichaeans

Chapter 2 - Why the Manichæans Should Be More Gently Dealt with 134

Chapter 3 - Augustin Once a Manichæan 135

Chapter 4 - Proofs of the Catholic Faith 135

Chapter 5 - Against the Title of the Epistle of Manichæus 136

Chapter 6 - Why Manichæus Called Himself an Apostle of Christ 137

Chapter 7 - In What Sense the Followers of Manichæus Believe Him to Be the Holy Spirit 137

Chapter 8 - The Festival of the Birth-Day of Manichæus 138

Chapter 9 - When the Holy Spirit Was Sent 138

Chapter 10 - The Holy Spirit Twice Given 139

Chapter 11 - Manichæus Promises Truth, But Does Not Make Good His Word 140

Chapter 12 - The Wild Fancies of Manichæus 140

Chapter 13 - Two Opposite Substances 141

Chapter 14 - Manichæus Promises the Knowledge of Undoubted Things, and Then Demands Faith in Doubtful Things 141

Chapter 15 - The Doctrine of Manichæus Not Only Uncertain, But False. His Absurd Fancy of a Land and Race of Darkness Bordering on the Holy Region and the Substance of God 142

Chapter 16 - The Soul, Though Mutable, Has No Material Form 143

Chapter 17 - The Memory Contains the Ideas of Places of the Greatest Size 144

Chapter 18 - The Understanding Judges of the Truth of Things, and of Its Own Action 144

Chapter 19 - If the Mind Has No Material Extension, Much Less Has God 144

Chapter 20 - Refutation of the Absurd Idea of Two Territories 145

Chapter 21 - This Region of Light Must Be Material If It is Joined to the Region of Darkness 145

Chapter 22 - The Form of the Region of Light the Worse of the Two 146

Chapter 23 - The Anthropomorphites Not So Bad as the Manichæans 146

Chapter 24 - Of the Number of Natures in the Manichæan Fiction 147

Chapter 25 - Omnipotence Creates Good Things Differing in Degree 148

Chapter 26 - The Manichæans are Reduced to the Choice of a Tortuous, or Curved, or Straight Line of Junction 149

Chapter 27 - The Beauty of the Straight Line Might Be Taken from the Region of Darkness Without Taking Anything from Its Substance 149

Chapter 28 - Manichæus Places Five Natures in the Region of Darkness 150

Chapter 29 - The Refutation of This Absurdity 151

Chapter 30 - The Number of Good Things in Those Natures Which Manichæus Places in the Region of Darkness 151

Chapter 31 - The Same Subject Continued 152

Chapter 32 - Manichæus Got the Arrangement of His Fanciful Notions from Visible Objects 153

Chapter 33 - Every Nature, as Nature, is Good 154

Chapter 34 - Nature Cannot Be Without Some Good 154

Chapter 35 - Evil Alone is Corruption 155

Chapter 36 - The Source of Evil or of Corruption of Good 156

Chapter 37 - God Alone Perfectly Good 157

- Chapter 38 - Nature Made by God; Corruption Comes from Nothing 158
- Chapter 39 - In What Sense Evils are from God 158
- Chapter 40 - Corruption Tends to Non-Existence 158
- Chapter 41 - Corruption is by God's Permission, and Comes from Us 159
- Chapter 42 - Exhortation to the Chief Good 159
- Chapter 43 - Conclusion 160
- Footnotes: 160

Reply to Faustus the Manichæan 162

- Book I - Who Faustus was 162
- Book II - Faustus claims to believe the Gospel, yet refuses to accept the genealogical tables on various grounds which Augustin seeks to set aside 163
- Book III - Faustus objects to the incarnation of God on the ground that the evangelists are at variance with each other, and that incarnation is unsuitable to deity 166
- Book IV - Faustus's reasons for rejecting the Old Testament, and Augustin's animadversions thereon 169
- Book V - Faustus claims that the Manichæans and not the Catholics are consistent believers in the Gospel, and seeks to establish this claim by comparing Manichæan and Catholic obedience to the precepts of the Gospel. Augustin exposes the hypocrisy of the Manichæans and praises the asceticism of Catholics 170
- Book VI - Faustus avows his disbelief in the Old Testament and his disregard of its precepts, and accuses Catholics of inconsistency in neglecting its ordinances, while claiming to accept it as authoritative. 176
- Book VII - The genealogical question is again taken up and argued on both sides 183
- Book VIII - Faustus maintains that to hold to the Old Testament after the giving of the New is putting new cloth on an old garment 185
- Book IX - Faustus argues that if the apostles born under the old covenant could lawfully depart from it, much more can he having been born a Gentile. Augustin explains the relation of Jews and Gentiles alike to the Gospel 186
- Book X - Faustus insists that the Old Testament promises are radically different from those of the New 187
- Book XI - Faustus quotes passages to show that the Apostle Paul abandoned belief in the incarnation, to which he earlier held 188
- Book XII - Faustus denies that the prophets predicted Christ 194
- Book XIII - Faustus asserts that even if the Old Testament could be shown to contain predictions, it would be of interest only to the Jews, pagan literature subserving the same purpose for Gentiles 213
- Book XIV - Faustus abhors Moses for the awful curse he has pronounced upon Christ 223
- Book XV - Faustus rejects the Old Testament because it leaves no room for Christ 228
- Book XVI - Faustus willing to believe not only that the Jewish but that all Gentile prophets wrote of Christ, if it should be proved; but he would none the less insist upon rejecting their superstitions 237
- Book XVII - Faustus rejects Christ's declaration that He came not to destroy the law and the prophets but to fulfill them, on the ground that it is found only in Matthew, who was not present when the words purport to have been spoken 254
- Book XVIII - The relation of Christ to prophecy, continued 257
- Book XIX - Faustus is willing to admit that Christ may have said that He came not to destroy the law and the prophets, but to fulfill them; but if He did, it was to pacify the Jews and in a modified sense 260

Book XX - Faustus repels the charge of sun-worship, and maintains that while the Manichæans believe that God's power dwells in the sun and his wisdom in the moon, they yet worship one deity, Father, Son, and Holy Spirit. They are not a schism of the Gentiles, nor a sect 276

Book XXI - Faustus denies that Manichæans believe in two gods 289

Book XXII - Faustus states his objections to the morality of the law and the prophets, and Augustin seeks by the application of the type and the allegory to explain away the moral difficulties of the Old Testament 299

Book XXIII - Faustus recurs to the genealogical difficulty and insists that even according to Matthew Jesus was not Son of God until His baptism. Augustin sets forth the Catholic view of the relation of the divine and the human in the person of Christ 343

Book XXIV - Faustus explains the Manichæan denial that man was made by God as applying to the fleshly man not to the spiritual 348

Book XXV - Faustus seeks to bring into ridicule the orthodox claim to believe in the infinity of God by caricaturing the anthropomorphic representations of the Old Testament 351

Book XXVI - Faustus insists that Jesus might have died though not born, by the exercise of divine power, yet he rejects birth and death alike. Augustin maintains that there are some things that even God cannot do, one of which is to die 352

Book XXVII - Faustus warns against pressing too far the argument, that if Jesus was not born He cannot have suffered 356

Book XXVIII - Faustus recurs to the genealogy and insists upon examining it as regards its consistency with itself 357

Book XXIX - Faustus seeks to justify the docetism of the Manichæans 359

Book XXX - Faustus repels the insinuation that the prophecy of Paul with reference to those that should forbid to marry, abstain from meats, etc., applies to the Manichæans more than to the Catholic ascetics, who are held in the highest esteem in the Church 361

Book XXXI - The scripture passage 364

Book XXXII - Faustus fails to understand why he should be required either to accept or reject the New Testament as a whole, while the Catholics accept or reject the various parts of the Old Testament at pleasure 366

Book XXXIII - Faustus does not think it would be a great honor to sit down with Abraham, Isaac and Jacob, whose moral characters as set forth in the Old Testament he detests 375

    Footnotes: 380

Concerning the Nature of Good, Against the Manichæans 388

    Chapter 1 - God the Highest and Unchangeable Good, from Whom are All Other Good Things, Spiritual and Corporeal 388

    Chapter 2 - How This May Suffice for Correcting the Manichæans 389

    Chapter 3 - Measure, Form, and Order, Generic Goods in Things Made by God 389

    Chapter 4 - Evil is Corruption of Measure, Form, or Order 389

    Chapter 5 - The Corrupted Nature of a More Excellent Order Sometimes Better Than an Inferior Nature Even Uncorrupted 389

    Chapter 6 - Nature Which Cannot Be Corrupted is the Highest Good; That Which Can, is Some Good 390

    Chapter 7 - The Corruption of Rational Spirits is on the One Hand Voluntary, on the Other Penal 390

    Chapter 8 - From the Corruption and Destruction of Inferior Things is the Beauty of the Universe 390

    Chapter 9 - Punishment is Constituted for the Sinning Nature that It May Be Rightly Ordered 390

    Chapter 10 - Natures Corruptible, Because Made of Nothing 390

Chapter 11 - God Cannot Suffer Harm, Nor Can Any Other Nature Except by His Permission 391

Chapter 12 - All Good Things are from God Alone 391

Chapter 13 - Individual Good Things, Whether Small or Great, are from God 391

Chapter 14 - Small Good Things in Comparison with Greater are Called by Contrary Names 391

Chapter 15 - In the Body of the Ape the Good of Beauty is Present, Though in a Less Degree 391

Chapter 16 - Privations in Things are Fittingly Ordered by God 392

Chapter 17 - Nature, in as Far as It is Nature, No Evil 392

Chapter 18 - Hyle, Which Was Called by the Ancients the Formless Material of Things, is Not an Evil 392

Chapter 19 - To Have True Existence is an Exclusive Prerogative of God 393

Chapter 20 - Pain Only in Good Natures 393

Chapter 21 - From Measure Things are Said to Be Moderate-Sized [1093] 393

Chapter 22 - Measure in Some Sense is Suitable to God Himself 393

Chapter 23 - Whence a Bad Measure, a Bad Form, a Bad Order May Sometimes Be Spoken of 394

Chapter 24 - It is Proved by the Testimonies of Scripture that God is Unchangeable 394

Chapter 25 - This Last Expression Misunderstood by Some 394

Chapter 26 - That Creatures are Made of Nothing 395

Chapter 27 - "From Him" And "Of Him" Do Not Mean The Same Thing 395

Chapter 28 - Sin Not From God, But From The Will of Those Sinning 395

Chapter 29 - That God is Not Defiled by Our Sins 396

Chapter 30 - That Good Things, Even the Least, and Those that are Earthly, are by God 396

Chapter 31 - To Punish and to Forgive Sins Belong Equally to God 396

Chapter 32 - From God Also is the Very Power to Be Hurtful 396

Chapter 33 - That Evil Angels Have Been Made Evil, Not by God, But by Sinning 397

Chapter 34 - That Sin is Not the Striving for an Evil Nature, But the Desertion of a Better .. 397

Chapter 35 - The Tree Was Forbidden to Adam Not Because It Was Evil, But Because It Was Good for Man to Be Subject to God 397

Chapter 36 - No Creature of God is Evil, But to Abuse a Creature of God is Evil 398

Chapter 37 - God Makes Good Use of the Evil Deeds of Sinners 398

Chapter 38 - Eternal Fire Torturing the Wicked, Not Evil 398

Chapter 39 - Fire is Called Eternal, Not as God Is, But Because Without End 398

Chapter 40 - Neither Can God Suffer Hurt, Nor Any Other, Save by the Just Ordination of God 398

Chapter 41 - How Great Good Things the Manichæans Put in the Nature of Evil, and How Great Evil Things in the Nature of Good 399

Chapter 42 - Manichæan Blasphemies Concerning the Nature of God 400

Chapter 43 - Many Evils Before His Commingling with Evil are Attributed to the Nature of God by the Manichæans 401

Chapter 44 - Incredible Turpitudes in God Imagined by Manichæus 402

Chapter 45 - Certain Unspeakable Turpitudes Believed, Not Without Reason, Concerning the

The Writings Against the Manichaeans and Against the Donatists: Part I - The Manichaeans
    Manichæans Themselves 403

    Chapter 46 - The Unspeakable Doctrine of the Fundamental Epistle 403

    Chapter 47 - He Compels to the Perpetration of Horrible Turpitudes 404

    Chapter 48 - Augustin Prays that the Manichæans May Be Restored to Their Senses 404

    Footnotes: 405

Writings in connection with the Manichæan controversy

translated by the Rev. Richard Stothert, M.A.,
Bombay;
and
Albert H. Newman, D.D., LL.D.
Professor of Church History and Comparative Religion, in Toronto
Baptist (Theological) College, Toronto, Canada.

Introductory Essay on the Manichæan Heresy,
By Albert H. Newman, D.D., LL.D.

Chapter I - Literature

I. Sources.

The following bibliography of Manichæism is taken from Schaff's History of the Christian Church, vol. II. pp. 498-500 (new edition).
Additions are indicated by brackets.

1. Oriental Sources:
The most important, though of comparatively late date.

(a) Mohammedan (Arabic):
Kitâb al Fihrist.
A history of Arabic literature to 987, by an Arab of Bagdad, usually called Ibn Abi Jakub An-Nadîm; brought to light by Flügel, and published after his death by Rödiger and Müller, in 2 vols. Leipz. 1871-'72.
Book IX. section first, treats of Manichæism.
Flügel's translation, see below.
Kessler calls the Fihrist a "Fündstätte allerersten Ranges."
Next to it comes the relation of the Mohammedan philosopher, Al-Shahrastani (d. 1153), in his History of Religious Parties and Philosophical Sects, Ed. Cureton, Lond. 1842, 2 vols. (I. 188-192); German translation by Haarbrücker, Halle, 1851.
On other Mohammedan sources, see Kessler in Herzog, IX., 225 sq.

(b) Persian Sources:
relating to the life of Mani, the Shâhnâmeh (the King's Book) of Firdausi; ed. by Jul. Mohl, Paris, 1866 (V. 472-475). See Kessler, ibid. 225.
[Albiruni's Chronology of Ancient Nations, tr. by E. Sachau, and published by the Oriental Translation Fund, Lond. 1879.
Albîrunî lived 973-1048, and is said to have possessed vast literary resources no longer available to us.
His work seems to be based on early Manichæan sources, and strikingly confirms the narrative preserved by the Fihrist.
See also articles by West and Thomas in Journal of the Asiatic Society, 1868, 1870, 1871.]

(c) Christian Sources:
In Arabic, the Alexandrian Patriarch Eutychius (d. 916). Annales, ed. Pococke, Oxon. 1628; Barhebræus (d. 1286), in his Historia Dynastiarum, ed. Pococke.
In Syriac:
Ephraem Syrus (d. 393), in various writings.
Esnig or Esnik, an Armenian bishop of the 5th Century, who wrote against Marcion and Mani

The Writings Against the Manichaeans and Against the Donatists: Part I - The Manichaeans (German translation from the Armenian by C. Fr. Neumann, in Illgen's Zeitschrift für die Hist. Theologie, 1834, pp.77-78).

2. Greek Sources:

[Alexander of Lycopolis:

The Tenets of the Manichæans (first published by Combefis, with a Latin version, in the Auctararium Novissimum, Bibl. S. S. Patrum; again by Gallandi, in his Bibl. Patrum, vol. IV. p. 73 sq.

An English translation by Rev. James B.H. Hawkins, M .A ., appeared in Clark's Ante-Nicene Library, Vol. XIV. p. 236 sq.; Am. ed. vol. VI. p. 237 sq.

Alexander represents himself as a convert from Paganism to Manichæism, and from Manichæism to Orthodoxy.

He claims to have learned Manichæism from those who were intimately associated with Mani himself, and is, therefore, one of the earliest witnesses. [1]]

Eusebius (H. E. VII. 31, a brief account). Epiphanius (Haer. 66).

Cyril of Jerusalem (Catech. VI. 20 sq.).

Titus of Bostra (πρὸσ Μανιχαίουσ, ed P. de Lagarde, 1859).

Photius: Adv. Manichæos (Cod. 179, Biblioth.).

John of Damascus:

De Haeres. and Dial.

[Petrus Siculus, Hist. Manichæorum.]

3. Latin Sources:

Archelaus (Bishop of Cascar in Mesopotamia, d. about 278):

Acta Disputationis cum Manete Hæresiarcha; first written in Syriac, and so far belonging to the Oriental Christian Sources (Comp. Jerome, de Vir. Ill. 72), but extant only in a Latin translation, which seems to have been made from the Greek, edited by Zacagni (Rome, 1698), and Routh (in Reliquiæ Sacræ, vol. V. 3-206); Eng. transl. in Clark's Ante-Nicene Library (vol. XX. 272-419).

[Am. ed. vol. VI. p. 173 sq.].

These Acts purport to contain the report of a disputation between Archelaus and Mani before a large assembly, which was in full sympathy with the orthodox bishop, but (as Beausobre first proved), they are in form a fiction from the first quarter of the fourth century (about 320), by a Syrian ecclesiastic (probably of Edessa), yet based upon Manichæan documents, and containing much information about Manichæan doctrines.

They consist of various pieces, and were the chief source of information to the West.

Mani is represented (ch. 12), as appearing in a many-colored cloak and trousers, with a sturdy staff of ebony, a Babylonian book under his left arm, and with a mien of an old Persian master.

In his defense he quotes freely from the N.T.

At the end, he makes his escape to Persia (ch. 55).

Comp. H. V. Zittwitz:

Die Acta Archelai et Manetis untersucht, in Kahnis' Zeitschrift für d. Hist. Theol. 1873, No. IV. Oblasinski:

Acta Disput. Arch., etc. Lips. 1874 (inaugural dissert.). Ad. Harnack:

Die Acta Archelai und das Diatessaron Tatians, in Texte und Untersuchungen zur Gesch. der altchristl. Lit. vol. I. Heft 3 (1883), p. 137-153.

Harnack tries to prove that the Gospel variations of Archelaus are taken from Tatian's Diatessaron.

St. Augustin (d. 430, the chief Latin authority next to the translation of Archelaus).

[Besides the treatises published in Clark's series, Contra Fortunatum quendam Manichæorum Presbyterum Disput. I. et II., Contra Adimantum Manichæi discipulum, Contra Secundinum Manichæum, De Natura Boni, De duabus Animabus, De Utilitate Credendi, De Haeres. XLVI.

Of these, De duabus Animabus, Contra Fortunatum, and De Natura Boni are added in the present edition, and De Utilitate Credendi has been included among Augustin's shorter theological treatises in vol. III. of the present series.

In the Confessions and the Letters, moreover, the Manichæans figure prominently.

The treatises included in the present series may be said to fairly represent Augustin's manner of dealing with Manichæism.

The Anti-Manichæan writings are found chiefly in vol. VIII. of the Benedictine edition, and in volumes I. and XI. of the Migne reprint.

Augustin's personal connection with the sect extending over a period of nine years, and his consummate ability in dealing with this form of error, together with the fact that he quotes largely from Manichæan literature, render his works the highest authority for Manichæism as it existed in the West at the close of the fifth century.]

Comp. also the Acts of Councils against the Manichæans from the fourth century onwards, in Mansi and Hefele [and Hardouin].

II. Modern Works.

Isaac de Beausobre (b. 1659 in France, pastor of the French church in Berlin, d. 1738):
Histoire Crit. de Manichée et du Manichéisme, Amst. 1634 and '39, 2 vols. 4to.
Part of the first volume is historical, the second doctrinal.
Very full and scholarly.
He intended to write a third volume on the later Manichæans.

F. Chr. Baur:
Das Manichäische Religions-system nach den Quellen neu untersucht und entwickelt, Tüb. 1831 (500 pages).
A comprehensive, philosophical and critical view. He calls the Manich. system a "glühend prächtiges Natur-und Weltgedicht."
[An able critique of Baur's work by Schneckenburger appeared in the "Theol. Studien u. Kritiken," 1833, p. 875 sq. Schneckenburger strives to make it appear that Baur unduly minifies the Christian element in Manichæism.
Later researches have tended to confirm Baur's main position.
The Oriental sources employed by Flügel and Kessler have thrown much light upon the character of primitive Manichæism, and have enabled us to determine more precisely than Beausobre and Baur were able to do the constituent elements of Mani's system.

A.V. Wegnern:
Manichæorum Indulgentiæ, Lips. 1827.
Wegnern points out the resemblance between the Manichæan system, in accordance with which the "hearers" participate in the merits of the "elect" without subjecting themselves to the rigorous asceticism practiced by the latter, and the later doctrine and practice of indulgences in the Roman Catholic church.]

Trechsel:
Ueber Kanon, Kritik und Exegese der Manichäer, Bern, 1832.

D. Chwolson:
Die Ssabier und der Ssabismus, Petersb. 1856, 2 vols.

G. Flugel:
Mani, seine Lehre und seine Scriften.
Aus dem Fihrist des Abî Jakub an-Nadîm (987), Leipz. 1862. Text, translation and commentary, 440 pages.
[Of the highest value, the principal document on which the work is based being, probably, the most authentic exposition of primitive Manichæan doctrine.]

K. Kessler:
Untersuchungen zur Genesis des Manich. Rel. Systems, Leipz. 1876.
By the same:
Mânî oder Beiträge zur Kenntniss der Religionsmischung im Semitismus, Leipz. 1887.
See also his thorough article, Mânî und die Manichæer, in "Herzog," new ed. vol. IX. 223-259 (abridged in Schaff's "Encyclop." II. 1396-1398).
[Kessler has done more than any other writer to establish the relation between the Manichæans and the earlier Oriental sects, and between these and the old Babylonian religion.
The author of this introduction wishes to express his deep obligation to Kessler.
The article on the "Mandäer" in "Herzog," by the same author, is valuable in this connection, though his attempt to exclude all historical connection between this Babylonian Gnostic sect and Palestine can hardly be pronounced a success.

J. B. Mozley:
Ruling Ideas in Early Ages; lecture on "The Manichæans and the Jewish Fathers," with special reference to Augustin's method of dealing with the cavils of the Manichæans.]

G. T. Stokes:
Manes and Manichæans, in "Smith and Wace," III. 792-801.

A. Harnack:
Manichæism in 9th ed. of the "Encycl. Britannica," vol. XV. (1883), 481-487.
[Also in German, as a Beigabe to his Lehrbuch d. Dogmengeschichte, vol. I. p. 681 sq.
Harnack follows Kessler in all essential particulars.
Of Kessler's article in "Herzog" he says: "This article contains the best that we possess on Manichæism."
In this we concur.

The Writings Against the Manichaeans and Against the Donatists: Part I - The Manichaeans
W. Cunningham:
S. Austin and his Place in the History of Christian Thought, Hulsean Lectures, 1885, p. 45-72, and passim, Lond. 1886.

This treatise is of considerable value, especially as it regards the philosophical attitude of Augustin towards Manichæism.] The accounts of Mosheim, Lardner, Schröckh, Walch, Neander, Gieseler [and Wolf].

Chapter II - Philosophical Basis, and Antecedents of Manichæism

"About 500 years before the commencement of the Christian era," writes Professor Monier Williams, [2] "a great stir seems to have taken place in Indo-Aryan, as in Grecian minds, and indeed in thinking minds everywhere throughout the then civilized world.

Thus when Buddha arose in India, Greece had her thinkers in Pythagoras, Persia in Zoroaster, and China in Confucius.

Men began to ask themselves earnestly such questions as--What am I?

Whence have I come?

Whither am I going?

How can I explain my consciousness of personal existence?

What is the relationship between my material and immaterial nature?

What is the world in which I find myself? did a wise, good and all-powerful Being create it out of nothing? or did it evolve out of an eternal germ? or did it come together by the combination of eternal atoms?

If created by a Being of infinite wisdom, how can I account for the inequality of condition in it--good and evil, happiness and misery.

Has the Creator form or is he formless?

Has he any qualities or none?"

It is true that such questions pressed themselves with special importunity upon the thinkers of the age mentioned, but we should be far astray if we should think for a moment that now for the first time they suggested themselves and demanded solution.

The fact is that the earliest literary records of the human race bear evidence of high thinking on the fundamental problems of God, man, and the world, and the relations of these to each other.

Recent scholars have brought to light facts of the utmost interest with reference to the pre-Babylonian (Accadian) religion.

A rude nature-worship, with a pantheistic basis, but assuming a polytheistic form, seems to have prevailed in Mesopotamia from a very early period.

"Spirit everywhere dispersed produced all the phenomena of nature, and directed and animated all created beings.

They caused evil and good, guided the movements of the celestial bodies, brought back the seasons in their order, made the wind to blow and the rain to fall, and produced by their influence atmospheric phenomena both beneficial and destructive; they also rendered the earth fertile, and caused plants to germinate and to bear fruit, presided over the births and preserved the lives of living beings, and yet at the same time sent death and disease.

There were spirits of this kind everywhere, in the starry heavens, in the earth, and in the intermediate region of the atmosphere; each element was full of them, earth, air, fire and water; and nothing could exist without them...As evil is everywhere present in nature side by side with good, plagues with favorable influences, death with life, destruction with fruitfulness; an idea of dualism as decided as in the religion of Zoroaster pervaded the conceptions of the supernatural world formed by the Accadian magicians, the evil beings of which they feared more than they valued the powers of good.

There were essentially good spirits, and others equally bad.

These opposing troops constituted a vast dualism, which embraced the whole universe and kept up a perpetual struggle in all parts of the creation." [3]This primitive Turanian quasi-dualism (it was not dualism in the strictest sense of the term) was not entirely obliterated by the Cushite and Semitic civilizations and cults that successively overlaid it.

So firmly rooted had this early mode of viewing the world become that it materially influenced the religions of the invaders rather than suffered extermination.

In the Babylonian religion of the Semitic period the dualistic element was manifest chiefly in the magical rites of the Chaldean priests who long continued to use Accadian as their sacred language.

"Upon this dualistic conception rested the whole edifice of sacred magic, of magic regarded as a holy and legitimate intercourse established by rites of divine origin, between man and the supernatural beings surrounding him on all sides.

Placed unhappily in the midst of this perpetual struggle between the good and bad spirits, man felt himself attacked by them at every moment; his fate depended upon them....He needed then some aid against the attacks of the bad spirits, against the plagues and diseases which they sent upon him.

This help he hoped to find in incantations, in mysterious and powerful words, the secret of which was known only to the priests of magic, in their prescribed rites and their talismans...The Chaldeans had such a great idea of the power and efficacy of their formulæ, rites and amulets, that they came to regard them as required to fortify the good spirits themselves in their combat with the demons, and as able to give them help by providing them with invincible weapons which should ensure success." [4] A large number of magical texts have been preserved and deciphered, and among them "the favorable Alad,' the favorable Lamma,' and the favorable Utuq,' are very frequently opposed...to the evil Alad,' the evil Lamma,' the evil Utuq.'" [5]

It would be interesting to give in detail the results of the researches of George Smith, Lenormant, A.H. Sayce, E. Schrader, Friedrich Delitzsch and others, with reference to the elaborate mythological and cosmological systems of the Babylonians.

Some of the features thereof will be brought out further on by way of comparison with the Manichæan mythology and cosmology.

Suffice it to say that the dualistic element is everywhere manifest, though not in so consistent and definite a form as in Zoroastrianism, to say nothing of Manichæism.

The Medo-Persian invasion brought into Babylonia the Zoroastrian system, already modified, no doubt, by the Elamitic (Cushite) cult. Yet the old Babylonian religion was too firmly rooted to be supplanted, even by the religion of such conquerors as Darius and Cyrus. Modifications, however, it undoubtedly underwent.

The dualism inherent in the system became more definite.

The influence of the Jews in Mesopotamia upon the ancient population cannot have been inconsiderable, especially as many of the former, including probably most of the captives of the Northern tribes, were absorbed by the latter.

As a result of this blending of old Babylonian, Persian, and Hebrew blood, traditions, and religious ideas, there was developed in Mesopotamia a type of religious thought that furnished a philosophical basis and a mythological and cosmological garnishing for the Manichæan system.

Dualism, therefore, arising from efforts of the unaided human mind to account for the natural phenomena that appear beneficent and malignant, partly of old Babylonian origin and partly of Persian, but essentially modified by Hebrew influence more or less pure, furnished to Mani the foundation of his system.

We shall attempt at a later stage of the discussion to determine more accurately the relations of Manichæism to the various systems with which correctly or incorrectly it has been associated.

Suffice it to say, at present, that no new problem presented itself to Mani, and that he furnished no essentially new solution of the problems that had occupied the attention of his countrymen for more than 2500 years.

Before proceeding to institute a comparison between Manichæism and the various systems of religious thought to which it stands related, it will be advantageous to have before us an exposition of the Manichæan system itself, based upon the most authentic sources.

Chapter III - The Manichæan System

Earlier writers on Manichæism have, for the most part, made the Acta Disp. Archelai et Manetis and the anti-Manichæan writings of Augustin the basis of their representations.

For later Manichæism in the West, Augustin is beyond question the highest authority, and the various polemical treatises which he put forth exhibit the system under almost every imaginable aspect. The "Acts of the Disputation of Archelaus and Manes," while it certainly rests upon a somewhat extensive and accurative knowledge of early Manichæism, is partially discredited by its generally admitted spuriousness--spuriousness in the sense that it is not a genuine record of a real debate.

It is highly probable that debates of this kind occurred between Mani and various Christian leaders in the East, and so Mani may at one time or other have given utterance to most of the statements that are attributed to him in this writing; or these statements may have been derived, for substance, from his numerous treatises, and have been artfully adapted to the purposes of the writer of the "Acts."

It is certain that most of the representations are correct.

But we can no longer rely upon it as an authentic first-hand authority.

Since Flügel published the treatise from the Fihrist entitled "The Doctrines of the

Manichæans, by Muhammad ben Ishâk," with a German translation and learned annotations, it has been admitted that this treatise must be made the basis for all future representations of Manichæism.

Kessler, while he has had access to many other Oriental documents bearing upon the subject, agrees with Flügel in giving the first place to this writing.

On this exposition of the doctrines of the Manichæans, therefore, as expounded by Flügel and Kessler, we must chiefly rely.

The highly poetical mythological form which Mani gave to his speculations renders it exceedingly difficult to arrive at assured results with reference to fundamental principles.

If we attempt to state in a plain matter-of-fact way just what Mani taught we are in constant danger of misrepresenting him.

In fact one of the favorite methods employed against Mani's doctrines by the writer of the "Acts of the Disputation," etc., as well as by Augustin and others, was to reduce Mani's poetical fancies to plain language and thus to show their absurdity.

The considerations which have led experts like Flügel and Kessler to put so high an estimate upon this document, and the discussions as to the original language in which the sources of the document were written, are beyond the scope of this essay.

Suffice it to say, that so far as we are able to form a judgment on the matter, the reasons for ascribing antiquity and authenticity to the representation of Manichæism contained in the document are decisive.

1. Mani's Life.

According to the Fihrist, Mani's father, a Persian by race, resided at Coche on the Tigris, about forty miles north of Babylon.

Afterwards he removed into Babylonia and settled at Modein, where he frequented an idol-temple like the rest of the people.

He next became associated with a party named Mugtasila (Baptizers), probably identical with or closely related to the Mandæans and Sabeans, both of which parties made much of ceremonial bathings.

Mani, who was born after the removal to Babylonia, is related to have been the recipient of angelic visitations at the age of twelve.

Even at this time he was forewarned that he must leave the religion of his father at the age of twenty-four.

At the appointed time the angel At-Taum appeared again and announced to him his mission.

"Hail, Mani, from me and the Lord, who has sent me to thee and chosen thee for his mission. But he commands thee to invite men to thy doctrine and to proclaim the glad tidings of truth that comes from him, and to bestow thereon all thy zeal."

Mani entered upon his work, according to Flügel's careful computation, April 1, 238, or, according to calculations based on another statement, in 252.

Mani maintained that he was the Paraclete promised by Jesus.

He is said, in this document, to have derived his teaching from the Magi and the Christians, and the characters in which he wrote his books, from the Syriac and the Persian.

After travelling in many lands for forty years and disseminating his doctrines in India, China, and Turkestan, he succeeded in impressing his views upon Fîrûz, brother of King Sapor, who had intended to put him to death.

Sapor became warmly attached to Mani and granted toleration to his followers.

Afterwards, according to some accounts, Mani was imprisoned by Sapor and liberated by his successor Hormizd.

He is said to have been crucified by order of King Bahraîm I. (276-'7), and his skin stuffed with straw is said to have been suspended at the city gate. Eusebius (H. E. VII. 31) describes Mani as "a barbarian in life, both in speech and conduct, who attempted to form himself into a Christ, and then also proclaimed himself to be the very Paraclete and the Holy Spirit.

Then, as if he had been Christ, he selected twelve disciples, the partners of his new religion, and after patching together false and ungodly doctrines collected from a thousand heresies long since extinct, he swept them off like a deadly poison from Persia, upon this part of the world."

The account given in the Acta Archel (written probably about 330-'40), is far more detailed than that of the Fihrist and differs widely therefrom.

It contains much that is highly improbable.

Mani is represented as having for his predecessors one Scythianus, an Egyptian heretic of Apostolic times, and Terebinthus, who went with him to Palestine and after the death of Scythianus removed to Babylonia.

The writings of Terebinthus or Scythianus came into the possession of a certain widow, who purchased Mani when seven years of age (then named Cubricus) and made him heir of her property and books.

He changed his name to Mani (Manes), and, having become imbued with the teachings of the books, began at about sixty years of age to promulgate their teachings, choosing three disciples, Thomas, Addas and Hermas, to whom he entrusted the writings mentioned above, along with some of his own.

Up to this time he knew little of Christianity, but having been imprisoned by the king for failure in a promised cure of the king's son, he studied the Christian Scriptures and derived therefrom the idea of the Paraclete, which he henceforth applied to himself.

After his escape the famous dialogue with Archelaus and that with Diodorus occurred.

Returning to Arabion he was arrested, carried to Persia, flayed alive, and his skin stuffed and suspended as above.

Some additional facts from an Oriental source used by Beausobre have more or less verisimilitude.

According to this, Mani was born of Magian parents about 240 A.D.

He became skilled in music, mathematics, geography, astronomy, painting, medicine, and in the Scriptures.

The account of his ascendancy over Sapor and his subsequent martyrdom is substantially the same as that of the Fihrist. Albîrunî's work (see bibliography preceding) confirms the account given by the Fihrist.

The conversion of Sapor to Manichæism (in A.D. 261) is said to be confirmed by Sassanian inscriptions (see Journal of Asiat. Soc. 1868 p. 310-'41, and ibid. p. 376, and 1871 p. 416).

The Fihrist's account contains a long list of the works of Mani, which is supplemented by other Oriental and Western notices.

The list is interesting as showing the wide range of Mani's literary activity, or at least of the literature that was afterwards connected with his name.

2. Mani's System.

As the life of Mani has been the subject of diversified and contradictory representations, so also have his doctrines.

Here, too, we must make the account given by the Fihrist fundamental.

It will be convenient to treat the subject under the following heads:

Theology, Cosmogony, Anthropology, Soteriology, Cultus, Eschatology, and Ethics.

(1.) Theology.

Mani taught dualism in the most unqualified sense. Zoroastrianism is commonly characterized as dualistic, yet it is so in no such sense as is Manichæism.

According to the Fihrist, "Mani teaches:

Two subsistences form the beginning of the world, the one light the other darkness; the two are separated from each other.

The light is the first most glorious being, limited by no number, God himself, the King of the Paradise of Light.

He has five members: meekness, knowledge, understanding, mystery, insight; and five other spiritual members:

love, faith, truth, nobleness, and wisdom.

He maintained furthermore that the God of light, with these his attributes, is without beginning, but with him two equally eternal things likewise exist, the one the atmosphere, the other the earth. Mani adds:

and the members of the atmosphere are five [the first series of divine attributes mentioned above are enumerated]; and the members of the earth are five [the second series].

The other being is the darkness, and his members are five:

cloud, burning, hot wind, poison, and darkness.

Mani teaches:

that the light subsistence borders immediately on the dark subsistence, without a dividing wall between them; the light touches with its (lowest) side the darkness, while upwards to the right and left it is unbounded.

Even so the darkness is endless downwards and to the right and left."

This represents Mani's view of the eternally existent status quo, before the conflict began, and the endless state after the conflict ceases.

What does Mani mean, when he enumerates two series of five attributes each as members of God, and straightway postulates the co-eternity of atmosphere and earth and divides these self-same attributes between the latter?

Doubtless Mani's theology was fundamentally pantheistic, i.e., pantheistic within the limits of each member of the dualism.

The God of Light himself is apparently conceived of as transcending thought.

Atmosphere and Earth (not the atmosphere and earth that we know, but ideal atmosphere and earth) are the æons derived immediately from the Ineffable One and coëternal with him.

The ten attributes are æons which all belong primarily to the Supreme Being and secondarily to the two great æons, half to each.

The question may arise, and has been often discussed, whether Mani meant to identify God (the Prince of Light) with the Kingdom of Light?

His language, in this treatise, is wavering.

He seems to struggle against such a representation, yet without complete success.

What do the other sources teach with reference to the absoluteness of the dualism and with reference to the identification of the Prince of Light with the Kingdom of Light?

According to the Acts of the Disputation of Archelaus and Manes, [6] Manes "worships two deities, unoriginated, self-existent, eternal, opposed the one to the other.

Of them he represents the one as good, and the other as evil, and assigned the name of Light to the former, and that of Darkness to the latter." Again, Manes is represented as saying:

"I hold that there are two natures, one good and another evil; and that the one which is good dwells in a certain part proper to it, but that the evil one is this world as well as all things in it, which are placed there like objects imprisoned in the portion of the wicked one" (1 John 5, 19).

According to Alexander of Lycopolis, [7] "Mani laid down two principles, God and matter (Hyle).

God he called good, and matter he affirmed to be evil. But God excelled more in good than matter in evil."

Alexander goes on to show how Mani used the word Hyle, comparing the Manichæan with the Platonic teaching.

Statements of substantially the same purport might be multiplied.

As regards the identification of God (the King of Light) with the Kingdom of Light, and of Satan (the King of Darkness) with the Kingdom of Darkness, the sensuous poetical way in which Mani expressed his doctrines may leave us in doubt.

The probability is, however, that he did pantheistically identify each element of the dualism with his Kingdom.

He personifies the Kingdom of Light and the Kingdom of Darkness, and peoples these Kingdoms with fanciful beings, which are to be regarded as personified attributes of the principles of darkness and light.

A word on the Manichæan conception of matter or Hyle may not be out of place in this connection.

It would seem that the Manichæans practically identified Hyle or matter with the Kingdom of Darkness.

At any rate Hyle is unoriginated and belongs wholly to this Kingdom.

(2.) Cosmogony.

So much for the Manichæan idea of the Kingdom of Light and the Kingdom of Darkness before the great conflict that resulted in the present order of things.

Why did not they remain separate?

Let us learn from the Fihrist's narrative:

"Mani teaches further:

Out of this dark earth [the Kingdom of Darkness] arose Satan, not that he was in himself eternal from the beginning, yet were his substances in his elements unoriginated.

These substances now united themselves out of his elements and went forth as Satan, his head as the head of a lion, his body as the body of a dragon, his wings as the wings of a bird, his tail as the tail of a great fish, and his four feet as the feet of creeping animals.

When this Satan under the name Iblis, the (temporally considered) eternal (primeval), had arisen out of the darkness, he devoured and consumed everything, spread destruction right and left, and plunged into the deep, in all these movements bringing down from above desolation and annihilation.

Then he strove for the height, and descried the beams of light; but they were opposed to him.

When he saw later how exalted these were, he was terrified, shrivelled up, and merged himself in his elements.

Hereupon he strove anew with such violence after the height, that the land of light descried the doings of Satan and how he was bent upon murder and destruction.

After they had been apprised thereof, the world of Insight learned of it, then the world of

Knowledge, then the world of Mystery, then the world of Understanding, then the world of Meekness. When at last, he further teaches, the King of the Paradise of Light had also learned of it, he thought how he might suppress Satan, and, Mani adds, those hosts of his would have been mighty enough to overpower Satan.

Yet he desired to do this by means of his own might. Accordingly, he produced by means of the spirit of his right hand [i.e., the Gentle Breeze], his five worlds, and his twelve elements, a creature, and this is the (temporally considered) Eternal Man [Primordial Man], and summoned him to do battle with the Darkness.

But Primordial Man, Mani adds, armed himself with the five races [natures], and these are the five gods, the Gentle Breeze, the Wind, the Light, the Water and the Fire.

Of them he made his armor, and the first that he put on was the Gentle Breeze.

He then covered the Gentle Breeze with the burning Light as with a mantle.

He drew over the Light Water filled with atoms, and covered himself with the blowing Wind.

Hereupon he took the Fire as a shield and as a lance in his hand, and precipitated himself suddenly out of Paradise until he reached the border of the region that is contiguous to the battle-field.

The Primordial Devil also took his five races [natures]:

Smoke, Burning, Darkness, Hot Wind and Cloud; armed himself with them; made of them a shield for himself; and went to meet Primordial Man.

After they had fought for a long time the Primordial Devil vanquished the Primordial Man, devoured some of his light, and surrounded him at the same time with his races and elements.

Then the King of the Paradise of Light sent other gods, freed him, and vanquished the Darkness.

But he who was sent by the King of Light to rescue Primordial Man is called the Friend of the Light.

This one made a precipitate descent, and Primordial Man was freed from the hellish substances, along with that which he had snatched from the spirit of Darkness and which had adhered to him.

When, therefore, Mani proceeds, Joyfulness and the Spirit of Life drew near to the border, they looked down into the abyss of this deep hell and saw Primordial Man and the angels [i.e., the races or natures with which he was armed], how Iblis, the Proud Oppressors, and the Dark Life surrounded them.

And the Spirit of Life, says Mani, called Primordial Man with a loud voice as quick as lightning and Primordial Man became another god.

When the Primordial Devil had ensnared Primordial Man in the battle, Mani further teaches, the five parts of the Light were mingled with the five parts of the Darkness."

Let us see if we can get at the meaning of this great cosmological poem as far as we have gone.

The thing to be accounted for is the mixture of good and evil.

The complete separation of the eternally existent Kingdoms of Light and Darkness has been posited.

How now are we to account for the mixture of light and darkness, of good and evil, in the present order of things?

Mani would account for it by supposing that a conflict had occurred between an insufficiently equipped representative of the King of Light and the fully equipped ruler of the Kingdom of Darkness.

His view of the vastly superior power of the King of Light would not allow him to suppose that the King of Light fully equipped had personally contended with the King of Darkness, and suffered the loss and contamination of his elements.

Yet he only clumsily obviates this difficulty; for Primordial Man is produced and equipped by the King of Light for the very purpose of combating the King of Darkness, and Mani saves the King of Light from personal contamination only by impugning his judgment.

We have now reached the point where, as a result of the conflict, good and evil are blended.

We must beware of supposing that Mani meant to ascribe any kind of materiality to the members of the Kingdom of Light.

The Kingdom of Light, on the contrary, he regarded as purely spiritual; the Kingdom of Darkness as material.

We have now the conditions for the creation of the present order of things, including man.

How does Mani picture the process and the results of this mixing of the elements?

"The smoke (or vapor) was mingled with the gentle breeze (zephyr), and the present atmosphere resulted.

So that whatever of agreeableness and power to quicken the soul and animal life is found in it [resultant air], is from the zephyr, and whatever of destructiveness and noisomeness is found in it, proceeds from the smoke.

The burning was mingled with the fire; therefore whatever of conflagration, destruction and ruin is found, is from the burning, but whatever of brightness and illumination is in it [the resultant fire], springs from the fire.

The light mingled itself with the darkness; therefore in dense bodies as gold, silver and the like, whatever of brightness, beauty, purity and other useful qualities occurs, is from the light, and whatever of tarnish, impurity, density and hardness occurs, springs from the darkness.

The hot wind was mingled with the wind; whatever now is useful and agreeable in this [resultant wind] springs from the wind, and whatever of uneasiness, hurtfulness and deleterious property is found in it [resultant wind] is from the hot wind.

Finally, the mist was mingled with the water, so that what is found in this [resultant water] of clearness, sweetness, and soul-satisfying property, is from the water; whatever, on the contrary, of overwhelming, suffocating, and destroying power, of heaviness, and corruption, is found in it, springs from the mist."

But we must from this point abbreviate the somewhat prolix account. Primordial Man, after the blending of the elements, ascended on high accompanied by "one of the angels of this intermingling;" in other words, snatching away a part of the imprisoned elements of the Kingdom of Light.

The next step is the creation of the present world, which Mani ascribes to the King of the World of Light, the object being to provide for the escape of the imprisoned elements of Light.

Through an angel he constructed ten heavens and eight earths, an angel being appointed to hold heavens and earths in their places.

A description of the stairways, doors, and halls of the heavens is given in the Fihrist's narrative.

The stairways lead to the "height of heaven."

The air was used as a medium for connecting heaven and earth.

A pit was formed to be the receptacle of darkness from which the light should be liberated.

The sun and the moon were created to be the receptacles of the light that should be liberated from the darkness, the sun for light that has been mingled with "hot devils," the moon for that which had been mingled with "cold devils."

The moon is represented as collecting light during the first half-month, and during the second pouring it into the sun.

When the sun and moon have liberated all the light they are able, there will be a fire kindled on the earth which will burn for 1468 years, when there will be no light left.

The King of Darkness and his hosts will thereupon withdraw into the pit prepared for them.

(3.) Anthropology.

So much for the liberation of the imprisoned light, which, according to Mani, was the sole object of creation.

As yet we have heard nothing of the creation of living creatures.

What place do man, the lower animals, and plants sustain in the Manichæan economy?

We are to keep constantly in mind that Primordial Man was not Adam, but a divine æon, and that he ascended into the heights immediately after the blending of parts of his armor with darkness. The creation of earthly man was an altogether different affair.

We must give the account of man's creation in Mani's own words, as preserved by the Fihrist:

"Hereupon one of those Arch-fiends and [one] of the Stars, and Overmastering Violence, Avarice, Lust, and Sin, copulated, and from their copulation sprang the first man, who is Adam, two Arch-fiends, a male and a female, directing the process.

A second copulation followed and from this sprang the beautiful woman who is Eve."

Man, therefore, unlike the world, is the creature of demons, the aim of the demons being to imprison in man, through the propagation of the race, as much as possible of the light, and so to hinder the separating process by the sun and the moon.

Avarice is represented as having secretly seized some of the divine light and imprisoned it in man.

The part played by the Star in the production of man is somewhat obscure in the narrative, yet the Star could hardly have been regarded as wholly evil.

Probably the Star was thought of as a detached portion of the light that had not entered into the sun or the moon.

"When, therefore, the five Angels saw what had taken place, they besought the Messenger of Joyful Knowledge, the Mother of Life, Primordial Man and the Spirit of Life, to send some one to liberate and save man, to reveal to him knowledge and righteousness, and to free him from the power of the devils.

They sent, accordingly, Jesus, whom a god accompanied.

These seized the two Arch-fiends, imprisoned them and freed the two creatures (Adam and Eve.)"

Jesus warned Adam of Eve's violent importunity, and Adam obeyed his injunction not to go near her.

One of the Arch-fiends, however, begat with her a son named Cain, who in turn begat Abel of his mother, and afterwards two maidens Worldly wise and Daughter-of-Avarice.

Cain took the first to wife and gave the other to Abel.

An angel having begotten of Worldly-wise two beautiful daughters (Raufarjâd and Barfarjâd), Abel accused Cain of the act.

Cain enraged by the false accusation slew Abel and took Worldly-wise to wife.

So far Adam had kept himself pure, but Eve was instructed by a demon in the art of enchanting, and she was enabled to excite his lust and to entrap him.

By Adam she bore a beautiful son, whom the demon urged Eve to destroy.

Adam stole the child away and brought it up on cow's milk and fruit.

This son was named Seth (Schatil).

Adam once more yielded to Eve's fascinations, but through Seth's exhortations was induced to flee "eastward to the light and the wisdom of God."

Adam, Seth, Raufarjâd, Barfarjâd, and Worldly-wise died and went to Paradise; while Eve, Cain, and Daughter-of-Avarice went into Hell.

This fantastic perversion of the Biblical narrative of the creation and fall of man has many parallels in Rabbinic literature, and doubtless Mani first became acquainted with the narrative in a corrupted form.

The teaching, however, of this mythologizing evidently is that the indulgence of the flesh and the begetting of children furnish the chief obstacle to the separation of light from darkness.

Adam is represented as striving to escape from the allurements of Eve, but Eve is aided by demonic craft in overcoming him.

Yet Adam does not become enslaved to lust, and so at last is saved.

Eve, lustful from the beginning, is lost along with those of like disposition.

(4.) Soteriology.

Such was, apparently, Mani's conception of the creation of man, and of the attempts to liberate the light that was in him.

What were his practical teachings to men of his time as to the means of escape from the Kingdom of Darkness into the Kingdom of Light?

What view did Mani take of the historical Jesus?

The Jesus who warned Adam against the seductions of Eve was evidently not the Jesus of the New Testament.

According to the narrative of the Fihrist, Mani "maintained that Jesus is a devil."

Such a statement occurs nowhere else, so far as we are aware, in the literature of Manichæism.

The sources, however, are unanimous in ascribing to Mani a completely docetical view of the person of Christ.

In using this blasphemous language, he probably referred to the representations of Jesus as God manifest in the flesh, which he regarded as Jewish and abominable.

The New Testament narratives Mani [or at least his followers] regarded as interpolated in the interest of Judaism.

Later Manichæans, under the influence of Marcionism (and orthodoxy) gave to Jesus a far more prominent place in the economy of man's salvation than did Mani himself.

How then is man to be saved according to Mani?

It is by rigorous asceticism, and by the practice of certain ceremonial observances. Mani does not rise above the plane of ordinary heathenism in his plan of salvation.

"It is incumbent upon him who will enter into the religion that he prove himself, and that if he sees that he is able to subdue lust and avarice, to leave off the eating of all kinds of flesh, the drinking of wine, and connubial intercourse, and to withhold himself from what is injurious in water, fire, magic and hypocrisy, he may enter into the religion; but if not let him abstain from entering. But if he loves religion, yet is not able to repress sensuality and avarice, yet he may make himself serviceable for the maintenance of religion and of the Truthful [i.e. the Elect'], and may meet (offset) his corrupt deeds through the use of opportunities where he wholly gives himself up to activity, righteousness, zealous watchfulness, prayer and pious humiliation; for this suffices him in this transitory world and in the future eternal world, and his form in the last day will be the second form, of which, God willing, we shall treat further below."

The doctrine of indulgences of which the germs appeared in the Catholic church even before the time of Mani, is here seen fully developed. What the Greek and Latin sources call the Elect or Perfect and the Hearers, are undoubtedly indicated here by those who are able to devote themselves to rigidly ascetical living, and those who, without such qualifications, are willing to exert themselves fully on behalf of the cause.

These latter evidently become partakers of the merits of those who carry out the ascetical regulations.

That this is primitive Manichæan doctrine is abundantly proved by the general agreement of ancient writers of all classes.

It is noteworthy that nothing Christian appears among the conditions of Manichæan discipleship.

It is not faith in Christ, but the ability to follow a particular kind of outward life that confers standing in the Manichæan society.

(5.) Cultus.

Let us next look at the precepts of Mani to the initiated:

"Mani imposed upon his disciples commandments, namely, ten commandments, and to these are attached three seals, and fasts of seven days in each month.

The commandments are:

Faith in the four most glorious essences:

God, his Light, his Power, and his Wisdom.

But God, whose name is glorious, is the King of the Paradise of Light; his Light is the sun and the moon, his Power the five angels:

Gentle Breeze, Wind, Light, Water and Fire; and his Wisdom the Sacred Religion.

This embraces five ideas:

that of teachers, the sons of Meekness; that of those enlightened by the Sun, sons of Knowledge; that of the presbyters, sons of Reason; that of the Truthful, sons of Mystery; that of Hearers, sons of Insight.

The ten commandments are: Abandoning of prayer to idols, of lies, avarice, murder, adultery, theft, of the teaching of jugglery and magic, of duplicity of mind, which betrays doubt on religion, of drowsiness and inertness in business; and the commandment of four or seven prayers.

In prayer one is to stand upright, rub himself with flowing water or with something else, and turn while standing to the great light (the Sun), then prostrate himself and in this position pray:

Blessed be our Leader, the Paraclete, the Ambassador of the Light, blessed be his angels, the Guardians, and highly praised be his resplendent hosts.... In the second prostration let him say:

Thou highly praised, O thou enlightening one, Mani, our Leader, thou root of enlightenment, stem of honorableness, thou great tree who art altogether the means of salvation.

In the third prostration let him say:

I fall down and praise with pure heart and upright tongue the great God, the Father of Light, and their element, highly praised, Blessed One, thou and thy whole glory and thy blessed world, which thou hast called into being. For he praises thee who praises thy Host, thy Righteous Ones, thy Word, thy Glory, and thy Good Pleasure, because thou art the God who is wholly truth, life and righteousness.

In the fourth prostration let him say:

I praise and fall down before all the gods, all the enlightening angels, before all Light and all Hosts, who are from the great God.

In the fifth prostration let him say:

I fall down and praise the great Host and the enlightening Gods, who with their wisdom assail the Darkness, drive it out and triumph over it.

In the sixth prostration let him say:

I fall down and praise the Father of Glory, the Exalted One, the Enlightening One, who has come forth from the two sciences (see note in Flügel p. 310), and so on to the twelfth prostration. *

* The first prayer is accomplished at mid-day, the second between this hour and sunset; then follows the prayer at eventide, after sunset, and hereupon the prayer in the first quarter of the night, three hours after sunset.

"As regards fasting, when the sun is in Sagittarius, and the moon has its full light, fasting is to take place for two days without interruption, also when the new moon begins to appear; likewise when the moon first becomes visible again after the sun has entered into the sign of Capricorn; then when the new moon begins to appear, the sun stands in Aquarius and from the moon eight days have flowed, a fast of thirty days occurs, broken, however, daily at sunset.

The common Manichæans celebrate Sunday, the consecrated ones (the Elect') Monday."

Here we have a somewhat detailed account of the cultus of the early Manichæans.

The forms of invocation do not differ materially from those of the Zoroastrians, of the early Indians, of the Babylonians, and of the Egyptians.

There is not the slightest evidence of Christian influence.

The times of worship and of fasting are determined by the sun and the moon, and practically these are the principal objects of worship.

It is certain that Mani himself was regarded by his followers as the most perfect revealer of God that had ever appeared among men, and, according to this account, he taught his followers to worship him.

We cannot fail to see in this Manichæan cult the old Oriental pantheism modified by a dualism, of which the most fully developed form was the Persian, but which, as we have seen, was by no means confined to Zoroastrianism.

(6.) Eschatology.

We must conclude our exposition of the doctrines of the Manichæans by quoting from the Fihrist Mani's teachings on eschatology.

"When death approaches a Truthful One (Elect'), teaches Mani, Primordial Man sends a Light-God in the form of a guiding Wise One, and with him three gods, and along with these the water-vessel, clothing, head-gear, crown, and garland of light.

With them comes the maiden, like the soul of this Truthful One.

There appears to him also the devil of avarice and lust, along with other devils.

As soon as the Truthful Man sees these he calls the goddess who has assumed the form of the Wise One and the three other gods to his help, and they draw near him.

As soon as the devils are aware of their presence they turn and flee.

The former, however, take this Truthful One, clothe him with the crown, the garland and the robe, put the water-vessel in his hand and mount with him upon the pillars of promise to the sphere of the moon, to Primordial Man, and to Nahnaha, the Mother of the Living, to the position in which he was at first in the Paradise of Light.

But his body remains lying as before in order that the sun, the moon, and the gods of Light may withdraw from it the powers, i.e., the water, the fire and the gentle breeze, and he rises to the sun and becomes a god. But the rest of his body, which is wholly darkness, is cast into hell."

In the case of Manichæans of the lower order, described above, the same divine personages appear at his summons.

"They free him also from devils, but he ceases not to be like a man in the world, who in his dreams sees frightful forms and sinks into filth and mire.

In this condition he remains, until his light and his spirit are liberated and he has attained to the place of union with the Truthful, and after a long period of wandering to and fro puts on their garments."

To the sinful man, on the other hand, the divine personages appear, not to free him from the devils that are tormenting him, but rather to "overwhelm him with reproaches, to remind him of his deeds, and strikingly to convince him that he has renounced help for himself, from the side of the Truthful.

Then wanders he round about in the world, unceasingly chased by torments, until this order of things ceases, and along with the world he is cast into hell."

There is nothing original about the eschatology of Mani, and scarcely anything Christian.

We see in it a fully developed doctrine of purgatory, somewhat like the Platonic, and still more like that of the later Catholic church.

Salvation consists simply in the liberation of the light from the darkness.

In the case of the Elect this takes place immediately after death; in the case of adherents who have not practiced the prescribed forms of asceticism, it takes place only after considerable torment.

In the case of the ordinary sensual man, there is no deliverance.

Doubtless Mani would have held that in his case, too, whatever particles of light may have been involved in his animal structure are liberated from the dead body.

(7.) Ethics.

As regards ceremonies we find little that enlightens us in the Fihrist's account.

Water (that is, water apart from the deleterious elements that have become blended with it) was regarded by Mani as one of the divine elements.

The ablutions in running water mentioned above in connection with the prayers may have sustained some relation to baptism, but can hardly be ascribed to Christian influence.

The connection of the Manichæans with the Mandæans, who made much of ceremonial bathing, will be considered below.

It is certain that Mani's father was connected with a baptizing party, viz., the Mugtasilah.

According to the Fihrist Mani was the author of an Epistle on Baptism.

The question whether Mani and his followers practised water-baptism or not is by no means an easy one to solve. The passage cited by Giesseler from Augustin to prove that the "Elect" were initiated by baptism is inconclusive.

Augustin acknowledges that God and the Manichæans themselves alone know what takes place in the secret meetings of the "Elect."

Whatever ceremonies they performed, whether baptism or the Lord's supper, or some other, were matters of profound secrecy, and so we need not wonder at the lack of definite information.

From a passage quoted by Augustin in his report of a discussion with Felix the Manichæan, we should certainly infer that both ordinances were practised in some form by the Manichæans of the West.

But Augustin himself says that Manichæans deny the saving efficacy of baptism, maintain that it is superfluous, do not require it of those whom they win to their views, etc.

It is certain, therefore, that if they practised baptism and the Lord's supper at all, they attached to it a meaning radically different from that of Augustin.

It is possible that a ceremonial anointing with oil took the place of baptism.

(Baur, p. 277 sq.).

Augustin mentions a disgusting ceremony in which human semen was partaken of by the Elect in order to deliver the imprisoned light contained therein (De Haeres. 46), and he calls this ceremony a sort of Eucharist.

But his confessed ignorance of the doings of the "Elect" discredits in some measure this accusation.

The Fihrist gives us no definite information about the three signacula.

The seals (not signs) of the mouth, the hand (or hands), and of the bosom.

In these are contained symbolically the Manichæan moral system.

In the book Sadder (Hyde, p. 492) we read:

"It is taught [by the Manichæans] to abstain from every sin, to eliminate every sin from hand, and tongue and thought."

Augustin explains the signacula more fully and represents the Manichæans as attaching great importance to them:

"When I name the mouth, I mean all the senses that are in the head; when I name the hand I mean every operation; when I name the bosom I mean every seminal lust."

It is confidently believed that the foregoing account of the Manichæan system, based upon the Arabic narratives preserved by the Fihrist, supplemented by the principal Eastern and Western sources, contains the essential facts with reference to this strange system of religious thought.

Our next task will to be to ascertain, as precisely as possible, the relations that Manichæism sustained to the various religious systems with which it has commonly been associated.

Chapter IV - Relation of Manichæism to Zoroastrianism

The very close connection of these two systems has commonly been presupposed, and is undeniable.

In fact Manichæism has frequently been represented as Zoroastrian dualism, slightly modified by contact with Christianity and other systems.

No one could possibly gain even a superficial view of the two systems without being strongly impressed with their points of resemblance.

A closer examination, however, will reveal points of antagonism just as striking, and will enable us to account for the fact that Mani was put to death by a zealous Zoroastrian ruler on account of his recognized hostility to the state religion.

The leading features of the Manichæan system are already before us.

Instead of quoting at length from the Zend-Avesta, which is now happily accessible in an excellent English translation, we may for the sake of brevity quote Tiele's description of Zoroastrian dualism as a basis of comparison: [8]

"Parsism is decidedly dualistic, not in the sense of accepting two hostile deities, for it recognizes no worship of evil beings, and teaches the adoration only of Ahura Mazda and the spirits subject to him; but in the sense of placing in hostility to each other two sharply divided kingdoms, that of light, of truth, and of purity, and that of darkness, of falsehood, and of impurity.

This division is carried through the whole creation, organic and inorganic, material and spiritual.

Above, in the highest sphere, is the domain of the undisputed sovereignty of the All-wise God; beneath, in the lowest abyss, the kingdom of his mighty adversary; midway between the two lies this world, the theatre of the contest.... This dualism further dominates the cosmogony, the cultus, and the entire view of the moral order of the world held by the Mazda worshippers.

Not only does Anro-Maînyus (Ahriman) spoil by his counter-creations all the good creations of Ahura-Mazda (Ormuzd), but by slaying the protoplasts of man and beast, he brings death into the world, seduces the first pair to sin, and also brings forth noxious animals and plants.

Man finds himself, in consequence, surrounded on all sides by the works of the spirits of darkness and by his hosts.

It is the object of worship to secure the pious against their influence."

Let us bring in review some of the points of resemblance between the two systems.

Both are in a sense dualistic.

In both the kingdoms of Light and Darkness are set over against each other in the sharpest antagonism.

In both we have similar emanations from these kingdoms (or kings).

Yet, while in the Manichæan system the dualism is absolute and eternal, in the later Zoroastrian system (as in the Jewish and Christian doctrine of Satan), Ahriman (Satan) if not merely a fallen creature [9] of Ormuzd (the good and supreme God) was at least an immeasurably inferior being.

The supreme control of the universe, to which it owes its perfect order, was ascribed by Zoroastrianism to Ormuzd.

The struggle between good and evil, beneficent and malevolent, was due to the opposition of the mighty, but not almighty, Ahriman. Whatever form of Mazdeism (Zoroastrianism) we take for purposes of comparison, we are safe in saying that the Manichæan dualism was by far the more absolute.

In both systems each side of the dualism is represented by a series (or rather several series) of personified principles.

These agree in the two systems in some particulars.

Yet the variations are quite as noticeable as the agreements.

There is much in common between the Manichæan and the Zoroastrian delineations of the fearful conflict between the Kingdom of Light and the Kingdom of Darkness, yet the beginning of the conflict is quite differently conceived of in the two systems.

In Manichæism the creation is accounted for by the conflict in which Primordial Man was beaten by the powers of Darkness and suffered the mixing of his elements with the elements of darkness.

The actual world was made by the good God, or rather by his subordinates, as a means of liberating the imprisoned light. The creation of man is ascribed, on the other hand, to the King of Darkness (or his subordinates), with a view to hindering the escape of the mingled light by diffusion thereof through propagation.

Mazdeism derives the creation solely from Ormuzd, from whose hand it issued "as pure and perfect as himself" (Lenormant, Anc. Hist. II. p. 30).

It was the work of Ahriman to "spoil it by his evil influence."

The appellation "Maker of the material world" is constantly applied to Ormuzd in the Vendîdâd and other sacred books. The most instructive Mazdean account of the creation that has come down to us is that contained in the Vendîdâd, Fargard I.

Ahura Mazda (Ormuzd) is represented here as naming one by one the sixteen good lands that he had created.

Angra Mainyu (Ahriman) is represented as coming to each, one by one, and creating in it noxious things.

Examples of these counter-creations are, the serpents, winter, venomous flies, sinful lusts, mosquitoes, pride, unnatural sin, burying the dead, witchcraft, the sin of unbelief, the burning of corpses, abnormal issues in women, oppression of foreign rulers, excessive heat, etc.

This jumble of physical evils and sins is characteristic of Mazdeism.

According to Mani matter is inherently evil, and it only ceases to be absolutely evil by the mixture with it of the elements of the Kingdom of Light.

Creation is a process forced upon the King of Light by the ravages of the King of Darkness, and is at best only partially good. Zoroastrianism looked upon earth, fire, water, as sacred elements, to defile which was sin of the most heinous kind.

Manichæism regarded actual fire and water as made up of a mixture of elements of light and darkness, and so, as by no means wholly pure.

Manichæans regarded earth, so far as it consisted of dead matter, with the utmost contempt.

The life-giving light in it was alone thought of with respect.

Zoroastrianism somewhat arbitrarily divided animals and plants between the kingdoms of Ormuzd and Ahriman; but the idea that all material things, so far as they are material, are evil, seems never to have occurred to the early Mazdeists.

Manichæans agreed with Mazdeists in their veneration for the sun, but the principles underlying this veneration seem to have been widely different in the two cases.

The most radical opposition of the two systems is seen in their views of human propagation.

Mani regarded the procreation of children as ministering directly to the designs of the King of Darkness to imprison the light, and so absolutely condemned it.

The Zend-Avesta says:

(Vendîdâd, Fargard IV.):

"Verily I say unto thee, O Spitama Zarathustra; the man who has a wife is far above him who begets no sons; he who keeps a house is far above him who has none; he who has children is far above a childless man."

Mani made great merit of voluntary poverty.

The Zend-Avesta (ibid.) says:

"He who has riches is far above him who has none."

Mani forbade the use of animal food as preventing the escape of the light contained in the bodies of animals. The Zend-Avesta (ibid.):

"And of two men, he who fills himself with meat is filled with the good spirit much more than he who does not do so; the latter is all but dead; the former is above him by the worth of an Asperena, by the worth of a sheep, by the worth of an ox, by the worth of a man." [10]

The eschatology of the two systems might be shown to present just as striking contrasts, and just as marked resemblances.

In both systems the consummation of the age is effected by means of a conflagration, the aim of the conflagration in Mazdeism being the punishment and the purging of wicked men, the destruction of wicked spirits, the renovation of the earth, and the inauguration of the sole sovereignty of Ormuzd, while in Manichæism the aim of the conflagration is to liberate the portions of light which the processes of animal and vegetable growth, with the aid of sun and the moon have proved unable to liberate.

But enough has been said to make it evident that Manichæism was by no means a slightly altered edition of Zoroastrianism.

The points of similarity between the two are certainly more apparent than real, though the historical relationship can by no means be denied.

Chapter V - The Relation of Manichæism to the Old Babylonian Religion as Seen in Mandæism and Sabeanism

It would have been strange indeed if the old Babylonian religion, after dominating the minds of the inhabitants of Mesopotamia for so many centuries, had given place completely to the religion of the Medo-Persian conquerors of the country.

Magism itself was a mixture of old Babylonian, Medic and Persian elements.

But there is much reason for believing that the primitive Babylonian faith, in a more or less pure form, persisted until long after the time of Mani, nay, that it has maintained its ground even till the present day.

The researches of Chwolson, Nöldeke, Kessler and others, in the literature and history of the Mandæans and the Sabeans, combined in the last case at least with accurate knowledge of old Babylonian literature and religion, have rendered it highly probable that representatives of the old Babylonian faith were numerous in Mesopotamia and the adjoining regions at the time of Mani, and that Mani himself was more or less closely connected with it.

The Mandæans were a Gnostic sect of the Ophitic type, without Christian elements.

It is the opinion of Kessler, who has devoted much attention to this sect and to the relations of occult religious matters in general in Mesopotamia, that "the source of all Gnosis, and especially the immediate source of Ophitic Gnosis, is not the doctrine of the Persian Zoroaster, not Phoenicean heathenism, not the theory and practise of Greek mysteries, but the old Babylonian-Chaldaic national religion, which maintained itself in Mesopotamia and Babylonia, the abode of the Ophites, Perates, Mandæans, until the post-Christian centuries, and was now opposed by the Gentiles in a mystical-ascetical form to Christianity."

The close connection of the Mandæans with the Ophites, and of both with the old Babylonian religion, would seem to be established beyond question.

The relation of Manichæism to Mandæism has been by no means so clearly shown.

Let us look at some of the supposed points of contact.

Mani's connection with the Mugtasilah sect (or Baptizers) has already been mentioned.

Kessler seeks to identify this party with the Mandæans, or at least to establish a community of origin and of fundamental principles in the two parties.

He would connect with the old Babylonian sect, of which ceremonial baptism seems to have been a common characteristic, the Palestinian Hemero-baptists, Elkesaites, Nazareans, Ebionites, etc.

There is nothing improbable about this supposition.

Certainly we find elements in Palestinian heresy during the early Christian centuries, which we can hardly suppose to have been indigenous.

And there is no more likely source of occult religious influence than Babylonia, unless it be Egypt, and there is much reason for supposing that even in Alexandria Babylonian influences were active before and after the beginning of the Christian era.

Besides, a large number of Gnostic elements different from these can be traced to Egypt.

How far the Mandæans of modern times, and as they are described in extant literature, correspond with representatives of the old Babylonian religion in the third century, cannot be determined with complete certainty.

Yet there is much about this party that has a primitive appearance, and the tenacity with which it has held aloof from Judaism, Manichæism, Mohammedanism, and Oriental Christianity, during centuries of conflict and oppression, says much for its conservatism.

It would extend this chapter unduly to describe the elaborate cosmogony, mythology, hierarchy, ceremonial, etc., of this interesting party.

For the illustration of Christian Gnosticism the facts that have been brought out are of the utmost value.

As compared with Manichæism, there is a remarkable parallelism between the two kingdoms and their subordinates or æons; the conflict between Primordial Man and the King of Darkness has its counterpart in Mandæism.

The close connection of the Mandæan and the Manichæan cosmogony, together with similar views about water in the two parties, would make it highly probable that the Manichæans, like the Mandæans, practised some kind of ceremonial ablutions.

What, now, are the grounds on which the connection of these systems with the old Babylonian religion is based?

The dualistic element in the old Babylonian system was pointed out above.

Kessler seeks to establish an almost complete parallelism between the Mandæan and Manichæan cosmological and mythological systems on the one hand, and the old Babylonian on the other.

That there are points of striking resemblance it is certain.

There is ground to suspect, however, that he has been led by partiality for a theory of his own to minimize unduly the Zoroastrian and Buddhist influence and to magnify unduly the old Babylonian.

Be that as it may, there remains an important residuum of solid fact which must be taken account of by all future students of Manichæism.

There is reason to hope that future work along the lines of Kessler's researches will bring to light much additional material.

Chapter VI - The Relation of Manichæism to Buddhism

The extent of Mani's dependence on Buddhism is a matter that has been much disputed.

The attention of scholars was first directed to this possible source of Manichæism by the discovery of important features that are radically opposed to Zoroastrianism, Judaism and Christianity, and by the traditional historical connection of Mani with India and Turkestan.

The antagonism of spirit and matter, of light and darkness, the mixture of spirit and light with matter and darkness in the formation of the world, the final catastrophe in which complete simplicity shall be re-established, only inert matter and darkness remaining to represent the Kingdom of Darkness, abstinence from bloody sacrifices, from marriage, from killing or eating animals--points in which Manichæism differs widely from the other systems with which it stands historically related--find their counterpart in Buddhism.

It is certain, moreover, that they were fully developed in Buddhism centuries before the time of Mani.

Baur,[11] though not the first to suggest a connection of the two systems, was the first to show by a somewhat detailed comparison the close parallelism that exists between Manichæism and Buddhism.

Baur's reasonings were still further elaborated and confirmed by Neander. [12]External grounds in favor of Mani's dependence on Buddhism are the traditions of Mani's journey to India and China, and of his prolonged stay in Turkestan, where Buddhism flourished at that time.

But it is on internal grounds that we chiefly rely.

If space permitted we could illustrate the close parallelism that undoubtedly exists between Manichæism and Buddhism, from Buddhist documents which have been made accessible through Professor Max Müller and his collaborators in The Sacred Book of the East, far more completely than was possible to Baur and Neander.

It is certain that parallels can be found in Buddhism for almost every feature of Manichæism that is sharply antagonistic to Zoroastrianism.

The Buddhist view of matter as antagonistic to spirit is fundamental.

It is the world of matter that deludes.

It is the body and its passions that prevent the longed-for Nirvana.

Buddhist asceticism is the direct outgrowth of the doctrine of the evil and delusive nature of matter. The Buddhist doctrine of metempsychosis has its precise counterpart in Manichæism, but it should be said that this doctrine was widely diffused in the West, through Pythagoreanism, before the time of Mani. The Buddhist tenderness for animal and plant life is paralleled by the Manichæan.

But there is considerable difference between the views on which this tenderness is based.

The Buddhist feeling was based, in part at least, upon the doctrine of metempsychosis, animals and plants being regarded as the abodes of human spirits awaiting their release into Nirvana.

The Manichæan looked upon the elements of light (life) contained in animals and plants as particles of God, and any injury done to them as a hindrance to the escape of these elements, to be conveyed away into the Kingdom of Light.

Both looked upon sexual intercourse as among the greatest of evils, though the theory in the two cases was slightly different.

So of the drinking of wine, the eating of animal food, etc.

The final state was conceived of in substantially the same way in the two systems.

Nirvana, the blowing out of man's life as an individual entity, is quite paralleled by the Manichæan view of the gradual escape of the imprisoned particles of light into the Kingdom of Light.

In both cases the divine pleroma is to be restored in such a way as to destroy individual consciousness.

The Buddhist Bhikkhus (or ascetical monks) correspond very closely with the Manichæan Truthful Ones (Elect), and the relations of these to ordinary adherents of the parties was much the same in the two cases. Both systems (like Christianity) had the proselyting spirit fully developed.

The position of Mani as a preacher or prophet corresponds with the Buddhist idea of the manifestations of Buddha.

The statement is attributed to Mani that "as Buddha came in the land of India, Zoroaster in the land of Persia, and Jesus in the land of the West, so at last in the epoch of the present this preaching came through me [Mani] in the land of Babylonia."

In the interest of his theory, which makes the old Babylonian religion the chief source of Manichæism, Kessler has attempted to detract from the significance of the Buddhist influence.

Yet he grants that the morality of the Manichæans (including many of the features mentioned above) was Buddhist.

The close connection of the two systems cannot, it would seem, be successfully gainsaid. [13]

Chapter VII - The Relation of Manichæism to Judaism

So far as a relation existed it was one of the intensest hostility. Like the Gnostics in general, Manichæism looked upon the God of the Old Testament as an evil, or at least imperfect being.

On this matter we do not learn so much from the Oriental as from the Western sources, but even from the former the radical antagonism is manifest.

The statement in the Fihrist's narrative, that "Mani treated all the prophets disparagingly in his books, degraded them, accused them of lying, and maintained that devils had possessed them and that these spoke out of their mouths; nay, he goes so far as expressly to assert in some passages of his books that the prophets were themselves devils," is precisely in the line of the later Manichæan polemics against the Judaistic element in Christianity.

The Manichæan account of the creation shows some acquaintance with the Jewish Scriptures or with Jewish tradition, yet the complete perversion of the Biblical account is one of the clearest indications of hostility.

It may be said in general that it is impossible to conceive of two systems of religion that have less in common, or more that is sharply antagonistic.

One of the principal points of controversy between Manichæans and Christians was the defense of the Jewish Scriptures and religion by the latter.

The Manichæan demanded the elimination from the current Christianity, and from the New Testament itself, of every vestige of Judaism.

Their objections to the Old Testament Scriptures and religion were in general substantially the same as those made by other Gnostics, especially by the Marcionites. The Old Testament anthropomorphic representations seem to have been offensive to them, notwithstanding their own crude conceptions of the conflict between light and darkness, of the creation, etc.

The relation of God to the conquest of Canaan is a point that those inclined to cavil have never failed to make the most of.

The Old Testament encouragement of race propagation, the narratives of polygamy as practised by those that enjoyed the favor of the God of the Old Testament, the seeming approval of prevarication in several well-known cases, the institution of animal sacrifices, the allowing of the use of animal food, were among the standard objections that they raised against Judaism and against Christians who accepted the Old Testament. Judaism had, since the captivity, had many representatives in Mesopotamia, and Mani was doubtless brought up to abominate the Jews. Some of his extreme positions may have been primarily due to his radical anti-Judaistic tendencies.

We shall see hereafter how Augustin met the Manichæan objections to the Old Testament.

Chapter VIII - The Relation of Manichæism to Christianity

Far more superficial are the relations of Manichæism to Christianity than to any of the heathen systems to which we have adverted.

In fact no Christian idea has been introduced into the system without being completely perverted.

If Christian language is used, it is utterly emptied of its meaning.

If Christian practices are introduced, a completely different motive lies at the basis.

Indeed the wildest of the Christian Gnostic systems kept immeasurably nearer to historical Christianity than did the Manichæans.

While he blasphemed against the historical Jesus, Mani claimed to believe in Christ, a purely spiritual and divine manifestation, whose teachings had been sadly perverted by the Jews.

It is scarcely possible to determine with any certainty what view Mani actually took of New Testament history.

That he claimed to be a follower of Christ, and the Paraclete whom Christ had promised to send, or at least the organ of the Paraclete, Eastern and Western authorities agree.

Mani is said, by Augustin, to have begun his Fundamental Epistle as follows:

"Manichæus, an Apostle of Jesus Christ, by the providence of God the Father.

These are wholesome words from the perennial and living fountain."

So also in the Act. Archel., Mani is represented as introducing a letter:

"Manichæus, an Apostle of Jesus Christ, and all the saints who are with me, and the virgins, to Marcellus, my beloved son:

Grace, mercy, and peace be with you from God the Father, and from our Lord Jesus Christ."

There can be no doubt but that Mani and his followers, whether from designed imposture or from less sinister motives, attempted to palm themselves off as Christians, nay, as the only true Christians.

It is certain, moreover, that in this guise they gained many proselytes from the Christian ranks.

As previously remarked, Mani and his followers professed to accept the New Testament Scriptures, yet they treated them in a purely subjective manner, eliminating as Judaistic interpolation whatever they could not reconcile with their own tenets.

Their adherence to the New Testament, as well as their adherence to Christ, was, therefore, virtually a mere pretence.

In common with Christianity, Manichæism laid much stress on redemption, yet there was nothing in common between the Christian idea of redemption through the atoning suffering of Jesus Christ and the Manichæan notion of redemption through the escape of imprisoned light.

Manichæans and Christians were at one in advocating self-denial and the due subordination of the flesh.

It need not be pointed out how radically different the Christian view was from the Manichæan view, already expounded.

Yet pagan ascetical ideas had already invaded the Church long before the time of Mani, and many Christians were in a position to be attracted strongly by the Manichæan theory and practice.

The later asceticism as it appeared in the hermit life of the fourth and following centuries was essentially pagan and had much in common with the Manichæan.

Still more manifest is the anatagonism between Manichæism and Christianity on the great fundamental principles of religion.

The Manichæan and Christian ideas of God are mutually contradictory.

Christianity holds fast at the same time to the unity, the omnipotence, the omniscience, the perfect wisdom, the holiness and the goodness of God.

If He permits sin to exist in the world it is not because He looks upon it with complacency, nor because He lacked wisdom to provide against its rise or power to annihilate it at once when it appeared, nor because He did not foresee its rise and its ravages, but because the permission of sin forms part of His all-wise plan for the education of moral and spiritual beings. If the forces of nature are under certain circumstances hurtful or destructive to man, Christianity does not regard them as the operations of a malevolent power thwarting God's purposes, but it sees underneath the destructive violence purposes of goodness and of grace; or if it fails to see them in any given instance it yet believes that God doeth all things well.

Christianity admits the existence of evil in men and in demons, yet of evil that ministers to the purposes of the Most High.

Christianity is the only religion that has been able to arrive at a perfectly satisfactory theology, cosmology, anthropology, and eschatology, and this is because Christianity alone has a true and satisfying soteriology.

It is God manifest in the flesh that meets all the conditions for the solution of the problem of human existence. Manichæism openly antagonized Christianity in its adherence to Old Testament revelation, including the Jewish and Christian monotheism. The good God could not, they maintained, be the creator of this world and of the universe of being.

That God should be looked upon as in any sense the creator of the devil and his angels, and of the material world, was in their view an absurdity--a monstrosity.

The unchristian character of the Manichæan view of matter, leading to unchristian asceticism, has already been sufficiently indicated.

The reader will only need to compare the principles and practices of Manichæism, as delineated above, with those of Christianity as they are delineated in the New Testament and in the evangelical churches of to-day, to be impressed with the completely anti-Christian character of the former.

How then, it may well be asked, could Manichæism succeed as it did in fascinating so many intelligent members of the Catholic Church during the third, fourth and fifth centuries?

In attempting to answer this question it should be premised that the later Western Manichæism took far more account of historical Christianity than did Mani and his immediate followers.

In the West, at least, Manichæism set itself up as the only genuine exponent of Christianity.

The Jewish-Alexandrian philosophy, and Gnosticism its product, had done much towards discrediting the Old Testament Scriptures, and the moral and religious teachings therein contained.

Devout Jewish and Christian thinkers who had adopted this mode of thought, had attempted by means of the allegorical method of interpretation to reconcile the seeming antagonism between Judaism and philosophy.

But the process was so forced that its results could not be expected to satisfy those that felt no special interest in the removal of the difficulties. Marcionism represents a stern refusal to apply the allegory, and a determination to exhibit the antagonism between Judaism and current thought, and especially the seeming antagonism between Judaism and Christianity, in the harshest manner.

Marcionism was still vigorous in the East when Manichæism arose, and through this party unfavorable views of the Old Testament were widely disseminated.

Many Christians doubtless felt that the Old Testament and its religion were burdensome and trammelling to Christianity.

The very fact that Mani set aside so summarily every element of Judaism that he encountered in the current Christianity, doubtless commended his views to a large and influential element in the East and the West alike.

Mani claimed to set forth a spiritual religion as opposed to a carnal.

The asceticism of Manichæism was in the line of a wide-spread popular ascetical movement that was already in progress, and so commended it to many.

The question as to the origin of evil, and as to the relation of the good, wise and powerful God to the evil that appears in the world, in man and in demons was never asked with more interest than during the early Christian centuries, and any party that should advance a moderately plausible theory was sure to receive its share of public attention. Mani professed to have a solution and the only possible solution of questions of this class, and however fantastic may have been the forms in which his speculations were set forth, they were doubtless all the more acceptable on this account in that semi-pagan age to many intelligent people.

The fact that these forms satisfied so able a thinker as Mani undoubtedly was, would guarantee their acceptance by a large number both East and West.

There was in the West at this time, and had been for centuries, a hankering after Oriental theosophy, the more extravagant the better.

The wide-spread worship of Mithra was an excellent preparation for the more complete system of Mani.

Manichæism and Neo-Platonism antagonized the Christianity of the fourth and fifth centuries from opposite sides, and those minds for whom Platonism had no charms were almost sure to be attracted by the theosophy of Mani. "How are we to explain," asks Harnack, [14] "the rapid spread of Manichæism, and the fact that it really became one of the great religions?

Our answer is, that Manichæism was the most complete Gnosis, the richest, most consequent and most artistic system formed on the basis of the ancient Babylonian religion.... What gave strength to Manichæism was... that it united its ancient mythology and a thorough-going materialistic dualism with an exceedingly simple spiritual worship and a strict morality.

On comparing it with the Semitic religions of nature, we perceive that it retained their mythologies, after transforming them into doctrines, but abolished all their sensuous cultus, substituting instead a spiritual worship as well as a strict morality.

Manichæism was thus able to satisfy the new wants of an old world.

It offered revelation, redemption, moral virtue, and immortality [this last is very doubtful, if conscious immortality be meant], spiritual benefits on the basis of the religion of nature.

A further source of strength lay in the simple, yet firm social organization which was given by Mani himself to his new institution.

The wise man and the ignorant, the enthusiast and the man of the world, could all find acceptance here, and there was laid on no one more than he was able and willing to bear."

The question as to the secret of the fascination that Manichæism was able to exercise even over the most intelligent Western minds, may receive a more concrete answer from the autobiographical account of Augustin's own relations to the party.

What was it that attracted and enthralled, for nine years, him who was to become the greatest theologian of the age?

In his Confessions (Book III. ch. 6) he gives this impassioned account of his first connection with Manichæism: "Therefore I fell among men proudly railing, very carnal and voluble, in whose mouth were the snares of the devil--the bird lime being composed of a mixture of the syllables of Thy Name, and of our Lord Jesus Christ, and of the Paraclete, the Holy Ghost, the Comforter. These names departed not out of their mouths, but so far forth as the sound and clatter of the tongue; for the heart was empty of truth. Still they cried Truth, Truth,' and spoke much about it to me, yet it was not in them, but they spake falsely not of Thee only--who, verily art the Truth--but also of the elements of this world, Thy creatures... O Truth, Truth! how inwardly even then did the marrow of my soul pant after Thee, when they frequently and in a multiplicity of ways, and in numerous and huge books, sounded out Thy Name to me, though it was but a voice.

And these were the dishes in which to me, hungering for Thee, they, instead of Thee, served up the sun and the moon, Thy beauteous works--but yet Thy works, not Thyself, nay, nor Thy first works...Woe, woe, by what steps was I dragged down to the depths of hell!--toiling and turmoiling through want of Truth, when I sought after Thee, my God,--to Thee I confess it, who hadst mercy on me when I had not yet confessed, sought after Thee not according to the understanding of the mind in which Thou desiredst that I should excel the beasts, but according to the sense of the flesh."

Chapter IX - Augustin and the Manichæans

In the preceding Chapter we have given in Augustin's own words some account of the process by which he became ensnared in Manichæan error. In reading Augustin's account of his experience among the Manichæans, we can not escape the conviction that he was never wholly a Manichæan, that he never surrendered himself absolutely to the system.

He held it rather as a matter of opinion than as a matter of heart-attachment. Doubtless the fact that he continued to occupy himself with rhetorical and philosophical studies prevented his complete enthrallment.

His mind was not naturally of an Oriental cast, and the study of the hard, common-sense philosophy of Aristotle, and of the Eclecticism of Cicero, could hardly have failed to make him more or less conscious of the absurdity of Manichæism.

The influence of scientific studies on his mind is very manifest from Confessions, Book V. ch. 3, where he compares the accurate astronomical knowledge with which he had become acquainted, with the absurd cosmological fancies of Faustus, the great Manichæan teacher who appeared at Carthage in Augustin's twenty-ninth year.

"Many truths, however, concerning the creation did I retain from these men [the philosophers], and the cause appeared to confirm calculations, the succession of seasons, and the visible manifestations of the stars; and I compared them with the sayings of Manichæus, who in his frenzy has written most extensively on these subjects, but discovered not any account either of the solstices, or the equinoxes, the eclipses of the luminaries, or anything of the kind I had learned in the books of secular philosophy.

But therein I was ordered to believe, and yet it corresponded not with those rules acknowledged by calculation and by our light, but was far different."

From this time Augustin's faith was shaken, and he was soon able to throw off completely the yoke that had become too grievous to be borne.

But to reject Manichæism was not necessarily to become an orthodox Christian.

Augustin finds himself still greatly perplexed about the nature of God and the origin of evil, problems the somewhat plausible Manichæan solutions of which had ensnared him.

It was through Platonism, or rather Neo-Platonism, that he was led to more just and satisfying views, and through Platonism, along with other influences, he was enabled at last to find peace in the bosom of the Catholic church.

"And Thou, willing to show me how Thou resistest the proud, but givest grace unto the humble,' and by how great an act of mercy Thou hadst pointed out to men the path of humility, in that Thy Word was made flesh and dwelt among men,'--Thou procuredst for me, by the instrumentality of one inflated with monstrous pride, certain books of the Platonists, translated from Greek into Latin.

And therein I read not indeed in the same words but to the self-same effect, enforced by many and divers reasons, that In the beginning was the Word, and the Word was with God, and the Word was God.

The same was in the beginning with God.

All things were made by Him; and without Him was not anything made that was made.'" [15]

In other words, Augustin thought that he discerned complete harmony between the prologue of John's gospel and the teachings of the Platonists, and in this teaching, thus corroborated, he found the solution of the problem that had caused him such anguish of soul.

In this connection Augustin points out in some detail the features that Platonism and Christianity have in common. Thus Neo-Platonism, not blindly followed, but adapted to his Christian purpose, became not only a means of deliverance to Augustin himself, but a mighty weapon for the combating of Manichæan error.

Neo-Platonism enters so largely and influentially into Augustin's polemics against Manichæism that it will be apposite here to inquire into the extent and the nature of Augustin's dependence on this system of thought.

Much has been written on this subject, especially by German and French scholars.

A brief statement of some of the more important points of contact is all that is allowable in an essay like this.

Premising, therefore, that Platonism essentially influenced the entire circle of Augustin's theological and philosophical thinking, let us first examine the Neo-Platonic and Augustinian conceptions of God. With Augustin God is absolutely simple and immutable, incomprehensible by men in their present state of existence, exalted above all human powers of thought or expression.

All things may be said of God, and yet nothing worthily; God is honored more by reverential silence than by any human voice.

He is better known by not being known; it is easier to say what He is not, than what He is.

God is wanting in qualities; has no variety and multitude of properties and attributes; is absolutely simple.

By no means is God to be called substance, for the word substance pertains to a certain accident; nor is it allowable to think of Him as composed of substance and of accidents.

Divine qualities are therefore purely subjective.

There is no discrimination in God of substance and accidents, of potency and act, of matter and form, of universal and singular, of superior and inferior.

To know, to will, to do, to be, are in God equivalent and identical.

Eternity itself is the substance of God, which has nothing mutable, nothing past, nothing future.

God makes new things, without being Himself new, unchangeable He makes changeable things, He always works and always rests.

The changes that take place in the world do not fall in the will of God, but solely in the things moved by God.

God changes them out of His unchangeable counsel.

For nearly every one of these statements an almost exact parallel can be pointed out in the writings of Plotinus, the Neo-Platonic writer with whom Augustin was most conversant. [16]It would be easy to point out that Augustin here goes to a dangerous extreme, and narrowly escapes fatalism on the one hand, and denial of the true personality of God on the other.

But the effectiveness of this type of teaching against Manichæism is what chiefly interests us in this connection.

Readers of the following treatises will have no difficulty in seeing for themselves how confidently and with what telling effect Augustin employs this view of God against the crudities of Manichæism, which thought of God as mutable, as capable of being successfully assailed by evil, as rent asunder, as suffering miserable contamination and imprisonment by mixture with matter, as painfully struggling for freedom, as suffering with the suffering of plants and animals, as liberated by their decay and by the digestive operations of the faithful, etc., etc.

Again, while still a Manichæan Augustin had thought and written much about beauty.

On this point also, the throwing off of Manichæism and the adoption of a Platonizing Christianity brought about a revolution in his conceptions.

The exactness with which he has followed Plotinus in his ideas of the beauty of God and of his creatures is remarkable. This we could fully illustrate by the citation of parallel passages. But we must content ourselves with remarking that Augustin himself acknowledged his indebtedness, and that his idea of beauty was an important factor in his polemics against Manichæism.

According to Augustin (and Plotinus) God is the most beautiful and splendid of all beings.

He is the beauty of all beauties; all the beautiful things that are the objects of our vision and love He Himself made.

If these are beautiful what is He?

All beauty is from the highest beauty, which is God.

Augustin follows Plato and Plotinus even in neglecting the distinction between the good and the beautiful.

The idea of Divine beauty Augustin applies to Christ also.

He speaks of Him as beautiful God, beautiful Word with God, beautiful on earth, beautiful in the womb, beautiful in the hands of his parents, beautiful in miracles, beautiful in being scourged, beautiful when inciting to life, beautiful when not caring for death, beautiful when laying down his life, beautiful when taking it up again, beautiful in the sepulchre, beautiful in Heaven.

The beauty of the creation, which is simply a reflection of the beauty of God, is not even disturbed by evil or sin. Beauty is with Augustin (and the Platonists) a comprehensive term, and is almost equivalent to perfect harmony or symmetry of parts, perfect adaptation of beings to the ends for which they exist.

It is patent that this view of the beauty of God and His creation is diametrically opposed to the crude conceptions of Mani, with reference to the disorder of the universe, a disorder not confined even to the Kingdom of Darkness, but invading the Realm of light itself.

So also Augustin's Platonizing views of the creation must be taken into consideration in judging of his attitude towards Manichæism.

It goes without saying that from Augustin's theological point of view, to account for creation is a matter of grave difficulty.

How can there be a relation between the infinite and the finite?

Any substantial connection is unthinkable.

The only thing left is a relation of causality.

The finite, according to Plotinus, is an accident, an image and shadow of God.

It is constituted, established, sustained, and nourished by the Divine potency, and is therefore absolutely dependent upon God.

The power that flows from God permeates each and every finite thing.

God as one, whole, and indivisible, is perpetually present with his eternal process, to everything, everywhere.

When Augustin teaches that God of his own free will, subject to no necessity, by His own Word created the world out of nothing, this statement might be taken in connection with his view of the absolute simplicity of God and the consequent denial of distinction between being, willing, doing, etc.

The easiest way to get over the difficulty involved in creation was to maintain the simultaneous creation of all things.

The six days of creation in Genesis are an accommodation to human modes of thinking.

In some expressions Augustin approaches the Platonic doctrine of the ideal or archetypal world.

Finite things, so far as they exist, are essence, i.e., God; so far as they are not essence they do not exist at all.

Thus the distinction between God and the world is almost obliterated.

Again, whatever is finite and derivative is subject to negation or nothingness.

Thus he goes along with Plato and Plotinus to the verge of denying the reality of derived existence, and so narrowly escapes pantheism.

It is easy to see how effectively this conception of creation might be employed against the Manichæan notion of the creation as something forced upon God by the powers of evil, and as a mere expedient for the gradual liberation of his imprisoned elements.

The Manichæan limitation of God and his domain by the bordering Kingdom of Darkness, was in sheer opposition to Augustin's view of the indivisibility of God and his presence as a whole everywhere and always.

Augustin's theory that nature or essence, as far as it has existence is God, is quite the antithesis of Mani's dualism, especially of his supposition that the Kingdom of Darkness is essentially and wholly evil.

Augustin argued that even the inhabitants of the Kingdom of Darkness, and the King of Darkness himself, according to Mani's own representations, are good so far as they have essence or nature, and evil only so far as they are non-existent.

With Augustin's Platonizing view of creation is closely connected his theory of evil and his doctrine of divine providence.

Evil with him, as with the Platonists, has no substantial existence.

It is only privation of good.

It is wanting in essence, substance, truth,--is in short mere negation, and so cannot have God for its efficient cause or author, or be referred to God.

God would not have permitted evil unless by His own supreme power he had been able to make good use of it.

He attempts, with some success, to show the advantages of the permission of evil in the world.

God made all things good from the angels of heaven to the lowest beasts and herbs of the earth.

Augustin delighted, with the Platonists, in dwelling upon the goodness of nature as shown in the animal and vegetable worlds, as well as in the great cosmical phenomena.

Each creature of God has its place, some a higher, some a lower, but all so far as they conform to the idea of their creation, or to their nature, are good.

So far as they fall short of this idea they are evil.

This principle Augustin applied with great force to the confutation of the Manichæan view of the substantiality and permanence of evil.

This may be regarded as the central point in Augustin's controversies with the Manichæans.

He evidently felt that the Manichæan view of evil was the citadel of their system, and he never wearied of assailing it.

It would be beyond the scope of the present essay to inquire whether and how far Augustin himself became involved in error, in his efforts to dislodge the Manichæans.

Far less satisfactory than his confutation of the fundamental principles of the Manichæan system were his answers to the Manichæan cavils against the Old Testament.

If we may judge from the prominence given in the extant literature to the Old Testament question, this must have been the favorite point of attack with the Manichæans.

The importance of the questions raised and the necessity of answering them was fully recognized by Augustin.

His principal reliance is the allegorical or typological method of interpretation. It would be hard to find examples of more perverse allegorizing than Augustin's Anti-Manichæan treatises furnish.

It will not be needful to adduce instances here, as readers of the treatises will discover them in abundance.

Nothing more wearisome and disgusting in Biblical interpretation can well be conceived of than certain sections of The Reply to Faustus, the Manichæan.

Yet Augustin did not fail entirely to recognize the distinction between Old Testament times and New, and he even suggests the theory "that God could in a former age and to a people of a lower moral standard, give commands to do actions, which we should think it wrong to do now.... There was a certain inward want, an unenlightenment, a rudeness of moral conception, in those to whom such commands were given; otherwise they would not have been given.

God would not have given a command to slaughter a whole nation to an enlightened people."
17

Yet with all the defects of Augustin's polemics against the Manichæans, they seem to have been adapted to the needs of the time.

Well does Canon Mozley declare Augustin to have been "the most marvellous controversial phenomenon which the whole history of the Church from first to last presents.... Armed with superabundant facility of expression,--so that he himself observes that one who had written so much must have a good deal to answer for,--he was able to hammer any point of view which he wanted, and which was desirable as a counteracting one to a pervading heresy, with endless repetition upon the ear of the Church; at the same time varying the forms of speech sufficiently to please and enliven."

Certainly he was one of the greatest debaters of any age.

He doubtless deserves the credit of completely checking the progress of Manichæism in the West, and of causing its gradual but almost complete overthrow.

His arguments were probably more effective in guarding Christians against perversion by Manichæan proselytizers, than in converting those that were already ensnared by Manichæan error.

Other controversies of a completely different character, especially the Pelagian, caused Augustin to look to other aspects of truth and so led to certain modifications in his own statements, nay led him on some occasions to the verge of Manichæan error itself.

But we are chiefly interested at present in knowing that his earnest efforts against the Manichæans from A.D. 388, the year of his baptism, to A.D. 405, were not in vain. [18]

Chapter X - Outline of Manichæan History [19]

In the East Mani's followers were involved in the persecution that resulted in his death, and many of them fled to Transoxiania.

Their headquarters and the residence of the chief of the sect continued to be Babylon.

They returned to Persia in 661, but were driven back, 908-32.

They seem to have become very numerous in the Transoxiania. Albîrûnî, 973-1048, speaks of the Manichæans as still existing in large numbers throughout all Mohammedan lands, and especially in the region of Samarkand, where they were known as Sabeans.

He also relates that they were prevalent among the Eastern Turks, in China, Thibet and India.

In Armenia and Cappadocia they gained many followers, and thence made their way into Europe.

The Paulicians are commonly represented as a Manichæan party, but the descriptions that have come down to us would seem to indicate Marcionitic rather than Manichæan elements.

Yet contemporary Catholic writers such as Peter Siculus and Photius constantly assail them as Manichæans.

In the West we have traces of their existence from 287 onwards. Diocletian, according to a somewhat doubtful tradition, condemned its leaders to the stake, and its adherents to decapitation with confiscation of goods.

The edict is supposed to have been directed to the pro-consul of Africa where Manichæans were making great progress. According to an early account, Mani sent a special envoy to Africa. Valentinian (372) and Theodosius (381) issued bloody edicts against them, yet we find them still aggressive in the time of Augustin.

From Africa Manichæism spread into Spain, Gaul and Aquitaine.

Leo the Great and Valentinian III. took measures against them in Italy (440 sq.). They appear, however, to have continued their work, for Gregory the Great mentions them (590 sq.).

From this time onwards their influence is to be traced in such parties as the Euchites, Enthusiasts, Bogomiles, Catharists, Beghards, etc.

But it is not safe to attach too much importance to the mere fact that these parties were stigmatized as Manichæans by their enemies.

Even in the Reformation time and since, individuals and small parties have appeared which in some features strongly resembled the ancient Manichæans.

Manichæism was a product of the East, and in the East it met with most acceptance.

To the spirit of the West it was altogether foreign, and only in a greatly modified form could it ever have flourished there.

It might persist for centuries as a secret society, but it could not endure the light.

Footnotes:

1. Baur discredits this claim on internal grounds (Das Manich. Religionssystem, p. 7).

2. Indian Wisdom, 3rd ed. (1876), p. 49.

3. Lenormant, Chaldean Magic (1877), p. 144-145.

4. Ibid. p. 146-147.

5. Ibid. p. 148.

6. Ante-Nicene Library, Am. ed. vol. vi. pp. 182 and 188.

7. Ibid. p. 241.

8. Outlines of the Hist. of Religion (1877), p. 173.

Cf. J. Darmsteter, Introduction to the Zend-Avesta, p. xliii., xliv., lvi., lxxii., lxxiv. sq.; and his article in the Contemporary Review (Oct. 1879), on "The Supreme God in the Indo-European Mythology."

9. This is confidently asserted by Kessler (Art. Mani in Herzog's RE, 2d ed. vol. IX. p. 258), and after him by Harnack, Encyclopædia Britannica, art. Manichæism.

On the other hand, Lenormant (Anc. Hist. II. p. 30), says:

"Ahriman had been eternal in the past, he had no beginning, and proceeded from no former being * * *.

This being who had no beginning would come to an end. * * *.

Evil then should be finally conquered and destroyed, the creation should become as pure as on its first day, and Ahriman should disappear forever."

Such, doubtless, was the original doctrine, but the form probably in vogue in the time of Mani was more pantheistic or monotheistic, both Ormuzd and Ahriman proceeding from boundless time (Zrvan akarana).

See on this matter, Darmsteter:

Introd. to the Zend-Avesta, p. lxxii, etc., and his art. in Contemp. Review; and Lenormant:

Anc. Hist. as above.

10. That meat is used in the sense of flesh may be inferred from Darmsteter's comment on this passage, which he suggests may be a bit of religious polemics against Manichæism.

See his Introd. to the Zend-Avesta, p. xl. sq.

11. Das Manichäische Religionssystem, p. 433 sq.

12. Church Hist. vol. I.

13. Cunningham, St. Austin and his Place in the History of Christian Thought (1886), has these remarks on the relation of Mani to Buddhism: "Mani was indeed a religious reformer:

deeply impregnated with the belief and practice which Buddhist monks were spreading in the East, he tried with some success to reform the religion of Zoroaster in Persia [i.e. the Persian Empire], his native land.

While his fundamental doctrine, the root of his system, was of Persian origin, and he figured the universe to himself as if it were given over to the unending conflict between the Powers of Light and Darkness, in regard to discipline his system very closely resembles that founded by Buddha; the elect of the Manichæans correspond to the Buddhist monks;

the precepts about abstinence from meat and things of sense are, if not borrowed from the rules Gotama gave for the conduct of his followers, the outcome of the same principles about the nature of man."

Harnack, art. Manichæism in Ency. Britannica, follows Kessler in attaching slight importance to the Buddhist influence on Manichæism, preferring, with him, to derive nearly all of the features ascribed by Baur, Neander and others to Buddhist influence, to the old Babylonian religion, the precise character of which, in the time of Mani, is imperfectly understood.

Harnack's (and Kessler's) statements must therefore be taken with some allowance.

There is no objection, however, to supposing that Mani derived from the old Babylonian party or parties with which he came in contact religious principles which were wrought out in detail under the influence of Buddhism.

This is in fact what probably occurred.

14. Encyclopædia Britannica, art. Manichæism.

15. Confessions, Book. VII. ch. 9, vol. 1. p. 108, of the present series.

16. See G. Loesche:

De Augustino Plotinizante in Doctrina de Deo Disserenda, Jenæ, 1880.

Also, Dorner:

Augustinus, Zeller, Ueberweg, Ritter, and Erdmann:

Histories of Philosophy, sections on Augustin and Neo-Platonism.

17. See J. B. Mozley's Ruling Ideas in Early Ages, art. The Manichæans and the Jewish Fathers.

The sentence quoted above is Mozley's.

18. For an account of the controversies in which Augustin was engaged with the Manichæans, and for the chronological order of the Anti-Manichæan treatises, see the Preface of the Edinburgh editor.

Cf. Bindemann, on the various controversies, in his Der h. Augustinus, passim.

See also, a good chronological list of St. Augustin's works in Cunningham:

St. Austin, p. 277 sq.

19. Compare Professor George T. Stokes' excellent article Manichæans, in Smith and Wace:

Dict. of Chr. Biography, vol. III. p. 798 sq.

Philip Schaff, D.D., LL.D.

Preface to the Anti-Manichæan Writings.

No reader of the accompanying volume can be expected to take a very lively interest in its contents, unless he has before his mind some facts regarding the extraordinary genius to whom the heresy of Manichæism owes its origin and its name.

His history is involved in considerable obscurity, owing to the suspicious nature of the documents from which it is derived, and the difficulty of constructing a consistent and probable account out of the contradictory statements of the Asiatics and the Greeks.

The ascertained facts, therefore, are few, and may be briefly stated. [20]

According to the Chronicle of Edessa, Mani was born A.D. 240. [21] From his original name, Corbicius or Carcubius, Beausobre conjectures that he was born in Carcub, a town of Chaldæa.

He belonged to a Magian family, and while still a youth won a distinguished place among the sages of Persia.

He was master of all the lore peculiar to his class, and was, besides, so proficient a mathematician and geographer, that he was able to construct a globe.

He was a skilled musician, and had some knowledge of the Greek language,--an accomplishment rare among his countrymen.

But his fame, and even his ultimate success as a teacher, was due in great measure to his skill in painting, which was so considerable as to earn for him among the Persians the distinctive title, Mani the painter.

His disposition was ardent and lively but patient and self-restrained.

His appearance was striking, as he wore the usual dress of a Persian sage:

the high-soled shoes, the one red, the other green; the mantle of azure blue, that changed color as he moved; the ebony staff in his right hand, and the Babylonish book under his left arm.

The meaning of his name, Mani, Manes, or Manichæus, has been the subject of endless conjectures.

Epiphanius supposes that he was providentially so named, that men might be warned against the mania of his heresy. [22]Hyde, whose opinion on any Oriental subject must have weight, tells us that in Persian mani means painter, and that he was so called from his profession.

Archbishop Usher conjectured that it was a form of Manaem or Menahem, which means Paraclete or Comforter; founding this conjecture on the fact that Sulpicius Severus calls the Israelitish king Menahem, [23] Mane.

Gataker supplements this idea by the conjecture that Mani took this name at his own instance, and in pursuance of his claim to be the Paraclete.

It is more probable that, if his name was really given on account of this meaning, he received it from the widow who seems to have adopted him when a boy, and may have called him her Consolation.

But it is also possible that Mani was not an uncommon Persian name, and that he adopted it for some reason too trifling to discover. [24]

While still a young man he was ordained as a Christian priest, and distinguished himself in that capacity by his knowledge of Scripture, and the zeal with which he discharged his sacred functions. [25]His heretical tendencies, however, were very soon manifested, stimulated, we may suppose, by his anxiety to make the Christian religion more acceptable to those who adhered to the Eastern systems.

Excommunicated from the Christian Church, Mani found asylum with Sapor, and won his confidence by presenting only the Magian side of his system.

But no sooner did he permit the Christian element to appear, and call himself the apostle of the Lord, and show a desire to reform Magianism, than his sovereign determined to put him to death as a revolutionist. Forced to flee, he took refuge in Turkestan, and gained influence there, partly by decorating the temples with paintings.

To lend his doctrines the appearance of divine authority, he adopted the same device as Zoroaster and Mohammed.

Having discovered a cave through which there ran a rill of water, he laid up in it a store of provisions, and retired there for a year, giving out that he was on a visit to heaven.

In this retirement he produced his Gospel, [26] --a work illustrated with symbolical drawings the

37

ingenuity of which has been greatly praised.

This book Mani presented to Hormizdas, the son and successor of Sapor, who professed himself favorable to his doctrine, and even built him a castle as a place of shelter and retirement.

Unfortunately for Mani, Hormizdas died in the second year of his reign; and though his successor, Varanes, was at first willing to shield him from persecution, yet, finding that the Magians were alarmed for their religion, he appointed a disputation to be held between the opposing parties.

Such trials of dialectic in Eastern courts have not unfrequently resulted in very serious consequences to the parties engaged in them.

In this instance the result was fatal to Mani.

Worsted in argument, he was condemned to die, and thus perished in some sense as a martyr.

The mode of his death is uncertain, [27] but it seems that his skin was stuffed with chaff, and hung up in public in terrorem.

This occurred in the year 277, and the anniversary was commemorated as the great religious festival of the Manichæans.

This is not the place to attempt any account or criticism of the strange eclecticism of Mani.[28] An adequate idea of the system may be gathered from the accompanying treatises.

It may, however, be desirable to give some account of the original sources of information regarding it.

We study the systems of heresiarchs at a disadvantage when our only means of ascertaining their opinions is from the fragmentary quotations and hostile criticism which occur in the writings of their adversaries.

Such, however, is our only source of information regarding the teaching of Mani.

Originally, indeed, this heresy was specially active in a literary direction, assailing the Christian Scriptures with an ingenuity of unbelief worthy of a later age, and apparently ambitious of promulgating a rival canon.

Certainly the writings of its early supporters were numerous; [29] and from the care and elegance with which they were transcribed, the sumptuous character of the manuscripts, and the mysterious emblems with which they were adorned, we should fancy it was intended to inspire the people with respect for an authoritative though as yet undefined code.

It is, indeed, nowhere said or implied that the sacred books of the Manichæans were reserved for the eye only of the initiated or elect; and their reception of the New Testament Scriptures (subject to their own revision and emendation) would make it difficult for them to establish any secret code apart from these writings.

They were certainly, however, doctrines of an esoteric kind, which were not divulged to the catechumens or hearers; and many of their books, being written in Persian, Syriac, or Greek, were practically unavailable for the instruction of the Latin speaking population.

It was not always easy, therefore, to obtain an accurate knowledge of their opinions. Commentaries on the whole of the Old and New Testaments were written by Hierax; [30] a Theosophy by Aristocritus; a book of memoirs, or rather Memorabilia, of Mani, and other works, by Heraclides, Aphthonius, Adas, and Agapius.

Unfortunately all of these books have perished, whether in the flames to which the Christian authorities commanded that all Manichæan books should be consigned, or by the slower if not more critical and impartial processes of time.

Mani himself was the author of several works:

a Gospel, the Treasury of Life (and probably an abridgment of the same), the Mysteries, the Foundation Fpistle, a book of Articles or heads of doctrine, one or two works on astronomy or astrology, and a collection of letters so dangerous, that Manichæans who sought restoration to the Church were required to anathematize them.

Probably the most important of these writings was the Foundation Epistle, so called because it contained the leading articles of doctrine on which the new system was built.

This letter was written in Greek or Syriac; but a Latin version of it was current in Africa, and came into the hands of Augustin, who undertook its refutation.

To accomplish this with the greater precision and effect, he quotes the entire text of each passage of the Epistle before proceeding to criticise it.

Had Augustin accomplished the whole of his task, we should accordingly have been in possession of the whole of this important document.

Unfortunately, for reasons unknown, Augustin stops short at an early point in the Epistle; and though he tells us he had notes on the remainder, and would some day expand and publish them, this promise lay unredeemed for thirty years till the day of his death.

Extracts from the same Epistle and from the Treasury are also given by Augustin in the treatise De Natura Boni. [31]

Next, we have in the Opus Imperfectum of Augustin some extracts from a letter of Mani to Menoch, which Julian had unearthed and republished to convict Augustin of being still tainted with Manichæan sentiments. These extracts give us some insight into the heresiarch's opinions regarding the corruption of nature and the evils of sexual love.

Again, we have Mani's letter to Marcel, preserved by Epiphanius, and given in full by Beausobre;[32] which, however, merely reiterates two of the doctrines most certainly identified with Mani,--the assertion of two principles, and the tenet that the Son of God was man only in appearance.

Finally, Fabricius has inserted in the fifth volume of his Bibliotheca Græca the fragments, such as they are, collected by Grabe.

Such is the fragmentary character of the literary remains of Mani:

for fuller information regarding his opinions we must depend on Theodoret, Epiphanius, Alexander of Lycopolis, Titus of Bostra, and Augustin. Beausobre is of opinion that the Fathers derived all that they knew of Manichæus from the Acts of Archelaus.[33] This professes to be a report of a disputation held between Manes and Archelaus, bishop of Caschar in Mesopotamia.

Grave doubts have been cast on the authenticity of this document, and Burton and Milman seem inclined to consider it an imaginary dialogue, and use it on the understanding that while some of its statements are manifestly untrustworthy, a discriminating reader may gather from it some reliable material.[34]

In the works of Augustin there are some other pieces which may well be reckoned among the original sources.

In the reply to Faustus, which is translated in this volume, the book of Faustus is not indeed reproduced; but there is no reason for doubting that his arguments are fairly represented, and we think there is evidence that even the original expression of them is preserved.[35] Augustin had been acquainted with Faustus for many years.

He first met him at Carthage in 383, and found him nothing more than a clever and agreeable talker, making no pretension to science or philosophy, and with only slender reading.[36] His cleverness is sufficiently apparent in his debate with Augustin; the objections he leads are plausible, and put with acuteness, but at the same time with a flippancy which betrays a want of earnestness and real interest in the questions.

In his reply to Faustus, Augustin is very much on the defensive, and his statements are apologetic rather than systematic.[37]

But in an age when the ability to read was by no means commensurate with the interest taken in theological questions, written discussions were necessarily supplemented by public disputations.

These theological contests seem to have been a popular entertainment in North Africa; the people attending in immense crowds, while reporters took down what was said on either side for the sake of appeal as well as for the information of the absent.

In two such disputations Augustin engaged in connection with Manichæism.[38] The first was held on the 28th and 29th of August, 392, with a Manichæan priest, Fortunatus.

To this encounter Augustin was invited by a deputation of Donatists and Catholics,[39] who were alike alarmed at the progress which this heresy was making in the district of Hippo.

Fortunatus at first showed some reluctance to meet so formidable an antagonist, but was prevailed upon by his own sectaries, and shows no nervousness during the debate. His incompetence, however, was manifest to the Manichæans themselves; and so hopeless was it to think of any further proselytizing in Hippo, that he left that city, and was too much ashamed of himself ever to return.

The character of his reasoning is shifty; he evades Augustin's questions and starts fresh ones. Augustin pushes his usual and fundamental objection to the Manichæan system.

If God is impassable and incorruptible, how could He be injured by the assaults of the kingdom of darkness?

In opposition to the statement of Fortunatus, that the Almighty produces no evil, he explains that God made no nature evil, but made man free, and that voluntary sin is the grand original evil.

The most remarkable circumstance in the discussion is the desire of Fortunatus to direct the conversation to the conduct of the Manichæans, and the refusal of Augustin to make good the charges which had been made against them, or to discuss anything but the doctrine.[40]

Twelve years after this, a similar disputation was held between Augustin and one of the elect among the Manichæans, who had come to Hippo to propagate his religion.

This man, Felix, is described by Augustin[41] as being ill-educated, but more adroit and subtle than Fortunatus.

After a keen discussion, which occupied two days, the proceedings terminated by Felix signing a recantation of his errors in the form of an anathema on Mani, his doctrines, and the seducing spirit that possessed him.

These two disputations are valuable, as exhibiting the points of the Manichæan system to which its own adherents were accustomed to direct attention, and the arguments on which they specially relied for their support.

The works given in the accompanying volume comprehend by no means the whole of Augustin's writings against this heresy.

Before his ordination he wrote five anti-Manichæan books, entitled, De Libero Arbitrio, De Genesi contra Manichæos, De Moribus Ecclesiæ Catholicæ, De Moribus Manichæorum, and De Vera Religione.

These Paulinus called his anti-Manichæan Pentateuch.

After his ordination he was equally diligent, publishing a little treatise in the year 391, under the title De Utilitate Credendi, [42] which was immediately followed by a small work, De Duabus Animabus.

In the following year the report of the Disputatio contra Fortunatum was published; and after this, at short intervals, there appeared the books Contra Adimantum, Contra Epistolam Manichæi quam vocant Fundamenti, Contra Faustum, Disputatio contra Felicem, De Naturo Boni, and Contra Secundinum.

Besides these writings, which are exclusively occupied with Manichæism, there are others in which the Manichæan doctrines are handled with more or less directness.

These are the Confessions, the 79th and 236th Letters, the Lecture on Psalm 140, Sermons 1, 2, 12, 50, 153, 182, 237, the Liber de Agone Christiano, and the De Continentia.

Of these writings, Augustin himself professed a preference for the reply to the letter of Secundinus. [43] It is a pleasing feature of the times, that a heretic whom he did not know even by sight should write to Augustin entreating him to abstain from writing against the Manichæans, and reconsider his position, and ally himself with those whom he had till now fancied to be in error.

His language is respectful, and illustrates the esteem in which Augustin was held by his contemporaries; though he does not scruple to insinuate that his conversion from Manichæism was due to motives not of the highest kind. We have not given this letter and its reply, because the preference of Augustin has not been ratified by the judgment of his readers.

The present volume gives a fair sample of Augustin's controversial powers.

His nine years' personal experience of the vanity of Manichæism made him thoroughly earnest and sympathetic in his efforts to disentangle other men from its snares, and also equipped him with the knowledge requisite for this task.

No doubt the Pelagian controversy was more congenial to his mind.

His logical acuteness and knowledge of Scripture availed him more in combating men who fought with the same weapons, than in dealing with a system which threw around its positions the mist of Gnostic speculation, or veiled its doctrine under a grotesque mythology, or based itself on a cosmogony too fantastic for a Western mind to tolerate. [44] But however Augustin may have misconceived the strange forms in which this system was presented, there is no doubt that he comprehended and demolished its fundamental principles; [45] that he did so as a necessary part of his own personal search for the truth; and that in doing so he gained possession, vitally and permanently of ideas and principles which subsequently entered into all he thought and wrote.

In finding his way through the mazes of the obscure region into which Mani had led him, he once for all ascertained the true relation subsisting between God and His creatures, formed his opinion regarding the respective provinces of reason and faith, and the connection of the Old and New Testaments, and found the root of all evil in the created will.

The Editor.

Some knowledge of the Magianism of the time of Mani may be obtained from the sacred books of the Parsis, especially from the Vendidad Sade, an account of which is given by Dr. Wilson, of Bombay, in his book on the Parsi Religion.--Tr.

Footnotes:

20. Beausobre (Histoire Critique de Manichée et du Manichéisme, Amst. 1734, 2 vols.) has collected everything that is known of Mani.

The original sources are here sifted with unusual acuteness, and with great and solid learning, though the author's strong "bias in favor of a heretic" frequently leads him to make unwarranted statements.

Burton's estimate of this entertaining and indispensable work (Heresies of Apostol. Age, p. xxi.), is much fairer than Pusey's (Aug. Conf. p. 314).

A brief account of Mani and his doctrines is given by Milman with his usual accuracy, impartiality and lucidity (Hist. of Christianity, ii. 259, ed. 1867).

For any one who wishes to investigate the subject further, ample references are there given.

A specimen of the confusion that involves the history of Mani will be found in the account given by Socrates (Hist. i. 22).

21. [For the Oriental accounts of Mani's parentage and youth, see the Introductory Essay, and the works there referred to.--A.H.N.]

22. See also Eusebius: Hist. Eccl. vii. 31, with Heinichen's note.

23. 2 Kings xv. 14.

24. "Peut-être cherchons nous du mystere, ou il n'y en a point."--Beausobre, i. 79.

25. [This is in the highest degree improbable.--A.H.N.]

26. Called Erteng or Arzeng, i.e., according to Renaudot, an illustrated book.

27. Böhringer adopts the more horrible tradition.

"Sein Schicksal war, dass er von den Christen, von den Magiern verfolgt, nach mannig fachem Wechsel unter Bahram lebendig geschunden wurde" (p. 386).

28. Böhringer characterizes it briefly in the words:

"Es ist der alte heidnische Dualismus mit seiner Naturtheologie, der in Mani's Systeme seine letzten Kräfte sammelt und unter der gleissenden Hülle christlicher Worte und Formen an den reinen Monotheismus des Christenthums und dessen reine Ethik sich heranwagt "

29. Aug. c. Faustum, xiii. 6 and 18. [See full list of Mani's writings in Kessler's art. in Herzog, R.E.--A.H.N.]

30. Lardner, however, seems to prove that Hierax was not a Manichæan, though some of his opinions approximated to this heresy.

The whole subject of the Manichæan literature is treated by Lardner (Works, iii. p. 374), with the learning of Beausobre and more than Beausobre's impartiality.

31. The De Natura Boni, written in the year 405, is necessarily very much a reproduction of what is elsewhere affirmed, that all natures are good, and created by God, who alone is immutable and incorruptible.

It presents concisely the leading positions of Augustin in this controversy, and concludes with an eloquent prayer that his efforts may be blessed to the conversion of the heretics,--not the only passage which demonstrates that he wrote not for the glory of victory so much as for the deliverance of men from fatal error.

32. Histoire, i. 91.

33. Published by Zaccagni in his Collectanea Monumentorum Veterum, Romæ, 1698; and by Routh his Reliquiæ Sacræ, vol. v., in which all the material for forming an opinion regarding it is collected.

34. Any one who consults Beausobre on this point will find that historical criticism is not of so recent an origin as some persons seem to think.

It is worth transcribing his own account of the spirit in which he means to do his work:

"Je traiterai mon sujet en Critique, suivant la Regle de S. Paul, Examinez toutes choses, et ne retenez que ce qui est bon.

L'Histoire en general, et l'Histoire Ecclesiastique en particulier, n'est bien souvent qu'un mélange confus de faux et de vrai, entassé par des Ecrivains mal instruits, credules ou passionez. Cela convient surtout a l'Histoire des Heretiques et des Heresies. C'est au Lecteur attentif et judicieux d'en faire le discernement, a l'aide d'une critique, qui ne soit trop timide, ni temeraire.

Sans le secours de cet art, on erre dans l'Histoire comme un Pilote sur les mers, lorsqu'il n'a ni boussole, ni carte marine" (i. 7).

35. Beausobre and Cave suppose that we have the whole of Faustus' book embodied in Augustin's review of it.

Lardner is of opinion that the commencement, and perhaps the greater part, of the work is given, but not the whole.

36. See the interesting account of Faustus in the Confessions, v. 10.

37. [This estimate of Faustus is somewhat too disparaging.

For fuller bibliography, see Introductory Essay.--A.H.N.]

38. His willingness to do so, and the success with which he encountered the most renowned champions of this heresy, should have prevented Beausobre from charging him with misunderstanding or misrepresenting the Manichæan doctrine.

The retractation of Felix tells strongly against this view of Augustin's incompetence to deal with Manichæism.

39. Possidius. Vita Aug. vi.

40. This cannot but make us cautious in receiving the statements of the tract, On the Morals of the Manichæans.

There can be little doubt that many of the Manichæans practiced the ascetic virtues, and were recognizable by the gauntness and pallor of their looks, so that Manichæan became a by-word for any one who did not appreciate the felicity of good living.

Thus Jerome says of a certain class of women, "quam viderint pallentem atque tristem, Miseram, Monacham, et Manichæan vocant" (De Custod. Virg. Ep. 18).

Lardner throws light on the practices of the Manichæans, and effectually disposes of some of the calumnies uttered regarding them.

Pusey's appendix to his translation of the Confessions may also be referred to with advantage.

41. Retract. ii. 8.

42. Epist. August. xxv.

43. Retract. ii. 10:

"quod, mea sententia, omnibus quoe adversus illam pestem scribere potui, facile præpono."

The reason of this preference is explained by Bindemann, Der heilige Augstinus, iii. 168.

44. "Wo Entwickelungen, dialektische Begriffe sein sollten, stellt sich ein Bild, ein Mythus ein."--Böhringer, p. 390.

45. Some have thought Augustin more successful here than elsewhere. Cassiodorus may have thought so when he said:

"diligentius atque vivacius adversus eos quam contra hæreses alias disseruit" (Instit. i. quoted by Lardner).

Philip Schaff, D.D., LL.D.

On the Morals of the Catholic Church
[de moribus ecclesiæ catholicæ].
A.D. 388.
translated by the rev. richard stothert, m.a., bombay

Of the Morals of the Catholic Church. [46]
[De Moribus Ecclesiæ Catholicæ]. a.d. 388.

It is laid down at the outset that the customs of the holy life of the Church should be referred to the chief good of man, that is, God.

We must seek after God with supreme affection; and this doctrine is supported in the Catholic Church by the authority of both Testaments. The four virtues get their names from different forms of this love. Then follow the duties of love to our neighbor.

In the Catholic Church we find examples of continence and of true Christian conduct.

Chapter 1 - How the Pretensions of the Manichæans are to Be Refuted. Two Manichæan Falsehoods

1.

Enough, probably, has been done in our other books [47] in the way of answering the ignorant and profane attacks which the Manichæans make on the law, which is called the Old Testament, in a spirit of vainglorious boasting, and with the approval of the uninstructed. Here, too, I may shortly touch upon the subject.

For every one with average intelligence can easily see that the explanation of the Scriptures should be sought for from those who are the professed teachers of the Scriptures; and that it may happen, and indeed always happens, that many things seem absurd to the ignorant, which, when they are explained by the learned, appear all the more excellent, and are received in the explanation with the greater pleasure on account of the obstructions which made it difficult to reach the meaning.

This commonly happens as regards the holy books of the Old Testament, if only the man who meets with difficulties applies to a pious teacher, and not to a profane critic, and if he begins his inquiries from a desire to find truth, and not in rash opposition.

And should the inquirer meet with some, whether bishops or presbyters, or any officials or ministers of the Catholic Church, who either avoid in all cases opening up mysteries, or, content with simple faith, have no desire for more recondite knowledge, he must not despair of finding the knowledge of the truth in a case where neither are all able to teach to whom the inquiry is addressed, nor are all inquirers worthy of learning the truth.

Diligence and piety are both necessary:
on the one hand, we must have knowledge to find truth, and, on the other hand, we must deserve to get the knowledge.

2.

But as the Manichæans have two tricks for catching the unwary, so as to make them take them as teachers,--one, that of finding fault with the Scriptures, which they either misunderstand or wish to be misunderstood, the other, that of making a show of chastity and of notable abstinence,--this book shall contain our doctrine of life and morals according to Catholic teaching, and will perhaps make it appear how easy it is to pretend to virtue, and how difficult to possess virtue.

I will refrain, if I can, from attacking their weak points, which I know well, with the violence with which they attack what they know nothing of; for I wish them, if possible, to be cured rather than conquered.

And I will quote such testimonies from the Scriptures as they are bound to believe, for they shall be from the New Testament; and even from this I will take none of the passages which the Manichæans when hard pressed are accustomed to call spurious, but passages which they are obliged to acknowledge and approve.

And for every testimony from apostolic teaching I will bring a similar statement from the Old Testament, that if they ever become willing to wake up from their persistent dreams, and to rise towards the light of Christian faith, they may discover both how far from being Christian is the life which they profess, and how truly Christian is the Scripture which they cavil at.

Chapter 2 - He Begins with Arguments, in Compliance with the Mistaken Method of the Manichæans

3.

Where, then, shall I begin?

With authority, or with reasoning?

In the order of nature, when we learn anything, authority precedes reasoning.

For a reason may seem weak, when, after it is given, it requires authority to confirm it.

But because the minds of men are obscured by familiarity with darkness, which covers them in the night of sins and evil habits, and cannot perceive in a way suitable to the clearness and purity of reason, there is most wholesome provision for bringing the dazzled eye into the light of truth under the congenial shade of authority.

But since we have to do with people who are perverse in all their thoughts and words and actions, and who insist on nothing more than on beginning with argument, I will, as a concession to them, take what I think a wrong method in discussion.

For I like to imitate, as far as I can, the gentleness of my Lord Jesus Christ, who took on Himself the evil of death itself, wishing to free us from it.

Chapter 3 - Happiness is in the Enjoyment of Man's Chief Good. Two Conditions of the Chief Good: 1st, Nothing is Better Than It; 2d, It Cannot Be Lost Against the Will.

4.

How then, according to reason, ought man to live?

We all certainly desire to live happily; and there is no human being but assents to this statement almost before it is made.

But the title happy cannot, in my opinion, belong either to him who has not what he loves, whatever it may be, or to him who has what he loves if it is hurtful or to him who does not love what he has, although it is good in perfection.

For one who seeks what he cannot obtain suffers torture, and one who has got what is not desirable is cheated, and one who does not seek for what is worth seeking for is diseased.

Now in all these cases the mind cannot but be unhappy, and happiness and unhappiness cannot reside at the same time in one man; so in none of these cases can the man be happy.

I find, then, a fourth case, where the happy life exists,--when that which is man's chief good is both loved and possessed.

For what do we call enjoyment but having at hand the objects of love?

And no one can be happy who does not enjoy what is man's chief good, nor is there any one who enjoys this who is not happy.

We must then have at hand our chief good, if we think of living happily.

5.

We must now inquire what is man's chief good, which of course cannot be anything inferior to man himself.

For whoever follows after what is inferior to himself, becomes himself inferior.

But every man is bound to follow what is best.

Wherefore man's chief good is not inferior to man.

Is it then something similar to man himself?

It must be so, if there is nothing above man which he is capable of enjoying. But if we find something which is both superior to man, and can be possessed by the man who loves it, who can doubt that in seeking for happiness man should endeavor to reach that which is more excellent than the being who makes the endeavor.

For if happiness consists in the enjoyment of a good than which there is nothing better, which we call the chief good, how can a man be properly called happy who has not yet attained to his chief good? or how can that be the chief good beyond which something better remains for us to arrive at?

Such, then, being the chief good, it must be something which cannot be lost against the will.

For no one can feel confident regarding a good which he knows can be taken from him, although he wishes to keep and cherish it.

But if a man feels no confidence regarding the good which he enjoys, how can he be happy while in such fear of losing it?

Chapter 4 - Man--What?

6.

Let us then see what is better than man.

This must necessarily be hard to find, unless we first ask and examine what man is.

I am not now called upon to give a definition of man.

The question here seems to me to be,--since almost all agree, or at least, which is enough, those I have now to do with are of the same opinion with me, that we are made up of soul and body,--What is man?

Is he both of these? or is he the body only, or the soul only?

For although the things are two, soul and body, and although neither without the other could be called man (for the body would not be man without the soul, nor again would the soul be man if there were not a body animated by it), still it is possible that one of these may be held to be man, and may be called so.

What then do we call man?

Is he soul and body, as in a double harness, or like a centaur?

Or do we mean the body only, as being in the service of the soul which rules it, as the word lamp denotes not the light and the case together, but only the case, yet it is on account of the light that it is so called?

Or do we mean only the mind, and that on account of the body which it rules, as horseman means not the man and the horse, but the man only, and that as employed in ruling the horse?

This dispute is not easy to settle; or, if the proof is plain, the statement requires time.

This is an expenditure of time and strength which we need not incur.

For whether the name man belongs to both, or only to the soul, the chief good of man is not the chief good of the body; but what is the chief good either of both soul and body, or of the soul only, that is man's chief good.

Chapter 5 - Man's Chief Good is Not the Chief Good of the Body Only, But the Chief Good of the Soul

7.

Now if we ask what is the chief good of the body, reason obliges us to admit that it is that by means of which the body comes to be in its best state.

But of all the things which invigorate the body, there is nothing better or greater than the soul.

The chief good of the body, then, is not bodily pleasure, not absence of pain, not strength, not beauty, not swiftness, or whatever else is usually reckoned among the goods of the body, but simply the soul.

For all the things mentioned the soul supplies to the body by its presence, and, what is above them all, life.

Hence I conclude that the soul is not the chief good of man, whether we give the name of man to soul and body together, or to the soul alone.

For as according to reason, the chief good of the body is that which is better than the body, and from which the body receives vigor and life, so whether the soul itself is man, or soul and body both, we must discover whether there is anything which goes before the soul itself, in following which the soul comes to the perfection of good of which it is capable in its own kind.

If such a thing can be found, all uncertainty must be at an end, and we must pronounce this to be really and truly the chief good of man.

8.

If, again, the body is man, it must be admitted that the soul is the chief good of man.

But clearly, when we treat of morals,--when we inquire what manner of life must be held in order to obtain happiness,--it is not the body to which the precepts are addressed, it is not bodily discipline which we discuss.

In short, the observance of good customs belongs to that part of us which inquires and learns, which are the prerogatives of the soul; so, when we speak of attaining to virtue, the question does not regard the body.

But if it follows, as it does, that the body which is ruled over by a soul possessed of virtue is ruled both better and more honorably, and is in its greatest perfection in consequence of the perfection of the soul which rightfully governs it, that which gives perfection to the soul will be man's chief good, though we call the body man.

For if my coachman, in obedience to me, feeds and drives the horses he has charge of in the most satisfactory manner, himself enjoying the more of my bounty in proportion to his good conduct, can any one deny that the good condition of the horses, as well as that of the coachman, is due to me?

So the question seems to me to be not, whether soul and body is man, or the soul only, or the body only, but what gives perfection to the soul; for when this is obtained, a man cannot but be either perfect, or at least much better than in the absence of this one thing.

Chapter 6 - Virtue Gives Perfection to the Soul; The Soul Obtains Virtue by Following God; Following God is the Happy Life

9.

No one will question that virtue gives perfection to the soul.

But it is a very proper subject of inquiry whether this virtue can exist by itself or only in the soul.

Here again arises a profound discussion, needing lengthy treatment; but perhaps my summary will serve the purpose.

God will, I trust, assist me, so that, notwithstanding our feebleness, we may give instruction on these great matters briefly as well as intelligibly.

In either case, whether virtue can exist by itself without the soul, or can exist only in the soul, undoubtedly in the pursuit of virtue the soul follows after something, and this must be either the soul itself, or virtue, or something else.

But if the soul follows after itself in the pursuit of virtue, it follows after a foolish thing; for before obtaining virtue it is foolish.

Now the height of a follower's desire is to reach that which he follows after. So the soul must either not wish to reach what it follows after, which is utterly absurd and unreasonable, or, in following after itself while foolish, it reaches the folly which it flees from.

But if it follows after virtue in the desire to reach it, how can it follow what does not exist? or how can it desire to reach what it already possesses? Either, therefore, virtue exists beyond the soul, or if we are not allowed to give the name of virtue except to the habit and disposition of the wise soul, which can exist only in the soul, we must allow that the soul follows after something else in order that virtue may be produced in itself; for neither by following after nothing, nor by following after folly, can the soul, according to my reasoning, attain to wisdom.

10.

This something else then, by following after which the soul becomes possessed of virtue and wisdom, is either a wise man or God. But we have said already that it must be something that we cannot lose against our will.

No one can think it necessary to ask whether a wise man, supposing we are content to follow after him, can be taken from us in spite of our unwillingness or our persistence.

God then remains, in following after whom we live well, and in reaching whom we live both well and happily.

If any deny God's existence, why should I consider the method of dealing with them, when it is doubtful whether they ought to be dealt with at all?

At any rate, it would require a different starting-point, a different plan, a different investigation from what we are now engaged in.

I am now addressing those who do not deny the existence of God, and who, moreover, allow that human affairs are not disregarded by Him.

For there is no one, I suppose, who makes any profession of religion but will hold that divine Providence cares at least for our souls.

Chapter 7 - The Knowledge of God to Be Obtained from the Scripture. The Plan and Principal Mysteries of the Divine Scheme of Redemption

11.

But how can we follow after Him whom we do not see? or how can we see Him, we who are not only men, but also men of weak understanding? For though God is seen not with the eyes but with the mind, where can such a mind be found as shall, while obscured by foolishness, succeed or even attempt to drink in that light?

We must therefore have recourse to the instructions of those whom we have reason to think wise.

Thus far argument brings us.

For in human things reasoning is employed, not as of greater certainty, but as easier from use.

But when we come to divine things, this faculty turns away; it cannot behold; it pants, and gasps, and burns with desire; it falls back from the light of truth, and turns again to its wonted obscurity, not from choice, but from exhaustion.

What a dreadful catastrophe is this, that the soul should be reduced to greater helplessness when it is seeking rest from its toil!

So, when we are hasting to retire into darkness, it will be well that by the appointment of adorable Wisdom we should be met by the friendly shade of authority, and should be attracted by the wonderful character of its contents, and by the utterances of its pages, which, like shadows, typify and attemper the truth.

12.

What more could have been done for our salvation?

What can be more gracious and bountiful than divine providence, which, when man had fallen from its laws, and, in just retribution for his coveting mortal things, had brought forth a mortal offspring, still did not wholly abandon him?

For in this most righteous government, whose ways are strange and inscrutable, there is, by means of unknown connections established in the creatures subject to it, both a severity of punishment and a mercifulness of salvation.

How beautiful this is, how great, how worthy of God, in fine, how true, which is all we are seeking for, we shall never be able to perceive, unless, beginning with things human and at hand, and holding by the faith and the precepts of true religion, we continue without turning from it in the way which God has secured for us by the separation of the patriarchs, by the bond of the law, by the foresight of the prophets, by the witness of the apostles, by the blood of the martyrs, and by the subjugation of the Gentiles.

From this point, then, let no one ask me for my opinion, but let us rather hear the oracles, and submit our weak inferences to the announcements of Heaven. [48]

Chapter 8 - God is the Chief Good, Whom We are to Seek After with Supreme Affection

13.

Let us see how the Lord Himself in the gospel has taught us to live; how, too, Paul the apostle,--for the Manichæans dare not reject these Scriptures.

Let us hear, O Christ, what chief end Thou dost prescribe to us; and that is evidently the chief end after which we are told to strive with supreme affection.

"Thou shalt love," He says, "the Lord thy God."

Tell me also, I pray Thee, what must be the measure of love; for I fear lest the desire enkindled in my heart should either exceed or come short in fervor.

"With all thy heart," He says.

Nor is that enough.

"With all thy soul."

Nor is it enough yet.

"With all thy mind." [49]

What do you wish more?

I might, perhaps, wish more if I could see the possibility of more.

What does Paul say on this?

"We know," he says, "that all things issue in good to them that love God."

Let him, too, say what is the measure of love.

"Who then," he says, "shall separate us from the love of Christ? shall tribulation, or distress, or persecution, or famine, or nakedness, or peril, or the sword?" [50]We have heard, then, what and how much we must love; this we must strive after, and to this we must refer all our plans.

The perfection of all our good things and our perfect good is God.

We must neither come short of this nor go beyond it:

the one is dangerous, the other impossible.

Chapter 9 - Harmony of the Old and New Testament on the Precepts of Charity. [51]

14.

Come now, let us examine, or rather let us take notice,--for it is obvious and can be seen, at once,--whether the authority of the Old Testament too agrees with those statements taken from the gospel and the apostle.

What need to speak of the first statement, when it is clear to all that it is a quotation from the law given by Moses?

For it is there written, "Thou shalt love the Lord thy God with all thy heart, and with all thy soul, and with all thy mind." [52]And not to go farther for a passage of the Old Testament to compare with that of the apostle, he has himself added one.

For after saying that no tribulation, no distress, no persecution, no pressure of bodily want, no peril, no sword, separates us from the love of Christ, he immediately adds, "As it is written, For Thy sake we are in suffering all the day long; we are accounted as sheep for the slaughter." [53] The Manichæans are in the habit of saying that this is an interpolation,--so unable are they to reply, that they are forced in their extremity to say this.

But every one can see that this is all that is left for men to say when it is proved that they are wrong.

15.

And yet I ask them if they deny that this is said in the Old Testament, or if they hold that the passage in the Old Testament does not agree with that of the apostle.

For the first, the books will prove it; and as for the second, those prevaricators who fly off at a tangent will be brought to agree with me, if they will only reflect a little and consider what is said, or else I will press upon them the opinion of those who judge impartially.

For what could agree more harmoniously than these passages?

For tribulation, distress, persecution, famine, nakedness, peril, cause great suffering to man while in this life.

So all these words are implied in the single quotation from the law, where it is said, "For Thy sake we are in suffering." [54]The only other thing is the sword, which does not inflict a painful life, but removes whatever life it meets with. Answering to this are the words, "We are accounted as sheep for the slaughter."

And love could not have been more plainly expressed than by the words, "For Thy sake."

Suppose, then, that this testimony is not found in the Apostle Paul, but is quoted by me, must you not prove, you heretic, either that this is not written in the old law, or that it does not harmonize with the apostle?

And if you dare not say either of these things (for you are shut up by the reading of the manuscript, which will show that it is written, and by common sense, which sees that nothing could agree better with what is said by the apostle), why do you imagine that there is any force in accusing the Scriptures of being corrupted?

And once more, what will you reply to a man who says to you, This is what I understand, this is my view, this is my belief, and I read these books only because I see that everything in them agrees with the Christian faith?

Or tell me at once if you will venture deliberately to tell me to the face that we are not to believe that the apostles and martyrs are spoken of as having endured great sufferings for Christ's sake, and as having been accounted by their persecutors as sheep for the slaughter?

If you cannot say this, why should you bring a charge against the book in which I find what you acknowledge I ought to believe?

Chapter 10 - What the Church Teaches About God. The Two Gods of the Manichæans.

16.

Will you say that you grant that we are bound to love God, but not the God worshipped by those who acknowledge the authority of the Old Testament?

In that case you refuse to worship the God who made heaven and earth, for this is the God set forth all through these books.

And you admit that the whole of the world, which is called heaven and earth, had God and a good God for its author and maker.

For in speaking to you about God we must make a distinction.

For you hold that there are two gods, one good and the other bad.

But if you say that you worship and approve of worshipping the God who made heaven and earth, but not the God supported by the authority of the Old Testament, you act impertinently in trying, though vainly, to attribute to us views and opinions altogether unlike the wholesome and profitable doctrine we really hold.

Nor can your silly and profane discourses be at all compared with the expositions in which learned and pious men of the Catholic Church open up those Scriptures to the willing and worthy.

Our understanding of the law and the prophets is quite different from what you suppose.

Mistake us no longer.

We do not worship a God who repents, or is envious, or needy, or cruel, or who takes pleasure in the blood of men or beasts, or is pleased with guilt and crime, or whose possession of the earth is limited to a little corner of it.

These and such like are the silly notions you are in the habit of denouncing at great length.

Your denunciation does not touch us.

The fancies of old women or of children you attack with a vehemence that is only ridiculous.

Any one whom you persuade in this way to join you shows no fault in the teaching of the Church, but only proves his own ignorance of it.

17.

If, then, you have any human feeling,--if you have any regard for your own welfare,--you should rather examine with diligence and piety the meaning of these passages of Scripture.

You should examine, unhappy beings that you are; for we condemn with no less severity and copiousness any faith which attributes to God what is unbecoming Him, and in those by whom these passages are literally understood we correct the mistake of ignorance, and look upon persistence in it as absurd. And in many other things which you cannot understand there is in the Catholic teaching a check on the belief of those who have got beyond mental childishness, not in years, but in knowledge and understanding--old in the progress towards wisdom.

For we learn the folly of believing that God is bounded by any amount of space, even though infinite; and it is held unlawful to think of God, or any part of Him, as moving from one place to another.

And should any one suppose that anything in God's substance or nature can suffer change or conversion, he will be held guilty of wild profanity.

There are thus among us children who think of God as having a human form, which they suppose He really has, which is a most degrading idea; and there are many of full age to whose mind the majesty of God appears in its inviolableness and unchangeableness as not only above the human body, but above their own mind itself.

These ages, as we said, are distinguished not by time, but by virtue and discretion. [55] Among you, again, there is no one who will picture God in a human form; but neither is there one who sets God apart from the contamination of human error.

As regards those who are fed like crying babies at the breast of the Catholic Church, if they are not carried off by heretics, they are nourished according to the vigor and capacity of each, and arrive at last, one in one way and another in another, first to a perfect man, and then to the maturity and hoary hairs of wisdom, when they may get life as they desire, and life in perfect happiness.

Chapter 11 - God is the One Object of Love; Therefore He is Man's Chief Good. Nothing is Better Than God. God Cannot Be Lost Against Our Will.

18.

Following after God is the desire of happiness; to reach God is happiness itself.

We follow after God by loving Him; we reach Him, not by becoming entirely what He is, but in nearness to Him, and in wonderful and immaterial contact with Him, and in being inwardly illuminated and occupied by His truth and holiness.

He is light itself; we get enlightenment from Him.

The greatest commandment, therefore, which leads to happy life, and the first, is this: "Thou shalt love the Lord thy God with all thy heart, and soul, and mind." For to those who love the Lord all things issue in good.

Hence Paul adds shortly after, "I am persuaded that neither death, nor life, nor angels, nor virtue, nor things present, nor things future, nor height, nor depth, nor any other creature, shall be able to separate us from the love of God, which is in Christ Jesus our Lord." [56]If, then, to those who love God all things issue in good, and if, as no one doubts, the chief or perfect good is not only to be loved, but to be loved so that nothing shall be loved better, as is expressed in the words, "With all thy soul, with all thy heart, and with all thy mind," who, I ask, will not at once conclude, when these things are all settled and most surely believed, that our chief good which we must hasten to arrive at in preference to all other things is nothing else than God?

And then, if nothing can separate us from His love, must not this be surer as well as better than any other good?

19.

But let us consider the points separately.

No one separates us from this by threatening death.

For that with which we love God cannot die, except in not loving God; for death is not to love God, and that is when we prefer anything to Him in affection and pursuit.

No one separates us from this in promising life; for no one separates us from the fountain in promising water.

Angels do not separate us; for the mind cleaving to God is not inferior in strength to an angel.

Virtue does not separate us; for if what is here called virtue is that which has power in this world, the mind cleaving to God is far above the whole world.

Or if this virtue is perfect rectitude of our mind itself, this in the case of another will favor our union with God, and in ourselves will itself unite us with God.

Present troubles do not separate us; for we feel their burden less the closer we cling to Him from whom they try to separate us.

The promise of future things does not separate us; for both future good of every kind is surest in the promise of God, and nothing is better than God Himself, who undoubtedly is already present to those who truly cleave to Him.

Height and depth do not separate us; for if the height and depth of knowledge are what is meant, I will rather not be inquisitive than be separated from God; nor can any instruction by which error is removed separate me from Him, by separation from whom it is that any one is in error.

Or if what is meant are the higher and lower parts of this world, how can the promise of heaven separate me from Him who made heaven?

Or who from beneath can frighten me into forsaking God, when I should not have known of things beneath but by forsaking Him?

In fine, what place can remove me from His love, when He could not be all in every place unless He were contained in none?

Chapter 12 - We are United to God by Love, in Subjection to Him

20.

"No other creature," he says, separates us.

O man of profound mysteries!

He thought it not enough to say, no creature:

but he says no other creature; teaching that with which we love God and by which we cleave to God, our mind, namely, and understanding, is itself a creature.

Thus the body is another creature; and if the mind is an object of intellectual perception, and is known only by this means, the other creature is all that is an object of sense, which as it were makes itself known through the eyes, or ears, or smell, or taste, or touch, and this must be inferior to what is perceived by the intellect alone.

Now, as God also can be known by the worthy, only intellectually, [57] exalted though He is above the intelligent mind as being its Creator and Author, there was danger lest the human mind, from being reckoned among invisible and immaterial things, should be thought to be of the same nature with Him who created it, and so should fall away by pride from Him to whom it should be united by love.

For the mind becomes like God, to the extent vouchsafed by its subjection of itself to Him for information and enlightenment.

And if it obtains the greatest nearness by that subjection which produces likeness, it must be far removed from Him by that presumption which would make the likeness greater.

It is this presumption which leads the mind to refuse obedience to the laws of God, in the desire to be sovereign, as God is.

21.

The farther, then, the mind departs from God, not in space, but in affection and lust after things below Him, the more it is filled with folly and wretchedness.

So by love it returns to God,--a love which places it not along with God, but under Him.

And the more ardor and eagerness there is in this, the happier and more elevated will the mind be, and with God as sole governor it will be in perfect liberty.

Hence it must know that it is a creature.

It must believe what is the truth,--that its Creator remains ever possessed of the inviolable and immutable nature of truth and wisdom, and must confess, even in view of the errors from which it desires deliverance, that it is liable to folly and falsehood.

But then again, it must take care that it be not separated by the love of the other creature, that is, of this visible world, from the love of God Himself, which sanctifies it in order to lasting happiness.

No other creature, then,--for we are ourselves a creature,--separates us from the love of God which is in Christ Jesus our Lord.

Chapter 13 - We are Joined Inseparably to God by Christ and His Spirit

22.

Let this same Paul tell us who is this Christ Jesus our Lord.

"To them that are called," he says, "we preach Christ the virtue of God, and the wisdom of God." [58] And does not Christ Himself say, "I am the truth?" [59] If, then, we ask what it is to live well,--that is, to strive after happiness by living well,--it must assuredly be to love virtue, to love wisdom, to love truth, and to love with all the heart, with all the soul, and with all the mind; virtue which is inviolable and immutable, wisdom which never gives place to folly, truth which knows no change or variation from its uniform character.

Through this the Father Himself is seen; for it is said, "No man cometh unto the Father but by me."

To this we cleave by sanctification.

For when sanctified we burn with full and perfect love, which is the only security for our not turning away from God, and for our being conformed to Him rather than to this world; for "He has predestinated us," says the same apostle, "that we should be conformed to the image of His Son."[60]

23.

It is through love, then, that we become conformed to God; and by this conformation, and configuration, and circumcision from this world we are not confounded with the things which are properly subject to us.

And this is done by the Holy Spirit.

"For hope," he says, "does not confound us; for the love of God is shed abroad in our hearts by the Holy Spirit, which is given unto us." [61] But we could not possibly be restored to perfection by the Holy Spirit, unless He Himself continued always perfect and immutable.

And this plainly could not be unless He were of the nature and of the very substance of God, who alone is always possessed of immutability and invariableness.

"The creature," it is affirmed, not by me but by Paul, "has been made subject to vanity."[62] And what is subject to vanity is unable to separate us from vanity, and to unite us to the truth.

But the Holy Spirit does this for us.

He is therefore no creature.

For whatever is, must be either God or the creature.

Chapter 14 - We Cleave to the Trinity, Our Chief Good, by Love

24.

We ought then to love God, the Trinity in unity, Father, Son, and Holy Spirit; for this must be said to be God Himself, for it is said of God, truly and in the most exalted sense, "Of whom are all things, by whom are all things, in whom are all things."

Those are Paul's words. And what does he add?

"To Him be glory." [63] All this is exactly true.

He does not say, To them; for God is one.

And what is meant by, To Him be glory, but to Him be chief and perfect and widespread praise?

For as the praise improves and extends, so the love and affection increases in fervor.

And when this is the case, mankind cannot but advance with sure and firm step to a life of perfection and bliss.

This, I suppose, is all we wish to find when we speak of the chief good of man, to which all must be referred in life and conduct. For the good plainly exists; and we have shown by reasoning, as far as we were able, and by the divine authority which goes beyond our reasoning, that it is nothing else but God Himself.

For how can any thing be man's chief good but that in cleaving to which he is blessed? Now this is nothing but God, to whom we can cleave only by affection, desire, and love.

Chapter 15 - The Christian Definition of the Four Virtues

25.

As to virtue leading us to a happy life, I hold virtue to be nothing else than perfect love of God.

For the fourfold division of virtue I regard as taken from four forms of love.

For these four virtues (would that all felt their influence in their minds as they have their names in their mouths!), I should have no hesitation in defining them:

that temperance is love giving itself entirely to that which is loved; fortitude is love readily bearing all things for the sake of the loved object; justice is love serving only the loved object, and therefore ruling rightly; prudence is love distinguishing with sagacity between what hinders it and what helps it.

The object of this love is not anything, but only God, the chief good, the highest wisdom, the perfect harmony.

So we may express the definition thus: that temperance is love keeping itself entire and incorrupt for God; fortitude is love bearing everything readily for the sake of God; justice is love serving God only, and therefore ruling well all else, as subject to man; prudence is love making a right distinction between what helps it towards God and what might hinder it. [64]

Chapter 16 - Harmony of the Old and New Testaments

26.

I will briefly set forth the manner of life according to these virtues, one by one, after I have brought forward, as I promised, passages from the Old Testament parallel to those I have been quoting from the New Testament.

For is Paul alone in saying that we should be joined to God so that there should be nothing between to separate us? Does not the prophet say the same most aptly and concisely in the words, "It is good for me to cleave to God?" [65] Does not this one word cleave express all that the apostle says at length about love? And do not the words, It is good, point to the apostle's statement, "All things issue in good to them that love God?"

Thus in one clause and in two words the prophet sets forth the power and the fruit of love.

27.

And as the apostle says that the Son of God is the virtue of God and the wisdom of God,--virtue being understood to refer to action, and wisdom to teaching (as in the gospel these two things are expressed in the words, "All things were made by Him," which belongs to action and virtue; and then, referring to teaching and the knowledge of the truth, he says, "The life was the light of men" [66]),--could anything agree better with these passages than what is said in the Old Testament [67] of wisdom, "She reaches from end to end in strength, and orders all things sweetly?"

For reaching in strength expresses virtue, while ordering sweetly expresses skill and method.

But if this seems obscure, see what follows:

"And of all," he says, "God loved her; for she teaches the knowledge of God, and chooses His works."

Nothing more is found here about action; for choosing works is not the same as working, so this refers to teaching.

There remains action to correspond with the virtue, to complete the truth we wish to prove. Read then what comes next:

"But if," he says, "the possession which is desired in life is honorable, what is more honorable than wisdom, which works all things?"

Could anything be brought forward more striking or more distinct than this, or even more fully expressed?

Or, if you wish more, hear another passage of the same meaning.

"Wisdom," he says, "teaches sobriety, and justice, and virtue." [68] Sobriety refers, I think, to the knowledge of the truth, or to teaching; justice and virtue to work and action.

And I know nothing comparable to these two things, that is, to efficiency in action and sobriety in contemplation, which the virtue of God and the wisdom of God, that is, the Son of God, gives to them that love Him, when the same prophet goes on to show their value; for it is thus stated:

"Wisdom teaches sobriety, and justice, and virtue, than which nothing is more useful in life to man." [69]

28.

Perhaps some may think that those passages do not refer to the Son of God.

What, then, is taught in the following words:

"She displays the nobility of her birth, having her dwelling with God?" [70] To what does birth refer but to parentage?

And does not dwelling with the Father claim and assert equality?

Again, as Paul says that the Son of God is the wisdom of God, [71] and as the Lord Himself says, "No man knoweth the Father save the only-begotten Son," [72] what could be more concordant than those words of the prophet:

"With Thee is wisdom which knows Thy works, which was present at the time of Thy making the world, and knew what would be pleasing in Thine eyes?" [73] And as Christ is called the truth, which is also taught by His being called the brightness of the Father [74] (for there is nothing round about the sun but its brightness which is produced from it), what is there in the Old Testament more plainly and obviously in accordance with this than the words, "Thy truth is round about Thee?"[75] Once more, Wisdom herself says in the gospel, "No man cometh unto the Father but by me;" [76] and the prophet says, "Who knoweth Thy mind, unless Thou givest wisdom?" and a little after, "The things pleasing to Thee men have learned, and have been healed by wisdom." [77]

29.

Paul says, "The love of God is shed abroad in our hearts by the Holy Spirit which is given unto us;" [78] and the prophet says, "The Holy Spirit of knowledge will shun guile." [79]For where there is guile there is no love.

Paul says that we are "conformed to the image of the Son of God;" [80] and the prophet says, "The light of Thy countenance is stamped upon us." [81]Paul teaches that the Holy Spirit is God, and therefore is no creature; and the prophet says, "Thou sendest Thy Spirit from the higher." [82]For God alone is the highest, than whom nothing is higher.

Paul shows that the Trinity is one God, when he says, "To Him be glory;" [83] and in the Old Testament it is said, "Hear, O Israel, the Lord thy God is one God." [84]

Chapter 17 - Appeal to the Manichæans, Calling on Them to Repent

30.

What more do you wish?
Why do you resist ignorantly and obstinately?
Why do you pervert untutored minds by your mischievous teaching?
The God of both Testaments is one.

For as there is an agreement in the passages quoted from both, so is there in all the rest, if you are willing to consider them carefully and impartially. But because many expressions are undignified, and so far adapted to minds creeping on the earth, that they may rise by human things to divine, [85] while many are figurative, that the inquiring mind may have the more profit from the exertion of finding their meaning, and the more delight when it is found, you pervert this admirable arrangement of the Holy Spirit for the purpose of deceiving and ensnaring your followers.

As to the reason why divine Providence permits you to do this, and as to the truth of the apostle's saying, "There must needs be many heresies, that they which are approved may be made manifest among you," [86] it would take long to discuss these things, and you, with whom we have now to do, are not capable of understanding them.

I know you well.

To the consideration of divine things, which are far higher than you suppose, you bring minds quite gross and sickly, from being fed with material images.

31.

We must therefore in your case try not to make you understand divine things, which is impossible, but to make you desire to understand.

This is the work of the pure and guileless love of God, which is seen chiefly in the conduct, and of which we have already said much.

This love, inspired by the Holy Spirit, leads to the Son, that is, to the wisdom of God, by which the Father Himself is known.

For if wisdom and truth are not sought for with the whole strength of the mind, it cannot possibly be found.

But when it is sought as it deserves to be, it cannot withdraw or hide itself from its lovers. Hence its words, which you too are in the habit of repeating, "Ask, and ye shall receive; seek, and ye shall find; knock, and it shall be opened unto you:" [87]"Nothing is hid which shall not be revealed." [88]It is love that asks, love that seeks, love that knocks, love that reveals, love, too, that gives continuance in what is revealed. From this love of wisdom, and this studious inquiry, we are not debarred by the Old Testament, as you always say most falsely, but are exhorted to this with the greatest urgency.

32.

Hear, then, at length, and consider, I pray you, what is said by the prophet:

"Wisdom is glorious, and never fadeth away; yea, she is easily seen of them that love her, and found of such as seek her.

She preventeth them that desire her, in making herself first known unto them.

Whoso seeketh her early shall have no great travail; for he shall find her sitting at his doors.

To think, therefore, upon her is perfection of wisdom; and whoso watcheth for her shall quickly be without care.

For she goeth about seeking such as are worthy of her, showeth herself favorably unto them in the ways, and meeteth them in every thought.

For the very true beginning of her is the desire of discipline; and the care of discipline is love; and love is the keeping of her laws; and the giving heed unto her laws is the assurance of incorruption; and incorruption maketh us near unto God.

Therefore the desire of wisdom bringeth to a kingdom." [89]Will you still continue in dogged hostility to these things?

Do not things thus stated, though not yet understood, make it evident to every one that they contain something deep and unutterable?

Would that you could understand the things here said!

Forthwith you would abjure all your silly legends and your unmeaning material imaginations, and with great alacrity, sincere love, and full assurance of faith, would betake yourselves bodily to the shelter of the most holy bosom of the Catholic Church.

Chapter 18 - Only in the Catholic Church is Perfect Truth Established on the Harmony of Both Testaments

33.

I could, according to the little ability I have, take up the points separately, and could expound and prove the truths I have learned, which are generally more excellent and lofty than words can express; but this cannot be done while you bark at it.

For not in vain is it said, "Give not that which is holy to dogs." [90]Do not be angry.

I too barked and was a dog; and then, as was right, instead of the food of teaching, I got the rod of correction.

But were there in you that love of which we are speaking, or should it ever be in you as much as the greatness of the truth to be known requires, may God vouchsafe to show you that neither is there among the Manichæans the Christian faith which leads to the summit of wisdom and truth, the attainment of which is the true happy life, nor is it anywhere but in the Catholic teaching.

Is not this what the Apostle Paul appears to desire when he says, "For this cause I bow my knees to the Father of our Lord Jesus Christ, from whom the whole family in heaven and earth is named, that He would grant unto you, according to the riches of His glory, to be strengthened with might by His Spirit in the inner man: that Christ may dwell in your hearts by faith; that ye, being rooted and grounded in love, may be able to comprehend with all saints what is the height, and length, and breadth, and depth, and to know the love of Christ, which passeth knowledge, that ye may be filled with all the fullness of God?" [91]Could anything be more plainly expressed?

34.

Wake up a little, I beseech you, and see the harmony of both Testaments, making it quite plain and certain what should be the manner of life in our conduct, and to what all things should be referred.

To the love of God we are incited by the gospel, when it is said, "Ask, seek, knock;" [92] by Paul, when he says, "That ye, being rooted and grounded in love, may be able to comprehend;" [93] by the prophet also, when he says that wisdom can easily be known by those who love it, seek for it, desire it, watch for it, think about it, care for it.

The salvation of the mind [94] and the way of happiness is pointed out by the concord of both Scriptures; and yet you choose rather to bark at these things than to obey them.

I will tell you in one word what I think.

Do you listen to the learned men of the Catholic Church with as peaceable a disposition, and with the same zeal, that I had when for nine years I attended on you: [95]there will be no need of so long a time as that during which you made a fool of me.

In a much, a very much, shorter time you will see the difference between truth and vanity.

Chapter 19 - Description of the Duties of Temperance, According to the Sacred Scriptures

35.

It is now time to return to the four virtues, and to draw out and prescribe a way of life in conformity with them, taking each separately.

First, then, let us consider temperance, which promises us a kind of integrity and incorruption in the love by which we are united to God.

The office of temperance is in restraining and quieting the passions which make us pant for those things which turn us away from the laws of God and from the enjoyment of His goodness, that is, in a word, from the happy life.

For there is the abode of truth; and in enjoying its contemplation, and in cleaving closely to it, we are assuredly happy; but departing from this, men become entangled in great errors and sorrows.

For, as the apostle says, "The root of all evils is covetousness; which some having followed, have made shipwreck of the faith, and have pierced themselves through with many sorrows." [96] And this sin of the soul is quite plainly, to those rightly understanding, set forth in the Old Testament in the transgression of Adam in Paradise.

Thus, as the apostle says, "In Adam we all die, and in Christ we shall all rise again." [97] Oh, the depth of these mysteries!

But I refrain; for I am now engaged not in teaching you the truth, but in making you unlearn your errors, if I can, that is, if God aid my purpose regarding you.

36.

Paul then says that covetousness is the root of all evils; and by covetousness the old law also intimates that the first man fell.

Paul tells us to put off the old man and put on the new. [98] By the old man he means Adam who sinned, and by the new man him whom the Son of God took to Himself in consecration for our redemption.

For he says in another place, "The first man is of the earth, earthy; the second man is from heaven, heavenly.

As is the earthy, such are they also that are earthy; and as is the heavenly, such are they also that are heavenly.

And as we have borne the image of the earthy, let us also bear the image of the heavenly,"[99] -- that is, put off the old man, and put on the new.

The whole duty of temperance, then, is to put off the old man, and to be renewed in God,--that is, to scorn all bodily delights, and the popular applause, and to turn the whole love to things divine and unseen.

Hence that following passage which is so admirable:

"Though our outward man perish, our inward man is renewed day by day." [100] Hear, too, the prophet singing, "Create in me a clean heart, O God, and renew a right spirit within me."[101] What can be said against such harmony except by blind barkers?

Chapter 20 - We are Required to Despise All Sensible Things, and to Love God Alone

37.

Bodily delights have their source in all those things with which the bodily sense comes in contact, and which are by some called the objects of sense; and among these the noblest is light, in the common meaning of the word, because among our senses also, which the mind uses in acting through the body, there is nothing more valuable than the eyes, and so in the Holy Scriptures all the objects of sense are spoken of as visible things.

Thus in the New Testament we are warned against the love of these things in the following words:

"While we look not at the things which are seen, but at the things which are not seen; for the things which are seen are temporal, but the things which are not seen are eternal." [102] This shows how far from being Christians those are who hold that the sun and moon are to be not only loved but worshipped.

For what is seen if the sun and moon are not?

But we are forbidden to regard things which are seen.

The man, therefore, who wishes to offer that incorrupt love to God must not love these things too.

This subject I will inquire into more particularly elsewhere. Here my plan is to write not of faith, but of the life by which we become worthy of knowing what we believe.

God then alone is to be loved; and all this world, that is, all sensible things, are to be despised,--while, however, they are to be used as this life requires.

Chapter 21 - Popular Renown and Inquisitiveness are Condemned in the Sacred Scriptures

38.
Popular renown is thus slighted and scorned in the New Testament: "If I wished," says St. Paul, "to please men, I should not be the servant of Christ." [103] Again, there is another production of the soul formed by imaginations derived from material things, and called the knowledge of things.

In reference to this we are fitly warned against inquisitiveness to correct which is the great function of temperance.

Thus it is said, "Take heed lest any one seduce you by philosophy."

And because the word philosophy originally means the love and pursuit of wisdom, a thing of great value and to be sought with the whole mind, the apostle, with great prudence, that he might not be thought to deter from the love of wisdom, has added the words, "And the elements of this world." [104] For some people, neglecting virtues, and ignorant of what God is, and of the majesty of nature which remains always the same, think that they are engaged in an important business when searching with the greatest inquisitiveness and eagerness into this material mass which we call the world.

This begets so much pride, that they look upon themselves as inhabitants of the heaven of which they often discourse.

The soul, then, which purposes to keep itself chaste for God must refrain from the desire of vain knowledge like this.

For this desire usually produces delusion, so that the soul thinks that nothing exists but what is material; or if, from regard to authority, it confesses that there is an immaterial existence, it can think of it only under material images, and has no belief regarding it but that imposed by the bodily sense.

We may apply to this the precept about fleeing from idolatry.

39.
To this New Testament authority, requiring us not to love anything in this world, [105] especially in that passage where it is said, "Be not conformed to this world," [106] --for the point is to show that a man is conformed to whatever he loves,--to this authority, then, if I seek for a parallel passage in the Old Testament, I find several; but there is one book of Solomon, called Ecclesiastes, which at great length brings all earthly things into utter contempt.

The book begins thus:

"Vanity of the vain, saith the Preacher, vanity of the vain; all is vanity.

What profit hath a man of all his labor which he taketh under the sun?" [107] If all these words are considered, weighed, and thoroughly examined, many things are found of essential importance to those who seek to flee from the world and to take shelter in God; but this requires time and our discourse hastens on to other topics.

But, after this beginning, he goes on to show in detail that the vain [108] are those who are deceived by things of this sort; and he calls this which deceives them vanity,--not that God did not create those things, but because men choose to subject themselves by their sins to those things, which the divine law has made subject to them in well-doing. For when you consider things beneath yourself to be admirable and desirable, what is this but to be cheated and misled by unreal goods? The man, then, who is temperate in such mortal and transient things has his rule of life confirmed by both Testaments, that he should love none of these things, nor think them desirable for their own sakes, but should use them as far as is required for the purposes and duties of life, with the moderation of an employer instead of the ardor of a lover.

These remarks on temperance are few in proportion to the greatness of the theme, but perhaps too many in view of the task on hand.

Chapter 22 - Fortitude Comes from the Love of God

40.
On fortitude we must be brief.

The love, then, of which we speak, which ought with all sanctity to burn in desire for God, is called temperance, in not seeking for earthly things, and fortitude in bearing the loss of them.

But among all things which are possessed in this life, the body is, by God's most righteous laws, for the sin of old, man's heaviest bond, which is well known as a fact but most incomprehensible in its mystery.

Lest this bond should be shaken and disturbed, the soul is shaken with the fear of toil and pain; lest it should be lost and destroyed, the soul is shaken with the fear of death.

For the soul loves it from the force of habit, not knowing that by using it well and wisely its resurrection and reformation will, by the divine help and decree, be without any trouble made subject to its authority.

But when the soul turns to God wholly in this love, it knows these things, and so will not only disregard death, but will even desire it.

41.
Then there is the great struggle with pain.
But there is nothing, though of iron hardness, which the fire of love cannot subdue.
And when the mind is carried up to God in this love, it will soar above all torture free and glorious, with wings beauteous and unhurt, on which chaste love rises to the embrace of God.
Otherwise God must allow the lovers of gold, the lovers of praise, the lovers of women, to have more fortitude than the lovers of Himself, though love in those cases is rather to be called passion or lust.
And yet even here we may see with what force the mind presses on with unflagging energy, in spite of all alarms, towards that it loves; and we learn that we should bear all things rather than forsake God, since those men bear so much in order to forsake Him.

Chapter 23 - Scripture Precepts and Examples of Fortitude

42.
Instead of quoting here authorities from the New Testament, where it is said, "Tribulation worketh patience; and patience, experience and experience, hope;" [109] and where, in addition to these words, there is proof and confirmation of them from the example of those who spoke them; I will rather summon an example of patience from the Old Testament, against which the Manichæans make fierce assaults.
Nor will I refer to the man who, in the midst of great bodily suffering, and with a dreadful disease in his limbs, not only bore human evils, but discoursed of things divine.
Whoever gives considerate attention to the utterances of this man, will learn from every one of them what value is to be attached to those things which men try to keep in their power, and in so doing are themselves brought by passion into bondage, so that they become the slaves of mortal things, while seeking ignorantly to be their masters.
This man, in the loss of all his wealth, and on being suddenly reduced to the greatest poverty, kept his mind so unshaken and fixed upon God, as to manifest that these things were not great in his view, but that he was great in relation to them, and God to him. [110] If this mind were to be found in men in our day, we should not be so strongly cautioned in the New Testament against the possession of these things in order that we may be perfect; for to have these things without cleaving to them is much more admirable than not to have them at all. [111]

43.
But since we are speaking here of bearing pain and bodily sufferings, I pass from this man, great as he was, indomitable as he was:
this is the case of a man.
But these Scriptures present to me a woman of amazing fortitude, and I must at once go on to her case.
This woman, along with seven children, allowed the tyrant and executioner to extract her vitals from her body rather than a profane word from her mouth, encouraging her sons by her exhortations, though she suffered in the tortures of their bodies, and was herself to undergo what she called on them to bear. [112] What patience could be greater than this?
And yet why should we be astonished that the love of God, implanted in her inmost heart, bore up against tyrant, and executioner, and pain, and sex, and natural affection?
Had she not heard, "Precious in the sight of the Lord is the death of His saints?" [113] Had she not heard, "A patient man is better than the mightiest?" [114] Had she not heard, "All that is appointed thee receive; and in pain bear it; and in abasement keep thy patience:
for in fire are gold and silver tried?" [115] Had she not heard, "The fire tries the vessels of the potter, and for just men is the trial of tribulation?" [116] These she knew, and many other precepts of fortitude written in these books, which alone existed at that time, by the same divine Spirit who writes those in the New Testament.

Chapter 24 - Of Justice and Prudence

44.

What of justice that pertains to God?

As the Lord says, "Ye cannot serve two masters," [117] and the apostle denounces those who serve the creature rather than the Creator, [118] was it not said before in the Old Testament, "Thou shalt worship the Lord thy God, and Him only shalt thou serve?" [119] I need say no more on this, for these books are full of such passages.

The lover, then, whom we are describing, will get from justice this rule of life, that he must with perfect readiness serve the God whom he loves, the highest good, the highest wisdom, the highest peace; [120] and as regards all other things, must either rule them as subject to himself, or treat them with a view to their subjection.

This rule of life, is, as we have shown, confirmed by the authority of both Testaments.

45.

With equal brevity we must treat of prudence, to which it belongs to discern between what is to be desired and what to be shunned. Without this, nothing can be done of what we have already spoken of. It is the part of prudence to keep watch with most anxious vigilance, lest any evil influence should stealthily creep in upon us.

Thus the Lord often exclaims, "Watch;" [121] and He says, "Walk while ye have the light, lest darkness come upon you." [122] And then it is said, "Know ye not that a little leaven leaveneth the whole lump?" [123] And no passage can be quoted from the Old Testament more expressly condemning this mental somnolence, which makes us insensible to destruction advancing on us step by step, than those words of the prophet, "He who despiseth small things shall fall by degrees."[124] On this topic I might discourse at length did our haste allow of it. And did our present task demand it, we might perhaps prove the depth of these mysteries, by making a mock of which profane men in their perfect ignorance fall, not certainly by degrees, but with a headlong overthrow.

Chapter 25 - Four Moral Duties Regarding the Love of God, of Which Love the Reward is Eternal Life and the Knowledge of the Truth

46.

I need say no more about right conduct.

For if God is man's chief good, which you cannot deny, it clearly follows, since to seek the chief good is to live well, that to live well is nothing else but to love God with all the heart, with all the soul, with all the mind; and, as arising from this, that this love must be preserved entire and incorrupt, which is the part of temperance; that it give way before no troubles, which is the part of fortitude; that it serve no other, which is the part of justice; that it be watchful in its inspection of things lest craft or fraud steal in, which is the part of prudence.

This is the one perfection of man, by which alone he can succeed in attaining to the purity of truth.

This both Testaments enjoin in concert; this is commended on both sides alike.

Why do you continue to cast reproaches on Scriptures of which you are ignorant?

Do you not see the folly of your attack upon books which only those who do not understand them find fault with, and which only those who find fault fail in understanding?

For neither can an enemy know them, nor can one who knows them be other than a friend to them.

47.

Let us then, as many as have in view to reach eternal life, love God with all the heart, with all the soul, with all the mind.

For eternal life contains the whole reward in the promise of which we rejoice; nor can the reward precede desert, nor be given to a man before he is worthy of it.

What can be more unjust than this, and what is more just than God?

We should not then demand the reward before we deserve to get it.

Here, perhaps, it is not out of place to ask what is eternal life; or rather let us hear the Bestower of it:

"This," He says, "is life eternal, that they should know Thee, the true God, and Jesus Christ whom Thou hast sent." [125] So eternal life is the knowledge of the truth.

See, then, how perverse and preposterous is the character of those who think that their teaching of the knowledge of God will make us perfect, when this is the reward of those already perfect!

What else, then, have we to do but first to love with full affection Him whom we desire to know? [126]Hence arises that principle on which we have all along insisted, that there is nothing more wholesome in the Catholic Church than using authority [127] before argument.

Chapter 26 - Love of Ourselves and of Our Neighbor

48.

To proceed to what remains.
It may be thought that there is nothing here about man himself, the lover.
But to think this, shows a want of clear perception.
For it is impossible for one who loves God not to love himself.
For he alone has a proper love for himself who aims diligently at the attainment of the chief and true good; and if this is nothing else but God, as has been shown, what is to prevent one who loves God from loving himself?
And then, among men should there be no bond of mutual love?
Yea, verily; so that we can think of no surer step towards the love of God than the love of man to man.

49.

Let the Lord then supply us with the other precept in answer to the question about the precepts of life; for He was not satisfied with one as knowing that God is one thing and man another, and that the difference is nothing less than that between the Creator and the thing created in the likeness of its Creator.
He says then that the second precept is, "Thou shalt love thy neighbor as thyself." [128]Now you love yourself suitably when you love God better than yourself.
What, then, you aim at in yourself you must aim at in your neighbor, namely, that he may love God with a perfect affection.
For you do not love him as yourself, unless you try to draw him to that good which you are yourself pursuing.
For this is the one good which has room for all to pursue it along with thee.
From this precept proceed the duties of human society, in which it is hard to keep from error.
But the first thing to aim at is, that we should be benevolent, that is, that we cherish no malice and no evil design against another.
For man is the nearest neighbor of man.

50.

Hear also what Paul says:
"The love of our neighbor," he says, "worketh no ill." [129]The testimonies here made use of are very short, but, if I mistake not, they are to the point, and sufficient for the purpose.
And every one knows how many and how weighty are the words to be found everywhere in these books on the love of our neighbor.
But as a man may sin against another in two ways, either by injuring him or by not helping him when it is in his power, and as it is for these things which no loving man would do that men are called wicked, all that is required is, I think, proved by these words, "The love of our neighbor worketh no ill."
And if we cannot attain to good unless we first desist from working evil, our love of our neighbor is a sort of cradle of our love to God, so that, as it is said, "the love of our neighbor worketh no ill," we may rise from this to these other words, "We know that all things issue in good to them that love God." [130]

51.

But there is a sense in which these either rise together to fullness and perfection, or, while the love of God is first in beginning, the love of our neighbor is first in coming to perfection. For perhaps divine love takes hold on us more rapidly at the outset, but we reach perfection more easily in lower things.
However that may be, the main point is this, that no one should think that while he despises his neighbor he will come to happiness and to the God whom he loves.
And would that it were as easy to seek the good of our neighbor, or to avoid hurting him, as it is for one well trained and kind-hearted to love his neighbor!

These things require more than mere good-will, and can be done only by a high degree of thoughtfulness and prudence, which belongs only to those to whom it is given by God, the source of all good.

On this topic--which is one, I think, of great difficulty--I will try to say a few words such as my plan admits of, resting all my hope in Him whose gifts these are.

Chapter 27 - On Doing Good to the Body of Our Neighbor

52.

Man, then, as viewed by his fellow-man, is a rational soul with a mortal and earthly body in its service.

Therefore he who loves his neighbor does good partly to the man's body, and partly to his soul. What benefits the body is called medicine; what benefits the soul, discipline.

Medicine here includes everything that either preserves or restores bodily health.

It includes, therefore, not only what belongs to the art of medical men, properly so called, but also food and drink, clothing and shelter, and every means of covering and protection to guard our bodies against injuries and mishaps from without as well as from within.

For hunger and thirst, and cold and heat, and all violence from without, produce loss of that health which is the point to be considered.

53.

Hence those who seasonably and wisely supply all the things required for warding off these evils and distresses are called compassionate, although they may have been so wise that no painful feeling disturbed their mind in the exercise of compassion. [131]No doubt the word compassionate implies suffering in the heart of the man who feels for the sorrow of another.

And it is equally true that a wise man ought to be free from all painful emotion when he assists the needy, when he gives food to the hungry and water to the thirsty, when he clothes the naked, when he takes the stranger into his house, when he sets free the oppressed, when, lastly, he extends his charity to the dead in giving them burial.

Still the epithet compassionate is a proper one, although he acts with tranquillity of mind, not from the stimulus of painful feeling, but from motives of benevolence.

There is no harm in the word compassionate when there is no passion in the case.

54.

Fools, again, who avoid the exercise of compassion as a vice, because they are not sufficiently moved by a sense of duty without feeling also distressful emotion, are frozen into hard insensibility, which is very different from the calm of a rational serenity.

God, on the other hand, is properly called compassionate; and the sense in which He is so will be understood by those whom piety and diligence have made fit to understand.

There is a danger lest, in using the words of the learned, we harden the souls of the unlearned by leading them away from compassion instead of softening them with the desire of a charitable disposition.

As compassion, then, requires us to ward off these distresses from others, so harmlessness forbids the infliction of them.

Chapter 28 - On Doing Good to the Soul of Our Neighbor. Two Parts of Discipline, Restraint and Instruction. Through Good Conduct We Arrive at the Knowledge of the Truth.

55.

As regards discipline, by which the health of the mind is restored, without which bodily health avails nothing for security against misery, the subject is one of great difficulty.

And as in the body we said it is one thing to cure diseases and wounds, which few can do properly, and another thing to meet the cravings of hunger and thirst, and to give assistance in all the other ways in which any man may at any time help another; so in the mind there are some things in which the high and rare offices of the teacher are not much called for,--as, for instance, in advice and exhortation to give to the needy the things already mentioned as required for the body.

To give such advice is to aid the mind by discipline, as giving the things themselves is aiding the body by our resources.

But there are other cases where diseases of the mind, many and various in kind, are healed in a way strange and indescribable.

Unless His medicine were sent from heaven to men, so heedlessly do they go on in sin, there would be no hope of salvation; and, indeed, even bodily health, if you go to the root of the matter, can have come to men from none but God, who gives to all things their being and their well-being.

56.

This discipline, then, which is the medicine of the mind, as far as we can gather from the sacred Scriptures, includes two things, restraint and instruction.

Restraint implies fear, and instruction love, in the person benefited by the discipline; for in the giver of the benefit there is the love without the fear.

In both of these God Himself, by whose goodness and mercy it is that we are anything, has given us in the two Testaments a rule of discipline.

For though both are found in both Testaments, still fear is prominent in the Old, and love in the New; which the apostle calls bondage in the one, and liberty in the other.

Of the marvellous order and divine harmony of these Testaments it would take long to speak, and many pious and learned men have discoursed on it.

The theme demands many books to set it forth and explain it as far as is possible for man.

He, then, who loves his neighbor endeavors all he can to procure his safety in body and in soul, making the health of the mind the standard in his treatment of the body.

And as regards the mind, his endeavors are in this order, that he should first fear and then love God.

This is true excellence of conduct, and thus the knowledge of the truth is acquired which we are ever in the pursuit of.

57.

The Manichæans agree with me as regards the duty of loving God and our neighbor, but they deny that this is taught in the Old Testament. How greatly they err in this is, I think, clearly shown by the passages quoted above on both these duties.

But, in a single word, and one which only stark madness can oppose, do they not see the unreasonableness of denying that these very two precepts which they commend are quoted by the Lord in the Gospel from the Old Testament, "Thou shalt love the Lord thy God with all thy heart, and with all thy soul, and with all thy mind;" and the other, "Thou shalt love thy neighbor as thyself?" [132]Or if they dare not deny this, from the light of truth being too strong for them, let them deny that these precepts are salutary; let them deny, if they can, that they teach the best morality; let them assert that it is not a duty to love God, or to love our neighbor; that all things do not issue in good to them that love God; that it is not true that the love of our neighbor worketh no ill (a two-fold regulation of human life which is most salutary and excellent).

By such assertions they cut themselves off not only from Christians, but from mankind.

But if they dare not speak thus, but must confess the divinity of the precepts, why do they not desist from assailing and maligning with horrible profanity the books from which they are quoted?

58.

Will they say, as they often do, that although we find these precepts in the books, it does not follow that all is good that is found there?

How to meet and refute this quibble I do not well see. Shall I discuss the words of the Old Testament one by one, to prove to stubborn and ignorant men their perfect agreement with the New Testament?

But when will this be done?

When shall I have time, or they patience?

What, then, is to be done?

Shall I desert the cause, and leave them to escape detection in an opinion which, though false and impious, is hard to disprove?

I will not.

God will Himself be at hand to aid me; nor will He suffer me in those straits to remain helpless or forsaken.

Chapter 29 - Of the Authority of the Scriptures

59.

Attend, then, ye Manichæans, if perchance there are some of you of whom your superstition has hold so as to allow you yet to escape. Attend, I say, without obstinacy, without the desire to oppose, otherwise your decision will be fatal to yourselves.

No one can doubt, and you are not so lost to the truth as not to understand that if it is good, as all allow, to love God and our neighbor, whatever hangs on these two precepts cannot rightly be pronounced bad.

What it is that hangs on them it would be absurd to think of learning from me.

Hear Christ Himself; hear Christ, I say; hear the Wisdom of God:

"On these two commandments," He says, "hang all the law and the prophets." [133]

60.

What can the most shameless obstinacy say to this?

That these are not Christ's words?

But they are written in the Gospel as His words. That the writing is false?

Is not this most profane blasphemy?

Is it not most presumptuous to speak thus?

Is it not most foolhardy?

Is it not most criminal?

The worshippers of idols, who hate even the name of Christ, never dared to speak thus against these Scriptures.

For the utter overthrow of all literature will follow, and there will be an end to all books handed down from the past, if what is supported by such a strong popular belief and established by the uniform testimony of so many men and so many times, is brought into such suspicion, that it is not allowed to have the credit and the authority of common history.

In fine, what can you quote from any writings of which I may not speak in this way if it is quoted against my opinion and my purpose? [134]

61.

And is it not intolerable that they forbid us to believe a book widely known and placed now in the hands of all, while they insist on our believing the book which they quote?

If any writing is to be suspected, what should be more so than one which has not merited notoriety, or which may be throughout a forgery, bearing a false name? If you force such a writing on me against my will, and make a display of authority to drive me into belief, shall I, when I have a writing which I see spread far and wide for a length of time, and sanctioned by the concordant testimony of churches scattered over all the world, degrade myself by doubting, and, worse degradation, by doubting at your suggestion?

Even if you brought forward other readings, I should not receive them unless supported by general agreement; and this being the case, do you think that now, when you bring forward nothing to compare with the text except your own silly and inconsiderate statement, mankind are so unreasonable and so forsaken by divine Providence as to prefer to those Scriptures not others quoted by you in refutation, but merely your own words?

You ought to bring forward another manuscript with the same contents, but incorrupt and more correct, with only the passage wanting which you charge with being spurious.

For example, if you hold that the Epistle of Paul to the Romans is spurious, you must bring forward another incorrupt, or rather another manuscript with the same epistle of the same apostle, free from error and corruption.

You say you will not, lest you be suspected of corrupting it.

This is your usual reply, and a true one.

Were you to do this, we should assuredly have this very suspicion; and all men of any sense would have it too. See then what you are to think of your own authority; and consider whether it is right to believe your words against these Scriptures, when the simple fact that a manuscript is brought forward by you makes it dangerous to put faith in it.

Chapter 30 - The Church Apostrophised as Teacher of All Wisdom. Doctrine of the Catholic Church

62.

But why say more on this?

For who but sees that men who dare to speak thus against the Christian Scriptures, though they may not be what they are suspected of being, are at least no Christians?

For to Christians this rule of life is given, that we should love the Lord Our God with all the heart, with all the soul, and with all the mind, and our neighbor as ourselves; for on these two commandments hang all the law and the prophets.

Rightly, then, Catholic Church, most true mother of Christians, dost thou not only teach that God alone, to find whom is the happiest life, must be worshipped in perfect purity and chastity, bringing in no creature as an object of adoration whom we should be required to serve; and from that incorrupt and inviolable eternity to which alone man should be made subject, in cleaving to which alone the rational soul escapes misery, excluding everything made, everything liable to change, everything under the power of time; without confounding what eternity, and truth, and peace itself keeps separate, or separating what a common majesty unites:

but thou dost also contain love and charity to our neighbor in such a way, that for all kinds of diseases with which souls are for their sins afflicted, there is found with thee a medicine of prevailing efficacy.

63.

Thy training and teaching are childlike for children, forcible for youths, peaceful for the aged, taking into account the age of the mind as well as of the body.

Thou subjectest women to their husbands in chaste and faithful obedience, not to gratify passion, but for the propagation of offspring, [135] and for domestic society.

Thou givest to men authority over their wives, not to mock the weaker sex, but in the laws of unfeigned love.

Thou dost subordinate children to their parents in a kind of free bondage, and dost set parents over their children in a godly rule.

Thou bindest brothers to brothers in a religious tie stronger and closer than that of blood.

Without violation of the connections of nature and of choice, thou bringest within the bond of mutual love every relationship of kindred, and every alliance of affinity.

Thou teachest servants to cleave to their masters from delight in their task rather than from the necessity of their position.

Thou renderest masters forbearing to their servants, from a regard to God their common Master, and more disposed to advise than to compel.

Thou unitest citizen to citizen, nation to nation, yea, man to man, from the recollection of their first parents, not only in society but in fraternity.

Thou teachest kings to seek the good of their peoples; thou counsellest peoples to be subject to their kings. Thou teachest carefully to whom honor is due, to whom regard, to whom reverence, to whom fear, to whom consolation, to whom admonition, to whom encouragement, to whom discipline, to whom rebuke, to whom punishment; showing both how all are not due to all, and how to all love is due, and how injury is due to none. [136]

64.

Then, after this human love has nourished and invigorated the mind cleaving to thy breast, and fitted it for following God, when the divine majesty has begun to disclose itself as far as suffices for man while a dweller on the earth, such fervent charity is produced, and such a flame of divine love is kindled, that by the burning out of all vices, and by the purification and sanctification of the man, it becomes plain how divine are these words, "I am a consuming fire," [137] and, "I have come to send fire on the earth." [138] These two utterances of one God stamped on both Testaments, exhibit with harmonious testimony, the sanctification of the soul, pointing forward to the accomplishment of that which is also quoted in the New Testament from the Old:

"Death is swallowed up in victory.

O death, where is thy sting?

Where, O death, is thy contest?" [139] Could these heretics understand this one saying, no longer proud but quite reconciled, they would worship God nowhere but with thee and in thy bosom.

In thee, as is fit, divine precepts are kept by widely-scattered multitudes.

In thee, as is fit, it is well understood how much more heinous sin is when the law is known than when it is unknown.

For "the sting of death is sin, and the strength of sin is the law," [140] which adds to the force with which the consciousness of disregard of the precept strikes and slays.

In thee it is seen, as is fit, how vain is effort under the law, when lust lays waste the mind, and is held in check by fear of punishment, instead of being overborne by the love of virtue.

Thine, as is fit, are the many hospitable, the many friendly, the many compassionate, the many learned, the many chaste, the many saints, the many so ardent in their love to God, that in perfect continence and amazing indifference to this world they find happiness even in solitude.

Chapter 31 - The Life of the Anachoretes and Coenobites Set Against the Continence of the Manichæans

65.

What must we think is seen by those who can live without seeing their fellow-creatures, though not without loving them?

It must be something transcending human things in contemplating which man can live without seeing his fellow-man.

Hear now, ye Manichæans, the customs and notable continence of perfect Christians, who have thought it right not only to praise but also to practise the height of chastity, that you may be restrained, if there is any shame in you, from vaunting your abstinence before uninstructed minds as if it were the hardest of all things.

I will speak of things of which you are not ignorant, though you hide them from us.

For who does not know that there is a daily increasing multitude of Christian men of absolute continence spread all over the world, especially in the East and in Egypt, as you cannot help knowing?

66.

I will say nothing of those to whom I just now alluded, who, in complete seclusion from the view of men, inhabit regions utterly barren, content with simple bread, which is brought to them periodically, and with water, enjoying communion with God, to whom in purity of mind they cleave, and most blessed in contemplating His beauty, which can be seen only by the understanding of saints.

I will say nothing of them, because some people think them to have abandoned human things more than they ought, not considering how much those may benefit us in their minds by prayer, and in their lives by example, whose bodies we are not permitted to see.

But to discuss this point would take long, and would be fruitless; for if a man does not of his own accord regard this high pitch of sanctity as admirable and honorable, how can our speaking lead him to do so?

Only the Manichæans, who make a boast of nothing, should be reminded that the abstinence and continence of the great saints of the Catholic Church has gone so far, that some think it should be checked and recalled within the limits of humanity,--so far above men, even in the judgment of those who disapprove, have their minds soared.

67.

But if this is beyond our tolerance, who can but admire and commend those who, slighting and discarding the pleasures of this world, living together in a most chaste and holy society, unite in passing their time in prayers, in readings, in discussions, without any swelling of pride, or noise of contention, or sullenness of envy; but quiet, modest, peaceful, their life is one of perfect harmony and devotion to God, an offering most acceptable to Him from whom the power to do those things is obtained?

No one possesses anything of his own; no one is a burden to another.

They work with their hands in such occupations as may feed their bodies without distracting their minds from God.

The product of their toil they give to the decans or tithesmen,--so called from being set over the tithes,--so that no one is occupied with the care of his body, either in food or clothes, or in anything else required for daily use or for the common ailments.

These decans, again, arranging everything with great care, and meeting promptly the demands made by that life on account of bodily infirmities, have one called "father," to whom they give in their accounts.

These fathers are not only more saintly in their conduct, but also distinguished for divine learning, and of high character in every way; and without pride they superintend those whom they call their children, having themselves great authority in giving orders, and meeting with willing obedience from those under their charge.

At the close of the day they assemble from their separate dwellings before their meal to hear their father, assembling to the number of three thousand at least for one father; for one may have even a much larger number than this.

They listen with astonishing eagerness in perfect silence, and give expression to the feelings of their minds as moved by the words of the preacher, in groans, or tears, or signs of joy without noise or shouting.

Then there is refreshment for the body, as much as health and a sound condition of the body requires, every one checking unlawful appetite, so as not to go to excess even in the poor, inexpensive fare provided.

So they not only abstain from flesh and wine, in order to gain the mastery over their passions, but also from those things which are only the more likely to whet the appetite of the palate and of the stomach, from what some call their greater cleanness, which often serves as a ridiculous and disgraceful excuse for an unseemly taste for exquisite viands, as distant from animal food. Whatever they possess in addition to what is required for their support (and much is obtained, owing to their industry and frugality), they distribute to the needy with greater care than they took in procuring it for themselves.

For while they make no effort to obtain abundance, they make every effort to prevent their abundance remaining with them,--so much so, that they send shiploads to places inhabited by poor people.

I need say no more on a matter known to all. [141]

68.

Such, too, is the life of the women, who serve God assiduously and chastely, living apart and removed as far as propriety demands from the men, to whom they are united only in pious affection and in imitation of virtue.

No young men are allowed access to them, nor even old men, however respectable and approved, except to the porch, in order to furnish necessary supplies.

For the women occupy and maintain themselves by working in wool, and hand over the cloth to the brethren, from whom, in return, they get what they need for food.

Such customs, such a life, such arrangements, such a system, I could not commend as it deserves, if I wished to commend it; besides, I am afraid that it would seem as if I thought it unlikely to gain acceptance from the mere description of it, if I considered myself obliged to add an ornamental eulogium to the simple narrative.

Ye Manichæans, find fault here if you can.

Do not bring into prominence our tares before men too blind to discriminate.

Chapter 32 - Praise of the Clergy

69.

There is not, however, such narrowness in the moral excellence of the Catholic Church as that I should limit my praise of it to the life of those here mentioned.

For how many bishops have I known most excellent and holy men, how many presbyters, how many deacons, and ministers of all kinds of the divine sacraments, whose virtue seems to me more admirable and more worthy of commendation on account of the greater difficulty of preserving it amidst the manifold varieties of men, and in this life of turmoil!

For they preside over men needing cure as much as over those already cured.

The vices of the crowd must be borne with in order that they may be cured, and the plague must be endured before it is subdued.

To keep here the best way of life and a mind calm and peaceful is very hard.

Here, in a word, we are among people who are learning to live.

There they live.

Chapter 33 - Another Kind of Men Living Together in Cities. Fasts of Three Days

70.

Still I would not on this account cast a slight upon a praiseworthy class of Christians,--those, namely, who live together in cities, quite apart from common life.

I saw at Milan a lodging-house of saints, in number not a few, presided over by one presbyter, a man of great excellence and learning.

At Rome I knew several places where there was in each one eminent for weight of character, and prudence, and divine knowledge, presiding over all the rest who lived with him, in Christian charity, and sanctity, and liberty.

These, too, are not burdensome to any one; but, in the Eastern fashion, and on the authority of the Apostle Paul, they maintain themselves with their own hands.

I was told that many practised fasts of quite amazing severity, not merely taking only one meal daily towards night, which is everywhere quite common, but very often continuing for three days or more in succession without food or drink.

And this among not men only, but women, who also live together in great numbers as widows or virgins, gaining a livelihood by spinning and weaving, and presided over in each case by a woman of the greatest judgment and experience, skilled and accomplished not only in directing and forming moral conduct, but also in instructing the understanding. [142]

71.

With all this, no one is pressed to endure hardships for which he is unfit; nothing is imposed on any one against his will; nor is he condemned by the rest because he confesses himself too feeble to imitate them:

for they bear in mind how strongly Scripture enjoins charity on all:

they bear in mind "To the pure all things are pure," [143] and "Not that which entereth into your mouth defileth you, but that which cometh out of it." [144] Accordingly, all their endeavors are concerned not about the rejection of kinds of food as polluted, but about the subjugation of inordinate desire and the maintenance of brotherly love.

They remember, "Meats for the belly, and the belly for meats; but God shall destroy both it and them;" [145] and again, "Neither if we eat shall we abound, nor if we refrain from eating shall we be in want;" [146] and, above all, this:

"It is good, my brethren, not to eat flesh, nor drink wine, nor anything whereby thy brother is offended;" for this passage shows that love is the end to be aimed at in all these things.

"For one man," he says, "believes that he can eat all things:

another, who is weak, eateth herbs.

He that eateth, let him not despise him that eateth not; and let not him that eateth not judge him that eateth:

for God hath approved him.

Who art thou that thou shouldest judge another man's servant?

To his own master he stands or fails; but he shall stand:

for God is able to make him to stand."

And a little after:

"He that eateth, to the Lord he eateth, and giveth God thanks; and he that eateth not, to the Lord he eateth not, and giveth God thanks."

And also in what follows:

"So every one of us shall give account of himself to God.

Let us not, then, any more judge one another:

but judge this rather, that ye place no stumbling-block, or cause of offence, in the way of a brother.

I know, and am confident in the Lord Jesus, that there is nothing common in itself:

but to him that thinketh anything to be common, to him it is common."

Could he have shown better that it is not in the things we eat, but in the mind, that there is a power able to pollute it, and therefore that even those who are fit to think lightly of these things, and know perfectly that they are not polluted if they take any food in mental superiority, without being gluttons, should still have regard to charity?

See what he adds:

"For if thy brother be grieved with thy meat, now walkest thou not charitably." [147]

72.

Read the rest:
it is too long to quote all.

You will find that those able to think lightly of such things,--that is, those of greater strength and stability,--are told that they must nevertheless abstain, lest those should be offended who from their weakness are still in need of such abstinence.

The people I was describing know and observe these things; for they are Christians, not heretics.

They understand Scripture according to the apostolic teaching, not according to the presumptuous and fictitious name of apostle. [148]"Him that eats not no one despises; him that eats no one judges; he who is weak eats herbs."

Many who are strong, however, do this for the sake of the weak; with many the reason for so doing is not this, but that they may have a cheaper diet, and may lead a life of the greatest tranquillity, with the least expensive provision for the support of the body.

"For all things are lawful for me," he says; "but I will not be brought under the power of any." [149]Thus many do not eat flesh, and yet do not superstitiously regard it as unclean.

And so the same people who abstain when in health take it when unwell without any fear, if it is required as a cure.

Many drink no wine; but they do not think that wine defiles them; for they cause it to be given with the greatest propriety and moderation to people of languid temperament, and, in short, to all who cannot have bodily health without it.

When some foolishly refuse it, they counsel them as brothers not to let a silly superstition make them weaker instead of making them holier.

They read to them the apostle's precept to his disciple to "take a little wine for his many infirmities." [150]Then they diligently exercise piety; bodily exercise, they know, profiteth for a short time, as the same apostle says. [151]

73.

Those, then who are able, and they are without number, abstain both from flesh and from wine for two reasons:
either for the weakness of their brethren, or for their own liberty.
Charity is principally attended to.
There is charity in their choice of diet, charity in their speech, charity in their dress, charity in their looks.
Charity is the point where they meet, and the plan by which they act.
To transgress against charity is thought criminal, like transgressing against God.
Whatever opposes this is attacked and expelled; whatever injures it is not allowed to continue for a single day.
They know that it has been so enjoined by Christ and the apostles; that without it all things are empty, with it all are fulfilled.

Chapter 34 - The Church is Not to Be Blamed for the Conduct of Bad Christians, Worshippers of Tombs and Pictures

74.

Make objections against these, ye Manichæans, if you can.
Look at these people, and speak of them reproachfully, if you dare, without falsehood.
Compare their fasts with your fasts, their chastity with yours; compare them to yourselves in dress, food, self-restraint, and, lastly, in charity.
Compare, which is most to the point, their precepts with yours.
Then you will see the difference between show and sincerity, between the right way and the wrong, between faith and imposture, between strength and inflatedness, between happiness and wretchedness, between unity and disunion; in short, between the sirens of superstition and the harbor of religion.

75.

Do not summon against me professors of the Christian name, who neither know nor give evidence of the power of their profession. [152]

Do not hunt up the numbers of ignorant people, who even in the true religion are superstitious, or are so given up to evil passions as to forget what they have promised to God.

I know that there are many worshippers of tombs and pictures.

I know that there are many who drink to great excess over the dead, and who, in the feasts which they make for corpses, bury themselves over the buried, and give to their gluttony and drunkenness the name of religion.

I know that there are many who in words have renounced this world, and yet desire to be burdened with all the weight of worldly things, and rejoice in such burdens.

Nor is it surprising that among so many multitudes you should find some by condemning whose life you may deceive the unwary and seduce them from Catholic safety; for in your small numbers you are at a loss when called on to show even one out of those whom you call the elect who keeps the precepts, which in your indefensible superstition you profess.

How silly those are, how impious, how mischievous, and to what extent they are neglected by most, nearly all of you, I have shown in another volume.

76.

My advice to you now is this:

that you should at least desist from slandering the Catholic Church, by declaiming against the conduct of men whom the Church herself condemns, seeking daily to correct them as wicked children.

Then, if any of them by good will and by the help of God are corrected, they regain by repentance what they had lost by sin.

Those, again, who with wicked will persist in their old vices, or even add to them others still worse, are indeed allowed to remain in the field of the Lord, and to grow along with the good seed; but the time for separating the tares will come. [153] Or if, from their having at least the Christian name, they are to be placed among the chaff rather than among thistles, there will also come One to purge the floor and to separate the chaff from the wheat, and to assign to each part (according to its desert) the due reward. [154]

Chapter 35 - Marriage and Property Allowed to the Baptized by the Apostles

77.

Meanwhile, why do you rage? why does party spirit blind your eyes?
Why do you entangle yourselves in a long defence of such great error?
Seek for fruit in the field, seek for wheat in the floor:
they will be found easily, and will present themselves to the inquirer.
Why do you look so exclusively at the dross?
Why do you use the roughness of the hedge to scare away the inexperienced from the fatness of the garden?

There is a proper entrance, though known to but a few; and by it men come in, though you disbelieve it, or do not wish to find it. In the Catholic Church there are believers without number who do not use the world, and there are those who "use it," in the words of the apostle, "as not using it," [155] as was proved in those times when Christians were forced to worship idols.

For then, how many wealthy men, how many peasant householders, how many merchants, how many military men, how many leading men in their own cities, and how many senators, people of both sexes, giving up all these empty and transitory things, though while they used them they were not bound down by them, endured death for the salutary faith and religion, and proved to unbelievers that instead of being possessed by all these things they really possessed them?

78.

Why do you reproach us by saying that men renewed in baptism ought no longer to beget children, or to possess fields, and houses, and money?

Paul allows it.

For, as cannot be denied, he wrote to believers, after recounting many kinds of evil-doers who shall not possess the kingdom of God:

"And such were you," he says:

"but ye are washed, but ye are sanctified, but ye are justified in the name of the Lord Jesus Christ and by the Spirit of our God."

By the washed and sanctified, no one, assuredly, will venture to think any are meant but believers, and those who have renounced this world.

But, after showing to whom he writes, let us see whether he allows these things to them. He goes on:

"All things are lawful for me, but all things are not expedient:

all things are lawful for me, but I will not be brought under the power of any.

Meat for the belly, and the belly for meats: but God will destroy both it and them.

Now the body is not for fornication, but for the Lord, and the Lord for the body.

But God raised up the Lord, and will raise us up also by His own power.

Know ye not that your bodies are the members of Christ? shall I then take the members of Christ, and make them the members of an harlot?

God forbid.

Know ye not that he which is joined to an harlot is made one body? for the twain, saith He, shall be one flesh.

But he that is joined to the Lord is one spirit.

Flee fornication.

Whatever sin a man doeth is without the body:

but he that committeth fornication sinneth against his own body.

Know ye not that your members are the temple of the Holy Spirit which is in you, which ye have of God, and ye are not your own?

For ye are bought with a great price:

glorify God, and carry Him in your body." [156]"But of the things concerning which ye wrote to me:

it is good for a man not to touch a woman. Nevertheless, to avoid fornication, let every man have his own wife, and let every woman have her own husband.

Let the husband render unto the wife due benevolence:

and likewise also the wife unto the husband.

The wife hath not power of her own body, but the husband: and likewise also the husband hath not power of his own body, but the wife.

Defraud ye not one the other, except it be with consent for a time, that ye may have leisure for prayer; and come together again, that Satan tempt you not for your incontinency.

But I speak this by permission, and not of commandment.

For I would that all men were even as I myself:

but every man hath his proper gift of God, one after this manner, and another after that." [157]

79.

Has the apostle, think you, both shown sufficiently to the strong what is highest, and permitted to the weaker what is next best?

Not to touch a woman he shows is highest when he says, "I would that all men were even as I myself."

But next to this highest is conjugal chastity, that man may not be the prey of fornication.

Did he say that these people were not yet believers because they were married?

Indeed, by this conjugal chastity he says that those who are united are sanctified by one another, if one of them is an unbeliever, and that their children also are sanctified.

"The unbelieving husband," he says, "is sanctified by the believing wife, and the unbelieving woman by the believing husband:

otherwise your children would be unclean; but now are they holy." [158]Why do you persist in opposition to such plain truth?

Why do you try to darken the light of Scripture by vain shadows?

80.

Do not say that catechumens are allowed to have wives, but not believers; that catechumens may have money, but not believers.

For there are many who use as not using.

And in that sacred washing the renewal of the new man is begun so as gradually to reach perfection, in some more quickly, in others more slowly.

The progress, however, to a new life is made in the case of many, if we view the matter without hostility, but attentively.

As the apostle says of himself, "Though the outward man perish, the inward man is renewed day by day." [159] The apostle says that the inward man is renewed day by day that it may reach perfection; and you wish it to begin with perfection!

And it were well if you did wish it.

In reality, you aim not at raising the weak, but at misleading the unwary.

You ought not to have spoken so arrogantly, even if it were known that you are perfect in your childish precepts.

But when your conscience knows that those whom you bring into your sect, when they come to a more intimate acquaintance with you, will find many things in you which nobody hearing you accuse others would suspect, is it not great impertinence to demand perfection in the weaker Catholics, to turn away the inexperienced from the Catholic Church, while you show nothing of the kind in yourself to those thus turned away?

But not to seem to inveigh against you without reason, I will now close this volume, and will proceed at last to set forth the precepts of your life and your notable customs.

Footnotes:

46. Written in the year 388.

In his Retractations (i. 7) Augustin says:

"When I was at Rome after my baptism, and could not bear in silence the vaunting of the Manichæans about their pretended and misleading continence or abstinence, in which, to deceive the inexperienced, they claim superiority over true Christians, to whom they are not to be compared, I wrote two books, one on the morals of the Catholic Church, the other on the morals of the Manichæans."

47. [This is commonly supposed to have been the first work of any importance written by the Author against Manichæism.

What he here refers to it is not easy to conjecture.--A.H.N.]

48. [Augustin's transition from his fine Platonizing discussion of virtue, the chief good, etc., to the patriarchs, the law, and the prophets is very fine rhetorically and apologetically.--A.H.N.]

49. Matt. xxii. 37.

50. Rom. viii. 28, 35.

51. [The most satisfactory feature of Augustin's apology for the Old Testament Scriptures is his demonstration of the substantial agreement of the Old Testament with undisputed portions of the New Testament.--A.H.N.]

52. Deut. vi. 5.

53. Rom. viii. 36; cf. Ps. xliv. 22.

54. Retract. i. 7, § 2:--"In the book on the morals of the Catholic Church, where I have quoted the words, For Thy sake we are in suffering all day long, we are accounted as sheep for the slaughter,' the inaccuracy of my manuscript misled me; for my recollection of the Scriptures was defective from my not being at that time familiar with them.

For the reading of the other manuscripts has a different meaning:

not, we suffer, but we suffer death, or, in one word, we are killed.

That this is the true reading is shown by the Greek text of the Septuagint, from which the Old Testament was translated into Latin.

I have indeed made a good many remarks on the words, For thy sake we suffer,' and the things said are not wrong in themselves; but, as regards the harmony of the Old and New Testaments, this case certainly does not prove it.

The error originated in the way mentioned above, and this harmony is afterwards abundantly proved from other passages."

55. [Augustin's virtus takes the place of the Greek δυνάμεις and the Vulgate virtutes.

It is not quite certain what meaning he attached to the expression.

He seems to waver between the idea of power and that of virtue in the ethical sense, and finally settles down to the use of the term in the latter sense.

That this does not accord with the meaning of the Apostle is evident.--A.H.N.]

56. Rom. viii. 38, 39.

57. [I.e. only by the use of the mental faculty of which God Himself is the Creator and Author; not by any independently existing power "of the same nature with Him who created it."--A.H.N.]

58. 1 Cor. i. 23, 24.

59. John xiv. 6.

60. Rom. viii. 29.

61. Rom. v. 5.

62. Rom. viii. 20.

63. Rom. xi. 36.

64. [It would be difficult to find in Christian literature a more beautiful and satisfactory exposition of love to God.

The Neo-Platonic influence is manifest, but it is Neo-Platonism thoroughly Christianized.--A.H.N.]

65. Ps. lxxiii. 28.

66. John i. 3, 4.

67. [Augustin seems to make no distinction between Apocryphal and Canonical books.

The book of Wisdom was evidently a favorite with him, doubtless on account of its decided Platonic quality.--A.H.N.]

68. Wisd. viii. 1, 4, 7.

69. Retract. i. 7, § 3:--"The quotation from the book of Wisdom is from my manuscript, where the reading is, Wisdom teaches sobriety, justice, and virtue.'

From these words I have made some remarks true in themselves, but occasioned by a false reading.

It is perfectly true that wisdom teaches truth of contemplation, as I have explained sobriety; and excellence of action, which is the meaning I give to justice and virtue.

And the reading in better manuscripts has the same meaning:

It teaches sobriety, and wisdom, and justice, and virtue.' These are the names given by the Latin translator to the four virtues which philosophers usually speak about.

Sobriety is for temperance, wisdom for prudence, virtue for fortitude, and justice only has its own name.

It was long after that we found these virtues called by their proper names in the Greek text of this book of Wisdom."

70. Wisd. viii. 3.
71. 1 Cor. i. 24.
72. Matt. xi. 27.
73. Wisd. ix. 9.
74. Heb. i. 3.
75. Ps. lxxxix. 8.
76. John xiv. 6.
77. Wisd. ix. 17-19.
78. Rom. v. 5.
79. Wisd. i. 5.
80. Rom. viii. 29.
81. Ps. iv. 6.
82. Wisd. ix. 17.
83. Rom. xi. 36.
84. Deut. vi. 4.
85. [Here we have the key to all that is best in Augustin's defense of the anthropomorphisms and the seemingly imperfect ethical representations of the Old Testament.

See Mozley's essay on "The Manichæans and the Jewish Fathers," in his Ruling Ideas in Early Ages. The entire volume represents an attempt to account for the elements in the Old Testament that offend the Christian consciousness.--A.H.N.]

86. 1 Cor. xi. 19.
87. Matt. vii. 7.
88. Matt. x. 26.
89. Wisd. vi. 12-20.
90. Matt. vii. 6.
91. Eph. iii. 14-19.
92. Matt. vii. 7.
93. Eph. iii. 7.
94. [Animi not mentis.--A.H.N.]
95. From his 19th to his 28th year.
96. 1 Tim. vi. 10.
97. 1 Cor. xv. 22.
98. Col. iii. 9, 10.
99. 1 Cor. xv. 47-49.
100. 2 Cor. iv. 16.
101. Ps. li. 10.
102. 2 Cor. iv. 18.
103. Gal. i. 10.
104. Col. ii. 8.
105. 1 John ii. 15.
106. Rom. xii. 2.
107. Eccles. i. 2, 3.
108. Retract. i. 7, § 3: --"I found in many manuscripts the reading, Vanity of the vain.'

But this is not in the Greek, which has Vanity of vanities.'

This I saw afterwards.

And I found that the best Latin manuscripts had vanities and not vain.

But the truths I have drawn from this false reading are self-evident."

109. Rom. v. 3, 4.
110. Job. i. 2.
111. [It is interesting to observe how remote Augustin was from attaching superior merit to voluntary poverty, or to other forms of asceticism as ends in themselves.

What he prized was the ability to use without abusing, to have without cleaving to the good things which God provides.--A.H.N.]

112. 2 Mac. vii.
113. Ps. cxvi. 15.
114. Prov. xvi. 32.
115. Ecclus. ii. 4, 5.
116. Ecclus. xxvii. 6.
117. Matt. vi. 24.
118. Rom. i. 25.
119. Deut. vi. 13.
120. A name given by Augustin to the Holy Spirit, v. xxx.
121. Matt. xxiv. 42.
122. John xii. 35.
123. 1 Cor. v. 6.
124. Ecclus. xix. 1.
125. John xvii. 3.
126. Retract. i. 7. § 4:--"I should have said sincere affection rather than full; or it might be thought that the love of God will be no greater when we shall see Him face to face.

Full, then, must be here understood as meaning that it cannot be greater while we walk by faith.

There will be greater, yea, perfect fullness, but only by sight."

127. [By authority Augustin does not mean the authority of the Church or of Scripture, but he refers to the loving recognition of the authority of God as the condition of true discipleship.--A.H.N.]

128. Matt. xxii. 39.
129. Rom. xiii. 10.
130. Rom. viii. 28.
131. Retract. i. 7. § 4:--"This does not mean that there are actually in this life wise men such as are here spoken of.

My words are not, although they are so wise,' but although they were so wise.'" [Augustin's ideal wise man was evidently the "Gnostic" of Clement of Alexandria.

The conception is Stoical and Neo-Platonic.--A.H.N.]

132. Deut. vi. 5; Lev. xix. 18; Matt. xxii. 37, 39.

133. Matt. xxii. 40.

134. [The strong testimony borne by Augustin against the perverse subjective criticism of the Manichæns has an important application to the present time.--A.H.N.]

135. [This view of the marriage relation seems to have been almost universal in the ancient Church.

Tertullian and Clement of Alexandria are fond of dwelling upon it.

For Augustin's views more fully stated see his De Bono Conjugali, 6.

See also an interesting excursus on "Continence in Married Life" in Cunningham's St. Austin, p. 168. sq.--A.H.N.]

136. [If this apostrophe had been addressed to "Christianity" rather than to the "Catholic Church," no Christian could fail to see in it one of the noblest tributes ever bestowed on the religion of Christ. Augustin identified Christianity with the organized body which was far from realizing the ideal that he here sets forth.

As an apostrophe to ideal Christianity nothing could be finer.--A.H.N.]

137. Deut. iv. 24.

Retract. i. 7, § 5:--"The Pelagians may think that I have spoken of perfection as attainable in this life.

But they must not think so.

For the fervor of charity which is fitted for following God, and of force enough to consume all vices, can have its origin and growth in this life; but it does not follow that it can here accomplish the purpose of its origin, so that no vice shall remain in the man; although this great effect is produced by this same fervor of charity, when and where this is possible, that as the laver of regeneration purifies from the guilt of all the sins which attach to man's birth, or come from his evil conduct, so this perfection may purify him from all stain from the vices which necessarily attend human infirmity in this world.

So we must understand the words of the apostle:

Christ loved the Church, and gave himself for it; cleansing it with the washing of water by the word, that He might present it to Himself a glorious Church, not having spot, or wrinkle, or any such thing' (Eph. v. 25-27).

For in this world there is the washing of water by the word which purifies the Church.

But as the whole Church, as long as it is here, says, Forgive us our debts,' it certainly is not while here without spot, or wrinkle, or any such thing; but from that which it here receives, it is led on to the glory which is not here, and to perfection."

138. Luke xii. 49.

139. Hos. xiii. 14; 1 Cor. xv. 54, 55.

140. 1 Cor. xv. 56.

141. [This picture of coenobitic life, even in its purest form, is doubtless idealized.

It is certain that the monasteries very soon became hot-beds of vice, and the refuge of the scum of society.--A.H.N.]

142. [Augustin ascribes a broadmindedness and charitableness to the ascetics of his time which was doubtless quite subjective.

The ascetics of that age with whose history we are acquainted were not of this type.

Jerome is an example.--A.H.N.]

143. Tit. i. 15.

144. Matt. xv. 11.

145. 1 Cor. vi. 13.

146. 1 Cor. viii. 8.

147. Rom. xiv. 2-21.

148. See title of the Epistle of Manichæus, Contra Faust. xiii. 4.

149. 1 Cor. vi. 12.

150. 1 Tim. v. 23.

151. 1 Tim. iv. 8.

152. [Augustin says nothing of the encouragement given to such pagan practices by men regarded in that age as possessed of almost superhuman sanctity, such as Sulpicius Severus, Paulinus of Nola, etc. He speaks of corruptions as if they were exceptional, whereas they seem to have been the rule.

Yet there is force in his contention that Christianity be judged by its best products rather than by the worst elements associated with it.--A.H.N.]

153. [Augustin's ideal representation of Christianity and his identification of the organized Catholic Church with Christianity is quite inconsistent with the practice of the Church which he here seeks to justify.

No duty is more distinctly enjoined upon believers in the New Testament than separation from unbelievers and evil doers.

But such separation is impracticable in an established Church such as that to which Augustin rejoiced to belong.--A.H.N.]

154. Matt. iii. 13, and xiii. 24-43.

155. 1 Cor. vii. 31.

156. 1 Cor. vi. 11-20.

157. 1 Cor. vii. 1-7.

158. 1 Cor. vii. 14.

159. 2 Cor. iv. 16.

On the Morals of the Manichæans
[de moribus manichæorum].
A.D. 388.
translated by the rev. richard stothert, m.a.,
bombay

Containing a particular refutation of the doctrine of these heretics regarding the origin and nature of evil; an exposure of their pretended symbolical customs of the mouth, of the hands, and of the breast; and a condemnation of their superstitious abstinence and unholy mysteries. Lastly, some crimes brought to light among the Manichæans are mentioned.

Chapter 1 - The Supreme Good is that Which is Possessed of Supreme Existence

1.
Every one, I suppose, will allow that the question of things good and evil belongs to moral science, in which such terms are in common use.

It is therefore to be wished that men would bring to these inquiries such a clear intellectual perfection as might enable them to see the chief good, than which nothing is better or higher, next in order to which comes a rational soul in a state of purity and perfection. [160]If this were clearly understood, it would also become evident that the chief good is that which is properly described as having supreme and original existence.

For that exists in the highest sense of the word which continues always the same, which is throughout like itself, which cannot in any part be corrupted or changed, which is not subject to time, which admits of no variation in its present as compared with its former condition.

This is existence in its true sense.

For in this signification of the word existence there is implied a nature which is self-contained, and which continues immutably.

Such things can be said only of God, to whom there is nothing contrary in the strict sense of the word.

For the contrary of existence is non-existence.

There is therefore no nature contrary to God.

But since the minds with which we approach the study of these subjects have their vision damaged and dulled by silly notions, and by perversity of will, let us try as we can to gain some little knowledge of this great matter by degrees and with caution, making our inquiries not like men able to see, but like men groping the dark.

Chapter 2 - What Evil is. That Evil is that Which is Against Nature. In Allowing This, the Manichæans Refute Themselves

2.
You Manichæans often, if not in every case, ask those whom you try to bring over to your heresy, Whence is evil?

Suppose I had now met you for the first time, I would ask you, if you please, to follow my example in putting aside for a little the explanation you suppose yourselves to have got of these subjects, and to commence this great inquiry with me as if for the first time.

You ask me, Whence is evil? I ask you in return, What is evil?

Which is the more reasonable question?

Are those right who ask whence a thing is, when they do not know what it is; or he who thinks it necessary to inquire first what it is, in order to avoid the gross absurdity of searching for the origin of a thing unknown?

Your answer is quite correct, when you say that evil is that which is contrary to nature; for no one is so mentally blind as not to see that, in every kind, evil is that which is contrary to the nature of the kind.

But the establishment of this doctrine is the overthrow of your heresy.
For evil is no nature, if it is contrary to nature.
Now, according to you, evil is a certain nature and substance.
Moreover, whatever is contrary to nature must oppose nature and seek its destruction.
For nature means nothing else than that which anything is conceived of as being in its own kind.
Hence is the new word which we now use derived from the word for being,--essence namely, or, as we usually say, substance,--while before these words were in use, the word nature was used instead.
Here, then, if you will consider the matter without stubbornness, we see that evil is that which falls away from essence and tends to non-existence.

3.
Accordingly, when the Catholic Church declares that God is the author of all natures and substances, those who understand this understand at the same time that God is not the author of evil.
For how can He who is the cause of the being of all things be at the same time the cause of their not being,--that is, of their falling off from essence and tending to non-existence?
For this is what reason plainly declares to be the definition of evil.
Now, how can that race of evil of yours, which you make the supreme evil, be against nature, that is, against substance, when it, according to you, is itself a nature and substance?
For if it acts against itself, it destroys its own existence; and when that is completely done, it will come at last to be the supreme evil.
But this cannot be done, because you will have it not only to be, but to be everlasting.
That cannot then be the chief evil which is spoken of as a substance. [161]

4.
But what am I to do?
I know that many of you can understand nothing of all this.
I know, too, that there are some who have a good understanding and can see these things, and yet are so stubborn in their choice of evil,--a choice that will ruin their understanding as well,--that they try rather to find what reply they can make in order to impose upon inactive and feeble minds, instead of giving their assent to the truth.
Still I shall not regret having written either what one of you may come some day to consider impartially, and be led to abandon your error, or what men of understanding and in allegiance to God, and who are still untainted with your errors, may read and so be kept from being led astray by your addresses.

Chapter 3 - If Evil is Defined as that Which is Hurtful, This Implies Another Refutation of the Manichæans

5.
Let us then inquire more carefully, and, if possible, more plainly.
I ask you again, What is evil?
If you say it is that which is hurtful, here, too, you will not answer amiss.
But consider, I pray you; be on your guard, I beg of you; be so good as to lay aside party spirit, and make the inquiry for the sake of finding the truth, not of getting the better of it.
Whatever is hurtful takes away some good from that to which it is hurtful; for without the loss of good there can be no hurt.
What, I appeal to you, can be plainer than this? what more intelligible?
What else is required for complete demonstration to one of average understanding, if he is not perverse?
But, if this is granted, the consequence seems plain.
In that race which you take for the chief evil, nothing can be liable to be hurt, since there is no good in it.
But if, as you assert, there are two natures,--the kingdom of light and the kingdom of darkness; since you make the kingdom of light to be God, attributing to it an uncompounded nature,[162] so that it has no part inferior to another, you must grant, however decidedly in opposition to yourselves, you must grant, nevertheless, that this nature, which you not only do not deny to be the chief good, but spend all your strength in trying to show that it is so, is immutable, incorruptible, impenetrable, inviolable, for otherwise it would not be the chief good; for the chief

good is that than which there is nothing better, and for such a nature to be hurt is impossible.

Again, if, as has been shown, to hurt is to deprive of good, there can be no hurt to the kingdom of darkness, for there is no good in it.

And as the kingdom of light cannot be hurt, as it is inviolable, what can the evil you speak of be hurtful to?

Chapter 4 - The Difference Between What is Good in Itself and What is Good by Participation

6.

Now, compare with this perplexity, from which you cannot escape, the consistency of the statements in the teaching of the Catholic Church, according to which there is one good which is good supremely and in itself, and not by the participation of any good, but by its own nature and essence; and another good which is good by participation, and by having something bestowed.

Thus it has its being as good from the supreme good, which, however, is still self-contained, and loses nothing. This second kind of good is called a creature, which is liable to hurt through falling away.

But of this falling away God is not the author, for He is author of existence and of being.

Here we see the proper use of the word evil; for it is correctly applied not to essence, but to negation or loss.

We see, too, what nature it is which is liable to hurt.

This nature is not the chief evil, for when it is hurt it loses good; nor is it the chief good, for its falling away from good is because it is good not intrinsically, but by possessing the good.

And a thing cannot be good by nature when it is spoken of as being made, which shows that the goodness was bestowed.

Thus, on the one hand, God is the good, and all things which He has made are good, though not so good as He who made them.

For what madman would venture to require that the works should equal the workman, the creatures the Creator?

What more do you want?

Could you wish for anything plainer than this?

Chapter 5 - If Evil is Defined to Be Corruption, This Completely Refutes the Manichæan Heresy

7.

I ask a third time, What is evil?

Perhaps you will reply, Corruption.

Undeniably this is a general definition of evil; for corruption implies opposition to nature, and also hurt.

But corruption exists not by itself, but in some substance which it corrupts; for corruption itself is not a substance.

So the thing which it corrupts is not corruption, is not evil; for what is corrupted suffers the loss of integrity and purity.

So that which has no purity to lose cannot be corrupted; and what has, is necessarily good by the participation of purity.

Again, what is corrupted is perverted; and what is perverted suffers the loss of order, and order is good.

To be corrupted, then, does not imply the absence of good; for in corruption it can be deprived of good, which could not be if there was the absence of good. Therefore that race of darkness, if it was destitute of all good, as you say it was, could not be corrupted, for it had nothing which corruption could take from it; and if corruption takes nothing away, it does not corrupt.

Say now, if you dare, that God and the kingdom of God can be corrupted, when you cannot show how the kingdom of the devil, such as you make it, can be corrupted.

Chapter 6 - What Corruption Affects and What It is

8.
What further does the Catholic light say?

What do you suppose, but what is the actual truth, that it is the created substance which can be corrupted, for the uncreated, which is the chief good, is incorruptible; and corruption, which is the chief evil, cannot be corrupted; besides, that it is not a substance?

But if you ask what corruption is, consider to what it seeks to bring the things which it corrupts; for it affects those things according to its own nature.

Now all things by corruption fall away from what they were, and are brought to non-continuance, to non-existence; for existence implies continuance.

Thus the supreme and chief existence is so called because it continues in itself, or is self-contained.

In the case of a thing changing for the better, the change is not from continuance, but from perversion to the worse, that is, from falling away from essence; the author of which falling away is not He who is the author of the essence.

So in some things there is change for the better, and so a tendency towards existence.

And this change is not called a perversion, but reversion or conversion; for perversion is opposed to orderly arrangement.

Now things which tend towards existence tend towards order, and, attaining order they attain existence, as far as that is possible to a creature.

For order reduces to a certain uniformity that which it arranges; and existence is nothing else than being one.

Thus, so far as anything acquires unity, so far it exists. For uniformity and harmony are the effects of unity, and by these compound things exist as far as they have existence.

For simple things exist by themselves, for they are one.

But things not simple imitate unity by the agreement of their parts; and so far as they attain this, so far they exist.

This arrangement is the cause of existence, disorder of non-existence; and perversion or corruption are the other names for disorder.

So whatever is corrupted tends to non-existence. You may now be left to reflect upon the effect of corruption, that you may discover what is the chief evil; for it is that which corruption aims at accomplishing.

Chapter 7 - The Goodness of God Prevents Corruption from Bringing Anything to Non-Existence. The Difference Between Creating and Forming

9.
But the goodness of God does not permit the accomplishment of this end, but so orders all things that fall away that they may exist where their existence is most suitable, till in the order of their movements they return to that from which they fell away. [163] Thus, when rational souls fall away from God, although they possess the greatest amount of free-will, He ranks them in the lower grades of creation, where their proper place is.

So they suffer misery by the divine judgment, while they are ranked suitably to their deserts.

Hence we see the excellence of that saying which you are always inveighing against so strongly, "I make good things, and create evil things." [164] To create is to form and arrange.

So in some copies it is written, "I make good things and form evil things."

To make is used of things previously not in existence; but to form is to arrange what had some kind of existence, so as to improve and enlarge it.

Such are the things which God arranges when He says, "I form evil things," meaning things which are falling off, and so tending to non-existence,--not things which have reached that to which they tend.

For it has been said, Nothing is allowed in the providence of God to go the length of non-existence. [165]

10.

These things might be discussed more fully and at greater length, but enough has been said for our purpose in dealing with you.

We have only to show you the gate which you despair of finding, and make the uninstructed despair of it too.

You can be made to enter only by good-will, on which the divine mercy bestows peace, as the song in the Gospel says, "Glory to God in the highest, and on earth peace to men of good-will."[166] It is enough, I say, to have shown you that there is no way of solving the religious question of good and evil, unless whatever is, as far as it is, is from God; while as far as it falls away from being it is not of God, and yet is always ordered by Divine Providence in agreement with the whole system.

If you do not yet see this, I know nothing else that I can do but to discuss the things already said with greater particularity.

For nothing save piety and purity can lead the mind to greater things.

Chapter 8 - Evil is Not a Substance, But a Disagreement Hostile to Substance

11.

For what other answer will you give to the question, What is evil? but either that it is against nature, or that it is hurtful, or that it is corruption, or something similar?

But I have shown that in these replies you make shipwreck of your cause, unless, indeed, you will answer in the childish way in which you generally speak to children, that evil is fire, poison, a wild beast, and so on.

For one of the leaders of this heresy, whose instructions we attended with great familiarity and frequency, used to say with reference to a person who held that evil was not a substance, "I should like to put a scorpion in the man's hand, and see whether he would not withdraw his hand; and in so doing he would get a proof, not in words but in the thing itself, that evil is a substance, for he would not deny that the animal is a substance."

He said this not in the presence of the person, but to us, when we repeated to him the remark which had troubled us, giving, as I said, a childish answer to children.

For who with the least tincture of learning or science does not see that these things hurt by disagreement with the bodily temperament, while at other times they agree with it, so as not only not to hurt, but to produce the best effects?

For if this poison were evil in itself, the scorpion itself would suffer first and most.

In fact, if the poison were quite taken from the animal, it would die.

So for its body it is evil to lose what it is evil for our body to receive; and it is good for it to have what it is good for us to want.

Is the same thing then both good and evil? By no means; but evil is what is against nature, for this is evil both to the animal and to us.

This evil is the disagreement, which certainly is not a substance, but hostile to substance.

Whence then is it?

See what it leads to, and you will learn, if any inner light lives in you.

It leads all that it destroys to non-existence.

Now God is the author of existence; and there is no existence which, as far as it is existing, leads to non-existence:

Thus we learn whence disagreement is not; as to whence it is, nothing can be said.

12.

We read in history of a female criminal in Athens, who succeeded in drinking the quantity of poison allotted as a fatal draught for the condemned with little or no injury to her health, by taking it at intervals.

So being condemned, she took the poison in the prescribed quantity like the rest, but rendered it powerless by accustoming herself to it, and did not die like the rest.

And as this excited great wonder, she was banished.

If poison is an evil, are we to think that she made it to be no evil to her?

What could be more absurd than this?

But because disagreement is an evil, what she did was to make the poisonous matter agree with her own body by a process of habituation.

For how could she by any amount of cunning have brought it about that disagreement should not hurt her?

Why so?

Because what is truly and properly an evil is hurtful both always and to all.
Oil is beneficial to our bodies, but very much the opposite to many six-footed animals.
And is not hellebore sometimes food, sometimes medicine, and sometimes poison.
Does not every one maintain that salt taken in excess is poisonous?
And yet the benefits to the body from salt are innumerable and most important.
Sea-water is injurious when drunk by land animals, but it is most suitable and useful to many who bathe their bodies in it and to fish it is useful and wholesome in both ways.
Bread nourishes man, but kills hawks.
And does not mud itself, which is offensive and noxious when swallowed or smelt, serve as cooling to the touch in hot weather, and as a cure for wounds from fire?
What can be nastier than dung, or more worthless than ashes? And yet they are of such use to the fields, that the Romans thought divine honors due to the discoverer, Stercutio, from whose name the word for dung [stercus] is derived.

13.
But why enumerate details which are countless?
We need not go farther than the four elements themselves, which, as every one knows, are beneficial when there is agreement, and bitterly opposed to nature when there is disagreement in the objects acted upon.
We who live in air die under earth or under water, while innumerable animals creep alive in sand or loose earth, and fish die in our air.
Fire consumes our bodies, but, when suitably applied, it both restores from cold, and expels diseases without number.
The sun to which you bow the knee, and than which, indeed, there is no fairer object among visible things, strengthens the eyes of eagles, but hurts and dims our eyes when we gaze on it; and yet we too can accustom ourselves to look upon it without injury.
Will you, then, allow the sun to be compared to the poison which the Athenian woman made harmless by habituating herself to it?
Reflect for once, and consider that if a substance is an evil because it hurts some one, the light which you worship cannot be acquitted of this charge.
See the preferableness of making evil in general to consist in this disagreement, from which the sun's ray produces dimness in the eyes, though nothing is pleasanter to the eyes than light. [167]

Chapter 9 - The Manichæan Fictions About Things Good and Evil are Not Consistent with Themselves

14.
I have said these things to make you cease, if that is possible, giving the name of evil to a region boundless in depth and length; to a mind wandering through the region; to the five caverns of the elements,--one full of darkness, another of waters, another of winds, another of fire, another of smoke; to the animals born in each of these elements,--serpents in the darkness, swimming creatures in the waters, flying creatures in the winds, quadrupeds in the fire, bipeds in the smoke.
For these things, as you describe them, cannot be called evil; for all such things, as far as they exist, must have their existence from the most high God, for as far as they exist they are good.
If pain and weakness is an evil, the animals you speak of were of such physical strength that their abortive offspring, after, as your sect believes, the world was formed of them, fell from heaven to earth, according to you, and could not die.
If blindness is an evil, they could see; if deafness, they could hear.
If to be nearly or altogether dumb is an evil, their speech was so clear and intelligible, that, as you assert, they decided to make war against God in compliance with an address delivered in their assembly.
If sterility is an evil, they were prolific in children.
If exile is an evil, they were in their own country, and occupied their own territories.
If servitude is an evil, some of them were rulers.
If death is an evil, they were alive, and the life was such that, by your statement, even after God was victorious, it was impossible for the mind ever to die.

15.
   Can you tell me how it is that in the chief evil so many good things are to be found, the opposites of the evils above mentioned? and if these are not evils, can any substance be an evil, as far as it is a substance?
   If weakness is not an evil, can a weak body be an evil?
   If blindness is not an evil, can darkness be an evil?
   If deafness is not an evil, can a deaf man be an evil?
   If dumbness is not an evil, can a fish be an evil?
   If sterility is not an evil, how can we call a barren animal an evil?
   If exile is not an evil, how can we give that name to an animal in exile, or to an animal sending some one into exile?
   If servitude is not an evil, in what sense is a subject animal an evil, or one enforcing subjection?
   If death is not an evil, in what sense is a mortal animal an evil, or one causing death?
   Or if these are evils, must we not give the name of good things to bodily strength, sight, hearing, persuasive speech, fertility, native land, liberty, life, all which you hold to exist in that kingdom of evil, and yet venture to call it the perfection of evil?

16.
   Once more, if, as has never been denied, unsuitableness is an evil, what can be more suitable than those elements to their respective animals,--the darkness to serpents, the waters to swimming creatures, the winds to flying creatures, the fire to voracious animals, the smoke to soaring animals?
   Such is the harmony which you describe as existing in the race of strife; such the order in the seat of confusion.
   If what is hurtful is an evil, I do not repeat the strong objection already stated, that no hurt can be suffered where no good exists; but if that is not so clear, one thing at least is easily seen and understood as following from the acknowledged truth, that what is hurtful is an evil.
   The smoke in that region did not hurt bipeds:
   it produced them, and nourished and sustained them without injury in their birth, their growth, and their rule.
   But now, when the evil has some good mixed with it, the smoke has become more hurtful, so that we, who certainly are bipeds, instead of being sustained by it, are blinded, and suffocated, and killed by it.
   Could the mixture of good have given such destructiveness to evil elements?
   Could there be such confusion in the divine government?

17.
   In the other cases, at least, how is it that we find that congruity which misled your author and induced him to fabricate falsehoods?
   Why does darkness agree with serpents, and waters with swimming creatures, and winds with flying creatures, though the fire burns up quadrupeds, and smoke chokes us?
   Then, again, have not serpents very sharp sight, and do they not love the sunshine, and abound most where the calmness of the air prevents the clouds from gathering much or often?
   How very absurd that the natives and lovers of darkness should live most comfortably and agreeably where the clearest light is enjoyed!
   Or if you say that it is the heat rather than the light that they enjoy, it would be more reasonable to assign to fire serpents, which are naturally of rapid motion, than the slow-going asp.[168]Besides, all must admit that light is agreeable to the eyes of the asp, for they are compared to an eagle's eyes.
   But enough of the lower animals.
   Let us, I pray, attend to what is true of ourselves without persisting in error, and so our minds shall be disentangled from silly and mischievous falsehoods.
   For is it not intolerable perversity to say that in the race of darkness, where there was no mixture of light, the biped animals had so sound and strong, so incredible force of eyesight, that even in their darkness they could see the perfectly pure light (as you represent it) of the kingdom of God? for, according to you, even these beings could see this light, and could gaze at it, and study it, and delight in it, and desire it; whereas our eyes, after mixture with light, with the chief good, yea, with God, have become so tender and weak, that we can neither see anything in the dark, nor bear to look at the sun, but, after looking, lose sight of what we could see before.

18.
    The same remarks are applicable if we take corruption to be an evil, which no one doubts. The smoke did not corrupt that race of animals, though it corrupts animals now.
    Not to go over all the particulars, which would be tedious, and is not necessary, the living creatures of your imaginary description were so much less liable to corruption than animals are now, that their abortive and premature offspring, cast headlong from heaven to earth, both lived and were productive, and could band together again, having, forsooth, their original vigor, because they were conceived before good was mixed with the evil; for, after this mixture, the animals born are, according to you, those which we now see to be very feeble and easily giving way to corruption.
    Can any one persist in the belief of error like this, unless he fails to see these things, or is affected by your habit and association in such an amazing way as to be proof against all the force of reasoning?

Chapter 10 - Three Moral Symbols Devised by the Manichæans for No Good

19.
    Now that I have shown, as I think, how much darkness and error is in your opinions about good and evil things in general, let us examine now those three symbols which you extol so highly, and boast of as excellent observances.
    What then are those three symbols?
    That of the mouth, that of the hands, and that of the breast.
    What does this mean?
    That man, we are told, should be pure and innocent in mouth, in hands, and in breast.
    But what if he sins with eyes, ears, or nose? What if he hurts some one with his heels, or perhaps kills him?
    How can he be reckoned criminal when he has not sinned with mouth, hands, or breast?
    But, it is replied, by the mouth we are to understand all the organs of sense in the head; by the hands, all bodily actions; by the breast, all lustful tendencies.
    To what, then, do you assign blasphemies?
    To the mouth or to the hand?
    For blasphemy is an action of the tongue.
    And if all actions are to be classed under one head, why should you join together the actions of the hands and the feet, and not those of the tongue.
    Do you wish to separate the action of the tongue, as being for the purpose of expressing something, from actions which are not for this purpose, so that the symbol of the hands should mean abstinence from all evil actions which are not for the purpose of expressing something?
    But then, what if some one sins by expressing something with his hands, as is done in writing or in some significant gesture?
    This cannot be assigned to the tongue and the mouth, for it is done by the hands.
    When you have three symbols of the mouth, the hands, and the breast, it is quite inadmissible to charge against the mouth sins found in the hands.
    And if you assign action in general to the hands, there is no reason for including under this the action of the feet and not that of the tongue.
    Do you see how the desire of novelty, with its attendant error, lands you in great difficulties? For you find it impossible to include purification of all sins in these three symbols, which you set forth as a kind of new classification.

Chapter 11 - The Value of the Symbol of the Mouth Among the Manichæans, Who are Found Guilty of Blaspheming God

20.
    Classify as you please, omit what you please, we must discuss the doctrines you insist upon most.
    You say that the symbol of the mouth implies refraining from all blasphemy.
    But blasphemy is speaking evil of good things.
    So usually the word blasphemy is applied only to speaking evil of God; for as regards man there is uncertainty, but God is without controversy good.
    If, then, you are proved guilty of saying worse things of God than any one else says, what

becomes of your famous symbol of the mouth?

The evidence is not obscure, but clear and obvious to every understanding, and irresistible, the more so that no one can remain in ignorance of it, that God is incorruptible, immutable, liable to no injury, to no want, to no weakness, to no misery.

All this the common sense of rational beings perceives, and even you assent when you hear it.

21.

But when you begin to relate your fables, that God is corruptible, and mutable, and subject to injury, and exposed to want and weakness, and not secure from misery, this is what you are blind enough to teach, and what some are blind enough to believe.

And this is not all; for, according to you, God is not only corruptible, but corrupted; not only changeable, but changed; not only subject to injury, but injured; not only liable to want, but in want; not only possibly, but actually weak; not only exposed to misery, but miserable.

You say that the soul is God, or a part of God.

I do not see how it can be part of God without being God.

A part of gold is gold; of silver silver; of stone stone; and, to come to greater things, part of earth is earth, part of water is water, and of air air; and if you take part from fire, you will not deny it to be fire; and part of light can be nothing but light.

Why then should part of God not be God?

Has God a jointed body, like man and the lower animals?

For part of man is not man.

22.

I will deal with each of these opinions separately.

If you view God as resembling light, you must admit that part of God is God. Hence, when you make the soul part of God, though you allow it to be corrupted as being foolish, and changed as having once been wise, and in want as needing health, and feeble as needing medicine, and miserable as desiring happiness, all these things you profanely attribute to God.

Or if you deny these things of the mind, it follows that the Spirit is not required to lead the soul into truth, since it is not in folly; nor is the soul renewed by true religion, since it does not need renewal; nor is it perfected by your symbols, since it is already perfect; nor does God give it assistance, since it does not need it; nor is Christ its physician, since it is in health; nor does it require the promise of happiness in another life.

Why then is Jesus called the deliverer, according to His own words in the Gospel, "If the Son shall make you free, ye shall be free indeed?" [169] And the Apostle Paul says, "Ye have been called to liberty." [170] The soul, then, which has not attained this liberty is in bondage.

Therefore, according to you, God, since part of God is God, is both corrupted by folly, and is changed by falling, and is injured by the loss of perfection, and is in need of help, and is weakened by disease, and bowed down with misery, and subject to disgraceful bondage.

23.

Again, if part of God is not God, still He is not incorrupt when His part is corrupted, nor unchanged when there is change in any part, nor uninjured when He is not perfect in every part, nor free from want when He is busily endeavoring to recover part of Himself, nor quite whole when He has a weak part, nor perfectly happy when any part is suffering misery, nor entirely free when any part is under bondage. These are conclusions to which you are driven, because you say that the soul, which you see to be in such a calamitous condition, is part of God.

If you can succeed in making your sect abandon these and many similar opinions, then you may speak of your mouth being free from blasphemies.

Better still, leave the sect; for if you cease to believe and to repeat what Manichæus has written, you will be no longer Manichæans.

24.

That God is the supreme good, and that than which nothing can be or can be conceived better, we must either understand or believe, if we wish to keep clear of blasphemy.

There is a relation of numbers which cannot possibly be impaired or altered, nor can any nature by any amount of violence prevent the number which comes after one from being the double of one.

This can in no way be changed; and yet you represent God as changeable!

This relation preserves its integrity inviolable; and you will not allow God an equality even in this!

Let some race of darkness take in the abstract the number three, consisting of indivisible units,

and divide it into two equal parts.
Your mind perceives that no hostility could effect this.
And can that which is unable to injure a numerical relation injure God?
If it could not, what possible necessity could there be for a part of him to be mixed with evil, and driven into such miseries?

Chapter 12 - Manichæan Subterfuge

25.
For this gives rise to the question, which used to throw us into great perplexity even when we were your zealous disciples, nor could we find any answer,--what the race of darkness would have done to God, supposing He had refused to fight with it at the cost of such calamity to part of Himself.
For if God would not have suffered any loss by remaining quiet, we thought it hard that we had been sent to endure so much.
Again, if He would have suffered, His nature cannot have been incorruptible, as it behoves the nature of God to be.
Sometimes the answer was, that it was not for the sake of escaping evil or avoiding injury, but that God in His natural goodness wished to bestow the blessing of order on a disturbed and disordered nature.
This is not what we find in the Manichæan books:
there it is constantly implied and constantly asserted that God guarded against an invasion of His enemies.
But supposing this answer, which was given from want of a better, to represent the opinion of the Manichæans, is God, in their view, vindicated from the charge of cruelty or weakness?
For this goodness of His to the hostile race proved most pernicious to His own subjects.
Besides, if God's nature could not be corrupted nor changed, neither could any destructive influence corrupt or change us; and the order to be bestowed on the race of strangers might have been bestowed without robbing us of it.

26.
Since those times, however, another answer has appeared which I heard recently at Carthage.
For one, whom I wish much to see brought out of this error, when reduced to this same dilemma, ventured to say that the kingdom had its own limits, which might be invaded by a hostile race, though God Himself could not be injured.
But this is a reply which your founder would never consent to give; for he would be likely to see that such an opinion would lead to a still speedier demolition of his heresy.
And in fact any one of average intellect, who hears that in this nature part is subject to injury and part not, will at once perceive that this makes not two but three natures,--one violable, a second inviolable, and a third violating.

Chapter 13 - Actions to Be Judged of from Their Motive, Not from Externals. Manichæan Abstinence to Be Tried by This Principle

27.
Having every day in your mouth these blasphemies which come from your heart, you ought not to continue holding up the symbol of the mouth as something wonderful, to ensnare the ignorant.
But perhaps you think the symbol of the mouth excellent and admirable because you do not eat flesh or drink wine.
But what is your end in this?
For according as the end we have in view in our actions, on account of which we do whatever we do, is not only not culpable but also praiseworthy, so only can our actions merit any praise.
If the end we have regard to in any performance is unlawful and blameworthy, the performance itself will be unhesitatingly condemned as improper.

28.

We are told of Catiline that he could bear cold, thirst, and hunger. [171]This the vile miscreant had in common with our apostles.

What then distinguishes the parricide from our apostles but the precisely opposite end which he followed?

He bore these things in order to gratify his fierce and ungoverned passions; they, on the other hand, in order to restrain these passions and subdue them to reason. You often say, when you are told of the great number of Catholic virgins, a she-mule is a virgin.

This, indeed, is said in ignorance of the Catholic system, and is not applicable.

Still, what you mean is that this continence is worthless unless it leads, on right principles, to an end of high excellence.

Catholic Christians might also compare your abstinence from wine and flesh to that of cattle and many small birds, as likewise of countless sorts of worms.

But, not to be impertinent like you, I will not make this comparison prematurely, but will first examine your end in what you do.

For I suppose I may safely take it as agreed on, that in such customs the end is the thing to look to.

Therefore, if your end is to be frugal and to restrain the appetite which finds gratification in eating and drinking, I assent and approve.

But this is not the case.

29.

Suppose, what is quite possible, that there is one so frugal and sparing in his diet, that, instead of gratifying his appetite or his palate, he refrains from eating twice in one day, and at supper takes a little cabbage moistened and seasoned with lard, just enough to keep down hunger; and quenches his thirst, from regard to his health, with two or three draughts of pure wine; and this is his regular diet: whereas another of different habits never takes flesh or wine, but makes an agreeable repast at two o'clock on rare and foreign vegetables, varied with a number of courses, and well sprinkled with pepper, and sups in the same style towards night; and drinks honey-vinegar, mead, raisin-wine, and the juices of various fruits, no bad imitation of wine, and even surpassing it in sweetness; and drinks not for thirst but for pleasure; and makes this provision for himself daily, and feasts in this sumptuous style, not because he requires it, but only gratifying his taste;--which of these two do you regard as living most abstemiously in food and drink?

You cannot surely be so blind as not to put the man of the little lard and wine above this glutton!

30.

This is the true view; but your doctrine sounds very differently. For one of your elect distinguished by the three symbols may live like the second person in this description, and though he may be reproved by one or two of the more sedate, he cannot be condemned as abusing the symbols.

But should he sup with the other person, and moisten his lips with a morsel of rancid bacon, or refresh them with a drink of spoilt wine, he is pronounced a transgressor of the symbol, and by the judgment of your founder is consigned to hell, while you, though wondering, must assent.

Will you not discard these errors?
Will you not listen to reason?
Will you not offer some little resistance to the force of habit?
Is not such doctrine most unreasonable?
Is it not insanity?

Is it not the greatest absurdity that one, who stuffs and loads his stomach every day to gratify his appetite with mushrooms, rice, truffles, cake, mead, pepper, and assafoetida, and who fares thus every day, cannot be convicted of transgressing the three symbols, that is, the rule of sanctity; whereas another, who seasons his dish of the commonest herbs with some smoky morsel of meat, and takes only so much of this as is needed for the refreshment of his body, and drinks three cups of wine for the sake of keeping in health, should, for exchanging the former diet for this, be doomed to certain punishment?

Chapter 14 - Three Good Reasons for Abstaining from Certain Kinds of Food

31.

But, you reply, the apostle says, "It is good, brethren, neither to eat flesh, nor to drink wine."[172] No one denies that this is good, provided that it is for the end already mentioned, of which it is said, "Make not provision for the flesh to fulfill the lusts thereof;"[173] or for the ends pointed out by the apostle, namely, either to check the appetite, which is apt to go to a more wild and uncontrollable excess in these things than in others, or lest a brother should be offended, or lest the weak should hold fellowship with an idol.

For at the time when the apostle wrote, the flesh of sacrifices was often sold in the market.

And because wine, too, was used in libations to the gods of the Gentiles, many weaker brethren, accustomed to purchase such things, preferred to abstain entirely from flesh and wine rather than run the risk of having fellowship, as they considered it, with idols, even ignorantly.

And, for their sakes, even those who were stronger, and had faith enough to see the insignificance of these things, knowing that nothing is unclean except from an evil conscience, and holding by the saying of the Lord, "Not that which entereth into your mouth defileth you, but that which cometh out of it,"[174] still, lest these weaker brethren should stumble, were bound to abstain from these things.

And this is not a mere theory, but is clearly taught in the epistles of the apostle himself.

For you are in the habit of quoting only the words, "It is good, brethren, neither to eat flesh, nor to drink wine," without adding what follows, "nor anything whereby thy brother stumbleth, or is offended or is made weak."

These words show the intention of the apostle in giving the admonition.

32.

This is evident from the preceding and succeeding context.

The passage is a long one to quote, but, for the sake of those who are indolent in reading and searching the sacred Scriptures, we must give the whole of it.

"Him that is weak in the faith," says the apostle, "receive ye, but not to doubtful disputations.

For one believeth that he may eat all things:

another, who is weak, eateth herbs.

Let not him that eateth despise him that eateth not; and let not him that eateth not judge him that eateth, for God hath received him.

Who art thou that judgest another man's servant? to his own master he standeth or falleth; yea, he shall be holden up:

for God is able to make him stand.

One man esteemeth one day above another; another esteemeth every day alike.

Let every man be fully persuaded in his own mind.

He that regardeth the day, regardeth it to the Lord.

He that eateth, eateth to the Lord, for he giveth God thanks; and he that eateth not, to the Lord he eateth not, and giveth God thanks.

For none of us liveth to himself, and no man dieth to himself.

For whether we live, we live unto the Lord; and whether we die, we die unto the Lord: whether we live, therefore, or die, we are the Lord's.

For to this end Christ both lived, and died and rose again, that He might be Lord both of the dead and living.

But why dost thou judge thy brother? or why dost thou set at nought thy brother? for we shall all stand before the judgment-seat of God.

For it is written, As I live, saith the Lord, every knee shall bow to me, and every tongue shall confess to God.[175] So then every one of us shall give account of himself to God. Let us not, therefore, judge one another any more:

but judge this rather, that no man put a stumbling-block, or occasion to fall, in his brother's way.

I know, and am persuaded in the Lord Jesus, that there is nothing common of itself:

but to him that esteemeth anything to be common, to him it is common.

But if thy brother be grieved with thy meat, now walkest thou not charitably.

Destroy not him with thy meat, for whom Christ died.

Let not then our good be evil spoken of.

For the kingdom of God is not meat and drink; but righteousness, and peace, and joy in the Holy Ghost.

For he who in this serveth Christ is acceptable to God, and approved of men.

Let us therefore follow after the things which make for peace, and things whereby one may edify another.

For meat destroys not the work of God.

All things indeed are pure; but it is evil for that man who eateth with offense.

It is good neither to eat flesh, nor to drink wine, nor anything whereby thy brother stumbleth, or is offended, or is made weak.

Hast thou faith? have it to thyself before God.

Happy is he who condemneth not himself in that thing which he alloweth.

And he that distinguishes is damned if he eats, because he eateth not of faith: for whatsoever is not of faith is sin.

We then that are strong ought to bear the infirmities of the weak, and not to please ourselves.

Let every one of us please his neighbor for his good to edification.

For even Christ pleased not Himself." [176]

33.

Is it not clear that what the apostle required was, that the stronger should not eat flesh nor drink wine, because they gave offense to the weak by not going along with them, and made them think that those who in faith judged all things to be pure, did homage to idols in not abstaining from that kind of food and drink?

This is also set forth in the following passage of the Epistle to the Corinthians:

"As concerning, therefore, the eating of those things that are offered in sacrifice unto idols, we know that an idol is nothing in the world, and that there is none other God but one.

For though there be that are called gods, whether in heaven or in earth, but to us there is but one God, the Father, of whom are all things, and we in Him; and one Lord Jesus Christ, by whom are all things, and we by Him.

Howbeit there is not in every man that knowledge:

for some, with conscience of the idol unto this hour, eat it as a thing offered to an idol; and their conscience being weak is defiled.

But meat commendeth us not to God: for neither, if we eat, shall we abound; neither, if we eat not, shall we suffer want.

But take heed, lest by any means this liberty of yours become a stumbling-block to them that are weak.

For if any man see one who has knowledge sit at meat in the idol's temple, shall not his conscience being weak be emboldened to eat those things which are offered to idols; and through thy knowledge shall the weak brother perish, for whom Christ died?

But when ye sin so against the brethren, and wound their weak conscience, ye sin against Christ.

Wherefore, if meat make my brother to offend, I will eat no flesh forever, lest I make my brother to offend." [177]

34.

Again, in another place:

"What say I then? that the idol is anything? or that which is offered in sacrifice to idols is anything? But the things which the Gentiles sacrifice they sacrifice to devils, and not to God:

and I would not that ye should have fellowship with devils.

Ye cannot drink the cup of the Lord, and the cup of devils: ye cannot be partakers of the Lord's table and of the table of devils. Do we provoke the Lord to jealousy? are we stronger than He?

All things are lawful for me, but all things are not expedient:

all things are lawful for me, but all things edify not.

Let no man seek his own, but every man what is another's.

Whatsoever is sold in the shambles, that eat, asking no question for conscience sake.

But if any man say unto you, This is offered in sacrifice unto idols, eat not for his sake that shows it, and for conscience sake:

conscience, I say, not thine own, but another's:

for why is my liberty judged of another man's conscience?

For if I be a partaker with thanksgiving, why am I evil spoken of for that for which I give thanks?

Whether, therefore, ye eat or drink, or whatsoever ye do, do all to the glory of God.

Give none offence, neither to the Jews, nor to the Greeks, nor to the Church of God:

even as I please all men in all things not seeking mine own profit, but the profit of many that

they may be saved.
Be ye followers of me, even as I also am of Christ." [178]

35.

It is clear, then, I think, for what end we should abstain from flesh and wine.

The end is threefold:

to check indulgence, which is mostly practised in this sort of food, and in this kind of drink goes the length of intoxication; to protect weakness, on account of the things which are sacrificed and offered in libation; and, what is most praiseworthy of all, from love, not to offend the weakness of those more feeble than ourselves, who abstain from these things.

You, again, consider a morsel of meat unclean; whereas the apostle says that all things are clean, but that it is evil to him that eateth with offence. And no doubt you are defiled by such food, simply because you think it unclean.

For the apostle says, "I know, and am persuaded by the Lord Jesus, that there is nothing common of itself:

but to him that esteemeth anything common, to him it is common."

And every one can see that by common he means unclean and defiled.

But it is folly to discuss passages of Scripture with you; for you both mislead people by promising to prove your doctrines, and those books which possess authority to demand our homage you affirm to be corrupted by spurious interpolations.

Prove then to me your doctrine that flesh defiles the eater, when it is taken without offending any one, without any weak notions, and without any excess. [179]

Chapter 15 - Why the Manichæans Prohibit the Use of Flesh

36.

It is worth while to take note of the whole reason for their superstitious abstinence, which is given as follows:--Since, we are told, the member of God has been mixed with the substance of evil, to repress it and to keep it from excessive ferocity,--for that is what you say,--the world is made up of both natures, of good and evil, mixed together.

But this part of God is daily being set free in all parts of the world, and restored to its own domain.

But in its passage upwards as vapor from earth to heaven, it enters plants, because their roots are fixed in the earth, and so gives fertility and strength to all herbs and shrubs.

From these animals get their food, and, where there is sexual intercourse, fetter in the flesh the member of God, and, turning it from its proper course, they come in the way and entangle it in errors and troubles.

So then, if food consisting of vegetables and fruits comes to the saints, that is, to the Manichæans by means of their chastity, and prayers, and psalms, whatever in it is excellent and divine is purified, and so is entirely perfected, in order to restoration, free from all hindrance, to its own domain.

Hence you forbid people to give bread or vegetables, or even water, which would cost nobody anything, to a beggar, if he is not a Manichæan, lest he should defile the member of God by his sins, and obstruct its return.

37.

Flesh, you say, is made up of pollution itself.

For, according to you, some portion of that divine part escapes in the eating of vegetables and fruits:

it escapes while they undergo the infliction of rubbing, grinding, or cooking, as also of biting or chewing.

It escapes, too, in all motions of animals, in the carriage of burdens, in exercise, in toil, or in any sort of action.

It escapes, too, in our rest, when digestion is going on in the body by means of internal heat.

And as the divine nature escapes in all these ways, some very unclean dregs remain, from which, in sexual intercourse, flesh is formed.

These dregs, however, fly off, in the motions above mentioned, along with what is good in the soul; for though it is mostly, it is not entirely good.

So, when the soul has left the flesh, the dregs are utterly filthy, and the soul of those who eat flesh is defiled.

Chapter 16 - Disclosure of the Monstrous Tenets of the Manichæans

38.

O the obscurity of the nature of things!

How hard to expose falsehood!

Who that hears these things, if he is one who has not learned the causes of things, and who, not yet illuminated by any ray of truth, is deceived by material images, would not think them true, precisely because the things spoken of are invisible, and are presented to the mind under the form of visible things, and can be eloquently expressed?

Men of this description exist in numbers and in droves, who are kept from being led away into these errors more by a fear grounded on religious feeling than by reason.

I will therefore endeavor, as God may please to enable me, so to refute these errors, as that their falsehood and absurdity will be manifest not only in the judgment of the wise, who reject them on hearing them, but also to the intelligence of the multitude.

39.

Tell me then, first, where you get the doctrine that part of God, as you call it, exists in corn, beans, cabbage, and flowers and fruits.

From the beauty of the color, say they, and the sweetness of the taste; this is evident; and as these are not found in rotten substances, we learn that their good has been taken from them.

Are they not ashamed to attribute the finding of God to the nose and the palate?

But I pass from this.

For I will speak, using words in their proper sense; and, as the saying is, this is not so easy in speaking to you.

Let us see rather what sort of mind is required to understand this; how, if the presence of good in bodies is shown by their color, the dung of animals, the refuse of flesh itself, has all kinds of bright colors, sometimes white, often golden; and so on, though these are what you take in fruits and flowers as proofs of the presence and indwelling of God.

Why is it that in a rose you hold the red color to be an indication of an abundance of good, while the same color in blood you condemn?

Why do you regard with pleasure in a violet the same color which you turn away from in cases of cholera, or of people with jaundice, or in the excrement of infants?

Why do you believe the light, shining appearance of oil to be a sign of a plentiful admixture of good, which you readily set about purifying by taking the oil into your throats and stomachs, while you are afraid to touch your lips with a drop of fat, though it has the same shining appearance as oil?

Why do you look upon a yellow melon as part of the treasures of God, and not rancid bacon fat or the yolk of an egg?

Why do you think that whiteness in a lettuce proclaims God, and not in milk?

So much for colors, as regards which (to mention nothing else) you cannot compare any flower-clad meadow with the wings and feathers of a single peacock, though these are of flesh and of fleshly origin.

40.

Again, if this good is discovered also by smell, perfumes of excellent smell are made from the flesh of some animals.

And the smell of food, when cooked along with flesh of delicate flavor, is better than if cooked without it.

Once more, if you think that the things that have a better smell than others are therefore cleaner, there is a kind of mud which you ought to take to your meals instead of water from the cistern; for dry earth moistened with rain has an odor most agreeable to the sense, and this sort of mud has a better smell than rain-water taken by itself.

But if we must have the authority of taste to prove the presence in any object of part of God, he must dwell in dates and honey more than in pork, but more in pork than in beans.

I grant that He dwells more in a fig than in a liver; but then you must allow that He is more in liver than in beet.

And, on this principle, must you not confess that some plants, which none of you can doubt to be cleaner than flesh, receive God from this very flesh, if we are to think of God as mixed with the flavor?

For both cabbages taste better when cooked along with flesh; and, while we cannot relish the plants on which cattle feed, when these are turned into milk we think them improved in color, and find them very agreeable to the taste.

41.
Or must we think that good is to be found in greater quantity where the three good qualities--a good color, and smell, and taste--are found together?

Then you must not admire and praise flowers so much, as you cannot admit them to be tried at the tribunal of the palate.

At least you must not prefer purslain to flesh, since flesh when cooked is superior in color, smell, and taste.

A young pig roasted (for your ideas on this subject force us to discuss good and evil with you as if you were cooks and confectioners, instead of men of reading or literary taste) is bright in color, and agreeable in smell, and pleasant in taste.

Here is a perfect evidence of the presence of the divine substance.

You are invited by this threefold testimony, and called on to purify this substance by your sanctity.

Make the attack.

Why do you hold back?

What objection have you to make.

In color alone the excrement of an infant surpasses lentils; in smell alone a roast morsel surpasses a soft green fig; in taste alone a kid when slaughtered surpasses the plant which it fed on when alive:

and we have found a kind of flesh in flavor of which all three give evidence.

What more do you require?

What reply will you make?

Why should eating meat make you unclean, if using such monstrosities in discussion does not?

And, above all, the rays of the sun, which you surely think more of than all animal or vegetable food, have no smell or taste, and are remarkable among other substances only by their eminently bright color; which is a loud call to you, and an obligation, in spite of yourselves, to place nothing higher than a bright color among the evidences of an admixture of good.

42.
Thus you are forced into this difficulty, that you must acknowledge the part of God as dwelling more in blood, and in the filthy but bright-colored animal refuse which is thrown out in the streets, than in the pale leaves of the olive.

If you reply, as you actually do, that olive leaves when burnt give out a flame, which proves the presence of light, while flesh when burnt does not, what will you say of oil, which lights nearly all the lamps in Italy?

What of cow dung (which surely is more unclean than the flesh), which peasants use when dry as fuel, so that the fire is always at hand, and the liberation of the smoke is always going on?

And if brightness and lustre prove a greater presence of the divine part, why do you yourselves not purify it, why not appropriate it, why not liberate it? For it is found chiefly in flowers, not to speak of blood and countless things almost the same as blood in flesh or coming from it, and yet you cannot feed on flowers.

And even if you were to eat flesh, you would certainly not take with your gruel the scales of fish, or some worms and flies, though these all shine with a light of their own in the dark.

43.
What then remains, but that you should cease saying that you have in your eyes, nose, and palate sufficient means of testing the presence of the divine part in material objects?

And, without these means, how can you tell not only that there is a greater part of God in plants than in flesh, but that there is any part in plants at all?

Are you led to think this by their beauty--not the beauty of agreeable color, but that of agreement of parts?

An excellent reason, in my opinion. For you will never be so bold as to compare twisted pieces of wood with the bodies of animals, which are formed of members answering to one another.

But if you choose the testimony of the senses, as those must do who cannot see with their mind the full force of existence, how do you prove that the substance of good escapes from bodies in course of time, and by some kind of attrition, but because God has gone out of it, according to your view, and has left one place for another?

The whole is absurd.

But, as far as I can judge, there are no marks or appearances to give rise to this opinion.

For many things plucked from trees, or pulled out of the ground, are the better of some interval of time before we use them for food, as leeks and endive, lettuce, grapes, apples, figs, and some pears; and there are many other things which get a better color when they are not used immediately after being plucked, besides being more wholesome for the body, and having a finer flavor to the palate.

But these things should not possess all these excellent and agreeable qualities, if, as you say, they become more destitute of good the longer they are kept after separation from their mother earth.

Animal food itself is better and more fit for use the day after the animal is killed; but this should not be, if, as you hold, it possessed more good immediately after the slaughter than next day, when more of the divine substance had escaped.

44.

Who does not know that wine becomes purer and better by age?

Nor is it, as you think, more tempting to the destruction of the senses, but more useful for invigorating the body,--only let there be moderation, which ought to control everything.

The senses are sooner destroyed by new wine.

When the must has been only a short time in the vat, and has begun to ferment, it makes those who look down into it fall headlong, affecting their brain, so that without assistance they would perish.

And as regards health, every one knows that bodies are swollen up and injuriously distended by new wine?

Has it these bad properties because there is more good in it?

Are they not found in wine when old because a good deal of the divine substance has gone?

An absurd thing to say, especially for you, who prove the divine presence by the pleasing effect produced on your eyes, nose, and palate!

And what a contradiction it is to make wine the poison of the princes of darkness, and yet to eat grapes!

Has it more of the poison when in the cup than when in the cluster?

Or if the evil remains unmixed after the good is gone, and that by the process of time, how is it that the same grapes, when hung up for awhile, become milder, sweeter, and more wholesome? or how does the wine itself, as already mentioned, become purer and brighter when the light has gone, and more wholesome by the loss of the beneficial substance?

45.

What are we to say of wood and leaves, which in course of time become dry, but cannot be the worse on that account in your estimation?

For while they lose that which produces smoke, they retain that from which a bright flame arises; and, to judge by the clearness, which you think so much of, there is more good in the dry than in the green.

Hence you must either deny that there is more of God in the pure light than in the smoky one, which will upset all your evidences; or you must allow it to be possible that, when plants are plucked up, or branches plucked off, and kept for a time, more of the nature of evil may escape from them than of the nature of good.

And, on the strength of this, we shall hold that more evil may go off from plucked fruits; and so more good may remain in animal food.

So much on the subject of time.

46.

As for motion, and tossing, and rubbing, if these give the divine nature the opportunity of escaping from these substances, many things of the same kind are against you, which are improved by motion.

In some grains the juice resembles wine, and is excellent when moved about.

Indeed, as must not be overlooked, this kind of drink produces intoxication rapidly; and yet you never called the juice of grain the poison of the princes of darkness.

There is a preparation of water, thickened with a little meal, which is the better of being shaken, and, strange to say, is lighter in color when the light is gone.

The pastry cook stirs honey for a long time to give it this light color, and to make its sweetness milder and less unwholesome:

you must explain how this can come from the loss of good.

Again, if you prefer to test the presence of God by the agreeable effects on the hearing, and not sight, or smell, or taste, harps get their strings and pipes their bones from animals; and these become musical by being dried, and rubbed, and twisted.

So the pleasures of music, which you hold to have come from the divine kingdom, are obtained from the refuse of dead animals, and that, too, when they are dried by time, and lessened by rubbing, and stretched by twisting.

Such rough treatment, according to you, drives the divine substance from living objects; even cooking them, you say, does this.

Why then are boiled thistles not unwholesome?

Is it because God, or part of God, leaves them when they are cooked?

47.

Why mention all the particulars, when it is difficult to enumerate them?

Nor is it necessary; for every one knows how many things are sweeter and more wholesome when cooked.

This ought not to be, if, as you suppose, things lose the good by being thus moved about.

I do not suppose that you will find any proof from your bodily senses that flesh is unclean, and defiles the souls of those who eat it, because fruits, when plucked and shaken about in various ways, become flesh; especially as you hold that vinegar, in its age and fermentation, is cleaner than wine, and the mead you drink is nothing else than cooked wine, which ought to be more impure than wine, if material things lose the divine members by being moved about and cooked.

But if not, you have no reason to think that fruits, when plucked, kept, handled, cooked, and digested, are forsaken by the good, and therefore supply most unclean matter for the formation of bodies.

48.

But if it is not from their color and appearance, and smell and taste, that you think the good to be in these things, what else can you bring forward?

Do you prove it from the strength and vigor which those things seem to lose when they are separated from the earth and put to use?

If this is your reason (though its erroneousness is seen at once, from the fact that the strength of some things is increased after their separation from the earth, as in the case already mentioned of wine, which becomes stronger from age),--if the strength, then, is your reason, it would follow that the part of God is to be found in no food more abundantly than in flesh.

For athletes, who especially require vigor and energy, are not in the habit of feeding on cabbage and fruit without animal food.

49.

Is your reason for thinking the bodies of trees better than our bodies, that flesh is nourished by trees and not trees by flesh.

You forget the obvious fact that plants, when manured with dung, become richer and more fertile and crops heavier, though you think it your gravest charge against flesh that it is the abode of dung.

This then gives nourishment to things you consider clean, though it is, according to you, the most unclean part of what you consider unclean.

But if you dislike flesh because it springs from sexual intercourse, you should be pleased with the flesh of worms, which are bred in such numbers, and of such a size, in fruits, in wood, and in the earth itself, without any sexual intercourse.

But there is some insincerity in this.

For if you were displeased with flesh because it is formed from the cohabitation of father and mother, you would not say that those princes of darkness were born from the fruits of their own trees; for no doubt you think worse of these princes than of flesh, which you refuse to eat.

50.

Your idea that all the souls of animals come from the food of their parents, from which confinement you pretend to liberate the divine substance which is held bound in your viands, is quite inconsistent with your abstinence from flesh, and makes it a pressing duty for you to eat animal food.

For if souls are bound in the body by those who eat animal food, why do you not secure their liberation by being beforehand in eating the food?

You reply, it is not from the animal food that the good part comes which those people bring into bondage, but from the vegetables which they take with their meat.

What will you say then of the souls of lions, who feed only on flesh?

They drink, is the reply, and so the soul is drawn in from the water and confined in flesh.
But what of birds without number?
What of eagles, which eat only flesh, and need no drink?
Here you are at a loss, and can find no answer.

For if the soul comes from food, and there are animals which neither drink anything nor have any food but flesh, and yet bring forth young, there must be some soul in flesh; and you are bound to try your plan of purifying it by eating the flesh.

Or will you say that a pig has a soul of light, because it eats vegetables, and drinks water; and that the eagle, because it eats only flesh, has a soul of darkness, though it is so fond of the sun?[180]

51.

What a confusion of ideas!
What amazing fatuity!

All this you would have escaped, if you had rejected idle fictions, and had followed what truth sanctions in abstinence from food, which would have taught you that sumptuous eating is to be avoided, not to escape pollution, as there is nothing of the kind, but to subdue the sensual appetite.

For should any one, from inattention to the nature of things, and the properties of the soul and body, allow that the soul is polluted by animal food, you will admit that it is much much more defiled by sensuality.

Is it reasonable, then, or rather, is it not most unreasonable, to expel from the number of the elect a man who, perhaps for his health's sake, takes some animal food without sensual appetite; while, if a man eagerly devours peppered truffles, you can only reprove him for excess, but cannot condemn him as abusing your symbol?

So one who has been induced, not by sensuality, but for health, to eat part of a fowl, cannot remain among your elect; though one may remain who has yielded voluntarily to an excessive appetite for comfits and cakes without animal matter.

You retain the man plunged in the defilements of sensuality, and dismiss the man polluted, as you think, by the mere food; though you allow that the defilement of sensuality is far greater than that of meat.

You keep hold of one who gloats with delight over highly-seasoned vegetables, unable to keep possession of himself; while you shut out one who, to satisfy hunger, takes whatever comes, if suitable for nourishment, ready either to use the food, or to let it go.

Admirable customs!
Excellent morals!
Notable temperance!

52.

Again, the notion that it is unlawful for any one but the elect to touch as food what is brought to your meals for what you call purification, leads to shameful and sometimes to criminal practices. For sometimes so much is brought that it cannot easily be eaten up by a few; and as it is considered sacrilege to give what is left to others, or, at least, to throw it away, you are obliged to eat to excess, from the desire to purify, as you call it, all that is given.

Then, when you are full almost to bursting, you cruelly use force in making the boys of your sect eat the rest.

So it was charged against some one at Rome that he killed some poor children, by compelling them to eat for this superstitious reason.

This I should not believe, did I not know how sinful you consider it to give this food to those who are not elect, or, at any rate, to throw it away.

So the only way is to eat it; and this leads every day to gluttony, and may sometimes lead to murder.

53.

For the same reason you forbid giving bread to beggars.
By way of showing compassion, or rather of avoiding reproach, you advise to give money.
The cruelty of this is equalled by its stupidity.

For suppose a place where food cannot be purchased:
the beggar will die of starvation, while you, in your wisdom and benevolence, have more mercy on a cucumber than on a human being!

This is in truth (for how could it be better designated) pretended compassion, and real cruelty.
Then observe the stupidity.
What if the beggar buys bread for himself with the money you give him?
Will the divine part, as you call it, not suffer the same in him when he buys the food as it

would have suffered if he had taken it as a gift from you?

So this sinful beggar plunges in corruption part of God eager to escape, and is aided in this crime by your money!

But you in your great sagacity think it enough that you do not give to one about to commit murder a man to kill, though you knowingly give him money to procure somebody to be killed.

Can any madness go beyond this?

The result is, that either the man dies if he cannot get food for his money, or the food itself dies if he gets it. The one is true murder; the other what you call murder:

though in both cases you incur the guilt of real murder.

Again, there is the greatest folly and absurdity in allowing your followers to eat animal food, while you forbid them to kill animals.

If this food does not defile, take it yourselves.

If it defiles, what can be more unreasonable than to think it more sinful to separate the soul of a pig from its body than to defile the soul of a man with the pig's flesh.

Chapter 17 - Description of the Symbol of the Hands Among the Manichæans

54.

We must now notice and discuss the symbol of the hands.

And, in the first place, your abstaining from the slaughter of animals and from injuring plants is shown by Christ to be mere superstition; for, on the ground that there is no community of rights between us and brutes and trees, He both sent the devils into an herd of swine, [181] and withered by His curse a tree in which He had found no fruit. [182] The swine assuredly had not sinned, nor had the tree.

We are not so insane as to think that a tree is fruitful or barren by its own choice.

Nor is it any reply to say that our Lord wished in these actions to teach some other truths; for every one knows that.

But assuredly the Son of God would not commit murder to illustrate truth, if you call the destruction of a tree or of an animal murder.

The signs which Christ wrought in the case of men, with whom we certainly have a community of rights, were in healing, not in killing them.

And it would have been the same in the case of beasts and trees, if we had that community with them which you imagine.

55.

I think it right to refer here to the authority of Scripture, because we cannot here enter on a profound discussion about the soul of animals, or the kind of life in trees.

But as you preserve the right to call the Scriptures corrupted, in case you should find them too strongly opposed to you,--although you have never affirmed the passages about the tree and the herd of swine to be spurious,--still, lest some day you should wish to say this of them too, when you find how much they are against you, I will adhere to my plan, and will ask you, who are so liberal in your promises of evidence and truth, to tell me first what harm is done to a tree, I say not by plucking a leaf or an apple,--for which, however, one of you would be condemned at once as having abused the symbol, if he did it intentionally, and not accidentally,--but if you tear it up by the root.

For the soul in trees, which, according to you, is a rational soul, is, in your theory, freed from bondage when the tree is cut down,--a bondage, too, where it suffered great misery and got no profit.

For it is well known that you, in the words of your founder, threaten as a great, though not the greatest punishment, the change from a man to a tree; and it is not probable that the soul in a tree can grow in wisdom as it does in a man.

There is the best reason for not killing a man, in case you should kill one whose wisdom or virtue might be of use to many, or one who might have attained to wisdom, whether by the advice of another without himself, or by divine illumination in his own mind.

And the more wisdom the soul has when it leaves the body, the more profitable is its departure, as we know both from well-grounded reasoning and from wide-spread belief.

Thus to cut down a tree is to set free the soul from a body in which it makes no progress in wisdom.

You--the holy men, I mean--ought to be mainly occupied in cutting down trees, and in leading the souls thus emancipated to better things by prayers and psalms.

Or can this be done only with the souls which you take into your belly, instead of aiding them by your understanding?

56.

And you cannot escape the admission that the souls in trees make no progress in wisdom while they are there, when you are asked why no apostle was sent to teach trees as well as men, or why the apostle sent to men did not preach the truth to trees also.

Your reply must be, that the souls while in such bodies cannot understand the divine precepts.

But this reply lands you in great difficulties; for you declare that these souls can hear your voices and understand what you say, and see bodies and their motions, and even discern thoughts.

If this is true, why could they learn nothing from the apostle of light? Why could they not learn even much better than we, since they can see into the mind?

Your master, who, as you say, has difficulty in teaching you by speech, might have taught these souls by thought; for they could see his ideas in his mind before he expressed them.

But if this is untrue, consider into what errors you have fallen.

57.

As for your not plucking fruits or pulling up vegetables yourselves, while you get your followers to pluck and pull and bring them to you, that you may confer benefits not only on those who bring the food but on the food which is brought, what thoughtful person can bear to hear this?

For, first, it matters not whether you commit a crime yourself, or wish another to commit it for you.

You deny that you wish this!

How then can relief be given to the divine part contained in lettuce and leeks, unless some one pull them and bring them to the saints to be purified.

And again, if you were passing through a field where the right of friendship permitted you to pluck anything you wished, what would you do if you saw a crow on the point of eating a fig?

Does not, according to your ideas, the fig itself seem to address you and to beg of you piteously to pluck it yourself and give it burial in a holy belly, where it may be purified and restored, rather than that the crow should swallow it and make it part of his cursed body, and then hand it over to bondage and torture in other forms?

If this is true, how cruel you are!

If not, how silly! What can be more contrary to your opinions than to break the symbol? What can be more unkind to the member of God than to keep it?

58.

This supposes the truth of your false and vain ideas.

But you can be shown guilty of plain and positive cruelty flowing from the same error.

For were any one lying on the road, his body wasted with disease, weary with journeying, and half-dead from his sufferings, and able only to utter some broken words, and if eating a pear would do him good as an astringent, and were he to beg you to help him as you passed by, and were he to implore you to bring the fruit from a neighboring tree, with no divine or human prohibition to prevent your doing so, while the man is sure to die for the want of it, you, a Christian man and a saint, will rather pass on and abandon a man thus suffering and entreating, lest the tree should lament the loss of its fruit, and you should be doomed to the punishment threatened by Manichæus for breaking the symbol.

Strange customs, and strange harmlessness!

59.

Now, as regards killing animals, and the reasons for your opinion, much that has been said will apply also to this.

For what harm will be done to the soul of a wolf by killing the wolf, since the wolf, as long as it lives, will be a wolf, and will not listen to any preacher, or give up, in the least, shedding the blood of sheep; and, by killing it, the rational soul, as you think, will be set free from its confinement in the body?

But you make this slaughter unlawful even for your followers; for you think it worse than that of trees.

And in this there is not much fault to be found with your senses,--that is, your bodily senses.

For we see and hear by their cries that animals die with pain, although man disregards this in a beast, with which, as not having a rational soul, we have no community of rights.

But as to your senses in the observation of trees, you must be entirely blind.

For not to mention that there are no movements in the wood expressive of pain, what is clearer than that a tree is never better than when it is green and flourishing, gay with flowers, and rich in fruit?

And this comes generally and chiefly from pruning.

But if it felt the iron, as you suppose, it ought to die of wounds so many, so severe, instead of sprouting at the places, and reviving with such manifest delight.

60.

But why do you think it a greater crime to destroy animals than plants, although you hold that plants have a purer soul than animals? There is a compensation, we are told, when part of what is taken from the fields is given to the elect and the saints to be purified.

This has already been refuted; and it has, I think, been proved sufficiently that there is no reason for saying that more of the good part is found in vegetables than in flesh.

But should any one support himself by selling butcher-meat, and spend the whole profit of his business in purchasing food for your elect, and bring larger supplies for those saints than any peasant or farmer, will he not plead this compensation as a warrant for his killing animals?

But there is, we are told, some other mysterious reason; for a cunning man can always find some resource in the secrets of nature when addressing unlearned people. The story, then, is that the heavenly princes who were taken from the race of darkness and bound, and have a place assigned them in this region by the Creator of the world, have animals on the earth specially belonging to them, each having those coming from his own stock and class; and they hold the slaughterers of those animals guilty, and do not allow them to leave the earth, but harass them as much as they can with pains and torments.

What simple man will not be frightened by this, and, seeing nothing in the darkness shrouding these things, will not think that the fact is as described?

But I will hold to my purpose, with God's help, to rebut mysterious falsehood by the plainest truth.

61.

Tell me, then, if animals on land and in water come in regular succession by ordinary generation from this race of princes, since the origin of animal life is traced to the abortive births in that race;--tell me, I say, whether bees and frogs, and many other creatures not sprung from sexual intercourse, [183] may be killed with impunity. We are told they cannot.

So it is not on account of their relation to certain princes that you forbid your followers to kill animals.

Or if you make a general relationship to all bodies, the princes would be equally concerned about trees, which you do not require your followers to spare.

You are brought back to the weak reply, that the injuries done in the case of plants are atoned for by the fruits which your followers bring to your church.

For this implies that those who slaughter animals, and sell their flesh in the market, if they are your followers, and if they bring to you vegetables bought with their gains, may think nothing of the daily slaughter, and are cleared of any sin that may be in it by your repasts.

62.

But if you say that, in order to expiate the slaughter, the thing must be given as food, as in the case of fruits and vegetables,--which cannot be done, because the elect do not eat flesh, and so your followers must not slaughter animals,--what reply will you give in the case of thorns and weeds, which farmers destroy in clearing their fields, while they cannot bring any food to you from them?

How can there be pardon for such destruction, which gives no nourishment to the saints?

Perhaps you also put away any sin committed, for the benefit of the fruits and vegetables, by eating some of these.

What then if the fields are plundered by locusts, mice, or rats, as we see often happen?

Can your rustic follower kill these with impunity, because he sins for the good of his crops?

Here you are at a loss; for you either allow your followers to kill animals, which your founder prohibited, or you forbid them to be cultivators, which he made lawful.

Indeed, you sometimes go so far as to say that an usurer is more harmless than a cultivator,--you feel so much more for melons than for men.

Rather than hurt the melons, you would have a man ruined as a debtor.

Is this desirable and praiseworthy justice, or not rather atrocious and damnable error?

Is this commendable compassion, or not rather detestable barbarity?

63.

What, again, of your not abstaining yourselves from the slaughter of lice, bugs, and fleas? You think it a sufficient excuse for this to say that these are the dirt of our bodies.

But this is clearly untrue of fleas and bugs; for every one knows that these animals do not come from our bodies.

Besides, if you abhor sexual intercourse as much as you pretend to do, you should think those animals all the cleaner which come from our bodies without any other generation; for although they produce offspring of their own, they are not produced in ordinary generation from us.

Again, if we must consider as most filthy the production of living bodies, still worse must be the production of dead bodies.

There must be less harm, therefore, in killing a rat, a snake, or a scorpion, which you constantly say come from our dead bodies.

But to pass over what is less plain and certain, it is a common opinion regarding bees that they come from the carcasses of oxen; so there is no harm in killing them.

Or if this too is doubted, every one allows that beetles, at least, are bred in the ball of mud which they make and bury. [184]You ought therefore to consider these animals, and others that it would be tedious to specify, more unclean than your lice; and yet you think it sinful to kill them, though it would be foolish not to kill the lice.

Perhaps you hold the lice cheap because they are small.

But if an animal is to be valued by its size, you must prefer a camel to a man.

64.

Here we may use the gradation which often perplexed us when we were your followers.

For if a flea may be killed on account of its small size, so may the fly which is bred in beans.

And if this, so also may one of a little larger size, for its size at birth is even less.

Then again, a bee may be killed, for its young is no larger than a fly.

So on to the young of a locust, and to a locust; and then to the young of a mouse, and to a mouse.

And, to cut short, it is clear we may come at last to an elephant; so that one who thinks it no sin to kill a flea, because of its small size, must allow that it would be no sin in him to kill this huge creature.

But I think enough has been said of these absurdities.

Chapter 18 - Of the Symbol of the Breast, and of the Shameful Mysteries of the Manichæans

65.

Lastly, there is the symbol of the breast, in which your very questionable chastity consists.

For though you do not forbid sexual intercourse, you, as the apostle long ago said, forbid marriage in the proper sense, although this is the only good excuse for such intercourse.

No doubt you will exclaim against this, and will make it a reproach against us that you highly esteem and approve perfect chastity, but do not forbid marriage, because your followers--that is, those in the second grade among you--are allowed to have wives.

After you have said this with great noise and heat, I will quietly ask, Is it not you who hold that begetting children, by which souls are confined in flesh, is a greater sin than cohabitation?

Is it not you who used to counsel us to observe as much as possible the time when a woman, after her purification, is most likely to conceive, and to abstain from cohabitation at that time, lest the soul should be entangled in flesh? This proves that you approve of having a wife, not for the procreation of children, but for the gratification of passion.

In marriage, as the marriage law declares, the man and woman come together for the procreation of children.

Therefore whoever makes the procreation of children a greater sin than copulation, forbids marriage, and makes the woman not a wife, but a mistress, who for some gifts presented to her is joined to the man to gratify his passion.

Where there is a wife there must be marriage.

But there is no marriage where motherhood is not in view; therefore neither is there a wife.

In this way you forbid marriage.

Nor can you defend yourselves successfully from this charge, long ago brought against you prophetically by the Holy Spirit.

66.
Moreover, when you are so eager in your desire to prevent the soul from being confined in flesh by conjugal intercourse, and so eager in asserting that the soul is set free from seed by the food of the saints, do you not sanction, unhappy beings, the suspicion entertained about you?

For why should it be true regarding corn and beans and lentils and other seeds, that when you eat them you wish to set free the soul, and not true of the seeds of animals?

For what you say of the flesh of a dead animal, that it is unclean because there is no soul in it, cannot be said of the seed of the animal; for you hold that it keeps confined the soul which will appear in the offspring, and you avow that the soul of Manichæus himself is thus confined.

And as your followers cannot bring these seeds to you for purification, who will not suspect that you make this purification secretly among yourselves, and hide it from your followers, in case they should leave you? [185] If you do not these things, as it is to be hoped you do not, still you see how open to suspicion your superstition is, and how impossible it is to blame men for thinking what your own profession suggests, when you maintain that you set free souls from bodies and from senses by eating and drinking.

I wish to say no more about this:
you see yourselves what room there is here for denunciation.

But as the matter is one rather to repress than to invite remark, and also as throughout my discourse my purpose appears of exaggerating nothing, and of keeping to bare facts and arguments, we shall pass on to other matters.

Chapter 19 - Crimes of the Manichæans

67.
We see then, now, the nature of your three symbols.
These are your customs.
This is the end of your notable precepts, in which there is nothing sure, nothing steadfast, nothing consistent, nothing irreproachable, but all doubtful, or rather undoubtedly and entirely false, all contradictory, abominable, absurd.

In a word, evil practices are detected in your customs so many and so serious, that one wishing to denounce them all, if he were at all able to enlarge, would require at least a separate treatise for each.

Were you to observe these, and to act up to your profession, no childishness, or folly, or absurdity would go beyond yours; and when you praise and teach these things without doing them, you display craft and deceit and malevolence equal to anything that can be described or imagined.

68.
During nine full years that I attended you with great earnestness and assiduity, I could not hear of one of your elect who was not found transgressing these precepts, or at least was not suspected of doing so.

Many were caught at wine and animal food, many at the baths; but this we only heard by report.

Some were proved to have seduced other men's wives, so that in this case I could not doubt the truth of the charge.

But suppose this, too, a report rather than a fact.

I myself saw, and not I only, but others who have either escaped from that superstition, or will, I hope, yet escape,--we saw, I say, in a square in Carthage, on a road much frequented, not one, but more than three of the elect walking behind us, and accosting some women with such indecent sounds and gestures as to outdo the boldness and insolence of all ordinary rascals.

And it was clear that this was quite habitual, and that they behaved in this way to one another, for no one was deterred by the presence of a companion, showing that most of them, if not all, were affected with this evil tendency.

For they did not all come from one house, but lived in quite different places, and quite accidentally left together the place where they had met.

It was a great shock to us, and we lodged a complaint about it.

But who thought of inflicting punishment,--I say not by separation from the church, but even by severe rebuke in proportion to the heinousness of the offence?

69.

All the excuse given for the impunity of those men was that, at that time, when their meetings were forbidden by law, it was feared that the persons suffering punishment might retaliate by giving information.

What then of their assertion that they will always have persecution in this world, for which they suppose that they will be thought the more of? for this is the application they make of the words about the world hating them. [186] And they will have it that truth must be sought for among them, because, in the promise of the Holy Spirit, the Paraclete, it is said that the world cannot receive Him. [187] This is not the place to discuss this question.

But clearly, if you are always to be persecuted, even to the end of the world, there will be no end to this laxity, and to the unchecked spread of all this immorality, from your fear of giving offence to men of this character.

70.

This answer was also given to us, when we reported to the very highest authorities that a woman had complained to us that in a meeting, where she was along with other women, not doubting of the sanctity of these people, some of the elect came in, and when one of them had put out the lamp, one, whom she could not distinguish, tried to embrace her, and would have forced her into sin, had she not escaped by crying out.

How common must we conclude the practice to have been which led to the misdeed on this occasion!

And this was done on the night when you keep the feast of vigils.

Forsooth, besides the fear of information being given, no one could bring the offender before the bishop, as he had so well guarded against being recognized.

As if all who entered along with him were not implicated in the crime; for in their indecent merriment they all wished the lamp to be put out.

71.

Then what wide doors were opened for suspicions, when we saw them full of envy, full of covetousness, full of greed for costly foods, constantly at strife, easily excited about trifles!

We concluded that they were not competent to abstain from the things they professed to abstain from, if they found an opportunity in secret or in the dark. There were two of sufficiently good character, of active minds, and leaders in their debates, with whom we had a more particular and intimate acquaintance than with the rest.

One of them was much associated with us, because he was also engaged in liberal studies; he is said to be now an elder there.

These two were very jealous of one another, and one accused the other--not openly, but in conversation, as he had opportunity, and in whispers--of having made a criminal assault on the wife of one of the followers.

He again, in clearing himself to us, brought the same charge against another of the elect, who lived with this follower as his most trusted friend.

He had, going in suddenly, caught this man with the woman, and his enemy and rival had advised the woman and her paramour to raise this false report about him, that he might not be believed if he gave any information.

We were much distressed, and took it greatly to heart, that although there was a doubt about the assault on the woman, the jealous feeling in those two men, than whom we found none better in the place, showed itself so keenly, and inevitably raised a suspicion of other things. [188]

72.

Another thing was, that we very often saw in theatres men belonging to the elect, men of years and, it was supposed, of character, along with a hoary-headed elder.

We pass over the youths, whom we used to come upon quarrelling about the people connected with the stage and the races; from which we may safely conclude how they would be able to refrain in secret, when they could not subdue the passion by which they were exposed in the eyes of their followers, bringing on them disgrace and flight.

In the case of the saint, whose discussions we attended in the street of the fig-sellers, would his atrocious crime have been discovered if he had been able to make the dedicated virgin his wife without making her pregnant?

The swelling womb betrayed the secret and unthought-of iniquity.

When her brother, a young man, heard of it from his mother, he felt keenly the injury, but refrained, from regard to religion, from a public accusation.

He succeeded in getting the man expelled from that church, for such conduct cannot always be tolerated; and that the crime might not be wholly unpunished, he arranged with some of his friends to have the man well beaten and kicked.

When he was thus assailed, he cried out that they should spare him, from regard to the authority of the opinion of Manichæus, that Adam the first hero had sinned, and was a greater saint after his sin.

73.

This, in fact, is your notion about Adam and Eve. [189]It is a long story; but I will touch only on what concerns the present matter. You say that Adam was produced from his parents, the abortive princes of darkness; that he had in his soul the most part of light, and very little of the opposite race.

So while he lived a holy life, on account of the prevalence of good, still the opposite part in him was stirred up, so that he was led away into conjugal intercourse.

Thus he fell and sinned, but afterwards lived in greater holiness.

Now, my complaint is not so much about this wicked man, who, under the garb of an elect and holy man, brought such shame and reproach on a family of strangers by his shocking immorality.

I do not charge you with this. Let it be attributed to the abandoned character of the man, and not to your habits.

I blame the man for the atrocity, and not you.

Still there is this in you all that cannot, as far as I can see, be admitted or tolerated, that while you hold the soul to be part of God, you still maintain that the mixture of a little evil prevailed over the superior force and quantity of good.

Who that believes this, when incited by passion, will not find here an excuse, instead of checking and controlling his passion?

Chapter 20 - Disgraceful Conduct Discovered at Rome

74.

What more shall I say of your customs?

I have mentioned what I found myself when I was in the city when the things were done.

To go through all that happened at Rome in my absence would take a long time.

I will, however, give a short account of it; for the matter became so notorious, that even the absent could not remain in ignorance of it.

And when I was afterwards in Rome, I ascertained the truth of all I had heard, although the story was told me by an eye-witness whom I knew so well and esteemed so highly, that I could not feel any doubt about it.

One of your followers, then, quite equal to the elect in their far-famed abstinence, for he was both liberally educated, and was in the habit of defending your sect with great zeal, took it very ill that he had cast in his teeth the vile conduct of the elect, who lived in all kinds of places, and went hither and thither for lodging of the worst description.

He therefore desired, if possible, to assemble all who were willing to live according to the precepts into his own house, and to maintain them at his own expense; for he was above the average in carelessness as to spending money, besides being above the average in the amount he had to spend.

He complained that his efforts were hindered by the remissness of the bishops, whose assistance he required for success.

At last one of your bishops was found,--a man, as I know, very rude and unpolished, but somehow, from his very moroseness, the more inclined to strict observance of morality.

The follower eagerly lays hold of this man as the person he had long wished for and found at last, and relates his whole plan.

He approves and assents, and agrees to be the first to take up his abode in the house.

When this was done, all the elect who could be at Rome were assembled there.

The rule of life in the epistle of Manichæus was laid before them.

Many thought it intolerable, and left; not a few felt ashamed, and stayed.

They began to live as they had agreed, and as this high authority enjoined.

The follower all the time was zealously enforcing everything on everybody, though never, in any case, what he did not undertake himself. Meanwhile quarrels constantly arose among the elect.

They charged one another with crimes, all which he lamented to hear, and managed to make them unintentionally expose one another in their altercations.

The revelations were vile beyond description.

Thus appeared the true character of those who were unlike the rest in being willing to bend to the yoke of the precepts.

What then is to be suspected, or rather, concluded, of the others?

To come to a close, they gathered together on one occasion and complained that they could not keep the regulations.

Then came rebellion.

The follower stated his case most concisely, that either all must be kept, or the man who had given such a sanction to such precepts, which no one could fulfill, must be thought a great fool.

But, as was inevitable, the wild clamor of the mob prevailed over the opinion of one man.

The bishop himself gave way at last, and took to flight with great disgrace; and he was said to have got in provisions by stealth, contrary to rule, which were often discovered.

He had a supply of money from his private purse, which he carefully kept concealed.

75.

If you say these things are false, you contradict what is too clear and public.

But you may say so if you like.

For, as the things are certain, and easily known by those who wish to know them, those who deny that they are true show what their habit of telling the truth is. But you have other replies with which I do not find fault.

For you either say that some do keep your precepts, and that they should not be mixed up with the guilty in condemning the others; or that the whole inquiry into the character of the members of your sect is wrong, for the question is of the character of the profession.

Should I grant both of these (although you can neither point out those faithful observers of the precepts, nor clear your heresy of all those frivolities and iniquities), still I must insist on knowing why you heap reproaches on Christians of the Catholic name on seeing the immoral life of some, while you either have the effrontery to repel inquiry about your members, or the still greater effrontery not to repel it, wishing it to be understood that in your scanty membership there are some unknown individuals who keep the precepts they profess, but that among the multitudes in the Catholic Church there are none.

Footnotes:

160. This statement has a complete parallel in Clement of Alexandria, and along with what follows, is Neo-Platonic.--A.H.N.]

161. [On Augustin's view of negativity of evil and on the relation of this view to Neo-Platonism, see Introduction, chapter IX.

Augustin's view seems to exclude the permanence of evil in the world, and so everlasting punishment and everlasting rebellion against God.--A.H.N.]

162. [It is probable that Mani thought of the Kingdom of Light pantheistically, and that the principles personified in his mythological system were the result of efforts on his part to connect the infinite with the finite.--A.H.N.]

163. In Retract. i. 7, § 6, it is said: "This must not be understood to mean that all things return to that from which they fell away, as Origen believed, but only those which do return.

Those who shall be punished in everlasting fire do not return to God, from whom they fell away.

Still they are in order as existing in punishment where their existence is most suitable."

[This does not really meet the difficulty suggested on a preceding page.--A.H.N.]

164. Isa. xlv. 7.

165. [That is to say nothing is absolutely evil, and conversely what is absolutely evil is ipso facto non-existent.--A.H.N.]

166. Luke ii. 14.

167. [The reasoning here is admirably adapted to Augustin's purpose, which is to refute the Manichæan notion of the evil nature of material substance.--A.H.N.]

168. [The text has asinum in this sentence but aspidem in the next.

The former is a mistake.--A.H.N.]

169. John viii. 36.

170. Gal. v. 13.

171. Sallust, in prolog. Catilin. § 3.

172. Rom. xiv. 21.

173. Rom. xiii. 14.

174. Matt. xv. 2.

175. Isa. xlv. 23, 24.

176. Rom. xiv. and xv. 1-3.

177. 1 Cor. viii. 4, etc.

178. 1 Cor. x. 19-25 and 28, xi. 1.

179. [Augustin's comparison of Manichæan with Christian asceticism is thoroughly just and admirable.--A.H.N.]

180. [Much of the foregoing, as well as of what follows, seems to the modern reader like mere trifling, but Augustin's aim was by introducing many familiar illustrations to show the utter absurdity of the Manichæan distinctions between clean and unclean.

It must be confessed that he does this

very effectively.--A.H.N.]

181. Matt. viii. 32.

182. Matt. xxi. 19.

183. [This is, of course, a physiological blunder, but Augustin doubtless states what was the common view at the time.--A.H.N.]

184. V. Retract. i. 7. § 6, where Augustin allows that this is doubtful, and that many have not even heard of it.

185. [Compare what is said about the disgusting ceremonial of Ischas by Cyril of Jerusalem (Cat. vi.), Augustin (Haeres. xlvi.), Pope Leo X. (Serm. V. de Jejuniis, X. Mens.).

These charges were probably unfounded, though they are not altogether out of harmony with the Manichæan principles.--A.H.N.]

186. John xv. 18.

187. John xiv. 17.

188. Doubtless Augustin exaggerates the immorality of the Manichæans; but there must have been a considerable basis of fact for his charges.--A.H.N.]

189. Compare the account from the Fihrist, in our Introduction, Chapter III.--A.H.N.]

On Two Souls, Against the Manichæans

[de duabus animabus contra manichæos].
A.D. 391. [190]
translated by albert h. newman, d.d., ll.d.,
professor of church history and comparative religion, in toronto baptist (theological) college, toronto, canada.

One Book

Chapter 1 - By What Course of Reasoning the Error of the Manichæans Concerning Two Souls, One of Which is Not from God, is Refuted. Every Soul, Inasmuch as It is a Certain Life, Can Have Its Existence Only from God the Source of Life.

1.
Through the assisting mercy of God, the snares of the Manichæans having been broken to pieces and left behind, having been restored at length to the bosom of the Catholic Church, I am disposed now at least to consider and to deplore my recent wretchedness.

For there were many things that I ought to have done to prevent the seeds of the most true religion wholesomely implanted in me from boyhood, from being banished from my mind, having been uprooted by the error and fraud of false and deceitful men.

For, in the first place, if I had soberly and diligently considered, with prayerful and pious mind, those two kinds of souls to which they attributed natures and properties so distinct that they wished one to be regarded as of the very substance of God, but were not even willing that God should be accepted as the author of the other; perhaps it would have appeared to me, intent on learning, that there is no life whatsoever, which, by the very fact of its being life and in so far as it is life at all, does not pertain to the supreme source and beginning of life, [191] which we must acknowledge to be nothing else than the supreme and only and true God.

Wherefore there is no reason why we should not confess, that those souls which the Manichæans call evil are either devoid of life and so not souls, neither will anything positively or negatively, neither follow after nor flee from anything; or, if they live so that they can be souls, and act as the Manichæans suppose, in no way do they live unless by life, and if it be an established fact, as it is, that Christ has said:

"I am the life," [192] that all souls seeing that they cannot be souls except by living were created and fashioned by Christ, that is, by the Life.

Chapter 2 - If the Light that is Perceived by Sense Has God for Its Author, as the Manichæans Acknowledge, Much More The Soul Which is Perceived by Intellect Alone

2.
But if at that time [193] my thought was not able to bear and sustain the question concerning life and partaking of life, which is truly a great question, and one that requires much calm discussion among the learned, I might perchance have had power to discover that which to every man considering himself, without a study of the individual parts, is perfectly evident, namely, that everything we are said to know and to understand, we comprehend either by bodily sense or by mental operation.

That the five bodily senses are commonly enumerated as sight, hearing, smell, taste, touch, than all of which intellect is immeasurably more noble and excellent, who would have been so ungrateful and impious as not to concede to me; which being established and confirmed, we should have seen how it follows, that whatsoever things are perceived by touch or sight or in any bodily manner at all, are by so much inferior to those things that we comprehend intellectually as the senses are inferior to the intellect. Wherefore, since all life, and so every soul, can be perceived by no bodily sense, but by the intellect alone, whereas while yonder sun and moon and every luminary that is beheld by these mortal eyes, the Manichæans themselves also say must be attributed to the true and good God, it is the height of madness to claim that that belongs to God which we observe bodily; but, on the other hand, to think that what we receive not only by the mind, but by the highest form of mind, [194] namely, reason and intellect, [195] that is life, whatsoever it may be called, nevertheless life, should be deprived and bereft of the same God as its author.

For if having invoked God, I had asked myself what living is, how inscrutable it is to every bodily sense, how absolutely incorporeal it is, could not I have answered?

Or would not the Manichæans also confess not only that the souls they detest live, but that they live also immortally? and that Christ's saying:

"Send the dead to bury their dead," [196] was uttered not with reference to those not living at all, but with reference to sinners, which is the only death of the immortal soul; as when Paul writes:

"The widow that giveth herself to pleasure is dead while she liveth," [197] he says that she at the same time is dead, and alive.

Wherefore I should have directed attention not to the great degree of contamination in which the sinful soul lives, but only to the fact itself that it lives.

But if I cannot perceive except by an act of intelligence, I believe it would have come into the mind, that by as much as any mind whatever is to be preferred to the light which we see through these eyes, by so much we should give to intellect the preference over the eyes themselves.

Chapter 3.--How It is Proved that Every Body Also is from God. That the Soul Which is Called Evil by the Manichæans is Better Than Light

They also affirm that the light is from the Father of Christ:
should I then have doubted that every soul is from Him?

But not even then, as a man forsooth so inexperienced and so youthful as I was, should I have been in doubt as to the derivation not only of the soul, but also of the body, nay of everything whatsoever, from Him, if I had reverently and cautiously reflected on what form is, or what has been formed, what shape is and what has been endued with shape.

3.

But not to speak at present concerning the body, I lament concerning the soul, concerning spontaneous and vivid movement, concerning action, concerning life, concerning immortality; in fine, I lament that I, miserable, should have believed that anything could have all these properties apart from the goodness of God, which properties, great as they are, I sadly neglected to consider; this I think, should be to me a matter of groaning and of weeping.

I should have inwardly pondered these things, I should have discussed them with myself, I should have referred them to others, I should have propounded the inquiry, what the power of knowing is, seeing there is nothing in man that we can compare to this excellency?

And as men, if only they had been men, would have granted me this, I should have inquired whether seeing with these eyes is knowing?

In case they had answered negatively, I should first have concluded, that mental intelligence is vastly inferior to ocular sensation; then I should have added, that what we perceive by means of a better thing must needs be judged to be itself better.

Who would not grant this?

I should have gone on to inquire, whether that soul which they call evil is an object of ocular sensation or of mental intelligence?

They would have acknowledged that the latter is the case.

All which things having been agreed upon and confirmed between us, I should have shown how it follows, that that soul forsooth which they execrate, is better than that light which they venerate, since the former is an object of mental knowledge, the latter an object of corporeal sense perception.

But here perhaps they would have halted, and would have refused to follow the lead of reason, so great is the power of inveterate opinion and of falsehood long defended and believed.

But I should have pressed yet more upon them halting, not harshly, not in puerile fashion, not obstinately; I should have repeated the things that had been conceded, and have shown how they must be conceded.

I should have exhorted that they consult in common, that they may see clearly what must be denied to us; whether they think it false that intellectual perception is to be preferred to these carnal organs of sight, or that what is known by means of the excellency of the mind is more excellent than what is known by vile corporeal sensation; whether they would be unwilling to confess that those souls which they think heterogenous, can be known only by intellectual perception, that is, by the excellency itself of the mind; whether they would wish to deny that the sun and the moon are made known to us only by means of these eyes.

But if they had replied that no one of these things could be denied otherwise than most absurdly and most impudently, I should have urged that they ought not to doubt but that the light whose worthiness of worship they proclaim, is viler than that soul which they admonish men to flee.

Chapter 4 - Even the Soul of a Fly is More Excellent Than the Light

4.

And here, if perchance in their confusion they had inquired of me whether I thought that the soul even of a fly [198] surpasses that light, I should have replied, yes, nor should it have troubled me that the fly is little, but it should have confirmed me that it is alive. For it is inquired, what causes those members so diminutive to grow, what leads so minute a body here and there according to its natural appetite, what moves its feet in numerical order when it is running, what regulates and gives vibration to its wings when flying?

This thing whatever it is in so small a creature towers up so prominently to one well considering, that it excels any lightning flashing upon the eyes.

Chapter 5 - How Vicious Souls, However Worthy of Condemnation They May Be, Excel the Light Which is Praiseworthy in Its Kind

Certainly nobody doubts that whatever is an object of intellectual perception, by virtue of divine laws surpasses in excellence every sensible object and consequently also this light.

For what, I ask, do we perceive by thought, if not that it is one thing to know with the mind, and another thing to experience bodily sensations, and that the former is incomparably more sublime than the latter, and so that intelligible things must needs be preferred to sensible things, since the intellect itself is so highly exalted above the senses?

5.

Hence this also I should perchance have known, which manifestly follows, since injustice and intemperance and other vices of the mind are not objects of sense, but of intellect, how it comes about that these too which we detest and consider condemnable, yet in as much as they are objects of intellect, can outrank this light however praiseworthy it may be in its kind.

For it is borne in upon the mind subjecting itself well to God, that, first of all, not everything that we praise is to be preferred to everything that we find fault with. For in praising the purest lead, I do not therefore put a higher value upon it than upon the gold that I find fault with.

For everything must be considered in its kind.

I disapprove of a lawyer ignorant of many statutes, yet I so prefer him to the most approved tailor, that I should think him incomparably superior.

But I praise the tailor because he is thoroughly skilled in his own craft, while I rightly blame the lawyer because he imperfectly fulfills the functions of his profession.

Wherefore I should have found out that the light which in its own kind is perfect, is rightly to be praised; yet because it is included in the number of sensible things, which class must needs yield to the class of intelligible things, it must be ranked below unjust and intemperate souls, since these are intelligible; although we may without injustice judge these to be most worthy of condemnation.

For in the case of these we ask that they be reconciled to God, not that they be preferred to that lightning.

Wherefore, if any one had contended that this luminary is from God, I should not have opposed; but rather I should have said, that souls, even vicious ones, not in so far as they are vicious, but in so far as they are souls, must be acknowledged to be creatures of God.

Chapter 6 - Whether Even Vices Themselves as Objects of Intellectual Apprehension are to Be Preferred to Light as an Object of Sense Perception, and are to Be Attributed to God as Their Author.

Vice of the Mind and Certain Defects are Not Rightly to Be Counted Among Intelligible Things.

Defects Themselves Even If They Should Be Counted Among Intelligible Things Should Never Be Put Before Sensible Things. If Light is Visible by God, Much More is the Soul, Even If Vicious, Which in So Far as It Lives is an Intelligible Thing.

Passages of Scripture are Adduced by the Manichæans to the Contrary.

At this point, in case some one of them, cautious and watchful, now also more studious than pertinacious, had admonished me that the inquiry is not about vicious souls but about vices themselves, which, seeing that they are not known by corporeal sense, and yet are known, can only be received as objects of intellectual apprehension, which if they excel all objects of sense, why can we not agree in attributing light to God as its author, but only a sacrilegious person would say that God is the author of vices; I should have replied to the man, if either on the spur of the moment, as is customary to the worshippers of the good God, a solution of this question had darted like lightning from on high, or a solution had been previously prepared.

If I had not deserved or was unable to avail myself of either of these methods, I should have deferred the undertaking, and should have confessed that the thing propounded was difficult to discern and arduous.

I should have withdrawn to myself, prostrated myself before God, groaned aloud asking Him not to suffer me to halt in mid space, when I should have moved forward with assured arguments, asking Him that I might not be compelled by a doubtful question either to subordinate intelligible things to sensible, and to yield, or to call Himself the author of vices; since either of these alternatives would have been absolutely full of falsehood and impiety.

I can by no means suppose that He would have deserted me in such a frame of mind.

Rather, in His own ineffable way, He would have admonished me to consider again and again whether vices of mind concerning which I was so troubled should be reckoned among intelligible things.

But that I might find out, on account of the weakness of my inner eye, which rightly befell me on account of my sins, I should have devised some sort of stage for gazing upon spiritual things in visible things themselves, of which we have by no means a surer knowledge, but a more confident familiarity.

Therefore I should straightway have inquired, what properly pertains to the sensation of the eyes.

I should have found that it is the color, the dominion of which the light holds.

For these are the things that no other sense touches, for the motions and magnitudes and intervals and figures of bodies, although they also can be perceived by the eyes, yet to perceive such is not their peculiar function, but belongs also to touch.

Whence I should have gathered that by as much as yonder light excels other corporeal and sensible things, by so much is sight more noble than the other senses.

The light therefore having been selected from all the things that are perceived by bodily sense, by this [light] I should have striven, and in this of necessity I should have placed that stage of my inquiry.

I should have gone on to consider what might be done in this way, and thus I should have reasoned with myself:

If yonder sun, conspicuous by its brightness and sufficing for day by its light, should little by little decline in our sight into the likeness of the moon, would we perceive anything else with our eyes than light however refulgent, yet seeking light by reason of not seeing what had been, and using it for seeing what was present?

Therefore we should not see the decline, but the light that should survive the decline. But since we should not see, we should not perceive; for whatever we perceive by sight must necessarily be seen; wherefore if that decline were perceived neither by sight nor by any other sense, it cannot be reckoned among objects of sense.

For nothing is an object of sense that cannot be perceived by sense.

Let us apply now the consideration to virtue, by whose intellectual light we most fittingly say the mind shines.

Again, a certain decline from this light of virtue, not destroying the soul, but obscuring it, is called vice.

Therefore also vice can by no means be reckoned among objects of intellectual perception, as that decline of light is rightly excluded from the number of objects of sense perception.

Yet what remains of soul, that is that which lives and is soul is just as much an object of intellectual perception as that is an object of sense perception which should shine in this visible luminary after any imaginable degree of decline.

And so the soul, in so far as it is soul and partakes of life, without which it can in no way be soul, is most correctly to be preferred to all objects of sense perception.

Wherefore it is most erroneous to say that any soul is not from God, from whom you boast that the sun and moon have their existence.

7.

But if now it should be thought fit to designate as objects of sense perception not only all those things that we perceive by the senses, but also all those things that though not perceiving by the senses we judge of by means of the body, as of darkness through the eyes, of silence through the ears,--for not by seeing darkness and not by hearing silence do we know of their existence,--and again, in the case of objects of intellectual perception, not those things only which we see illuminated by the mind, as is wisdom itself, but also those things which by the illumination itself we avoid, such as foolishness, which I might fittingly designate mental darkness; I should have made no controversy about a word, but should have dissolved the whole question by an easy division, and straightway I should have proved to those giving good attention, that by the divine law of truth intelligible subsistences are to be preferred to sensible subsistences, not the decline of these subsistences, even though we should choose to call these intelligible, those sensible.

Wherefore, that those who acknowledge that these visible luminaries and those intelligible souls are subsistences, are in every way compelled to grant and to attribute the sublimer part to souls; but that defects of either kind cannot be preferred the one to the other, for they are only privative and indicate nonexistence, and therefore have precisely the same force as negations themselves.

For when we say, It is not gold, and, It is not virtue, although there is the greatest possible difference between gold and virtue, yet there is no difference between the negations that we adjoin to them.

But that it is worse indeed not to be virtue than not to be gold, no sane man doubts.

Who does not know that the difference lies not in the negations themselves, but in the things to which they are adjoined?

For by as much as virtue is more excellent than gold, by so much is it more wretched to be in want of virtue than of gold. Wherefore, since intelligible things excel sensible things, we rightly feel greater repugnance towards defect in intelligible than in sensible things, esteeming not the defects, but the things that are deficient more or less precious.

From which now it appears, that defect of light, which is intelligible, is far more wretched than defect of the sensible light, because, forsooth, life which is known is by far more precious than yonder light which is seen.

8.

This being the case, who will dare, while attributing sun and moon, and whatever is refulgent in the stars, nay in this fire of ours and in this visible earthly life, to God, to decline to grant that any souls whatsoever, which are not souls except by the fact of their being perfectly alive, since in this fact alone life has the precedence of light, are from God.

And since he speaks truth who says, In as far as a thing shines it is from God, would I speak falsely, mighty God, if I should say, In so far as a thing lives it is from God?

Let not, I beseech thee, blindness of intellect and perversions of mind be increased to such an extent that men may fail to know these things. But however great their error and pertinacity might have been, trusting in these arguments and armed therewith, I believe that when I should have laid the matter before them thus considered and canvassed, and should have calmly conferred with them, I should have feared lest any one of them should have seemed to me to be of any consequence, should he endeavor to subordinate or even to compare to bodily sense, or to those things that pertain to bodily sense as objects of knowledge, either intellect or those things that are perceived (not by way of defect) by the intellect.

Which point having been settled, how would he or any other have dared to deny that such souls as he would consider evil, yet since they are souls, are to be reckoned in the number of intelligible things, nor are objects of intellectual perception by way of defect?

This is on the supposition that souls are souls only by being alive.

For if they were intellectually perceived as vicious through defect, being vicious by lack of virtue, yet they are perceived as souls not through defect, for they are souls by reason of being alive.

Nor can it be maintained that presence of life is a cause of defect, for by as much as anything is defective, by so much is it severed from life.

9.

Since therefore it would have been every way evident that no souls can be separated from that Author from whom yonder light is not separated, whatever they might have now adduced I should not have accepted, and should rather have admonished them that they should choose with me to follow those who maintain that whatever is, since it is, and in whatever degree it is, has its existence from the one God.

Chapter 7 - How Evil Men are of God, and Not of God

They might have cited against me those words of the gospel:
"Ye therefore do not hear, because ye are not of God;" "Ye are of your father the devil."[199]I also should have cited:
"All things were made by Him and without Him was not anything made," [200] and this of the Apostle:
"One God of whom are all things, and one Lord Jesus Christ through whom are all things,"[201] and again from the same Apostle:
"Of whom are all things, through whom are all things, in whom are all things, to Him be glory." [202]I should have exhorted those men (if indeed I had found them men), that we should presume upon nothing as if we had found it out, but should rather inquire of the masters who would demonstrate the agreement and harmony of those passages that seem to be discordant.

For when in one and the same Scriptural authority we read:
"All things are of God," [203] and elsewhere:
"Ye are not of God," since it is wrong rashly to condemn books of Scripture, who would not have seen that a skilled teacher should be found who would know a solution of this problem, from whom assuredly if endowed with good intellectual powers, and a "spiritual man," as is said by divine inspiration [204] (for he would necessarily have favored the true arguments concerning the intelligible and sensible nature, which, as far as I can, I have conducted and handled, nay he would have disclosed them far better and more convincingly); we should have heard nothing else concerning this problem, except, as might happen, that there is no class of souls but has its existence from God, and that it is yet rightly said to sinners and unbelievers: "Ye are not of God."

For we also, perchance, Divine aid having been implored, should have been able easily to see, that it is one thing to live and another to sin, and (although life in sin may be called death in comparison with just life, [205] and while in one man it may be found, that he is at the same time alive and a sinner) that so far as he is alive, he is of God, so far as he is a sinner he is not of God. In which division we use that alternative that suits our sentiment; so that when we wish to insist upon the omnipotence of God as Creator, we may say even to sinners that they are of God.

For we are speaking to those who are contained in some class, we are speaking to those having animal life, we are speaking to rational beings, we are speaking lastly--and this applies especially to the matter in hand--to living beings, all which things are essentially divine functions.

But when our purpose is to convict evil men, we rightly say:
"Ye are not of God."

For we speak to them as averse to truth, unbelieving, criminal, infamous, and, to sum up all in one term--sinners, all of which things are undoubtedly not of God.

Therefore what wonder is it, if Christ says to sinners, convicting them of this very thing that they were sinners and did not believe in Him:

"Ye are not of God;" and on the other hand, without prejudice to the former statement:
"All things were made through Him," and "All things are of God?"

For if not to believe Christ, to repudiate Christ's advent, not to accept Christ, was a sure mark of souls that are not of God; and so it was said:

"Ye therefore hear not, because ye are not of God;" how would that saying of the apostle be true that occurs in the memorable beginning of the gospel:

"He came unto his own things, and his own people did not receive him?" [206]Whence his own if they did not receive him; or whence therefore not his own because they did not receive him, unless that sinners by virtue of being men belong to God, but by virtue of being sinners belong to the devil?

He who says:

"His own people received him not" had reference to nature; but he who says:

"Ye are not of God." had reference to will; for the evangelist was commending the works of God, Christ was censuring the sins of men.

Chapter 8 - The Manichæans Inquire Whence is Evil and by This Question Think They Have Triumphed

Let Them First Know, Which is Most Easy to Do, that Nothing Can Live Without God.

Consummate Evil Cannot Be Known Except by the Knowledge of Consummate Good, Which is God.

Here perchance some one may say:

Whence are sins themselves, and whence is evil in general?

If from man, whence is man? if from an angel, whence is the angel?

When it is said, however truly and rightly, that these are from God, it nevertheless seems to those unskillful and possessed of little power to look into recondite matters, that evils and sins are thereby connected, as by a sort of chain, to God.

By this question they think themselves triumphant, as if forsooth to ask were to know;--would it were so, for in that case no one would be more knowing than myself.

Yet very often in controversy the propounder of a great question, while impersonating the great teacher, is himself more ignorant in the matter concerning which he would frighten his opponent, than he whom he would frighten.

These therefore suppose that they are superior to the common run, because the former ask questions that the latter cannot answer.

If therefore when I most unfortunately was associated with them, not in the position in which I have now for some time been, they had raised these objections when I had brought forward this argument, I should have said:

I ask that you meanwhile agree with me, which is most easy, that if nothing can shine without God, much less can anything live without God.

Let us not persist in such monstrous opinions as to maintain that any souls whatsoever have life apart from God.

For perchance it may so happen that with me you are ignorant as to this thing, namely whence is evil, let us then learn either simultaneously or in any order, I care not what.

For what if knowledge of the perfection of evil is impossible to man without knowledge of the perfection of good?

For we should not know darkness if we were always in darkness.

But the notion of light does not allow its opposite to be unknown.

But the highest good is that than which there is nothing higher.

But God is good and than Him nothing can be higher.

God therefore is the highest good.

Let us therefore together so recognize God, and thus what we seek too hastily will not be hidden from us.

Do you suppose then that the knowledge of God is a matter of small account or desert.

For what other reward is there for us than life eternal, which is to know God?

For God the Master says:

"But this is life eternal, that they might know Thee the only and true God, and Jesus Christ whom thou hast sent." [207] For the soul, although it is immortal, yet because aversion from the knowledge of God is rightly called its death, when it is converted to God, the reward of eternal life to be attained is that knowledge; so that this is, as has been said, eternal life.

But no one can be converted to God, except he turn himself away from this world.

This for myself I feel to be arduous and exceedingly difficult, whether it is easy to you, God Himself would have seen.

I should have been inclined to think it easy to you, had I not been moved by the fact, that, since the world from which we are commanded to turn away is visible, and the apostle says:

"The things that are seen are temporal, but the things that are unseen are eternal," [208] you ascribe more importance to the judgment of these eyes than to that of the mind, asserting and believing as you do that there is no shining feather that does not shine from God; and that there are living souls that do not live from God.

These and like things I should either have said to them or considered with myself, for even then, supplicating God with all my bowels, so to speak, and examining as attentively as possible the Scriptures, I should perchance have been able either to say such things or to think them, so far as was necessary for my salvation.

Chapter 9 - Augustin Deceived by Familiarity with the Manichæans, and by the Succession of Victories Over Ignorant Christians Reported by Them

The Manichæans are Likewise Easily Refuted from the Knowledge of Sin and the Will.
But two things especially, which easily lay hold upon that unwary age, urged me through wonderful circuits.
One of these was familiarity, suddenly, by a certain false semblance of goodness, wrapped many times around my neck as a certain sinuous chain.
The other was, that I was almost always noxiously victorious in arguing with ignorant Christians who yet eagerly attempted, each as he could, to defend their faith. [209]By which frequent success the ardor of youth was kindled, and by its own impulse rashly verged upon the great evil of stubbornness. For this kind of wrangling, after I had become an auditor among them, whatever I was able to do either by my own genius, such as it was, or by reading the works of others, I most gladly devoted to them alone. Accordingly from their speeches ardor in disputations was daily increased, from success in disputations love for them [the Manichæans].
Whence it resulted that whatever they said, as if affected by certain strange disorders, I approved of as true, not because I knew it to be true, but because I wished it to be.
So it came about that, however slowly and cautiously, yet for a long time I followed men that preferred a sleek straw to a living soul.

12.
So be it, I was not able at that time to distinguish and discern sensible from intelligible things, carnal forsooth from spiritual.
It did not belong to age, nor to discipline, nor even to any habit, nor, finally, to any deserts; for it is a matter of no small joy and felicitation:
had I not thus been able at length even to grasp that which in the judgment of all men nature itself by the laws of the most High God has established?

Chapter 10 - Sin is Only from the Will

His Own Life and Will Best Known to Each Individual.
What Will is.
For let any men whatever, if only no madness has broken them loose from the common sense of the human race, bring whatever zeal they like for judging, whatever ignorance, nay whatever slowness of mind, I should like to find out what they would have replied to me had I asked, whether a man would seem to them to have sinned by whose hand while he was asleep another should have written something disgraceful?
Who doubts that they would have denied that it is a sin, and have exclaimed against it so vehemently that they might perchance have been enraged that I should have thought them proper objects of such a question?
Of whom reconciled and restored to equanimity, as best I could do it, I should have begged that they would not take it amiss if I asked them another thing just as manifest, just as completely within the knowledge of all.
Then I should have asked, if some stronger person had done some evil thing by the hand of one not sleeping but conscious, yet with the rest of his members bound and in constraint, whether because he knew it, though absolutely unwilling, he should be held guilty of any sin?
And here all marvelling that I should ask such questions, would reply without hesitation, that he had absolutely not sinned at all. Why so?
Because whoever has done anything evil by means of one unconscious or unable to resist, the latter can by no means be justly condemned.
And precisely why this is so, if I should inquire of the human nature in these men, I should easily bring out the desired answer, by asking in this manner:
Suppose that the sleeper already knew what the other would do with his hand, and of purpose aforethought, having drunk so much as would prevent his being awakened, should go to sleep, in order to deceive some one with an oath.
Would any amount of sleep suffice to prove his innocence?
What else than a guilty man would one pronounce him?

But if he has also willingly been bound that he may deceive some one by this pretext, in what respect then would those chains profit as a means of relieving him of sin? Although bound by these he was really not able to resist, as in the other case the sleeper was absolutely ignorant of what he was then doing.

Is there therefore any possibility of doubting that both should be judged to have sinned?

Which things having been conceded, I should have argued, that sin is indeed nowhere but in the will, [210] since this consideration also would have helped me, that justice holds guilty those sinning by evil will alone, although they may have been unable to accomplish what they willed.

13.

For who could have said that, in adducing these considerations, I was dwelling upon obscure and recondite things, where on account of the fewness of those able to understand, either fraud or suspicion of ostentation is accustomed to arise?

Let that distinction between intelligible and sensible things withdraw for a little:

let me not be found fault with for following up slow minds with the stimuli of subtle disputations.

Permit me to know that I live, permit me to know that I will to live.

If in this the human race agrees, as our life is known to us, so also is our will.

Nor when we become possessed of this knowledge, is there any occasion to fear lest any one should convince us that we may be deceived; for no one can be deceived as to whether he does not live, or wishes nothing.

I do not think that I have adduced anything obscure, and my concern is rather lest some should find fault with me for dwelling on things that are too manifest.

But let us consider the bearing of these things.

14.

Sinning therefore takes place only by exercise of will.

But our will is very well known to us; for neither should I know that I will, if I did not know what will itself is.

Accordingly, it is thus defined:

will is a movement of mind, no one compelling, either for not losing or for obtaining something. [211] Why therefore could not I have so defined it then?

Was it difficult to see that one unwilling is contrary to one willing, just as the left hand is contrary to the right, not as black to white?

For the same thing cannot be at the same time black and white.

But whoever is placed between two men is on the left hand with reference to one, on the right with reference to the other.

One man is both on the right hand and on the left hand at the same time, but by no means both to the one man.

So indeed one mind may be at the same time unwilling and willing, but it cannot be at the same time unwilling and willing with reference to one and the same thing. For when any one unwillingly does anything; if you ask him whether he wished to do it, he says that he did not.

Likewise if you ask whether he wished not to do it, he replies that he did.

So you will find him unwilling with reference to doing, willing with reference to not doing, that is to say, one mind at the same time having both attitudes, but each referring to different things.

Why do I say this?

Because if we should again ask wherefore though unwilling he does this, he will say that he is compelled.

For every one also who does a thing unwillingly is compelled, and every one who is compelled, if he does a thing, does it only unwillingly.

It follows that he that is willing is free from compulsion, even if any one thinks himself compelled.

And in this manner every one who willingly does a thing is not compelled, and whoever is not compelled, either does it willingly or not at all. Since nature itself proclaims these things in all men whom we can interrogate without absurdity, from the boy even to the old man, from literary sport even to the throne of the wise, why then should I not have seen that in the definition of will should be put, "no one compelling," which now as if with greater experience most cautiously I have done.

But if this is everywhere manifest, and promptly occurs to all not by instruction but by nature, what is there left that seems obscure, unless perchance it be concealed from some one, that when we wish for something, we will, and our mind is moved towards it, and we either have it or do not have it, and if we have it we will to retain it, if we have it not, to acquire it?

Wherefore everyone who wills, wills either not to lose something or to obtain it.

Hence if all these things are clearer than day, as they are, nor are they given to my conception alone, but by the liberality of truth itself to the whole human race, why could I not have said even at that time:

Will is a movement of the mind, no one compelling, either for not losing or for obtaining something?

Chapter 11 - What Sin is

Some one will say:
What assistance would this have furnished you against the Manichæans?
Wait a moment; permit me first also to define sin, which, every mind reads divinely written in itself, cannot exist apart from will.
Sin therefore is the will to retain and follow after what justice forbids, and from which it is free to abstain. [212] Although if it be not free, it is not will.
But I have preferred to define more roughly than precisely.
Should I not also have carefully examined those obscure books, whence I might have learned that no one is worthy of blame or punishment who either wills what justice does not prohibit him from willing, or does not do what he is not able to do? Do not shepherds on mountains, poets in theatres, unlearned in social intercourse, learned in libraries, masters in schools, priests in consecrated places, and the human race throughout the whole world, sing out these things?
But if no one is worthy of blame and condemnation, who either does not act against the prohibition of justice, or who does not do what he cannot do, yet every sin is blameworthy and condemnable, who doubts then that it is sin, when willing is unjust, and not willing is free.
And hence that definition is both true and easy to understand, and not only now but then also could have been spoken by me:
Sin is the will of retaining or of obtaining, what justice forbids, and whence it is free to abstain?

Chapter 12 - From the Definitions Given of Sin and Will, He Overthrows the Entire Heresy of the Manichæans

Likewise from the Just Condemnation of Evil Souls It Follows that They are Evil Not by Nature But by Will.
That Souls are Good By Nature, to Which the Pardon of Sins is Granted.

16.
Come now, let us see in what respect these things would have aided us.
Much every way, so that I should have desired nothing more; for they end the whole cause; for whoever consulting in the inner mind, where they are more pronounced and assured, the secrets of his own conscience, and the divine laws absolutely imposed upon nature, grants that these two definitions of will and sin are true, condemns without any hesitation by the fewest and the briefest, but plainly the most invincible reasons, the whole heresy of the Manichæans.
Which can be thus considered.
They say that there are two kinds of souls, the one good, which is in such a way from God, that it is said not to have been made by Him out of any material or out of nothing, but to have proceeded as a certain part from the very substance itself of God; the other evil, which they believe and strive to get others to believe pertains to God in no way whatever; and so they maintain that the one is the perfection of good, but the other the perfection of evil, and that these two classes were at one time distinct but are now commingled.
The character and the cause of this commingling I had not yet heard; but nevertheless I could have inquired whether that evil kind of souls, before it was mingled with the good, had any will.
For if not, it was without sin and innocent, and so by no means evil. [213]
But if evil in such a way, that though without will, as fire, yet if it should touch the good it would violate and corrupt it; how impious it is to believe that the nature of evil is powerful enough to change any part of God, and that the Highest Good is corruptible and violable!
But if the will was present, assuredly there was present, no one compelling, a movement of the mind either towards not losing something or obtaining something.
But this something was either good, or was thought to be good, for not otherwise could it be earnestly desired.
But in supreme evil, before the commingling which they maintain, there never was any good.
Whence then could there be in it either the knowledge or the thought of good?

Did they wish for nothing that was in themselves, and earnestly desire that true good which was without?

That will must truly be declared worthy of distinguished and great praise by which is earnestly desired the supreme and true good. Whence then in supreme evil was this movement of mind most worthy of so great praise?

Did they seek it for the sake of injuring it?

In the first place, the argument comes to the same thing.

For he who wishes to injure, wishes to deprive another of some good for the sake of some good of his own.

There was therefore in them either a knowledge of good or an opinion of good, which ought by no means to belong to supreme evil.

In the second place, whence had they known, that good placed outside of themselves, which they designed to injure, existed at all.

If they had intellectually perceived it, what is more excellent than such a mind?

Is there anything else for which the whole energy of good men is put forth except the knowledge of that supreme and sincere good?

What therefore is now scarcely conceded to a few good and just men, was mere evil, no good assisting, then able to accomplish?

But if those souls bore bodies and saw the supreme good with their eyes, what tongues, what hearts, what intellects suffice for lauding and proclaiming those eyes, with which the minds of just men can scarcely be compared?

How great good things we find in supreme evil!

For if to see God is evil, God is not a good; but God is a good; therefore to see God is good; and I know not what can be compared to this good.

Since to see anything is good, whence can it be made out that to be able to see is evil?

Therefore whatever in those eyes or in those minds brought it about, that the divine essence could be seen by them, brought about a great thing and a good thing most worthy of ineffable praise.

But if it was not brought about, but it was such in itself and eternal, it is difficult to find anything better than this evil.

17.

Lastly, that these souls may have nothing of these praiseworthy things which by the reasonings of the Manichæans they are compelled to have, I should have asked, whether God condemns any or no souls.

If none, there is no judgment of rewards and punishments, no providence, and the world is administered by chance rather than by reason, or rather is not administered at all.

For the name administration must not be given to chances.

But if it is impious for all those that are bound by any religion to believe this, it remains either that there is condemnation of some souls, or that there are no sins.

But if there are no sins, neither is there any evil.

Which if the Manichæans should say, they would slay their heresy with a single blow.

Therefore they and I agree that some souls are condemned by divine law and judgment. But if these souls are good, what is that justice?

If evil, are they so by nature, or by will?

But by nature souls can in no way be evil. Whence do we teach this.

From the above definitions of will and sin. For to speak of souls, and that they are evil, and that they do not sin, is full of madness; but to say that they sin without will, is great craziness, and to hold any one guilty of sin for not doing what he could not do, belongs to the height of iniquity and insanity. Wherefore whatever these souls do, if they do it by nature not by will, that is, if they are wanting in a movement of mind free both for doing and not doing, if finally no power of abstaining from their work is conceded to them; we cannot hold that the sin is theirs. [214]But all confess both that evil souls are justly, and souls that have not sinned are unjustly condemned; therefore they confess that those souls are evil that sin.

But these, as reason teaches, do not sin. Therefore the extraneous class of evil souls of the Manichæans, whatever it may be, is a non-entity.

18.

Let us now look at that good class of souls, which again they exalt to such a degree as to say that it is the very substance of God. But how much better it is that each one should recognize his own rank and merit, nor be so puffed up with sacrilegious pride as to believe that as often as he experiences a change in himself it is the substance of that supreme good, which devout reason holds and teaches to be unchangeable!

For behold! since it is manifest that souls do not sin in not being such as they cannot be; it follows that these supposititious souls, whatever they may be, do not sin at all, and moreover that they are absolutely non-existent; it remains that since there are sins, they find none to whom to attribute them except the good class of souls and the substance of God.

But especially are they pressed by Christian authority; for never have they denied that forgiveness of sins is granted when any one has been converted to God; never have they said (as they have said of many other passages) that some corrupter has interpolated this into the divine Scriptures.

To whom then are sins attributed?

If to those evil souls of the alien class, these also can become good, can possess the kingdom of God with Christ.

Which denying, they [the Manichæans] have no other class except those souls which they maintain are of the substance of God.

It remains that they acknowledge that not only these latter also, but these alone sin.

But I make no contention about their being alone in sinning; yet they sin.

But are they compelled to sin by being commingled with evil?

If so compelled that there was no power of resisting, they do not sin.

If it is in their power to resist, and they voluntarily consent, we are compelled to find out through their [the Manichæan] teaching, why so great good things in supreme evil, why this evil in supreme good, unless it be that neither is that which they bring into suspicion evil, nor is that which they pervert by superstition supreme good?

Chapter 13 - From Deliberation on the Evil and on the Good Part It Results that Two Classes of Souls are Not to Be Held to

A Class of Souls Enticing to Shameful Deeds Having Been Conceded, It Does Not Follow that These are Evil by Nature, that the Others are Supreme Good.

19.

But if I had taught, or at any rate had myself learned, that they rave and err regarding those two classes of souls, why should I have thenceforth thought them worthy of being heard or consulted about anything?

That I might learn hence, that these two kinds of souls are pointed out, which in the course of deliberation assent puts now on the evil side, now on the good?

Why is not this rather the sign of one soul which by free will can be borne here and there, swayed hither and thither?

For it was my own experience to feel that I am one, considering evil and good and choosing one or the other, but for the most part the one pleases, the other is fitting, placed in the midst of which we fluctuate.

Nor is it to be wondered at, for we are now so constituted that through the flesh we can be affected by sensual pleasure, and through the spirit by honorable considerations.

Am I not therefore compelled to acknowledge two souls?

Nay, we can better and with far less difficulty recognize two classes of good things, of which neither is alien from God as its author, one soul acted upon from diverse directions, the lower and the higher, or to speak more correctly, the external and the internal.

These are the two classes which a little while ago we considered under the names sensible and intelligible, which we now prefer to call more familiarly carnal and spiritual.

But it has been made difficult for us to abstain from carnal things, since our truest bread is spiritual.

For with great labor we now eat this bread.

For neither without punishment for the sin of transgression have we been changed from immortal into mortal. So it happens, that when we strive after better things, habit formed by connection with the flesh and our sins in some way begin to militate against us and to put obstacles in our way, some foolish persons with most obtuse superstition suspect that there is another kind of souls which is not of God.

20.

However even if it be conceded to them that we are enticed to shameful deeds by another inferior kind of souls, they do not thence make it evident that those enticing are evil by nature, or those enticed, supremely good.

For it may be, the former of their own will, by striving after what was not lawful, that is, by sinning, from being good have become evil; and again they may be made good, but in such manner that for a long time they remain in sin, and by a certain occult suasion traduce to themselves other souls.

Then, they may not be absolutely evil, but in their own kind, however inferior, they may exercise their own functions without any sin.

But those superior souls to whom justice, the directress of things, has assigned a far more excellent activity, if they should wish to follow and to imitate those inferior ones, become evil, not because they imitate evil souls, but because they imitate in an evil way.

By the evil souls is done what is proper to them, by the good what is alien to them is striven after. Hence the former remain in their own grade, the latter are plunged into a lower.

It is as when men copy after beasts.

For the four-footed horse walks beautifully, but if a man on all fours should imitate him, who would think him worthy even of chaff for food?

Rightly therefore we generally disapprove of one who imitates, while we approve of him whom he imitates.

But we disapprove not because he has not succeeded, but for wishing to succeed at all.

For in the horse we approve of that to which by as much as we prefer man, by so much are we offended that he copies after inferior creatures.

So among men, however well the crier may do in sending forth his voice, would not the senator be insane, if he should do it even more clearly and better than the crier?

Take an illustration from the heavenly bodies:

The moon when shining is praised, and by its course and its changes is quite pleasing to those that pay attention to such things.

But if the sun should wish to imitate it (for we may feign that it has desires of this sort [215]), who would not be greatly and rightly displeased.

From which illustrations I wish it to be understood, that even if there are souls (which meanwhile is left an open question [216]) devoted to bodily offices not by sin but by nature, and even if they are related to us, however inferior they may be, by some inner affinity, they should not be esteemed evil simply because we are evil ourselves in following them and in loving corporeal things.

For we sin by loving corporeal things, because by justice we are required and by nature we are able to love spiritual things, and when we do this we are, in our kind, the best and the happiest.[217]

21.

Wherefore what proof does deliberation, violently urged in both directions, now prone to sin, now borne on toward right conduct, furnish, that we are compelled to accept two kinds of souls, the nature of one of which is from God, of the other not; when we are free to conjecture so many other causes of alternating states of mind?

But that these things are obscure and are to no purpose pried into by blear-eyed minds, whoever is a good judge of things sees.

Wherefore those things rather which have been said regarding the will and sin, those things, I say, that supreme justice permits no man using his reason to be ignorant of, those things which if they were taken from us, there is nothing whence the discipline of virtue may begin, nothing whence it may rise from the death of vices, those things I say considered again and again with sufficient clearness and lucidity convince us that the heresy of the Manichæans is false.

Chapter 14 - Again It is Shown from the Utility of Repenting that Souls are Not by Nature Evil

So Sure a Demonstration is Not Contradicted Except from the Habit of Erring.

22.

Like the foregoing considerations is what I shall now say about repenting.

For as among all sane people it is agreed, and this the Manichæans themselves not only confess but also teach, that to repent of sin is useful.

Why shall I now, in this matter, collect the testimonies of the divine Scriptures, which are scattered throughout their pages?

It is also the voice of nature; notice of this thing has escaped no fool.

We should be undone, if this were not deeply imbedded in our nature.

Some one may say that he does not sin; but no barbarity will dare to say, that if one sins he should not repent of it.

This being the case, I ask to which of the two kinds of souls does repenting pertain?

I know indeed that it can pertain neither to him who does ill nor to him who cannot do well.

Wherefore, that I may use the words of the Manichæans, if a soul of darkness repent of sin, it is not of the substance of supreme evil, if a soul of light, it is not of the substance of supreme good; that disposition of repenting which is profitable testifies alike that the penitent has done ill, and that he could have done well.

How, therefore, is there from me nothing of evil, if I have acted unadvisedly, or how can I rightly repent if I have not so done?

Hear the other part.

How is there from me nothing of good, if in me there is good will, or how do I rightly repent if there is not?

Wherefore, either let them deny that there is great utility in repenting, so that they may be driven not only from the Christian name, but from every even imaginary argument for their views, or let them cease to say and to teach that there are two kinds of souls, one of which has nothing of evil, the other nothing of good; for that whole sect is propped up by this two-headed [218] or rather headlong [219] variety of souls.

23.

And to me indeed it is sufficient thus to know that the Manichæans err, that I know that sin must be repented of; and yet if now by right of friendship I should accost some one of my friends who still thinks that they are worthy of being listened to, and should say to him:

Do you not know that it is useful, when any one has sinned, to repent? Without hesitation he will swear that he knows.

If then I shall have convinced you that Manichæism is false, will you not desire anything more?

Let him reply what more he can desire in this matter.

Very well, so far.

But when I shall have begun to show the sure and necessary arguments which, bound to it with adamantine chains, as the saying is, follow that proposition, and shall have conducted to its conclusion the whole process by which that sect is overthrown, he will deny perhaps that he knows the utility of repenting, which no learned man, no unlearned, is ignorant of, and will rather contend, when we hesitate and deliberate, that two souls in us furnish each its own proper help to the solution of the different parts of the question.

O habit of sin!

O accompanying penalty of sin!

Then you turned me away from the consideration of things so manifest, but you injured me when I did not discern.

But now, among my most familiar acquaintances who do not discern, you wound and torment me discerning.

Chapter 15 - He Prays for His Friends Whom He Has Had as Associates in Error

24.

Give heed to these things, I beseech you, dearly beloved.

Your dispositions I have well known.

If you now concede to me the mind and the reason of any sort of man, these things are far more certain than the things that we seemed to learn or rather were compelled to believe.

Great God, God omnipotent, God of supreme goodness, whose right it is to be believed and known to be inviolable and unchangeable.

Trinal Unity, whom the Catholic Church worships, as one who have experienced in myself Thy mercy, I supplicate Thee, that Thou wilt not permit those with whom from boyhood I have lived most harmoniously in every relation to dissent from me in Thy worship.

I see how it was especially to be expected in this place that I should either even then have defended the Catholic Scriptures attacked by the Manichæans, if as I say, I had been cautious; or I should now show that they can be defended.

But in other volumes God will aid my purpose, for the moderate length of this, as I suppose, already asks to be spared. [220]

Footnotes:

190. Scarcely any one of his earlier treatises was more unsatisfactory to Augustin in his later Anti-Pelagian years than that Concerning Two Souls.

In his Retractations, Book I., chapter xv., he recognizes the rashness of some of his statements and points out the sense in which they are tenable or the reverse.

As regards the occasion of the writing, the following may be quoted:

"After this book [De Utilitate Credendi] I wrote, while still a presbyter, against the Manichæans Concerning Two Souls, of which they say that one part is of God, the other from the race of darkness, which God did not found, and which is coeternal with God, and they rave about both these souls, the one good, the other evil, being in one man, saying forsooth that the evil soul on the one hand belongs to the flesh, which flesh also they say is of the race of darkness; but that the good soul is from the part of God that came forth, combated the race of darkness, and mingled with the latter; and they attribute all good things in man to that good soul, and all evil things to that evil soul."--A.H.N.

191. In his Retractations, Augustin explains this proposition as follows:

"I said this in the sense in which the creature is known to pertain to the Creator, but not in the sense that it is of Him, so as to be regarded as part of Him."--A.H.N.

192. John xiv. 6.

193. It will aid the reader in following the thread of Augustin's argument, if he will bear in mind that throughout this treatise the writer considers the points of antagonism between Manichæism and Catholicism from the point of view of his early entanglement in Manichæan error.

Considering the opportunities that he had for knowing the truth, the helps to have been expected from God in answer to prayer, the capacities of the unperverted intellect to arrive at truth, he inquires how he should have guarded himself from the insinuation of Manichæan error, how he should have defended the truth, and how he should have been the means of liberating others.--A.H.N.

194. Sublimitate animi.

195. Mente atque intelligentia.

196. Matt. viii. 22.

197. 1 Tim. v. 6.

198. Neither Augustin nor the Manichæans seem to have recognized the distinction in kind between the human soul and animal life.--A.H.N.

199. John viii. 47 and 44.

200. John i. 3.

201. 1 Cor. viii. 6.

202. Rom. xi. 36.

203. 1 Cor. xi. 12.

204. 1 Cor. ii. 15.

205. 1 Tim. v. 6.

206. John i. 11.

207. John xvii. 3.

208. 2 Cor. iv. 18.

209. Nothing is more certain than that Christianity has suffered more at the hands of injudicious and ignorant defenders than from its most astute and determined foes.

Little attention would be paid to the blatant infidels of the present day were it not for the interest aroused and sustained by weak attempts to refute their arguments.

And as the youthful, ardent Augustin was encouraged and confirmed in his errors by the inability of his opponents, so are errors confirmed at the present day.

The philosophical defence of Christianity is a matter of the utmost delicacy, and should be undertaken with fear and trembling.--A.H.N.

210. The Pelagians used this statement with considerable effect in their polemics against its author.

In his Retractations Augustin has this to say by way of explanation:

"The Pelagians may think that thus was said in their interest, on account of young children whose sin which is remitted to them in baptism they deny on the ground that they do not yet use the power of will.

As if indeed the sin, which we say they derive originally from Adam, that is, that they are implicated in his guilt and on this account are held obnoxious to punishment, could ever be otherwise than in will, by which will it was committed when the transgression of the divine precept was accomplished.

Our statement, that there is never sin but in will,' may be thought false for the reason that the apostle says:

If what I will not this I do, it is no longer I that do it, but sin that dwelleth in me.'

For this sin is to such an extent involuntary, that he says:

What I will not this I do.'

How, therefore, is there never sin but in the will?

But this sin concerning which the apostle has spoken is called sin, because by sin it was done, and it is the penalty of sin; since this is said concerning carnal concupiscence, which he discloses in what follows saying:

I know that in me, that is in my flesh, dwelleth no good; for to will is present to me, but to accomplish that which is good, is not.' (Rom. vii. 16-18).

Since the perfection of good is, that not even the concupiscence of sin should be in man, to which indeed when one lives well the will does not consent; nevertheless man does not accomplish the good because as yet concupiscence is in him, to which the will is antagonistic, the guilt of which concupiscence is loosed by baptism, but the infirmity remains, against which until it is healed every believer who advances well most earnestly struggles.

But sin, which is never but in will, must especially be known as that which is followed by just condemnation.

For this through one man entered into the world; although that sin also by which consent is yielded to concupiscence is not committed but by will.

Wherefore also in another place I have said:

Not therefore except by will is sin committed.'"--A.H.N. On this matter Augustin's still earlier treatise De Libero Arbitrio, and his interesting Retractations on the same, should be compared.

The reader of these earlier treatises in comparison with the Anti-Pelagian treatises can hardly fail to recognize a marked change of base on Augustin's part.

His efforts to show the consistency of his earlier with his later modes of thought are to be pronounced only partially successful.

The fact is, that in the Anti-Manichæan time he went too far in maintaining the absolute freedom of the will and the impossibility of sin apart from personal will in the sinner; while in the Anti-Pelagian time he ventured too near to the fatalism that he so earnestly combated in the Manichæans.--A.H.N.

211. This dictum also Augustin thought it needful to explain:

"This was said that by this definition a willing person might be distinguished from one not willing, and so the intention might be referred to those who first in Paradise were the origin of evil to the human race, by sinning no one compelling, that is by sinning with free will, because also knowingly they sinned against the command, and the tempters persuaded, did not compel, that this should be done.

For he who ignorantly sinned may not incongruously be said to have sinned unwillingly, although not knowing what he did, yet willingly he did it.

So not even the sin of such a one could be without will, which will assuredly, as it has been defined, was a movement of the mind, no one compelling, either for not losing or for obtaining something.'

For he was not compelled to do what if he had been unwilling he would not have done.

Because he willed, therefore he did it, even if he did not sin because he willed, being ignorant that what he did is sin.

So not even such a sin could be without will, but by will of deed not by will of sin, which deed was yet sin; for this deed is what ought not to have taken place.

But whoever knowingly sins, if he can without sin resist the one compelling him to sin, yet resists not, assuredly sins willingly.

For he who can resist is not compelled to yield.

But he who cannot by good will resist cogent covetousness, and therefore does what is contrary to the precepts of righteousness, this now is sin in the sense of being the penalty of sin.

Wherefore it is most true that sin cannot be apart from will." It is needless to say that such reasoning would not have answered Augustin's purpose in writing against the Manichæans.--A.H.N.

212. Here also Augustin guards himself in his Retractations:

"The definition is true, inasmuch as that is defined which is only sin, and not also that which is the penalty of sin."--A.H.N.

213. In his Retractations, Augustin replies to the Pelagian denial of the sinfulness of infants, in support of which they had quoted the above sentence.

"They [infants] are held guilty not by propriety of will but by origin.

For what is every earthly man in origin but Adam?"

The will of the whole human race was in Adam, and when Adam sinned the whole race voluntarily sinned, seems to be his meaning.--A.H.N.

214. In his Retractations, Augustin explains that by nature is to be understood the state in which we were created without vice.

He transfers the entire argument from the actual condition of man to the primitive Adamic condition.

It is evident, however, that this was not his meaning when he combated the Manichæans.

The question of infant sinfulness arises here also, and is discussed in the usual Anti-Pelagian way.--A.H.N.

215. Augustin's carefulness to explain that he is only indulging in personification is doubtless due to the fact that with the Manichæans the sun and the moon were

objects of worship.--A.H.N.

216. In his Retractations, Augustin explains that he did not really regard this as an open question, but speaks of it as such only so far as this particular discussion is concerned.

He simply declines to enter upon a consideration of it in this connection.--A.H.N.

217. Here also the use of the word "nature" gave Augustin trouble in his later years.

He claims in the Retractations that he uses the word in the sense of "nature that has been healed" and that "cannot be vitiated," and seeks to show that he did not mean to exclude divine grace.--A.H.N.

218. Bicipiti.

219. Præcipiti.

220. This purpose Augustin accomplished in several works.

See especially Contra Adimantum, and Contra Faustum Manichæum.

On Augustin's defense of the Old Testament Scriptures, see Mozley's Ruling Ideas in Early Ages, last chapter.--A.H.N.

Acts or Disputation Against Fortunatus the Manichæan

[acta seu disputatio contra fortunatum manichæum].
A.D. 392. [221]
translated by albert h. newman, d.d., ll.d.,
professor of church history and comparative religion, in toronto baptist (theological) college, toronto, canada.

Disputation of the First Day

On the fifth of September, the most renowned men Arcadius Augustus (the second time) and Rufinus being consuls, a disputation against Fortunatus, an elder of the Manichæans, was held in the city of Hippo Regius, in the baths of Sossius, in the presence of the people.

1.

Augustin said:

I now regard as error what formerly I regarded as truth.

I desire to hear from you who are present whether my supposition is correct.

First of all I regard it as the height of error to believe that Almighty God, in whom is our one hope, is in any part either violable, or contaminable, or corruptible.

This I know your heresy affirms, not indeed in the words that I now use; for when you are questioned you confess that God is incorruptible, and absolutely inviolable, and incontaminable; but when you begin to expound the rest of your system, we are compelled to declare Him corruptible, penetrable, contaminable.

For you say that another race of darkness, whatever it may be, has rebelled against the kingdom of God; but that Almighty God, when He saw what ruin and desolation threatened his domains, unless he should make some opposition to the adverse race and resist it, sent this virtue, from whose commingling with evil and the race of darkness the world was framed.

Hence it is that here good souls labor, serve, err, are corrupted:

that they may see the need of a liberator, who should purge them from error, loose them from this commingling with evil, and liberate them from servitude.

I think it impious to believe that Almighty God ever feared any adverse race, or was under necessity to precipitate us into afflictions.

Fortunatus said:

Because I know that you have been in our midst, that is, have lived as an adherent among the Manichæans, these are the principles of our faith.

The matter now to be considered is our mode of living, the falsely alleged crimes for which we are maltreated. Therefore let the good men present hear from you whether these things with which we are charged and which we have thrown in our teeth are true or false.

For from your instruction, and from your exposition and explanation, they will have been able to gain more correct information about our mode of life, if it shall have been set forth by you.

2.

Augustin said:

I was among you, but faith and morals are different questions.

I proposed to discuss faith.

But if those present prefer to hear about morals, I do not decline that question.

Fortunatus said:

I wish first to purge myself in your conscience in which we are polluted, by the testimony of a competent man, (who even now is competent for me), and in view of the future examination of Christ, the just judge, whether he saw in us, or himself practiced by imitation, the things that are now thrown in our teeth?

3.

Augustin said:

You call me to something else, when I had proposed to discuss faith, but concerning your morals only those who are your Elect can fully know.

But you know that I was not your Elect, but an Auditor.

Hence though I was present at your prayer meetings, [222] as you have asked (whether separately among yourselves you have any prayer meetings, God alone and yourselves can know); yet in your prayer meetings where I have been present I have seen nothing shameful take place; but only that the faith that I afterwards learned and approved is denounced, and that you perform your services facing the sun. Besides this I found out nothing new in your meetings, but whoever raises any question of morals against you, raises it against your Elect.

But what you who are Elect do among yourselves, I have no means of knowing.

For I have often heard from you that you receive the Eucharist.

But since the time of receiving it was concealed from me, how could I know what you receive? [223] So keep the question about morals, if you please, for discussion among your Elect, if it can be discussed.

You gave me a faith that I today disapprove.

This I proposed to discuss.

Let a response be made to my proposition.

Fortunatus said:

And our profession is this very thing:

that God is incorruptible, lucid, unapproachable, intenible, impassible, that He inhabits His own eternal lights, that nothing corruptible proceeds from Him, neither darkness, demons, Satan, nor anything adverse can be found in His kingdom.

But that He sent forth a Saviour like Himself; that the Word born from the foundation of the world, when He had formed the world, after the formation of the world came among men; that He has chosen souls worthy of Himself according to His own holy will, sanctified by celestial command, imbued with the faith and reason of celestial things; that under His leadership those souls will return hence again to the kingdom of God according to the holy promise of Him who said:

"I am the way, the truth, and the door;" [224] and "No one can come unto the Father, except through me."

These things we believe because otherwise, that is, through another mediator, souls cannot return to the kingdom of God, unless they find Him as the way, the truth, and the door.

For Himself said:

"He that hath seen me, hath seen my Father also;" [225] and "whosoever shall have believed on me shall not taste death forever, but has passed from death unto life, and shall not come into judgment." [226] These things we believe and this is the reason of our faith, and according to the strength of our mind we endeavor to act according to His commandments, following after the one faith of this Trinity, Father and Son and Holy Spirit. [227]

4.

Augustin said:

What was the cause of those souls being precipitated into death, whom you confess come through Christ from death to life?

Fortunatus said:

Hence now deign to go on and to contradict, if there is nothing besides God.

5.

Augustin said:

Nay, do you deign to answer the question put to you:

What cause has given these souls to death?

Fortunatus said:

Nay but do you deign to say whether there is anything besides God, or all things are in God.

6.

Augustin said:

This I can reply, that the Lord wished me to know that God cannot suffer any necessity, nor be violated or corrupted in any part.

Which, since you also acknowledge, I ask by what necessity He sent hither souls that you say return through Christ?

Fortunatus said:

What you have said:

that thus far God has revealed to you, that He is incorruptible, as He has also revealed to me; the reason must be sought, how and wherefore souls have come into this world, so that now of right God should liberate them from this world through his Son only begotten and like Himself, if besides Himself there is nothing?

7.

Augustin said:

We ought not to disappoint those present, being men of note, and from the question proposed for discussion go to another. So we both confess, so we concede to ourselves, that God is incorruptible and inviolable, and could have in no way suffered.

From which it follows, that your heresy is false, which says that God, when He saw desolation and ruin threaten His kingdom, sent forth a power that should do battle with the race of darkness, and that out of this commingling our souls are laboring.

My argument is brief, and as I suppose, perfectly clear to any one.

If God could have suffered nothing from the race of darkness because He is inviolable, without cause He sent us hither that we might here suffer distress.

But if anything can suffer, it is not inviolable, and you deceive those to whom you say that God is inviolable.

For this your heresy denies when you expound the rest of it.

Fortunatus said:

We are of that mind in which the Apostle Paul instructs us, who says:

"Let this mind be in you that was also in Christ Jesus, who when He had been constituted in the form of God, thought it not robbery to be equal with God; but emptied Himself receiving the form of a servant, having been made in the likeness of men, and having been found in fashion as a man, He humbled Himself, and was made obedient even unto death." [228] We have this mind therefore about ourselves, which we have also about Christ, who when He was constituted in the form of God, was made obedient even unto death that He might show the similitude of our souls.

And like as He showed in Himself the similitude of death, and having been raised from the midst of the dead showed that He was from the Father, in the same manner we think it will be with our souls, because through Him we shall have been able to be freed from this death, which is either alien from God, or if it belongs to God, His mercy ceases, and the name of liberator, and the works of Him who liberates. [229]

8.

Augustin said:

I ask how we came into death, and you tell how we may be liberated from death.

Fortunatus said:

So the apostle said that we ought to have that mind concerning ourselves which Christ has shown us.

If Christ was in suffering and death, so also are we.

9.

Augustin said:

It is known to all that the Catholic faith is to the effect that our Lord, that is the Power and Wisdom of God, [230] and the Word through whom all things have been made and without whom was not anything made, [231] took upon Himself man to liberate us.

In the man whom He took upon Himself, He demonstrated those things that you spoke of.

But we now ask concerning the substance of God Himself and of Unspeakable Majesty, whether anything can injure it or not.

For if anything can injure it, He is not inviolable.

If nothing can injure the substance of God, what was the race of darkness about to do to it, against which you say war was waged by God before the foundation of the world; in which war you assert that we, that is souls that are now manifestly in need of a liberator, have been commingled with every evil and implicated in death.

For I return to that very brief statement: If He could be injured, He is not inviolable; if He could not, He acted cruelly in sending us hither to suffer these things.

Fortunatus said:

Does the soul belong to God, or not?

10.

Augustin said:

If it is just that you should fail to respond to my questions, and that I should be questioned, I will reply.

Fortunatus said:
Does the soul act independently?
This I ask of you.

11.

Augustin said:
I indeed will tell what you have asked; only remember this, that while you have refused to respond to my questions, I have responded to yours.

If you ask whether the soul descended from God, it is indeed a great question; but whether it descends from God or not, I make this reply concerning the soul, that it is not God; that God is one thing, the soul another.

That God is inviolable, incorruptible, and impenetrable, and incontaminable, who also could be corrupted in no part and to whom no injury can be done in any part. But we see also that the soul is sinful, and is conversant with misery, and seeks the truth, and is in want of a liberator.

This changing condition of the soul shows me that the soul is not God.

For if the soul is the substance of God, the substance of God errs, the substance of God is corrupted, the substance of God is violated, the substance of God is deceived; which it is impious to say.

Fortunatus said:
Therefore you have denied that the soul is of God, so long as it serves sins, and vices, and earthly things, and is led by error, because it cannot happen that either God or His substance should suffer this thing.

For God is incorruptible and His substance immaculate and holy.

But here it is inquired of you whether the soul is of God, or not?

Which we confess, and show from the advent of the Saviour, from His holy preaching, from His election; while He pitied souls, and the soul is said to have come according to His will, that He might free it from death and might bring it to eternal glory, and restore it to the Father.

But what do you say and hope concerning the soul; is it from God or not?

Can the substance of God, from which you deny that the soul has its being, be subject to no passions?

12.

Augustin said:
I have denied that the soul is the substance of God in the sense of its being God; but yet I hold that it is from God as its author, because it was made by God.

The Maker is one thing, the thing made is another.

He who made cannot be corruptible at all, but what He made cannot be at all equal to Him who made it.

Fortunatus said:
Nor have I said that the soul is like God.

But because you have said that the soul is an artificial thing, and that there is nothing besides God, I ask whence then God invented the substance of the soul?

13.

Augustin said:
Only bear in mind that I reply to your interrogations, but that you do not reply to mine.

I say that the soul was made by God as all other things that were made by God; and that among the things that God Almighty made the principal place was given to the soul.

But if you ask whence God made the soul, remember that you and I agree in confessing that God is almighty.

But he is not almighty who seeks the assistance of any material whence he may make what he will.

From which it follows, that according to our faith, all things that God made through His Word and Wisdom, He made out of nothing.

For so we read:

"He ordered and they were made; He commanded and they were created." [232]

Fortunatus said:
Do all things have their existence from God's command?

14.

Augustin said:
So I believe, but all things which were made.

Fortunatus said:
As things made they agree, but because they are unsuitable to themselves, therefore on this account it follows, that there is not one substance, although from the same order of the One they came to the composition and fashioning of this world.

But it is plain in the things themselves that there is no similarity between darkness and light, truth and falsehood, death and life, soul and body, and other similar things which differ from each other both in names and appearances.

And for good reason did our Lord say:
"The tree which my heavenly Father has not planted shall be rooted up and cast into the fire, because it brings not forth good fruit:" [233] ^

and that the tree has been rooted up.

Hence truly it follows from the reason of things that there are two substances in this world which agree in forms and in names, of which one belongs to corporeal natures, but the other is the eternal substance of the omnipotent Father, which we believe to be God's substance.

15.

Augustin said:
Those contrary things that move you so that we think adversely, have happened on account of our sin, that is, on account of the sin of man.

For God made all things good, and ordered them well; but He did not make sin, and our voluntary sin is the only thing that is called evil.

There is another kind of evil, which is the penalty of sin.

Since therefore there are two kinds of evil, sin and the penalty of sin, sin does not pertain to God; the penalty of sin pertains to the avenger.

For as God is good who constituted all things, so He is just in taking vengeance on sin.

Since therefore all things are ordered in the best possible way, which seem to us now to be adverse, it has deservedly happened to fallen man who was unwilling to keep the law of God.

For God gave free will to the rational soul which is in man.

For thus it would have been possible to have merit, if we should be good voluntarily and not of necessity.

Since therefore it behooves us to be good not of necessity but voluntarily, it behooved God to give to the soul free will.

But to this soul obeying His laws, He subjected all things without adversity, so that the rest of the things that God made should serve it, if also the soul itself had willed to serve God.

But if it should refuse to serve God, those things that served it should be converted into its punishment. Wherefore if all things are rightly ordered by God, and are good, neither does God suffer evil.

Fortunatus said:
He does not suffer, but prevents evil.

16.

Augustin said:
From whom then was He about to suffer it?

Fortunatus said:
This is my point, that He wished to prevent it, not rashly, but by power and prescience.

But deny evil to be apart from God, when other precepts can be shown which are done apart from His will.

A precept is not introduced, unless where there is contrariety. The free faculty of living is not given except where there is a fall according to the argument of the apostle who says:

"And you did he quicken, when ye were dead in your trespasses and sins, wherein aforetime ye walked according to the rulership of this world, according to the prince of the power of the air, of the spirit that now worketh in the souls of disobedience; among whom we also all once lived in the lusts of our flesh, doing the desires of the counsels of the flesh, and were by nature children of wrath, even as the rest:

but God, who is rich in all mercy, had mercy on us.

And when we were dead by sins, quickened us together in Christ, by whose grace ye have been saved; and at the same time also raised us up, and made us to sit with Him in the heavenly places with Christ Jesus, that in the ages to come He might show the exceeding riches of his grace in kindness toward us in Christ Jesus.

For by grace have ye been saved through faith; and that not of yourselves, for it is a gift of God; not of works, lest any one should glory.

For we are his workmanship created in Christ Jesus in good works, which God prepared that we should walk in them.

Wherefore remember, that aforetime ye were Gentiles in the flesh, who are called uncircumcision, by that which is called circumcision in flesh made by hands, because ye were at that time without Christ, alienated from the commonwealth of Israel, and strangers of the covenant, having no hope of the promise, and without God in this world.

But now in Christ Jesus, ye that once were far off are made nigh in the blood of Christ. For He is our peace, who made both one, and breaking down the middle wall of partition, the enmities in His flesh, making void by His decrees the law of commandments, that in Himself He might unite the two into one new man, making peace, that He might reconcile them both in one body unto God through the cross, slaying the enmities in Himself. And He came and preached peace unto you that were far off, and peace to them that were nigh.

For through Him we both have our access in one Spirit unto the Father." [234]

17.

Augustin said:

This passage from the apostle, which you have thought fit to recite, if I mistake not, makes very strongly for my faith and against yours.

In the first place, because free will itself, on which I have said that the possibility of the soul's sinning depends, is here sufficiently expressed, when sins are mentioned, and it is said that our reconciliation with God takes place through Jesus Christ.

For by sinning we were brought into opposition to God; but by holding to the precepts of Christ we are reconciled to God; so that we who were dead in sins may be made alive by keeping His precepts, and may have peace with Him in one Spirit, from whom we were alienated, by failure to keep His precepts; as is set forth in our faith concerning the man who was first created.

I ask of you, therefore, according to that passage which has been read, how can we have sins if contrary nature compels us to do what we do?

For he who is compelled by nature to do anything, does not sin.

But he who sins, sins by free will. Wherefore would repentance be enjoined upon us, if we have done nothing evil, but only the race of darkness?

Likewise, I ask, to whom is forgiveness of sins granted, to us or to the race of darkness?

If to the race of darkness, their race will also reign with Him, receiving the forgiveness of sin; but if to us it is manifest that we have sinned voluntarily.

For it is the height of folly for him to be pardoned who has done no evil.

But he has done no evil, who has done nothing of his own will.

Therefore the soul that today promises itself forgiveness of sins and reconciliation to God, if it should cease to sin, and repent past sins:

if it should answer according to your faith and should say:

In what have I sinned?

In what am I guilty?

Why hast Thou expelled me from Thy domains, that I might do battle with some sort of race?

I have been trodden under foot, I have been mixed up, I have been corrupted, I am worn out,[235] my free will has not been preserved.

Thou knowest the necessity by which I am preserved:

Why dost Thou impute to me the wounds that I have received?

Wherefore dost Thou compel me to repentance when Thou art the cause of my wounds; when Thou knowest what I have suffered, what the race of darkness has done against me, Thou being the author who couldst suffer no harm and yet wishing to save the domains which nothing could injure, Thou didst thrust me down into these miseries.

If indeed I am a part of Thee, who have proceeded from Thy bowels, if I am from Thy kingdom and Thy mouth, I ought not to suffer anything in this race of darkness, so that I being uncorrupted that race should be subjected, if I was a part of the Lord.

But now since it cannot be controlled except by my corruption, how can I either be said to be a part of Thee, or Thou remain inviolable, or not be cruel in wishing me to suffer for those domains, that could in no way be injured by that race of darkness?

Respond to this if you please, and deign also to explain to me how it was said by the apostle, "We were by nature children of wrath," who, he says, have been reconciled to God.

If therefore they were by nature children of wrath, how do you say that the soul is by nature a daughter and portion of God?

Fortunatus said:

If with regard to the soul the apostle had said that we are by nature children of wrath, the soul would have been alienated by the mouth of the apostle from God.

From this argument you only show that the soul does not belong to God, because, the apostle says, "We are by nature children of wrath."

But if it is said in view of the fact that the apostle [236] was held by the law, descending as he himself testifies, from the seed of Abraham, it follows that he has said corporeally, that we [i.e., Jews] were children of wrath even as the rest of mankind.

But he shows that the substance of the soul is of God, and that the soul cannot otherwise be reconciled to God than through the Master, who is Christ Jesus.

For the enmity having been slain, the soul seemed to God unworthy to have existed.

But that it was sent, this we confess, by God yet omnipotent, both deriving its origin from Him and sent for the sealing of His will.

In the same way we believe also that Christ the Saviour came from heaven to fulfill the will of the Father.

Which will of the Father was this, to free our souls from the same enmity, this enmity having been slain, which if it had not been opposed to God could neither be called enmity where there was unity, nor could slaying be spoken of or take place where there was life.

18.

Augustin said:

Remember that the apostle said that we are alienated from God by our manner of life.

Fortunatus said:

I submit, that there were two substances.

In the substance of light, as we have above said, God is to be held incorruptible; but that there was a contrary nature of darkness, that which I also today confess is vanquished by the power of God, and that Christ has been sent forth as a Saviour for my restoration, as previously the same apostle says.

19.

Augustin said:

That we should discuss on rational grounds the belief in two natures, has been made obligatory by those who are hearing us.

But inasmuch as you have again betaken yourself to the Scriptures, I descend to them, and demand that nothing be passed by, lest using certain statements we should bring confusion into the minds of those to whom the Scriptures are not well known.

Let us therefore consider a statement that the apostle has in his epistle to the Romans.

For on the first page is what is strongly against you.

For he says:

"Paul, a servant of Jesus Christ, called to be an apostle, separated unto the gospel of God, which He promised aforetime by His prophets in the Holy Scriptures, concerning his Son, who was made unto Him of the seed of David according to the flesh, who was predestinated to be the Son of God with power, according to the spirit of holiness from the resurrection from the dead of our Lord Jesus Christ." [237] We see that the apostle teaches us concerning our Lord Jesus Christ that before the flesh he was predestinated by the power of God, and according to the flesh was made unto Him of the seed of David.

Since you have always denied and always will deny this, how do you so earnestly demand the Scriptures that we should discuss rather according to them.

Fortunatussaid:

You assert that according to the flesh Christ was of the seed of David, when it should be asserted that he was born of a virgin, [238] and should be magnified as Son of God.

For this cannot be, unless as what is from spirit may be held to be spirit, so also what is from flesh may be known to be flesh. [239] Against which is the authority of the Gospel in which it is said, that "flesh and blood shall not inherit the kingdom of God, neither shall corruption inherit incorruption." [240]

Here a clamor was made by the audience who wished the argument to be conducted on rational grounds, because they saw that Fortunatus was not willing to receive all things that are written in the Codex of the apostle.

Then little discussions began to be held here and there by all, until Fortunatus said that the Word of God has been fettered in the race of darkness.

At which, when those present had expressed their horror, the meeting was closed. [241]

Disputation of the Second Day

The next day, a notary having again been summoned, the discussion was conducted as follows:

Fortunatus said:

I say that God Almighty brings forth from Himself nothing evil, and that the things that are His remain incorrupt, having sprung and being born from an inviolable source; but other contrary things which have their being in this world, do not flow from God nor have appeared in this world with God as their author; that is to say, they do not derive their origin from God.

These things therefore we have received in the belief that evil things are foreign to God.

20.

Augustin said:

And our faith is this, that God is not the progenitor of evil things, neither has He made any evil nature.

But since both of us agree that God is incorruptible and incontaminable, it is the part of the prudent and faithful to consider, which faith is purer and worthier of the majesty of God; that in which it is asserted that either the power of God, or some part of God, or the Word of God, can be changed, violated, corrupted, fettered; or that in which it is said that Almighty God and His entire nature and substance can never be corrupted in any part, but that evils have their being by the voluntary sin of the soul, to which God gave free will.

Which free will if God had not given, there could be no just penal judgment, nor merit of righteous conduct, nor divine instruction to repent of sins, nor the forgiveness of sins itself which God has bestowed upon us through our Lord Jesus Christ.

Because he who sins not voluntarily, sins not at all.

This I suppose to be open and perspicuous to all.

Wherefore it ought not to trouble us if according to our deserts we suffer some inconveniences in the things God has made.

For as He is good, that He should constitute all things; so He is just, that He may not spare sins, which sins, as I have said, unless free will were in us, would not be sins.

For if any one, so to speak, should be bound by some one in his other members, and with his hand something false should be written without his own will, I ask whether if this were laid open before a judge, he could condemn this one for the crime of falsehood. Wherefore, if it is manifest that there is no sin where there is not free exercise of will, [242] I wish to hear what evil the soul which you call either part, or power, or word, or something else, of God, has done, that it should be punished by God, or repent of sin, or merit forgiveness, since it has in no way sinned?

Fortunatus said:

I proposed concerning substances, that God is to be regarded as creator only of good things, but as the avenger of evil things, for the reason that evil things are not of Him.

Therefore for good reason I think this, and that God avenges evil things because they are not of Himself.

But if they were from Him, either He would give them license to sin, as you say that God has given free will, He would be already found a participator in my fault, because He would be the author of my fault; or ignorant what I should be, he left me whom he did not constitute worthy of Himself.

This therefore is proposed by me, and what I ask now is, whether God instituted evil or not? and whether He Himself instituted the end of evils.

For it appears from these things, and the evangelical faith teaches, that the things which we have said were made by God Himself as God the Creator, as having been created and begotten by Him, are to be esteemed incorruptible. These things I also proposed which belong to our belief, and which can be confirmed by you in that profession of ours, without prejudice to the authority of the Christian faith.

And because I can in no way show that I rightly believe, unless I should confirm that belief by the authority of the Scriptures, this is therefore what I have insinuated, what I have said.

Either if evil things have appeared in the world with God as their author, deign to say so yourself; or if it is right to believe that evil things are not of God, this also the contemplation of those present ought to honor and receive.

I have spoken about substances, not about sin that dwells in us.

For if what we think to make faults had no origin, we should not be compelled to come to sin or to fault.

For because we sinned unwillingly, and are compelled by a substance contrary and hostile to ourselves, therefore we follow the knowledge of things.

By which knowledge the soul admonished and restored to pristine memory, recognizes the source from which it derives its existence, in what evil it dwells, by what good works emending again that in which unwillingly it sinned, it may be able through the emendation of its faults, for the sake of good works, to secure for itself the merit of reconciliation with God, our Saviour being the author of it, who teaches us also to practice good things and to flee from evil.

For you ask us to believe that not by some contrary nature, but by his own choice, man either serves righteousness or becomes involved in sins; since, no contrary race existing, if the soul, to which as you say God has given free will, having been constituted in the body, dwells alone, it would be without sin, nor would it become involved in sins.

21.
Augustin said:
I say it is not sin, if it be not committed by one's own will; hence also there is reward, because of our own will we do right.

Or if he who sins unwillingly deserves punishment, he who unwillingly does well ought to deserve reward.

But who doubts that reward is only bestowed upon him who does something of good will?

From which we know that punishment also is inflicted upon him who does something of ill will.

But since you recall me to primordial natures and substances, my faith is that God Almighty--which must especially be attended to and fixed in the mind--that God Almighty has made good things.

But the things made by Him cannot be such as is He who made them.

For it is unjust and foolish to believe that works are equal to the workman, things made to the maker.

Wherefore if it is reverential to believe that God made all good things, than which nevertheless He is by far more excellent and by far more pre-eminent; the origin and head of evil is sin, as the apostle said:

"Covetousness is the root of all evils; which some following after have made shipwreck of the faith, and have pierced themselves through with many sorrows." [243] For if you seek the root of all evils, you have the apostle saying that covetousness is the root of all evils.

But the root of a root I cannot seek.

Or if there is another evil, whose root covetousness is not, covetousness will not be the root of all evils.

But if it is true that covetousness is the root of all evils, in vain do we seek some other kind of evil.

But as regards that contrary nature of yours which you introduce, since I have responded to your objections, I ask that you deign to tell me whether it is wholly evil, whether there can be no sin apart from it, whether by this alone punishment is deserved, not by the soul by which no sin has been committed.

But if you say that this contrary nature alone deserves punishment, and not the soul, I ask to which is repentance, which is commanded, vouchsafed.

If the soul is commanded to repent, sin is from the soul, and the soul has sinned voluntarily.

For if the soul is compelled to do evil, that which it does is not evil.

Is it not foolish and most absurd to say that the race of darkness has sinned and that I repent of the sins.

Is it not most absurd to say that the race of darkness has sinned and that forgiveness of sins is vouchsafed to me, who according to your faith may well say:

What have I done?
What have I committed?
I was with Thee, I was in a state of integrity, I was contaminated with no pollution.

Thou didst send me hither, Thou didst suffer necessity, Thou didst protect Thy domains when great pollution and desolation threatened them.

Since therefore Thou knowest the necessity by which I have been here oppressed, by reason of which I could not breathe, which I could not resist; why dost Thou accuse me as if sinning? or why dost Thou promise forgiveness of sins?

Reply to this without evasion, if you please, as I have replied to you.

Fortunatus said:

We say this, that the soul is compelled by contrary nature to transgress, for which transgression you maintain there is no root save the evil that dwells in us; for it is certain that apart from our bodies evil things dwell in the whole world.

For not those things alone that we have in our bodies, dwell in the whole world, and are known by their names as good; an evil root also inheres.

For your dignity said that this covetousness that dwells in our bodies is the root of evils; since therefore there is no desire of evil out of our bodies, from that source contrary nature dwells in the whole world. For the apostle designated that, namely covetousness, as the root of evils, not one evil which you have called the root of all evils.

But not in one manner is covetousness, which you have said is the root of all evils, understood, as if of that which dwells in our bodies alone; for it is certain that this evil which dwells in us descends from an evil author and that this root as you call it is a small portion of evil, so that it is not the root itself, but is a small portion of evil, of that evil which dwells everywhere.

Which root and tree our Lord called evil, as never bearing good fruit, which his Father did not plant, and which is deservedly rooted up and cast into the fire. [244]

For as you say, that sin ought to be imputed to the contrary nature, that nature belongs to evil; and that this is sin of the soul, if after the warning of our Saviour and his wholesome instruction, the soul shall have segregated itself from its contrary and hostile race, adorning itself also with purer things; that otherwise it cannot be restored to its own substance.

For it is said:

"If I had not come and spoken unto them, they had not had sin.

But now that I have come and spoken, and they have refused to believe me, they shall have no excuse for their sin." [245]

Whence it is perfectly plain, that repentance has been given after the Saviour's advent, and after this knowledge of things, by which the soul can, as if washed in a divine fountain from the filth and vices as well of the whole world as of the bodies in which the same soul dwells, be restored to the kingdom of God whence it has gone forth.

For it is said by the apostle, that "the mind of the flesh is hostile to God; is not subject to the law of God, neither indeed can be." [246] Therefore it is evident from these things that the good soul seems to sin not voluntarily, but by the doing of that which is not subject to the law of God.

For it likewise follows that "the flesh lusteth against the spirit and the spirit against the flesh; so that ye may not do the things that ye will." [247] Again:

"I see another law in my members, warring against the law of my mind and leading me captive in the law of sin and of death.

Therefore I am a miserable man; who shall deliver me from the body of this death, unless it be the grace of God through our Lord Jesus Christ," [248] "through whom the world has been crucified to me and I to the world?" [249]

22.

Augustin said:

I recognize and embrace the testimonies of the divine Scriptures, and I will show in a few words, as God may deign to grant, how they are consistent with my faith.

I say that there was free exercise of will in that man who was first formed.

He was so made that absolutely nothing could resist his will, if he had willed to keep the precepts of God.

But after he voluntarily sinned, we who have descended from his stock were plunged into necessity.

But each one of us can by a little consideration find that what I say is true.

For today in our actions before we are implicated by any habit, we have free choice of doing anything or not doing it.

But when by that liberty we have done something and the pernicious sweetness and pleasure of that deed has taken hold upon the mind, by its own habit the mind is so implicated that afterwards it cannot conquer what by sinning it has fashioned for itself.

We see many who do not wish to swear, but because the tongue has already become habituated, they are not able to prevent those things from going forth from the mouth which we cannot but ascribe to the root of evil.

For that I may discuss with you those words, which as they do not withdraw from your mouth so may they be understood by your heart:

you swear by the Paraclete.

If therefore you wish to find out experimentally whether what I say is true, determine not to swear.

You will see, that that habit is borne along as it has become accustomed to be.

And this is what wars against the soul, habit formed in the flesh.

This is indeed the mind of the flesh, which, as long as it cannot thus be subject to the law of God, so long is it the mind of the flesh; but when the soul has been illuminated it ceases to be the mind of the flesh.

For thus it is said the mind of the flesh cannot be subject to the law of God, just as if it were said, that snow cannot be warm.

For so long as it is snow, it can in no way be warm.

But as the snow is melted by heat, so that it may become warm, so the mind of the flesh, that is, habit formed with the flesh, when our mind has become illuminated, that is, when God has subjected for Himself the whole man to the choice of the divine law, instead of the evil habit of the soul, makes a good habit.

Accordingly it is most truly said by the Lord of the two trees, the one good and the other evil, which you have called to mind, that they have their own fruits; that is, neither can the good tree yield evil fruit, nor the evil tree good fruit, but so long as it is evil.

Let us take two men, a good and a bad.

As long as he is good he cannot yield evil fruit; as long as he is bad he cannot yield good fruit.

But that you may know that those two trees are so placed by the Lord, that free choice may be there signified, that these two trees are not natures but our wills, He Himself says in the gospel:

"Either make the tree good, or make the tree evil." [250] Who is it that can make nature?

If therefore we are commanded to make a tree either good or evil, it is ours to choose what we will.

Therefore concerning that sin of man and concerning that habit of soul formed with the flesh the apostle says:

"Let no one seduce you;" [251] "Every creature that has been made by God is good."[252] The same apostle whom you also have cited says:

"As through the disobedience of the one the many were constituted sinners; so also through the obedience of the one the many are constituted righteous." [253] "Since through man is death, through man also is resurrection of the dead."

As long therefore as we bear the image of the earthly man, [254] that is, as long as we live according to the flesh, which is also called the old man, we have the necessity of our habit, so that we may not do what we will.

But when the grace of God has breathed the divine love into us and has made us subject to His will, to us it is said:

"Ye are called for freedom," [255] and "the grace of God has made me free from the law of sin and of death." [256] But the law of sin is that whoever has sinned shall die.

From this law we are freed when we have begun to be righteous.

The law of death is that by which it was said to man:

"Earth thou art and into earth thou shalt go." [257] For from this very fact we are all so born, because we are earth, and from the fact that we are all so born because we are earth, we shall all go into earth on account of the desert of the sins of the first man.

But on account of the grace of God, which frees us from the law of sin and of death, having been converted to righteousness we are freed; so that afterwards this same flesh tortures us with its punishment so long as we remain in sins, is subjected to us in resurrection, and shakes us by no adversity from keeping the law of God and His precepts.

Whence, since I have replied to your questions, deign to reply as I desire, how it can happen, that if nature is contrary to God, sin should be imputed to us, who were sent into that nature not voluntarily, but by God Himself, whom nothing could injure?

Fortunatus said:

Just as also the Lord said to His disciples:

"Behold I send you as sheep in the midst of wolves." [258] Hence it must be known that not with hostile intent did our Saviour send forth His lambs, that is His disciples, into the midst of wolves, unless there had been some contrariety, which He would indicate by the similitude of wolves, where also He had sent His disciples; that the souls which perchance might be deceived in the midst of wolves might be recalled to their proper substance.

Hence also may appear the antiquity of our times to which we return, and of our years, that before the foundation of the world souls were sent in this way against the contrary nature, that subjecting the same by their passion, victory might be restored to God.

For the same apostle said, that not only there should be a struggle against flesh and blood, but also against principalities and powers, and the spiritual things of wickedness, and the domination of darkness." [259] If therefore in both places evils dwell and are esteemed wickednesses, not only now is evil in our bodies, but in the whole world, where souls appear to dwell, which dwell beneath yonder heaven and are fettered.

23.

Augustin said:

The Lord sent His lambs into the midst of wolves, that is, just men into the midst of sinners for the preaching of the gospel received in the time of man from the inestimable divine Wisdom, that He might call us from sin to righteousness.

But what the apostle says, that our struggle is not against flesh and blood, but against principalities and powers, and the other things that have been quoted, this signifies that the devil and his angels, as also we, have fallen and lapsed by sin, and have secured possession of earthly things, that is, sinful men, who, as long as we are sinners, are under their yoke, just as when we shall be righteous, we shall be under the yoke of righteousness; and against them we have a struggle, that passing over to righteousness we may be freed from their dominion.

Do you also therefore deign to reply to the one question that I ask:

Could God suffer injury, or not?

But I ask you to reply:

He could not.

Fortunatus said:

He could not suffer injury.

24.

Augustin said:

Wherefore then did He send us hither, according to your faith?

Fortunatus said:

My profession is this, that God could not be injured, and that He directed us hither.

But since this is contrary to your view, do you tell how you account for the soul being here, which our God desires to liberate both by His commandments and by His own Son whom He has sent.

25.

Augustin said:

Since I see that you cannot answer my inquiries, and wish to ask me something, behold I satisfy you, provided only that you bear in mind that you have not replied to my question.

Why the soul is here in this world involved in miseries has been explained by me not just now, but again and again a little while ago.

The soul sinned, and therefore is miserable.

It accepted free choice, used free choice, as it willed; it fell, was cast out from blessedness, was implicated in miseries.

As bearing upon this I recited to you the testimony of the apostle who says:

"As through one man death, so also through one man came the resurrection of the dead."

What more do you ask?

Hence do you reply, wherefore did He, who could not suffer injury, send us hither?

Fortunatus said:

The cause must be sought, why the soul came hither, or wherefore God desires hence to liberate the soul that lives in the midst of evils?

26.

Augustin said:

This cause I ask of you, that is, if God could not suffer injury, wherefore He sent us hither?

Fortunatus said:

It is inquired of us, if evil cannot injure God, wherefore the soul was sent hither, or for what reason was it mingled with the world?

Which is manifest in what the apostle says:

"Shall the thing formed say to him that formed it, why hast thou formed me thus?" [260]If therefore this cause must be pleaded, He must be asked, why He sent the soul, no necessity compelling Him.

But if there was necessity for sending the soul, of right is there also the will of liberating it.

27.

Augustin said:
Then God is pressed by necessity, is He?
Fortunatus said:
Now this is it.
Do not seek to bring odium upon what has been said because we do not make God subject to necessity, but to have voluntarily sent the soul.

28.

Augustin said:
Recall what was said above.
And it runs:
"But if there was necessity for sending the soul, of right is there also the will of liberating it."
Augustin said:
We have heard:
But if there was necessity for sending the soul, of right is there also the will of liberating it."
You, therefore, said that there was necessity for sending the soul.
But if you only wish to say "a will to send," I add this also:
He who could suffer no injury, had the cruel will to send the soul to so great miseries.
Because I speak for the sake of refuting this statement, I ask pardon from the mercy of that One in whom we have hope of liberation from all the errors of heretics.
Fortunatus said:
You asseverate that we say that God is cruel in sending the soul, but that God made man, breathed into him a soul which assuredly He foreknew to be involved in future misery, and not to be able by reason of evils to be restored to its inheritance.
This belongs either to one who is ignorant, or who gives the soul up to these aforesaid evils.
This I have cited because you said not long since, that God adopted the soul, not that it is from Him; for to adopt is a different matter.

29.

Augustin said:
Concerning adoption I remember that I spoke some days ago according to the testimony of the apostle, who says that we have been called into the adoption of sons. [261]This was not my reply, therefore, but the apostle's, concerning which thing, that is, that adoption, we may inquire, if we please, in its own time; and concerning that I will reply without delay, when you shall have answered my objections.
Fortunatus said:
I say that there was a going forth of the soul against a contrary nature, which nature could not injure God.

30.

Augustin said:
What need was there for that going forth, when God whom nothing could injure had nothing to protect?
Fortunatus said:
Do you conscientiously hold that Christ came from God?

31.

Augustin said:
Again you are questioning me. Reply to my inquiries.
Fortunatus said:
So I have received in faith, that by the will of God He came hither.

32.

Augustin said:
And I say:
Why did God, omnipotent, inviolable, immutable, whom nothing could injure, send hither the soul, to miseries, to error, to those things that we suffer?
Fortunatussaid:
For it has been said:
"I have power to lay down my soul and I have power to take it again." [262]Now He said that by the will of God the soul went forth.

33.
> Augustin said:
> I ask for the reason why God, when He can in no way suffer injury, sent the soul hither?

> Fortunatus said:
> We have already said that God can in no way suffer injury, and we have said that the soul is in a contrary nature, therefore that it imposes a limit on the contrary nature.
> The restraint having been imposed on the contrary nature, God takes the same.
> For He Himself said, "I have power to lay down my soul and power to take it."
> The Father gave to me the power of laying down my soul, and of taking it.
> To what soul, therefore, did God who spoke in the Son refer?
> Evidently our soul, which is held in these bodies, which came of His will, and of His will is again taken up.

34.
> Augustin said:
> Why our Lord said:
> "I have power to lay down my soul and power to take it," is known to all; because He was about to suffer and to rise again.
> But I ask of you again and again, If God could in no way suffer injury, why did he send souls hither?

> Fortunatus said:
> To impose a limit on contrary nature.

35.
> Augustin said:
> And did God omnipotent, merciful and supreme, that He might impose a restraint on contrary nature, wish it to be limited so that He might make us unrestrained?

> Fortunatus said:
> But so He calls us back to Himself.

36.
> Augustin said:
> If He recalls to Himself from an unrestrained state, if from sin, from error, from misery, what need was there for the soul to suffer so great evils through so long a time till the world ends? since God by whom you say it was sent could in no way suffer injury.

> Fortunatus said:
> What then am I to say?

37.
> Augustin said:
> I know that you have nothing to say, and that I, when I was among you, never found anything to say on this question, and that I was thus admonished from on high to leave that error and to be converted to the Catholic faith or rather to recall it, by the indulgence of Him who did not permit me to inhere forever in this fallacy.
> But if you confess that you have nothing to reply, I will expound the Catholic faith to all those hearing and investigating, seeing that they are believers, if they permit and wish.

> Fortunatus said:
> Without prejudice to my profession I might say:
> when I shall have reconsidered with my superiors the things that have been opposed by you, if they fail to respond to this question of mine, which is now in like manner proposed to me by you, it will be in my contemplation (since I desire my soul to be liberated by an assured faith) to come to the investigation of this thing that you have proposed to me and that you promise you will show.

> Augustin said:
> Thanks be to God.

Footnotes:

221. This Disputation seems to have occurred shortly after the writing of the preceding treatise.

It appears from the Retractations that Fortunatus had lived for a considerable time at Hippo, and had secured so large a number of followers that it was a delight to him to dwell there.

The Disputation is supposed to be a verbatim report of what Augustin and Fortunatus said during a two days' discussion.

The subject is the origin of evil.

Augustin maintains that evil, so far as man is concerned, has arisen from a free exercise of the will on man's part; Fortunatus, on the other hand, maintains that the nature of evil is co-eternal with God.

Fortunatus shows considerable knowledge of the New Testament, but no remarkable dialectic powers.

He appears at great disadvantage beside his great antagonist.

In fact, he is far from saying the best that can be said in favor of dualism.

We may say that he was fairly vanquished in the argument, and at the close confessed himself at a loss what to say, and expressed an intention of more carefully examining the problems discussed, in view of what Augustin had said.

Augustin is more guarded in this treatise than in the preceding in his statements about free will.

He found little occasion here, therefore, to retract or explain.

Fortunatus often expresses himself vaguely and obscurely.

If some sentences are difficult to understand in the translation, they will be found equally so in the Latin.--A.H.N.

222. The word used is oratio, by which is evidently meant the religious services to which Auditors were admitted, prayer (oratio) being the prominent feature.--A.H.N.

223. The allusion here is doubtless to the probably slanderous charge that the Manichæans were accustomed to partake of human semen as a Eucharist.

The Manichæan view of the relation of the substance mentioned to the light, and their well-known opposition to procreation, give a slight plausibility to the charge.

Compare the Morals of the Manichæans, ch. xviii., where Augustin expresses his suspicions of Manichæan shamelessness.

See also further references in the Introduction.--A.H.N.

224. This is, of course, a mixture of two passages of Scripture.--A.H.N.

225. John xiv. 8, 9.

226. John v. 24.

227. As remarked in the Introduction, the Manichæans of the West, in Augustin's time, sustained a far more intimate relation to Christianity than did Mani and his immediate followers.

Far as Fortunatus may have been from using the above language in the ordinary Christian sense, yet he held, by profession at least, enough of Christian truth to beguile the unwary.--A.H.N.

228. Philipp. ii. 5-8.

229. Fortunatus could not surely have used this language with any proper conception of its meaning.

He seems, against Mani, to have identified in some sense the Jesus that suffered with Christ.

Yet even in this statement his docetism is manifest.--A.H.N.

230. 1 Cor. i. 24.

231. John i. 3.

232. Ps. cxlviii. 5.

233. Matt. xv. 13, and iii. 10.

234. Eph. ii. 1-18.

There are several somewhat important variations from the Greek text in this long extract.

The attentive reader can get a good idea of the nature of the variations by comparing this literal translation with the revised English version.--A.H.N.

235. There are three readings here, "wearied out," "deceived," and "worn out."

The latter is preferred by the Benedictine editors.--A.H.N.

236. Rom. xi. 1.

237. Rom. i. 1-4.

238. Isa. vii. 14.

239. John iii. 6.

240. 1 Cor. xv. 50.

241. This little side remark lends reality to the discussion, and enables us to form a vivid conception of what doctrinal debates were in the age of Augustin.--A.H.N.

242. Liberum voluntatis arbitrium.

243. 1 Tim. vi. 10.

244. Matt. xv. 13, and iii. 10.

245. John xv. 22.

246. Rom. viii. 7.

247. Gal. v. 17.

248. Rom. vii. 23-25.

249. Gal. v. 14.

250. Matt. xii. 35.

251. Eph. v. 6.

252. 1 Tim. iv. 4.

253. Rom. v. 19.

254. 1 Cor. xv. 21, 49.

255. Gal. v. 13.

256. Rom. viii. 2.

257. Gen. iii. 19.

258. Matt. x. 16.

259. Eph. v. 12.

260. Rom. ix. 20.

261. Eph. i. 5.

262. John x. 18.

Against the Epistle of Manichæus, Called Fundamental

[contra epistolam manichæi quam vocant fundamentum]. [263]
A.D. 397.
translated by rev. richard stothert, m.a.,
bombay

Chapter 1 - To Heal Heretics is Better Than to Destroy Them

1.

My prayer to the one true, almighty God, of whom, and through whom, and in whom are all things, has been, and is now, that in opposing and refuting the heresy of you Manichæans, as you may after all be heretics more from thoughtlessness than from malice, He would give me a mind calm and composed, and aiming at your recovery rather than at your discomfiture.

For while the Lord, by His servants, overthrows the kingdoms of error, His will concerning erring men, as far as they are men, is that they should be amended rather than destroyed.

And in every case where, previous to the final judgment, God inflicts punishment, whether through the wicked or the righteous, whether through the unintelligent or through the intelligent, whether in secret or openly, we must believe that the designed effect is the healing of men, and not their ruin; while there is a preparation for the final doom in the case of those who reject the means of recovery.

Thus, as the universe contains some things which serve for bodily punishment, as fire, poison, disease, and the rest, and other things, in which the mind is punished, not by bodily distress, but by the entanglements of its own passions, such as loss, exile, bereavement, reproach, and the like; while other things, again, without tormenting are fitted to comfort and soothe the languishing, as, for example, consolations, exhortations, discussions, and such things; in all these the supreme justice of God makes use sometimes even of wicked men, acting in ignorance, and sometimes of good men, acting intelligently.

It is ours, accordingly, to desire in preference the better part, that we might attain our end in your correction, not by contention, and strife, and persecutions, but by kindly consolation, by friendly exhortation, by quiet discussion; as it is written, "The servant of the Lord must not strive; but be gentle toward all men, apt to teach, patient; in meekness instructing those that oppose themselves." [264]It is ours, I say, to desire to obtain this part in the work; it belongs to God to give what is good to those who desire it and ask for it.

Chapter 2 - Why the Manichæans Should Be More Gently Dealt with

2.

Let those rage against you who know not with what labor the truth is to be found and with what difficulty error is to be avoided.

Let those rage against you who know not how rare and hard it is to overcome the fancies of the flesh by the serenity of a pious disposition.

Let those rage against you who know not the difficulty of curing the eye of the inner man that he may gaze upon his Sun,--not that sun which you worship, and which shines with the brilliance of a heavenly body in the eyes of carnal men and of beasts,--but that of which it is written through the prophet, "The Sun of righteousness has arisen upon me;" [265] and of which it is said in the gospel, "That was the true Light, which lighteth every man that cometh into the world." [266]Let those rage against you who know not with what sighs and groans the least particle of the knowledge of God is obtained.

And, last of all, let those rage against you who have never been led astray in the same way that they see that you are.

Chapter 3 - Augustin Once a Manichæan

3.

For my part, I,--who, after much and long-continued bewilderment, attained at last, to the discovery of the simple truth, which is learned without being recorded in any fanciful legend; who, unhappy that I was, barely succeeded, by God's help, in refuting the vain imaginations of my mind, gathered from theories and errors of various kinds; who so late sought the cure of my mental obscuration, in compliance with the call and the tender persuasion of the all-merciful Physician; who long wept that the immutable and inviolable Existence would vouchsafe to convince me inwardly of Himself, in harmony with the testimony of the sacred books; by whom, in fine, all those fictions which have such a firm hold on you, from your long familiarity with them, were diligently examined, and attentively heard, and too easily believed, and commended at every opportunity to the belief of others, and defended against opponents with determination and boldness,--I can on no account rage against you; for I must bear with you now as formerly I had to bear with myself, and I must be as patient towards you as my associates were with me, when I went madly and blindly astray in your beliefs.

4.

On the other hand, all must allow that you owe it to me, in return, to lay aside all arrogance on your part too, that so you may be the more disposed to gentleness, and may not oppose me in a hostile spirit, to your own hurt.

Let neither of us assert that he has found truth; let us seek it as if it were unknown to us both.

For truth can be sought with zeal and unanimity if by no rash presumption it is believed to have been already found and ascertained.

But if I cannot induce you to grant me this, at least allow me to suppose myself a stranger now for the first time hearing you, for the first time examining your doctrines.

I think my demand a just one.

And it must be laid down as an understood thing that I am not to join you in your prayers, or in holding conventicles, or in taking the name of Manichæus, unless you give me a clear explanation, without any obscurity, of all matters touching the salvation of the soul.

Chapter 4 - Proofs of the Catholic Faith

5.

For in the Catholic Church, not to speak of the purest wisdom, to the knowledge of which a few spiritual men attain in this life, so as to know it, in the scantiest measure, indeed, because they are but men, still without any uncertainty (since the rest of the multitude derive their entire security not from acuteness of intellect, but from simplicity of faith,)--not to speak of this wisdom, which you do not believe to be in the Catholic Church, there are many other things which most justly keep me in her bosom.

The consent of peoples and nations keeps me in the Church; so does her authority, inaugurated by miracles, nourished by hope, enlarged by love, established by age.

The succession of priests keeps me, beginning from the very seat of the Apostle Peter, to whom the Lord, after His resurrection, gave it in charge to feed His sheep, down to the present episcopate.

And so, lastly, does the name itself of Catholic, which, not without reason, amid so many heresies, the Church has thus retained; so that, though all heretics wish to be called Catholics, yet when a stranger asks where the Catholic Church meets, no heretic will venture to point to his own chapel or house.

Such then in number and importance are the precious ties belonging to the Christian name which keep a believer in the Catholic Church, as it is right they should, though from the slowness of our understanding, or the small attainment of our life, the truth may not yet fully disclose itself.

But with you, where there is none of these things to attract or keep me, the promise of truth is the only thing that comes into play.

Now if the truth is so clearly proved as to leave no possibility of doubt, it must be set before all the things that keep me in the Catholic Church; but if there is only a promise without any fulfillment, no one shall move me from the faith which binds my mind with ties so many and so strong to the Christian religion.

Chapter 5 - Against the Title of the Epistle of Manichæus

6.

Let us see then what Manichæus teaches me; and particularly let us examine that treatise which he calls the Fundamental Epistle, in which almost all that you believe is contained.

For in that unhappy time when we read it we were in your opinion enlightened.

The epistle begins thus:--"Manichæus, an apostle of Jesus Christ, by the providence of God the Father.

These are wholesome words from the perennial and living fountain."

Now, if you please, patiently give heed to my inquiry.

I do not believe Manichæus to be an apostle of Christ.

Do not, I beg of you, be enraged and begin to curse.

For you know that it is my rule to believe none of your statements without consideration. Therefore I ask, who is this Manichæus?

You will reply, An apostle of Christ.

I do not believe it.

Now you are at a loss what to say or do; for you promised to give knowledge of the truth, and here you are forcing me to believe what I have no knowledge of.

Perhaps you will read the gospel to me, and will attempt to find there a testimony to Manichæus.

But should you meet with a person not yet believing the gospel, how would you reply to him were he to say, I do not believe? For my part, I should not believe the gospel except as moved by the authority of the Catholic Church. [267] So when those on whose authority I have consented to believe in the gospel tell me not to believe in Manichæus, how can I but consent?

Take your choice.

If you say, Believe the Catholics:

their advice to me is to put no faith in you; so that, believing them, I am precluded from believing you;--If you say, Do not believe the Catholics:

you cannot fairly use the gospel in bringing me to faith in Manichæus; for it was at the command of the Catholics that I believed the gospel;--Again, if you say, You were right in believing the Catholics when they praised the gospel, but wrong in believing their vituperation of Manichæus:

do you think me such a fool as to believe or not to believe as you like or dislike, without any reason?

It is therefore fairer and safer by far for me, having in one instance put faith in the Catholics, not to go over to you, till, instead of bidding me believe, you make me understand something in the clearest and most open manner.

To convince me, then, you must put aside the gospel.

If you keep to the gospel, I will keep to those who commanded me to believe the gospel; and, in obedience to them, I will not believe you at all.

But if haply you should succeed in finding in the gospel an incontrovertible testimony to the apostleship of Manichæus, you will weaken my regard for the authority of the Catholics who bid me not to believe you; and the effect of that will be, that I shall no longer be able to believe the gospel either, for it was through the Catholics that I got my faith in it; and so, whatever you bring from the gospel will no longer have any weight with me.

Wherefore, if no clear proof of the apostleship of Manichæus is found in the gospel, I will believe the Catholics rather than you.

But if you read thence some passage clearly in favor of Manichæus, I will believe neither them nor you:

not them, for they lied to me about you; nor you, for you quote to me that Scripture which I had believed on the authority of those liars.

But far be it that I should not believe the gospel; for believing it, I find no way of believing you too.

For the names of the apostles, as there recorded, [268] do not include the name of Manichæus.

And who the successor of Christ's betrayer was we read in the Acts of the Apostles; [269] which book I must needs believe if I believe the gospel, since both writings alike Catholic authority commends to me.

The same book contains the well-known narrative of the calling and apostleship of Paul.[270] Read me now, if you can, in the gospel where Manichæus is called an apostle, or in any other book in which I have professed to believe.

Will you read the passage where the Lord promised the Holy Spirit as a Paraclete, to the apostles? Concerning which passage, behold how many and how great are the things that restrain and deter me from believing in Manichæus.

Chapter 6 - Why Manichæus Called Himself an Apostle of Christ

7.

For I am at a loss to see why this epistle begins, "Manichæus, an apostle of Jesus Christ," and not Paraclete, an apostle of Jesus Christ.

Or if the Paraclete sent by Christ sent Manichæus, why do we read, "Manichæus, an apostle of Jesus Christ," instead of Manichæus, an apostle of the Paraclete?

If you say that it is Christ Himself who is the Holy Spirit, you contradict the very Scripture, where the Lord says, "And I will send you another Paraclete." [271] Again, if you justify your putting of Christ's name, not because it is Christ Himself who is also the Paraclete, but because they are both of the same substance,--that is, not because they are one person, but one existence [non quia unus est, sed quia unum sunt],--Paul too might have used the words, Paul, an apostle of God the Father; for the Lord said, "I and the Father are one." [272] Paul nowhere uses these words; nor does any of the apostles write himself an apostle of the Father.

Why then this new fashion?

Does it not savor of trickery of some kind or other?

For if he thought it made no difference, why did he not for the sake of variety in some epistles call himself an apostle of Christ, and in others of the Paraclete?

But in every one that I know of, he writes, of Christ; and not once, of the Paraclete.

What do we suppose to be the reason of this, but that pride, the mother of all heretics, impelled the man to desire to seem to have been sent by the Paraclete, but to have been taken into so close a relation as to get the name of Paraclete himself?

As the man Jesus Christ was not sent by the Son of God, that is, the power and wisdom of God--by which all things were made, but, according to the Catholic faith, was taken into such a relation as to be Himself the Son of God--that is, that in Himself the wisdom of God was displayed in the healing of sinners,--so Manichæus wished it to be thought that he was so taken up by the Holy Spirit, whom Christ promised, that we are henceforth to understand that the names Manichæus and Holy Spirit alike signify the apostle of Jesus Christ,--that is, one sent by Jesus Christ, who promised to send him. Singular audacity this! and unutterable sacrilege!

Chapter 7 - In What Sense the Followers of Manichæus Believe Him to Be the Holy Spirit

8.

Besides, you should explain how it is that, while the Father, Son, and Holy Spirit are united in equality of nature, as you also acknowledge, you are not ashamed to speak of Manichæus, a man taken into union with the Holy Spirit, as born of ordinary generation; and yet you shrink from believing that the man taken into union with the only-begotten Wisdom of God was born of a Virgin.

If human flesh, if generation [concubitus viri], if the womb of a woman could not contaminate the Holy Spirit, how could the Virgin's womb contaminate the Wisdom of God?

This Manichæus, then, who boasts of a connection with the Holy Spirit, and of being spoken of in the gospel, must produce his claim to either of these two things,--that he was sent by the Spirit, or that he was taken into union with the Spirit.

If he was sent, let him call himself the apostle of the Paraclete; if taken into union, let him allow that He whom the only-begotten Son took upon Himself had a human mother, since he admits a human father as well as mother in the case of one taken up by the Holy Spirit.

Let him believe that the Word of God was not defiled by the virgin womb of Mary, since he exhorts us to believe that the Holy Spirit could not be defiled by the married life of his parents.

But if you say that Manichæus was united to the Spirit, not in the womb or before conception, but after his birth, still you must admit that he had a fleshly nature derived from man and woman.

And since you are not afraid to speak of the blood and the bodily substance of Manichæus as coming from ordinary generation, or of the internal impurities contained in his flesh, and hold that the Holy Spirit, who took on Himself, as you believe, this human being, was not contaminated by all those things, why should I shrink from speaking of the Virgin's womb and body undefiled, and not rather believe that the Wisdom of God in union with the human being in his mother's flesh still remained free from stain and pollution? Wherefore, as, whether your Manichæus professes to be sent by or to be united with the Paraclete, neither statement can hold good, I am on my guard, and refuse to believe either in his mission or in his susception.

Chapter 8 - The Festival of the Birth-Day of Manichæus

9.

In adding the words, "by the providence of God the Father," what else did Manichæus design but that, having got the name of Jesus Christ, whose apostle he calls himself, and of God the Father, by whose providence he says he was sent by the Son, we should believe himself, as the Holy Spirit, to be the third person?

is words are: "Manichæus, an apostle of Jesus Christ, by the providence of God the Father."

The Holy Spirit is not named, though He ought specially to have been named by one who quotes to us in favor of his apostleship the promise of the Paraclete, that he may prevail upon ignorant people by the authority of the gospel.

In reply to this, you of course say that in the name of the Apostle Manichæus we have the name of the Holy Spirit, the Paraclete, because He condescended to come into Manichæus. Why then, I ask again, should you cry out against the doctrine of the Catholic Church, that He in whom divine Wisdom came was born of a virgin, when you do not scruple to affirm the birth by ordinary generation of him in whom you say the Holy Spirit came?

I cannot but suspect that this Manichæus, who uses the name of Christ to gain access to the minds of the ignorant, wished to be worshipped instead of Christ Himself.

I will state briefly the reason of this conjecture.

At the time when I was a student of your doctrines, to my frequent inquiries why it was that the Paschal feast of the Lord was celebrated generally with no interest, though sometimes there were a few languid worshippers, but no watchings, no prescription of any unusual fast,--in a word, no special ceremony,--while great honor is paid to your Bema, that is, the day on which Manichæus was killed, when you have a platform with fine steps, covered with precious cloth, placed conspicuously so as to face the votaries,--the reply was, that the day to observe was the day of the passion of him who really suffered, and that Christ, who was not born, but appeared to human eyes in an unreal semblance of flesh, only feigned suffering, without really bearing it. Is it not deplorable, that men who wish to be called Christians are afraid of a virgin's womb as likely to defile the truth, and yet are not afraid of falsehood?

But to go back to the point, who that pays attention can help suspecting that the intention of Manichæus in denying Christ's being born of a woman, and having a human body, was that His passion, the time of which is now a great festival all over the world, might not be observed by the believers in himself, so as to lessen the devotion of the solemn commemoration which he wished in honor of the day of his own death?

For to us it was a great attraction in the feast of the Bema that it was held during Pascha, since we used all the more earnestly to desire that festal day [the Bema], that the other which was formerly most sweet had been withdrawn.

Chapter 9 - When the Holy Spirit Was Sent

10.

Perhaps you will say to me, When, then, did the Paraclete promised by the Lord come?

As regards this, had I nothing else to believe on the subject, I should rather look for the Paraclete as still to come, than allow that He came in Manichæus.

But seeing that the advent of the Holy Spirit is narrated with perfect clearness in the Acts of the Apostles, where is the necessity of my so gratuitously running the risk of believing heretics?

For in the Acts it is written as follows:

"The former treatise have we made, O Theophilus, of all that Jesus began both to do and teach, in the day in which He chose the apostles by the Holy Spirit, and commanded them to preach the gospel.

By those to whom He showed Himself alive after His passion by many proofs in the daytime, He was seen forty days, teaching concerning the kingdom of God.

And how He conversed with them, and commanded them that they should not depart from Jerusalem, but wait for the promise of the Father, which, saith He, ye have heard of me.

For John indeed baptized with water, but ye shall begin to be baptized with the Holy Spirit, whom also ye shall receive after not many days, that is, at Pentecost. When they had come, they asked him, saying, Lord, wilt Thou at this time manifest Thyself?

And when will be the kingdom of Israel?

And He said unto them, No one can know the time which the Father hath put in His own power.

But ye shall receive the power of the Holy Ghost coming upon you, and ye shall be witnesses unto me both in Jerusalem, and in all Judæa, and in Samaria, and unto the uttermost part of the earth." [273] Behold you have here the Lord reminding His disciples of the promise of the Father, which they had heard from His mouth, of the coming of the Holy Spirit.

Let us now see when He was sent; for shortly after we read as follows:

"And when the day of Pentecost was fully come, they were all with one accord in one place.

And suddenly there came a sound from heaven, as of a rushing mighty wind, and it filled all the house where they were sitting.

And there appeared unto them cloven tongues, like as of fire, and it sat upon each of them. And they were all filled with the Holy Ghost, and began to speak with other tongues, as the Spirit gave them utterance.

And there were dwelling at Jerusalem Jews, devout men, out of every nation under heaven.

And when the sound was heard, the multitude came together, and were confounded, because every man heard them speak in his own language.

And they were all amazed, and marvelled, saying one to another, Are not all these which speak Galilæans? and how heard we every man in our own tongue, wherein we were born?

Parthians, and Medes, and Elamites, and the dwellers in Mesopotamia, in Armenia, and in Cappadocia, in Pontus, Asia, Phrygia, and Pamphylia, in Egypt, and in the regions of Africa about Cyrene, and strangers of Rome, Jews, natives, Cretes, and Arabians, they heard them speak in their own tongues the wonderful works of God.

And they were all amazed, and were in doubt on account of what had happened, saying, What meaneth this? But others, mocking, said, These men are full of new wine." [274] You see when the Holy Spirit came.

What more do you wish?

If the Scriptures are credible, should not I believe most readily in these Acts, which have the strongest testimony in their support, and which have had the advantage of becoming generally known, and of being handed down and of being publicly taught along with the gospel itself, which contains the promise of the Holy Spirit, which also we believe?

On reading, then, these Acts of the Apostles, which stand, as regards authority, on a level with the gospel, I find that not only was the Holy Spirit promised to these true apostles, but that He was also sent so manifestly, that no room was left for errors on this subject.

Chapter 10 - The Holy Spirit Twice Given

11.

For the glorification of our Lord among men is His resurrection from the dead and His ascension to heaven.

For it is written in the Gospel according to John:

"The Holy Ghost was not yet given, because that Jesus was not yet glorified." [275] Now if the reason why He was not given was that Jesus was not yet glorified, He was given immediately on the glorification of Jesus.

And since that glorification was twofold, as regards man and as regards God, twice also was the Holy Spirit given:

once, when, after His resurrection from the dead, He breathed on the face of His disciples, saying, "Receive ye the Holy Ghost;" [276] and again, ten days after His ascension to heaven.

This number ten signifies perfection; for to the number seven which embraces all created things, is added the trinity of the Creator. [277] On these things there is much pious and sober discourse among spiritual men.

But I must keep to my point; for my business at present is not to teach you, which you might think presumptuous, but to take the part of an inquirer, and learn from you, as I tried to do for nine years without success.

Now, therefore, I have a document to believe on the subject of the Holy Spirit's advent; and if you bid me not to believe this document, as your usual advice is not to believe ignorantly, without consideration, [278] much less will I believe your documents.

Away, then, with all books, and disclose the truth with logical clearness, so as to leave no doubt in my mind; or bring forward books where I shall find not an imperious demand for my belief, but a trustworthy statement of what I may learn.

Perhaps you say this epistle is also of this character.

Let me, then, no longer stop at the threshold:

let us see the contents.

Chapter 11 - Manichæus Promises Truth, But Does Not Make Good His Word

12.

"These," he says, "are wholesome words from the perennial and living fountain; and whoever shall have heard them, and shall have first believed them, and then shall have observed the truths they set forth, shall never suffer death, but shall enjoy eternal life in glory.

For he is to be judged truly blessed who has been instructed in this divine knowledge, by which he is made free and shall abide in everlasting life."

And this, as you see, is a promise of truth, but not the bestowal of it.

And you yourselves can easily see that any errors whatever might be dressed up in this fashion, so as under cover of a showy exterior to steal in unawares into the minds of the ignorant.

Were he to say, These are pestiferous words from a poisonous fountain; and whoever shall have heard them, and shall have first believed them, and then have observed what they set forth, shall never be restored to life, but shall suffer a woful death as a criminal;

for assuredly he is to be pronounced miserable who falls into this infernal error, in which he will sink so as to abide in everlasting torments;--were he to say this, he would say the truth; but instead of gaining any readers for his book, he would excite the greatest aversion in the minds of all into whose hands the book might come.

Let us then pass on to what follows; nor let us be deceived by words which may be used alike by good and bad, by learned and unlearned.

What, then, comes next?

13.

"May the peace," he says, "of the invisible God, and the knowledge of the truth, be with the holy and beloved brethren who both believe and also yield obedience to the divine precepts."

Amen, say we.

For the prayer is a most amiable and commendable one.

Only we must bear in mind that these words might be used by false teachers as well as by good ones.

So, if he said nothing more than this, all might safely read and embrace it.

Nor should I disapprove of what follows:

"May also the right hand of light protect you, and deliver you from every hostile assault, and from the snares of the world."

In fact, I have no fault to find with the beginning of this epistle, till we come to the main subject of it.

For I wish not to spend time on minor points. Now, then, for this writer's plain statement of what is to be expected from him.

Chapter 12 - The Wild Fancies of Manichæus

The Battle Before the Constitution of the World.

14.

"Of that matter," he says, "beloved brother of Patticus, of which you told me, saying that you desired to know the manner of the birth of Adam and Eve, whether they were produced by a word or sprung from matter, I will answer you as is fit.

For in various writings and narratives we find different assertions made and different descriptions given by many authors.

Now the real truth on the subject is unknown to all peoples, even to those who have long and frequently treated of it. For had they arrived at a clear knowledge of the generation of Adam and Eve, they would not have remained liable to corruption and death." Here, then, is a promise to us of clear knowledge of this matter, so that we shall not be liable to corruption and death.

And if this does not suffice, see what follows:

"Necessarily," he says, "many things have to be said by way of preface, before a discovery of this mystery free from all uncertainty can be made."

This is precisely what I asked for, to have such evidence of the truth as to free my knowledge of it from all uncertainty.

And even were the promise not made by this writer himself, it was proper for me to demand and to insist upon this, so that no opposition should make me ashamed of becoming a Manichæan from a Catholic Christian, in view of such a gain as that of perfectly clear and certain truth.

Philip Schaff, D.D., LL.D.

Now, then, let us hear what he has to state.

15.
"Accordingly," he says, "hear first, if you please, what happened before the constitution of the world, and how the battle was carried on, that you may be able to distinguish the nature of light from that of darkness."

Such are the utterly false and incredible statements which this writer makes.

Who can believe that any battle was fought before the constitution of the world?

And even supposing it credible, we wish now to get something to know, not to believe.

For to say that the Persians and Scythians long ago fought with one another is a credible statement; but while we believe it when we read or hear it, we cannot know it as a fact of experience or as a truth of the understanding.

So, then, as I would repudiate any such statement on the ground that I have been promised something, not that I must believe on authority, but that I shall understand without any ambiguity; still less will I receive statements which are not only uncertain, but incredible.

But what if he have some evidence to make these things clear and intelligible?

Let us hear, then, if we can, what follows with all possible patience and forbearance.

Chapter 13 - Two Opposite Substances

The Kingdom of Light.
Manichæus Teaches Uncertainties Instead of Certainties.

16.
"In the beginning, then," he says, "these two substances were divided.

The empire of light was held by God the Father, who is perpetual in holy origin, magnificent in virtue, true in His very nature, ever rejoicing in His own eternity, possessing in Himself wisdom and the vital senses, by which He also includes the twelve members of His light, which are the plentiful resources of his kingdom.

Also in each of His members are stored thousands of untold and priceless treasures.

But the Father Himself, chief in praise, incomprehensible in greatness, has united to Himself happy and glorious worlds, incalculable in number and duration, along with which this holy and illustrious Father and Progenitor resides, no poverty or infirmity being admitted in His magnificent realms.

And these matchless realms are so founded on the region of light and bliss, that no one can ever move or disturb them." [279]

17.
Where is the proof of all this?
And where did Manichæus learn it?
Do not frighten me with the name of the Paraclete.
For, in the first place, I have come not to put faith in unknown things, but to get the knowledge of undoubted truths, according to the caution enjoined on me by yourselves.
For you know how bitterly you taunt those who believe without consideration.
And what is more, this writer, who here begins to tell of very doubtful things, himself promised a little before to give complete and well-grounded knowledge.

Chapter 14 - Manichæus Promises the Knowledge of Undoubted Things, and Then Demands Faith in Doubtful Things

In the next place, if faith is what is required of me, I should prefer to keep to the Scripture, which tells me that the Holy Spirit came and inspired the apostles, to whom the Lord had promised to send Him.

You must therefore prove, either that what Manichæus says is true, and so make clear to me what I am unable to believe; or that Manichæus is the Holy Spirit, and so lead me to believe in what you cannot make clear. For I profess the Catholic faith, and by it I expect to attain certain knowledge.

Since, then, you try to overthrow my faith, you must supply me with certain knowledge, if you can, that you may convict me of having adopted my present belief without consideration.

141

You make two distinct propositions,--one when you say that the speaker is the Holy Spirit, and another when you say that what the speaker teaches is evidently true.

I might fairly ask undeniable proof for both propositions.

But I am not greedy and require to be convinced only of one.

Prove this person to be the Holy Spirit, and I will believe what he says to be true, even without understanding it; or prove that what he says is true, and I will believe him to be the Holy Spirit, even without evidence.

Could anything be fairer or kinder than this?

But you cannot prove either one or other of these propositions.

You can find nothing better than to praise your own faith and ridicule mine. So, after having in my turn praised my belief and ridiculed yours, what result do you think we shall arrive at as regards our judgment and our conduct, but to part company with those who promise the knowledge of indubitable things, and then demand from us faith in doubtful things? while we shall follow those who invite us to begin with believing what we cannot yet fully perceive, that, strengthened by this very faith, we may come into a position to know what we believe by the inward illumination and confirmation of our minds, due no longer to men, but to God Himself.

18.

And as I have asked this writer to prove these things to me, I ask him now where he learned them himself.

If he replies that they were revealed to him by the Holy Spirit, and that his mind was divinely enlightened that he might know them to be certain and evident, he himself points to the distinction between knowing and believing.

The knowledge is his to whom these things are fully made known as proved; but in the case of those who only hear his account of these things, there is no knowledge imparted, but only a believing acquiescence required.

Whoever thoughtlessly yields this becomes a Manichæan, not by knowing undoubted truth, but by believing doubtful statements.

Such were we when in our inexperienced youth we were deceived.

Instead, therefore, of promising knowledge, or clear evidence, or the settlement of the question free from all uncertainty, Manichæus ought to have said that these things were clearly proved to him, but that those who hear his account of them must believe him without evidence.

But were he to say this, who would not reply to him, If I must believe without knowing, why should I not prefer to believe those things which have a widespread notoriety from the consent of learned and unlearned, and which among all nations are established by the weightiest authority? From fear of having this said to him, Manichæus bewilders the inexperienced by first promising the knowledge of certain truths, and then demanding faith in doubtful things.

And then, if he is asked to make it plain that these things have been proved to himself, he fails again, and bids us believe this too.

Who can tolerate such imposture and arrogance?

Chapter 15 - The Doctrine of Manichæus Not Only Uncertain, But False. His Absurd Fancy of a Land and Race of Darkness Bordering on the Holy Region and the Substance of God

The Error, First of All, of Giving to the Nature of God Limits and Borders, as If God Were a Material Substance, Having Extension in Space.

19.

What if I shall have shown, with the help of God and of our Lord, that this writer's statements are false as well as uncertain?

What more unfortunate thing can be found than that superstition which not only fails to impart the knowledge and the truth which it promises, but also teaches what is directly opposed to knowledge and truth?

This will appear more clearly from what follows:

"In one direction on the border of this bright and holy land there was a land of darkness deep and vast in extent, where abode fiery bodies, destructive races.

Here was boundless darkness, flowing from the same source in immeasurable abundance, with the productions properly belonging to it.

Beyond this were muddy turbid waters with their inhabitants; and inside of them winds terrible and violent with their prince and their progenitors. Then again a fiery region of destruction, with its chiefs and peoples. And similarly inside of this a race full of smoke and gloom, where abode the dreadful prince and chief of all, having around him innumerable princes, himself the mind and source of them all.

Such are the five natures of the pestiferous land."

20.

To speak of God as an aerial or even as an ethereal body is absurd in the view of all who, with a clear mind, possessing some measure of discernment, can perceive the nature of wisdom and truth as not extended or scattered in space, but as great, and imparting greatness without material size, nor confined more or less in any direction, but throughout co-extensive with the Father of all, nor having one thing here and another there, but everywhere perfect, everywhere present. [280]

Chapter 16 - The Soul, Though Mutable, Has No Material Form

It is All Present in Every Part of the Body.

But why speak of truth and wisdom which surpass all the powers of the soul, when the nature of the soul itself, which is known to be mutable, still has no kind of material extension in space?

For whatever consists of any kind of gross matter must necessarily be divisible into parts, having one in one place, and another in another.

Thus, the finger is less than the whole hand, and one finger is less than two; and there is one place for this finger, and another for that, and another for the rest of the hand.

And this applies not to organized bodies only, but also to the earth, each part of which has its own place, so that one cannot be where the other is.

So in moisture, the smaller quantity occupies a smaller space, and the larger quantity a larger space; and one part is at the bottom of the cup, and another part near the mouth.

So in air, each part has its own place; and it is impossible for the air in this house to have along with itself, in the same house at the same moment, the air that the neighbors have.

And even as regards light itself, one part pours through one window, and another through another; and a greater through the larger, and a smaller through the smaller.

Nor, in fact, can there be any bodily substance, whether celestial or terrestrial, whether aerial or moist, which is not less in part than in whole, or which can possibly have one part in the place of another at the same time; but, having one thing in one place and another in another, its extension in space is a substance which has distinct limits and parts, or, so to speak, sections.

The nature of the soul, on the other hand, though we leave out of account its power of perceiving truth, and consider only its inferior power of giving unity to the body, and of sensation in the body, does not appear to have any material extension in space.

For it is all present in each separate part of its body when it is all present in any sensation. There is not a smaller part in the finger, and a larger in the arm, as the bulk of the finger is less than that of the arm; but the quantity everywhere is the same, for the whole is present everywhere.

For when the finger is touched, the whole mind feels, though the sensation is not through the whole body.

No part of the mind is unconscious of the touch, which proves the presence of the whole.

And yet it is not so present in the finger or in the sensation as to abandon the rest of the body, or to gather itself up into the one place where the sensation occurs.

For when it is all present in the sensation in a finger, if another part, say the foot, be touched, it does not fail to be all present in this sensation too:

so that at the same moment it is all present in different places, without leaving one in order to be in the other, and without having one part in one, and another in the other; but by this power showing itself to be all present at the same moment in separate places.

Since it is all present in the sensations of these places, it proves that it is not bound by the conditions of space. [281]

Chapter 17 - The Memory Contains the Ideas of Places of the Greatest Size

Again, if we consider the mind's power of remembering not the objects of the intellect, but material objects, such as we see brutes also remembering (for cattle find their way without mistake in familiar places, and animals return to their cribs, and dogs recognize the persons of their masters, and when asleep they often growl, or break out into a bark, which could not be unless their mind retained the images of things before seen or perceived by some bodily sense), who can conceive rightly where these images are contained, where they are kept, or where they are formed?

If, indeed, these images were no larger than the size of our body, it might be said that the mind shapes and retains them in the bodily space which contains itself.

But while the body occupies a small material space, the mind revolves images of vast extent, of heaven and earth, with no want of room, though they come and go in crowds; so that clearly, the mind is not diffused through space:

for instead of being contained in images of the largest spaces, it rather contains them; not, however, in any material receptacle, but by a mysterious faculty or power, by which it can increase or diminish them, can contract them within narrow limits, or expand them indefinitely, can arrange or disarrange them at pleasure, can multiply them or reduce them to a few or to one.

Chapter 18 - The Understanding Judges of the Truth of Things, and of Its Own Action

What, then, must be said of the power of perceiving truth, and of making a vigorous resistance against these very images which take their shape from impressions on the bodily senses, when they are opposed to the truth?

This power discerns the difference between, to take a particular example, the true Carthage and its own imaginary one, which it changes as it pleases with perfect ease.

It shows that the countless worlds of Epicurus, in which his fancy roamed without restraint, are due to the same power of imagination, and, not to multiply examples, that we get from the same source that land of light, with its boundless extent, and the five dens of the race of darkness, with their inmates, in which the fancies of Manichæus have dared to usurp for themselves the name of truth.

What then is this power which discerns these things?

Clearly, whatever its extent may be, it is greater than all these things, and is conceived of without any such material images.

Find, if you can, space for this power; give it a material extension; provide it with a body of huge size.

Assuredly if you think well, you cannot.

For of everything of this corporeal nature your mind forms an opinion as to its divisibility, and you make of such things one part greater and another less, as much as you like; while that by which you form a judgment of these things you perceive to be above them, not in local loftiness of place, but in dignity of power.

Chapter 19 - If the Mind Has No Material Extension, Much Less Has God

21.

So then, if the mind, so liable to change, whether from a multitude of dissimilar desires, or from feelings varying according to the abundance or the want of desirable things, or from these endless sports of the fancy, or from forgetfulness and remembrance, or from learning and ignorance; if the mind, I say, exposed to frequent change from these and the like causes, is perceived to be without any local or material extension, and to have a vigor of action which surmounts these material conditions, what must we think or conclude of God Himself, who remains superior to all intelligent beings in His freedom from perturbation and from change, giving to every one what is due?

Him the mind dares to express more easily than to see; and the clearer the sight, the less is the power of expression.

And yet this God, if, as the Manichæan fables are constantly asserting, He were limited in extension in one direction and unlimited in others, could be measured by so many subdivisions or fractions of greater or less size, as every one might fancy; so that, for example, a division of the extent of two feet would be less by eight parts than one of ten feet.

For this is the property of all natures which have extension in space, and therefore cannot be all in one place.

But even with the mind this is not the case; and this degrading and perverted idea of the mind is found among people who are unfit for such investigations.

Chapter 20 - Refutation of the Absurd Idea of Two Territories

22.
But perhaps, instead of thus addressing carnal minds, we should rather descend to the views of those who either dare not or are as yet unfit to turn from the consideration of material things to the study of an immaterial and spiritual nature, and who thus are unable to reflect upon their own power of reflection, so as to see how it forms a judgment of material extension without itself possessing it.

Let us descend then to these material ideas, and let us ask in what direction, and on what border of the shining and sacred territory, to use the expressions of Manichæus, was the region of darkness?

For he speaks of one direction and border, without saying which, whether the right or the left.

In any case, it is clear that to speak of one side implies that there is another.

But where there are three or more sides, either the figure is bounded in all directions, or if it extends infinitely in one direction, still it must be limited in the directions where it has sides.

If, then, on one side of the region of light there was the race of darkness, what bounded it on the other side or sides?

The Manichæans say nothing in reply to this; but when pressed, they say that on the other sides the region of light, as they call it, is infinite, that is, extends throughout boundless space.

They do not see, what is plain to the dullest understanding, that in that case there could be no sides?

For the sides are where it is bounded.

What, then, he says, though there are no sides?

But what you said of one direction or side, implied of necessity the existence of another direction and side, or other directions and sides.

For if there was only one side, you should have said, on the side, not on one side; as in reference to our body we say properly, By one eye, because there is another; or on one breast, because there is another.

But if we spoke of a thing as being on one nose, or one navel, we should be ridiculed by learned and unlearned, since there is only one.

But I do not insist on words, for you may have used one in the sense of the only one.

Chapter 21 - This Region of Light Must Be Material If It is Joined to the Region of Darkness

The Shape of the Region of Darkness Joined to the Region of Light.
What, then, bordered on the side of the region which you call shining and sacred?
The region, you reply, of darkness.
Do you then allow this latter region to have been material?
Of course you must, since you assert that all bodies derive their origin from it.
How then is it that, dull and carnal as you are, you do not see that unless both regions were material, they could not have their sides joined to one another?
How could you ever be so blinded in mind as to say that only the region of darkness was material, and that the so-called region of light was immaterial and spiritual?
My good friends, let us open our eyes for once, and see, now that we are told of it, what is most obvious, that two regions cannot be joined at their sides unless both are material.

23.
Or if we are too dull and stupid to see this, let us hear whether the region of darkness too has one side, and is boundless in the other directions, like the region of light.
They do not hold this from fear of making it seem equal to God.
Accordingly they make it boundless in depth and in length; but upwards, above it, they maintain that there is an infinity of empty space.
And lest this region should appear to be a fraction equal in amount to half of that representing

the region of light, they narrow it also on two sides.

As if, to give the simplest illustration, a piece of bread were made into four squares, three white and one black; then suppose the three white pieces joined as one, and conceive them as infinite upwards and downwards, and backwards in all directions:

this represents the Manichæan region of light.

Then conceive the black square infinite downwards and backwards, but with infinite emptiness above it:

this is their region of darkness.

But these are secrets which they disclose to very eager and anxious inquirers.

Chapter 22 - The Form of the Region of Light the Worse of the Two

Well, then, if this is so, the region of darkness is clearly touched on two sides by the region of light.

And if it is touched on two sides, it must touch on two.

So much for its being on one side, as we were told before.

24.

And what an unseemly appearance is this of the region of light!--like a cloven arch, with a black wedge inserted below, bounded only in the direction of the cleft, and having a void space interposed where the boundless emptiness stretches above the region of darkness. Indeed, the form of the region of darkness is better than that of the region of light:

for the former cleaves, the latter is cloven; the former fills the gap which is made in the latter; the former has no void in it, while the latter is undefined in all directions, except that where it is filled up by the wedge of darkness.

In an ignorant and greedy notion of giving more honor to a number of pans than to a single one, so that the region of light should have six, three upwards and three downwards, they have made this region be split up, instead of sundering the other.

For, according to this figure, though there may be no commixture of darkness with light, there is certainly penetration.

Chapter 23 - The Anthropomorphites Not So Bad as the Manichæans

25.

Compare, now, not spiritual men of the Catholic faith, whose mind, as far as is possible in this life, perceives that the divine substance and nature has no material extension, and has no shape bounded by lines, but the carnal and weak of our faith, who, when they hear the members of the body used figuratively, as, when God's eyes or ears are spoken of, are accustomed, in the license of fancy, to picture God to themselves in a human form; compare these with the Manichæans, whose custom it is to make known their silly stories to anxious inquirers as if they were great mysteries:

and consider who have the most allowable and respectable ideas of God, --those who think of Him as having a human form which is the most excellent of its kind, or those who think of Him as having boundless material extension, yet not in all directions, but with three parts infinite and solid, while in one part He is cloven, with an empty void, and with undefined space above, while the region of darkness is inserted wedge-like below.

Or perhaps the proper expression is, that He is unconfined above in His own nature, but encroached on below by a hostile nature.

I join with you in laughing at the folly of carnal men, unable as yet to form spiritual conceptions, who think of God as having a human form.

Do you too join me, if you can, in laughing at those whose unhappy conceptions represent God as having a shape cloven or cut in such an unseemly and unbecoming way, with such an empty gap above, and such a dishonorable curtailment below.

Besides, there is this difference, that these carnal people, who think of God as having a human form, if they are content to be nourished with milk from the breast of the Catholic Church, and do not rush headlong into rash opinions, but cultivate in the Church the pious habit of inquiry, and there ask that they may receive, and knock that it may be opened to them, begin to understand spiritually the figures and parables of the Scriptures, and gradually to perceive that the divine energies are suitably set forth under the name, sometimes of ears, sometimes of eyes, sometimes of hands or feet, or even of wings and feathers a shield too, and sword, and helmet, and all the other innumerable things.

And the more progress they make in this understanding, the more are they confirmed as Catholics.

The Manichæans, on the other hand, when they abandon their material fancies, cease to be Manichæans.

For this is the chief and special point in their praises of Manichæus, that the divine mysteries which were taught figuratively in books from ancient times were kept for Manichæus, who was to come last, to solve and demonstrate; and so after him no other teacher will come from God, for he has said nothing in figures or parables, but has explained ancient sayings of that kind, and has himself taught in plain, simple terms.

Therefore, when the Manichæans hear these words of their founder, on one side and border of the shining and sacred region was the region of darkness, they have no interpretations to fall back on.

Wherever they turn, the wretched bondage of their own fancies brings them upon clefts or sudden stoppages and joinings or sunderings of the most unseemly kind, which it would be shocking to believe as true of any immaterial nature, even though mutable, like the mind, not to speak of the immutable nature of God.

And yet if I were unable to rise to higher things, and to bring my thoughts from the entanglement of false imaginations which are impressed on the memory by the bodily senses, into the freedom and purity of spiritual existence, how much better would it be to think of God as in the form of a man, than to fasten that wedge of darkness to His lower edge, and, for want of a covering for the boundless vacuity above to leave it void and unoccupied throughout infinite space!

What notion could be worse than this?

What darker error can be taught or imagined?

Chapter 24 - Of the Number of Natures in the Manichæan Fiction

26.

Again, I wish to know, when I read of God the Father and His kingdoms founded on the shining and happy region, whether the Father and His kingdoms, and the region, are all of the same nature and substance.

If they are, then it is not another nature or sort of body of God which the wedge of the race of darkness cleaves and penetrates, which itself is an unspeakably revolting thing, but it is actually the very nature of God which undergoes this.

Think of this, I beseech you:

as you are men, think of it, and flee from it; and if by tearing open your breasts you can cast out by the roots such profane fancies from your faith, I pray you to do it.

Or will you say that these three are not of one and the same nature, but that the Father is of one, the kingdoms of another, and the region of another, so that each has a peculiar nature and substance, and that they are arranged according to their degree of excellence?

If this is true, Manichæus should have taught that there are four natures, not two; or if the Father and the kingdoms have one nature, and the region only one of its own, he should have made three.

Or if he made only two, because the region of darkness does not belong to God, in what sense does the region of light belong to God?

For if it has a nature of its own, and if God neither generated nor made it, it does not belong to Him, and the seat of His kingdom is in what belongs to another.

Or if it belongs to Him because of its vicinity, the region of darkness must do so too; for it not only borders on the region of light, but penetrates it so as to sever it in two.

Again, if God generated it, it cannot have a separate nature. For what is generated by God must be what God is, as the Catholic Church believes of the only begotten Son.

So you are brought back of necessity to that shocking and detestable profanity, that the wedge of darkness sunders not a region distinct and separate from God, but the very nature of God.

Or if God did not generate, but make it, of what did He make it?

Or if of Himself, what is this but to generate?

If of some other nature, was this nature good or evil?

If good, there must have been some good nature not belonging to God; which you will scarcely have the boldness to assert.

If evil, the race of darkness cannot have been the only evil nature.

Or did God take a part of that region and turn it into a region of light, in order to found His kingdom upon it?

If He had, He would have taken the whole, and there would have been no evil nature left.

If God, then, did not make the region of light of a substance distinct from His own, He must have made it of nothing. [282]

Chapter 25 - Omnipotence Creates Good Things Differing in Degree

In Every Description Whatsoever of the Junction of the Two Regions There is Either Impropriety or Absurdity.

27.

If, then, you are now convinced that God is able to create some good thing out of nothing, come into the Catholic Church, and learn that all the natures which God has created and founded in their order of excellence from the highest to the lowest are good, and some better than others; and that they were made of nothing, though God, their Maker, made use of His own wisdom as an instrument, so to speak, to give being to what was not, and that as far as it had being it might be good, and that the limitation of its being might show that it was not begotten by God, but made out of nothing.

If you examine the matter, you will find nothing to keep you from agreeing to this.

For you cannot make your region of light to be what God is, without making the dark section an infringement on the very nature of God.

Nor can you say that it was generated by God, without being reduced to the same enormity, from the necessity of concluding that as begotten of God, it must be what God is.

Nor can you say that it was distinct from Him, lest you should be forced to admit that God placed His kingdom in what did not belong to Him, and that there are three natures.

Nor can you say that God made it of a substance distinct from His own, without making something good besides God, or something evil besides the race of darkness.

It remains, therefore that you must confess that God made the region of light out of nothing: and you are unwilling to believe this; because if God could make out of nothing some great good which yet was inferior to Himself, He could also, since He is good, and grudges no good, make another good inferior to the former, and again a third inferior to the second, and so on, in order down to the lowest good of created natures, so that the whole aggregate, instead of extending indefinitely without number or measure should have a fixed and definite consistency.

Again, if you will not allow this either, that God made the region of light out of nothing, you will have no escape from the shocking profanities to which your opinions lead.

28.

Perhaps, since the carnal imagination can fancy any shapes it likes, you might be able to devise some other form for the junction of the two regions, instead of presenting to the mind such a disagreeable and painful description as this, that the region of God, whether it be of the same nature as God or not, where at least God's kingdoms are founded, lies through immensity in such a huge mass that its members stretch loosely to an infinite extent, and that on their lower part that wedge of the region of darkness, itself of boundless size encroaches upon them.

But whatever other form you contrive for the junction of these two regions, you cannot erase what Manichæus has written.

I refer not to other treatises where a more particular description is given,--for perhaps, because they are in the hands of only a few, there might not be so much difficulty with them,--but to this Fundamental Epistle which we are now considering, with which all of you who are called enlightened are usually quite familiar.

Here the words are:

"On one side the border of the shining and sacred region was the region of darkness, deep and boundless in extent."

Chapter 26 - The Manichæans are Reduced to the Choice of a Tortuous, or Curved, or Straight Line of Junction

The Third Kind of Line Would Give Symmetry and Beauty Suitable to Both Regions. What more is to be got? we have now heard what is on the border.

Make what shape you please, draw any kind of lines you like, it is certain that the junction of this boundless mass of the region of darkness to the region of light must have been either by a straight line, or a curved, or a tortuous one.

If the line of junction is tortuous the side of the region of light must also be tortuous; otherwise its straight side joined to a tortuous one would leave gaps of infinite depth, instead of having vacuity only above the land of darkness, as we were told before.

And if there were such gaps, how much better it would have been for the region of light to have been still more distant, and to have had a greater vacuity between, so that the region of darkness might not touch it at all!

Then there might have been such a gap of bottomless depth, that, on the rise of any mischief in that race, although the chiefs of darkness might have the foolhardy wish to cross over, they would fall headlong into the gap (for bodies cannot fly without air to support them); and as there is infinite space downwards, they could do no more harm, though they might live for ever, for they would be for ever falling.

Again, if the line of junction was a curved one, the region of light must also have had the disfigurement of a curve to answer it.

Or if the land of darkness were curved inwards like a theatre, there would be as much disfigurement in the corresponding line in the region of light.

Or if the region of darkness had a curved line, and the region of light a straight one, they cannot have touched at all points.

And certainly, as I said before, it would have been better if they had not touched, and if there was such a gap between that the regions might be kept distinctly separate, and that rash evildoers might fall headlong so as to be harmless.

If, then, the line of junction was a straight one, there remain, of course, no more gaps or grooves, but, on the contrary, so perfect a junction as to make the greatest possible peace and harmony between the two regions.

What more beautiful or more suitable than that one side should meet the other in a straight line, without bends or breaks to disturb the natural and permanent connection throughout endless space and endless duration?

And even though there was a separation, the straight sides of both regions would be beautiful in themselves, as being straight; and besides, even in spite of an interval, their correspondence, as running parallel, though not meeting, would give a symmetry to both.

With the addition of the junction, both regions become perfectly regular and harmonious; for nothing can be devised more beautiful in description or in conception than this junction of two straight lines. [283]

Chapter 27 - The Beauty of the Straight Line Might Be Taken from the Region of Darkness Without Taking Anything from Its Substance

So Evil Neither Takes from Nor Adds to the Substance of the Soul.
The Straightness of Its Side Would Be So Far a Good Bestowed on the Region of Darkness by God the Creator.

29.
What is to be done with unhappy minds, perverse in error, and held fast by custom?
These men do not know what they say when they say those things; for they do not consider.
Listen to me; no one forces you, no one quarrels with you, no one taunts you with past errors, unless some one who has not experienced the divine mercy in deliverance from error:
all we desire is that the errors should some time or other be abandoned.
Think a little without animosity or bitterness.
We are all human beings:
let us hate, not one another, but errors and lies. Think a little, I pray you.
God of mercy, help them to think, and kindle in the minds of inquirers the true light.

If anything is plain, is not this, that right is better than wrong?

Give me, then, a calm and quiet answer to this, whether making crooked the right line of the region of darkness which joins on to the right line of the region of light, would not detract from its beauty.

If you will not be dogged, you must confess that not only is beauty taken from it by its being made crooked, but also the beauty which it might have had from connection with the right line of the region of light.

Is it the case, then, that in this loss of beauty, in which right is made crooked, and harmony becomes discord, and agreement disagreement, there is any loss of substance?

Learn, then, from this that substance is not evil; but as in the body, by change of form for the worse, beauty is lost, or rather lessened, and what was called fair before is said to be ugly, and what was pleasing becomes displeasing, so in the mind the seemliness of a right will, which makes a just and pious life, is injured when the will changes for the worse; and by this sin the mind becomes miserable, instead of enjoying as before the happiness which comes from the ornament of a right will, without any gain or loss of substance.

30.

Consider, again, that though we admit that the border of the region of darkness was evil for other reasons, such as that it was dim and dark, or any other reason, still it was not evil in being straight.

So, if I admit that there was some evil in its color, you must admit that there was some good in its straightness.

Whatever the amount of this good, it is not allowable to attribute it to any other than God the Maker, from whom we must believe that all good in whatsoever nature comes, if we are to escape deadly error.

It is absurd, then, to say that this region is perfect evil, when in its straightness of border is found the good of not a little beauty of a material kind; and also to make this region to be altogether estranged, from the almighty and good God, when this good which we find in it can be attributed to no other but the author of all good things.

But this border, too, we are told, was evil.

Well, suppose it evil:

it would surely have been worse had it been crooked instead of straight.

And how can that be the perfection of evil than which something worse than itself can be thought of?

And to be worse implies that there is some good, the want of which makes the thing worse.

Here the want of straightness would make the line worse.

Therefore its straightness is something good.

And you will never answer the question whence this goodness comes, without reference to Him from whom we must acknowledge that all good things come, whether small or great.

But now we shall pass on from considering this border to something else.

Chapter 28 - Manichæus Places Five Natures in the Region of Darkness

31.

"There dwelt," he says, "in that region fiery bodies, destructive races."

By speaking of dwelling, he must mean that those bodies were animated and in life.

But, not to appear to cavil at a word, let us see how he divides into five classes all these inhabitants of this region.

"Here," he says, "was boundless darkness, flowing from the same source in immeasurable abundance, with the productions properly belonging to it. Beyond this were muddy turbid waters, with their inhabitants; and inside of them winds terrible and violent, with their prince and their progenitors.

Then, again, a fiery region of destruction, with its chiefs and peoples.

And, similarly, inside of this a race full of smoke and gloom, where abode the dreadful prince and chief of all, having around him innumerable princes, himself the mind and source of them all.

Such are the five natures of the pestiferous region."

We find here five natures mentioned as part of one nature, which he calls the pestiferous region.

The natures are darkness, waters, winds, fire, smoke; which he so arranges as to make darkness first, beginning at the outside.

Inside of darkness he puts the waters; inside of the waters, the winds; inside of the winds, the fire; inside of the fire, the smoke.

And each of these natures had its peculiar kind of inhabitants, which were likewise five in number.

For to the question, Whether there was only one kind in all, or different kinds corresponding to the different natures; the reply is, that they were different:

as in other books we find it stated that the darkness had serpents; the waters swimming creatures, such as fish; the winds flying creatures, such as birds; the fire quadrupeds, such as horses, lions, and the like; the smoke bipeds, such as men.

Chapter 29 - The Refutation of This Absurdity

32.

Whose arrangement, then, is this?
Who made the distinctions and the classification?
Who gave the number, the qualities, the forms, the life?

For all these things are in themselves good, nor could each of the natures have them except from the bestowal of God, the author of all good things.

For this is not like the descriptions or suppositions of poets about an imaginary chaos, as being a shapeless mass, without form, without quality, without measurement, without weight and number, without order and variety; a confused something, absolutely destitute of qualities, so that some Greek writers call it ἄποιον.

So far from being like this is the Manichæan description of the region of darkness, as they call it, that, in a directly contrary style, they add side to side, and join border to border; they number five natures; they separate, arrange, and assign to each its own qualities.

Nor do they leave the natures barren or waste, but people them with their proper inhabitants; and to these, again, they give suitable forms, and adapted to their place of habitation, besides giving the chief of all endowments, life.

To recount such good things as these, and to speak of them as having no connection with God, the author of all good things, is to lose sight of the excellence of the order in the things, and of the great evil of the error which leads to such a conclusion.

Chapter 30 - The Number of Good Things in Those Natures Which Manichæus Places in the Region of Darkness

33.

"But," is the reply, "the orders of beings inhabiting those five natures were fierce and destructive."

As if I were praising their fierceness and destructiveness.

I, you see, join with you in condemning the evils you attribute to them; join you with me in praising the good things which you ascribe to them:

so it will appear that there is a mixture of good and evil in what you call the last extremity of evil.

If I join you in condemning what is mischievous in this region, you must join with me in praising what is beneficial.

For these beings could not have been produced, or nourished, or have continued to inhabit that region, without some salutary influence.

I join with you in condemning the darkness; join with me in praising the productiveness.

For while you call the darkness immeasurable, you speak of "suitable productions."

Darkness, indeed, is not a real substance, and means no more than the absence of light, as nakedness means the want of clothing, and emptiness the want of material contents:

so that darkness could produce nothing, although a region in darkness--that is, in the absence of light--might produce something. But passing over this for the present, it is certain that where productions arise there must be a beneficent adaptation of substances, as well as a symmetrical arrangement and construction in unity of the members of the beings produced,--a wise adjustment making them agree with one another.

And who will deny that all these things are more to be praised than darkness is to be condemned?

If I join with you in condemning the muddiness of the waters, you must join with me in praising the waters as far as they possessed the form and quality of water, and also the agreement of the members of the inhabitants swimming in the waters, their life sustaining and directing their body, and every particular adaptation of substances for the benefit of health.

For though you find fault with the waters as turbid and muddy, still, in allowing them the quality of producing and maintaining their living inhabitants, you imply that there was some kind of bodily form, and similarity of parts, giving unity and congruity of character; otherwise there could be no body at all:

and, as a rational being, you must see that all these things are to be praised.

And however great you make the ferocity of these inhabitants, and their massacrings and devastations in their assaults, you still leave them the regular limits of form, by which the members of each body are made to agree together, and their beneficial adaptations, and the regulating power of the living principle binding together the parts of the body in a friendly and harmonious union.

And if all these are regarded with common sense it will be seen that they are more to be commended than the faults are to be condemned.

I join with you in condemning the frightfulness of the winds; join with me in praising their nature, as giving breath and nourishment, and their material form in its continuousness and diffusion by the connection of its parts:

for by these things these winds had the power of producing and nourishing, and sustaining in vigor these inhabitants you speak of; and also in these inhabitants--besides the other things which have already been commended in all animated creatures--this particular power of going quickly and easily whence and whither they please, and the harmonious stroke of their wings in flight, and their regular motion.

I join with you in condemning the destructiveness of fire; join with me in commending the productiveness of this fire, and the growth of these productions, and the adaptation of the fire to the beings produced, so that they had coherence, and came to perfection in measure and shape, and could live and have their abode there:

for you see that all these things deserve admiration and praise, not only in the fire which is thus habitable, but in the inhabitants too.

I join with you in condemning the denseness of smoke, and the savage character of the prince who, as you say, abode in it; join with me in praising the similarity of all the parts in this very smoke, by which it preserves the harmony and proportion of its parts among themselves, according to its own nature, and has an unity which makes it what it is:

for no one can calmly reflect on these things without wonder and praise.

Besides, even to the smoke you give the power and energy of production, for you say that princes inhabited it; so that in that region the smoke is productive, which never happens here, and, moreover, affords a wholesome dwelling place to its inhabitants.

Chapter 31 - The Same Subject Continued

34.

And even in the prince of smoke himself, instead of mentioning only his ferocity as a bad quality, ought you not to have taken notice of the other things in his nature which you must allow to be commendable?

For he had a soul and a body; the soul life-giving, and the body endowed with life.

Since the soul governed and the body obeyed, the soul took the lead and the body followed; the soul gave consistency, the body was not dissolved; the soul gave harmonious motion, and the body was constructed of a well-proportioned framework of members.

In this single prince are you not induced to express approval of the orderly peace or the peaceful order?

And what applies to one applies to all the rest.

You say he was fierce and cruel to others.

This is not what I commend, but the other important things which you will not take notice of.

Those things, when perceived and considered,--after advice by any one who has without consideration put faith in Manichæus,--lead him to a clear conviction that, in speaking of those natures, he speaks of things good in a sense, not perfect and un-created, like God the one Trinity, nor of the higher rank of created things, like the holy angels and the ever-blessed powers; but of the lowest class, and ranked according to the small measure of their endowments.

These things are thought to be blameworthy by the uninstructed when they compare them with higher things; and in view of their want of some good, the good they have gets the name of evil, because it is defective.

My reason also for thus discussing the natures enumerated by Manichæus is that the things named are things familiar to us in this world.

We are familiar with darkness, waters, winds, fire, smoke; we are familiar, too, with animals, creeping, swimming, flying; with quadrupeds and biped.

Philip Schaff, D.D., LL.D.

With the exception of darkness (which, as I have said already, is nothing but the absence of light, and the perception of it is only the absence of sight, as the perception of silence is the absence of hearing; not that darkness is anything, but that light is not, as neither that silence is anything, but that sound is not), all the other things are natural qualities and are familiar to all; and the form of those natures, which is commendable and good as far as it exists, no wise man attributes to any other author than God, the author of all good things. [284]

Chapter 32 - Manichæus Got the Arrangement of His Fanciful Notions from Visible Objects

35.

For in giving to these natures which he has learned from visible things, an arrangement according to his fanciful ideas, to represent the race of darkness, Manichæus is clearly in error.

First of all, he makes darkness productive, which is impossible.

But, he replies, this darkness was unlike what you are familiar with.

How, then, can you make me understand about it?

After so many promises to give knowledge, will you force me to take your word for it?

Suppose I believe you, this at least is certain, that if the darkness had no form, as darkness usually has not, it could produce nothing; if it had form, it was better than ordinary darkness: whereas, when you call it different from the ordinary kind, you wish us to believe that it is worse.

You might as well say that silence, which is the same to the ear as darkness to the eyes, produced some deaf or dumb animals in that region; and then, in reply to the objection that silence is not a nature, you might say that it was different silence from ordinary silence; in a word, you might say what you pleased to those whom you have once misled into believing you.

No doubt, the obvious facts relating to the origin of animal life led Manichæus to say that serpents were produced in darkness.

However, there are serpents which have such sharp sight, and such pleasure in light, that they seem to give evidence of the most weighty kind against this idea.

Then the idea of swimming things in the water might easily be got here, and applied to the fanciful objects in that region; and so of flying things in the winds, for the motion of the lower air in this world, where birds fly, is called wind.

Where he got the idea of the quadrupeds in fire, no one can tell.

Still he said this deliberately, though without sufficient thought, and from great misconception.

The reason usually given is, that quadrupeds are voracious and salacious.

But many men surpass any quadruped in voracity, though they are bipeds, and are called children of the smoke, and not of fire.

Geese, too, are as voracious as any animal; and though he might place them in fire as bipeds, or in the water because they love to swim, or in the winds because they have wings and sometimes fly, they certainly have nothing to do with fire in this classification.

As regards salaciousness, I suppose he was thinking of neighing horses, which sometimes bite through the bridle and rush at the mares; and writing hastily, with this in his mind, he forgot the common sparrow, in comparison of which the hottest stallion is cold.

The reason they give for assigning bipeds to the smoke is, that bipeds are conceited and proud, for men are derived from this class; and the idea, which is a plausible one, is that smoke resembles proud people in rising up into the air, round and swelling.

This idea might warrant a figurative description of proud men, or an allegorical expression or explanation, but not the belief that bipeds are born in smoke and of smoke.

They might with equal reason be said to be born in dust, for it often rises up to the heaven with a similar circling and lofty motion; or in the clouds, for they are often drawn up from the earth in such a way, that those looking from a distance are uncertain whether they are clouds or smoke.

Once more, why, in the case of the waters and the winds, does he suit the inhabitants to the character of the place, as we see swimming things in water, and flying things in the wind; whereas, in the face of fire and smoke, this bold liar is not ashamed to assign to these places the most unlikely inhabitants?

For fire burns quadrupeds, and consumes them, and smoke suffocates and kills bipeds.

At least he must acknowledge that he has made these natures better in the race of darkness than they are here, though he wishes us to think everything to be worse.

For, according to this, the fire there produced and nourished quadrupeds, and gave them a lodging not only harmless, but most convenient.

The smoke, too, provided room for the offspring of its own benign bosom, and cherished them up to the rank of prince.

Thus we see that these lies, which have added to the number of heretics, arose from the perception by carnal sense, only without care or discernment, of visible objects in this world, and when thus conceived, were brought forth by fancy, and then presumptuously written and published.

Chapter 33 - Every Nature, as Nature, is Good

36.

But the consideration we wish most to urge is the truth of the Catholic doctrine, if they can understand it, that God is the author of all natures.

I urged this before when I said, I join with you in your condemnation of destructiveness, of blindness, of dense muddiness, of terrific violence, of perishableness, of the ferocity of the princes, and so on; join with me in commending form, classification, arrangement, harmony, unity of structure, symmetry and correspondence of members, provision for vital breath and nourishment, wholesome adaptation, regulation and control by the mind, and the subjection of the bodies, and the assimilation and agreement of parts in the natures, both those inhabiting and those inhabited, and all the other things of the same kind.

From this, if they would only think honestly, they would understand that it implies a mixture of good and evil, even in the region where they suppose evil to be alone and in perfection:

so that if the evils mentioned were taken away, the good things will remain, without anything to detract from the commendation given to them; whereas, if the good things are taken away, no nature is left. From this every one sees, who can see, that every nature, as far as it is nature, is good; since in one and the same thing in which I found something to praise, and he found something to blame, if the good things are taken away, no nature will remain; but if the disagreeable things are taken away, the nature will remain unimpaired.

Take from waters their thickness and muddiness, and pure clear water remains; take from them the consistence of their parts, and no water will be left.

If then, after the evil is removed, the nature remains in a purer state, and does not remain at all when the good is taken away, it must be the good which makes the nature of the thing in which it is, while the evil is not nature, but contrary to nature.

Take from the winds their terribleness and excessive force, with which you find fault, you can conceive of winds as gentle and mild; take from them the similarity of their parts which gives them continuity of substance, and the unity essential to material existence, and no nature remains to be conceived of.

It would be tedious to go through all the cases; but all who consider the subject free from party spirit must see that in their list of natures the disagreeable things mentioned are additions to the nature; and when they are removed, the natures remain better than before.

This shows that the natures, as far as they are natures, are good; for when you take from them the good instead of the evil, no natures remain.

And attend, you who wish to arrive at a correct judgment, to what is said of the fierce prince himself.

If you take away his ferocity, see how many excellent things will remain; his material frame, the symmetry of the members on one side with those on the other, the unity of his form, the settled continuity of his parts, the orderly adjustment of the mind as ruling and animating, and the body as subject and animated.

The removal of these things, and of others I may have omitted to mention, will leave no nature remaining.

Chapter 34 - Nature Cannot Be Without Some Good

The Manichæans Dwell Upon the Evils.

37.

But perhaps you will say that these evils cannot be removed from the natures, and must therefore be considered natural.

The question at present is not what can be taken away, and what cannot; but it certainly helps to a clear perception that these natures, as far as they are natures, are good, when we see that the good things can be thought of without these evil things, while without these good things no nature can be conceived of.

I can conceive of waters without muddy commotion; but without settled continuity of parts no material form is an object of thought or of sensation in any way.

Therefore even these muddy waters could not exist without the good which was the condition of their material existence.

As to the reply that these evil things cannot be taken from such natures, I rejoin that neither can the good things be taken away.

Why, then, should you call these things natural evils, on account of the evil things which you suppose cannot be taken away, and yet refuse to call them natural good things, on account of the good things which, as has been proved, cannot be taken away?

38.

You may next ask, as you usually do for a last resource, whence come these evils which I have said that I too disapprove of.

I shall perhaps tell you, if you first tell me whence are those good things which you too are obliged to commend, if you would not be altogether unreasonable.

But why should I ask this, when we both acknowledge that all good things whatever, and how great soever, are from the one God, who is supremely good?

You must therefore yourselves oppose Manichæus who has placed all these important good things which we have mentioned and justly commended,--the continuity and agreement of parts in each nature, the health and vigor of the animated creatures, and the other things which it would be wearisome to repeat,--(in an imaginary region of darkness, so as to separate them altogether from that God whom he allows to be the author of all good things.)

He lost sight of those good things, while taking notice only of what was disagreeable; as if one, frightened by a lion's roaring, and seeing him dragging away and tearing the bodies of cattle or human beings which he had seized, should from childish pusillanimity be so overpowered with fear as to see nothing but the cruelty and ferocity of the lion; and overlooking or disregarding all the other qualities, should exclaim against the nature of this animal as not only evil, but a great evil, his fear adding to his vehemence.

But were he to see a tame lion, with its ferocity subdued, especially if he had never been frightened by a lion, he would have leisure, in the absence of danger and terror, to observe and admire the beauty of the animal.

My only remark on this is one closely connected with our subject:

that any nature may be in some case disagreeable, so as to excite hatred towards the whole nature; though it is clear that the form of a real living beast, even when it excites terror in the woods, is far better than that of the artificial imitation which is commended in a painting on the wall.

We must not then be misled into this error by Manichæus, or be hindered from observing the forms of the natures, by his finding fault with some things in them in such a way as to make us disapprove of them entirely, when it is impossible to show that they deserve entire disapproval. And when our minds are thus composed and prepared to form a just judgment, we may ask whence come those evils which I have said that I condemn.

It will be easier to see this if we class them all under one name.

Chapter 35 - Evil Alone is Corruption

Corruption is Not Nature, But Contrary to Nature.
Corruption Implies Previous Good.

39.

For who can doubt that the whole of that which is called evil is nothing else than corruption? Different evils may, indeed, be called by different names; but that which is the evil of all things in which any evil is perceptible is corruption.

So the corruption of an educated mind is ignorance; the corruption of a prudent mind is imprudence; the corruption of a just mind, injustice; the corruption of a brave mind, cowardice; the corruption of a calm, peaceful mind, cupidity, fear, sorrow, pride.

Again, in a living body, the corruption of health is pain and disease; the corruption of strength is exhaustion; the corruption of rest is toil.

Again, in any corporeal thing, the corruption of beauty is ugliness; the corruption of straightness is crookedness; the corruption of order is confusion; the corruption of entireness is disseverance, or fracture, or diminution. It would be long and laborious to mention by name all the corruptions of the things here mentioned, and of countless other things; for in many cases the words may apply to the mind as well as to the body, and in innumerable cases the corruption has a distinct name of its own. But enough has been said to show that corruption does harm only as displacing the natural condition; and so, that corruption is not nature, but against nature.

And if corruption is the only evil to be found anywhere, and if corruption is not nature, no nature is evil.

40.

But if, perchance, you cannot follow this, consider again, that whatever is corrupted is deprived of some good:

for if it were not corrupted, it would be incorrupt; or if it could not in any way be corrupted, it would be incorruptible.

Now, if corruption is an evil, both incorruption and incorruptibility must be good things.

We are not, however, speaking at present of incorruptible nature, but of things which admit of corruption, and which, while not corrupted, may be called incorrupt, but not incorruptible.

That alone can be called incorruptible which not only is not corrupted, but also cannot in any part be corrupted.

Whatever things, then, being incorrupt, but liable to corruption, begin to be corrupted, are deprived of the good which they had as incorrupt.

Nor is this a slight good, for corruption is a great evil.

And the continued increase of corruption implies the continued presence of good, of which they may be deprived. Accordingly, the natures supposed to exist in the region of darkness must have been either corruptible or incorruptible.

If they were incorruptible, they were in possession of a good than which nothing is higher.

If they were corruptible, they were either corrupted or not corrupted.

If they were not corrupted, they were incorrupt, to say which of anything is to give it great praise.

If they were corrupted, they were deprived of this great good of incorruption; but the deprivation implies the previous possession of the good they are deprived of; and if they possessed this good, they were not the perfection of evil, and consequently all the Manichæan story is a falsehood.

Chapter 36 - The Source of Evil or of Corruption of Good

41.

After thus inquiring what evil is, and learning that it is not nature, but against nature, we must next inquire whence it is.

If Manichæus had done this, he might have escaped falling into the snare of these serious errors.

Out of time and out of order, he began with inquiring into the origin of evil, without first asking what evil was; and so his inquiry led him only to the reception of foolish fancies, of which the mind, much fed by the bodily senses, with difficulty rids itself.

Perhaps, then, some one, desiring no longer argument, but delivery from error, will ask, Whence is this corruption which we find to be the common evil of good things which are not incorruptible?

Such an inquirer will soon find the answer if he seeks for truth with great earnestness, and knocks reverently with sustained assiduity.

For while man can use words as a kind of sign for the expression of his thoughts, teaching is the work of the incorruptible Truth itself, who is the one true, the one internal Teacher.

He became external also, that He might recall us from the external to the internal; and taking on Himself the form of a servant, that He might bring down His height to the knowledge of those rising up to Him, He condescended to appear in lowliness to the low.

In His name let us ask, and through Him let us seek mercy of the Father while making this inquiry.

For to answer in a word the question, Whence is corruption? it is hence, because these natures that are capable of corruption were not begotten by God, but made by Him out of nothing; and as we already proved that those natures are good, no one can say with propriety that they were not good as made by God.

If it is said that God made them perfectly good, it must be remembered that the only perfect good is God Himself, the maker of those good things.

Chapter 37 - God Alone Perfectly Good

42.

What harm, you ask, would follow if those things too were perfectly good?

Still, should any one, who admits and believes the perfect goodness of God the Father, inquire what source we should reverently assign to any other perfectly good thing, supposing it to exist, our only correct reply would be, that it is of God the Father, who is perfectly good.

And we must bear in mind that what is of Him is born of Him, and not made by Him out of nothing, and that it is therefore perfectly, that is, incorruptibly, good like God Himself.

So we see that it is unreasonable to require that things made out of nothing should be as perfectly good as He who was begotten of God Himself, and who is one as God is one, otherwise God would have begotten something unlike Himself.

Hence it shows ignorance and impiety to seek for brethren for this only-begotten Son through whom all good things were made by the Father out of nothing, except in this, that He condescended to appear as man.

Accordingly in Scripture He is called both only-begotten and first-begotten; only-begotten of the Father, and first-begotten from the dead.

"And we beheld," says John, "His glory, the glory as of the only-begotten of the Father, full of grace and truth." [285] And Paul says, "that He might be the first-born among many brethren." [286]

43.

But should we say, These things made out of nothing are not good things, but only God's nature is good, we shall be unjust to good things of great value.

And there is impiety in calling it a defect in anything not to be what God is, and in denying a thing to be good because it is inferior to God.

Pray submit then, thou nature of the rational soul, to be somewhat less than God, but only so far less, that after Him nothing else is above thee.

Submit, I say, and yield to Him, lest He drive thee still lower into depths where the punishment inflicted will continually detract more and more from the good which thou hast.

Thou exaltest thyself against God, if thou art indignant at His preceding thee; and thou art very contumacious in thy thoughts of Him, if thou dost not rejoice unspeakably in the possession of this good, that He alone is above thee.

This being settled as certain, thou art not to say, God should have made me the only nature: there should be no good thing after me.

It could not be that the next good thing to God should be the last.

And in this is seen most clearly how great dignity God conferred on thee, that He who in the order of nature alone rules over thee, made other good things for thee to rule over.

Nor be surprised that they are not now in all respects subject to thee, and that sometimes they pain thee; for thy Lord has greater authority over the things subject to thee than thou hast, as a master over the servants of his servants.

What wonder, then, if, when thou sinnest, that is, disobeyest thy Lord, the things thou before ruledst over are made instrumental in thy punishment?

For what is so just, or what is more just than God?

For this befell human nature in Adam, of whom this is not the place to speak.

Suffice it to say, the righteous Ruler acts in character both in just rewards and in just punishments, in the happiness of those who live rightly, and in the penalty inflicted on sinners.

Nor yet art thou [287] left without mercy, since by an appointed distribution of things and times thou art called to return. Thus the righteous control of the supreme Creator extends even to earthly good things, which are corrupted and restored, that thou mightest have consolations mingled with punishments; that thou mightest both praise God when delighted by the order of good things, and mightest take refuge in Him when tried by experience of evils.

So, as far as earthly things are subject to thee, they teach thee that thou art their ruler; as far as they distress thee, they teach thee to be subject to thy Lord.

Chapter 38 - Nature Made by God; Corruption Comes from Nothing

44.

In this way, though corruption is an evil, and though it comes not from the Author of natures, but from their being made out of nothing, still, in God's government and control over all that He has made, even corruption is so ordered that it hurts only the lowest natures, for the punishment of the condemned, and for the trial and instruction of the returning, that they may keep near to the incorruptible God, and remain incorrupt, which is our only good; as is said by the prophet, "But it is good for me that I keep near to God." [288] And you must not say, God did not make corruptible natures:

for, as far as they are natures, God made them; but as far as they are corruptible, God did not make them:

for corruption cannot come from Him who alone is incorruptible. If you can receive this, give thanks to God; if you cannot, be quiet and do not condemn what you do not yet understand, but humbly wait on Him who is the light of the mind that thou mayest know.

For in the expression "corruptible nature" there are two words, and not one only. So, in the expression, God made out of nothing, "God" and "nothing" are two separate words.

Render therefore to each of these words that which belongs to each, so that the word "nature" may go with the word "God," and the word "corruptible" with the word "nothing."

And yet even the corruptions, though they have not their origin from God, are to be overruled by Him in accordance with the order of inanimate things and the deserts of His intelligent creatures.

Thus we say rightly that reward and punishment are both from God.

For God's not making corruption is consistent with His giving over to corruption the man who deserves to be corrupted, that is, who has begun to corrupt himself by sinning, that he who has wilfully yielded to the allurements of corruption may, against his will, suffer its pains.

Chapter 39 - In What Sense Evils are from God

45.

Not only is it written in the Old Testament, "I make good, and create evil;" [289] but more clearly in the New Testament, where the Lord says, "Fear not them which kill the body, and have no more that they can do; but fear him who, after he has killed the body, has power to cast the soul into hell." [290] And that to voluntary corruption penal corruption is added in the divine judgment, is plainly declared by the Apostle Paul, when he says, "The temple of God is holy, which temple ye are; whoever corrupts the temple of God, him will God corrupt." [291] If this had been said in the Old Law, how vehemently would the Manichæans have denounced it as making God a corrupter!

And from fear of the word, many Latin translators make it, "him shall God destroy," instead of corrupt, avoiding the offensive word without any change of meaning.

Although these would inveigh against any passage in the Old Law or the prophets if God was called in it a destroyer.

But the Greek original here shows that corrupt is the true word; for it is written distinctly, "Whoever corrupts the temple of God, him will God corrupt."

If the Manichæans are asked to explain the words, they will say, to escape making God a corrupter, that corrupt here means to give over to corruption, or some such explanation.

Did they read the Old Law in this spirit, they would both find many admirable things in it; and instead of spitefully attacking passages which they did not understand, they would reverently postpone the inquiry.

Chapter 40 - Corruption Tends to Non-Existence

46.

But if any one does not believe that corruption comes from nothing, let him place before himself existence and non-existence--one, as it were, on one side, and the other on the other (to speak so as not to outstrip the slow to understand); then let him set something, say the body of an animal, between them, and let him ask himself whether, while the body is being formed and produced, while its size is increasing, while it gains nourishment, health, strength, beauty, stability, it is tending, as regards its duration and permanence, to this side or that, to existence or non-existence.

He will see without difficulty, that even in the rudimentary form there is an existence, and that the more the body is established and built up in form, and figure and strength, the more does it come to exist, and to tend to the side of existence.

Then, again, let the body begin to be corrupted; let its whole condition be enfeebled, let its vigor languish, its strength decay, its beauty be defaced, its framework be sundered, the consistency of its parts give way and go to pieces; and let him ask now where the body is tending in this corruption, whether to existence or non-existence:

he will not surely be so blind or stupid as to doubt how to answer himself, or as not to see that, in proportion as anything is corrupted, in that proportion it approaches decease.

But whatever tends to decease tends to non-existence.

Since, then, we must believe that God exists immutably and incorruptibly, while what is called nothing is clearly altogether nonexistent; and since, after setting before yourself existence and non-existence, you have observed that the more a visible object increases the more it tends towards existence, while the more it is corrupted the more it tends towards non-existence, why are you at a loss to tell regarding any nature what in it is from God, and what from nothing; seeing that visible form is natural, and corruption against nature?

The increase of form leads to existence, and we acknowledge God as supreme existence; the increase of corruption leads to non-existence, and we know that what is non-existent is nothing.

Why then, I say, are you at a loss to tell regarding a corruptible nature, when you have both the words nature and corruptible, what is from God, and what from nothing?

And why do you inquire for a nature contrary to God, since, if you confess that He is the supreme existence, it follows that non-existence is contrary to Him? [292]

Chapter 41 - Corruption is by God's Permission, and Comes from Us

47.

You ask, Why does corruption take from nature what God has given to it?

It takes nothing but where God permits; and He permits in righteous and well-ordered judgment, according to the degrees of non-intelligent and the deserts of intelligent creatures.

The word uttered passes away as an object of sense, and perishes in silence; and yet the coming and going of these passing words make our speech, and the regular intervals of silence give pleasing and appropriate distinction; and so it is with temporal natures which have this lowest form of beauty, that transition gives them being, and the death of what they give birth to gives them individuality.

And if our sense and memory could rightly take in the order and proportions of this beauty, it would so please us, that we should not dare to give the name of corruptions to those imperfections which give rise to the distinction. And when distress comes to us through their peculiar beauty, by the loss of beloved temporal things passing away, we both pay the penalty of our sins, and are exhorted to set our affection on eternal things.

Chapter 42 - Exhortation to the Chief Good

48.

Let us, then, not seek in this beauty for what has not been given to it (and from not having what we seek for, this is the lowest form of beauty); and in that which has been given to it, let us praise God, because He has bestowed this great good of visible form even on the lowest degree of beauty.

And let us not cleave as lovers to this beauty, but as praisers of God let us rise above it; and from this superior position let us pronounce judgment on it, instead of so being bound up in it as to be judged along with it.

And let us hasten on to that good which has no motion in space or advancement in time, from which all natures in space and time receive their sensible being and their form.

To see this good let us purify our heart by faith in our Lord Jesus Christ, who says, "Blessed are the pure in heart, for they shall see God." [293] For the eyes needed in order to see this good are not those with which we see the light spread through space, which has part in one place and part in another, instead of being all in every place.

The sight and the discernment we are to purify is that by which we see, as far as is allowed in this life, what is just, what is pious, what is the beauty of wisdom.

He who sees these things, values them far above the fullness of all regions in space, and finds that the vision of these things requires not the extension of his perception through distances in space, but its invigoration by an immaterial influence. [294]

Chapter 43 - Conclusion

49.

And as this vision is greatly hindered by those fancies which are originated by the carnal sense, and are retained and modified by the imagination, let us abhor this heresy which has been led by faith in its fancies to represent the divine substance as extended and diffused through space, even through infinite space, and to cut short one side so as to make room for evil,--not being able to perceive that evil is not nature, but against nature; and to beautify this very evil with such visible appearance, and forms, and consistency of parts prevailing in its several natures, not being able to conceive of any nature without those good things, that the evils found fault with in it are buried under a countless abundance of good things.

Here let us close this part of the treatise.

The other absurdities of Manichæus will be exposed in what follows, by the permission and help of God. [295]

Footnotes:

263. Written about the year 397.

In his Retractations (ii. 2) Augustin says:

"The book against the Epistle of Manichæus, called Fundamental, refutes only its commencement; but on the other parts of the epistle I have made notes, as required, refuting the whole, and sufficient to recall the argument, had I ever had leisure to write against the whole."

[The Fundamental Epistle seems to have been a sort of hand-book for Manichæan catechumens or Auditors.

In making this document the basis of his attack, Augustin felt that he had selected the best-known and most generally accepted standard of the Manichæan faith.

The tone of the work is conciliatory, yet some very sharp thrusts are made at Manichæan error.

The claims of Mani to be the Paraclete are set aside, and the absurd cosmological fancies of Mani are ruthlessly exposed.

Dualism is combated with substantially the same weapons as in the treatise Concerning Two Souls.

We could wish that the author had found time to finish the treatise, and had thus preserved for us more of the Fundamental Epistle itself.

This work was written after the author had become Bishop of Hippo.--A.H.N.]

264. 2 Tim. ii. 24, 25.
265. Mal. iv. 2.
266. John i. 9.
267. [This is one of the earliest distinct assertions of the dependence of the Scriptures for authority on the Church.--A.H.N.]
268. Matt. x. 2-4; Mark iii. 13-19; Luke vi. 13-18.
269. Acts i. 26.
270. Acts ix.
271. John xiv. 16.
272. John x. 30.
273. Acts i. 1-8.
274. Acts ii. 1-13.
275. John vii. 39.
276. John xx. 22.
277. [This is, of course, fanciful; but is quite in accordance with the exegetical methods of the time.--A.H.N.]
278. [The Manichæans assumed the role of rationalists, and scorned the credulity of ordinary believers.

Yet they required in their followers an amount of credulity which only persons of a peculiar turn of mind could furnish.

The same thing applies to modern rationalistic anti-Christian systems.

The fact is, that it requires infinitely less credulity to believe in historical Christianity than to disbelieve in it.--A.H.N.]
279. [Compare the fuller account from the Fihrist in the Introduction.--A.H.N.]
280. [This exalted view of God Augustin held in common with the Neo-Platonists.--A.H.N.]
281. [Modern mental physiologists differ among themselves as regards the presence of the mind throughout the entire nervous system; some maintaining the view here presented, and others making the brain to be the seat of sensation, and the nerves telegraphic lines, so to speak, for the communication of impressions from the various parts of the body to the brain.

Compare Carpenter:

Mental Physiology, and Calderwood: Mind and Brain.--A.H.N.]
282. [There is sufficient reason to think that Mani identified God with the kingdom and the region of light.

See Introduction.--A.H.N.]
283. [This discussion of the lines bounding the Kingdom of Light and the Kingdom of Darkness seems very much like trifling, but Augustin's aim was to bring the Manichæan representations into ridicule.--

A.H.N.]

284. [This portion of the argument is conducted with great adroitness.

Augustin takes the inhabitants of the region of darkness, as Mani describes them, and proves that they possess so much of good that they can have no other author than God.--A.H.N.]

285. John i. 14.

286. Rom. viii. 29.

287. [Augustin still addresses himself to the "nature of the rational soul."--A.H.N.]

288. Ps. lxxiii. 28.

289. Ps. xlv. 7.

290. Matt. x. 28, and Luke xii. 4.

291. 1 Cor. iii. 17.

292. [We have already encountered in the treatise Concerning two Souls, substantially the same course of argumentation here pursued. The doctrine of the negativity of evil may be said to have been fundamental with Augustin, and he uses it very effectually against Manichæan dualism.--A.H.N.]

293. Matt. v. 8.

294. [The Neo-Platonic quality of this section cannot escape the attention of the philosophical student.--A.H.N.]

295. Vide Preface.

Reply to Faustus the Manichæan

[contra faustum manichæum].
A.D. 400.
translated by rev. richard stothert, m.a.,
bombay

[Faustus was undoubtedly the acutest, most determined and most unscrupulous opponent of orthodox Christianity in the age of Augustin.

The occasion of Augustin's great writing against him was the publication of Faustus' attack on the Old Testament Scriptures, and on the New Testament so far as it was at variance with Manichæan error.

Faustus seems to have followed in the footsteps of Adimantus, against whom Augustin had written some years before, but to have gone considerably beyond Adimantus in the recklessness of his statements.

The incarnation of Christ, involving his birth from a woman, is one of the main points of attack.

He makes the variations in the genealogical records of the Gospels a ground for rejecting the whole as spurious.

He supposed the Gospels, in their present form, to be not the works of the Apostles, but rather of later Judaizing falsifiers.

The entire Old Testament system he treats with the utmost contempt, blaspheming the Patriarchs, Moses, the Prophets, etc., on the ground of their private lives and their teachings.

Most of the objections to the morality of the Old Testament that are now current were already familiarly used in the time of Augustin.

Augustin's answers are only partially satisfactory, owing to his imperfect view of the relation of the old dispensation to the new; but in the age in which they were written they were doubtless very effective.

The writing is interesting from the point of view of Biblical criticism, as well as from that of polemics against Manichæism.--A.H.N.]

Book I - Who Faustus was

Faustus's object in writing the polemical treatise that forms the basis of Augustin's reply. Augustin's remarks thereon.

1.

Faustus was an African by race, a citizen of Mileum; he was eloquent and clever, but had adopted the shocking tenets of the Manichæan heresy.

He is mentioned in my Confessions, [296] where there is an account of my acquaintance with him.

This man published a certain volume against the true Christian faith and the Catholic truth.

A copy reached us, and was read by the brethren, who called for an answer from me, as part of the service of love which I owe to them. Now, therefore, in the name and with the help of our Lord and Saviour Jesus Christ, I undertake the task, that all my readers may know that acuteness of mind and elegance of style are of no use to a man unless the Lord directs his steps. [297] In the mysterious equity of divine mercy, God often bestows His help on the slow and the feeble; while from the want of this help, the most acute and eloquent run into error only with greater rapidity and willfulness.

I will give the opinions of Faustus as if stated by himself, and mine as if in reply to him.

2.

Faustus said:
As the learned Adimantus, the only teacher since the sainted Manichæus deserving of our

attention, has plentifully exposed and thoroughly refuted the errors of Judaism and of semi-Christianity, I think it not amiss that you should be supplied in writing with brief and pointed replies to the captious objections of our adversaries, that when, like children of the wily serpent, they try to bewilder you with their quibbles, you may be prepared to give intelligent answers.

In this way they will be kept to the subject, instead of wandering from one thing to another.

And I have placed our opinions and those of our opponent over against one another, as plainly and briefly as possible, so as not to perplex the reader with a long and intricate discourse.

3.

Augustin replies:

You warn against semi-Christians, which you say we are; but we warn against pseudo-Christians, which we have shown you to be.

Semi-Christianity may be imperfect without being false.

So, then, if the faith of those whom you try to mislead is imperfect, would it not be better to supply what is lacking than to rob them of what they have?

It was to imperfect Christians that the apostle wrote, "joying and beholding your conversation," and "the deficiency in your faith in Christ." [298] The apostle had in view a spiritual structure, as he says elsewhere, "Ye are God's building;" [299] and in this structure he found both a reason for joy and a reason for exertion.

He rejoiced to see part already finished; and the necessity of bringing the edifice to perfection called for exertion.

Imperfect Christians as we are, you pursue us with the desire to pervert what you call our semi-Christianity by false doctrine; while even those who are so deficient in faith as to be unable to reply to all your sophisms, are wise enough at least to know that they must not have anything at all to do with you.

You look for semi-Christians to deceive:

we wish to prove you pseudo-Christians, that Christians may learn something from your refutation, and that the less advanced may learn to avoid you.

Do you call us children of the serpent?

You have surely forgotten how often you have found fault with the prohibition in Paradise, and have praised the serpent for opening Adam's eyes.

You have the better claim to the title which you give us.

The serpent owns you as well when you blame him as when you praise him.

Book II - Faustus claims to believe the Gospel, yet refuses to accept the genealogical tables on various grounds which Augustin seeks to set aside

1.

Faustus said:

Do I believe the gospel?

Certainly.

Do I therefore believe that Christ was born?

Certainly not.

It does not follow that because I believe the gospel, as I do, I must therefore believe that Christ was born.

This I do not believe; because Christ does not say that He was born of men, and the gospel, both in name and in fact, begins with Christ's preaching.

As for the genealogy, the author himself does not venture to call it the gospel.

For what did he write?

"The book of the generation of Jesus Christ the Son of David." [300] The book of the generation is not the book of the gospel.

It is more like a birth-register, the star confirming the event.

Mark, on the other hand, who recorded the preaching of the Son of God, without any genealogy, begins most suitably with the words, "The gospel of Jesus Christ the Son of God."

It is plain that the genealogy is not the gospel.

Matthew himself says, that after John was put in prison, Jesus began to preach the gospel of the kingdom; so that what is mentioned before this is the genealogy, and not the gospel.

Why did not Matthew begin with, "The gospel of Jesus Christ the Son of God," but because he thought it sinful to call the genealogy the gospel? Understand, then, what you have hitherto overlooked --the distinction between the genealogy and the gospel.

Do I then admit the truth of the gospel?

Yes; understanding by the gospel the preaching of Christ.

I have plenty to say about the generations too, if you wish.

But you seem to me now to wish to know not whether I accept the gospel, but whether I accept the generations.

2.

Augustin replied:

Well, in answer to your own questions, you tell us first that you believe the gospel, and next, that you do not believe in the birth of Christ; and your reason is, that the birth of Christ is not in the gospel.

What, then, will you answer the apostle when he says, "Remember that Christ Jesus rose from the dead, of the seed of David, according to my gospel?" [301]You surely are ignorant, or pretend to be ignorant, what the gospel is.

You use the word, not as the apostle teaches, but as suits your own errors.

What the apostles call the gospel you depart from; for you do not believe that Christ was of the seed of David.

This was Paul's gospel; and it was also the gospel of the other apostles, and of all faithful stewards of so great a mystery.

For Paul says elsewhere, "Whether, therefore, I or they, so we preach, and so ye believed." [302]They did not all write the gospel, but they all preached it.

The name evangelist is properly given to the narrators of the birth, the actions, the words, the sufferings of our Lord Jesus Christ.

The word gospel means good news, and might be used of any good news, but is properly applied to the narrative of the Saviour.

If, then, you teach something different, you must have departed from the gospel.

Assuredly those babes whom you despise as semi-Christians will oppose you, when they hear their mother Charity declaring by the mouth of the apostle, "If any one preach another gospel than that which we have preached to you, let him be accursed." [303]Since, then, Paul, according to his gospel, preached that Christ was of the seed of David, and you deny this and preach something else, may you be accursed!

And what can you mean by saying that Christ never declares Himself to have been born of men, when on every occasion He calls Himself the Son of man?

3.

You learned men, forsooth, dress up for our benefit some wonderful First Man, who came down from the race of light to war with the race of darkness, armed with his waters against the waters of the enemy, and with his fire against their fire, and with his winds against their winds.

And why not with his smoke against their smoke, and with his darkness against their darkness?

According to you, he was armed against smoke with air, and against darkness with light.

So it appears that smoke and darkness are bad, since they could not belong to his goodness.

The other three, again--water, wind, and fire--are good. How, then, could these belong to the evil of the enemy?

You reply that the water of the race of darkness was evil, while that which the First Man brought was good; and so, too, his good wind and fire fought against the evil wind and fire of the adversary.

But why could he not bring good smoke against evil smoke?

Your falsehoods seem to vanish in smoke.

Well, your First Man warred against an opposite nature.

And yet only one of the five things he brought was the opposite of what the hostile race had. The light was opposed to the darkness, but the four others are not opposed to one another.

Air is not the opposite of smoke, and still less is water the opposite of water, or wind of wind, or fire of fire.

4.

One is shocked at your wild fancies about this First Man changing the elements which he brought, that he might conquer his enemies by pleasing them.

So you make what you call the kingdom of falsehood keep honestly to its own nature, while truth is changeable in order to deceive.

Jesus Christ, according to you, is the son of this First Man.

Truth springs, forsooth, from your fiction.

You praise this First Man for using changeable and delusive forms in the contest.

If you, then, speak the truth, you do not imitate him.

If you imitate him, you deceive as he did.

But our Lord and Saviour Jesus Christ, the true and truthful Son of God, the true and truthful Son of man, both of which He testifies of Himself, derived the eternity of His godhead from true God, and His incarnation from true man.

Your First Man is not the first man of the apostle.

"The first man," he says, "was of the earth, earthy; the second man is from heaven, heavenly.

As is the earthy, such are they also that are earthy; as is the heavenly, such are they also that are heavenly.

As we have borne the image of the earthy, let us also bear the image of the heavenly."[304]The first man of the earth, earthy, is Adam, who was made of dust.

The second man from heaven, heavenly, is the Lord Jesus Christ; for, being the Son of God, He became flesh that He might be a man outwardly, while He remained God within; that He might be both the true Son of God, by whom we were made, and the true Son of man, by whom we are made anew.

Why do you conjure up this fabulous First Man of yours, and refuse to acknowledge the first man of the apostle?

Is this not a fulfillment of what the apostle says:

"Turning away their ears from the truth, they will give heed to fables?" [305]According to Paul, the first man is of the earth, earthy; according to Manichæus, he is not earthy, and is equipped with five elements of some unreal, unintelligible kind.

Paul says:

"If any one should have announced to you differently from what we have announced let him be accursed."

Therefore lest Paul be a liar, let Manichæus be accursed.

5.

Again, you find fault with the star by which the Magi were led to worship the infant Christ, which you should be ashamed of doing, when you represent your fabulous Christ, the son of your fabulous First Man not as announced by a star, but as bound up in all the stars. [306] For you say that he mingled with the principles of darkness in his conflict with the race of darkness, that by capturing these principles the world might be made out of the mixture.

So that, by your profane fancies, Christ is not only mingled with heaven and all the stars, but conjoined and compounded with the earth and all its productions, [307] --a Saviour no more, but needing to be saved by you, by your eating and disgorging Him.

This foolish custom of making your disciples bring you food, that your teeth and stomach may be the means of relieving Christ, who is bound up in it, is a consequence of your profane fancies.

You declare that Christ is liberated in this way--not, however, entirely; for you hold that some tiny particles of no value still remain in the excrement, to be mixed up and compounded again and again in various material forms, and to be released and purified at any rate by the fire in which the world will be burned up, if not before.

Nay, even then, you say, Christ is not entirely liberated; but some extreme particles of His good and divine nature, which have been so defiled that they cannot be cleansed, are condemned to stay for ever in the horrid mass of darkness.

And these people pretend to be offended with our saying that a star announced the birth of the Son of God, as if this were placing His birth under the influence of a constellation; while they subject Him not to stars only, but to such polluting contact with all material things, with the juices of all vegetables, and with the decay of all flesh, and with the decomposition of all food, in which He is bound up, that the only way of releasing Him, at least one great means, is that men, that is the Elect of the Manichæans, should succeed in digesting their dinner.

We, too, deny the influence of the stars upon the birth of any man; for we maintain that, by the just law of God, the free-will of man, which chooses good or evil, is under no constraint of necessity.

How much less do we subject to any constellation the incarnation of the eternal Creator and Lord of all!

When Christ was born after the flesh, the star which the Magi saw had no power as governing, but attended as a witness.

Instead of assuming control over Him, it acknowledged Him by the homage it did.

Besides, this star was not one of those which from the beginning of the world continue in the course ordained by the Creator.

Along with the new birth from the Virgin appeared a new star, which served as a guide to the Magi who were themselves seeking for Christ; for it went before them till they reached the place where they found the Word of God in the form of a child.

But what astrologer ever thought of making a star leave its course, and come down to the child that is born, as they imagine, under it?

They think that the stars affect the birth, not that the birth changes the course of the stars; so, if the star in the Gospel was one of those heavenly bodies, how could it determine Christ's action, when it was compelled to change its own action at Christ's birth?

But if, as is more likely, a star which did not exist before appeared to point out Christ, it was the effect of Christ's birth, and not the cause of it.

Christ was not born because the star was there; but the star was there because Christ was born.

If there was any fate, it was in the birth, and not in the star.

The word fate is derived from a word which means to speak; and since Christ is the Word of God by which all things were spoken before they were, the conjunction of stars is not the fate of Christ, but Christ is the fate of the stars.

The same will that made the heavens took our earthly nature.

The same power that ruled the stars laid down His life and took it again.

6.

Why, then, should the narrative of the birth not be the gospel, since it conveys such good news as heals our malady?

Is it because Matthew begins, not like Mark, with the words, "The beginning of the gospel of Jesus Christ," but, "The book of the generation of Jesus Christ?"

In this way, John, too, might be said not to have written the gospel, for he has not the words, Beginning of the gospel, or Book of the gospel, but, "In the beginning was the Word."

Perhaps the clever word-maker Faustus will call the introduction in John a Verbidium, as he called that in Matthew a Genesidium.

The wonder is, that you are so impudent as to give the name of gospel to your silly stories.

What good news is there in telling us that, in the conflict against some strange hostile nation, God could protect His own kingdom only by sending part of His own nature into the greedy jaws of the former, and to be so defiled, that after all those toils and tortures it cannot all be purged?

Is this bad news the gospel?

Every one who has even a slender knowledge of Greek knows that gospel means good news.

But where is your good news, when your God himself is said to weep as under eclipse till the darkness and defilement are removed from his members? And when he ceases to weep, it seems he becomes cruel.

For what has that part of him which is to be involved in the mass done to deserve this condemnation?

This part must go on weeping for ever.

But no; whoever examines this news will not weep because it is bad, but will laugh because it is not true.

Book III - Faustus objects to the incarnation of God on the ground that the evangelists are at variance with each other, and that incarnation is unsuitable to deity

Augustin attempts to remove the critical and theological difficulties.

1.

Faustus said:

Do I believe in the incarnation?

For my part, this is the very thing I long tried to persuade myself of, that God was born; but the discrepancy in the genealogies of Luke and Matthew stumbled me, as I knew not which to follow.

For I thought it might happen that, from not being omniscient, I might take the true for false, and the false for true.

So, in despair of settling this dispute, I betook myself to Mark and John, two authorities still, and evangelists as much as the others.

I approved with good reason of the beginning of Mark and John, for they have nothing of David, or Mary, or Joseph.

John says, "In the beginning was the Word, and the Word was with God, and the Word was God," meaning Christ.

Mark says, "The gospel of Jesus Christ, the Son of God," as if correcting Matthew, who calls him the Son of David.

Perhaps, however, the Jesus of Matthew is a different person from the Jesus of Mark.

This is my reason for not believing in the birth of Christ.

Remove this difficulty, if you can, by harmonizing the accounts, and I am ready to yield.

In any case, however, it is hardly consistent to believe that God, the God of Christians, was born from the womb.

2.

Augustin replied:

Had you read the Gospel with care, and inquired into those places where you found opposition, instead of rashly condemning them, you would have seen that the recognition of the authority of the evangelists by so many learned men all over the world, in spite of this most obvious discrepancy, proves that there is more in it than appears at first sight.

Any one can see, as well as you, that the ancestors of Christ in Matthew and Luke are different; while Joseph appears in both, at the end in Matthew and at the beginning in Luke. Joseph, it is plain, might be called the father of Christ, on account of his being in a certain sense the husband of the mother of Christ; and so his name, as the male representative, appears at the beginning or end of the genealogies.

Any one can see as well as you that Joseph has one father in Matthew and another in Luke, and so with the grandfather and with all the rest up to David.

Did all the able and learned men, not many Latin writers certainly, but innumerable Greek, who have examined most attentively the sacred Scriptures, overlook this manifest difference?

Of course they saw it.

No one can help seeing it.

But with a due regard to the high authority of Scripture, they believed that there was something here which would be given to those that ask, and denied to those that snarl; would be found by those that seek, and taken away from those that criticise; would be open to those that knock, and shut against those that contradict.

They asked, sought, and knocked; they received, found, and entered in.

3.

The whole question is how Joseph had two fathers.

Supposing this possible, both genealogies may be correct.

With two fathers, why not two grandfathers, and two great-grandfathers, and so on, up to David, who was the father both of Solomon, who is mentioned in Matthew's list, and of Nathan, who occurs in Luke?

This is the difficulty with many people who think it impossible that two men should have one and the same son, forgetting the very obvious fact that a man may be called the son of the person who adopted him as well as of the person who begot him.

Adoption, we know, was familiar to the ancients; for even women adopted the children of other women, as Sarah adopted Ishmael, and Leah her handmaid's son, and Pharaoh's daughter Moses.

Jacob, too, adopted his grandsons, the children of Joseph.

Moreover, the word adoption is of great importance in the system of our faith, as is seen from the apostolic writings.

For the Apostle Paul, speaking of the advantages of the Jews, says:

"Whose are the adoption, and the glory, and the covenants, and the giving of the law; whose are the fathers, and of whom, according to the flesh, Christ came, who is over all, God blessed for ever." [308] And again:

"We ourselves also groan within ourselves, waiting for the adoption of the sons of God, even the redemption of the body." [309] Again, elsewhere:

"But in the fullness of time, God sent His Son, made of a woman, made under the law, that we might receive the adoption of sons." [310] These passages show clearly that adoption is a significant symbol.

God has an only Son, whom He begot from His own substance, of whom it is said, "Being in the form of God, He thought it not robbery to be equal to God." [311]Us He begot not of His own substance, for we belong to the creation which is not begotten, but made; but that He might make us the brothers of Christ, He adopted us.

That act, then, by which God, when we were not born of Him, but created and formed, begot us by His word and grace, is called adoption.

So John says, "He gave them power to become the sons of God." [312]

Since, therefore; the practice of adoption is common among our fathers, and in Scripture, is there not irrational profanity in the hasty condemnation of the evangelists as false because the genealogies are different, as if both could not be true, instead of considering calmly the simple fact that frequently in human life one man may have two fathers, one of whose flesh he is born, and another of whose will he is afterwards made a son by adoption?

If the second is not rightly called father, neither are we right in saying, "Our Father which art in heaven," to Him of whose substance we were not born, but of whose grace and most merciful will we were adopted, according to apostolic doctrine, and truth most sure.

For one is to us God, and Lord, and Father:

God, for by Him we are created, though of human parents; Lord, for we are His subjects; Father, for by His adoption we are born again.

Careful students of sacred Scripture easily saw, from a little consideration, how, in the different genealogies of the two evangelists, Joseph had two fathers, and consequently two lists of ancestors.

You might have seen this too, if you had not been blinded by the love of contradiction.

Other things far beyond your understanding have been discovered in the careful investigation of all parts of these narratives.

The familiar occurrence of one man begetting a son and another adopting him, so that one man has two fathers, you might, in spite of Manichæan error, have thought of as an explanation, if you had not been reading in a hostile spirit.

4.

But why Matthew begins with Abraham and descends to Joseph, while Luke begins with Joseph and ascends, not to Abraham, but to God, who made man, and, by giving a commandment, gave him power to become, by believing, a son of God; and why Matthew records the generations at the commencement of his book, Luke after the baptism of the Saviour by John; and what is the meaning of the number of the generations in Matthew, who divides them into three sections of fourteen each, though in the whole sum there appears to be one wanting; while in Luke the number of generations recorded after the baptism amount to seventy-seven, which number the Lord Himself enjoins in connection with the forgiveness of sins, saying, "Not only seven times, but seventy-seven times;"--these things you will never understand, unless either you are taught by some Catholic of superior stamp, who has studied the sacred Scriptures, and has made all the progress possible, or you yourselves turn from your error, and in a Christian spirit ask that you may receive, seek that you may find, and knock that it may be opened to you.

5.

Since, then, this double fatherhood of nature and adoption removes the difficulty arising from the discrepancy of the genealogies, there is no occasion for Faustus to leave the two evangelists and betake himself to the other two, which would be a greater affront to those he betook himself to than to those he left.

For the sacred writers do not desire to be favored at the expense of their brethren.

For their joy is in union, and they are one in Christ; and if one says one thing, and another another, or one in one way and another in another, still they all speak truth, and in no way contradict one another; only let the reader be reverent and humble, not in an heretical spirit seeking occasion for strife, but with a believing heart desiring edification. Now, in this opinion that the evangelists give the ancestors of different fathers, as it is quite possible for a man to have two fathers, there is nothing inconsistent with truth.

So the evangelists are harmonized, and you, by Faustus's promise are bound to yield at once.

6.

You may perhaps be troubled by that additional remark which he makes:

"In any case, however, it is hardly consistent to believe that God, the God of Christians, was born from the womb."

As if we believed that the divine nature came from the womb of a woman.

Have I not just quoted the testimony of the apostle, speaking of the Jews:

"Whose are the fathers, and of whom, according to the flesh, Christ came, who is God over all, blessed for ever?"

Christ, therefore, our Lord and Saviour, true Son of God in His divinity, and true son of man according to the flesh, not as He is God over all was born of a woman, but in that feeble nature which He took of us, that in it He might die for us, and heal it in us:

not as in the form of God, in which He thought it not robbery to be equal to God, was He born of a woman, but in the form of a servant, in taking which He emptied Himself.

He is therefore said to have emptied Himself because He took the form of a servant, not because He lost the form of God.

For in the unchangeable possession of that nature by which in the form of God He is equal to the Father, He took our changeable nature, by which He might be born of a virgin. You, while you protest against putting the flesh of Christ in a virgin's womb, place the very divinity of God in the womb not only of human beings, but of dogs and swine.

You refuse to believe that the flesh of Christ was conceived in the Virgin's womb, in which God was not found nor even changed; while you assert that in all men and beasts, in the seed of male and in the womb of female, in all conceptions on land or in water, an actual part of God and the divine nature is continually bound, and shut up, and contaminated, never to be wholly set free.[313]

Book IV - Faustus's reasons for rejecting the Old Testament, and Augustin's animadversions thereon

1.

Faustus said:

Do I believe the Old Testament?

If it bequeaths anything to me, I believe it; if not, I reject it.

It would be an excess of forwardness to take the documents of others which pronounce me disinherited.

Remember that the promise of Canaan in the Old Testament is made to Jews, that is, to the circumcised, who offer sacrifice, and abstain from swine's flesh, and from the other animals which Moses pronounces unclean, and observe Sabbaths, and the feast of unleavened bread, and other things of the same kind which the author of the Testament enjoined.

Christians have not adopted these observances, and no one keeps them; so that if we will not take the inheritance, we should surrender the documents.

This is my first reason for rejecting the Old Testament, unless you teach me better.

My second reason is, that this inheritance is such a poor fleshly thing, without any spiritual blessings, that after the New Testament, and its glorious promise of the kingdom of heaven and eternal life, I think it not worth the taking.

2.

Augustin replied:

No one doubts that promises of temporal things are contained in the Old Testament, for which reason it is called the Old Testament; or that the kingdom of heaven and the promise of eternal life belong to the New Testament.

But that in these temporal things were figures of future things which should be fulfilled in us upon whom the ends of the ages are come, is not my fancy, but the judgment of the apostle, when he says of such things, "These things were our examples;" and again, "These things happened to them for an example, and they are written for us on whom the ends of the ages are come." [314]We receive the Old Testament, therefore, not in order to obtain the fulfillment of these promises, but to see in them predictions of the New Testament; for the Old bears witness to the New.

Whence the Lord, after He rose from the dead, and allowed His disciples not only to see but to handle Him, still, lest they should doubt their mortal and fleshly senses, gave them further confirmation from the testimony of the ancient books, saying, "It was necessary that all things should be fulfilled which were written in the law of Moses, and in the Prophets and Psalms, concerning me." [315]

Our hope, therefore, rests not on the promise of temporal things.

Nor do we believe that the holy and spiritual men of these times--the patriarchs and prophets--were taken up with earthly things.

For they understood, by the revelation of the Spirit of God, what was suitable for that time, and how God appointed all these sayings and actions as types and predictions of the future. Their great desire was for the New Testament; but they had a personal duty to perform in those predictions, by which the new things of the future were foretold.

So the life as well as the tongue of these men was prophetic.

The carnal people, indeed, thought only of present blessings, though even in connection with the people there were prophecies of the future.

These things you do not understand, because, as the prophet said, "Unless you believe, you shall not understand." [316]For you are not instructed in the kingdom of heaven,--that is, in the true Catholic Church of Christ.

If you were, you would bring forth from the treasure of the sacred Scriptures things old as well as new.

For the Lord Himself says, "Therefore every scribe instructed in the kingdom of heaven is like an householder who brings forth from his treasure things new and old." [317]And so, while you profess to receive only the new promises of God, you have retained the oldness of the flesh, adding only the novelty of error; of which novelty the apostle says, "Shun profane novelties of words, for they increase unto more ungodliness, and their speech eats like a cancer.

Of whom is Hymenæus and Philetus, who concerning the faith have erred, saying that the resurrection is past already, and have overthrown the faith of some." [318]Here you see the source of your false doctrine, in teaching that the resurrection is only of souls by the preaching of the truth, and that there will be no resurrection of the body.

But how can you understand spiritual things of the inner man, who is renewed in the knowledge of God, when in the oldness of the flesh, if you do not possess temporal things, you concoct fanciful notions about them in those images of carnal things of which the whole of your false doctrine consists?

You boast of despising as worthless the land of Canaan, which was an actual thing, and actually given to the Jews; and yet you tell of a land of light cut asunder on one side, as by a narrow wedge, by the land of the race of darkness,--a thing which does not exist, and which you believe from the delusion of your minds; so that your life is not supported by having it, and your mind is wasted in desiring it. [319]

Book V - Faustus claims that the Manichæans and not the Catholics are consistent believers in the Gospel, and seeks to establish this claim by comparing Manichæan and Catholic obedience to the precepts of the Gospel. Augustin exposes the hypocrisy of the Manichæans and praises the asceticism of Catholics

1.
    Faustus said:
    Do I believe the gospel?
    You ask me if I believe it, though my obedience to its commands shows that I do.
    I should rather ask you if you believe it, since you give no proof of your belief.
    I have left my father, mother, wife, and children, and all else that the gospel requires; [320] and do you ask if I believe the gospel?
    Perhaps you do not know what is called the gospel.
    The gospel is nothing else than the preaching and the precept of Christ.
    I have parted with all gold and silver, and have left off carrying money in my purse; content

with daily food; without anxiety for tomorrow; and without solicitude about how I shall be fed, or where-withal I shall be clothed:

and do you ask if I believe the gospel?

You see in me the blessings of the gospel; [321] and do you ask if I believe the gospel? You see me poor, meek, a peacemaker, pure in heart, mourning, hungering, thirsting, bearing persecutions and enmity for righteousness' sake; and do you doubt my belief in the gospel?

One can understand now how John the Baptist, after seeing Jesus, and also hearing of His works, yet asked whether He was Christ.

Jesus properly and justly did not deign to reply that He was; but reminded him of the works of which he had already heard:

"The blind see, the deaf hear, the dead are raised." [322] In the same way, I might very well reply to your question whether I believe the gospel, by saying, I have left all, father, mother, wife, children, gold, silver, eating, drinking, luxuries, pleasures; take this as a sufficient answer to your questions, and believe that you will be blessed if you are not offended in me. [323]

2.

But, according to you, to believe the gospel is not only to obey its commands, but also to believe in all that is written in it; and, first of all, that God was born.

But neither is believing the gospel only to believe that Jesus was born, but also to do what He commands. So, if you say that I do not believe the gospel because I disbelieve the incarnation, much more do you not believe because you disregard the commandments.

At any rate, we are on a par till these questions are settled.

If your disregard of the precepts does not prevent you from professing faith in the gospel, why should my rejection of the genealogy prevent me?

And if, as you say, to believe the gospel includes both faith in the genealogies and obedience to the precepts, why do you condemn me, since we both are imperfect?

What one wants the other has.

But if, as there can be no doubt, belief in the gospel consists solely in obedience to the commands of God, your sin is twofold.

As the proverb says, the deserter accuses the soldier.

But suppose, since you will have it so, that there are these two parts of perfect faith, one consisting in word, or the confession that Christ was born, the other in deed or the observance of the precepts; it is plain that my part is hard and painful, yours light and easy.

It is natural that the multitude should flock to you and away from me, for they know not that the kingdom of God is not in word, but in power. Why, then, do you blame me for taking the harder part, and leaving to you, as to a weak brother, the easy part?

You have the idea that your part of faith, or confessing that Christ was born, has more power to save the soul than the other parts.

3.

Let us then ask Christ Himself, and learn from His own mouth, what is the chief means of our salvation.

Who shall enter, O Christ, into Thy kingdom?

He that doeth the will of my Father in heaven, [324] is His reply; not, "He that confesses that I was born."

And again, He says to His disciples, "Go, teach all nations, baptizing them in the name of the Father, and of the Son, and of the Holy Ghost, teaching them to observe all things which I have commanded you." [325] It is not, "teaching them that I was born," but, "to observe my commandments."

Again, "Ye are my friends if ye do what I command you;" [326] not, "if you believe that I was born."

Again, "If ye keep my commandments, ye shall abide in my love," [327] and in many other places.

Also in the sermon on the mount, when He taught, "Blessed are the poor, blessed are the meek, blessed are the peacemakers, blessed are the pure in heart, blessed are they that mourn, blessed are they that hunger, blessed are they that are persecuted for righteousness' sake," [328] He nowhere says, "Blessed are they that confess that I was born."

And in the separation of the sheep from the goats in the judgment, He says that He will say to them on the right hand, "I was hungry, and ye gave me meat; I was thirsty, and ye gave me drink," [329] and so on; therefore "inherit the kingdom."

Not, "Because ye believe that I was born, inherit the kingdom."

Again, to the rich man seeking for eternal life, He says, "Go, sell all that thou hast, and follow me;"[330] not, "Believe that I was born, that you may have eternal life."

You see, the kingdom, life, happiness, are everywhere promised to the part I have chosen of what you call the two parts of faith, and nowhere to your part.

Show, if you can, a place where it is written that whoso confesses that Christ was born of a woman is blessed, or shall inherit the kingdom, or have eternal life.

Even supposing, then, that there are two parts of faith, your part has no blessing.

But what if we prove that your part is not a part of faith at all?

It will follow that you are foolish, which indeed will be proved beyond a doubt.

At present, it is enough to have shown that our part is crowned with the beatitudes.

Besides, we have also a beatitude for a confession in words:

for we confess that Jesus Christ is the Son of the living God; and Jesus declares with His own lips that this confession has a benediction, when He says to Peter, "Blessed art thou, Simon Barjona; for flesh and blood hath not revealed this unto thee, but my Father which is in heaven."[331] So that we have not one, but both these parts of faith, and in both alike are we pronounced blessed by Christ; for in one we reduce faith to practice, while in the other our confession is unmixed with blasphemy.

4.

Augustin replied:

I have already said that the Lord Jesus Christ repeatedly calls Himself the Son of man, and that the Manichæans have contrived a silly story about some fabulous First Man, who figures in their impious heresy, not earthly, but combined with spurious elements, in opposition to the apostle, who says, "The first man is of the earth, earthy;"[332] and that the apostle carefully warns us, "If any one preaches to you differently from what we have preached, let him be accursed."[333] So that we must believe Christ to be the Son of man according to apostolic truth, not according to Manichæan error.

And since the evangelists assert that Christ was born of a woman, of the seed of David, and Paul writing to Timothy says, "Remember that Jesus Christ, of the seed of David, was raised from the dead, according to my gospel,"[334] it is clear what sense we must believe Christ to be the Son of man; for being the Son of God by whom we were made, He also by His incarnation became the Son of man, that He might die for our sins, and rise again for our justification.[335] Accordingly He calls Himself both Son of God and Son of man.

To take only one instance out of many, in the Gospel of John it is written, "Verily, verily, I say unto you, The hour cometh, and now is, when the dead shall hear the voice of the Son of God; and they that hear shall live.

For as the Father hath life in Himself, so He hath given to the Son to have life in Himself; and hath given Him power to execute judgment also, because He is the Son of man."[336] He says, "They shall hear the voice of the Son of God;" and He says, "because He is the Son of man."

As the Son of man, He has received power to execute judgment, because He will come to judgment in human form, that He may be seen by the good and the wicked.

In this form He ascended into heaven, and that voice was heard by His disciples, "He shall so come as ye have seen Him go into heaven."[337] As the Son of God, as God equal to and one with the Father, He will not be seen by the wicked; for "blessed are the pure in heart, for they shall see God."

Since, then, He promises eternal life to those that believe in Him, and since to believe in Him is to believe in the true Christ, such as He declares Himself and His apostles declare Him to be, true Son of God and true Son of man; you, Manichæans, who believe on a false and spurious son of a false and spurious man, and teach that God Himself, from fear of the assault of the hostile race, gave up His own members to be tortured, and after all not to be wholly liberated, are plainly far from that eternal life which Christ promises to those who believe in Him.

It is true, He said to Peter when he confessed Him to be the Son of God, "Blessed art thou, Simon. Barjona."

But does He promise nothing to those who believe Him to be the Son of man, when the Son of God and the Son of man are the same?

Besides, eternal life is expressly promised to those who believe in the Son of man.

"As Moses," He says, "lifted up the serpent in the wilderness, so must the Son of man be lifted up, that whosoever believeth in Him should not perish, but have eternal life."[338] What more do you wish?

Believe then in the Son of man, that you may have eternal life; for He is also the Son of God, who can give eternal life:

for He is "the true God and eternal life," as the same John says in his epistle.

John also adds, that he is antichrist who denies that Christ has come in the flesh.[339]

5.

There is no need, then that you should extol so much the perfection of Christ's commands, because you obey the precepts of the gospel.

For the precepts, supposing you really to fulfill them, would not profit you without true faith.

Do you not know that the apostle says, "If I distribute all my goods to the poor, and give my body to be burned, and have not charity, it profiteth me nothing?" [340]Why do you boast of having Christian poverty, when you are destitute of Christian charity? Robbers have a kind of charity to one another, arising from a mutual consciousness of guilt and crime; but this is not the charity commended by the apostle.

In another passage he distinguishes true charity from all base and vicious affections, by saying, "Now the end of the commandment is charity out of a pure heart, and a good conscience, and faith unfeigned." [341]How then can you have true charity from a fictitious faith? [342]You persist in a faith corrupted by falsehood:

for your First Man, according to you, used deceit in the conflict by changing his form, while his enemies remained in their own nature; and, besides, you maintain that Christ, who says, "I am the truth," feigned His incarnation, His death on the cross, the wounds of His passion, the marks shown after His resurrection.

If you speak the truth, and your Christ speaks falsehood, you must be better than he. But if you really follow your own Christ, your truthfulness may be doubted, and your obedience to the precepts you speak of may be only a pretence.

Is it true, as Faustus says, that you have no money in your purses?

He means, probably, that your money is in boxes and bags; nor would we blame you for this, if you did not profess one thing and practise another.

Constantius, who is still alive, and is now our brother in Catholic Christianity, once gathered many of your sect into his house at Rome, to keep these precepts of Manichæus, which you think so much of, though they are very silly and childish.

The precepts proved too much for your weakness, and the gathering was entirely broken up.

Those who persevered separated from your communion, and are called Mattarians, because they sleep on mats,--a very different bed from the feathers of Faustus and his goatskin coverlets, and all the grandeur that made him despise not only the Mattarians, but also the house of his poor father in Mileum.

Away, then, with this accursed hypocrisy from your writing, if not from your conduct; or else your language will conflict with your life by your deceitful words, as your First Man with the race of darkness by his deceitful elements.

6.

I am, however, addressing not merely men who fail to do what they are commanded, but the members of a deluded sect.

For the precepts of Manichæus are such that, if you do not keep them, you are deceivers; if you do keep them, you are deceived.

Christ never taught you that you should not pluck a vegetable for fear of committing homicide; for when His disciples were hungry when passing through a field of corn, He did not forbid them to pluck the ears on the Sabbath-day; which was a rebuke to the Jews of the time since the action was on Sabbath; and a rebuke in the action itself to the future Manichæans.

The precept of Manichæus, however, only requires you to do nothing while others commit homicide for you; though the real homicide is that of ruining miserable souls by such doctrines of devils.

7.

The language of Faustus has the typhus of heresy in it, and is the language of overweening arrogance.

"You see in me" he says, "the beatitudes of the gospel; and do you ask if I believe the gospel?

You see me poor, meek, a peacemaker, pure in heart, mourning, hungering, thirsting, bearing persecution and enmity for righteousness' sake; and do you doubt my belief in the gospel?"

If to justify oneself were to be just, Faustus would have flown to heaven while uttering these words.

I say nothing of the luxurious habits of Faustus, known to all the followers of the Manichæans, and especially to those at Rome.

I shall suppose a Manichæan such as Constantius sought for, when he enforced the observance of these precepts with the sincere desire to see them observed.

How can I see him to be poor in spirit, when he is so proud as to believe that his own soul is God, and is not ashamed to speak of God as in bondage?

How can I see him meek, when he affronts all the authority of the evangelists rather than believe?

How a peacemaker, when he holds that the divine nature itself by which God is whatever is, and is the only true existence, could not remain in lasting peace?

How pure in heart, when his heart is filled with so many impious notions?

How mourning, unless it is for his God captive and bound till he be freed and escape, with the loss, however, of a part which is to be united by the Father to the mass of darkness, and is not to be mourned for?

How hungering and thirsting for righteousness, which Faustus omits in his writings lest, no doubt, he should be thought destitute of righteousness?

But how can they hunger and thirst after righteousness, whose perfect righteousness will consist in exulting over their brethren condemned to darkness, not for any fault of their own, but for being irremediably contaminated by the pollution against which they were sent by the Father to contend?

8.

How do you suffer persecution and enmity for righteousness' sake, when, according to you, it is righteous to preach and teach these impieties?

The wonder is, that the gentleness of Christian times allows such perverse iniquity to pass wholly or almost unpunished.

And yet, as if we were blind or silly, you tell us that your suffering reproach and persecution is a great proof of your righteousness.

If people are just according to the amount of their suffering, atrocious criminals of all kinds suffer much more than you.

But, at any rate, if we are to grant that suffering endured on account of any sort of profession of Christianity proves the sufferer to be in possession of true faith and righteousness, you must admit that any case of greater suffering that we can show proves the possession of truer faith and greater righteousness.

Of such cases you know many among our martyrs, and chiefly Cyprian himself, whose writings also bear witness to his belief that Christ was born of the Virgin Mary.

For this faith, which you abhor, he suffered and died along with many Christian believers of that day, who suffered as much, or more.

Faustus, when shown to be a Manichæan by evidence, or by his own confession, on the intercession of the Christians themselves, who brought him before the proconsul, was, along with some others, only banished to an island, which can hardly be called a punishment at all, for it is what God's servants do of their own accord every day when they wish to retire from the tumult of the world.

Besides, earthly sovereigns often by a public decree give release from this banishment as an act of mercy.

And in this way all were afterwards released at once.

Confess, then, that they were in possession of a truer faith and a more righteous life, who were accounted worthy to suffer for it much more than you ever suffered.

Or else, cease boasting of the abhorrence which many feel for you, and learn to distinguish between suffering for blasphemy and suffering for righteousness.

What it is you suffer for, your own books will show in a way that deserves your most particular attention.

9.

Those evangelical precepts of peculiar sublimity which you make people who know no better believe that you obey, are really obeyed by multitudes in our communion.

Are there not among us many of both sexes who have entirely refrained from sexual intercourse, and many formerly married who practise continence?

Are there not many others who give largely of their property, or give it up altogether, and many who keep the body in subjection by fasts, either frequent or daily, or protracted beyond belief?

Then there are fraternities whose members have no property of their own, but all things common, including only things necessary for food and clothing, living with one soul and one heart towards God, inflamed with a common feeling of charity.

In all such professions many turn out to be deceivers and reprobates, while many who are so are never discovered; many, too, who at first walk well, fall away rapidly from willfulness.

Many are found in times of trial to have adopted this kind of life with another intention than they professed; and again, many in humility and steadfastness persevere in their course to the end,

Philip Schaff, D.D., LL.D.

and are saved.

There are apparent diversities in these societies; but one charity unites all who, from some necessity, in obedience to the apostle's injunction, have their wives as if they had them not, and buy as if they bought not, and use this world as if they used it not.

With these are joined, in the abundant riches of God's mercy, the inferior class of those to whom it is said, "Defraud not one another, except it be with consent for a time, that ye may give yourselves to prayer; and come together again, that Satan tempt you not for your incontinency.

But I speak this by permission, and not of commandment." [343] To such the same apostle also says, "Now therefore there is utterly a fault among you, that ye go to law one with another;" while, in consideration of their infirmity, he adds, "If ye have judgments of things pertaining to this life, set them to judge who are least esteemed in the Church." [344] For in the kingdom of heaven there are not only those who, that they may be perfect, sell or leave all they have and follow the Lord; but others in the partnership of charity are joined like a mercenary force to the Christian army, to whom it will be said at last, "I was hungry, and ye gave me meat," and so on.

Otherwise, there would be no salvation for those to whom the apostle gives so many anxious and particular directions about their families, telling the wives to be obedient to their husbands, and husbands to love their wives; children to obey their parents, and parents to bring up their children in the instruction and admonition of the Lord; servants to obey with fear their masters according to the flesh, and masters to render to their servants what is just and equal.

The apostle is far from condemning such people as regardless of gospel precepts, or unworthy of eternal life.

For where the Lord exhorts the strong to attain perfection, saying, "If any man take not up his cross and follow me, he cannot be my disciple," He immediately adds, for the consolation of the weak, "Whoso receiveth a just man in the name of a just man shall receive a just man's reward; and whoso receiveth a prophet in the name of a prophet, shall receive a prophet's reward."

So that not only he who gives Timothy a little wine for his stomach's sake, and his frequent infirmities, but he who gives to a strong man a cup of cold water only in the name of a disciple, shall not lose his reward. [345]

10.

If it is true that a man cannot receive the gospel without giving up everything, why do you delude your followers, by allowing them to keep in your service their wives, and children, and households, and houses, and fields?

Indeed, you may well allow them to disregard the precepts of the gospel:

for all you promise them is not a resurrection, but a change to another mortal existence, in which they shall live the silly, childish, impious life of those you call the Elect, the life you live yourself, and are so much praised for; or if they possess greater merit, they shall enter into melons or cucumbers, or some eatables which you will masticate, that they may be quickly purified by your digestion.

Least of all should you who teach such doctrines profess any regard for the gospel.

For if the faith of the gospel had any connection with such nonsense, the Lord should have said, not, "I was hungry, and ye gave me meat;" but, "Ye were hungry, and ye ate me," or, "I was hungry, and I ate you." For, by your absurdities, a man will not be received into the kingdom of God for the service of giving food to the saints, but, because he has eaten them and belched them out, or has himself been eaten and belched into heaven.

Instead of saying, "Lord, when saw we Thee hungry, and fed Thee?" the righteous must say, "When saw we Thee hungry, and were eaten by Thee?"

And He must answer, not, "When ye gave food to one of the least of these my brethren, you gave to me;" but, "When you were eaten by one of the least of these my brethren, you were eaten by me."

11.

Believing and teaching such monstrosities, and living accordingly, you yet have the boldness to say that you obey the precepts of the gospel, and to decry the Catholic Church, which includes many weak as well as strong, both of whom the Lord blesses, because both according to their measure obey the precepts of the gospel and hope in its promises.

The blindness of hostility makes you see only the tares in our harvest:

for you might easily see wheat too, if you were willing that there should be any.

But among you, those who are pretended Manichæans are wicked, and those who are really Manichæans are silly. For where the faith itself is false, he who hypocritically professes it acts deceitfully, while he who truly believes is deceived.

Such a faith cannot produce a good life, for every man's life is good or bad according as his heart is engaged.

If your affections were set upon spiritual and intellectual good, instead of material forms, you would not pay homage to the material sun as a divine substance, and as the light of wisdom, which every one knows you do, though I now only mention it in passing.

Book VI - Faustus avows his disbelief in the Old Testament and his disregard of its precepts, and accuses Catholics of inconsistency in neglecting its ordinances, while claiming to accept it as authoritative.

Augustin explains the Catholic view of the relation of the Old Testament to the New.

1.

Faustus said:
You ask if I believe the Old Testament.
Of course not, for I do not keep its precepts.
Neither, I imagine, do you.
I reject circumcision as disgusting; and if I mistake not, so do you.
I reject the observance of Sabbaths as superfluous:
I suppose you do the same.
I reject sacrifice as idolatry, as doubtless you also do. Swine's flesh is not the only flesh I abstain from; nor is it the only flesh you eat.
I think all flesh unclean:
you think none unclean. Both alike, in these opinions, throw over the Old Testament.
We both look upon the weeks of unleavened bread and the feast of tabernacles as unnecessary and useless.
Not to patch linen garments with purple; to count it adultery to make a garment of linen and wool; to call it sacrilege to yoke together an ox and an ass when necessary; not to appoint as priest a bald man, or a man with red hair, or any similar peculiarity, as being unclean in the sight of God, are things which we both despise and laugh at, and rank as of neither first nor second importance; and yet they are all precepts and judgments of the Old Testament.
You cannot blame me for rejecting the Old Testament; for whether it is right or wrong to do so, you do it as much as I.
As for the difference between your faith and mine, it is this, that while you choose to act deceitfully, and meanly to praise in words what in your heart you hate, I, not having learned the art of deception, frankly declare that I hate both these abominable precepts and their authors.

2.

Augustin replied:
How and for what purpose the Old Testament is received by the heirs of the New Testament has been already explained. [346]But as the remarks of Faustus were then about the promises of the Old Testament, and now he speaks of the precepts, I reply that he displays ignorance of the difference between moral and symbolical precepts.

For example, "Thou shalt not covet" is a moral precept; "Thou shalt circumcise every male on the eighth day" is a symbolical precept.

From not making this distinction, the Manichæans, and all who find fault with the writings of the Old Testament, not seeing that whatever observance God appointed for the former dispensation was a shadow of future things, because these observances are now discontinued, condemn them, though no doubt what is unsuitable now was perfectly suitable then as prefiguring the things now revealed.

In this they contradict the apostle who says, "All these things happened to them for an example, and they were written for our learning, on whom the end of the world is come." [347]The apostle here explains why these writings are to be received, and why it is no longer necessary to continue the symbolical observances.

For when he says, "They were written for our learning," he clearly shows that we should be very diligent in reading and in discovering the meaning of the Old Testament Scriptures, and that we should have great veneration for them, since it was for us that they were written.

Again, when he says, "They are our examples," and "these things happened to them for an example," he shows that, now that the things themselves are clearly revealed, the observance of the actions by which these things were prefigured is no longer binding.

So he says elsewhere, "Let no man judge you in meat, or in drink, or in respect of an holy day, or of the new moon or of the sabbath-days, which are a shadow of things to come." [348]Here also, when he says, "Let no one judge you" in these things, he shows that we are no longer bound to observe them.

And when he says, "which are a shadow of things to come," he explains how these observances were binding at the time when the things fully disclosed to us were symbolized by these shadows of future things.

3.

Assuredly, if the Manichæans were justified by the resurrection of the Lord,--the day of whose resurrection, the third after His passion, was the eighth day, coming after the Sabbath, that is, after the seventh day,--their carnal minds would be delivered from the darkness of earthly passions which rests on them; and rejoicing in the circumcision of the heart, they would not ridicule it as prefigured in the Old Testament by circumcision in the flesh, although they should not enforce this observance under the New Testament.

But, as the apostle says, "To the pure all things are pure."

But to the impure and unbelieving nothing is pure, but both their mind and conscience are defiled." [349]So these people, who are so pure in their own eyes, that they regard, or pretend to regard, as impure these members of their bodies, are so defiled with unbelief and error, that, while they abhor the circumcision of the flesh,--which the apostle calls a seal of the righteousness of faith,--they believe that the divine members of their God are subjected to restraint and contamination in these very carnal members of theirs.

For they say that flesh is unclean; and it follows that God, in the part which is detained by the flesh, is made unclean:

for they declare that He must be cleansed, and that till this is done, as far as it can be done, He undergoes all the passions to which flesh is subject, not only in suffering pain and distress, but also in sensual gratification.

For it is for His sake, they say, that they abstain from sexual intercourse, that He may not be bound more closely in the bondage of the flesh, nor suffer more defilement.

The apostle says, "To the pure all things are pure."

And if this is true of men, who may be led into evil by a perverse will, how much more must all things be pure to God, who remains for ever immutable and immaculate!

In those books which you defile with your violent reproaches, it is said of the divine wisdom, that "no defiled thing falleth into it, and it goeth everywhere by reason of its pureness." [350]It is mere prurient absurdity to find fault with the sign of human regeneration appointed by that God, to whom all things are pure, to be put on the organ of human generation, while you hold that your God, to whom nothing is pure, is in a part of his nature subjected to taint and corruption by the vicious actions in which impure men employ the members of their body.

For if you think there is pollution in conjugal intercourse, what must there be in all the practices of the licentious?

If you ask, then, as you often do, whether God could not find some other way of sealing the righteousness of faith, the answer is, Why not this way, since all things are pure to the pure, much more to God?

And we have the authority of the apostle for saying that circumcision was the seal of the righteousness of the faith of Abraham.

As for you, you must try not to blush when you are asked whether your God had nothing better to do than to entangle part of his nature with these members that you revile so much.

These are delicate subjects to speak of, on account of the penal corruption attending the propagation of man.

They are things which call into exercise the modesty of the chaste, the passions of the impure, and the justice of God.

4.
    The rest of the Sabbath we consider no longer binding as an observance, now that the hope of our eternal rest has been revealed. But it is a very useful thing to read of, and to reflect on.

    In prophetic times, when things now manifested were prefigured and predicted by actions as well as words, this sign of which we read was a presage of the reality which we possess.

    But I wish to know why you observe a sort of partial rest.

    The Jews, on their Sabbath, which they still keep in a carnal manner, neither gather any fruit in the field, nor dress and cook it at home.

    But you, in your rest, wait till one of your followers takes his knife or hook to the garden, to get food for you by murdering the vegetables, and brings back, strange to say, living corpses.

    For if cutting plants is not murder, why are you afraid to do it?

    And yet, if the plants are murdered, what becomes of the life which is to obtain release and restoration from your mastication and digestion?

    Well, you take the living vegetables, and certainly you ought, if it could be done to swallow them whole; so that after the one wound your follower has been guilty of inflicting in pulling them, of which you will no doubt consent to absolve him, they may reach without loss or injury your private laboratory, where your God may be healed of his wound.

    Instead of this, you not only tear them with your teeth, but, if it pleases your taste, mince them, inflicting a multitude of wounds in the most criminal manner.

    Plainly it would be a most advantageous thing if you would rest at home too, and not only once a week, like the Jews, but every day of the week. The cucumbers suffer while you are cooking them, without any benefit to the life that is in them:

    for a boiling pot cannot be compared to a saintly stomach.

    And yet you ridicule as superfluous the rest of the Sabbath.

    Would it not be better, not only to refrain from finding fault with the fathers for this observance, in whose case it was not superfluous, but, even now that it is superfluous, to observe this rest yourselves instead of your own, which has no symbolical use, and is condemned as grounded on falsehood?

    According to your own foolish opinions, you are guilty of a defective observance of your own rest, though the observance itself is foolish in the judgment of truth.

    You maintain that the fruit suffers when it is pulled from the tree, when it is cut and scraped, and cooked, and eaten.

    So you are wrong in eating anything that can not be swallowed raw and unhurt, so that the wound inflicted might not be from you, but from your follower in pulling them.

    You declare that you could not give release to so great a quantity of life, if you were to eat only things which could be swallowed without cooking or mastication.

    But if this release compensates for all the pains you inflict, why is it unlawful for you to pull the fruit?

    Fruit may be eaten raw, as some of your sect make a point of eating raw vegetables of all kinds.

    But before it can be eaten at all, it must be pulled or fall off, or be taken in some way from the ground or from the tree.

    You might well be pardoned for pulling it, since nothing can be done without that, but not for torturing the members of your God to the extent you do in dressing your food.

    One of your silly notions is that the tree weeps when the fruit is pulled.

    Doubtless the life in the tree knows all things, and perceives who it is that comes to it.

    If the elect were to come and pull the fruit, would not the tree rejoice to escape the misery of having its fruit plucked by others, and to gain felicity by enduring a little momentary pain?

    And yet, while you multiply the pains and troubles of the fruit after it is plucked, you will not pluck it. Explain that, if you can!

    Fasting itself is a mistake in your case. There should be no intermission in the task of purging away the dross of the excrements from the spiritual gold, and of releasing the divine members from confinement.

    The most merciful man among you is he who keeps himself always in good health, takes raw food, and eats a great deal.

    But you are cruel when you eat, in making your food undergo so much suffering; and you are cruel when you fast, in desisting from the work of liberating the divine members. [351]

5.

With all this, you venture to denounce the sacrifices of the Old Testament, and to call them idolatry, and to attribute to us the same impious notion.

To answer for ourselves in the first place, while we consider it no longer a duty to offer sacrifices, we recognize sacrifices as part of the mysteries of Revelation, by which the things prophesied were foreshadowed.

For they were our examples, and in many and various ways they all pointed to the one sacrifice which we now commemorate.

Now that this sacrifice has been revealed, and has been offered in due time, sacrifice is no longer binding as an act of worship, while it retains its symbolical authority.

For these things "were written for our learning, upon whom the end of the world is come."[352] What you object to in sacrifice is the slaughter of animals, though the whole animal creation is intended conditionally in some way for the use of man.

You are merciful to beasts, believing them to contain the souls of human beings, while you refuse a piece of bread to a hungry beggar.

The Lord Jesus, on the other hand, was cruel to the swine when He granted the request of the devils to be allowed to enter into them. [353] The same Lord Jesus, before the sacrifice of His passion, said to a leper whom He had cured, "Go, show thyself to the priest, and give the offering, as Moses commanded, for a testimony unto them." [354] When God, by the prophets, repeatedly declares that He needs no offering, as indeed reason teaches us that offerings cannot be needed by Him who stands in need of nothing, the human mind is led to inquire what God wished to teach us by these sacrifices.

For, assuredly, He would not have required offerings of which He had no need, except to teach us something that it would profit us to know, and which was suitably set forth by means of these symbols.

How much better and more honorable it would be for you to be still bound by these sacrifices, which have an instructive meaning, though they are not now necessary, than to require your followers to offer to you as food what you believe to be living victims.

The Apostle Paul says most appropriately of some who preached the gospel to gratify their appetite, that their "god was their belly." [355] But the arrogance of your impiety goes much beyond this; for, instead of making your belly your god, you do what is far worse in making your belly the purifier of God.

Surely it is great madness to make a pretence of piety in not slaughtering animals, while you hold that the souls of animals inhabit all the food you eat, and yet make what you call living creatures suffer such torture from your hands and teeth.

6.

If you will not eat flesh why should you not slay animals in sacrifice to your God, in order that their souls, which you hold to be not only human, but so divine as to be members of God Himself, may be released from the confinement of flesh, and be saved from returning by the efficacy of your prayers?

Perhaps, however, your stomach gives more effectual aid than your intellect, and that part of divinity which has had the advantage of passing through your bowels is more likely to be saved than that which has only the benefit of your prayers.

Your objection to eating flesh will be that you cannot eat animals alive, and so the operation of your stomach will not avail for the liberation of their souls.

Happy vegetables, that, torn up with the hand, cut with knives, tortured in fire, ground by teeth, yet reach alive the altars of your intestines!

Unhappy sheep and oxen, that are not so tenacious of life, and therefore are refused entrance into your bodies!

Such is the absurdity of your notions.

And you persist in making out an opposition in us to the Old Testament, because we consider no flesh unclean:

according to the opinion of the apostle, "To the pure all things are pure;" [356] and according to the saying of our Lord Himself, "Not that which goeth into your mouth defileth you, but that which cometh out." [357] This was not said to the crowd only, as your Adimantus, whom Faustus, in his attack on the Old Testament, praises as second only to Manichæus, wishes us to understand; but when retired from the crowd, the Lord repeated this still more plainly and pointedly to His disciples.

Adimantus quotes this saying of our Lord in opposition to the Old Testament, where the people are prohibited from eating some animals which are pronounced unclean; and doubtless he was afraid that he should be asked why, since he quotes a passage from the Gospel about man not being defiled by what enters into his mouth and passes into his belly, and out into the draft, he yet considers not some only, but all flesh unclean, and abstains from eating it.

It is in order to escape from this strait, when the plain truth is too much for his error, that he makes the Lord say this to the crowd; as if the Lord were in the habit of speaking the truth only in small companies, while He blurted out falsehoods in public.

To speak of the Lord in this way is blasphemy.

And all who read the passage can see that the Lord said the same thing more plainly to His disciples in private.

Since Faustus praises Adimantus so much at the beginning of this book of his, placing him next to Manichæus, let him say in a word whether it is true or false that a man is not defiled by what enters into his mouth.

If it is false, why does this great teacher Adimantus quote it against the Old Testament?

If it is true, why, in spite of this, do you believe that eating any flesh will defile you?

It is true, if you choose this explanation, that the apostle does not say that all things are pure to heretics, but, "to the pure all things are pure."

The apostle also goes on to explain why all things are not pure to heretics:

"To the impure and unbelieving nothing is pure, but both their mind and conscience are defiled." [358]

So to the Manichæans there is absolutely nothing pure; for they hold that the very substance or nature of God not only may be, but has actually been defiled, and so defiled that it can never be wholly restored and purified.

What do they mean when they call animals unclean, and refrain from eating them, when it is impossible for them to think anything, whether food or whatever it may be, clean? According to them, vegetables too, fruits, all kinds of crops, the earth and sky, are defiled by mixture with the race of darkness.

Why do they not act up to their opinions about other things as well as about animals?

Why do they not abstain altogether, and starve themselves to death, instead of persisting in their blasphemies?

If they will not repent and reform, this is evidently the best thing that they could do.

7.

The saying of the apostle, that "to the pure all things are pure," and that "every creature of God is good," is not opposed to the prohibitions of the Old Testament; and the explanation, if they can understand it, is this.

The apostle speaks of the natures of the things, while the Old Testament calls some animals unclean, not in their nature, but symbolically, on account of the prefigurative character of that dispensation.

For instance, a pig and a lamb are both clean in their nature, for every creature of God is good; but symbolically, a lamb is clean, and a pig unclean.

So the words wise and fool are both clean in their nature, as words composed of letters but fool may be called symbolically unclean, because it means an unclean thing.

Perhaps a pig is the same among symbols as a fool is among real things.

The animal, and the four letters which compose the word, may mean the same thing.

No doubt the animal is pronounced unclean by the law, because it does not chew the cud; which is not a fault but its nature.

But the men of whom this animal is a symbol are unclean, not by nature, but from their own fault; because, though they gladly hear the words of wisdom, they never reflect on them afterwards.

For to recall, in quiet repose, some useful instruction from the stomach of memory to the mouth of reflection, is a kind of spiritual rumination.

The animals above mentioned are a symbol of those people who do not do this.

And the prohibition of the flesh of these animals is a warning against this fault.

Another passage of Scripture speaks of the precious treasure of wisdom, and describes ruminating as clean, and not ruminating as unclean:

"A precious treasure resteth in the mouth of a wise man; but a foolish man swallows it up."[359] Symbols of this kind, either in words or in things, give useful and pleasant exercise to intelligent minds in the way of inquiry and comparison.

But formerly people were required not only to hear, but to practise many such things.

For at that time it was necessary that, by deeds as well as by words, those things should be foreshadowed which were in after times to be revealed.

After the revelation by Christ and in Christ, the community of believers is not burdened with the practice of the observances, but is admonished to give heed to the prophecy.

This is our reason for accounting no animals unclean, in accordance with the saying of the

Lord and of the apostle, while we are not opposed to the Old Testament, where some animals are pronounced unclean.

Now let us hear why you consider all animal food unclean.

8.

One of your false doctrines is, that flesh is unclean on account of mixture with the race of darkness.

But this would make not only flesh unclean, but your God himself, in that part which he sent to become subject to absorption and contamination, in order that the enemy might be conquered and taken captive.

Besides, on account of this mixture, all that you eat must be unclean.

But you say flesh is especially unclean.

It requires patience to listen to all their absurd reasons for this peculiar impurity of flesh.

I will mention only what will suffice to show the inveterate folly of these critics of the Old Testament, who, while they denounce flesh, savor only fleshly things, and have no sort of spiritual perception.

And a lengthy discussion of this question may perhaps enable us to dispense with saying much on some other points.

The following, then, is an account of their vain delusions in this matter:--In that battle, when the First Man ensnared the race of darkness by deceitful elements, princes of both sexes belonging to this race were taken.

By means of these princes the world was constructed; and among those used in the formation of the heavenly bodies, were some pregnant females.

When the sky began to rotate, the rapid circular motion made these females give birth to abortions, which, being of both sexes, fell on the earth, and lived, and grew, and came together, and produced offspring.

Hence sprang all animal life in earth, air, and sea. [360]Now if the origin of flesh is from heaven, that is no reason for thinking it especially unclean.

Indeed, in this construction of the world, they hold that these principles of darkness were arranged higher or lower, according to the greater or less amount of good mixed with them in the construction of the various parts of the world.

So flesh ought to be cleaner than vegetables which come out of the earth, for it comes from heaven.

And how irrational to suppose that the abortions, before becoming animate, were so lively, though in an abortive state, that after falling from the sky, they could live and multiply; whereas, after becoming animate, they die if brought forth prematurely, and a fall from a very moderate height is enough to kill them!

The kingdom of life in contest with the kingdom of death ought to have improved them, by giving them life instead of making them more perishable than before.

If the perishableness is a consequence of a change of nature, it is wrong to say that there is a bad nature.

The change is the only cause of the perishableness.

Both natures are good, though one is better than the other.

Whence then comes the peculiar impurity of flesh as it exists in this world, sprung, as they say, from heaven?

They tell us, indeed, of the first bodies of these principles of darkness being generated like worms from trees of darkness; and the trees, they say, are produced from the five elements.

But supposing that the bodies of animals come in the first place from trees, and afterwards from heaven, why should they be more unclean than the fruit of trees?

Perhaps it will be said that what remains after death is unclean, because the life is no longer there.

For the same reason fruits and vegetables must be unclean, for they die when they are pulled or cut.

As we saw before, the elect get others to bring their food to them, that they may not be guilty of murder.

Perhaps, since they say that every living being has two souls, one of the race of light, and the other of the race of darkness, the good soul leaves at death, and the bad soul remains.

But, in that case, the animal would be as much alive as it was in the kingdom of darkness, when it had only the soul of its own race, with which it had rebelled against the kingdom of God.

So, since both souls leave at death, why call the flesh unclean, as if only the good soul had left?

Any life that remains must be of both kinds; for some remains of the members of God are found, we are told, even in filth.

There is therefore no reason for making flesh more unclean than fruits.

The truth is, they pretend to great chastity in holding flesh unclean because it is generated. But if the divine body is more grossly shut in by flesh, there is all the more reason that they should liberate it by eating.

And there are innumerable kinds of worms not produced from sexual intercourse; some in the neighborhood of Venice come from trees, which they should eat, since there is not the same reason for their being unclean.

Besides, there are the frogs produced by the earth after a shower of rain. [361]

Let them liberate the members of their God from these.

Let them rebuke the mistake of mankind in preferring fowls and pigeons produced from males and females to the pure frogs, daughters of heaven and earth.

By this theory, the first principles of darkness produced from trees must be purer than Manichæus, who was produced by generation; and his followers, for the same reason, must be less pure than the lice which spring from the perspiration of their bodies.

But if everything that comes from flesh is unclean, because the origin of flesh itself is unclean, fruits and vegetables must also be unclean, because they are manured with dung.

After this, what becomes of the notion that fruits are cleaner than flesh?

Dung is the most unclean product of flesh, and also the most fertilizing manure.

Their doctrine is, that the life escapes in the mastication and digestion of the food, so that only a particle remains in the excrement.

How is it, then, that this particle of life has such an effect on the growth and the quality of your favorite food?

Flesh is nourished by the productions of the earth, not by its excrements; while the earth is nourished by the excrements of flesh, not by its productions.

Let them say which is the cleaner.

Or let them turn from being unbelieving and impure to whom nothing is clean, and join with us in embracing the doctrine of the apostle, that to the pure all things are pure; that the earth is the Lord's, and the fullness thereof; that every creature of God is good.

All things in nature are good in their own order; and no one sins in using them, unless, by disobedience to God, he transgresses his own order, and disturbs their order by using them amiss.

9.

The elders who pleased God kept their own order by their obedience, in observing, according to God's arrangement, what was appointed as suitable to certain times.

So, although all animals intended for food are by nature clean, they abstained from some which had then a symbolical uncleanness, in preparation for the future revelation of the things signified.

And so with regard to unleavened bread and all such things, in which the apostle says there was a shadow of future things, neglect of their observance under the old dispensation, when this observance was enjoined, and was employed to prefigure what was afterwards to be revealed, would have been as criminal, as it would now be foolish in us, after the light of the New Testament has arisen, to think that these predictive observances could be of any use to us.

On the other hand, since the Old Testament teaches us that the things now revealed were so long ago prefigured, that we may be firm and faithful in our adherence to them, it would be blasphemy and impiety to discard these books, simply because the Lord requires of us now not a literal, but a spiritual and intelligent regard to their contents.

They were written, as the apostle says, for our admonition, on whom the end of the world is come. [362] "For whatsoever things were written aforetime were written for our learning." [363] Not to eat unleavened bread in the appointed seven days was a sin in the time of the Old Testament; in the time of the New Testament it is not a sin.

But having the hope of a future world through Christ, who makes us altogether new by clothing our souls with righteousness and our bodies with immortality, to believe that the bondage and infirmity of our original corruption will prevail over us or over our actions, must continue to be a sin, till the seven days of the course of time are accomplished.

In the time of the Old Testament, this, under the disguise of a type, was perceived by some saints.

In the time of the New Testament it is fully declared and publicly preached. [364]

What was then a precept of Scripture is now a testimony.

Formerly, not to keep the feast of tabernacles was a sin, which is not the case now. But not to form part of the building of God's tabernacle, which is the Church, is always a sin.

Formerly this was acted in a figure; now the record serves as testimony.

The ancient tabernacle, indeed, would not have been called the tabernacle of the testimony, unless as an appropriate symbol it had borne testimony to some truth which was to be revealed in its own time.

To patch linen garments with purple, or to wear a garment of woollen and linen together, is not a sin now.

But to live intemperately, and to wish to combine opposite modes of life,--as when a woman devoted to religion wears the ornaments of married women, or when one who has not abstained from marriage dresses like a virgin,--is always sin.

So it is sin whenever inconsistent things are combined in any man's life.

This, which is now a moral truth, was then symbolized in dress.

What was then a type is now revealed truth.

So the same Scripture which then required symbolical actions, now testifies to the things signified.

The prefigurative observance is now a record for the confirmation of our faith.

Formerly it was unlawful to plough with an ox and an ass together; now it is lawful.

The apostle explains this when he quotes the text about not muzzling the ox that is treading out the corn.

He says, "Does God care for oxen?" What, then, have we to do with an obsolete prohibition? The apostle teaches us in the following words, "For our sakes it is written." [365]

It must be impiety in us not to read what was written for our sakes; for it is more for our sakes, to whom the revelation belongs, than for theirs who had only the figure.

There is no harm in joining an ox with an ass where it is required.

But to put a wise man and a fool together, not that one should teach and the other obey, but that both with equal authority should declare the word of God, cannot be done without causing offence.

So the same Scripture which was once a command enjoining the shadow in which future things were veiled, is now an authoritative witness to the unveiled truth.

In what he says of the uncleanness of a man that is bald or has red hair, Faustus is inaccurate, or the manuscript he has used is incorrect. [366]Would that Faustus were not ashamed to bear on his forehead the cross of Christ, the want of which is baldness, instead of maintaining that Christ, who says, "I am the truth," showed unreal marks, after His resurrection, of unreal wounds!

Faustus says he has not learned the art of deceiving, and speaks what he thinks.

He cannot therefore be a disciple of his Christ, whom he madly declares to have shown false marks of wounds to his disciples when they doubted.

Are we to believe Faustus, not only in his other absurdities, but also when he tells us that he does not deceive us in calling Christ a deceiver?

Is he better than Christ?

Is he not a deceiver, while Christ is?

Or does he prove himself to be a disciple not of the truthful Christ, but of the deceiver Manichæus, by this very falsehood, when he boasts that he has not learned the art of deceiving?

Book VII - The genealogical question is again taken up and argued on both sides

1.

Faustus said:

You ask why I do not believe in the genealogy of Jesus.

There are many reasons; but the principal is, that He never declares with His own lips that He had an earthly father or descent, but on the contrary, that he is not of this world, that He came forth from God the Father, that He descended from heaven, that He has no mother or brethren except those who do the will of His Father in heaven.

Besides, the framers of these genealogies do not seem to have known Jesus before His birth or soon after it, so as to have the credibility of eye-witnesses of what they narrate.

They became acquainted with Jesus as a young man of about thirty years of age, if it is not blasphemy to speak of the age of a divine being.

Now the question regarding a witness is always whether he has seen or heard what he testifies to.

But the writers of these genealogies never assert that they heard the account from Jesus Himself, nor even the fact of His birth; nor did they see Him till they came to know Him after his baptism, many years after the time of His birth.

To me, therefore, and to every sensible man, it appears as foolish to believe this account, as it would be to call into court a blind and deaf witness.

2.

Augustin replied:

As regards what Faustus calls his principal reason for not receiving the genealogy of Jesus Christ, a complete refutation is found in the passages formerly quoted, where Christ declares Himself to be the Son of man, and in what we have said of the identity of the Son of man with the Son of God:

that in His Godhead He has no earthly descent, while after the flesh He is of the seed of David, as the apostle teaches.

We are to believe, therefore, that He came forth from the Father, that He descended from heaven, and also that the Word was made flesh and dwelt amongst men.

If the words, "Who is my mother, and who are my brethren?" [367] are quoted to show that Christ had no earthly mother or descent, it follows that we must believe that His disciples, whom He here teaches by His own example to set no value on earthly relationship, as compared with the kingdom of heaven, had no fathers, because Christ says to them, "Call no man father upon earth; for one is your Father, even God." [368] What He taught them to do with reference to their fathers, He Himself first did in reference to His own mother and brethren; as in many other things He condescended to set us an example, and to go before that we might follow in His footsteps.

Faustus' principal objection to the genealogy fails completely; and after the defeat of this invincible force, the rest is easily routed.

He says that the apostles who declared Christ to be the Son of man as well as the Son of God are not to be believed, because they were not present at the birth of Christ, whom they joined when He had reached manhood, nor heard of it from Christ Himself.

Why then do they believe John when he says, "In the beginning was the Word, and the Word was with God, and the Word was God.

The same was in the beginning with God.

All things were made by Him, and without Him was not anything made," [369] and such passages, which they agree to, without understanding them?

Where did John see this, or did he ever hear it from the Lord Himself?

In whatever way John learned this, those who narrate the nativity may have learned also.

Again, how do they know that the Lord said, "Who is my mother, and who are my brethren?"

If on the authority of the evangelist, why do they not also believe that the mother and the brethren of Christ were seeking for Him?

They believe that Christ said these words, which they misunderstand, while they deny a fact resting on the same authority. Once more, if Matthew could not know that Christ was born, because he knew Him only in His manhood, how could Manichæus, who lived so long after, know that He was not born?

They will say that Manichæus knew this from the Holy Spirit which was in him.

Certainly the Holy Spirit would make him speak the truth.

But why not rather believe what Christ's own disciples tell us, who were personally acquainted with Him, and who not only had the gift of inspiration to supply defects in their knowledge, but in a purely natural way obtained information of the birth of Christ, and of His descent, when the event was fresh in memory?

And yet he dares to call the apostles deaf and blind.

Why were you not deaf and blind, to prevent you from learning such profane nonsense, and dumb too, to prevent you from uttering it?

Book VIII - Faustus maintains that to hold to the Old Testament after the giving of the New is putting new cloth on an old garment

Augustin further explains the relation of the Old Testament to the New, and reproaches the Manichæans with carnality.

1.

Faustus said:
Another reason for not receiving the Old Testament is, that I am provided with the New; and Scripture says that old and new do not agree.

For "no one putteth a piece of new cloth unto an old garment, otherwise the rent is made worse." [370] To avoid making a worse rent, as you have done, I do not mix Christian newness with Hebrew oldness.

Every one accounts it mean, when a man has got a new dress, not to give the old one to his inferiors.

So, even if I were a Jew by birth, as the apostles were, it would be proper for me, on receiving the New Testament, to discard the Old, as the apostles did. And having the advantage of being born free from the yoke of bondage, and being early introduced into the full liberty of Christ, what a foolish and ungrateful wretch I should be to put myself again under the yoke!

This is what Paul blames the Galatians for; because, going back to circumcision, they turned again to the weak and beggarly elements, whereunto they desired again to be in bondage. [371] Why should I do what I see another blamed for doing?

My going into bondage would be worse than their returning to it.

2.

Augustin replied:
We have already shown sufficiently why and how we maintain the authority of the Old Testament, not for the imitation of Jewish bondage, but for the confirmation of Christian liberty.

It is not I, but the apostle, who says, "All these things happened to them as an example, and they were written for our admonition, on whom the ends of the world are come." [372]

We do not therefore, as bondmen, observe what was enjoined as predictive of us; but as free, we read what was written to confirm us.

So any one may see that the apostle remonstrates with the Galatians not for devoutly reading what Scripture says of circumcision, but for superstitiously desiring to be circumcised.

We do not put a new cloth to an old garment, but we are instructed in the kingdom of heaven, like the householder, whom the Lord describes as bringing out of his treasure things new and old. [373] He who puts a new cloth to an old garment is the man who attempts spiritual self-denial before he has renounced fleshly hope. Examine the passage, and you will see that, when the Lord was asked about fasting, He replied, "No man putteth a new cloth to an old garment."

The disciples had still a carnal affection for the Lord; for they were afraid that, if He died, they would lose Him.

So He calls Peter Satan for dissuading Him from suffering, because he understood not the things of God, but the things of men. [374] The fleshly character of your hope is evident from your fancies about the kingdom of God, and from your paying homage and devotion to the light of the sun, which the carnal eye perceives, as if it were an image of heaven. So your carnal mind is the old garment to which you join your fasts. Moreover, if a new cloth and an old garment do not agree, how do the members of your God come to be not only joined or fastened, but to be united far more intimately by mixture and coherence to the principles of darkness?

Perhaps both are old, because both are false, and both of the carnal mind.

Or perhaps you wish to prove that one was new and the other old, by the rent being made worse, in tearing away the unhappy piece of the kingdom of light, to be doomed to eternal imprisonment in the mass of darkness.

So this pretended artist in the fashions of the sacred Scriptures is found stitching together absurdities, and dressing himself in the rags of his own invention.

The Writings Against the Manichaeans and Against the Donatists: Part I - The Manichaeans

Book IX - Faustus argues that if the apostles born under the old covenant could lawfully depart from it, much more can he having been born a Gentile. Augustin explains the relation of Jews and Gentiles alike to the Gospel

1.

Faustus said:
Another reason for not receiving the Old Testament is, that if it was allowable for the apostles, who were born under it, to abandon it, much more may I, who was not born under it, be excused for not thrusting myself into it.

We Gentiles are not born Jews, nor Christians either.

Out of the same Gentile world some are induced by the Old Testament to become Jews, and some by the New Testament to become Christians.

It is as if two trees, a sweet and a bitter, drew from one soil the sap which each assimilates to its own nature.

The apostle passed from the bitter to the sweet; it would be madness in me to change from the sweet to the bitter.

2.

Augustin replied:
You say that the apostle, in leaving Judaism, passed from the bitter to the sweet.

But the apostle himself says that the Jews, who would not believe in Christ, were branches broken off, and that the Gentiles, a wild olive tree, were grafted into the good olive, that is, the holy stock of the Hebrews, that they might partake of the fatness of the olive.

For, in warning the Gentiles not to be proud on account of the fall of the Jews, he says:

"For I speak to you Gentiles, inasmuch as I am the apostle of the Gentiles.

I magnify my office; if by any means I may provoke to emulation them which are my flesh, and might save some of them.

For if the casting away of them be the reconciling of the world, what shall the receiving of them be, but life from the dead?

For if the first fruit be holy, the lump is also holy; and if the root be holy, so are the branches.

And if some of the branches are broken off, and thou, being a wild olive tree, were grafted in among them, and with them partakest of the root and fatness of the olive tree; boast not against the branches:

but if thou boast, thou bearest not the root, but the root thee.

Thou wilt say then, The branches were broken off, that I might be grafted in.

Well; because of unbelief they were broken off, and thou standest by faith.

Be not high-minded, but fear; for if God spared not the natural branches, take heed lest He also spare not thee.

Behold therefore the goodness and severity of God:

on them which fell, severity; but toward thee, goodness, if thou continue in His goodness; otherwise thou also shalt be cut off.

And they also, if they abide not still in unbelief, shall be grafted in; for God is able to graft them in again.

For if thou wert cut out of the olive tree, which is wild by nature, and wert grafted contrary to nature into a good olive tree; how much more shall these, which be the natural branches, be grafted into their own olive tree?

For I would not, brethren, that ye should be ignorant of this mystery (lest ye should be wise in your own conceits), that blindness in part is happened to Israel, until the fullness of the Gentiles be come in; and so all Israel shall be saved." [375]It appears from this, that you, who do not wish to be graffed into this root, though you are not broken off, like the carnal unbelieving Jews, remain still in the bitterness of the wild olive.

Your worship of the sun and moon has the true Gentile flavor.

You are none the less in the wild olive of the Gentiles, because you have added thorns of a new kind, and worship along with the sun and moon a false Christ, the fabrication not of your hands, but of your perverse heart.

Come, then, and be grafted into the root of the olive tree, in his return to which the apostle rejoices, after by unbelief he had been among the broken branches.

He speaks of himself as set free, when he made the happy transition from Judaism to Christianity.

For Christ was always preached in the olive tree, and those who did not believe on Him when He came were broken off, while those who believed were grafted in.

These are thus warned against pride:

"Be not high-minded, but fear; for if God spared not the natural branches, neither will He spare thee."

And to prevent despair of those broken off, he adds:

"And they also, if they abide not still in unbelief, shall be grafted in; for God is able to graft them in again.

For if thou wert cut out of the olive tree, which is wild by nature, and wert grafted contrary to nature into a good olive tree, how much more shall these, which be the natural branches, be grafted into their own olive tree."

The apostle rejoices in being delivered from the condition of a broken branch, and in being restored to the fatness of the olive tree.

So you who have been broken off by error should return and be grafted in again.

Those who are still in the wild olive should separate themselves from its barrenness, and become partakers of fertility.

Book X - Faustus insists that the Old Testament promises are radically different from those of the New

Augustin admits a difference, but maintains that the moral precepts are the same in both.

1.

Faustus said:

Another reason for not receiving the Old Testament is, that both the Old and the New teach us not to covet what belongs to others.

Everything in the Old Testament is of this kind.

It promises riches, and plenty, and children, and children's children, and long life, and withal the land of Canaan; but only to the circumcised, the Sabbath observers, those offering sacrifices, and abstaining from swine's flesh.

Now I, like every other Christian, pay no attention to these things, as being trifling and useless for the salvation of the soul.

I conclude, therefore, that the promises do not belong to me. And mindful of the commandment, Thou shall not covet, I gladly leave to the Jews their own property, and content myself with the gospel, and with the bright inheritance of the kingdom of heaven.

If a Jew were to claim part in the gospel, I should justly reproach him with claiming what he had no right to, because he does not obey its precepts.

And a Jew might say the same to me if I professed to receive the Old Testament while I disregard its requirements.

2.

Augustin replied:

Faustus is not ashamed to repeat the same nonsense again and again.

But it is tiresome to repeat the same answers, though it is to repeat truth.

What Faustus says here has already been answered. [376]But if a Jew asks me why I profess to believe the Old Testament while I do not observe its precepts, my reply is this:

The moral precepts of the law are observed by Christians; the symbolical precepts were properly observed during the time that the things now revealed were prefigured.

Accordingly, those observances, which I regard as no longer binding, I still look upon as a testimony, as I do also the carnal promises from which the Old Testament derives its name.

For although the gospel teaches me to hope for eternal blessings, I also find a confirmation of the gospel in those things which "happened to them for an example, and were written for our admonition, on whom the ends of the world are come."

So much for our answer to the Jews.

And now we have something to say to the Manichæans.

3.

By showing the way in which we regard the authority of the Old Testament we have answered the Jews, by whose question about our not observing the precepts Faustus thought we would be puzzled.

But what answer can you give to the question, why you deceive simple-minded people by professing to believe in the New Testament, while you not only do not believe it, but assail it with all your force?

It will be more difficult for you to answer this than it was for us to answer the Jews.

We hold all that is written in the Old Testament to be true, and enjoined by God for suitable times.

But in your inability to find a reason for not receiving what is written in the New Testament, you are obliged, as a last resource, to pretend that the passages are not genuine.

This is the last gasp of a heretic in the clutches of truth; or rather it is the breath of corruption itself.

Faustus, however, confesses that the Old Testament as well as the New teaches him not to covet.

His own God could never have taught him this.

For if this God did not covet what belonged to another, why did he construct new worlds in the region of darkness?

Perhaps the race of darkness first coveted his kingdom.

But this would be to imitate their bad example.

Perhaps the kingdom of light was previously of small extent, and war was desirable in order to enlarge it by conquest.

In that case, no doubt, there was covetousness, though the hostile race was allowed to begin the wars to justify the conquest.

If there had been no such desire, there was no necessity to extend the kingdom beyond its old limits into the region of the conquered foe.

If the Manichæans would only learn from these Scriptures the moral precepts, one of which is, Do not covet, instead of taking offence at the symbolical precept, they would acknowledge in meekness and candor that they suited the time then present.

We do not covet what belongs to another, when we read in the Old Testament what "happened to them for examples, and was written for our admonition, on whom the ends of the world are come."

It is surely not coveting when a man reads what is written for his benefit.

Book XI - Faustus quotes passages to show that the Apostle Paul abandoned belief in the incarnation, to which he earlier held

Augustin shows that the apostle was consistent with himself in the utterances quoted.

1.

Faustus said:
Assuredly I believe the apostle.

And yet I do not believe that the Son of God was born of the seed of David according to the flesh, [377] because I do not believe that God's apostle could contradict himself, and have one opinion about our Lord at one time, and another at another.

But, granting that he wrote this,--since you will not hear of anything being spurious in his writings,--it is not against us.

For this seems to be Paul's old belief about Jesus, when he thought, like everybody else, that Jesus was the son of David. Afterwards, when he learned that this was false, he corrects himself; and in his Epistle to the Corinthians he says:

"We know no man after the flesh; yea, though we have known Christ after the flesh, yet now henceforth know we Him no more." [378] Observe the difference between these two verses.

In one he asserts that Jesus was the son of David after the flesh; in the other he says that now he knows no man after the flesh.

If Paul wrote both, it can only have been in the way I have stated.

Philip Schaff, D.D., LL.D.

In the next verse he adds:

"Therefore, if any man be in Christ, he is a new creature; old things are passed away; behold, all things are become new."

The belief that Jesus was born of the seed of David according to the flesh is of this old transitory kind; whereas the faith which knows no man after the flesh is new and permanent.

So, he says elsewhere:

"When I was a child, I spoke as a child, I understood as a child, I thought as a child; but when I became a man, I put away childish things." [379]We are thus warranted in preferring the new and amended confession of Paul to his old and faulty one.

And if you hold by what is said in the Epistle to the Romans, why should not we hold by what is said to the Corinthians?

But it is only by your insisting on the correctness of the text that we are made to represent Paul as building again the things which he destroyed, in spite of his own repudiation of such prevarication.

If the verse is Paul's, he has corrected himself.

If Paul should not be supposed to have written anything requiring correction, the verse is not his.

2.

Augustin replied:

As I said a little ago, when these men are beset by clear testimonies of Scripture, and cannot escape from their grasp, they declare that the passage is spurious.

The declaration only shows their aversion to the truth, and their obstinacy in error.

Unable to answer these statements of Scripture, they deny their genuineness.

But if this answer is admitted, or allowed to have any weight, it will be useless to quote any book or any passage against your errors.

It is one thing to reject the books themselves, and to profess no regard for their authority, as the Pagans reject our Scriptures, and the Jews the New Testament, and as we reject any books peculiar to your sect, or any other heretical sect, and also the apocryphal books, which are so called, not because of any mysterious regard paid to them, but because they are mysterious in their origin, and in the absence of clear evidence, have only some obscure presumption to rest upon; and it is another thing to say, This holy man wrote only the truth, and this is his epistle, but some verses are his, and some are not.

And then, when you are asked for a proof, instead of referring to more correct or more ancient manuscripts, or to a greater number, or to the original text, your reply is, This verse is his, because it makes for me; and this is not his, because it is against me.

Are you, then, the rule of truth? Can nothing be true that is against you?

But what answer could you give to an opponent as insane as yourself, if he confronts you by saying, The passage in your favor is spurious, and that against you is genuine?

Perhaps you will produce a book, all of which can be explained so as to support you.

Then, instead of rejecting a passage, he will reply by condemning the whole book as spurious.

You have no resource against such an opponent.

For all the testimony you can bring in favor of your book from antiquity or tradition will avail nothing. In this respect the testimony of the Catholic Church is conspicuous, as supported by a succession of bishops from the original seats of the apostles up to the present time, and by the consent of so many nations.

Accordingly, should there be a question about the text of some passage, as there are a few passages with various readings well known to students of the sacred Scriptures, we should first consult the manuscripts of the country where the religion was first taught; and if these still varied, we should take the text of the greater number, or of the more ancient.

And if any uncertainty remained, we should consult the original text.

This is the method employed by those who, in any question about the Scriptures, do not lose sight of the regard due to their authority, and inquire with the view of gaining information, not of raising disputes. [380]

3.

As regards the passage from Paul's epistle which teaches, in opposition to your heresy, that the Son of God was born of the seed of David, it is found in all manuscripts both new and old of all Churches, and in all languages.

So the profession which Faustus makes of believing the apostle is hypocritical.

Instead of saying, "Assuredly I believe," he should have said, Assuredly I do not believe, as he would have said if he had not wished to deceive people.

What part of his belief does he get from the apostle?

Not the first man, of whom the apostle says that he is of the earth, earthy; and again, "The first man Adam was made a living soul."

Faustus' First Man is neither of the earth, earthy, nor made a living soul, but of the substance of God, and the same in essence as God; and this being is said to have mixed up with the race of darkness his members, or vesture, or weapons, that is, the five elements, which also are part of the substance of God, so that they became subject to confinement and pollution.

Nor does Faustus get from Paul his Second Man, of whom Paul says that He is from heaven, and that He is the last Adam, and a quickening spirit; and also that He was born of the seed of David after the flesh, that He was made of a woman, made under the law, that He might redeem them that were under the law. [381]Of Him Paul says to Timothy:

"Remember that Jesus Christ, of the seed of David, was raised from the dead, according to my gospel." [382]And this resurrection he quotes as an example of our resurrection:

"I delivered unto you first of all that which I also received, how that Christ died for our sins, according to the Scriptures; and that He was buried, and that He rose again the third day, according to the Scriptures."

And a little further on he draws an inference from this doctrine:

"Now, if Christ be preached that He rose from the dead, how say some among you that there is no resurrection of the dead?" [383]Our professed believer in Paul believes nothing of all this.

He denies that Jesus was born of the seed of David, that He was made of a woman (by the word woman is not meant a wife in the common sense of the word, but merely one of the female sex, as in the book of Genesis, where it is said that God made a woman before she was brought to Adam [384]); he denies His death, His burial, and His resurrection.

He holds that Christ had not a mortal body, and therefore could not really die; and that the marks of His wounds which He showed to His disciples when He appeared to them alive after His resurrection, which Paul also mentions, [385] were not real.

He denies, too, that our mortal body will be raised again, changed into a spiritual body; as Paul teaches:

"It is sown a natural body, it is raised a spiritual body."

To illustrate this distinction between the natural and the spiritual body, the apostle adds what I have quoted already about the first and the last Adam.

Then he goes on:

"But this I say, brethren, that flesh and blood cannot inherit the kingdom of God."

And to explain what he means by flesh and blood, that it is not the bodily substance, but corruption, which will not enter into the resurrection of the just, he immediately says, "Neither shall corruption inherit incorruption."

And in case any one should still suppose that it is not what is buried that is to rise again, but that it is as if one garment were laid aside and a better taken instead, he proceeds to show distinctly that the same body will be changed for the better, as the garments of Christ on the mount were not displaced, but transfigured:

"Behold, I show you a mystery; we shall not all be changed, but we shall all rise." [386]Then he shows who are to be changed:

"In a moment, in the twinkling of an eye, at the last trumpet:

for the trumpet shall sound, and the dead shall rise incorruptible, and we shall be changed."

And if it should be said that it is not as regards our mortal and corruptible body, but as regards our soul, that we are to be changed, it should be observed that the apostle is not speaking of the soul, but of the body, as is evident from the question he starts with:

"But some one will say, How are the dead raised, and with what body do they come?"

So also, in the conclusion of his argument, he leaves no doubt of what he is speaking: "This corruptible must put on incorruption, and this mortal must put on immortality." [387]Faustus denies this; and the God whom Paul declares to be "immortal, incorruptible, to whom alone is glory and honor," [388] he makes corruptible.

For in this monstrous and horrible fiction of theirs, the substance and nature of God was in danger of being wholly corrupted by the race of darkness, and to save the rest part actually was corrupted.

And to crown all this, he tries to deceive the ignorant who are not learned in the sacred Scriptures, by making this profession:

I assuredly believe the Apostle Paul; when he ought to have said, I assuredly do not believe.

4.

But Faustus has a proof to show that Paul changed his mind, and, in writing to the Corinthians, corrected what he had written to the Romans; or else that he never wrote the passage which appears as his, about Jesus Christ being born of the seed of David according to the flesh.

And what is this proof?

If the passage, he says, in the Epistle to the Romans is true, "the Son of God, who was made of the seed of David according to the flesh," what he says to the Corinthians cannot be true, "Henceforth know we no man after the flesh; yea, though we have known Christ after the flesh, yet now henceforth know we Him no more."

We must therefore show that both these passages are true, and not opposed to one another.

The agreement of the manuscripts proves both to be genuine.

In some Latin versions the word "born" [389] is used instead of "made," [390] which is not so literal a rendering, but gives the same meaning.

For both these translations, as well as the original, teach that Christ was of the seed of David after the flesh. We must not for a moment suppose that Paul corrected himself on account of a change of opinion.

Faustus himself felt the impropriety and impiety of such an explanation, and preferred to say that the passage was spurious, instead of that Paul was mistaken.

5.

As regards our writings, which are not a rule of faith or practice, but only a help to edification, we may suppose that they contain some things falling short of the truth in obscure and recondite matters, and that these mistakes may or may not be corrected in subsequent treatises.

For we are of those of whom the apostle says:

"And if ye be otherwise minded, God shall reveal even this unto you." [391] Such writings are read with the right of judgment, and without any obligation to believe.

In order to leave room for such profitable discussions of difficult questions, there is a distinct boundary line separating all productions subsequent to apostolic times from the authoritative canonical books of the Old and New Testaments.

The authority of these books has come down to us from the apostles through the successions of bishops and the extension of the Church, and, from a position of lofty supremacy, claims the submission of every faithful and pious mind.

If we are perplexed by an apparent contradiction in Scripture, it is not allowable to say, The author of this book is mistaken; but either the manuscript is faulty, or the translation is wrong, or you have not understood.

In the innumerable books that have been written latterly we may sometimes find the same truth as in Scripture, but there is not the same authority.

Scripture has a sacredness peculiar to itself.

In other books the reader may form his own opinion, and perhaps, from not understanding the writer, may differ from him, and may pronounce in favor of what pleases him, or against what he dislikes.

In such cases, a man is at liberty to withhold his belief, unless there is some clear demonstration or some canonical authority to show that the doctrine or statement either must or may be true.

But in consequence of the distinctive peculiarity of the sacred writings, we are bound to receive as true whatever the canon shows to have been said by even one prophet, or apostle, or evangelist. Otherwise, not a single page will be left for the guidance of human fallibility, if contempt for the wholesome authority of the canonical books either puts an end to that authority altogether, or involves it in hopeless confusion. [392]

6.

With regard, then, to this apparent contradiction between the passage which speaks of the Son of God being of the seed of David, to the words, "Though we have known Christ after the flesh, yet now henceforth know we Him no more," even though both quotations were not from the writings of one apostle,--though one were from Paul, and the other from Peter, or Isaiah, or any other apostle or prophet,--such is the equality of canonical authority, that it would not be allowable to doubt of either.

For the utterances of Scripture, harmonious as if from the mouth of one man, commend themselves to the belief of the most accurate and clear-sighted piety, and demand for their discovery and confirmation the calmest intelligence and the most ingenious research. In the case before us both quotations are from the canonical, that is, the genuine epistles of Paul.

We cannot say that the manuscript is faulty, for the best Latin translations substantially agree;

or that the translations are wrong, for the best texts have the same reading. So that, if any one is perplexed by the apparent contradiction, the only conclusion is that he does not understand.

Accordingly it remains for me to explain how both passages, instead of being contradictory, may be harmonized by one rule of sound faith.

The pious inquirer will find all perplexity removed by a careful examination.

7.

That the Son of God was made man of the seed of David, is not only said in other places by Paul, but is taught elsewhere in sacred Scripture.

As regards the words, "Though we have known Christ after the flesh, yet now henceforth know we Him no more," the context shows what is the apostle's meaning.

Here, or elsewhere, he views with an assured hope, as if it were already present and in actual possession, our future life, which is now fulfilled in our risen Head and Mediator, the man Christ Jesus.

This life will certainly not be after the flesh, even as Christ's life is now not after the flesh.

For by flesh the apostle here means not the substance of our bodies, in which sense the Lord used the word when, after His resurrection, He said, "Handle me, and see, for a spirit hath not flesh and bones, as ye see me have," [393] but the corruption and mortality of flesh, which will then not be in us, as now it is not in Christ.

The apostle uses the word flesh in the sense of corruption in the passage about the resurrection quoted before:

"Flesh and blood cannot inherit the kingdom of God, neither shall corruption inherit incorruption."

So, after the event described in the next verse, "Behold, I show you a mystery; we shall all rise, but we shall not all be changed.

In a moment, in the twinkling of an eye, at the last trump (for the trumpet shall sound); and the dead shall be raised incorruptible, and we shall be changed.

For this corruptible must put on incorruption, and this mortal must put on immortality," [394] -- then flesh, in the sense of the substance of the body, will, after this change, no longer have flesh, in the sense of the corruption of mortality; and yet, as regards its own nature, it will be the same flesh, the same which rises and which is changed. What the Lord said after His resurrection is true, "Handle me, and see; for a spirit hath not flesh and bones, as ye see me have;" and what the apostle says is true, "Flesh and blood cannot inherit the kingdom of God."

The first is said of the bodily substance, which exists as the subject of the change:

the second is said of the corruption of the flesh, which will cease to exist, for, after its change, flesh will not be corrupted.

So, "we have known Christ after the flesh," that is, after the mortality of flesh, before His resurrection; "now henceforth we know Him no more," because, as the same apostle says, "Christ being risen from the dead, dieth no more, and death hath no more dominion over Him." [395] The words, "we have known Christ after the flesh," strictly speaking, imply that Christ was after the flesh, for what never was cannot be known.

And it is not "we have supposed," but "we have known."

But not to insist on a word, in case some one should say that known is used in the sense of supposed, it is astonishing, if one could be surprised at want of sight in a blind man, that these blind people do not perceive that if what the apostle says about not knowing Christ after the flesh proves that Christ had not flesh, then what he says in the same place of not knowing any one henceforth after the flesh proves that all those here referred to had not flesh.

For when he speaks of not knowing any one, he cannot intend to speak only of Christ; but in his realization of the future life with those who are to be changed at the resurrection, he says, "Henceforth we know no man after the flesh;" that is, we have such an assured hope of our future incorruption and immortality, that the thought of it makes us rejoice even now.

So he says elsewhere:

"If ye then be risen with Christ, seek those things that are above, where Christ sitteth at the right hand of God.

Set your affections upon things above, and not on things on the earth." [396] It is true we have not yet risen as Christ has, but we are said to have risen with Him on account of the hope which we have in Him.

So again he says:

"According to His mercy He saved us, by the washing of regeneration." [397] Evidently what we obtain in the washing of regeneration is not the salvation itself, but the hope of it.

And yet, because this hope is certain, we are said to be saved, as if the salvation were already bestowed.

Philip Schaff, D.D., LL.D.

Elsewhere it is said explicitly:
"We groan within ourselves, waiting for the adoption, even the redemption of our body.
For we are saved by hope.
But hope which is seen is not hope; for what a man seeth, why doth he yet hope for? But if we hope for what we see not, then do we with patience wait for it." [398]The apostle says not, "we are to be saved," but, "We are now saved," that is, in hope, though not yet in reality.
And in the same way it is in hope, though not yet in reality, that we now know no man after the flesh.
This hope is in Christ, in whom what we hope for as promised to us has already been fulfilled.
He is risen, and death has no more dominion over Him.
Though we have known Him after the flesh, before His death, when there was in His body that mortality which the apostle properly calls flesh, now henceforth know we Him no more; for that mortal of His has now put on immortality, and His flesh, in the sense of mortality, no longer exists.

8.

The context of the passage containing this clause of which our adversaries make such a bad use, brings out its real meaning.
"The love of Christ," we read, "constrains us, because we thus judge, that if one died for all, then all died; and He died for all, that they which live should not henceforth live unto themselves, but to Him who died for them, and rose again.
Therefore henceforth know we no man after the flesh; and though we have known Christ after the flesh, yet now henceforth know we Him no more."
The words, "that they which live should not henceforth live unto themselves, but unto Him who died for them, and rose again," show plainly that the resurrection of Christ is the ground of the apostle's statement.
To live not to themselves, but to Him, must mean to live not after the flesh, in the hope of earthly and perishable goods, but after the spirit, in the hope of resurrection,--a resurrection already accomplished in Christ.
Of those, then, for whom Christ died and rose again, and who live henceforth not to themselves, but to Him, the Apostle says that he knows no one after the flesh, on account of the hope of future immortality to which they were looking forward,--a hope which in Christ was already a reality.
So, though he has known Christ after the flesh, before His death, now he knows Him no more; for he knows that He has risen, and that death has no more dominion over Him.
And because in Christ we all are even now in hope, though not in reality, what Christ is, he adds:
"Therefore if any man be in Christ, he is a new creature:
old things are passed away; behold, all things are become new.
And all things are of God, who has reconciled us to Himself by Christ." [399]What the new creature--that is, the people renewed by faith--hopes for regarding itself, it has already in Christ; and the hope will also hereafter be actually realized.
And, as regards this hope, old things have passed away, because we are no longer in the times of the Old Testament, expecting a temporal and carnal kingdom of God; and all things are become new, making the promise of the kingdom of heaven, where there shall be no death or corruption, the ground of our confidence.
But in the resurrection of the dead it will not be as a matter of hope, but in reality, that old things shall pass away, when the last enemy, death, shall be destroyed; and all things shall become new when this corruptible has put on incorruption, and this mortal has put on immortality.
This has already taken place in Christ, whom Paul accordingly, in reality, knew no longer after the flesh.
But not yet in reality, but only in hope, did he know no one after the flesh of those for whom Christ died and rose again.
For, as he says to the Ephesians, we are already saved by grace.
The whole passage is to the purpose:
"But God, who is rich in mercy, for His great love wherewith He loved us, even when we were dead in sins, hath quickened us together with Christ, by whose grace we have been saved."
The words, "hath quickened us together with Christ," correspond to what he said to the Corinthians, "that they which live should no longer live to themselves, but to Him that died for them and rose again."
And in the words, "by whose grace we have been saved," he speaks of the thing hoped for as already accomplished.

193

So, in the passage quoted above, he says explicitly, "We have been saved by hope."

And here he proceeds to specify future events as if already accomplished.

"And has raised us up together," he says, "and has made us sit together in heavenly places in Christ Jesus."

Christ is certainly already seated in heavenly places, but we not yet.

But as in an assured hope we already possess the future, he says that we sit in heavenly places, not in ourselves, but in Him.

And to show that it is still future, in case it should be thought that what is spoken of as accomplished in hope has been accomplished in reality, he adds, "that He might show in the ages to come the exceeding riches of His grace in His kindness towards us in Christ Jesus." [400] So also we must understand the following passage:

"For when we were in the flesh, the motions of sins, which were by the law, did work in our members to bring forth fruit unto death." [401] He says, "when we were in the flesh," as if they were no longer in the flesh.

He means to say, when we were in the hope of fleshly things, referring to the time when the law, which can be fulfilled only by spiritual love, was in force, in order that by transgression the offence might abound, that after the revelation of the New Testament, grace and the gift by grace might much more abound. And to the same effect he says elsewhere, "They which are in the flesh cannot please God;" and then, to show that he does not mean those not yet dead, he adds, "But ye are not in the flesh, but in the Spirit." [402] The meaning is, those who are in the hope of fleshly good cannot please God; but you are not in the hope of fleshly things, but in the hope of spiritual things, that is, of the kingdom of heaven, where the body itself, which now is natural, will, by the change in the resurrection, be, according to the capacity of its nature, a spiritual body.

For "it is sown a natural body, it will be raised a spiritual body."

If, then, the apostle knew no one after the flesh of those who were said to be not in the flesh, because they were not in the hope of fleshly things, although they still were burdened with corruptible and mortal flesh; how much more significantly could he say of Christ that he no longer knew Him after the flesh, seeing that in the body of Christ what they hoped for had already been accomplished!

Surely it is better and more reverential to examine the passages of sacred Scripture so as to discover their agreement with one another, than to accept some as true, and condemn others as false, whenever any difficulty occurs beyond the power of our weak intellect to solve.

As to the apostle in his childhood understanding as a child, this is said merely as an illustration. [403] And when he was a child he was not a spiritual man, as he was when he produced for the edification of the churches those writings which are not, as other books, merely a profitable study, but which authoritatively claim our belief as part of the ecclesiastical canon.

Book XII - *Faustus denies that the prophets predicted Christ*

Augustin proves such prediction from the New Testament, and expounds at length the principal types of Christ in the Old Testament.

1.

Faustus said:

Why do I not believe the prophets?

Rather why do you believe them?

On account, you will reply, of their prophecies about Christ.

For my part, I have read the prophets with the most eager attention, and have found no such prophecies.

And surely it shows a weak faith not to believe in Christ without proofs and testimonies.

Indeed, you yourselves are accustomed to teach that Christian faith is so simple and absolute as not to admit of laborious investigations.

Why, then, should you destroy the simplicity of faith by buttressing it with evidences, and Jewish evidences too?

Or if you are changing your opinion about evidences, what more trustworthy witness could you have than God Himself testifying to His own Son when He sent Him on earth,--not by a prophet or an interpreter,--by a voice immediately from heaven:

"This is my beloved Son, believe Him?" [404]

And again He testifies of Himself:

"I came forth from the Father, and am come into the world;" [405] and in many similar passages.

When the Jews quarrelled with this testimony, saying "Thou bearest witness of thyself, thy witness is not true," He replied:

"Although I bear witness of myself, my witness is true.

It is written in your law, The witness of two men is true.

I am one that bear witness of myself, and the Father who sent me beareth witness of me."[406] He does not mention the prophets.

Again He appeals to the testimony of His own works, saying, "If ye believe not me, believe the works;" [407] not, "If ye believe not me, believe the prophets."

Accordingly we require no testimonies concerning our Saviour.

All we look for in the prophets is prudence and virtue, and a good example, which, you are well aware, are not to be found in the Jewish prophets.

This, no doubt, explains your referring me at once to their predictions as a reason for believing them, without a word about their actions.

This may be good policy, but it is not in harmony with the declaration of Scripture, that it is impossible to gather grapes from thorns, or figs from thistles.

This may serve meanwhile as a brief and sufficient reply to the question, why we do not believe the prophets.

The fact that they did not prophesy of Christ is abundantly proved in the writings of our fathers.

I shall only add this, that if the Hebrew prophets knew and preached Christ, and yet lived such vicious lives, what Paul says of the wise men among the Gentiles might be applied to them:

"Though they knew God, they glorified Him not as God, nor were thankful; but they became vain in their imaginations, and their foolish heart was darkened." [408] You see the knowledge of great things is worth little, unless the life corresponds.

2.

Augustin replied:

The meaning of all this is, that the Hebrew prophets foretold nothing of Christ, and that, if they did, their predictions are of no use to us, and they themselves did not live suitably to the dignity of such prophecies.

We must therefore prove the fact of the prophecies; and their use for the truth and steadfastness of our faith; and that the lives of the prophets were in harmony with their words.

In this threefold discussion, it would take a long time under the first head to quote from all the books the passages in which Christ may be shown to have been predicted.

Faustus' frivolity may be met effectually by the weight of one great authority. Although Faustus does not believe the prophets, he professes to believe the apostles.

Above, as if to satisfy the doubts of some opponent, he declares that he assuredly believes the Apostle Paul. [409] Let us then hear what Paul says of the prophets.

His words are:

"Paul, a servant of Jesus Christ, called to be an apostle, separated unto the gospel of God, which He had promised before by His prophets in the holy Scriptures, concerning His Son, who was made of the seed of David according to the flesh." [410] What more does Faustus wish?

Will he maintain that the apostle is speaking of some other prophets, and not of the Hebrew prophets?

In any case, the gospel spoken of as promised was concerning the Son of God, who was made for Him of the seed of David according to the flesh:

and to this gospel the apostle says that he was separated.

So that the Manichæan heresy is opposed to faith in the gospel, which teaches that the Son of God was made of the seed of David according to the flesh.

Besides, there are many passages where the apostle plainly testifies in behalf of the Hebrew prophets, with an authority by which the necks of these proud Manichæans are broken.

3.

"I speak the truth in Christ," says the apostle, "I lie not, my conscience bearing me witness in the Holy Ghost, that I have great heaviness and continual sorrow of heart.

For I could wish that myself were accursed from Christ, for my brethren, my kinsmen according to the flesh:

who are Israelites; to whom pertaineth the adoption, and the glory, and the covenants, and the giving of the law, and the service and the promises; whose are the fathers, and of whom, as concerning the flesh, Christ came, who is over all, God blessed for ever." [411] Here is the most abundant and express testimony and the most solemn commendation.

The adoption here spoken of is evidently through the Son of God; as the apostle says to the Galatians:

"In the fullness of time, God sent forth His Son, made of a woman, made under the law, that He might redeem them that were under the law, that we might receive the adoption of sons."[412] And the glory spoken of is chiefly that of which he says in the same Epistle to the Romans:

"What advantage hath the Jew? or what profit is there in circumcision?

Much every way: chiefly, because unto them were committed the oracles of God." [413] Can the Manichæans tell us of any oracles of God committed to the Jews besides those of the Hebrew prophets?

And why are the covenants said to belong especially to the Israelites, but because not only was the Old Testament given to them, but also the New was prefigured in the Old?

Our opponents often display much ignorant ferocity in attacking the dispensation of the law given to the Israelites, not understanding that God wishes us to be not under the law, but under grace.

They are here answered by the apostle himself, who, in speaking of the advantages of the Jews, mentions this as one, that they had the giving of the law.

If the law had been bad, the apostle would not have referred to it in praise of the Jews.

And if Christ had not been preached by the law, the Lord Himself would not have said, "If ye believe Moses, ye would have believed me, for he wrote of me;" [414] nor would He have borne the testimony He did after His resurrection, saying, "All things must needs be fulfilled that were written in the law of Moses, and in the Prophets, and in the Psalms, concerning me." [415]

4.

But because the Manichæans preach another Christ, and not Him whom the apostles preached, but a false Christ of their own false contrivance, in imitation of whose falsehood they themselves speak lies, though they may perhaps be believed when they are not ashamed to profess to be the followers of a deceiver, that has befallen them which the apostle asserts of the unbelieving Jews:

"When Moses is read, a veil is upon their heart."

Neither will this veil which keeps them from understanding Moses be taken away from them till they turn to Christ; not a Christ of their own making, but the Christ of the Hebrew prophets.

For, as the apostle says, "When thou shalt turn to the Lord, the veil shall be taken away."[416] We cannot wonder that they do not believe in the Christ who rose from the dead, and who said, "All things must needs be fulfilled which were written in the law of Moses, and in the prophets, and in the Psalms, concerning me;" for this Christ has Himself told us what Abraham said to a hard-hearted rich man when he was in torment in hell, and asked Abraham to send some one to his brothers to teach them, that they might not come too into that place of torment.

Abraham's reply was:

"They have Moses and the prophets, let them hear them."

And when the rich man said that they would not believe unless some one rose from the dead, he received this most truthful answer:

"If they hear not Moses and the prophets, neither will they believe even though one rose from the dead." [417] Wherefore, the Manichæans will not hear Moses and the prophets, and so they do not believe Christ, though He rose from the dead.

Indeed, they do not even believe that Christ rose from the dead.

For how can they believe that He rose, when they do not believe that He died?

For, again, how can they believe that He died, when they deny that He had a mortal body?

5.

But we reject those false teachers whose Christ is false, or rather, whose Christ never existed.

For we have a Christ true and truthful, foretold by the prophets, preached by the apostles, who in innumerable places refer to the testimonies of the law and the prophets in support of their preaching.

Paul, in one short sentence, gives the right view of this subject.

"Now," he says, "the righteousness of God without the law is manifested, being witnessed by the law and the prophets." [418] What prophets, if not of Israel, to whom, as he expressly says, pertain the covenants, and the giving of the law, and the promises?

And what promises, but about Christ?

Elsewhere, speaking of Christ, he says concisely:

"All the promises of God are in Him yea." [419] Paul tells me that the giving of the law pertained to the Israelites.

He also tells me that Christ is the end of the law for righteousness to every one that believeth.

He also tells me that all the promises of God are in Christ yea.

And you tell me that the prophets of Israel foretold nothing of Christ.

Shall I believe the absurdities of Manichæus relating a vain and long fable in opposition to Paul? or shall I believe Paul when he forewarns us:

"If any man preach to you another gospel than that which we have preached, let him be accursed?"

6.

Our opponents may perhaps ask us to point out passages where Christ is predicted by the prophets of Israel.

One would think they might be satisfied with the authority of the apostles, who declare that what we read in the writings of the Hebrew prophets was fulfilled in Christ, or with that of Christ Himself, who says that these things were written of Him.

Whoever is unable to point out the passages should lay the blame on his own ignorance; for the apostles and Christ and the sacred Scriptures are not chargeable with falsehood.

However, one instance out of many may be adduced.

The apostle, in the verses following the passage quoted above, says:

"The word of God cannot fail.

For they are not all Israel which are of Israel; neither, because they are the seed of Abraham, are they all children:

but, In Isaac shall thy seed be called:

that is, they which are the children of the flesh, these are not the children of God; but the children of promise are counted for the seed." [420] What can our opponent say against this, in view of the declaration made to Abraham:

"In thy seed shall all the nations of the earth be blessed?"

At the time when the apostle gave the following exposition of this promise, "To Abraham and to his seed were the promises made.

He saith not, To seed, as of many, but as of one, To thy seed, which is Christ," [421] a doubt on this point might then have been less inexcusable, for at that time all nations had not yet believed on Christ, who is preached as of the seed of Abraham.

But now that we see the fulfillment of what we read in the ancient prophecy,--now that all nations are actually blessed in the seed of Abraham, to whom it was said thousands of years ago, "In thy seed shall all nations be blessed,"--it is mere obstinate folly to try to bring in another Christ, not of the seed of Abraham, or to hold that there are no predictions of Christ in the prophetical books of the children of Abraham.

7.

To enumerate all the passages in the Hebrew prophets referring to our Lord and Saviour Jesus Christ, would exceed the limits of a volume, not to speak of the brief replies of which this treatise consists.

The whole contents of these Scriptures are either directly or indirectly about Christ.

Often the reference is allegorical or enigmatical, perhaps in a verbal allusion, or in a historical narrative, requiring diligence in the student, and rewarding him with the pleasure of discovery.

Other passages, again, are plain; for, without the help of what is clear, we could not understand what is obscure.

And even the figurative passages, when brought together, will be found so harmonious in their testimony to Christ as to put to shame the obtuseness of the sceptic.

8.

In the creation God finished His works in six days, and rested on the seventh.

The history of the world contains six periods marked by the dealings of God with men.

The first period is from Adam to Noah; the second, from Noah to Abraham; the third, from Abraham to David; the fourth, from David to the captivity in Babylon; the fifth, from the captivity to the advent of lowliness of our Lord Jesus Christ; the sixth is now in progress, and will end in the coming of the exalted Saviour to judgment.

What answers to the seventh day is the rest of the saints,--not in this life, but in another, where the rich man saw Lazarus at rest while he was tormented in hell; where there is no evening, because there is no decay.

On the sixth day, in Genesis, man is formed after the image of God; in the sixth period of the world there is the clear discovery of our transformation in the renewing of our mind, according to the image of Him who created us, as the apostle says. [422] As a wife was made for Adam from his side while he slept, the Church becomes the property of her dying Saviour, by the sacrament of the blood which flowed from His side after His death.

The woman made out of her husband's side is called Eve, or Life, and the mother of living beings; and the Lord says in the Gospel:

"Except a man eat my flesh and drink my blood, he has no life in him." [423]The whole narrative of Genesis, in the most minute details, is a prophecy of Christ and of the Church with reference either to the good Christians or to the bad.

There is a significance in the words of the apostle when he calls Adam "the figure of Him that was to come;" [424] and when he says, "A man shall leave his father and mother, and shall cleave to his wife, and they two shall be one flesh.

This is a great mystery; but I speak concerning Christ and the Church." [425]This points most obviously to the way in which Christ left His Father; for "though He was in the form of God, and thought it not robbery to be equal with God, He emptied Himself, and took upon Him the form of a servant." [426]And so, too, He left His mother, the synagogue of the Jews which cleaved to the carnality of the Old Testament, and was united to the Church His holy bride, that in the peace of the New Testament they two might be one flesh.

For though with the Father He was God, by whom we were made, He became in the flesh partaker of our nature, that we might become the body of which He is the head.

9.

As Cain's sacrifice of the fruit of the ground is rejected, while Abel's sacrifice of his sheep and the fat thereof is accepted, so the faith of the New Testament praising God in the harmless service of grace is preferred to the earthly observances of the Old Testament. For though the Jews were right in practising these things, they were guilty of unbelief in not distinguishing the time of the New Testament when Christ came, from the time of the Old Testament.

God said to Cain, "If thou offerest well, yet if thou dividest not well, thou hast sinned."[427]If Cain had obeyed God when He said, "Be content, for to thee shall be its reference, and thou shalt rule over it," he would have referred his sin to himself, by taking the blame of it, and confessing it to God; and so assisted by supplies of grace, he would have ruled over his sin, instead of acting as the servant of sin in killing his innocent brother.

So also the Jews, of whom all these things are a figure, if they had been content, instead of being turbulent, and had acknowledged the time of salvation through the pardon of sins by grace, and heard Christ saying, "They that are whole need not a physician, but they that are sick; I came not to call the righteous, but sinners to repentance;" [428] and, "Every one that committeth sin is the servant of sin;" and, "If the Son make you free, ye shall be free indeed," [429] --they would in confession have referred their sin to themselves, saying to the Physician, as it is written in the Psalm, "I said, Lord, be merciful to me; heal my soul, for I have sinned against Thee." [430]And being made free by the hope of grace, they would have ruled over sin as long as it continued in their mortal body.

But now, being ignorant of God's righteousness, and wishing to establish a righteousness of their own, proud of the works of the law, instead of being humbled on account of their sins, they have not been content; and in subjection to sin reigning in their mortal body, so as to make them obey it in the lusts thereof, they have stumbled on the stone of stumbling, and have been inflamed with hatred against him whose works they grieved to see accepted by God.

The man who was born blind, and had been made to see, said to them, "We know that God heareth not sinners; but if any man serve Him, and do His will, him He heareth;" [431] as if he had said, God regardeth not the sacrifice of Cain, but he regards the sacrifice of Abel.

Abel, the younger brother, is killed by the elder brother; Christ, the head of the younger people, is killed by the elder people of the Jews.

Abel dies in the field; Christ dies on Calvary.

10.

God asks Cain where his brother is, not as if He did not know, but as a judge asks a guilty criminal.

Cain replies that he knows not, and that he is not his brother's keeper.

And what answer can the Jews give at this day, when we ask them with the voice of God, that is, of the sacred Scriptures, about Christ, except that they do not know the Christ that we speak of?

Cain's ignorance was pretended, and the Jews are deceived in their refusal of Christ.

Moreover, they would have been in a sense keepers of Christ, if they had been willing to receive and keep the Christian faith.

For the man who keeps Christ in his heart does not ask, like Cain, Am I my brother's keeper?

Then God says to Cain, "What hast thou done?

The voice of thy brother's blood crieth unto me from the ground."

So the voice of God in the Holy Scriptures accuses the Jews.

For the blood of Christ has a loud voice on the earth, when the responsive Amen of those who believe in Him comes from all nations.

This is the voice of Christ's blood, because the clear voice of the faithful redeemed by His blood is the voice of the blood itself.

11.

Then God says to Cain:

"Thou art cursed from the earth, which hath opened its mouth to receive thy brother's blood at thy hand.

For thou shalt till the earth, and it shall no longer yield unto thee its strength.

A mourner and an abject shalt thou be on the earth."

It is not, Cursed is the earth, but, Cursed art thou from the earth, which hath opened its mouth to receive thy brother's blood at thy hand.

So the unbelieving people of the Jews is cursed from the earth, that is, from the Church, which in the confession of sins has opened its mouth to receive the blood shed for the remission of sins by the hand of the people that would not be under grace, but under the law.

And this murderer is cursed by the Church; that is, the Church admits and avows the curse pronounced by the apostle:

"Whoever are of the works of the law are under the curse of the law." [432]Then, after saying, Cursed art thou from the earth, which has opened its mouth to receive thy brother's blood at thy hand, what follows is not, For thou shalt till it, but, Thou shalt till the earth, and it shall not yield to thee its strength.

The earth he is to till is not necessarily the same as that which opened its mouth to receive his brother's blood at his hand. From this earth he is cursed, and so he tills an earth which shall no longer yield to him its strength.

That is, the Church admits and avows the Jewish people to be cursed, because after killing Christ they continue to till the ground of an earthly circumcision, an earthly Sabbath, an earthly passover, while the hidden strength or virtue of making known Christ, which this tilling contains, is not yielded to the Jews while they continue in impiety and unbelief, for it is revealed in the New Testament.

While they will not turn to God, the veil which is on their minds in reading the Old Testament is not taken away.

This veil is taken away only by Christ, who does not do away with the reading of the Old Testament, but with the covering which hides its virtue.

So, at the crucifixion of Christ, the veil was rent in twain, that by the passion of Christ hidden mysteries might be revealed to believers who turn to Him with a mouth opened in confession to drink His blood.

In this way the Jewish people, like Cain, continue tilling the ground, in the carnal observance of the law, which does not yield to them its strength, because they do not perceive in it the grace of Christ.

So too, the flesh of Christ was the ground from which by crucifying Him the Jews produced our salvation, for He died for our offences.

But this ground did not yield to them its strength, for they were not justified by the virtue of His resurrection, for He arose again for our justification.

As the apostle says:

"He was crucified in weakness, but He liveth by the power of God." [433]This is the power of that ground which is unknown to the ungodly and unbelieving. When Christ rose, He did not appear to those who had crucified Him.

So Cain was not allowed to see the strength of the ground which he tilled to sow his seed in it; as God said, "Thou shalt till the ground, and it shall no longer yield unto thee its strength."

12.

"Groaning and trembling shalt thou be on the earth."

Here no one can fail to see that in every land where the Jews are scattered they mourn for the loss of their kingdom, and are in terrified subjection to the immensely superior number of Christians.

So Cain answered, and said:

"My case is worse, if Thou drivest me out this day from the face of the earth, and from Thy face shall I be hid, and I shall be a mourner and an outcast on the earth; and it shall be that every one that findeth me shall slay me."

Here he groans indeed in terror, lest after losing his earthly possession he should suffer the death of the body.

This he calls a worse case than that of the ground not yielding to him its strength, or than that of spiritual death.

For his mind is carnal; for he thinks little of being hid from the face of God, that is, of being under the anger of God, were it not that he may be found and slain.

This is the carnal mind that tills the ground, but does not obtain its strength.

To be carnally minded is death; but he, in ignorance of this, mourns for the loss of his earthly possession, and is in terror of bodily death.

But what does God reply?

"Not so," He says; "but whosoever shall kill Cain, vengeance shall be taken on him sevenfold."

That is, It is not as thou sayest; not by bodily death shall the ungodly race of carnal Jews perish.

For whoever destroys them in this way shall suffer sevenfold vengeance, that is, shall bring upon himself the sevenfold penalty under which the Jews lie for the crucifixion of Christ.

So to the end of the seven days of time, the continued preservation of the Jews will be a proof to believing Christians of the subjection merited by those who, in the pride of their kingdom, put the Lord to death.

13.

"And the Lord God set a mark upon Cain, lest any one finding him should slay him."

It is a most notable fact, that all the nations subjugated by Rome adopted the heathenish ceremonies of the Roman worship; while the Jewish nation, whether under Pagan or Christian monarchs, has never lost the sign of their law, by which they are distinguished from all other nations and peoples.

No emperor or monarch who finds under his government the people with this mark kills them, that is, makes them cease to be Jews, and as Jews to be separate in their observances, and unlike the rest of the world.

Only when a Jew comes over to Christ, he is no longer Cain, nor goes out from the presence of God, nor dwells in the land of Nod, which is said to mean commotion.

Against this evil of commotion the Psalmist prays, "Suffer not my feet to be moved;" [434] and again, "Let not the hands of the wicked remove me;" [435] and, "Those that trouble me will rejoice when I am moved:" [436] and, "The Lord is at my right hand, that I should not be moved;" [437] and so in innumerable places.

This evil comes upon those who leave the presence of God, that is, His loving-kindness.

Thus the Psalmist says, "I said in my prosperity, I shall never be moved."

But observe what follows, "Lord, by Thy favor Thou hast given strength to my honor; Thou didst hide Thy face, and I was troubled;" [438] which teaches us that not in itself, but by participation in the light of God, can any soul possess beauty, or honor, or strength.

The Manichæans should think of this, to keep them from the blasphemy of identifying themselves with the nature and substance of God.

But they cannot think, because they are not content.

The Sabbath of the heart they are strangers to.

If they were content, as Cain was told to be, they would refer their sin to themselves; that is, they would lay the blame on themselves, and not on a race of darkness that no one ever heard of, and so by the grace of God they would prevail over their sin.

But now the Manichæans, and all who oppose the truth by their various heresies, leave the presence of God, like Cain and the scattered Jews, and inhabit the land of commotion, that is, of carnal disquietude, instead of the enjoyment of God, that is instead of Eden, which is interpreted Feasting, where Paradise was planted.

But not to depart too much from the argument of this treatise I must limit myself to a few, short remarks under this head.

14.

Omitting therefore many passages in these Books where Christ may be found, but which require longer explanation and proof, although the most hidden meanings are the sweetest, convincing testimony may be obtained from the enumeration of such things as the following:--That Enoch, the seventh from Adam, pleased God, and was translated, as there is to be a seventh day of rest into which all will be translated who, during the sixth day of the world's history, are created anew by the incarnate Word.

That Noah, with his family is saved by water and wood, as the family of Christ is saved by baptism, as representing the suffering of the cross.

That this ark is made of beams formed in a square, as the Church is constructed of saints

prepared unto every good work:
for a square stands firm on any side.

That the length is six times the breadth, and ten times the height, like a human body, to show that Christ appeared in a human body.

That the breadth reaches to fifty cubits; as the apostle says, "Our heart is enlarged," [439] that is, with spiritual love, of which he says again, "The love of God is shed abroad in our heart by the Holy Ghost, which is given unto us." [440] For in the fiftieth day after His resurrection, Christ sent His Holy Spirit to enlarge the hearts of His disciples.

That it is three hundred cubits long, to make up six times fifty; as there are six periods in the history of the world during which Christ has never ceased to be preached,--in five foretold by the prophets, and in the sixth proclaimed in the gospel.

That it is thirty cubits high, a tenth part of the length; because Christ is our height, who in his thirtieth year gave His sanction to the doctrine of the gospel, by declaring that He came not to destroy the law, but to fulfil it.

Now the ten commandments are to be the heart of the law; and so the length of the ark is ten times thirty.

Noah himself, too, was the tenth from Adam. That the beams of the ark are fastened within and without with pitch, to signify by compact union the forbearance of love, which keeps the brotherly connection from being impaired, and the bond of peace from being broken by the offences which try the Church either from without or from within.

For pitch is a glutinous substance, of great energy and force, to represent the ardor of love which, with great power of endurance, beareth all things in the maintenance of spiritual communion.

15.

That all kinds of animals are inclosed in the ark; as the Church contains all nations, which was also set forth in the vessel shown to Peter.

That clean and unclean animals are in the ark; as good and bad take part in the sacraments of the Church.

That the clean are in sevens, and the unclean in twos; not because the bad are fewer than the good, but because the good preserve the unity of the Spirit in the bond of peace; and the Spirit is spoken of in Scripture as having a sevenfold operation, as being "the Holy Spirit of wisdom and understanding, of counsel and might, of knowledge and piety, and of the fear of God." [441] So also the number fifty, which is connected with the advent of the Holy Spirit, is made up of seven times seven, and one over; whence it is said, "Endeavoring to keep the unity of the Spirit in the bond of peace." [442] The bad, again, are in twos, as being easily divided, from their tendency to schism.

That Noah, counting his family, was the eighth; because the hope of our resurrection has appeared in Christ, who rose from the dead on the eighth day, that is, on the day after the seventh, or Sabbath day.

This day was the third from His passion; but in the ordinary reckoning of days, it is both the eighth and the first.

16.

That the whole ark together is finished in a cubit above; as the Church, the body of Christ gathered into unity, is raised to perfection.

So Christ says in the Gospel:

"He that gathereth not with me, scattereth." [443] That the entrance is on the side; as no man enters the Church except by the sacrament of the remission of sins which flowed from Christ's opened side.

That the lower spaces of the ark are divided into two and three chambers:

as the multitude of all nations in the Church is divided into two, as circumcised and uncircumcised; or into three, as descended from the three sons of Noah.

And these parts of the ark are called lower, because in this earthly state there is a difference of races, and above we are completed in one.

Above there is no diversity; for Christ is all and in all, finishing us, as it were, in one cubit above with heavenly unity.

17.
That the flood came seven days after Noah entered the ark; as we are baptized in the hope of the future rest, which was denoted by the seventh day.

That all flesh on the face of the earth, outside the ark, was destroyed by the flood; as, beyond the communion of the Church, though the water of baptism is the same, it is efficacious only for destruction, and not for salvation.

That it rained for forty days and forty nights; as the sacrament of heavenly baptism washes away all the guilt of the sins against the ten commandments throughout all the four quarters of the world (four times ten is forty), whether that guilt has been contracted in the day of prosperity or in the night of adversity.

18.
That Noah was five hundred years old when God told him to make the ark, and six hundred when he entered the ark; which shows that the ark was made during one hundred years, which seem to correspond to the years of an age of the world.

So the sixth age is occupied with the construction of the Church by the preaching of the gospel.

The man who avails himself of the offer of salvation is made like a square beam, fitted for every good work, and forms part of the sacred fabric. Again, it was the second month of the six hundredth year when Noah entered the ark, and in two months there are sixty days; so that here, as in every multiple of six, we have the number denoting the sixth age.

19.
That mention is made of the twenty seventh day of the month; as we have already seen the significance of the square in the beams.

Here especially it is significant; for as twenty-seven is the cube of three, there is a trinity in the means by which we are, as it were, squared, or fitted for every good work.

By the memory we remember God; by the understanding we know Him; by the will we love Him.

That in the seventh month the ark rested; reminding us again of the seventh day of rest.

And here again, to denote the perfection of those at rest, the twenty-seventh day of the month is mentioned for the second time.

So what is promised in hope is realized in experience.

There is here a combination of seven and eight; for the water rose fifteen cubits above the mountains, pointing to a profound mystery in baptism,--the sacrament of our regeneration.

For the seventh day of rest is connected with the eighth of resurrection.

For when the saints receive again their bodies after the rest of the intermediate state, the rest will not cease; but rather the whole man, body and soul united, renewed in the immortal health, will attain to the realization of his hope in the enjoyment of eternal life.

Thus the sacrament of baptism, like the waters of Noah, rises above all the wisdom of the proud.

Seven and eight are also combined in the number of one hundred and fifty, made up of seventy and eighty, which was the number of days during which the water prevailed, pointing out the deep import of baptism in consecrating the new man to hold the faith of rest and resurrection.

20.
That the raven sent out after forty days did not return, being either prevented by the water or attracted by some floating carcase; as men defiled by impure desire, and therefore eager for things outside in the world, are either baptized, or are led astray into the company of those to whom, as they are outside the ark, that is, outside the Church, baptism is destructive.

That the dove when sent forth found no rest, and returned; as in the New Testament rest is not promised to the saints in this world.

The dove was sent forth after forty days, a period denoting the length of human life.

When again sent forth after seven days, denoting the sevenfold operation of the Spirit, the dove brought back a fruitful olive branch; as some even who are baptized outside of the Church, if not destitute of the fatness of charity, may come after all, as it were in the evening, and be brought into the one communion by the mouth of the dove in the kiss of peace.

That, when again sent forth after seven days, the dove did not return; as, at the end of the world, the rest of the saints shall no longer be in the sacrament of hope, as now, while in the communion of the Church, they drink what flowed from the side of Christ, but in the perfection of eternal safety, when the kingdom shall be delivered up to God and the Father, and when, in that unclouded contemplation of unchangeable truth, we shall no longer need natural symbols.

21.

There are many other points which we cannot take notice of even in this cursory manner.

Why in the six hundred and first year of Noah's life--that is, after six hundred years were completed--the covering of the ark is removed, and the hidden mystery, as it were, disclosed.

Why the earth is said to have dried on the twenty-seventh day of the second month; as if the number fifty-seven denoted the completion of the rite of baptism.

For the twenty-seventh day of the second month is the fifty-seventh day of the year; and the number fifty-seven is seven times eight, which are the numbers of the spirit and the body, with one over, to denote the bond of unity.

Why they leave the ark together, though they entered separately.

For it is said:

"Noah went in, and his sons, and his wife, and his sons' wives with him, into the ark;" the men and the women being spoken of separately; which denotes the time when the flesh lusteth against the spirit, and the spirit against the flesh.

But they go forth, Noah and his wife, and his sons and their wives,--the men and women together.

For in the end of the world, and in the resurrection of the just, the body will be united to the spirit in perfect harmony, undisturbed by the wants and the passions of mortality.

Why, after leaving the ark, only clean animals are offered in sacrifice to God, though both clean and unclean were in the ark.

22.

Then, again, it is significant that when God speaks to Noah, and begins anew, as it were, in order, by repetition in various forms, to draw attention to the figure of the Church, the sons of Noah are blessed, and told to replenish the earth, and all animals are given to them for food; as was said to Peter of the vessel, "Kill and eat." That they are told to pour out the blood when they eat; that the former life may not be kept shut up in the conscience, but may be, as it were, poured out in confession.

That God makes the bow, which appears in the clouds only when the sun shines, the sign of His covenant with men, and with every living thing, that He will not destroy them with a flood; as those do not perish by the flood, in separation from the Church, who in the clouds of God--that is, in the prophets and in all the sacred Scriptures--discern the glory of Christ, instead of seeking their own glory.

The worshippers of the sun, however, need not pride themselves on this; for they must understand that the sun, as also a lion, a lamb, and a stone, are used as types of Christ because they have some resemblance, not because they are of the same substance.

23.

Again, the sufferings of Christ from His own nation are evidently denoted by Noah being drunk with the wine of the vineyard he planted, and his being uncovered in his tent.

For the mortality of Christ's flesh was uncovered, to the Jews a stumbling-block, and to the Greeks foolishness; but to them that are called, both Jews and Greeks, both Shem and Japhet, the power of God and the wisdom of God.

Because the foolishness of God is wiser than men, and the weakness of God is stronger than men. [444]

Moreover, the two sons, the eldest and the youngest, carrying the garment backwards, are a figure of the two peoples, and the sacrament of the past and completed passions of the Lord.

They do not see the nakedness of their father, because they do not consent to Christ's death; and yet they honor it with a covering, as knowing whence they were born.

The middle son is the Jewish people, for they neither held the first place with the apostles, nor believed subsequently with the Gentiles.

They saw the nakedness of their father, because they consented to Christ's death; and they told it to their brethren outside, for what was hidden in the prophets was disclosed by the Jews.

And thus they are the servants of their brethren.

For what else is this nation now but a desk for the Christians, bearing the law and the prophets, and testifying to the doctrine of the Church, so that we honor in the sacrament what they disclose in the letter?

24.

Again, every one must be impressed, and be either enlightened or confirmed in the faith, by the blessing of the two sons who honored the nakedness of their father, though they turned away their faces, as displeased with the evil done by the vine.

"Blessed," he says, "be the Lord God of Shem."

For although God is the God of all nations, even the Gentiles acknowledge Him to be in a peculiar sense the God of Israel.

And how is this to be explained but by the blessing of Japhet?

The occupation of all the world by the Church among the Gentiles was exactly foretold in the words:

"Let God enlarge Japhet, and let him dwell in the tents of Shem."

That is for the Manichæan to attend to.

You see what the state of the world actually is.

The very thing that you are astonished and grieved at in us is this, that God is enlarging Japhet.

Is He not dwelling in the tents of Shem?--that is, in the churches built by the apostles, the sons of the prophets.

Hear what Paul says to the believing Gentiles:

"Ye were at that time without Christ, being aliens from the commonwealth of Israel, and strangers from the covenants; having no hope of the promise, and without God in the world."

In these words there is a description of the state of Japhet before he dwelt in the tents of Shem.

But observe what follows:

"Now then;" he says, "ye are no more strangers and foreigners, but fellow-citizens with the saints, and of the household of God, being built upon the foundation of the apostles and prophets, Jesus Christ Himself being the chief corner-stone." [445] Here we have Japhet enlarged, and dwelling in the tents of Shem.

These testimonies are taken from the epistles of the apostles, which you yourselves acknowledge, and read, and profess to follow.

You occupy an unhappy middle position in a building of which Christ is not the chief corner-stone.

For you do not belong to the wall of those who, like the apostles, being of the circumcision, believed in Christ; nor to the wall of those who, being of the uncircumcision, like all the Gentiles, are joined in the unity of faith, as in the fellowship of the corner-stone.

However, all who accept and read any books of our canon in which Christ is spoken of as having been born and having suffered in the flesh, and who do not unite with us in a common veiling with the sacrament of the mortality, uncovered by the passion, but without the knowledge of piety and charity make known that from which we all are born,--although they differ among themselves, whether as Jews and heretics, or as heretics of one kind or other,--are still all useful to the Church, as being all alike servants, either in bearing witness to or in proving some truth.

For of heretics it is said:

"There must be heresies, that those who are approved among you may be manifested."[446] Go on, then, with your objections to the Old Testament Scriptures!

Go on, ye servants of Ham!

You have despised the flesh from which you were born when uncovered.

For you could not have called yourselves Christians unless Christ had come into the world, as foretold by the prophets, and had drunk of His own vine that cup which could not pass from Him, and had slept in His passion, as in the drunkenness of the folly which is wiser than men; and so, in the hidden counsel of God, the disclosure had been made of that infirmity of mortal flesh which is stronger than men.

For unless the Word of God had taken on Himself this infirmity, the name of Christian, in which you also glory, would not exist in the earth.

Go on, then, as I have said.

Declare in mockery what we may honor with reverence.

Let the Church use you as her servants to make manifest those members who are approved.

So particular are the predictions of the prophets regarding the state and the sufferings of the Church, that we can find a place even for you in what is said of the destructive error by which the reprobate are to perish, while the approved are to be manifested.

25.

You say that Christ was not foretold by the prophets of Israel, when, in fact, their Scriptures teem with such predictions, if you would only examine them carefully, instead of treating them with levity.

Who in Abraham leaves his country and kindred that he may become rich and prosperous among strangers, but He who, leaving the land and country of the Jews, of whom He was born in the flesh, is now extending His power, as we see, among the Gentiles?

Who in Isaac carried the wood for His own sacrifice, but He who carried His own cross?

Who is the ram for sacrifice, caught by the horns in a. bush, but He who was fastened to the cross as an offering for us?

26.

Who in the angel striving with Jacob, on the one hand is constrained to give him a blessing, as the weaker to the stronger, the conquered to the conqueror, and on the other hand puts his thigh-bone out of joint, but He who, when He suffered the people of Israel to prevail against Him, blessed those among them who believed, while the multitude, like Jacob's thigh-bone, halted in their carnality?

Who is the stone placed under Jacob's head, but Christ the head of man?

And in its anointing the very name of Christ is expressed, for, as all know, Christ means anointed.

Christ refers to this in the Gospel, and declares it to be a type of Himself, when He said of Nathanael that he was an Israelite indeed, in whom was no guile, and when Nathanael, resting his head, as it were, on this Stone, or on Christ, confessed Him as the Son of God and the King of Israel anointing the Stone by his confession, in which he acknowledged Jesus to be Christ.

On this occasion the Lord made appropriate mention of what Jacob saw in his dream "Verily I say unto you, Ye shall see heaven opened, and the angels of God ascending and descending upon the Son of man." [447] This Jacob saw, who in the blessing was called Israel, when he had the stone for a pillow, and had the vision of the ladder reaching from earth to heaven, on which the angels of God were ascending and descending. [448] The angels denote the evangelists, or preachers of Christ.

They ascend when they rise above the created universe to describe the supreme majesty of the divine nature of Christ as being in the beginning God with God, by whom all things were made.

They descend to tell of His being made of a woman, made under the law, that He might redeem them that were under the law.

Christ is the ladder reaching from earth to heaven, or from the carnal to the spiritual:

for by His assistance the carnal ascend to spirituality; and the spiritual may be said to descend to nourish the carnal with milk when they cannot speak to them as to spiritual, but as to carnal.[449] There is thus both an ascent and a descent upon the Son of man.

For the Son of man is above as our head, being Himself the Saviour; and He is below in His body, the Church.

He is the ladder, for He says, "I am the way."

We ascend to Him to see Him in heavenly places; we descend to Him for the nourishment of His weak members.

And the ascent and descent are by Him as well as to Him.

Following His example, those who preach Him not only rise to behold Him exalted, but let themselves down to give a plain announcement of the truth.

So the apostle ascends, "Whether we be beside ourselves, it is to God;" and descends, "Whether we be sober, it is for your sake."

And by whom did he ascend and descend?

"For the love of Christ constraineth us:

for we thus judge, that if one died for all, then all died; and that He died for all, that they which live should no longer live unto themselves, but unto Him that died for them, and rose again."[450]

27.

The man who does not find pleasure in these views of sacred Scripture is turned away to fables, because he cannot bear sound doctrine.

The fables have an attraction for childish minds in people of all ages; but we who are of the body of Christ should say with the Psalmist; "O Lord, the wicked have spoken to me pleasing things, but they are not after Thy law." [451] In every page of these Scriptures, while I pursue my search as a son of Adam in the sweat of my brow, Christ either openly or covertly meets and refreshes me.

Where the discovery is laborious my ardor is increased, and the spoil obtained is eagerly devoured, and is hidden in my heart for my nourishment.

28.

Christ appears to me in Joseph, who was persecuted and sold by his brethren, and after his troubles obtained honor in Egypt.

We have seen the troubles of Christ in the world, of which Egypt was a figure, in the sufferings of the martyrs.

And now we see the honor of Christ in the same world which He subdues to Himself, in exchange for the food which He bestows.

Christ appears to me in the rod of Moses, which became a serpent when cast on the earth as a figure of His death, which came from the serpent.

Again, when caught by the tail it became a rod, as a figure of His return after the accomplishment of His work in His resurrection to what He was before, destroying death by His new life, so as to leave no trace of the serpent.

We, too, who are His body, glide along in the same mortality through the folds of time; but when at last the tail of this course of things is laid hold of by the hand of judgment that it shall go no further, we shall be renewed, and rising from the destruction of death, the last enemy, we shall be the sceptre of government in the right hand of God.

29.

Of the departure of Israel from Egypt, let us hear what the apostle himself says:

"I would not, brethren, that ye should be ignorant that all our fathers were under the cloud, and all passed through the sea, and were all baptized into Moses in the cloud and in the sea, and did all eat the same spiritual meat, and did all drink of the same spiritual drink.

For they drank of the spiritual rock which followed them, and that rock was Christ." [452] The explanation of one thing is a key to the rest.

For if the rock is Christ from its stability, is not the manna Christ, the living bread which came down from heaven, which gives spiritual life to those who truly feed on it? The Israelites died because they received the figure only in its carnal sense.

The apostle, by calling it spiritual food, shows its reference to Christ, as the spiritual drink is explained by the words, "That rock was Christ," which explain the whole.

Then is not the cloud and the pillar Christ, who by His uprightness and strength supports our feebleness; who shines by night and not by day, that they who see not may see, and that they who see may be made blind?

In the clouds and the Red Sea there is the baptism consecrated by the blood of Christ. The enemies following behind perish, as past sins are put away.

30.

The Israelites are led through the wilderness, as those who are baptized are in the wilderness while on the way to the promised land, hoping and patiently waiting for that which they see not.

In the wilderness are severe trials, lest they should in heart return to Egypt.

Still Christ does not leave them; the pillar does not go away. The bitter waters are sweetened by wood, as hostile people become friendly by learning to honor the cross of Christ.

The twelve fountains watering the seventy palm trees are a figure of apostolic grace watering the nations.

As seven is multiplied by ten, so the decalogue is fulfilled in the sevenfold operation of the Spirit.

The enemy attempting to stop them in their way is overcome by Moses stretching out his hands in the figure of the cross.

The deadly bites of serpents are healed by the brazen serpent, which was lifted up that they might look at it.

The Lord Himself gives the explanation of this:

"As Moses lifted up the serpent in the wilderness, so must the Son of man be lifted up, that whosoever believeth in Him may not perish, but have everlasting life." [453] So in many other things we may find a protest against the obstinacy of unbelieving hearts.

In the passover a lamb is killed, representing Christ, of whom it is said in the Gospel, "Behold the Lamb of God, who taketh away the sin of the world!" [454] In the passover the bones of the lamb were not to be broken; and on the cross the bones of the Lord were not broken.

The evangelist, in reference to this, quotes the words, "A bone of Him shall not be broken."[455] The posts were marked with blood to keep away destruction, as people are marked on their foreheads with the sign of the Lord's passion for their salvation.

The law was given on the fiftieth day after the passover; so the Holy Spirit came on the

Philip Schaff, D.D., LL.D.

fiftieth day after the passion of the Lord.

The law is said to have been written with the finger of God; and the Lord says of the Holy Spirit, "With the finger of God I cast out devils." [456] Such are the Scriptures in which Faustus, after shutting his eyes, declares that he can see no prediction of Christ.

But we need not wonder that he should have eyes to read and yet no heart to understand, since, instead of knocking in devout faith at the door of the heavenly secret, he dares to act in profane hostility.

So let it be, for so it ought to be.

Let the gate of salvation be shut to the proud.

The meek, to whom God teaches His ways, will find all these things in the Scriptures, and those things which he does not see he will believe from what he sees.

31.

He will see Jesus leading the people into the land of promise; for this name was given to the leader of Israel, not at first, or by chance, but on account of the work to which he was called.

He will see the cluster from the land of promise hanging from a wooden pole.

He will see in Jericho, as in this perishing world, an harlot, one of those of whom the Lord says that they go before the proud into the kingdom of heaven, putting out of her window a scarlet line symbolical of blood, as confession is made with the mouth for the remission of sins.

He will see the walls of Jericho, like the frail defences of the world, fall when compassed seven times by the ark of the covenant; as now in the course of the seven days of time the covenant of God compasses the whole globe, that in the end, death, the last enemy, may be destroyed, and the Church, like one single house, be saved from the destruction of the ungodly, purified from the defilement of fornication by the window of confession in the blood of remission.

32.

He will see the times of the judges precede those of the kings, as the judgment will precede the kingdom.

And under both the judges and the kings he will see Christ and the Church repeatedly prefigured in many and various ways.

Who was in Samson, when he killed the lion that met him as he went to get a wife among strangers, but He who, when going to call His Church from among the Gentiles, said, "Be of good cheer, I have overcome the world?" [457] What means the hive in the mouth of the slain lion, but that, as we see, the very laws of the earthly kingdom which once raged against Christ have now lost their fierceness, and have become a protection for the preaching of gospel sweetness?

What is that woman boldly piercing the temples of the enemy with a wooden nail, but the faith of the Church casting down the kingdom of the devil by the cross of Christ?

What is the fleece wet while the ground was dry, and again the fleece dry while the ground was wet, but the Hebrew nation at first possessing alone in its typical institution Christ the mystery of God, while the whole world was in ignorance?

And now the whole world has this mystery revealed, while the Jews are destitute of it.

33.

To mention only a few things in the times of the kings, at the very outset does not the change in the priesthood when Eli was rejected and Samuel chosen, and in the kingdom when Saul was rejected and David chosen, clearly predict the new priesthood and kingdom to come in our Lord Jesus Christ, when the old, which was a shadow of the new, was rejected?

Did not David, when he ate the shew-bread, which it was not lawful for any but the priests to eat, prefigure the union of the kingdom and priesthood in one person, Jesus Christ?

In the separation of the ten tribes from the temple while two were left, is there not a figure of what the apostle asserts of the whole nation:

"A remnant is saved by the election of grace."? [458]

34.

In the time of famine, Elijah is fed by ravens bringing bread in the morning and flesh in the evening; but the Manichæans cannot in this perceive Christ, who, as it were, hungers for our salvation, and to whom sinners come in confession, having now the first-fruits of the Spirit, while in the end, that is to say in the evening of the age, they will have the resurrection of their bodies also.

Elijah is sent to be fed by a widow woman of another nation, who was going to gather two sticks before she died, denoting the two wooden beams of the cross.

Her meal and oil are blessed, as the fruit and cheerfulness of charity do not diminish by expenditure, for God loveth a cheerful giver. [439]

35.

The children that mocked Elisha by calling out Baldhead, are devoured by wild beasts, as those who in childish folly scoff at Christ crucified on Calvary are destroyed by devils.

Elisha sends his servants to lay his staff on the dead body, but it does not revive; he comes himself, and lays himself exactly upon the dead body, and it revives:

as the Word of God sent the law by His servant, without any profit to mankind dead in sins; and yet it was not sent without purpose by Him who knew the necessity of its being first sent.

Then He Himself came, conformed Himself to us by participation in our death, and we were revived.

When they were cutting down wood with axes, the iron, flying off the wood, sank to the bottom of the river, and came up again when the wood was thrown in by Elisha.

So, when Christ's bodily presence was cutting down the unfruitful trees among the unbelieving Jews, according to the saying of John, "Behold, the axe is laid to the roots of the tree,"[460] by the death they inflicted, Christ was separated from His body, and descended to the depths of the infernal world; and then, when His body was laid in the tomb, like the wood on the water, His spirit returned, like the iron to the handle, and He rose.

The reader will observe how many things of this kind are omitted for the sake of brevity.

36.

As regards the departure to Babylon, where the Spirit of God by the prophet Jeremiah enjoins them to go, telling them to pray for the people in whose land they dwell as strangers, because in their peace they would find peace, and to build houses, and plant vineyards and gardens,--the figurative meaning is plain, when we consider that the true Israelites, in whom is no guile, passed over in the ministry of the apostles with the ordinances of the gospel into the kingdom of the Gentiles.

So the apostle, like an echo of Jeremiah, says to us, "I will first of all that prayer, supplications, intercessions and giving of thanks be made for all men, and for those in authority, that we may live a quiet and peaceable life in all godliness and charity; for this is good and acceptable in the sight of God our Saviour, who will have all men to be saved, and to come to the knowledge of the truth." [461]

Accordingly the basilicas of Christian congregations have been built by believers as abodes of peace, and vineyards of the faithful have been renewed, and gardens planted, where chief among the plants is the mustard tree, in whose wide-spreading branches the pride of the Gentiles, like the birds of heaven, in its soaring ambition, takes shelter.

Again, in the return from captivity after seventy years, according to Jeremiah's prophecy, and in the restoration of the temple, every believer in Christ must see a figure of our return as the Church of God from the exile of this world to the heavenly Jerusalem, after the seven days of time have fulfilled their course.

Joshua the high priest, after the captivity, who rebuilt the temple, was a figure of Jesus Christ, the true High Priest of our restoration.

The prophet Zechariah saw this Joshua in a filthy garment; and after the devil who stood by to accuse him was defeated, the filthy garment was taken from him, and a dress of honor and glory given him.

So the body of Jesus Christ, which is the Church, when the adversary is conquered in the judgment at the end of the world, will pass from the pains of exile to the glory of everlasting safety.

This is the song of the Psalmist at the dedication of his house:

"Thou hast turned for me my mourning into gladness; Thou hast removed my sackcloth, and girded me with gladness, that my glory may sing praise unto Thee, and not be silent." [462]

37.

It is impossible, in a digression like this, to refer, however briefly, to all the figurative predictions of Christ which are to be found in the law and the prophets.

Will it be said that these things happened in the regular course of things, and that it is a mere ingenious fancy to make them typical of Christ?

Such an objection might come from Jews and Pagans; but those who wish to be considered Christians must yield to the authority of the apostle when he says, "All these things happened to them for an example;" and again, "These things are our examples." [463] For if two men, Ishmael and Isaac, are types of the two covenants, can it be supposed that there is no significance in the vast number of particulars which have no historical or natural value?

Suppose we were to see some Hebrew characters written on the wall of a noble building, should we be so foolish as to conclude that, because we cannot understand the characters, they are not intended to be read, and are mere painting, without any meaning? So, whoever with a candid mind reads all these things that are contained in the Old Testament Scriptures, must feel constrained to acknowledge that they have a meaning.

38.

As an example of those particulars which have no meaning at all if not a symbolical one:
Granting that it was necessary that woman should be made as an help meet for man, what natural reason can be assigned for her being taken from his side while he slept?

Granting that an ark was required in order to escape from the flood, why should it have precisely these dimensions, and why should they be recorded for the devout study of future generations?

Granting that the animals were brought into the ark to preserve the various races, why should there be seven clean and two unclean?

Granting that the ark must have a door, why should it be in the side, and why should this fact be committed to writing?

Abraham is commanded to sacrifice his son:
we may allow that this proof of his obedience was required in order to make it conspicuous in all ages; we may allow, too, that it was a proper thing for the son to carry the wood instead of the aged father, and that in the end the fatal stroke was forbidden, lest the father should be left childless.

But what had the shedding of the ram's blood to do with Abraham's trial? or if it was necessary to complete the sacrifice, was the ram any the better of being caught by the horns in a bush?

The human mind, that is to say, a rational mind, is led by the consideration of the way in which these apparently superfluous things are blended with what is necessary, first to acknowledge their significance, and then to try to discover it.

39.

The Jews themselves, who scoff at the crucified Saviour in whom we believe, and who consequently will not allow that Christ is predicted in the sayings and actions recorded in the Old Testament, are compelled to come to us for an explanation of those things which, if not explained, must appear trifling and ridiculous.

This led Philo, a Jew of great learning, whom the Greeks speak of as rivalling Plato in eloquence, to attempt to explain some things without any reference to Christ, in whom he did not believe.

His attempt only shows the inferiority of all ingenious speculations, when made without keeping Christ in view, to whom all the predictions really point.

So true is that saying of the apostle:
"When they shall turn to the Lord, the veil shall be taken away." [464]For instance, Noah's ark is, according to Philo, a type of the human body, member by member:
with this view, he shows that the numerical proportions agree perfectly. For there is no reason why a type of Christ should not be a type of the human body, too, since the Saviour of mankind appeared in a human body, though what is typical of a human body is not necessarily typical of Christ.

Philo's explanation fails, however, as regards the door in the side of the ark.

He actually, for the sake of saying something, makes this door represent the lower apertures of the body.

He has the hardihood to put this in words, and on paper.

Indeed, he knew not the door and could not understand the symbol.

Had he turned to Christ the veil would have been taken away, and he would have found the sacraments of the Church flowing from the side of Christ's human body.

For, according to the announcement, "They two shall be one flesh," some things in the ark which is a type of Christ, refer to Christ, and some to the Church.

This contrast between the explanations which keep Christ in view, and all other ingenious perversions, is the same in every particular of all the figures in Scripture.

40.

The Pagans, too, cannot deny our right to give a figurative meaning to both words and things, especially as we can point to the fulfillment of the types and figures.

For the Pagans themselves try to find in their own fables figures of natural and religious truth. Sometimes they give clear explanations, while at other times they disguise their meaning, and what is sacred in the temples becomes a jest in the theatres.

They unite a disgraceful licentiousness to a degrading superstition.

41.

Besides this wonderful agreement between the types and the things typified, the adversary may be convinced by plain prophetic intimations, such as this:

"In thy seed shall all nations be blessed."

This was said to Abraham, [465] and again to Isaac, [466] and again to Jacob. [467] Hence the significance of the words "I am the God of Abraham, and Isaac, and Jacob." [468] God fulfills His promise to their seed in blessing all nations.

With a like significance, Abraham himself, when he made his servant swear, told him to put his hand under his thigh; [469] for he knew that thence would come the flesh of Christ, in whom we have now, not the promise of blessing to all nations, but the promise fulfilled.

42.

I should like to know, or rather, it would be well not to know, with what blindness of mind Faustus reads the passage where Jacob calls his sons, and says, "Assemble, that I may tell you the things that are to happen in the last day.

Assemble and hear, ye sons of Jacob; give ear to Israel, your father."

Surely these are the words of a prophet. What, then, does he say of his son Judah, of whose tribe Christ came of the seed of David according to the flesh, as the apostle teaches? "Judah," he says, "thy brethren shall praise thee:

thy hand shall be upon the backs of thine enemies; the sons of thy father shall bow down to thee.

Judah is a lion's whelp; my son and offspring:

bowing down, thou hast gone up:

thou sleepest as a lion, and as a young lion, who will rouse him up?

A prince shall not depart from Judah, nor a leader from his loins, till those things come which have been laid up for him.

He also is the desire of nations:

binding his foal unto the vine, and his ass's colt with sackcloth, he shall wash his garment in wine, and his clothes in the blood of grapes:

his eyes are bright with wine, and his teeth whiter than milk." [470] There is no falsehood or obscurity in these words when we read them in the clear light of Christ.

We see His brethren the apostles and all His joint-heirs praising Him, seeking, not their own glory, but His.

We see His hands on the backs of His enemies, who are bent and bowed to the earth by the growth of the Christian communities in spite of their opposition.

We see Him worshipped by the sons of Jacob, the remnant saved according to the election of grace.

Christ, who was born as an infant, is the lion's whelp, as it is added, My son and offspring, to show why this whelp, in whose praise it is said, "The lion's whelp is stronger than the herd," [471] is even in infancy stronger than its elders.

We see Christ ascending the cross, and bowing down when He gave up His spirit.

We see Him sleeping as a lion, because in death itself He was not the conquered, but the conqueror, and as a lion's whelp; for the reason of His birth and of His death was the same.

And He is raised from the dead by Him whom no man hath seen or can see; for the words, "Who will raise Him up?" point to an unknown power.

A prince did not depart from Judah, nor a leader from his loins, till in due time those things came which had been laid up in the promise.

For we learn from the authentic history of the Jews themselves, that Herod, under whom Christ was born, was their first foreign king.

So the sceptre did not depart from the seed of Judah till the things laid up for him came. Then, as the promise is not only to the believing Jews, it is added: "He is the desire of the nations."

Christ bound His foal--that is, His people--to the vine, when He preached in sackcloth, crying, "Repent, for the kingdom of heaven is at hand."

The Gentiles made subject to Him are represented by the ass's colt, on which He also sat, leading it into Jerusalem, that is, the vision of peace teaching the meek His ways.

We see Him washing His garments in wine; for He is one with the glorious Church, which He presents to Himself, not having spot or wrinkle; to whom also it is said by Isaiah:

"Though your sins be as scarlet, I will make them white as snow." [472] How is this done but by the remission of sins?

And the wine is none other than that of which it is said that it is "shed for many, for the remission of sins."

Christ is the cluster that hung on the pole.

So it is added, "and His clothes in the blood of the grape."

Again, what is said of His eyes being bright with wine, is understood by those members of His body who are enabled, in holy aberration of mind from the current of earthly things, to gaze on the eternal light of wisdom.

So Paul says in a passage quoted before:

"If we be beside ourselves, it is to God."

Those are the eyes bright with wine.

But he adds:

"If we be sober, it is for your sakes."

The babes needing to be fed with milk are not forgotten, as is denoted by the words, "His teeth are whiter than milk."

43.

What can our deluded adversaries say to such plain examples, which leave no room for perverse denial, or even for sceptical uncertainty? I call on the Manichæans to begin to inquire into these subjects, and to admit the force of these evidences, on which I have no time to dwell; nor do I wish to make a selection, in case the ignorant reader should think there are no others, while the Christian student might blame me for the omission of many points more striking than those which occur to me at the moment.

You will find many passages which require no such explanation as has been given here of Jacob's prophecy.

For instance, every reader can understand the words, "He was led as a lamb to the slaughter," and the whole of that plain prophecy, "With His stripes we are healed"--"He bore our sins."[473]We have a poetical gospel in the words:

"They pierced my hands and feet.

They have told all my bones.

They look and stare upon me.

They divided my garments among them, and cast lots on my vesture." [474]The blind even may now see the fulfillment of the words:

"All the ends of the earth shall remember and turn unto the Lord, and all kingdoms of the nations shall worship before Him."

The words in the Gospel, "My soul is sorrowful, even unto death," "My soul is troubled," are a repetition of the words in the Psalm, "I slept in trouble." [475]And who made Him sleep? Whose voices cried, Crucify him, crucify him?

The Psalm tells us: "The sons of men, their teeth are spears and arrows, and their tongue a sharp sword." [476]But they could not prevent His resurrection, or His ascension above the heavens, or His filling the earth with the glory of His name; for the Psalm says:

"Be Thou exalted, O God, above the heavens, and let Thy glory be above all the earth."

Every one must apply these words to Christ:

"The Lord said unto me, Thou art my Son, this day have I begotten Thee.

Ask of me, and I will give Thee the heathen for Thine inheritance, and the uttermost parts of the earth for Thy possession." [477]And what Jeremiah says of wisdom plainly applies to Christ:

"Jacob delivered it to his son, and Israel to his chosen one.

Afterwards He appeared on earth, and conversed with men." [478]

44.

The same Saviour is spoken of in Daniel, where the Son of man appears before the Ancient of days, and receives a kingdom without end, that all nations may serve Him. [479]In the passage quoted from Daniel by the Lord Himself, "When ye shall see the abomination of desolation, spoken of by Daniel the prophet, standing in the holy place, let him that readeth understand," [480] the number of weeks points not only to Christ, but to the very time of His advent.

With the Jews, who look to Christ for salvation as we do, but deny that He has come and suffered, we can argue from actual events.

Besides the conversion of the heathen, now so universal, as prophesied of Christ in their own Scriptures, there are the events in the history of the Jews themselves.

Their holy place is thrown down, the sacrifice has ceased, and the priest, and the ancient anointing; which was all clearly foretold by Daniel when he prophesied of the anointing of the Most Holy. [481]Now, that all these things have taken place, we ask the Jews for the anointed Most Holy, and they have no answer to give.

But it is from the Old Testament that the Jews derive all the knowledge they have of Christ and His advent.

Why do they ask John whether he is Christ?

Why do they say to the Lord, "How long dost thou make us to doubt? If thou art the Christ, tell us plainly."

Why do Peter and Andrew and Philip say to Nathanael, "We have found Messias, which is interpreted Christ," but because this name was known to them from the prophecies of their Scriptures?

In no other nation were the kings and priests anointed, and called Anointed or Christs.

Nor could this symbolical anointing be discontinued till the coming of Him who was thus prefigured.

For among all their anointed ones the Jews looked for one who was to save them.

But in the mysterious justice of God they were blinded; and thinking only of the power of the Messiah, they did not understand His weakness, in which He died for us.

In the book of Wisdom it is prophesied of the Jews:

"Let us condemn him to an ignominious death; for he will be proved in his words.

If he is truly the Son of God, He will aid him; and deliver him from the hand of his enemies.

Thus they thought, and erred; for their wickedness blinded them." [482] These words apply also to those who, in spite of all these evidences, in spite of such a series of prophecies, and of their fulfillment, still deny that Christ is foretold in the Scriptures.

As often as they repeat this denial, we can produce fresh proofs, with the help of Him who has made such provision against human perversity, that proofs already given need not be repeated.

45.

Faustus has an evasive objection, which he no doubt thinks a most ingenious way of eluding the force of the clearest evidence of prophecy, but of which one is unwilling to take any notice, because answering it may give it an appearance of importance which it does not really possess.

What could be more irrational than to say that it is weak faith which will not believe in Christ without evidence?

Do our adversaries, then, believe in testimony about Christ?

Faustus wishes us to believe the voice from heaven as distinguished from human testimony.

But did they hear this voice?

Has not the knowledge of it come to us through human testimony?

The apostle describes the transmission of this knowledge, when he says:

"How shall they call on Him on whom they have not believed? and how shall they believe on Him of whom they have not heard? and how shall they hear without a preacher? and how shall they preach except they be sent?

As it is written, "How beautiful are the feet of them who publish peace, who bring good tidings!" [483] Clearly, in the preaching of the apostles there was a reference to prophetic testimony.

The apostles quoted the predictions of the prophets, to prove the truth and importance of their doctrines.

For although their preaching was accompanied with the power of working miracles, the miracles would have been ascribed to magic, as some even now venture to insinuate, unless the apostles had shown that the authority of the prophets was in their favor.

The testimony of prophets who lived so long before could not be ascribed to magical arts.

Perhaps the reason why Faustus will not have us believe the Hebrew prophets as witnesses of the true Christ, is because he believes Persian heresies about a false Christ.

46.

According to the teaching of the Catholic Church, the Christian mind must first be nourished in simple faith, in order that it may become capable of understanding things heavenly and eternal.

Thus it is said by the prophet:

"Unless ye believe, ye shall not understand." [484] Simple faith is that by which, before we attain to the height of the knowledge of the love of Christ, that we may be filled with all the fullness of God, we believe that not without reason was the dispensation of Christ's humiliation, in which He was born and suffered as man, foretold so long before by the prophets through a prophetic race, a prophetic people, a prophetic kingdom.

This faith teaches us, that in the foolishness which is wiser than men, and in the weakness which is stronger than men, is contained the hidden means of our justification and glorification.

There are hid all the treasures of wisdom and knowledge, which are opened to no one who despises the nourishment transmitted through the breast of his mother that is, the milk of apostolic and prophetic instruction; or who, thinking himself too old for infantile nourishment, devours heretical poison instead of the food of wisdom, for which he rashly thought himself prepared.

To require simple faith is quite consistent with requiring faith in the prophets.

The very use of simple faith is to believe the prophets at the outset, while the understanding of the person who speaks in the prophets is attained after the mind has been purified and strengthened.

47.

But, it is said, if the prophets foretold Christ, they did not live in a way becoming their office. How can you tell whether they did or not?

You are bad judges of what it is to live well or ill, whose justice consists in giving relief to an inanimate melon by eating it, instead of giving food to the starving beggar.

It is enough for the babes in the Catholic Church, who do not yet know the perfect justice of the human soul, and the difference between the justice aimed at and that actually attained, to think of those men according to the wholesome doctrine of the apostles, that the just lives by faith. "Abraham believed God, and it was counted to him for righteousness. For the scripture, foreseeing that God would justify the Gentiles by faith, preached before the gospel unto Abraham, saying, In thy seed shall all nations be blessed." [485] These are the words of the apostle.

If you would, at his clear well-known voice, wake up from your unprofitable dreams, you would follow in the footsteps of our father Abraham, and would be blessed, along with all nations, in his seed.

For, as the apostle says, "He received the sign of circumcision, a seal of the righteousness of the faith which he had, yet being uncircumcised, that he might be the father of all that believe in uncircumcision; that he might be the father of circumcision not only to those who are of the circumcision, but also to those who follow the footsteps of the faith of our father Abraham in uncircumcision." [486]

Since the righteousness of Abraham's faith is thus set forth as an example to us, that we too, being justified by faith, may have peace with God, we ought to understand his manner of life, without finding fault with it; lest, by a premature separation from mother-Church, we prove abortions, instead of being brought forth in due time, when the conception has arrived at completeness.

48.

This is a brief reply to Faustus in behalf of the character of the patriarchs and prophets.

It is the reply of the babes of our faith, among whom I would reckon myself, inasmuch as I would not find fault with the life of the ancient saints, even if I did not understand its mystical character.

Their life is proclaimed to us with approval by the apostles in their Gospel, as they themselves in their prophecy foretold the future apostles, that the two Testaments, like the seraphim, might cry to one another, "Holy, holy, holy is the Lord God of hosts." [487] When Faustus, instead of the vague general accusation which he makes here, condemns particular actions in the lives of the patriarchs and the prophets, the Lord their God, and ours also, will assist me to reply suitably and appropriately to the separate charges.

For the present, the reader must choose whether to believe the commendation of the Apostle Paul or the accusations of Faustus the Manichæan. [488]

Book XIII - Faustus asserts that even if the Old Testament could be shown to contain predictions, it would be of interest only to the Jews, pagan literature subserving the same purpose for Gentiles

Augustin shows the value of prophesy for Gentiles and Jews alike.

1.

Faustus said:

We are asked how we worship Christ when we reject the prophets, who declared the promise of His advent.

It is doubtful whether, on examination, it can be shown that the Hebrew prophets foretold our Christ, that is, the Son of God.

But were it so, what does it matter to us?

If these testimonies of the prophets that you speak of were the means of converting any one from Judaism to Christianity, and if he should afterwards neglect these prophets, he would certainly be in the wrong, and would be chargeable with ingratitude.

But we are by nature Gentiles, of the uncircumcision; as Paul says, born under another law.

Those whom the Gentiles call poets were our first religious teachers, and from them we were afterwards converted to Christianity.

We did not first become Jews, so as to reach Christianity through faith in their prophets; but were attracted solely by the fame, and the virtues, and the wisdom of our liberator Jesus Christ.

If I were still in the religion of my fathers, and a preacher were to come using the prophets as evidence in favor of Christianity, I should think him mad for attempting to support what is doubtful by what is still more doubtful to a Gentile of another religion altogether.

He would require first to persuade me to believe the prophets, and then through the prophets to believe Christ.

And to prove the truth of the prophets, other prophets would be necessary. For if the prophets bear witness to Christ, who bears witness to the prophets?

You will perhaps say that Christ and the prophets mutually support each other.

But a Pagan, who has nothing to do with either, would believe neither the evidence of Christ to the prophets, nor that of the prophets to Christ.

If the Pagan becomes a Christian, he has to thank his own faith, and nothing else.

Let us, for the sake of illustration, suppose ourselves conversing with a Gentile inquirer.

We tell him to believe in Christ, because He is God.

He asks for proof. We refer him to the prophets.

He asks, What prophets?

We reply, The Hebrew.

He smiles, and says that he does not believe them.

We remind him that Christ testifies to them.

He replies, laughing, that we must first make him believe in Christ.

The result of such a conversation is that we are silenced, and the inquirer departs, thinking us more zealous than wise.

Again, I say, the Christian Church, which consists more of Gentiles than of Jews, can owe nothing to Hebrew witnesses. If, as is said, any prophecies of Christ are to be found in the Sibyl,[489] or in Hermes,[490] called Trismegistus, or Orpheus, or any heathen poet, they might aid the faith of those who, like us, are converts from heathenism to Christianity.

But the testimony of the Hebrews is useless to us before conversion, for then we cannot believe them; and superfluous after, for we believe without them.

2.

Augustin replied:

After the long reply of last book, a short answer may suffice here.

To one who has read that reply, it must seem insanity in Faustus to persist in denying that Christ was foretold by the Hebrew prophets, when the Hebrew nation was the only one in which the name Christ had a peculiar sacredness as applied to kings and priests; in which sense it continued to be applied till the coming of Him whom those kings and priests typified.

Where did the Manichæan learn the name of Christ?

If from Manichæus, it is very strange that Africans, not to speak of others, should believe the Persian Manichæus, since Faustus finds fault with the Romans and Greeks, and other Gentiles, for believing the Hebrew prophets as belonging to another race.

According to Faustus, the predictions of the Sibyl, or Orpheus, or any heathen poet, are more suitable for leading Gentiles to believe in Christ.

He forgets that none of these are read in the churches, whereas the voice of the Hebrew prophets, sounding everywhere, draws swarms of people to Christianity.

When it is so evident that men are everywhere led to Christ by the Hebrew prophets, it is great absurdity to say that those prophets are not suitable for the Gentiles.

3.

Christ as foretold by the Hebrew prophets does not please you; but this is the Christ in whom the Gentile nations believe, with whom, according to you, Hebrew prophecy should have no weight.

They receive the gospel which, as Paul says, "God had promised before by His prophets in the Holy Scriptures of His Son, who was made of the seed of David according to the flesh."[491] So we read in Isaiah:

"There shall be a Root of Jesse, which shall rise to reign in the nations; in Him shall the Gentiles trust." [492] And again:

"Behold, a virgin shall conceive and bear a son, and they shall call His name Emmanuel,"[493] which is, being interpreted, God with us.

Nor let the Manichæan think that Christ is foretold only as a man by the Hebrew prophets; for this is what Faustus seems to insinuate when he says, "Our Christ is the Son of God," as if the Christ of the Hebrews was not the Son of God.

We can prove Christ the virgin's son of Hebrew prophecy to be God.

For the Lord Himself teaches the carnal Jews not to think that, because He is foretold as the son of David, He is therefore no more than that.

He asks:

"What think ye of Christ?

Whose son is He?" They reply:

"Of David."

Then, to remind them of the name Emmanuel, God with us, He says:

"How does David in the Spirit call Him Lord, saying, The Lord said unto my Lord, Sit Thou at my right hand, till I make Thine enemies Thy footstool?"[494] Here, then, Christ appears as God in Hebrew prophecy.

What prophecy can the Manichæans show with the name of Christ in it?

4.

Manichæus indeed was not a prophet of Christ, but calls himself an apostle, which is a shameless falsehood; for it is well known that this heresy began not only after Tertullian, but after Cyprian.

In all his letters Manichæus begins thus:

"Manichæus, an apostle of Jesus Christ."

Why do you believe what Manichæus says of Christ?

What evidence does he give of his apostleship?

This very name of Christ is known to us only from the Jews, who, in their application of it to their kings and priests, were not individually, but nationally, prophets of Christ and Christ's kingdom.

What right has he to use this name, who forbids you to believe the Hebrew prophets, that he may make you the heretical disciples of a false Christ, as he himself is a false and heretical apostle?

And if Faustus quotes as evidence in his own support some prophets who, according to him, foretell Christ, how will he satisfy his supposed inquirer, who will not believe either the prophets or Faustus?

Will he take our apostles as witnesses?

Unless he can find some apostles in life, he must read their writings; and these are all against him.

They teach our doctrine that Christ was born of the Virgin Mary, that He was the Son of God, of the seed of David according to the flesh.

He cannot pretend that the writings have been tampered with, for that would be to attack the credit of his own witnesses.

Or if he produces his own manuscripts of the apostolic writings, he must also obtain for them the authority of the churches founded by the apostles themselves, by showing that they have been preserved and transmitted with their sanction.

It will be difficult for a man to make me believe him on the evidence of writings which derive all their authority from his own word, which I do not believe.

5.

But perhaps you believe the common report about Christ.

Faustus makes a feeble suggestion of this kind as a last resource, to escape being obliged either to produce his worthless authorities, or to come under the power of those opposed to him.

Well, if report is your authority, you should consider the consequences of trusting to such evidence.

There are many bad things reported of you which you do not wish people to believe.

Is it reasonable to make the same evidence true about Christ and false about yourselves?

In fact, you deny the common report about Christ.

For the report most widely spread, and which every one has heard repeated, is that which distinctly asserts that Christ was born of the seed of David, according to the promise made in the Hebrew Scriptures to Abraham and Isaac and Jacob:

"In thy seed shall all nations be blessed."

You will not admit this Hebrew testimony, but you do not seem to have any other.

The authority of our books, which is confirmed by the agreement of so many nations, supported by a succession of apostles, bishops, and councils, is against you.

Your books have no authority, for it is an authority maintained by only a few, and these the worshippers of an untruthful God and Christ.

If they are not following the example of the beings they worship, their testimony must be against their own false doctrine.

And, once more, common report gives a very bad account of you, and invariably asserts, in opposition to you, that Christ was of the seed of David.

You did not hear the voice of the Father from heaven.

You did not see the works by which Christ bore witness to Himself.

The books which tell of these things you profess to receive, that you may maintain a delusive appearance of Christianity; but when anything is quoted against you, you say that the books have been tampered with.

You quote the passage where Christ says, "If ye believe not me, believe the works;" and again, "I am one that bear witness of myself, and the Father that sent me beareth witness of me;" but you will not let us quote in reply such passages as these:

"Search the Scriptures; for in them ye think that ye have eternal life, and they are they that testify of me;" "If ye believed Moses, ye would believe me, for he wrote of me;" "They have Moses and the prophets, let them hear them;" "If they hear not Moses and the prophets, neither will they believe though one rose from the dead."

What have you to say for yourselves?

Where is your authority?

If you reject these passages of Scripture, in spite of the weighty authority in their favor, what miracles can you show?

However, if you did work miracles, we should be on our guard against receiving their evidence in your case; for the Lord has forewarned us:

"Many false Christs and false prophets shall arise, and shall do many signs and wonders, that they may deceive, if it were possible, the very elect:

behold, I have told you before." [495]This shows that the established authority of Scripture must outweigh every other; for it derives new confirmation from the progress of events which happen, as Scripture proves, in fulfillment of the predictions made so long before their occurrence.

6.

Are, then, your doctrines so manifestly true, that they require no support from miracles or from any testimony?

Show us these self-evident truths, if you have anything of the kind to show.

Your legends, as we have already seen, are long and silly, old wives fables for the amusement of women and children.

The beginning is detached from the rest, the middle is unsound, and the end is a miserable failure.

If you begin with the immortal, invisible, incorruptible God, what need was there of His fighting with the race of darkness?

And as for the middle of your theory, what becomes of the incorruptibility and unchangeableness of God, when His members in fruits and vegetables are purified by your mastication and digestion?

And for the end, is it just that the wretched soul should be punished with lasting confinement in the mass of darkness, because its God is unable to cleanse it of the defilement contracted from evil external to itself in the fulfillment of His own commission?

You are at a loss for a reply.

See the worthlessness of your boasted manuscripts, numerous and valuable as you say they are!

Alas for the toils of the antiquaries!

Alas for the property of the unhappy owners!

Alas for the food of the deluded followers!

Destitute as you are of Scripture authority, of the power of miracles, of moral excellence, and of sound doctrine, depart ashamed, and return penitent, confessing that true Christ, who is the Saviour of all who believe in Him, whose name and whose Church are now displayed as they were of old foretold, not by some being issuing from subterranean darkness, but by a nation in a distinct kingdom established for this purpose, that there those things might be figuratively predicted of Christ which are now in reality fulfilled, and the prophets might foretell in writing what the apostles now exhibit in their preaching.

7.

Let us suppose, then, a conversation with a heathen inquirer, in which Faustus described us as making a poor appearance, though his own appearance was much more deplorable.

If we say to the heathen, Believe in Christ, for He is God, and, on his asking for evidence, produce the authority of the prophets, if he says that he does not believe the prophets, because they are Hebrew and he is a Gentile, we can prove the truth of the prophets from the actual fulfillment of their prophecies. He could scarcely be ignorant of the persecutions suffered by the early Christians from the kings of this world; or if he was ignorant, he could be informed from history and the records of imperial laws.

But this is what we find foretold long ago by the prophet, saying, "Why do the heathen rage, and the people imagine a vain thing?

The kings of the earth set themselves, and the princes take counsel together against the Lord, and against His Christ."

The rest of the Psalm shows that this is not said of David.

For what follows might convince the most stubborn unbeliever:

"The Lord said unto me, Thou art my Son; this day have I begotten Thee.

Ask of me, and I will give Thee the heathen for Thine inheritance, and the ends of the earth for Thy possession." [496]

This never happened to the Jews, whose king, David was, but is now plainly fulfilled in the subjection of all nations to the name of Christ.

This and many similar prophecies, which it would take too long to quote, would surely impress the mind of the inquirer.

He would see these very kings of the earth now happily subdued by Christ, and all nations serving Him; and he would hear the words of the Psalm in which this was so long before predicted:

"All the kings of the earth shall bow down to Him; all nations shall serve Him." [497] And if he were to read the whole of that Psalm, which is figuratively applied to Solomon, he would find that Christ is the true King of peace, for Solomon means peaceful; and he would find many things in the Psalm applicable to Christ, which have no reference at all to the literal King Solomon.

Then there is that other Psalm where God is spoken of as anointed by God, the very word anointed pointing to Christ, showing that Christ is God, for God is represented as being anointed.[498] In reading what is said in this Psalm of Christ and of the Church, he would find that what is there foretold is fulfilled in the present state of the world.

He would see the idols of the nations perishing from off the earth, and he would find that this is predicted by the prophets, as in Jeremiah, "Then shall ye say unto them, The gods that have not made the heavens and the earth shall perish from the earth, and from under heaven;" [499] and again, "O Lord, my strength, and my fortress, and my refuge in the day of affliction, the Gentiles shall come unto Thee from the ends of the earth, and shall say, Surely our fathers have inherited lies, vanity, and things wherein there is no profit.

Shall a man make gods unto himself, and they are no gods? Therefore, behold, I will at that time cause them to know, I will cause them to know mine hand and my might; and they shall know that I am the Lord." [500] Hearing these prophecies, and seeing their actual fulfillment, I need not say that he would be affected; for we know by experience how the hearts of believers are confirmed by seeing ancient predictions now receiving their accomplishment.

8.

In the same prophet the inquirer would find clear proof that Christ is not merely one of the great men that have appeared in the world. For Jeremiah goes on to say:

"Cursed be the man that trusteth in man, and maketh flesh his arm, and whose heart departeth from the Lord:

for he shall be like the heath in the desert, and shall not see when good cometh; but shall inhabit the parched places of the wilderness, in a salt land not inhabited.

Blessed is the man that trusteth in the Lord, and whose hope the Lord is:

for he shall be as a tree beside the water, that spreadeth out its roots by the river:

he shall not fear when heat cometh, but his leaf shall be green; he shall not be careful in the year of drought, neither shall cease from yielding fruit." [501]

On hearing this curse pronounced in the figurative language of prophecy on him that trusts in man, and the blessing in similar style on him that trusts in God, the inquirer might have doubts about our doctrine, in which we teach not only that Christ is God, so that our trust is not in man, but also that He is man because He took our nature.

So some err by denying Christ's humanity, while they allow His divinity.

Others, again, assert His humanity, but deny His divinity, and so either become infidels or incur the guilt of trusting in man. The inquirer, then, might say that the prophet says only that Christ is God, without any reference to His human nature; whereas, in our apostolic doctrine, Christ is not only God in whom we may safely trust, but the Mediator between God and man--the man Jesus.

The prophet explains this in the words in which he seems to check himself, and to supply the omission:

"His heart," he says "is sorrowful throughout; and He is man, and who shall know Him?"[502]He is man, in order that in the form of a servant He might heal the hard in heart, and that they might acknowledge as God Him who became man for their sakes, that their trust might be not in man, but in God-man.

He is man taking the form of a servant.

And who shall know Him?

For "He was in the form of God, and thought it not robbery to be equal to God." [503]He is man, for "the Word was made flesh, and dwelt among us."

And who shall know Him?

For "in the beginning was the Word, and the Word was with God, and the Word was God."[504] And truly His heart was sorrowful throughout.

For even as regards His own disciples His heart was sorrowful, when He said, "Have I been so long time with you, and yet have ye not known me?"

"Have I been so long time with you" answers to the words "He is man," and "Have ye not known me?" to "Who shall know Him?"

And the person is none other but He who says, "He that hath seen me hath seen the Father."[505]So that our trust is not in man, to be under the curse of the prophet, but in God-man, that is, in the Son of God, the Saviour Jesus Christ, the Mediator between God and man.

In the form of a servant the Father is greater than He; in the form of God He is equal with the Father.

9.

In Isaiah we read:

"The pride of man shall be brought low; and the Lord alone shall be exalted in that day.

And they shall hide the workmanship of their hands in the clefts of the rocks, and in dens and caves of the earth, from fear of the Lord, and from the glory of His power, when He shall arise to shake terribly the earth.

For in that day a man shall cast away his idols of gold and silver, which they have made to worship, as useless and hurtful." [506]Perhaps the inquirer himself, who, as Faustus supposes, would laugh and say that he does not believe the Hebrew prophets, has hid idols made with hands in some cleft, or cave, or den.

Or he may know a friend, or neighbor, or fellow-citizen who has done this from the fear of the Lord, who by the severe prohibition of the kings of the earth, now serving and bowing down to him, as the prophet predicted, shakes the earth, that is, breaks the stubborn heart of worldly men.

The inquirer is not likely to disbelieve the Hebrew prophets, when he finds their predictions fulfilled, perhaps in his own person.

10.

One might rather fear that the inquirer, in the midst of such copious evidence, would say that the Christians composed those writings when the events described had already begun to take place, in order that those occurrences might appear to be not due to a merely human purpose, but as if divinely foretold.

One might fear this, were it not for the widely spread and widely known people of the Jews; that Cain, with the mark that he should not be killed by any one; that Ham, the servant of his brethren, carrying as a load the books for their instruction.

From the Jewish manuscripts we prove that these things were not written by us to suit the event, but were long ago published and preserved as prophecies in the Jewish nation.

These prophecies are now explained in their accomplishment:

for even what is obscure in them--because these things happened to them as an example, and were written for our benefit, on whom the ends of the world are come--is now made plain; and what was hidden in the shadows of the future is now visible in the light of actual experience.

11.

The inquirer might bring forward as a difficulty the fact that those in whose books these prophecies are found are not united with us in the gospel.

But when convinced that this also is foretold, he would feel how strong the evidence is.

The prophecies of the unbelief of the Jews no one can avoid seeing, no one can pretend to be blind to them. No one can doubt that Isaiah spoke of the Jews when he said, "The ox knoweth his owner, and the ass his master's crib; but Israel hath not known, and my people hath not considered;"[507] or again, in the words quoted by the apostle, "I have stretched out my hands all the day to a wicked and gainsaying people;" [508] and especially where he says, "God has given them the spirit of remorse, eyes that they should not see, and ears that they should not hear, and should not understand," [509] and many similar passages.

If the inquirer objected that it was not the fault of the Jews if God blinded them so that they did not know Christ, we should try in the simplest manner possible to make him understand that this blindness is the just punishment of other secret sins known to God.

We should prove that the apostle recognizes this principle when he says of some persons, "God gave them up to the lusts of their own hearts, and to a reprobate mind, to do things not convenient;" [510] and that the prophets themselves speak of this. For, to revert to the words of Jeremiah, "He is man, and who shall know Him?" lest it should be an excuse for the Jews that they did not know,--for if they had known, as the apostle says, "they would not have crucified the Lord of glory," [511] --the prophet goes on to show that their ignorance was the result of secret criminality; for he says:

"I the Lord search the heart and try the reins, to give to every one according to his ways, and according to the fruits of his doings."

12.

If the next difficulty in the mind of the inquirer arose from the divisions and heresies among those called Christians, he would learn that this too is taken notice of by the prophets.

For, as if it was natural that, after being satisfied about the blindness of the Jews, this objection from the divisions among Christians should occur, Jeremiah, observing this order in his prophecy, immediately adds in the passage already quoted:

"The partridge is clamorous, gathering what it has not brought forth, making riches without judgment."

For the partridge is notoriously quarrelsome, and is often caught from its eagerness in quarreling.

So the heretics discuss not to find the truth, but with a dogged determination to gain the victory one way or another, that they may gather, as the prophet says, what they have not brought forth.

For those whom they lead astray are Christians already born of the gospel, whom the Christian profession of the heretics misleads.

Thus they make riches not with judgment, but with inconsiderate haste.

For they do not consider that the followers whom they gather as their riches are taken from the genuine original Christian society, and deprived of its benefits; and as the apostle describes these heretics in the words:

"As Jannes and Jambres withstood Moses, so they also resist the truth:
men of corrupt minds, reprobate concerning the faith.

But they shall proceed no further: for their folly shall be manifest to all men, as theirs also was." [512]So the prophet goes on to say of the partridge, which gathers what it has not brought forth:

"In the midst of his days they shall leave him, and in the end he shall be a fool;" that is, he who at first misled people by a promising display of superior wisdom, shall be a fool, that is, shall be seen to be a fool.

He will be seen when his folly is manifest to all men, and to those to whom he was at first a wise man he will then be a fool.

13.

As if anticipating that the inquirer would ask next by what plain mark a young disciple, not yet able to distinguish the truth among so many errors, might find the true Church of Christ, since the clear fulfillment of so many predictions compelled him to believe in Christ, the prophet answers this question in what follows, and teaches that the Church of Christ, which he describes prophetically, is conspicuously visible.

His words are:

"A glorious high throne is our sanctuary." [513]This glorious throne is the Church of which the apostle says: "The temple of God is holy, which temple ye are." [514]The Lord also, foreseeing the conspicuousness of the Church as a help to young disciples who might be misled, says, "A city that is set on an hill cannot be hid." [515]Since, then, a glorious high throne is our sanctuary, no attention is to be paid to those who would lead us into sectarianism, saying, "Lo, here is Christ," or "Lo there."

Lo here, lo there, speaks of division; but the true city is on a mountain, and the mountain is that which, as we read in the prophet Daniel, grew from a little stone till it filled the whole earth.[516] And no attention should be paid to those who, professing some hidden mystery confined to a small number, say, Behold, He is in the chamber; behold, in the desert:

for a city set on an hill cannot be hid, and a glorious high throne is our sanctuary.

14.

After considering these instances of the fulfillment of prophecy about kings and people acting as persecutors, and then becoming believers, about the destruction of idols, about the blindness of the Jews, about their testimony to the writings which they have preserved, about the folly of heretics, about the dignity of the Church of true and genuine Christians, the inquirer would most reasonably receive the testimony of these prophets about the divinity of Christ.

No doubt, if we were to begin by urging him to believe prophecies yet unfulfilled, he might justly answer, What have I to do with these prophets, of whose truth I have no evidence?

But, in view of the manifest accomplishment of so many remarkable predictions, no candid person would despise either the things which were thought worthy of being predicted in those early times with so much solemnity, or those who made the predictions. To none can we trust more safely, as regards either events long past or those still future, than to men whose words are supported by the evidence of so many notable predictions having been fulfilled.

15.

If any truth about God or the Son of God is taught or predicted in the Sibyl or Sibyls, or in Orpheus, or in Hermes, if there ever was such a person, or in any other heathen poets, or theologians, or sages, or philosophers, it may be useful for the refutation of Pagan error, but cannot lead us to believe in these writers.

For while they spoke, because they could not help it, of the God whom we worship, they either taught their fellow-countrymen to worship idols and demons, or allowed them to do so without daring to protest against it.

But our sacred writers, with the authority and assistance of God, were the means of establishing and preserving among their people a government under which heathen customs were condemned as sacrilege.

If any among this people fell into idolatry or demon-worship, they were either punished by the laws, or met by the awful denunciations of the prophets.

They worshipped one God, the maker of heaven and earth.

They had rites; but these rites were prophetic, or symbolical of things to come, and were to cease on the appearance of the things signified.

The whole state was one great prophet, with its king and priest symbolically anointed which was discontinued, not by the wish of the Jews themselves, who were in ignorance through unbelief, but only on the coming of Him who was God, anointed with spiritual grace above His fellows, the holy of holies, the true King who should govern us, the true Priest who should offer Himself for us.

In a word, the predictions of heathen ingenuity regarding Christ's coming are as different from sacred prophecy as the confession of devils from the proclamation of angels.

16.

By such arguments, which might be expanded if we were discussing with one brought up in heathenism, and might be supported by proofs in still greater number, the inquirer whom Faustus has brought before us would certainly be led to believe, unless he preferred his sins to his salvation.

As a believer, he would be taken to be cherished in the bosom of the Catholic Church, and would be taught in due course the conduct required of him.

He would see many who do not practise the required duties; but this would not shake his faith, even though these people should belong to the same Church and partake of the same sacraments as himself.

He would understand that few share in the inheritance of God, while many partake in its outward signs; that few are united in holiness of life, and in the gift of love shed abroad in our hearts by the Holy Spirit who is given to us, which is a hidden spring that no stranger can approach; and that many join in the solemnity of the sacrament, which he that eats and drinks unworthily eats and drinks judgment to himself, while he who neglects to eat it shall not have life in him, [517] and so shall never reach eternal life.

He will understand, too, that the good are called few as compared with the multitude of the evil, but that as scattered over the world there are very many growing among the tares, and mixed with the chaff, till the day of harvest and of purging.

As this is taught in the Gospel, so is it foretold by the prophets.

We read, "As a lily among thorns, so is my beloved among the daughters;" [518] and again, "I have dwelt in the tabernacles of Kedar; peaceful among them that hated peace;" [519] and again, "Mark in the forehead those who sigh and cry for the iniquities of my people, which are done in the midst of them." [520] The inquirer would be confirmed by such passages; and being now a fellow-citizen with the saints and of the household of God, no longer an alien from Israel, but an Israelite indeed, in whom is no guile, would learn to utter from a guileless heart the words which follow in the passage of Jeremiah already quoted, "O Lord, the patience of Israel:

let all that forsake Thee be dismayed."

After speaking of the partridge that is clamorous, and gathers what it has not brought forth; and after extolling the city set on an hill which cannot be hid, to prevent heretics from drawing men away from the Catholic Church; after the words, "A glorious high throne is our sanctuary," he seems to ask himself, What do we make of all those evil men who are found mixed with the Church, and who become more numerous as the Church extends, and as all nations are united in Christ?

And then follow the words, "O Lord, the patience of Israel."

Patience is necessary to obey the command, "Suffer both to grow together till the harvest."[521] Impatience towards the evil might lead to forsaking the good, who in the strict sense are the body of Christ, and to forsake them would be to forsake Him.

So the prophet goes on to say, "Let all that forsake Thee be dismayed; let those who have departed to the earth be confounded."

The earth is man trusting in himself, and inducing others to trust in him.

So the prophet adds:

"Let them be overthrown, for they have forsaken the Lord, the fountain of life."

This is the cry of the partridge, that it has got the fountain of life, and will give it; and so men are gathered to it, and depart from Christ, as if Christ, whose name they had professed, had not fulfilled His promise.

The partridge gathers those whom it has not brought forth.

And in order to do this, it declares, The salvation which Christ promises is with me; I will give it.

In opposition to this the prophet says:

"Heal me, O Lord, and I shall be healed; save me, and I shall be saved."

So we read in the apostle, "Let no man glory in men;" [522] or in the words of the prophet, "Thou art my praise." [523] Such is a specimen of instruction in apostolic and prophetic doctrine, by which a man may be built on the foundation of the apostles and prophets.

17.

Faustus has not told us how he would prove the divinity of Christ to the heathen, whom he makes to say:

I believe neither the prophets in support of Christ, nor Christ in support of the prophets.

It would be absurd to suppose that such a man would believe what Christ says of Himself, when he disbelieves what He says of others.

For if he thinks Him unworthy of credit in one case, he must think Him so in all, or at least more so when speaking of Himself than when speaking of others. Perhaps, failing this, Faustus would read to him the Sibyls and Orpheus, and any heathen prophecies about Christ that he could find. But how could he do this, when he confesses that he knows none?

His words are:

"If, as is said, any prophecies of Christ are to be found in the Sibyl, or in Hermes, called Trismegistus, or Orpheus, or any heathen poet."

How could he read writings of which he knows nothing, and which he supposes to exist only from report, to one who will not believe either the prophets or Christ?

What, then, would he do?

Would he bring forward Manichæus as a witness to Christ?

The opposite of this is what the Manichæans do.

They take advantage of the widespread fragrance of the name of Christ to gain acceptance for Manichæus, that the edge of their poisoned cup may be sweetened with this honey. Taking hold of the promises of Christ to His disciples that He would send the Paraclete, that is, the Comforter or Advocate, they say that this Paraclete is Manichæus, or in Manichæus, and so steal an entrance into the minds of men who do not know when He who was promised by Christ really came.

Those who have read the canonical book called the Acts of the Apostles find a reference to

Christ's promise, and an account of its fulfillment.

Faustus, then, has no proof to give to the inquirer.

It is not likely that any one will be so infatuated as to take the authority of Manichæus when he rejects that of Christ.

Would he not reply in derision, if not in anger, Why do you ask me to believe Persian books, when you forbid me to believe Hebrew books?

The Manichæan has no hold on the inquirer, unless he is already in some way convinced of the truth of Christianity.

When he finds him willing to believe Christ, then he deludes him with the representation of Christ given by Manichæus.

So the partridge gathers what it has not brought forth.

When will you whom he gathers leave him?

When will you see him to be a fool, who tells you that Hebrew testimony is worthless in the case of unbelievers, and superfluous to believers?

18.

If believers are to throw away all the books which have led them to believe, I see no reason why they should continue reading the Gospel itself.

The Gospel, too, must be worthless to this inquirer, who, according to Faustus' pitiful supposition, rejects with ridicule the authority of Christ.

And to the believer it must be superfluous, if true notices of Christ are superfluous to believers.

And if the Gospel should be read by the believer, that he may not forget what he has believed, so should the prophets, that he may not forget why he believed.

For if he forgets this his faith cannot be firm.

By this principle, you should throw away the books of Manichæus, on the authority of which you already believe that light--that is, God--fought with darkness, and that, in order to bind darkness, the light was first swallowed up and bound, and polluted and mangled by darkness, to be restored, and liberated, and purified, and healed by your eating, for which you are rewarded by not being condemned to the mass of darkness for ever, along with that part of the light which cannot be extricated.

This fiction is sufficiently published by your practice and your words.

Why do you seek for the testimony of books, and add to the embarrassment of your God by the consumption of strength in the needless task of writing manuscripts?

Burn all your parchments, with their finely-ornamented binding; so you will be rid of a useless burden, and your God who suffers confinement in the volume will be set free.

What a mercy it would be to the members of your God, if you could boil your books and eat them!

There might be a difficulty, however, from the prohibition of animal food.

Then the writing must share in the impurity of the sheepskin.

Indeed, you are to blame for this, for, like what you say was done in the first war between light and darkness, you brought what was clean in the pen in contact with the uncleanness of the parchment.

Or perhaps, for the sake of the colors, we may put it the other way; and so the darkness would be yours, in the ink which you brought against the light of the white pages.

If these remarks irritate you, you should rather be angry with yourselves for believing doctrines of which these are the necessary consequences.

As for the books of the apostles and prophets, we read them as a record of our faith, to encourage our hope and animate our love.

These books are in perfect harmony with one another; and their harmony, like the music of a heavenly trumpet, wakens us from the torpor of worldliness, and urges us on to the prize of our high calling.

The apostle, after quoting from the prophets the words, "The reproaches of them that reproached Thee fell on me," goes on to speak of the benefit of reading the prophets:

"For whatsoever things were written beforetime were written for our learning; that we, through patience and comfort of the Scriptures, might have hope." [524] If Faustus denies this, we can only say with Paul, "If any one shall preach to you another doctrine than that ye have received, let him be accursed." [525]

Book XIV - Faustus abhors Moses for the awful curse he has pronounced upon Christ

Augustin expounds the Christian doctrine of the suffering Saviour by comparing Old and New Testament passages.

1.

Faustus said:

If you ask why we do not believe Moses, it is on account of our love and reverence for Christ. The most reckless man cannot regard with pleasure a person who has cursed his father.

So we abhor Moses, not so much for his blasphemy of everything human and divine, as for the awful curse he has pronounced upon Christ the Son of God, who for our salvation hung on the tree.

Whether Moses did this intentionally or not is your concern.

Either way, he cannot be excused, or considered worthy of belief.

His words are, "Cursed is every one that hangeth on a tree." [526] You tell me to believe this man, though, if he was inspired, he must have cursed Christ knowingly and intentionally; and if he did it in ignorance, he cannot have been divine.

Take either alternative.

Moses was no prophet, and while cursing in his usual manner, he fell ignorantly into the sin of blasphemy against God.

Or he was indeed divine, and foresaw the future; and from ill-will to our salvation, he directs the venom of his malediction against Him who was to accomplish that salvation on a tree.

He who thus injures the Son cannot surely have seen or known the Father.

He who knew nothing of the final ascension of the Son, cannot surely have foretold His advent.

Moreover, the extent of the injury inflicted by this curse is to be considered.

For it denounces all the righteous men and martyrs, and sufferers of every kind, who have died in this way, as Peter and Andrew, and the rest.

Such a cruel denunciation could never have come from Moses if he had been a prophet, unless he was a bitter enemy of these sufferers.

For he pronounces them cursed not only of men but of God.

What hope, then, of blessing remains to Christ, or his apostles, or to us if we happen to be crucified for Christ's sake?

It indicates great thoughtlessness in Moses, and the want of all divine inspiration, that he overlooked the fact that men are hung on a tree for very different reasons, some for their crimes, and others who suffer in the cause of God and of righteousness.

In this thoughtless way lie heaps all together without distinction under the same curse; whereas if he had had any sense, not to say inspiration, if he wished to single out the punishment of the cross from all others as specially detestable, he would have said, Cursed is every guilty and impious person that hangeth on a tree.

This would have made a distinction between the guilty and the innocent.

And yet even this would have been incorrect, for Christ took the malefactor from the cross along with himself into the Paradise of his Father. What becomes of the curse on every one that hangeth on a tree?

Was Barabbas, the notorious robber, who certainly was not hung on a tree, but was set free from prison at the request of the Jews, more blessed than the thief who accompanied Christ from the cross to heaven?

Again, there is a curse on the man that worships the sun or the moon.

Now if under a heathen monarch I am forced to worship the sun, and if from fear of this curse I refuse, shall I incur this other curse by suffering the punishment of crucifixion?

Perhaps Moses was in the habit of cursing everything good.

We think no more of his denunciation than of an old wife's scolding.

So we find him pronouncing a curse on all youths of both sexes, when he says: "Cursed is every one that raiseth not up a seed in Israel." [527] This is aimed directly at Jesus, who, according to you, was born among the Jews, and raised up no seed to continue his family.

It points too at his disciples, some of whom he took from the wives they had married, and some who were unmarried he forbade to take wives.

We have good reason, you see, for expressing our abhorrence of the daring style in which Moses hurls his maledictions against Christ, against light, against chastity, against everything divine.

You cannot make much of the distinction between hanging on a tree and being crucified, as you often try to do by way of apology; for Paul repudiates such a distinction when he says, "Christ hath redeemed us from the curse of the law, being made a curse for us; as it is written, Cursed is every one that hangeth on a tree." [528]

2.

Augustin replied:

The pious Faustus is pained because Christ is cursed by Moses.

His love for Christ makes him hate Moses.

Before explaining the sacred import and the piety of the words, "Cursed is every one that hangeth on a tree," I would ask these pious people why they are angry with Moses, since his curse does not affect their Christ.

If Christ hung on the tree, He must have been fastened to it with nails, the marks of which He showed to His doubting disciple after His resurrection.

Accordingly He must have had a vulnerable and mortal body, which the Manichæans deny.

Call the wounds and the marks false, and it follows that His hanging on the tree was false.

This Christ is not affected by the curse, and there is no occasion for this indignation against the person uttering the curse.

If they pretend to be angry with Moses for cursing what they call the false death of Christ, what are we to think of themselves, who do not curse Christ, but, what is much worse, make Him a liar?

If it is wrong to curse mortality, it is a much more heinous offense to sully the purity of truth.

But let us make these heretical cavils an occasion for explaining this mystery to believers.

3.

Death comes upon man as the punishment of sin, and so is itself called sin; not that a man sins in dying, but because sin is the cause of his death.

So the word tongue, which properly means the fleshy substance between the teeth and the palate, is applied in a secondary sense to the result of the tongue's action.

In this sense we speak of a Latin tongue and a Greek tongue.

The word hand, too, means both the members of the body we use in working, and the writing which is done with the hand.

In this sense we speak of writing as being proved to be the hand of a certain person, or of recognizing the hand of a friend. The writing is certainly not a member of the body, but the name hand is given to it because it is the hand that does it.

So sin means both a bad action deserving punishment, and death the consequence of sin. Christ has no sin in the sense of deserving death, but He bore for our sakes sin in the sense of death as brought on human nature by sin. This is what hung on the tree; this is what was cursed by Moses.

Thus was death condemned that its reign might cease, and cursed that it might be destroyed.

By Christ's taking our sin in this sense, its condemnation is our deliverance, while to remain in subjection to sin is to be condemned.

4.

What does Faustus find strange in the curse pronounced on sin, on death, and on human mortality, which Christ had on account of man's sin, though He Himself was sinless?

Christ's body was derived from Adam, for His mother the Virgin Mary was a child of Adam.

But God said in Paradise, "On the day that ye eat, ye shall surely die."

This is the curse which hung on the tree.

A man may deny that Christ was cursed who denies that He died.

But the man who believes that Christ died, and acknowledges that death is the fruit of sin, and is itself called sin, will understand who it is that is cursed by Moses, when he hears the apostle saying "For our old man is crucified with Him." [529]

The apostle boldly says of Christ, "He was made a curse for us;" for he could also venture to say, "He died for all."

"He died," and "He was cursed," are the same.

Death is the effect of the curse; and all sin is cursed, whether it means the action which merits punishment, or the punishment which follows.

Christ, though guiltless, took our punishment, that He might cancel our guilt, and do away with our punishment.

5.

These things are not my conjectures, but are affirmed constantly by the apostle, with an emphasis sufficient to rouse the careless and to silence the gainsayers.

"God," he says, "sent His Son in the likeness of sinful flesh, that by sin He might condemn sin in the flesh." [530]

Christ's flesh was not sinful, because it was not born of Mary by ordinary generation; but because death is the effect of sin, this flesh, in being mortal, had the likeness of sinful flesh.

This is called sin in the following words, "that by sin He might condemn sin in the flesh."

Again he says:

"He hath made Him to be sin for us who knew no sin, that we might be made the righteousness of God in Him." [531] Why should not Moses call accursed what Paul calls sin?

In this prediction the prophet claims a share with the apostle in the reproach of the heretics.

For whoever finds fault with the word cursed in the prophet, must find fault with the word sin in the apostle; for curse and sin go together.

6.

If we read, "Cursed of God is every one that hangeth on a tree," the addition of the words "of God" creates no difficulty.

For had not God hated sin and our death, He would not have sent His Son to bear and to abolish it.

And there is nothing strange in God's cursing what He hates.

For His readiness to give us the immortality which will be had at the coming of Christ, is in proportion to the compassion with which He hated our death when it hung on the cross at the death of Christ. And if Moses curses every one that hangeth on a tree, it is certainly not because he did not foresee that righteous men would be crucified, but rather because He foresaw that heretics would deny the death of the Lord to be real, and would try to disprove the application of this curse to Christ, in order that they might disprove the reality of His death.

For if Christ's death was not real, nothing cursed hung on the cross when He was crucified, for the crucifixion cannot have been real.

Moses cries from the distant past to these heretics:

Your evasion in denying the reality of the death of Christ is useless. Cursed is every one that hangeth on a tree; not this one or that, but absolutely every one.

What! the Son of God?

Yes, assuredly.

This is the very thing you object to, and that you are so anxious to evade. You will not allow that He was cursed for us, because you will not allow that He died for us.

Exemption from Adam's curse implies exemption from his death.

But as Christ endured death as man, and for man; so also, Son of God as He was, ever living in His own righteousness, but dying for our offences, He submitted as man, and for man, to bear the curse which accompanies death.

And as He died in the flesh which He took in bearing our punishment, so also, while ever blessed in His own righteousness, He was cursed for our offences, in the death which He suffered in bearing our punishment.

And these words "every one" are intended to check the ignorant officiousness which would deny the reference of the curse to Christ, and so, because the curse goes along with death, would lead to the denial of the true death of Christ.

7.

The believer in the true doctrine of the gospel will understand that Christ is not reproached by Moses when he speaks of Him as cursed, not in His divine majesty, but as hanging on the tree as our substitute, bearing our punishment, any more than He is praised by the Manichæans when they deny that He had a mortal body, so as to suffer real death.

In the curse of the prophet there is praise of Christ's humility, while in the pretended regard of the heretics there is a charge of falsehood.

If, then, you deny that Christ was cursed, you must deny that He died; and then you have to meet, not Moses, but the apostles.

Confess that He died, and you may also confess that He, without taking our sin, took its punishment.

Now the punishment of sin cannot be blessed, or else it would be a thing to be desired.

The curse is pronounced by divine justice, and it will be well for us if we are redeemed from it.

Confess then that Christ died, and you may confess that He bore the curse for us; and that when Moses said, "Cursed is every one that hangeth on a tree," he said in fact, To hang on a tree is to be mortal, or actually to die.

He might have said, "Cursed is every one that is mortal," or "Cursed is every one dying;" but the prophet knew that Christ would suffer on the cross, and that heretics would say that He hung on the tree only in appearance, without really dying.

So he exclaims, Cursed; meaning that He really died.

He knew that the death of sinful man, which Christ though sinless bore, came from that curse, "If ye touch it, ye shall surely die."

Thus also, the serpent hung on the pole was intended to show that Christ did not feign death, but that the real death into which the serpent by his fatal counsel cast mankind was hung on the cross of Christ's passion. The Manichæans turn away from the view of this real death, and so they are not healed of the poison of the serpent, as we read that in the wilderness as many as looked were healed.

8.

It is true, some ignorantly distinguish between hanging on a tree and being crucified.

So some explain this passage as referring to Judas.

But how do they know whether he hung himself from wood or from stone?

Faustus is right in saying that the apostle obliges us to refer the words to Christ.

Such ignorant Catholics are the prey of the Manichæans.

Such they get hold of and entangle in their sophistry. Such were we when we fell into this heresy, and adhered to it.

Such were we, when, not by our own strength, but by the mercy of God, we were rescued.

9.

What attacks on divine things does Faustus speak of when he charges Moses with sparing nothing human or divine?

He makes the charge without stopping to prove it.

We know, on the contrary, that Moses gave due praise to everything really divine, and in human affairs was a just ruler, considering his times and the grace of his dispensation. It will be time to prove this when we see any proof of Faustus' charges.

It may be clever to make such charges cautiously, but there is great incaution in the cleverness which ruins its possessor.

It is good to be clever on the side of truth, but it is a poor thing to be clever in opposition to the truth.

Faustus says that Moses spared nothing human or divine; not that he spared no god or man.

If he said that Moses did not spare God, it could easily be shown in reply that Moses everywhere does honor to the true God, whom he declares to be the Maker of heaven and earth.

Again, if he said that Moses spared none of the gods, he would betray himself to Christians as a worshipper of the false gods that Moses denounces; and so he would be prevented from gathering what he has not brought forth, by the brood taking refuge under the wings of the Mother Church.

Faustus tries to ensnare the babes, by saying that Moses spared nothing divine, wishing not to frighten Christians with a profession of belief in the gods, which would be plainly opposed to Christianity, and at the same time appearing to take the side of the Pagans against us; for they know that Moses has said many plain and pointed things against the idols and gods of the heathen, which are devils.

10.

If the Manichæans disapprove of Moses on this account, let them confess that they are worshippers of idols and devils.

This, indeed, may be the case without their being aware of it.

The apostle tells us that "in the last days some shall depart from the faith, giving heed to seducing spirits, and to doctrines of devils, speaking lies in hypocrisy." [532] Whence but from devils, who are fond of falsehood, could the idea have come that Christ's sufferings and death were unreal, and that the marks which He showed of His wounds were unreal? Are these not the doctrines of lying devils, which teach that Christ, the Truth itself, was a deceiver?

Besides, the Manichæans openly teach the worship, if not of devils, still of created things, which the apostle condemns in the words, "They worshipped and served the creature rather than the Creator." [533]

11.

As there is an unconscious worship of idols and devils in the fanciful legends of the Manichæans, so they knowingly serve the creature in their worship of the sun and moon.

And in what they call their service of the Creator they really serve their own fancy, and not the Creator at all.

For they deny that God created those things which the apostle plainly declares to be the creatures of God, when he says of food, "Every creature of God is good, and nothing to be refused, if it is received with thanksgiving." [534]This is sound doctrine, which you cannot bear, and so turn to fables.

The apostle praises the creature of God, but forbids the worship of it; and in the same way Moses gives due praise to the sun and moon, while at the same time he states the fact of their having been made by God, and placed by Him in their courses,--the sun to rule the day, and the moon to rule the night.

Probably you think Moses spared nothing divine, simply because he forbade the worship of the sun and moon, whereas you turn towards them in all directions in your worship.

But the sun and moon take no pleasure in your false praises.

It is the devil, the transgressor, that delights in false praises.

The powers of heaven, who have not fallen by sin, wish their Creator to be praised in them; and their true praise is that which does no wrong to their Creator.

He is wronged when they are said to be His members, or parts of His substance.

For He is perfect and independent, underived, not divided or scattered in space, but unchangeably self-existent, self-sufficient, and blessed in Himself.

In the abundance of His goodness, He by His word spoke, and they were made: He commanded, and they were created.

And if earthly bodies are good, of which the apostle spoke when he said that no food is unclean, because every creature of God is good, much more the heavenly bodies, of which the sun and moon are the chief; for the apostle says again, "The glory of the terrestrial is one, and the glory of the celestial is another." [535]

12.

Moses, then, casts no reproach on the sun and moon when he prohibits their worship.

He praises them as heavenly bodies; while he also praises God as the Creator of both heavenly and earthly, and will not allow of His being insulted by giving the worship due to Him to those who are praised only as dependent upon Him.

Faustus prides himself on the ingenuity of his objection to the curse pronounced by Moses on the worship of the sun and moon.

He says, "If under a heathen monarch I am forced to worship the sun, and if from fear of this curse I refuse, shall I incur this other curse by suffering the punishment of crucifixion?"

No heathen monarch is forcing you to worship the sun: nor would the sun itself force you, if it were reigning on the earth, as neither does it now wish to be worshipped.

As the Creator bears with blasphemers till the judgment, so these celestial bodies bear with their deluded worshippers till the judgment of the Creator.

It should be observed that no Christian monarch could enforce the worship of the sun.

Faustus instances a heathen monarch, for he knows that their worship of the sun is a heathen custom.

Yet, in spite of this opposition to Christianity, the partridge takes the name of Christ, that it may gather what it has not brought forth.

The answer to this objection is easy, and the force of truth will soon break the horns of this dilemma.

Suppose, then, a Christian threatened by royal authority with being hung on a tree if he will not worship the sun.

If I avoid, you say, the curse pronounced by the law on the worshipper of the sun, I incur the curse pronounced by the same law on him that hangs on a tree.

So you will be in a difficulty; only that you worship the sun without being forced by anybody.

But a true Christian, built on the foundation of the apostles and prophets, distinguishes the curses, and the reasons of them.

He sees that one refers to the mortal body which is hung on the tree, and the other to the mind which worships the sun. For though the body bows in worship,--which also is a heinous offence,-- the belief or imagination of the object worshipped is an act of the mind.

The death implied in both curses is in one case the death of the body, and in the other the death of the soul.

It is better to have the curse in bodily death,--which will be removed in the resurrection,--than the curse in the death of the soul, condemning it along with the body to eternal fire.

The Lord solves this difficulty in the words:

"Fear not them that kill the body, but cannot kill the soul; but fear him who has power to cast both soul and body into hell-fire." [536] In other words, fear not the curse of bodily death, which in time is removed; but fear the curse of spiritual death, which leads to the eternal torment of both soul and body.

Be assured, Cursed is every one that hangeth on a tree is no old wife's railing, but a prophetical utterance.

Christ, by the curse, takes the curse away, as He takes away death by death, and sin by sin.

In the words, "Cursed is every one that hangeth on a tree," there is no more blasphemy than in the words of the apostle, "He died," or, "Our old man was crucified along with Him," [537] or, "By sin He condemned sin," [538] or, "He made Him to be sin for us who knew no sin," [539] and in many similar passages.

Confess, then, that when you exclaim against the curse of Christ, you exclaim against His death.

If this is not an old wife's railing on your part, it is devilish delusion, which makes you deny the death of Christ because your own souls are dead.

You teach people that Christ's death was feigned, making Christ your leader in the falsehood with which you use the name of Christian to mislead men.

13.

If Faustus thinks Moses an enemy of continence or virginity because he says, "Cursed is everyone that raiseth not up seed in Israel," let them hear the words of Isaiah:

"Thus saith the Lord to all eunuchs; To them who keep my precepts, and choose the things that please me, and regard my covenant, will I give in my house and within my walls a place and a name better than of sons and of daughters; I will give them an everlasting name, that shall not be cut off." [540] Though our adversaries disagree with Moses, if they agree with Isaiah it is something gained.

It is enough for us to know that the same God spoke by both Moses and Isaiah, and that every one is cursed who raiseth not up seed in Israel, both then when begetting children in marriage (for the continuation of the people was a civil duty), and now because no one spiritually born should rest content without seeking spiritual increase in the production of Christians by preaching Christ, each one according to his ability.

So that the times of both Testaments are briefly described in the words, "Cursed is every one that raiseth not up seed in Israel." [541]

Book XV - Faustus rejects the Old Testament because it leaves no room for Christ

Christ the one Bridegroom suffices for His Bride the Church. Augustin answers as well as he can, and reproves the Manichæans with presumption in claiming to be the Bride of Christ.

1.

Faustus said:

Why do we not receive the Old Testament?

Because when a vessel is full, what is poured on it is not received, but allowed to run over; and a full stomach rejects what it cannot hold. So the Jews, satisfied with the Old Testament, reject the New; and we who have received the New Testament from Christ, reject the Old.

You receive both because you are only half filled with each, and the one is not completed, but corrupted by the other.

For vessels half filled should not be filled up with anything of a different nature from what they already contain.

If it contains wine, it should be filled up with wine, honey with honey, vinegar with vinegar.

For to pour gall on honey, or water on wine, or alkalies on vinegar, is not addition, but adulteration.

This is why we do not receive the Old Testament.

Our Church, the bride of Christ, the poor bride of a rich bridegroom, is content with the possession of her husband, and scorns the wealth of inferior lovers, and despises the gifts of the Old Testament and of its author, and from regard to her own character, receives only the letters of her husband.

We leave the Old Testament to your Church, that, like a bride faithless to her spouse, delights in the letters and gifts of another.

This lover who corrupts your chastity, the God of the Hebrews in his stone tablets promises you gold and silver, and abundance of food, and the land of Canaan.

Such low rewards have tempted you to be unfaithful to Christ, after all the rich dowry bestowed by him.

By such attractions the God of the Hebrews gains over the bride of Christ.

You must know that you are cheated, and that these promises are false.

This God is in poverty and beggary, and cannot do what he promises.

For if he cannot give these things to the synagogue, his proper wife, who obeys him in all things like a servant, how can he bestow them on you who are strangers, and who proudly throw off his yoke from your necks?

Go on, then, as you have begun, join the new cloth to the old garment, put the new wine in old bottles, serve two masters without pleasing either, make Christianity a monster, half horse and half man; but allow us to serve only Christ, content with his immortal dower, and imitating the apostle who says, "Our sufficiency is of God, who has made us able ministers of the New Testament."[542] In the God of the Hebrews we have no interest whatever; for neither can he perform his promises, nor do we desire that he should.

The liberality of Christ has made us indifferent to the flatteries of this stranger.

This figure of the relation of the wife to her husband is sanctioned by Paul, who says: "The woman that has a husband is bound to her husband as long as he liveth; but if her husband die, she is freed from the law of her husband.

So, then, if while her husband liveth she be joined to another man, she shall be called an adulteress; but if her husband be dead, she is not an adulteress, though she be married to another man."[543] Here he shows that there is a spiritual adultery in being united to Christ before repudiating the author of the law, and counting him, as it were, as dead.

This applies chiefly to the Jews who believe in Christ, and who ought to forget their former superstition.

We who have been converted to Christ from heathenism, look upon the God of the Hebrews not merely as dead, but as never having existed, and do not need to be told to forget him.

A Jew, when he believes, should regard Adonai as dead; a Gentile should regard his idol as dead; and so with everything that has been held sacred before conversion.

One who, after giving up idolatry, worships both the God of the Hebrews and Christ, is like an abandoned woman, who after the death of one husband marries two others.

2.

Augustin replied:

Let all who have given their hearts to Christ say whether they can listen patiently to these things, unless Christ Himself enable them.

Faustus, full of the new honey, rejects the old vinegar; and Paul, full of the old vinegar, has poured out half that the new honey may be poured in, not to be kept, but to be corrupted. When the apostle calls himself a servant of Jesus Christ, called to be an apostle, separated unto the gospel of God, this is the new honey. But when he adds, "which He promised before by His prophets in the Holy Scriptures of His Son, who was made of the seed of David according to the flesh,"[544] this is the old vinegar.

Who could bear to hear this, unless the apostle himself consoled us by saying: "There must be heresies, that they which are approved may be made manifest among you?"[545] Why should we repeat what we said already?[546] --that the new cloth and the old garment, the new wine and the old bottles, mean not two Testaments, but two lives and two hopes,--that the relation of the two Testaments is figuratively described by the Lord when He says: "Therefore every scribe instructed in the kingdom of God is like an householder bringing out of his treasure things new and old."[547] The reader may remember this as said before, or he may find it on looking back.

For if any one tries to serve God with two hopes, one of earthly felicity, and the other of the kingdom of heaven, the two hopes cannot agree; and when the latter is shaken by some affliction, the former will be lost too.

Thus it is said, No man can serve two masters; which Christ explains thus: "Ye cannot serve God and Mammon."[548] But to those who rightly understand it, the Old Testament is a prophecy of the New.

Even in that ancient people, the holy patriarchs and prophets, who understood the part they performed, or which they were instrumental in performing, had this hope of eternal life in the New Testament.

They belonged to the New Testament, because they understood and loved it, though revealed only in figure.

Those belonging to the Old Testament were the people who cared for nothing else but the temporal promises, without understanding them as significant of eternal things.

But all this has already been more than enough insisted on.

3.

It is amazingly bold in the impious and impure sect of the Manichæans to boast of being the chaste bride of Christ.

All the effect of such a boast on the really chaste members of the holy Church is to remind them of the apostle's warning against deceivers:

"I have joined you to one husband, to present you as a chaste virgin to Christ.

But I fear lest, as the serpent deceived Eve by his guile, so your minds also should be corrupted from the purity which is in Christ." [549] What else do those preachers of another gospel than that which we have received try to do, but to corrupt us from the purity which we preserve for Christ, when they stigmatize the law of God as old, and praise their own falsehoods as new, as if all that is new must be good, and all that is old bad?

The Apostle John, however, praises the old commandment, and the Apostle Paul bids us avoid novelties in doctrine.

As an unworthy son and servant of the Catholic Church, the true bride of the true Christ, I too, as appointed to give out food to my fellow-servants, would speak to her a word of counsel. Continue ever to shun the profane errors of the Manichæans, which have been tried by the experience of thine own children, and condemned by their recovery.

By that heresy I was once separated from thy fellowship, and after running into danger which ought to have been avoided, I escaped.

Restored to thy service, my experience may perhaps be profitable to thee.

Unless thy true and truthful Bridegroom, from whose side thou wert made, had obtained the remission of sins through His own real blood, the gulf of error would have swallowed me up; I should have become dust, and been devoured by the serpent.

Be not misled by the name of truth.

The truth is in thine own milk, and in thine own bread.

They have the name only, and not the thing.

Thy full-grown children, indeed, are secure; but I speak to thy babes, my brothers, and sons, and masters, whom thou, the virgin mother, fertile as pure, dost cherish into life under thine anxious wings, or dost nourish with the milk of infancy.

I call upon these, thy tender offspring, not to be seduced by noisy vanities, but rather to pronounce accursed any one that preaches to them another gospel than that which they have received in thee.

I call upon these not to leave the true and truthful Christ, in whom are hid all the treasures of wisdom and knowledge; not to forsake the abundance of His goodness which He has laid up for them that fear Him, and has wrought for them that trust in Him. [550] How can they expect to find truthful words in one who preaches an untruthful Christ?

Scorn the reproaches cast on thee, for thou knowest well that the gift which thou desirest from thy Bridegroom is eternal life, for He Himself is eternal life.

4.

It is a silly falsehood that thou hast been seduced to another God, who promises abundance of food and the land of Canaan.

For thou canst perceive how the saints of old, who were also thy children, were enlightened by these figures which were prophecies of thee.

Thou needest not regard the poor jest against the stone tablets, for the stony heart of which they were in old times a figure is not in thee. For thou art an epistle of the apostles, "written not with ink, but with the Spirit of the living God; not on tables of stone, but on the fleshy tables of the heart." [551] Our opponents ignorantly think that these words are in their favor, and that the apostle finds fault with the dispensation of the Old Testament, whereas they are the words of the prophet.

This utterance of the apostles was a fulfillment of the long anterior utterances of the prophet whom the Manichæans reject, for they believe the apostles without understanding them.

The prophet says:

"I will take away from them the stony heart, and I will give them a heart of flesh." [552] What is this but "Not on tables of stones but on the fleshy tables of the heart"?

For by the heart of flesh and the fleshy tables is not meant a carnal understanding:

but as flesh feels, whereas a stone cannot, the insensibility of stone signifies an unintelligent heart, and the sensibility of flesh signifies an intelligent heart.

Instead, then, of scoffing at thee, they deserve to be ridiculed who say that earth, and wood, and stones have sense, and that their life is more intelligent than animal life. So, not to speak of the truth, even their own fiction obliges them to confess that the law written on tables of stone was purer than their sacred parchments.

Or perhaps they prefer sheepskin to stone, because their legends make stones the bones of princes.

In any case, the ark of the Old Testament was a cleaner covering for the tables of stone than the goatskin of their manuscripts.

Laugh at these things, while pitying them, to show their falsehood and absurdity.

With a heart no longer stony, thou canst see in these stone tablets a suitableness to that hard-hearted people; and at the same time thou canst find even there the stone, thy Bridegroom, described by Peter as "a living stone, rejected by men, but chosen of God, and precious."

To them He was "a stone of stumbling and a rock of offence;" but to thee, "the stone which the builders rejected has become the head of the corner." [553] This is all explained by Peter, and is quoted from the prophets, with whom these heretics have nothing to do.

Fear not, then, to read these tablets--they are from thy Husband; to others the stone was a sign of insensibility, but to thee of strength and stability.

With the finger of God these tablets were written; with the finger of God thy Lord cast out devils; with the finger of God drive thou away the doctrines of lying devils which sear the conscience.

With these tablets thou canst confound the seducer who calls himself the Paraclete, that he may impose upon thee by a sacred name.

For on the fiftieth day after the passover the tables were given; and on the fiftieth day after the passion of thy Bride-groom--of whom the passover was a type--the finger of God, the Holy Spirit, the promised Paraclete, was given.

Fear not the tablets which convey to thee ancient writings now made plain.

Only be not under the law, lest fear prevent thy fulfilling it; but be under grace, that love, which is the fulfilling of the law, may be in thee. For it was in a review of these very tablets that the friend of thy Bridegroom said:

"For thou shalt not commit adultery, Thou shalt not murder, Thou shalt not covet, and if there be any other commandment, it is contained in this word, Thou shalt love thy neighbor as thyself. Love worketh no ill to his neighbor; therefore love is the fulfilling of the law." [554] One table contains the precept of love to God, and the other of love to man.

And He who first sent these tablets Himself came to enjoin those precepts on which hang the law and the prophets. [555]

In the first precept is the chastity of thy espousals; in the second is the unity of thy members.

In the one thou art united to divinity; in the other thou dost gather a society.

And these two precepts are identical with the ten, of which three relate to God, and seven to our neighbor.

Such is the chaste tablet in which thy Lover and thy Beloved of old prefigured to thee the new song on a psaltery of ten strings; Himself to be extended on the cross for thee, that by sin He might condemn sin in the flesh, and that the righteousness of the law might be fulfilled in thee.

Such is the conjugal tablet, which may well be hated by the unfaithful wife.

5.

I turn now to thee, thou deluded and deluding congregation of Manichæus,--wedded to so many elements, or rather prostituted to so many devils, and impregnated with blasphemous falsehoods,--dost thou dare to slander as unchaste the marriage of the Catholic Church with thy Lord?

Behold thy lovers, one balancing creation, and the other bearing it up like Atlas.

For one, by thy account, holds the sources of the elements, and hangs the world in space; while the other keeps him up by kneeling down and carrying the weight on his shoulders. Where are those beings?

And if they are so occupied, how can they come to visit thee, to spend an idle hour in getting their shoulders or their fingers relieved by thy soft, soothing touch?

But thou art deceived by evil spirits which commit adultery with thee, that thou mayest conceive falsehoods and bring forth vanities.

Well mayest thou reject the message of the true God, as opposed to thy parchments, where in the vain imaginations of a wanton mind thou hast gone after so many false gods.

The fictions of the poets are more respectable than thine, in this at least, that they deceive no one; while the fables in thy books, by assuming an appearance of truth, mislead the childish, both young and old, and pervert their minds.

As the apostle says, they have itching ears, and turn away from hearing the truth to listen to fables. [556] How shouldest thou bear the sound doctrine of these tables, where the first commandment is, "Hear, O Israel, the Lord thy God is one Lord," [557] when thy corrupt affections find shameful delight in so many false deities?

Dost thou not remember thy love-song, where thou describest the chief ruler in perennial majesty, crowned with flowers, and of fiery countenance?

To have even one such lover is shameful; for a chaste wife seeks not a husband crowned with flowers. And thou canst not say that this description or representation has a typical meaning, for thou art wont to praise Manichæus for nothing more than for speaking to thee the simple naked truth without the disguise of figures.

So the God of thy song is a real king, bearing a sceptre and crowned with flowers.

When he wears a crown of flowers, he ought to put aside his sceptre; for effeminacy and majesty are incongruous. And then he is not thy only lover; for the song goes on to tell of twelve seasons clothed in flowers, and filled with song, throwing their flowers at their father's face.

These are twelve great gods of thine, three in each of the four regions surrounding the first deity.

How this deity can be infinite, when he is thus circumscribed, no one can say.

Besides, there are countless principalities, and hosts of gods, and troops of angels, which thou sayest were not created by God, but produced from His substance.

6.

Thou art thus convicted of worshipping gods without number; for thou canst not bear the sound doctrine which teaches that there is one Son of one God, and one Spirit of both.

And these, instead of being without number, are not three Gods; for not only is their substance one and the same, but their operation by means of this substance is also one and the same, while they have a separate manifestation in the material creation.

These things thou dost not understand, and canst not receive.

Thou art full, as thou sayest, for thou art steeped in blasphemous absurdities.

Will thou continue burying thyself under such crudities?

Sing on, then, and open thine eyes, if thou canst, to thine own shame.

In this doctrine of lying devils thou art invited to fabulous dwellings of angels in a happy clime, and to fragrant fields where nectar flows for ever from trees and hills, in seas and rivers. These are the fictions of thy foolish heart, which revels in such idle fancies.

Such expressions are sometimes used as figurative descriptions of the abundance of spiritual enjoyments; and they lead the mind of the student to inquire into their hidden meaning. Sometimes there is a material representation to the bodily senses, as the fire in the bush, the rod becoming a serpent, and the serpent a rod, the garment of the Lord not divided by His persecutors, the anointing of His feet or of His head by a devout woman, the branches of the multitude preceding and following Him when riding on the ass. Sometimes, either in sleep or in a trance, the spirit is informed by means of figures taken from material things, as Jacob's ladder, and the stone in Daniel cut out without hands and growing into a mountain, and Peter's vessel, and all that John saw.

Sometimes the figures are only in the language; as in the Song of Songs, and in the parable of a householder making a marriage for his son, or that of the prodigal son, or that of the man who planted a vineyard and let it out to husbandmen.

Thou boastest of Manichæus as having come last, not to use figures, but to explain them.

His expositions throw light on ancient types, and leave no problem unsolved.

This idea is supported by the assertion that the ancient types, in vision or in action or in words, had in view the coming of Manichæus, by whom they were all to be explained; while he, knowing that no one is to follow him, makes use of a style free from all figurative expressions.

What, then, are those fields, and shady hills, and crowns of flowers, and fragrant odors, in which the desires of thy fleshly mind take pleasure?

If they are not significant figures, they are either idle fancies or delirious dreams. If they are figures, away with the impostor who seduces thee with the promise of naked truth, and then mocks thee with idle tales.

His ministers and his wretched deluded followers are wont to bait their hook with that saying of the apostle, "Now we see through a glass in a figure, but then face to face." [558] As if, forsooth, the Apostle Paul knew in part, and prophesied in part, and saw through a glass in a figure; whereas all this is removed at the coming of Manichæus, who brings that which is perfect, and reveals the truth face to face.

O fallen and shameless! still to continue uttering such folly, still feeding on the wind, still embracing the idols of thine own heart. Hast thou, then, seen face to face the king with the sceptre, and the crown of flowers, and the hosts of gods, and the great worldholder with six faces and radiant with light, and that other exalted ruler surrounded with troops of angels, and the invincible warrior with a spear in his right hand and a shield in his left, and the famous sovereign who moves the three wheels of fire, water, and wind, and Atlas, chief of all, bearing the world on his shoulders, and supporting himself on his arms?

These, and a thousand other marvels, hast thou seen face to face, or are thy songs doctrines learned from lying devils, though thou knowest it not?

Alas! miserable prostitute to these dreams, such are the vanities which thou drinkest up instead of the truth; and, drunk with this deadly poison, thou darest with this jest of the tablets to affront the matronly purity of the spouse of the only Son of God; because no longer under the tutorship of the law, but under the control of grace, neither proud in activity nor crouching in fear, she lives by faith, and hope, and love, the Israel in whom there is no guile, who hears what is written:

"The Lord thy God is one God."

This thou hearest not, and art gone a whoring after a multitude of false gods.

7.

Of necessity these tables are against thee, for the second commandment is, "Thou shalt not take the name of the Lord thy God in vain;" whereas thou dost attribute the vanity of falsehood to Christ Himself, who, to remove the vanity of the fleshly mind, rose in a true body, visible to the bodily eye.

So also the third commandment about the rest of the Sabbath is against thee, for thou art tossed about by a multitude of restless fancies.

How these three commandments relate to the love of God, thou hast neither the power nor the will to understand.

Shamefully headstrong and turbulent, thou hast reached the height of folly, vanity, and worthlessness; thy beauty is spoiled, and thine order perished.

I know thee, for I was once the same.

How shall I now teach thee that these three precepts relate to the love of God, of whom, and by whom, and in whom are all things?

How canst thou understand this, when thy pernicious doctrines prevent thee from understanding and from obeying the seven precepts relating to the love of our neighbor, which is the bond of human society?

The first of these precepts is, "Honor thy father and mother;" which Paul quotes as the first commandment with promise, and himself repeats the injunction.

But thou art taught by thy doctrine of devils to regard thy parents as thine enemies, because their union brought thee into the bonds of flesh, and laid impure fetters even on thy god.

The doctrine that the production of children is an evil, directly opposes the next precept, "Thou shall not commit adultery;" for those who believe this doctrine, in order that their wives may not conceive, are led to commit adultery even in marriage.

They take wives, as the law declares, for the procreation of children; but from this erroneous fear of polluting the substance of the deity, their intercourse with their wives is not of a lawful character; and the production of children, which is the proper end of marriage, they seek to avoid.

As the apostle long ago predicted of thee, thou dost indeed forbid to marry, for thou seekest to destroy the purpose of marriage.

Thy doctrine turns marriage into an adulterous connection, and the bed-chamber into a brothel.

This false doctrine leads in a similar way to the transgression of the commandment, "Thou shall not kill."

For thou dost not give bread to the hungry, from fear of imprisoning in flesh the member of thy God. From fear of fancied murder, thou dost actually commit murder.

For if thou wast to meet a beggar starving for want of food, by the law of God to refuse him food would be murder; while to give food would be murder by the law of Manichæus.

Not one commandment in the decalogue dost thou observe.

If thou wert to abstain from theft, thou wouldst be guilty of allowing bread or food, whatever it might be, to undergo the misery of being devoured by a man of no merit, instead of running off with it to the laboratory of the stomach of thine elect; and so by theft saving thy god from the imprisonment with which he is threatened, and also from that from which he already suffers.

Then, if thou art caught in the theft, wilt thou not swear by this god that thou art not guilty?

For what will he do to thee when thou sayest to him, I swore by thee falsely, but it was for thy benefit; a regard for thine honor would have been fatal to thee?

So the precept, Thou shall not bear false witness, will be broken, not only in thy testimony, but in thine oath, for the sake of the liberation of the members of thy god.

The commandment, "Thou shall not covet thy neighbor's wife," is the only one which thy false doctrine does not oblige thee to break.

But if it is unlawful to covet our neighbor's wife, what must it be to excite covetousness in others?

Remember thy beautiful gods and goddesses presenting themselves with the purpose of exciting desire in the male and female leaders of darkness, in order that the gratification of this passion might effect the liberation of this god, who is in confinement everywhere, and who requires the assistance of such self-degradation. The last commandment, "Thou shall not covet the possessions of thy neighbor," it is wholly impossible for thee to obey.

Does not this god of thine delude thee with the promise of making new worlds in a region belonging to another, to be the scene of thine imaginary triumph after thine imaginary conquest?

In the desire for the accomplishment of these wild fancies, while at the same time thou believest that this land of darkness is in the closest neighborhood with thine own substance, thou certainly covetest the possessions of thy neighbor. Well indeed mayest thou dislike the tables which contain such good precepts in opposition to thy false doctrine.

The three relating to the love of God thou dost entirely set aside.

The seven by which human society is preserved thou keepest only from a regard to the opinion of men, or from fear of human laws; or good customs make thee averse to some crimes; or thou art restrained by the natural principle of not doing to another what thou wouldst not have done to thyself.

But whether thou doest what thou wouldst not have done to thyself, or refrainest from doing what thou wouldst not have done to thyself, thou seest the opposition of the heresy to the law, whether thou actest according to it or not.

8.

The true bride of Christ, whom thou hast the audacity to taunt with the stone tablets, knows the difference between the letter and the spirit, or in other words, between law and grace; and serving God no longer in the oldness of the letter, but in newness of spirit, she is not under the law, but under grace.

She is not blinded by a spirit of controversy, but learns meekly from the apostle what is this law which we are not to be under; for "it was given," he says, "on account of transgression, till the seed should come to whom the promise was made." [559] And again:

"It entered, that the offence might abound; but where sin abounded, grace has much more abounded." [560] Not that the law is sin, though it cannot give life without grace, but rather increases the guilt; for "where there is no law, there is no transgression." [561] The letter without the spirit, the law without grace, can only condemn.

So the apostle explains his meaning, in case any should not understand:

"What shall we say then?

Is the law sin? God forbid.

For I had not known sin but by the law.

For I had not known lust unless the law had said, Thou shalt not covet.

But sin, taking occasion by the commandment, deceived me, and by it slew me. Therefore the law is holy, and the commandment holy, and just, and good.

Was then that which is good made death unto me?

God forbid. But sin, that it might appear sin, wrought death in me by that which is good."[562] She at whom thou scoffest knows what this means; for she asks earnestly, and seeks humbly, and knocks meekly.

She sees that no fault is found with the law, when it is said, "The letter killeth, but the spirit giveth life," any more than with knowledge, when it is said, "Knowledge puffeth up, but love edifieth." [563] The passage runs thus:

"We know that we all have knowledge.

Knowledge puffeth up, but love edifieth."

The apostle certainly had no desire to be puffed up; but he had knowledge, because knowledge joined with love not only does not puff up, but strengthens.

So the letter when joined with the spirit, and the law when joined with grace, is no longer the letter and the law in the same sense as when by itself it kills by abounding sin. In this sense the law is even called the strength of sin, because its strict prohibitions increase the fatal pleasure of sin.

Even thus, however, the law is not evil; but "sin, that it may appear sin, works death by that which is good."

So things that are not evil may often be hurtful to certain people.

The Manichæans, when they have sore eyes, will shut out their god the sun.

The bride of Christ, then, is dead to the law, that is, to sin, which abounds more from the prohibition of the law; for the law apart from grace commands, but does not enable. Being dead to the law in this sense, that she may be married to another who rose from the dead, she makes this distinction without any reproach to the law, which would be blasphemy against its author.

This is thy crime; for though the apostle tells thee that the law is holy, and the commandment holy, and just, and good, thou dost not acknowledge it as the production of a good being.

Its author thou makest to be one of the princes of darkness.

Here the truth confronts thee.

They are the words of the Apostle Paul:

"The law is holy, and the commandment holy, and just, and good."

Such is the law given by Him who appointed for a great symbolical use the tablets which thou foolishly deridest.

The same law which was given by Moses becomes through Jesus Christ grace and truth; for the spirit is joined to the letter, that the righteousness of the law might begin to be fulfilled, which when unfulfilled only added the guilt of transgression.

The law which is holy, and just, and good, is the same law by which sin works death, and to which we must die, that we may be married to another who rose from the dead.

Hear what the apostle adds:

"But sin, that it might appear sin, wrought death in me by that which is good, that sin by the commandment might become exceeding sinful."

Deaf and blind, dost thou not now hear and see?

"Sin wrought death in me," he says, "by that which is good."

The law is always good:

whether it hurts those who are destitute of grace, or benefits those who are filled with grace, itself is always good; as the sun is always good, for every creature of God is good, whether it hurts weak eyes or gladdens the sight of the healthy.

Grace fits the mind for keeping the law, as health fits the eyes for seeing the sun.

And as healthy eyes die not to the pleasure of seeing the sun, but to that painful effect of the rays which beat upon the eye so as to increase the darkness; so the mind, healed by the love of the spirit, dies not to the justice of the law, but to the guilt and transgression which followed on the law in the absence of grace.

So it is said "The law is good, if used lawfully;" and immediately after of the same law, "Knowing this, that the law is not made for a righteous man."

The man who delights in righteousness itself, does not require the restraint of the letter.

9.

The bride of Christ rejoices in the hope of full salvation, and desires for thee a happy conversion from fables to truth.

She desires that the fear of Adoneus, as if he were a strange lover, may not prevent thy escape from the seductions of the wily serpent.

Adonai is a Hebrew word, meaning Lord, as applied only to God.

In the same way the Greek word latria means service, in the sense of the service of God; and Amen means true, in a special sacred sense.

This is to be learned only from the Hebrew Scriptures, or from a translation.

The Church of Christ understands and loves these names, without regarding the evils of those who scoff because they are ignorant.

What she does not yet understand, she believes may be explained, as similar things have already been explained to her.

If she is charged with loving Emmanuel, she laughs at the ignorance of the accuser, and holds fast by the truth of this name.

If she is charged with loving Messiah, she scorns her powerless adversary, and clings to her anointed Master.

Her prayer for thee is, that thou also mayest be cured of thy errors, and be built upon the foundation of the apostles and prophets.

The monstrosity with which thou ignorantly chargest the true doctrine, is really to be found in the world which, according to thy fanciful stories, is made partly of thy god and partly of the world of darkness.

This world, half savage and half divine, is worse than monstrous.

The view of such follies should make thee humble and penitent, and should lead thee to shun the serpent, who seduces thee into such errors.

If thou dost not believe what Moses says of the guile of the serpent, thou mayest be warned by Paul, who, when speaking of presenting the Church as a chaste virgin to Christ, says, "I fear lest, as the serpent beguiled Eve through his craftiness, your minds also should be corrupted from the simplicity and purity which is in Christ." [564] In spite of this warning, thou hast been so misled, so infatuated by the serpent's fatal enchantments, that while he has persuaded other heretics to believe various falsehoods, he has persuaded thee to believe that he is Christ.

Others, though fallen into the maze of manifold error, still admit the truth of the apostle's warning.

But thou art so far gone in corruption, and so lost to shame, that thou holdest as Christ the very being by whom the apostle declares that Eve was beguiled, and against whom he thus seeks to put the virgin bride of Christ on her guard.

Thy heart is darkened by the deceiver, who intoxicates thee with dreams of glittering groves.

What are these promises but dreams?

What reason is there to believe them true?

O drunken, but not with wine!

10.

Thou hast the impious audacity to accuse the God of the prophets of not fulfilling His promises even to His servants the Jews.

Thou dost not mention, however, any promise that is unfulfilled; otherwise it might be shown, either that the promise has been fulfilled, and so that thou dost not understand it, or that it is yet to be fulfilled, and so that thou dost not believe it.

What promise has been fulfilled to thee, to make it probable that thou wilt obtain new worlds gained from the region of darkness?

If there are prophets who predict the Manichæans with praise, and if it is said that the existence of the sect is a fulfillment of this prediction, it must first be proved that these predictions were not forged by Manichæus in order to gain followers.

He does not consider falsehood sinful.

If he declares in praise of Christ that He showed false marks of wounds in His body, he can have no scruple about showing false predictions in his sheepskin volumes.

Assuredly there are predictions of the Manichæans, less clear in the prophets, and most explicit in the apostle.

For example:

"The Spirit," he says, "speaketh expressly, that in the last times some shall depart from the faith, giving heed to seducing spirits, and to doctrines of devils, speaking lies in hypocrisy, having their conscience seared, forbidding to marry, abstaining from meats, which God has created to be received with thanksgiving by believers, and those who know the truth.

For every creature of God is good, and nothing to be refused, if it be received with thanksgiving." [565] The fulfillment of this in the Manichæans is as clear as day to all that know them, and has already been proved as fully as time permits.

11.

She whom the apostle warns against the guile of the serpent by which thou hast been corrupted, that he may present her as a chaste virgin to Christ, her only husband, acknowledges the God of the prophets as the true God, and her own God.

So many of His promises have already been fulfilled to her, that she looks confidently for the fulfillment of the rest.

Nor can any one say that these prophecies have been forged to suit the present time, for they are found in the books of the Jews.

What could be more unlikely than that all nations should be blessed in Abraham's seed, as it was promised?

And yet how plainly is this promise now fulfilled!

The last promise is made in the following short prophecy:

"Blessed are they that dwell in Thy house: they shall ever praise Thee." [566] When trial is past, and death, the last enemy, is destroyed, there will be rest in the constant occupation of praising God, where there shall be no arrivals and no departures.

So the prophet says elsewhere:

"Praise the Lord, O Jerusalem; celebrate thy God, O Zion:

for He hath strengthened the bars of thy gates; He hath blessed thy children within thee."[567] The gates are shut, so that none can go in or out.

The Bridegroom Himself says in the Gospel, that He will not open to the foolish virgins though they knock.

This Jerusalem, the holy Church, the bride of Christ, is described fully in the Revelation of John.

And that which commends the promises of future bliss to the belief of this chaste virgin is, that now she is in possession of what was foretold of her by the same prophets.

For she is thus described:

"Hearken, O daughter, and regard, and incline thine ear; forget also thine own people, and thy father's house.

For the King hath greatly desired thy beauty; and He is thy God.

The daughters of Tyre shall worship Him with gifts; the rich among the people shall entreat thy favor.

The daughter of the King is all glorious within; her clothing is of wrought gold.

The virgins following her shall be brought unto the King:

her companions shall be brought unto thee; with gladness and rejoicing shall they be brought into the temple of the King.

Instead of thy fathers, children shall be born to thee, whom thou shall make princes over all the earth.

Thy name shall be remembered to all generations: therefore shall the people praise thee for ever and ever." [568] Unhappy victim of the serpent's guile, the inward beauty of the daughter of the King is not for thee even to think of.

For this purity of mind is that which thou hast lost in opening thine eyes to love and worship the sun and moon.

And so by the just judgment of God thou art estranged from the tree of life, which is eternal and internal wisdom; and with thee nothing is called or accounted truth or wisdom but that light which enters the eyes opened to evil, and which in thy impure mind expands and shapes itself into fanciful images.

These are thy abominable whoredoms.

Still the truth calls on thee to reflect and return.

Return to me, and thou shall be cleansed and restored, if thy shame leads thee to repentance.

Hear these words of the true Truth, who neither with feigned shapes fought against the race of darkness, nor with feigned blood redeemed thee.

Book XVI - Faustus willing to believe not only that the Jewish but that all Gentile prophets wrote of Christ, if it should be proved; but he would none the less insist upon rejecting their superstitions

Augustin maintains that all Moses wrote is of Christ, and that his writings must be either accepted or rejected as a whole.

1.

Faustus said:

You ask why we do not believe Moses, when Christ says, "Moses wrote of me; and if ye believed Moses, ye would also believe me."

I should be glad if not only Moses, but all prophets, Jew and Gentile, had written of Christ.

It would be no hindrance, but a help to our faith, if we could cull testimonies from all hands agreeing in favor of our God.

You could extract the prophecies of Christ out of the superstition which we should hate as much as ever.

I am quite willing to believe that Moses, though so much the opposite of Christ, may seem to have written of Him.

No one but would gladly find a flower in every thorn, and food in every plant, and honey in every insect, although we would not feed on insects or on grass, nor wear thorns as a crown.

No one but would wish pearls to be found in every deep, and gems in every land, and fruit on every tree.

We may eat fish from the sea without drinking the water.

We may take the useful, and reject what is hurtful.

And why may we not take the prophecies of Christ from a religion the rites of which we condemn as useless?

This need not make us liable to be led into the bondage of the errors; for we do not hate the unclean spirits less because they confessed plainly and openly that Jesus was the Son of God.

If any similar testimony is found in Moses, I will accept it.

But I will not on this account be brought into subjection to his law, which to my mind is pure Paganism.

There is no reason whatever for thinking that I can have any objections to receiving prophecies of Christ from every spirit.

2.

Since you have proved that Christ declared that Moses wrote of him, I should be very grateful if you would show me what he has written.

I have searched the Scriptures, as we are told to do, and have found no prophecies of Christ, either because there are none, or because I could not understand them.

The only escape from this perplexity was in one or other of two conclusions.

Either this verse must be spurious, or Jesus a liar.

As it is not consistent with piety to suppose God a liar, I preferred to attribute falsehood to the writers, rather than to the Author, of truth.

Moreover, He Himself tells that those who came before him were thieves and robbers, which applies first of all to Moses.

And when, on the occasion of His speaking of His own majesty, and calling Himself the light of the world, the Jews angrily rejoined, "Thou bearest witness of thyself, thy witness is not true," I do not find that He appealed to the prophecies of Moses, as might have been expected.

Instead of this, as having no connection with the Jews, and receiving no testimony from their fathers, He replied:

"It is written in your law, that the testimony of two men is true.

I am one who bear witness of myself, and the Father who sent me beareth witness of me."[569]He referred to the voice from heaven which all had heard: "This is my beloved Son, believe Him."

I think it likely that if Christ had said that Moses wrote of Him, the ingenious hostility of the Jews would have led them at once to ask what He supposed Moses to have written.

The silence of the Jews is a proof that Jesus never made such a statement.

3.

My chief reason, however, for suspecting the genuineness of this verse is what I said before, that in all my search of the writings of Moses I have found no prophecy of Christ.

But now that I have found in you a reader of superior intelligence, I hope to learn something; and I promise to be grateful if no feeling of ill-will prevents you from giving me the benefit of your higher attainments, as your lofty style of reproof entitles me to expect from you.

I ask for instruction in whatever the writings of Moses contain about our God and Lord which has escaped me in reading.

I beseech you not to use the ignorant argument that Christ affirms Moses to have written of Him.

For suppose you had not to deal with me, as in my case there is an obligation to believe Him whom I profess to follow, but with a Jew or a Gentile, in reply to the statement that Moses wrote of Christ, they will ask for proofs. What shall we say to them?

We cannot quote Christ's authority, for they do not believe in Him.

We must point out what Moses wrote.

4.

What, then, shall we point to?

Shall it be that passage which you often quote where the God of Moses says to him:

"I will raise up unto them from among their brethren a prophet like unto thee?"[570]But the Jew can see that this does not refer to Christ, and there is every reason against our thinking that it does.

Christ was not a prophet, nor was He like Moses:

for Moses was a man, and Christ was God; Moses was a sinner, and Christ sinless; Moses was born by ordinary generation, and Christ of a virgin according to you, or, as I hold, not born at all:

Moses, for offending his God, was put to death on the mountain; and Christ suffered voluntarily, and the Father was well pleased in Him.

If we were to assert that Christ was a prophet like Moses, the Jew would either deride us as ignorant or pronounce us untruthful.

5.

Or shall we take another favorite passage of yours:
"They shall see their life hanging, and shall not believe their life?" [571] You insert the words "on a tree," which are not in the original.

Nothing can be easier than to show that this has no reference to Christ.

Moses is uttering dire threatenings in case the people should depart from his law, and says among other things that they would be taken captive by their enemies, and would be expecting death day and night, having no confidence in the life allowed them by their conquerors, so that their life would hang in uncertainty from fear of impending danger.

This passage will not do, we must try others.

I cannot admit that the words, "Cursed is every one that hangeth on a tree," refer to Christ, or when it is said that the prince or prophet must be killed who should try to turn away the people from their God, or should break any of the commandments. [572]

That Christ did this I am obliged to grant.

But if you assert that these things were written of Christ, it may be asked in reply, What spirit dictated these prophecies in which Moses curses Christ and orders him to be killed?

If he had the Spirit of God, these things are not written of Christ; if they are written of Christ, he had not the Spirit of God.

The Spirit of God would not curse Christ, or order Him to be killed.

To vindicate Moses, you must confess that these passages too have no reference to Christ.

So, if you have no others to show, there are none.

If there are none, Christ could not have said that there were; and if Christ did not say so, that verse is spurious.

6.

The next verse too is suspicious, "If ye believed Moses, ye would also believe me;" for the religion of Moses is so entirely different from that of Christ, that if the Jews believed one, they could not believe the other.

Moses strictly forbids any work to be done on Sabbath, and gives as a reason for this prohibition that God made the world and all that is therein in six days, and rested on the seventh day, which is Sabbath; and therefore blessed or sanctified it as His haven of repose after toil, and commanded that breaking the Sabbath should be punished with death.

The Jews, in obedience to Moses, insisted strongly on this, and so would not even listen to Christ when He told them that God always works, and that no day is appointed for the intermission of His pure and unwearied energy, and that accordingly He Himself had to work incessantly even on Sabbath.

"My Father," he says, "worketh always, and I too must work." [573] Again, Moses places circumcision among the rites pleasing to God, and commands every male to be circumcised in the foreskin of his flesh, and declares that this is a necessary sign of the covenant which God made with Abraham, and that every male not circumcised would be cut off from his tribe, and from his part in the inheritance promised to Abraham and to his seed. [574] In this observance, too, the Jews were very zealous, and consequently could not believe in Christ, who made light of these things, and declared that a man when circumcised became twofold a child of hell. [575] Again, Moses is very particular about the distinction in animal foods, and discourses like an epicure on the merits of fish, and birds, and quadrupeds, and orders some to be eaten as clean, and others which are unclean not to be touched.

Among the unclean he reckons the swine and the hare, and fish without scales, and quadrupeds that neither divide the hoof nor chew the cud.

In this also the Jews carefully obeyed Moses, and so could not believe in Christ, who taught that all food is alike, and though he allowed no animal food to his own disciples, gave full liberty to the laity to eat whatever they pleased, and taught that men are polluted not by what goes into the mouth, but by the evil things which come out of it.

In these and many other things the doctrine of Jesus, as everybody knows, contradicts that of Moses.

7.

Not to enumerate all the points of difference, it is enough to mention this one fact, that most Christian sects, and, as is well known, the Catholics, pay no regard to what is prescribed in the writings of Moses.

If this does not originate in some error, but in the doctrine correctly transmitted from Christ and His disciples, you surely must acknowledge that the teaching of Jesus is opposed to that of Moses, and that the Jews did not believe in Christ on account of their attachment to Moses.

How can it be otherwise than false that Jesus said to the Jews, "If ye believed Moses, ye would believe me also," when it is perfectly clear that their belief in Moses prevented them from believing in Jesus, which they might have done if they had left off believing in Moses?

Again I ask you to show me anything that Moses wrote of Christ.

8.

Elsewhere Faustus says:

When you find no passage to point to, you use this weak and inappropriate argument, that a Christian is bound to believe Christ when he says that Moses wrote of Him, and that whoever does not believe this is not a Christian.

It would be far better to confess at once that you cannot find any passage.

This argument might be used with me, because my reverence for Christ compels me to believe what He says.

Still it may be a question whether this is Christ's own declaration, requiring absolute belief, or only the writer's, to be carefully examined.

And disbelief in falsehood is no offence to Christ, but to impostors.

But of whatever use this argument may be with Christians, it is wholly inapplicable in the case of the Jew or Gentile, with whom we are supposed to be discussing.

And even with Christians the argument is objectionable.

When the Apostle Thomas was in doubt, Christ did not spurn him from Him.

Instead of saying, "Believe, if thou art a disciple; whoever does not believe is not a disciple," Christ sought to heal the wounds of his mind by showing him the marks of the wounds in His own body.

Does it become you then to tell me that I am not a Christian because I am in doubt, not about Christ, but about the genuineness of a remark attributed to Christ? But, you say, He calls those especially blessed, who have not seen, and yet have believed.

If you think that this refers to believing without the use of judgment and reason, you are welcome to this blind blessedness.

I shall be content with rational blessedness.

9.

Augustin replied:

Your idea of taking any prophecies of Christ to be found in Moses, as a fish out of the sea, while you throw away the water from which the fish is taken, is a clever one.

But since all that Moses wrote is of Christ, or relates to Christ, either as predicting Him by words and actions, or as illustrating His grace and glory, you, with your faith in the untrue and untruthful Christ from the writings of Manichæus, and your unbelief in Moses, will not even eat the fish.

Moreover, though you are sincere in your hostility to Moses, you are hypocritical in your praise of fish.

For how can you say that there is no harm in eating a fish taken out of the sea, when your doctrine is that such food is so hurtful, that you would rather starve than make use of it?

If all flesh is unclean, as you say it is, and if the wretched life of your god is confined in all water or plants, from which it is liberated by your using them for food, according to your own vile superstition, you must throw away the fish you have praised, and drink the water and eat the thistles you speak of as useless.

As for your comparison of the servant of God to devils, as if his prophecies of Christ resembled their confession, the servant does not refuse to bear the reproach of his master.

If the Master of the house was called Beelzebub, how much more they of His household![576] You have learned this reproach from Christ's enemies; and you are worse than they were.

They did not believe that Jesus was Christ, and therefore thought Him an impostor.

But the only doctrine you believe in is that which dares to make Christ a liar.

10.

What reason have you for saying that the law of Moses is pure Paganism?

Is it because it speaks of a temple, and an altar of sacrifices, and priests?

But all these names are found also in the New Testament.

"Destroy," Christ says, "this temple, and in three days I will raise it up;" [577] and again, "When thou offerest thy gift at the altar;" [578] and again, "Go, show thyself to the priest, and offer for thyself a sacrifice as Moses commanded, for a testimony unto them." [579] What these things prefigured the Lord Himself partly tells us, when He calls His own body the temple; and we learn also from the apostle, who says, "The temple of God is holy, which temple ye are;" [580] and again, "I beseech you therefore by the mercies of God, that ye present your bodies a living sacrifice, holy, acceptable to God;" [581] and in similar passages.

As the same apostle says, in words which cannot be too often quoted, these things were our examples, for they were not the work of devils, but of the one true God who made heaven and earth, and who, though not needing such things, yet, suiting His requirements to the time, made ancient observances significant of future realities.

Since you pretend to abhor Paganism, though it is only that you may lead astray by your deception unlearned Christians or those not established in the faith, show us any authority in Christian books for your worship and service of the sun and moon.

Your heresy is liker Paganism than the law of Moses is.

For you do not worship Christ, but only something that you call Christ, a fiction of your own fancy; and the gods you serve are either the bodies visible in the heavens, or hosts of your own contrivance.

If you do not build shrines for these worthless idols, the creatures of the imagination, you make your hearts their temple.

11.

You ask me to show what Moses wrote of Christ.

Many passages have already been pointed out.

But who could point out all?

Besides, when any quotation is made, you are ready perversely to try to give the words another meaning; or if the evidence is too strong to be resisted, you will say that you take the passage as a sweet fish out of the salt water, and that you will not therefore consent to drink all the brine of the books of Moses.

It will be enough, then, to take those passages in the Hebrew law which Faustus has chosen for criticism, and to show that, when rightly understood, they apply to Christ.

For if the things which our adversary ridicules and condemns are made to prove that he himself is condemned by Christian truth, it will be evident that either the mere quotation or the careful examination of the other passages will be enough to show their agreement with Christian faith.

Well, then, O thou full of all subtilty, when the Lord in the Gospel says, "If ye believed Moses, ye would believe me also, for he wrote of me," [582] there is no occasion for the great perplexity you pretend to be in, or for the alternative of either pronouncing this verse spurious or calling Jesus a liar.

The verse is as genuine as its words are true. I preferred, says Faustus, to attribute falsehood to the writers, rather than to the Author of truth.

What sort of faith can you have in Christ as the author of truth, when your doctrine is that His flesh and His death, His wounds and their marks, were feigned?

And where is your authority for saying that Christ is the author of truth, if you dare to attribute falsehood to those who wrote of Him, whose testimony has come down to us with the confirmation of those immediately succeeding them? You have not seen Christ, nor has He conversed with you as with the apostles, nor called you from heaven as He did Saul.

What knowledge or belief can we have of Christ, but on the authority of Scripture?

Or if there is falsehood in the Gospel which has been widely published among all nations, and has been held in such high sacredness in all churches since the name of Christ was first preached, where shall we find a trustworthy record of Christ?

If the Gospel is called in question in spite of the general consent regarding it, there can be no writing which a man may not call spurious if he does not wish to believe it.

12.

You go on to quote Christ's words, that all who came before Him were thieves and robbers.

How do you know that these were Christ's words, but from the Gospel?

You profess faith in these words, as if you had heard them from the mouth of the Lord Himself.

But if any one declares the verse to be spurious, and denies that Christ said this, you will have, in reply, to exert yourself in vindication of the authority of the Gospel.

Unhappy being! what you refuse to believe is written in the same place as that which you quote as spoken by the Lord Himself.

We believe both, for we believe the sacred narrative in which both are contained.

We believe both that Moses wrote of Christ, and that all that came before Christ were thieves and robbers.

By their coming He means their not being sent.

Those who were sent, as Moses and the holy prophets, came not before Him, but with Him.

They did not proudly wish to precede Him, but were the humble bearers of the message which He uttered by them.

According to the meaning which you give to the Lord's words, it is plain that with you there can be no prophets. And so you have made a Christ for yourselves who should prophesy a Christ to come.

If you have any prophets of your own, they will have, of course, no authority, as not being recognized by any others; but if there are any that you dare to quote as prophesying that Christ would come in an unreal body, and would suffer an unreal death, and would show to His doubting disciples unreal marks of wounds, not to speak of the abominable nature of such prophecies, and of the evident untruthfulness of those who commend falsehood in Christ, by your own interpretation those prophets must have been thieves and robbers, for they could not have spoken of Christ as coming in any manner unless they had come before Him.

If by those who came before Christ we understand those who would not come with Him,--that is, with the Word of God,--but without being sent by God brought their own falsehoods to men, you yourselves, although you are born in this world after the death and the resurrection of Christ, are thieves and robbers.

For, without waiting for His illumination that you might preach His truth, you have come before Him to preach up your own deceits.

13.

In the passage where we read of the Jews saying to Christ, Thou bearest witness of thyself, thy witness is not true, you do not see that Christ replies by saying that Moses wrote of Him, simply because you have not got the eye of piety to see with.

The answer of Christ is this:

"It is written in your law, that the testimony of two men is true; I am one who bear witness of myself, and the Father that sent me beareth witness of me." [583] What does this mean, if rightly understood, but that this number of witnesses required by the law was fixed upon and consecrated in the spirit of prophecy, that even thus might be prefigured the future revelation of the Father and Son, whose spirit is the Holy Spirit of the inseparable Trinity?

So it is written:

"In the mouth of two or three witnesses shall every word be established." [584] As a matter of fact, one witness generally speaks the truth, while a number tell lies.

And the world, in its conversion to Christianity, believed one apostle preaching the gospel rather than the mistaken multitude who persecuted him.

There was a special reason for requiring this number of witnesses, and in His answer the Lord implied that Moses prophesied of Him.

Do you carp at His saying your law instead of the law of God?

But, as every one knows, this is the common expression in Scripture.

Your law means the law given to you. So the apostle speaks of his gospel, while at the same time he declares that he received it not from man, but by the revelation of Jesus Christ.

You might as well say that Christ denies God to be His Father, when He uses the words your Father instead of our Father.

Again, you should refuse to believe the voice which you allude to as having come from heaven, This is my beloved Son, believe Him, because you did not hear it.

But if you believe this because you find it in the sacred Scriptures, you will also find there what you deny, that Moses wrote of Christ, besides many other things that you do not acknowledge as true. Do you not see that your own mischievous argument may be used to prove that this voice never came from heaven?

To your own destruction, and to the detriment of the welfare of mankind, you try to weaken the authority of the gospel, by arguing that it cannot be true that Christ said that Moses wrote of Him; because if He had said this, the ingenious hostility of the Jews would have led them at once to ask what He supposed Moses to have written of Him.

In the same way, it might be impiously argued that if that voice had really come from heaven, all the Jews who heard it would have believed.

Why are you so unreasonable as not to consider that, as it was possible for the Jews to remain hardened in unbelief after hearing the voice from heaven, so it was possible for them, when Christ said that Moses wrote of Him, to refrain from asking what Moses wrote, because in their ingenious hostility they were afraid of being proved to be in the wrong?

14.

Besides that this argument is an impious assault on the gospel, Faustus himself is aware of its feebleness, and therefore insists more on what he calls his chief difficulty,--that in all his search of the writings of Moses he has found no prophecies of Christ.

The obvious reply is, that he does not understand.

And if any one asks why he does not understand, the answer is that he reads with a hostile, unbelieving mind; he does not search in order to know, but thinks he knows when he is ignorant.

This vainglorious presumption either blinds the eye of his understanding so as to prevent his seeing anything, or distorts his vision, so that his remarks of approval or disapproval are misdirected.

I ask, he says, for instruction in whatever the writings of Moses contain about our God and Lord, which has escaped me in reading.

I reply at once that it has all escaped him, for all is written of Christ.

As we cannot go through the whole, I will, with the help of God, comply with your request, to the extent I have already promised, by showing that the passages which you specially criticise refer to Christ.

You tell me not to use the ignorant argument that Christ affirms Moses to have written of Him.

But if I use this argument, it is not because I am ignorant, but because I am a believer.

I acknowledge that this argument will not convince a Gentile or a Jew.

But, in spite of all your evasions, you are obliged to confess that it tells against you, who boast of possessing a kind of Christianity.

You say, Suppose you had not to deal with me, as in my case there is an obligation to believe Him whom I profess to follow, but with a Jew or a Gentile.

This is as much as to say that you, at any rate, with whom I have at present to do, are satisfied that Moses wrote of Christ; for you are not bold enough to discard altogether the well-grounded authority of the Gospel where Christ's own declaration is recorded.

Even when you attack this authority indirectly, you feel that you are attacking your own position.

You are aware that if you refuse to believe the Gospel, which is so generally known and received, you must fail utterly in the attempt to substitute for it any trustworthy record of the sayings and doings of Christ.

You are afraid that the loss of the Christian name might lead to the exposure of your absurdities to universal scorn and condemnation.

Accordingly you try to recover yourself, by saying that your profession of Christianity obliges you to believe these words of the Gospel.

So you, at any rate, which is all that we need care for just now, are caught and slain in this death blow to your errors.

You are forced to confess that Moses wrote of Christ, because the Gospel, which your profession obliges you to believe, states that Christ said so.

As regards a discussion with a Jew or a Gentile, I have already shown as well as I could how I think it should be conducted.

15.

I still hold that there is a reference to Christ in the passage which you select for refutation, where God says to Moses, "I will raise up unto them from among their brethren a prophet like unto thee." [585]

The string of showy antitheses with which you try to ornament your dull discourse does not at all affect my belief of this truth.

You attempt to prove, by a comparison of Christ and Moses, that they are unlike, and that therefore the words, "I will raise up a prophet like unto thee," cannot be understood of Christ.

You specify a number of particulars in which you find a diversity:

that the one is man, and the other God; that one is a sinner, the other sinless; that one is born of ordinary generation, the other, as we hold, of a virgin, and, as you hold, not even of a virgin; the one incurs God's anger, and is put to death on a mountain, the other suffers voluntarily, having throughout the approval of His Father.

But surely things may be said to be like, although they are not like in every respect.

Besides the resemblance between things of the same nature, as between two men, or between parents and children, or between men in general, or any species of animals, or in trees, between one olive and another, or one laurel and another, there is often a resemblance in things of a different nature, as between a wild and a tame olive, or between wheat and barley.

These things are to some extent allied.

But there is the greatest possible distance between the Son of God, by whom all things were made, and a beast or a stone.

And yet in the Gospel we read, "Behold the Lamb of God,"[586] and in the apostle, "That rock was Christ."[587] This could not be said except on the supposition of some resemblance.

What wonder, then, if Christ condescended to become like Moses, when He was made like the lamb which God by Moses commanded His people to eat as a type of Christ, enjoining that its blood should be used as a means of protection, and that it should be called the Passover, which every one must admit to be fulfilled in Christ?

The Scripture, I acknowledge, shows points of difference; and the Scripture also, as I call on you to acknowledge, shows points of resemblance. There are points of both kinds, and one can be proved as well as the other.

Christ is unlike man, for He is God; and it is written of Him that He is "over all, God blessed for ever."[588] Christ is also like man, for He is man; and it is likewise written of Him, that He is the "Mediator between God and man, the man Christ Jesus."[589] Christ is unlike a sinner, for He is ever holy; and He is like a sinner, for "God sent His Son in the likeness of sinful flesh, that by sin He might condemn sin in the flesh."[590] Christ is unlike a man born in ordinary generation, for He was born of a virgin; and yet He is like, for He too was born of a woman, to whom it was said, "That holy thing which shall be born of thee shall be called the Son of God."[591] Christ is unlike a man, who dies on account of his own sin, for He died without sin, and of His own free-will; and again, He is like, for He too died a real death of the body.

16.

You ought not to say, in disparagement of Moses, that he was a sinner, and that he was put to death on a mountain because his God was angry with him.

For Moses could glory in the Lord as his Saviour, who is also the Saviour of him who says, "Christ Jesus came into the world to save sinners, of whom I am chief."[592] Moses, indeed, is accused by the voice of God, because his faith showed signs of weakness when he was commanded to draw water out of the rock.[593] In this he may have sinned as Peter did, when from the weakness of his faith he became afraid in the midst of the waves.[594] But we cannot think from this, that he who, as the Gospel tells us, was counted worthy to be present with the Lord along with holy Elias on the mount of transfiguration, was separated from the eternal fellowship of the saints.

The sacred history shows in what favor he was with God even after his sin.

But since you may ask why God speaks of this sin as deserving the punishment of death, and as I have promised to point out prophecies of Christ in those passages which you select for criticism, I will try, with the Lord's help, to show that what you object to in the death of Moses is, when rightly understood, prophetical of Christ.

17.

We often find in the symbolical passages of Scripture, that the same person appears in different characters on different occasions. So, on this occasion, Moses represents and prefigures the Jewish people as placed under the law.

As, then, Moses, when he struck the rock with his rod, doubted the power of God, so the people who were under the law given by Moses, when they nailed Christ to the cross, did not believe Him to be the power of God.

And as water flowed from the smitten rock for those that were athirst, so life comes to believers from the stroke of the Lord's passion.

The testimony of the apostle is clear and decisive on this point, when he says, "This rock was Christ."[595] In the command of God, that the death of the flesh of Moses should take place on the mountain, we see the divine appointment that the carnal doubt of the divinity of Christ should die on Christ's exaltation.

As the rock is Christ, so is the mountain.

The rock is the fortitude of His humiliation; the mountain the height of His exaltation.

For as the apostle says, "This rock was Christ," so Christ Himself says, "A city set upon an hill cannot be hid,"[596] showing that He is the hill, and believers the city built upon the glory of His name.

The carnal mind lives when, like the smitten rock, the humiliation of Christ on the cross is despised.

For Christ crucified is to the Jews a stumbling-block, and to the Greeks foolishness.

And the carnal mind dies when, like the mountain-top, Christ is seen in His exaltation. "For to them that are called, both Jews and Greeks, Christ is the power of God, and the wisdom of God."[597] Moses therefore ascended the mount, that in the death of the flesh he might be received by the living spirit.

If Faustus had ascended, he would not have uttered carnal objections from a dead mind.

It was the carnal mind that made Peter dread the smiting of the rock, when, on the occasion of the Lord's foretelling His passion, he said, "Be it far from Thee, Lord; spare Thyself."

And this sin too was severely rebuked, when the Lord replied, "Get thee behind me, Satan; thou art an offense unto me:

for thou savorest not the things which be of God, but those which be of men." [598] And where did this carnal distrust die but in the glorification of Christ, as on a mountain height?

If it was alive when Peter timidly denied Christ, it was dead when he fearlessly preached Him.

It was alive in Saul, when, in his aversion to the offense of the cross, he made havoc of the Christian faith, and where but on this mountain had it died, when Paul was able to say, "I live no longer, but Christ liveth in me?" [599]

18.

What other reason has your heretical folly to give for thinking that there is no prophecy of Christ in the words, "I will raise up unto them a Prophet from among their brethren, like unto thee?"

Your showing Christ to be unlike Moses is no reason; for we can show that in other respects He is like.

How can you object to Christ's being called a prophet, since He condescended to be a man, and actually foretold many future events?

What is a prophet, but one who predicts events beyond human foresight?

So Christ says of Himself:

"A prophet is not without honor, save in his own country." [600] But, turning from you, since you have already acknowledged that your profession of Christianity obliges you to believe the Gospel, I address myself to the Jew, who enjoys the poor privilege of liberty from the yoke of Christ, and who therefore thinks it allowable to say:

Your Christ spoke falsely; Moses wrote nothing of him.

19.

Let the Jews say what prophet is meant in this promise of God to Moses:

"I will raise up unto them a Prophet from among their brethren, like unto thee."

Many prophets appeared after Moses; but one in particular is here pointed out.

The Jews will perhaps naturally think of the successor of Moses, who led into the promised land the people that Moses had brought out of Egypt.

Having this successor of Moses in his mind, he may perhaps laugh at me for asking to what prophet the words of the promise refer, since it is recorded who followed Moses in ruling and leading the people.

When he has laughed at my ignorance, as Faustus supposes him to do, I will still continue my inquiries, and will desire my laughing opponent to give me a serious answer to the question why Moses changed the name of this successor, who was preferred to himself as the leader of the people into the promised land, to show that the law given by Moses not to save, but to convince the sinner, cannot lead us into heaven, but only the grace and truth which are by Jesus Christ.

This successor was called Osea, and Moses gave him the name of Jesus.

Why then did he give him this name when he sent him from the valley of Pharan into the land into which he was to lead the people? [601] The true Jesus says, "If I go and prepare a place for you, I will come again, and receive you unto myself." [602] I will ask the Jew if the prophet does not show the prophetical meaning of these things when he says, "God shall come from Africa, and the Holy One from Pharan."

Does this not mean that the holy God would come with the name of him who came from Africa by Pharan, that is, with the name of Jesus?

Then, again, it is the Word of God Himself who speaks when He promises to provide this successor to Moses, speaking of him as an angel,--a name commonly given in Scripture to those carrying any message.

The words are:

"Behold I send my angel before thy face, to preserve thee in the way, and to bring thee into the land which I have sworn to give thee.

Take heed unto him, and obey, and beware of unbelief in him; for he will not take anything from thee wrongfully, for my name is in him." [603] Consider these words.

Let the Jew, not to speak of the Manichæan, say what other angel he can find in Scripture to whom these words apply, but this leader who was to bring the people into the land of promise.

Then let him inquire who it was that succeeded Moses, and brought in the people.

He will find that it was Jesus, and that this was not his name at first, but after his name was changed.

It follows that He who said, "My name is in him," is the true Jesus, the leader who brings His people into the inheritance of eternal life, according to the New Testament, of which the Old was a figure.

No event or action could have a more distinctly prophetical character than this, where the very name is a prediction.

20.

It follows that this Jew, if he wishes to be a Jew inwardly, in the spirit, and not in the letter, if he wishes to be thought a true Israelite, in whom is no guile, will recognize in this dead Jesus, who led the people into the land of mortality, a figure of the true living Jesus, whom he may follow into the land of life.

In this way, he will no longer in a hostile spirit resist so plain a prophecy, but, influenced by the allusion to the Jesus of the Old Testament, he will be prepared to listen meekly to Him whose name he bore, and who leads to the true land of promise; for He says, "Blessed are the meek, for they shall inherit the land." [604] The Gentile also, if his heart is not too stony, if he is one of those stones from which God raises up children unto Abraham, must allow it to be wonderful that in the ancient books of the people of whom Jesus was born, so plain a prophecy, including His very name, is found recorded; and must remark at the same time, that it is not any man of the name of Jesus who is prophesied of, but a divine person, because God said that His name was in that man who was appointed to rule the people, and to lead them into the kingdom, and who by a change of name was called Jesus.

In His being sent with this new name, He brings a great and divine message, and is therefore called an Angel, which, as every tyro in Greek knows, means messenger.

No Gentile, therefore, if he were not perverse and obstinate, would despise these books merely because he is not subject to the law of the Hebrews, to whom the books belong; but would think highly of the books, no matter whose they were, on finding in them prophecies of such ancient date, and of what he sees now taking place. Instead of despising Christ Jesus because He is foretold in the Hebrew Scriptures, he would conclude that one thought worthy of being the subject of prophetic description, whoever the writers might be, for so many ages before His coming into the world,--sometimes in plain announcements, sometimes in figure by symbolic actions and utterances,--must claim to be regarded with profound admiration and reverence, and to be followed with implicit reliance.

Thus the facts of Christian history would prove the truth of the prophecy, and the prophecy would prove the claims of Christ.

Call this fancy, if it is not actually the case that men all over the world have been led, and are now led, to believe in Christ by reading these books.

21.

In view of the multitudes from all nations who have become zealous believers in these books, it is laughably absurd to tell us that it is impossible to persuade a Gentile to learn the Christian faith from Jewish books.

Indeed, it is a great confirmation of our faith that such important testimony is borne by enemies.

The believing Gentiles cannot suppose these testimonies to Christ to be recent forgeries; for they find them in books held sacred for so many ages by those who crucified Christ, and still regarded with the highest veneration by those who every day blaspheme Christ.

If the prophecies of Christ were the production of the preachers of Christ, we might suspect their genuineness.

But now the preacher expounds the text of the blasphemer.

In this way the Most High God orders the blindness of the ungodly for the profit of the saint, in His righteous government bringing good out of evil, that those who by their own choice live wickedly may be, in His just judgment, made the instruments of His will.

So, lest those that were to preach Christ to the world should be thought to have forged the prophecies which speak of Christ as to be born, to work miracles, to suffer unjustly, to die, to rise again, to ascend to heaven, to publish the gospel of eternal life among all nations, the unbelief of the Jews has been made of signal benefit to us; so that those who do not receive in their heart for their own good these truths, carry, in their hands for our benefit the writings in which these truths are contained.

And the unbelief of the Jews increases rather than lessens the authority of the books, for this blindness is itself foretold.

They testify to the truth by their not understanding it.

By not understanding the books which predict that they would not understand, they prove these books to be true.

22.

In the passage, "Thou shalt see thy life hanging, and shalt not believe thy life," [605] Faustus is deceived by the ambiguity of the words.

The words may be differently interpreted; but that they cannot be understood of Christ is not said by Faustus, nor can be said by anyone who does not deny that Christ is life, or that He was seen by the Jews hanging on the cross, or that they did not believe Him.

Since Christ Himself says, "I am the life," [606] and since there is no doubt that He was seen hanging by the unbelieving Jews, I see no reason for doubting that this was written of Christ; for, as Christ says, Moses wrote of Him.

Since we have already refuted Faustus' arguments by which he tries to show that the words, "I will raise up from among their brethren a prophet like unto thee," do not apply to Christ, because Christ is not like Moses, we need not insist on this other prophecy.

Since, in the one case, his argument is that Christ is unlike Moses, so here he ought to argue that Christ is not the life, or that He was not seen hanging by the unbelieving Jews.

But as he has not said this, and as no one will now venture to say so, there should be no difficulty in accepting this too as a prophecy of our Lord and Saviour Jesus Christ, uttered by His servant.

These words, says Faustus, occur in a chapter of curses.

But why should it be the less a prophecy because it occurs in the midst of prophecies?

Or why should it not be a prophecy of Christ, although the context does not seem to refer to Christ?

Indeed, among all the curses which the Jews brought on themselves by their sinful pride, nothing could be worse than this, that they should see their Life--that is, the Son of God --hanging, and should not believe their Life.

For the curses of prophecy are not hostile imprecations, but announcements of coming judgment.

Hostile imprecations are forbidden, for it is said, "Bless, and curse not." [607]But prophetic announcements are often found in the writings of the saints, as when the Apostle Paul says:

"Alexander the coppersmith has done me much evil; the Lord shall reward him according to his works." [608]So it might be thought that the apostle was prompted by angry feeling to utter this imprecation:

"I would that they were even made eunuchs that trouble you." [609]But if we remember who the writer is, we may see in this ambiguous expression an ingenious style of benediction.

For there are eunuchs which have made themselves eunuchs for the kingdom of heaven's sake. [610]If Faustus had a pious appetite for Christian food, he would have found a similar ambiguity in the words of Moses.

By the Jews the declaration, "Thou shalt see thy life hanging, and shalt not believe thy life," may have been understood to mean that they would see their life to be in danger from the threats and plots of their enemies, and would not expect to live.

But the child of the Gospel, who has heard Christ say, "He wrote of me," distinguishes in the ambiguity of the prophecy between what is thrown to swine and what is addressed to man.

To his mind the thought immediately suggests itself of Christ hanging as the life of man, and of the Jews not believing in Him for this very reason, that they saw Him hanging.

As to the objection that these words, "Thou shalt see thy life hanging, and shalt not believe thy life," are the only words referring to Christ in a passage containing maledictions not applicable to Christ, some might grant that this is true.

For this prophecy might very well occur among the curses pronounced by the prophet upon the ungodly people, for these curses are of different kinds.

But I, and those who with me consider more closely the saying of the Lord in His Gospel, which is not, He wrote also of me, as admitting that Moses wrote other things not referring to Christ, but, "He wrote of me," as teaching that in searching the Scriptures we should view them as intended solely to illustrate the grace of Christ, see a reference to Christ in the rest of the passage also.

But it would take too much time to explain this here.

23.

So far from these words of Faustus' quotation being proved not to refer to Christ by their occurring among the other curses, these curses cannot be rightly understood except as prophecies of the glory of Christ, in which lies the happiness of man.

And what is true of these curses is still more true of this quotation.

If it could be said of Moses that his words have a different meaning from what was in his mind, I would rather suppose him to have prophesied without knowing it, than allow that the words, "Thou shalt see thy life hanging, and shalt not believe thy life," are not applicable to Christ.

So the words of Caiaphas had a different meaning from what he intended, when, in his hostility to Christ, he said that it was expedient that one man should die for the people, and that the whole nation should not perish, where the Evangelist added that he said this not of himself, but, since he was high priest, he prophesied. [611]But Moses was not Caiaphas; and therefore when Moses said to the Hebrew people, "Thou shalt see thy life hanging, and shalt not believe thy life," he not only spoke of Christ, as he certainly did, even though he spoke without knowing the meaning of what he said, but he knew that he spoke of Christ.

For he was a most faithful steward of the prophetic mystery, that is, of the priestly unction which gives the knowledge of the name of Christ; and in this mystery even Caiaphas, wicked as he was, was able to prophesy without knowing it.

The prophetic unction enabled him to prophesy, though his wicked life prevented him from knowing it.

Who then can say that there are no prophecies of Christ in Moses, with whom began that unction to which we owe the knowledge of Christ's name, and by which even Caiaphas, the persecutor of Christ, prophesied of Christ without knowing it?

24.

We have already said as much as appeared desirable of the curse pronounced on every one that hangs on a tree.

Enough has been said to show that the command to kill any prophet or prince who tried to turn away the children of Israel from their God, or to break any commandment, is not directed against Christ.

The more we consider the words and actions of our Lord Jesus Christ, the more clearly will this appear; for Christ never tried to turn away any of the Israelites from their God.

The God whom Moses taught the people to love and serve, is the God of Abraham, of Isaac, and of Jacob, whom the Lord Jesus Christ speaks of by this name, using the name in refutation of the Sadducees, who denied the resurrection of the dead.

He says, "Of the resurrection of the dead, have ye not read what God said from the bush to Moses, I am the God of Abraham, the God of Isaac, and the God of Jacob?

God is not the God of the dead, but of the living; for all live unto Him." [612]In the same words with which Christ answered the Sadducees we may answer the Manichæans, for they too deny the resurrection, though in a different way.

Again, when Christ said, in praise of the centurion's faith, "Verily I say unto you, I have not found so great faith, no, not in Israel," He added, "And I say unto you, that many shall come from the east and from the west, and shall sit down with Abraham, and Isaac, and Jacob, in the kingdom of heaven; but the children of the kingdom shall go into outer darkness." [613]If, then, as Faustus must admit, the God of whom Moses spoke was the God of Abraham, and Isaac, and Jacob, of whom Christ also spoke, as these passages prove, it follows that Christ did not try to turn away the people from their God.

On the contrary, He warned them that they would go into outer darkness, because He saw that they were turned away from their God, in whose kingdom He says the Gentiles called from the whole world will sit down with Abraham, and Isaac, and Jacob; implying that they would believe in the God of Abraham, and of Isaac, and of Jacob. So the apostle also says:

"The Scripture, foreseeing that God would justify the Gentiles by faith, preached the gospel beforehand to Abraham, saying, In thy seed shall all nations be blessed." [614]It is implied that those who are blessed in the seed of Abraham shall imitate the faith of Abraham.

Christ, then, did not try to turn away the Israelites from their God, but rather charged them with being turned away.

The idea that Christ broke one of the commandments given by Moses is not a new one, for the Jews thought so; but it is a mistake, for the Jews were in the wrong.

Let Faustus mention the commandment which he supposes the Lord to have broken, and we will point out his mistake, as we have done already, when it was required. Meanwhile it is enough to say, that if the Lord had broken any commandment, He could not have found fault with the Jews for doing so. For when the Jews blamed His disciples for eating with unwashen hands, in which they transgressed not a commandment of God, but the traditions of the elders, Christ said, "Why do ye also transgress the commandment of God, that ye may observe your traditions?"

He then quotes a commandment of God, which we know to have been given by Moses.

"For God said," He adds, "Honor thy father and mother, and he that curseth father or mother shall die the death.

But ye say, Whoever shall say to his father or mother, It is a gift, by whatsoever thou mightest be profited by me, is not obliged to honor his father.

So ye make the word of God of none effect by your traditions." [615]From this several things maybe learned:

that Christ did not turn away the Jews from their God; that He not only did not Himself break God's commandments, but found fault with those who did so; and that it was God Himself who gave these commandments by Moses.

25.

In fulfillment of our promise that we would prove the reference to Christ in those passages selected by Faustus from the writings of Moses for adverse criticism, since we cannot here point out the reference to Christ which we believe to exist in all the writings of Moses, it becomes our duty to show that this commandment of Moses, that every prophet or prince should be killed who tried to turn away the people from their God, or to break any commandment, refers to the preservation of the faith which is taught in the Church of Christ.

Moses no doubt knew in the spirit of prophecy, and from what he himself heard from God, that many heretics would arise to teach errors of all kinds against the doctrine of Christ, and to preach another Christ than the true Christ.

For the true Christ is He that was foretold in the prophecies uttered by Moses himself, and by the other holy men of that nation.

Moses accordingly commanded that whoever tried to teach another Christ should be put to death.

In obedience to this command, the voice of the Catholic Church, as with the spiritual two-edged sword of both Testaments, puts to death all who try to turn us away from our God, or to break any of the commandments.

And chief among these is Manichæus himself; for the truth of the law and the prophets convinces him of error as trying to turn us away from our God, the God of Abraham, and Isaac, and Jacob, whom Christ acknowledges, and as trying to break the commandments of the law, which, even when they are only figurative, we regard as prophetic of Christ.

26.

Faustus uses an argument which is either very deceitful or very stupid.

And as Faustus is not stupid, it is probable that he used the argument intentionally, with the design of misleading the careless reader.

He says:

If these things are not written of Christ, and if you cannot show any others, it follows that there are none at all.

The proposition is true; but it remains to be proved, both that these things are not written of Christ, and that no other can be shown. Faustus has not proved this; for we have shown both how these things are to be understood of Christ, and that there are many other things which have no meaning but as applied to Christ.

So it does not follow, as Faustus says, that nothing was written by Moses of Christ.

Let us repeat Faustus' argument:

If these things are not written of Christ, and if you cannot show any others, it follows that there are none at all.

Perfectly so.

But as both these things and many others have been shown to be written of Christ, or with reference to Christ, the true conclusion is that Faustus' argument is worthless.

In the passages quoted by Faustus, he has tried, though without success, to show that they were not written of Christ.

But in order to draw the conclusion that there are none at all, he should first have proved that no others can be shown.

Instead of this, he takes for granted that the readers of his book will be blind, or the hearers deaf, so that the omission will be overlooked, and runs on thus:

If there are none, Christ could not have asserted that there were any.

And if Christ did not make this assertion, it follows that this verse is spurious.

Here is a man who thinks so much of what he says himself, that he does not consider the possibility of another person saying the opposite.

Where is your wit? Is this all you could say for a bad cause?

But if the badness of the cause made you utter folly, the bad cause was your own choice.

To prove your antecedent false, we have only to show some other things written of Christ.

If there are some, it will not be true that there are none.

And if there are some, Christ may have asserted that there were.

And if Christ may have asserted this, it follows that this verse of the Gospel is not spurious.

Coming back, then, to Faustus' proposition, If you cannot show any other, it follows that there are none at all, it requires to be proved that we cannot show any other. We need only refer to what we showed before, as sufficient to prove the truth of the text in the Gospel, in which Christ says, "If ye believed Moses, ye would also believe me; for he wrote of me."

And even though from dullness of mind we could find nothing written of Christ by Moses, still, so strong is the evidence in support of the authority of the Gospel, that it would be incumbent on us to believe that not only some things, but everything written by Moses, refers to Christ; for He says not, He wrote also of me, but, He wrote of me.

The truth then is this, that even though there were doubts, which God forbid, of the genuineness of this verse, the doubt would be removed by the number of testimonies to Christ which we find in Moses; while, on the other hand, even if we could find none, we should still be bound to believe that these are to be found, because no doubts can be admitted regarding any verse in the Gospel.

27.

As to your argument that the doctrine of Moses was unlike that of Christ, and that therefore it was improbable that if they believed Moses, they would believe Christ too; and that it would rather follow that their belief in one would imply of necessity opposition to the other,--you could not have said this if you had turned your mind's eye for a moment to see men all the world over, when they are not blinded by a contentious spirit, learned and unlearned, Greek and barbarian, wise and unwise, to whom the apostle called himself a debtor, [616] believing in both Christ and Moses.

If it was improbable that the Jews would believe both Christ and Moses, it is still more improbable that all the world would do so.

But as we see all nations believing both, and in a common and well-grounded faith holding the agreement of the prophecy of the one with the gospel of the other, it was no impossible thing to which this one nation was called, when Christ said to them, "If ye believed Moses, ye would also believe me."

Rather we should be amazed at the guilty obstinacy of the Jews, who refused to do what we see the whole world has done.

28.

Regarding the Sabbath and circumcision, and the distinction in foods, in which you say the teaching of Moses differs from what Christians are taught by Christ, we have already shown that, as the apostle says, "all those things were our examples." [617] The difference is not in the doctrine, but in the time.

There was a time when it was proper that these things should be figuratively predicted; and there is now a different time when it is proper that they should be openly declared and fully accomplished.

It is not surprising that the Jews, who understood the Sabbath in a carnal sense, should oppose Christ, who began to open up its spiritual meaning.

Reply, if you can, to the apostle, who declares that the rest of the Sabbath was a shadow of something future. [618] If the Jews opposed Christ because they did not understand what the true Sabbath is, there is no reason why you should oppose Him, or refuse to learn what true innocence is.

For on that occasion when Jesus appears especially to set aside the Sabbath, when His disciples were hungry, and pulled the ears of corn through which they were passing, and ate them, Jesus, in replying to the Jews, declared His disciples to be innocent.

"If you knew," He said "what this meaneth, I will have mercy, and not sacrifice, you would not have condemned the innocent." [619] They should rather have pitied the wants of the disciples, for hunger forced them to do what they did. But pulling ears of corn, which is innocence in the teaching of Christ, is murder in the teaching of Manichæus.

Or was it an act of charity in the apostles to pull the ears of corn, that they might in eating set free the members of God, as in your foolish notions?

Then it must be cruelty in you not to do the same.

Faustus' reason for setting aside the Sabbath is because he knows that God's power is exercised without cessation, and without weariness.

It is for those to say this, who believe that all times are the production of an eternal act of God's will.

But you will find it difficult to reconcile this with your doctrine, that the rebellion of the race of darkness broke your god's rest, which was also disturbed by a sudden attack of the enemy; or perhaps God never had rest, as he foresaw this from eternity, and could not feel at ease in the prospect of so dire a conflict, with such loss and disaster to his members.

29.

Unless Christ had considered this Sabbath--which in your want of knowledge and of piety you laugh at--one of the prophecies written of Himself, He would not have borne such a testimony to it as He did.

For when, as you say in praise of Christ, He suffered voluntarily, and so could choose His own time for suffering and for resurrection, He brought it about that His body rested from all its works on Sabbath in the tomb, and that His resurrection on the third day, which we call the Lord's day, the day after the Sabbath, and therefore the eighth, proved the circumcision of the eighth day to be also prophetical of Him.

For what does circumcision mean, but the eradication of the mortality which comes from our carnal generation?

So the apostle says:

"Putting off from Himself His flesh, He made a show of principalities and powers, triumphing over them in Himself." [620] The flesh here said to be put off is that mortality of flesh on account of which the body is properly called flesh.

The flesh is the mortality, for in the immortality of the resurrection there will be no flesh; as it is written, "Flesh and blood shall not inherit the kingdom of God."

You are accustomed to argue from these words against our faith in the doctrine of the resurrection of the body, which has already taken place in the Lord Himself.

You keep out of view the following words, in which the apostle explains his meaning.

To show what he here means by flesh, he adds, "Neither shall corruption inherit incorruption."

For this body, which from its mortality is properly called flesh, is changed in the resurrection, so as to be no longer corruptible and mortal.

This is the apostle's statement, and not a supposition of ours, as his next words prove.

"Lo" he says, "I show you a mystery:

we shall all rise again, but we shall not all be changed.

In a moment, in the twinkling of an eye, at the last trump; for the last trumpet shall sound, and the dead shall rise incorruptible, and we shall be changed.

For this corruptible must put on incorruption, and this mortal must put on immortality."[621] To put on immortality, the body puts off mortality.

This is the mystery of circumcision, which by the law took place on the eighth day; and on the eighth day, the Lord's day, the day after the Sabbath, was fulfilled in its true meaning by the Lord. Hence it is said, "Putting off His flesh, He made a show of principalities and powers."

For by means of this mortality the hostile powers of hell ruled over us.

Christ is said to have made a show or example of these, because in Himself, our Head, He gave an example which will be fully realized in the liberation of His whole body, the Church, from the power of the devil at the last resurrection.

This is our faith.

And according to the prophetic declaration quoted by Paul, "The just shall live by faith." This is our justification. [622] Even Pagans believe that Christ died.

But only Christians believe that Christ rose again.

"If thou confess with thy mouth," says the apostle, "that Jesus is the Lord, and believest in thy heart that God raised Him from the dead, thou shalt be saved." [623] Again, because we are justified by faith in Christ's resurrection, the apostle says, "He died for our offenses, and rose again for our justification." [624] And because this resurrection by faith in which we are justified was prefigured by the circumcision of the eighth day, the apostle says of Abraham, with whom the observance began, "He received the sign of circumcision, a seal of the righteousness of faith." [625] Circumcision, then, is one of the prophecies of Christ, written by Moses, of whom Christ said, "He wrote of me."

In the words of the Lord, "Woe unto you, scribes and Pharisees, hypocrites! for ye compass sea and land to make one proselyte; and when he is made, ye make him twofold more the child of hell than yourselves," [626] it is not the circumcision of the proselyte which is meant, but his imitation of the conduct of the scribes and Pharisees, which the Lord forbids His disciples to imitate, when He says:

"The scribes and Pharisees sit on Moses' seat:

what they say unto you, do; but do not after their works; for they say, and do not." [627]These words of the Lord teach us both the honor due to the teaching of Moses, in whose seat even bad men were obliged to teach good things, and the reason of the proselyte becoming a child of hell, which was not that he heard from the Pharisees the words of the law, but that he copied their example.

Such a circumcised proselyte might have been addressed in the words of Paul: "Circumcision verily profiteth, if thou keep the law." [628] His imitation of the Pharisees in not keeping the law made him a child of hell.

And he was twofold more than they, probably because of his neglecting to fulfill what he voluntarily undertook, when, not being born a Jew, he chose to become a Jew.

30.
Your scoff is very inappropriate, when you say that Moses discusses like a glutton what should be eaten, and commands some things to be freely used as clean, and other things as unclean to be not even touched.

A glutton makes no distinction, except in choosing the sweetest food.

Perhaps you wish to commend to the admiration of the uninitiated the innocence of your abstemious habits, by appearing not to know, or to have forgotten, that swine's flesh tastes better than mutton.

But as this too was written by Moses of Christ in figurative prophecy, in which the flesh of animals signifies those who are to be united to the body of Christ, which is the Church, or who are to be cast out, you are typified by the unclean animals; for your disagreement with the Catholic faith shows that you do not ruminate on the word of wisdom, and that you do not divide the hoof, in the sense of making a correct distinction between the Old Testament and the New. But you show still more audacity in adopting the erroneous opinions of your Adimantus.

31.
You follow Adimantus in saying that Christ made no distinction in food, except in entirely prohibiting the use of animal food to His disciples, while He allowed the laity to eat anything that is eatable; and declared that they were not polluted by what enters into the mouth, but that the unseemly things which come out of the mouth are the things which defile a man.

These words of yours are unseemly indeed, for they express notorious falsehood.

If Christ taught that the evil things which come out of the mouth are the only things that defile a man, why should they not be the only things to defile His disciples, so as to make it unnecessary that any food should be forbidden or unclean?

Is it only the laity that are not polluted by what goes into the mouth, but by what comes out of it?

In that case, they are better protected from impurity than the saints, who are polluted both by what goes in and by what comes out.

But as Christ, comparing Himself with John, who came neither eating nor drinking, says that He came eating and drinking, I should like to know what He ate and drank.

When exposing the perversity which found fault with both, He says:

"John came neither eating nor drinking; and ye say, He hath a devil.

The Son of man cometh eating and drinking; and ye say, Behold a glutton and a wine-bibber, a friend of publicans and sinners." [629]We know what John ate and drank.

For it is not said that he drank nothing, but that he drank no wine or strong drink; so he must have drunk water.

He did not live without food, but his food was locusts and wild honey. [630] When Christ says that John did not eat or drink, He means that he did not use the food which the Jews used.

And because the Lord used this food, He is spoken of, in contrast with John, as eating and drinking. Will it be said that it was bread and vegetables which the Lord ate, and which John did not eat?

It would be strange if one was said not to eat, because he used locusts and honey, while the other is said to eat simply because he used bread and vegetables.

But whatever may be thought of the eating, certainly no one could be called a wine-bibber unless he used wine.

Why then do you call wine unclean?

It is not in order to subdue the body by abstinence that you prohibit these things, but because they are unclean, for you say that they are the poisonous filth of the race of darkness; whereas the apostle says, "To the pure all things are pure." [631]Christ, according to this doctrine, taught that all food was alike, but forbade His disciples to use what the Manichæans call unclean.

Where do you find this prohibition?

You are not afraid to deceive men by falsehood; but in God's righteous providence, you are so blinded that you provide us with the means of refuting you.

For I cannot resist quoting for examination the whole of that passage of the Gospel which Faustus uses against Moses; that we may see from it the falsehood of what was said first by Adimantus, and here by Faustus, that the Lord Jesus forbade the use of animal food to His disciples, and allowed it to the laity.

After Christ's reply to the accusation that His disciples ate with unwashen hands, we read in the Gospel as follows:

"And He called the multitude, and said unto them, Hear and understand.

Not that which goeth into the mouth defileth a man:

but that which cometh out of the mouth, this defileth a man.

Then came His disciples, and said unto Him, Knowest Thou that the Pharisees were offended after they heard this saying?"

Here, when addressed by His disciples, He ought certainly, according to the Manichæans, to have given them special instructions to abstain from animal food, and to show that His words, "Not that which goeth into the mouth defileth a man, but that which goeth out of the mouth," applied to the multitude only.

Let us hear, then, what, according to the evangelist, the Lord replied, not to the multitude, but to His disciples:

"But He answered and said, Every plant which my heavenly Father hath not planted shall be rooted up.

Let them alone:

they be blind leaders of the blind.

And if the blind lead the blind, both shall fall into the ditch."

The reason of this was, that in their desire to observe their own traditions, they did not understand the commandments of God.

As yet the disciples had not asked the Master how they were to understand what He had said to the multitude.

But now they do so; for the evangelist adds:

"Then answered Peter and said unto Him, Declare unto us this parable."

This shows that Peter thought that when the Lord said, "Not that which goeth into the mouth defileth a man, but that which goeth out of the mouth," He did not speak plainly and literally, but, as usual, wished to convey some instruction under the guise of a parable.

When His disciples, then, put this question in private, does He tell them, as the Manichæans say, that all animal food is unclean, and that they must never touch it?

Instead of this, He rebukes them for not understanding His plain language, and for thinking it a parable when it was not.

We read:

"And Jesus said, Are ye also yet without understanding?

Do not ye yet understand, that whatsoever entereth in at the mouth goeth into the belly, and is cast out into the drought?

But those things which proceed out of the mouth come forth from the heart, and they defile the man.

For out of the heart proceed evil thoughts, murders, adulteries, fornications, thefts, false witness, blasphemies.

These are the things which defile a man:

but to eat with unwashen hands defileth not a man." [632]

32.

Here we have a complete exposure of the falsehood of the Manichæans:

for it is plain that the Lord did not in this matter teach one thing to the multitude, and another in private to His disciples. Here is abundant evidence that the error and deceit are in the Manichæans, and not in Moses, nor in Christ, nor in the doctrine taught figuratively in one Testament and plainly in the other,--prophesied in one, and fulfilled in the other.

How can the Manichæans say that the Catholics regard none of the things that Moses wrote, when in fact they observe them all, not now in the figures, but in what the figures were intended to foretell?

No one would say that one who reads the Scripture subsequently to its being written does not observe it because he does not form the letters which he reads.

The letters are the figures of the sounds which he utters; and though he does not form the letters, he cannot read without examining them.

The reason why the Jews did not believe in Christ, was because they did not observe even the plain literal precepts of Moses.

So Christ says to them:

"Ye pay tithe of mint and cummin, and omit the weightier matters of the law, mercy and judgment.

Ye strain out a gnat and swallow a camel.

These ought ye to have done, and not to leave the other undone." [633]So also He told them that by their traditions they made of none effect the commandment of God to give honor to parents.

On account of this pride and perversity in neglecting what they understood, they were justly blinded, so that they could not understand the other things.

33.

You see, my argument is not that if you are a Christian you must believe Christ when He says that Moses wrote of Him, and that if you do not believe this you are no Christian.

The account you give of yourself in asking to be dealt with as a Jew or a Gentile is your own affair.

My endeavor is to leave no avenue of error open to you.

I have shut you out, too, from that precipice to which you rush as a last resort, when you say that these are spurious passages in the Gospel; so that, freed from the pernicious influence of this opinion, you may be reduced to the necessity of believing in Christ.

You say you wish to be taught like the Christian Thomas, whom Christ did not spurn from Him because he doubted of Him, but, in order to heal the wounds of his mind, showed him the marks of the wounds in His own body.

These are your own words.

It is well that you desire to be taught as Thomas was.

I feared you would make out this passage too to be spurious. Believe, then, the marks of Christ's wounds.

For if the marks were real, the wounds must have been real.

And the wounds could not have been real, unless His body had been capable of real wounds; which upsets at once the whole error of the Manichæans.

If you say that the marks were unreal which Christ showed to His doubting disciple, it follows that He must be a deceitful teacher, and that you wish to be deceived in being taught by Him.

But as no one wishes to be deceived, while many wish to deceive, it is probable that you would rather imitate the teaching which you ascribe to Christ than the learning you ascribe to Thomas.

If, then, you believe that Christ deceived a doubting inquirer by false marks of wounds, you must yourself be regarded, not as a safe teacher, but as a dangerous impostor.

On the other hand, if Thomas touched the real marks of Christ's wounds, you must confess that Christ had a real body.

So, if you believe as Thomas did, you are no more a Manichæan.

If you do not believe even with Thomas, you must be left to your infidelity.

Book XVII - Faustus rejects Christ's declaration that He came not to destroy the law and the prophets but to fulfill them, on the ground that it is found only in Matthew, who was not present when the words purport to have been spoken.

Augustin rebukes the folly of refusing to believe Matthew and yet believing Manichæus, and shows what the passage of scripture really means.

1.

Faustus said:

You ask why we do not receive the law and the prophets, when Christ said that he came not to destroy them, but to fulfill them.

Where do we learn that Jesus said this?

Philip Schaff, D.D., LL.D.

From Matthew, who declares that he said it on the mount.

In whose presence was it said?

In the presence of Peter, Andrew, James, and John--only these four; for the rest, including Matthew himself, were not yet chosen.

Is it not the case that one of these four--John, namely--wrote a Gospel? It is.

Does he mention this saying of Jesus?

No.

How, then, does it happen that what is not recorded by John, who was on the mount, is recorded by Matthew, who became a follower of Christ long after He came down from the mount?

In the first place, then, we must doubt whether Jesus ever said these words, since the proper witness is silent on the matter, and we have only the authority of a less trustworthy witness. But, besides this, we shall find that it is not Matthew that has imposed upon us, but some one else under his name, as is evident from the indirect style of the narrative.

Thus we read:

"As Jesus passed by, He saw a man, named Matthew, sitting at the receipt of custom, and called him; and he immediately rose up, and followed Him." [634]No one writing of himself would say, He saw a man, and called him; and he followed Him; but, He saw me, and called me, and I followed Him. Evidently this was written not by Matthew himself, but by some one else under his name.

Since, then, the passage already quoted would not be true even if it had been written by Matthew, since he was not present when Jesus spoke on the mount; much more is its falsehood evident from the fact that the writer was not Matthew himself, but some one borrowing the names both of Jesus and of Matthew.

2.

The passage itself, in which Christ tells the Jews not to think that He came to destroy the law, is rather designed to show that He did destroy it.

For, had He not done something of the kind, the Jews would not have suspected Him.

His words are:

"Think not that I am come to destroy the law."

Suppose the Jews had replied, What actions of thine might lead us to suspect this?

Is it because thou exposest circumcision, breakest the Sabbath, discardest sacrifices, makest no distinction in foods? this would be the natural answer to the words, Think not.

The Jews had the best possible reason for thinking that Jesus destroyed the law.

If this was not to destroy the law, what is? But, indeed, the law and the prophets consider themselves already so faultlessly perfect, that they have no desire to be fulfilled.

Their author and father condemns adding to them as much as taking away anything from them; as we read in Deuteronomy:

"These precepts which I deliver unto thee this day, O Israel, thou shalt observe to do; thou shalt not turn aside from them to the right hand or to the left; thou shalt not add thereto nor diminish from it, that thy God may bless thee." [635]Whether, therefore, Jesus turned aside to the right by adding to the law and the prophets in order to fulfill them, or to the left in taking away from them to destroy them, either way he offended the author of the law.

So this verse must either have some other meaning, or be spurious.

3.

Augustin replied:

What amazing folly, to disbelieve what Matthew records of Christ, while you believe Manichæus!

If Matthew is not to be believed because he was not present when Christ said, "I came not to destroy the law and the prophets, but to fulfill," was Manichæus present, was he even born, when Christ appeared among men?

According, then, to your rule, you should not believe anything that Manichæus says of Christ.

On the other hand, we refuse to believe what Manichæus says of Christ; not because he was not present as a witness of Christ's words and actions, but because he contradicts Christ's disciples, and the Gospel which rests on their authority.

The apostle, speaking in the Holy Spirit, tells us that such teachers would arise.

With reference to such, he says to believers:

"If any man preaches to you another gospel than that ye have received, let him be accursed."[636]

If no one can say what is true of Christ unless he has himself seen and heard Him, no one now can be trusted.

But if believers can now say what is true of Christ because the truth has been handed down in word or writing by those who saw and heard, why might not Matthew have heard the truth from his fellow-disciple John, if John was present and he himself was not, as from the writings of John both we who are born so long after and those who shall be born after us can learn the truth about Christ?

In this way, the Gospels of Luke and Mark, who were companions of the disciples, as well as the Gospel of Matthew, have the same authority as that of John.

Besides, the Lord Himself might have told Matthew what those called before him had already been witnesses of.

Your idea is, that John should have recorded this saying of the Lord, as he was present on the occasion.

As if it might not happen that, since it was impossible to write all that be heard from the Lord, he set himself to write some, omitting this among others.

Does he not say at the close of his Gospel:

"And there are also many other things which Jesus did, the which, if they should be written every one, I suppose that even the world itself could not contain the books that should be written"?[637] This proves that he omitted many things intentionally.

But if you choose John as an authority regarding the law and the prophets, I ask you only to believe his testimony to them. It is John who writes that Isaiah saw the glory of Christ.[638] It is in his Gospel we find the text already treated of:

"If ye believed Moses, ye would also believe me; for he wrote of me."[639] Your evasions are met on every side.

You ought to say plainly that you do not believe the gospel of Christ.

For to believe what you please, and not to believe what you please, is to believe yourselves, and not the gospel.

4.

Faustus thinks himself wonderfully clever in proving that Matthew was not the writer of this Gospel, because, when speaking of his own election, he says not, He saw me, and said to me, Follow me; but, He saw him, and said to him, Follow me.

This must have been said either in ignorance or from a design to mislead.

Faustus can hardly be so ignorant as not to have read or heard that narrators, when speaking of themselves, often use a construction as if speaking of another.

It is more probable that Faustus wished to bewilder those more ignorant than himself, in the hope of getting hold on not a few unacquainted with these things.

It is needless to resort to other writings to quote examples of this construction from profane authors for the information of our friends, and for the refutation of Faustus.

We find examples in passages quoted above from Moses by Faustus himself, without any denial, or rather with the assertion, that they were written by Moses, only not written of Christ.

When Moses, then, writes of himself, does he say, I said this, or I did that, and not rather, Moses said, and Moses did?

Or does he say, The Lord called me, The Lord said to me, and not rather, The Lord called Moses, The Lord said to Moses, and so on?

So Matthew, too, speaks of himself in the third person.

And John does the same; for towards the end of his book he says:

"Peter, turning, saw the disciple whom Jesus loved, who also lay on His breast at supper, and who said to the Lord, Who is it that shall betray Thee?"

Does he say, Peter, turning, saw me?

Or will you argue from this that John did not write this Gospel?

But he adds a little after: "This is the disciple that testifies of Jesus, and has written these things; and we know that his testimony is true."[640] Does he say, I am the disciple who testify of Jesus, and who have written these things, and we know that my testimony is true?

Evidently this style is common in writers of narratives.

There are innumerable instances in which the Lord Himself uses it.

"When the Son of man," He says, "cometh, shall He find faith on the earth?"[641] Not, When I come, shall I find?

Again, "The Son of man came eating and drinking;"[642] not, I came.

Again, "The hour shall come, and now is, when the dead shall hear the voice of the Son of God, and they that hear shall live;"[643] not, My voice.

And so in many other places.

This may suffice to satisfy inquirers and to refute scoffers.

5.

Every one can see the weakness of the argument that Christ could not have said, "Think not that I am come to destroy the law and the prophets:

I came not to destroy, but to fulfill," unless He had done something to create a suspicion of this kind.

Of course, we grant that the unenlightened Jews may have looked upon Christ as the destroyer of the law and the prophets; but their very suspicion makes it certain that the true and truthful One, in saying that He came not to destroy the law and the prophets, referred to no other law than that of the Jews.

This is proved by the words that follow:

"Verily, verily, I say unto you, Till heaven and earth pass, one jot or one tittle shall in no wise pass from the law till all be fulfilled.

Whosoever therefore shall break one of the least of these commandments, and shall teach men so, shall be called the least in the kingdom of heaven.

But whosoever shall do and teach them, shall be called great in the kingdom of heaven."

This applied to the Pharisees, who taught the law in word, while they broke it in deed.

Christ says of the Pharisees in another place, "What they say, that do; but do not after their works:

for they say, and do not." [644]So here also He adds, "For I say unto you, Except your righteousness exceed the righteousness of the scribes and Pharisees, ye shall not enter into the kingdom of heaven;" [645] that is, Unless ye shall both do and teach what they teach without doing, ye shall not enter into the kingdom of heaven.

This law, therefore, which the Pharisees taught without keeping it, Christ says He came not to destroy, but to fulfill; for this was the law connected with the seat of Moses in which the Pharisees sat, who because they said without doing, are to be heard, but not to be imitated.

6.

Faustus does not understand, or pretends not to understand, what it is to fulfill the law.

He supposes the expression to mean the addition of words to the law, regarding which it is written that nothing is to be added to or taken away from the Scriptures of God.

From this Faustus argues that there can be no fulfillment of what is spoken of as so perfect that nothing can be added to it or taken from it.

Faustus requires to be told that the law is fulfilled by living as it enjoins. "Love is the fulfilling of the law," [646] as the apostle says.

The Lord has vouchsafed both to manifest and to impart this love, by sending the Holy Spirit to His believing people.

So it is said by the same apostle:

"The love of God is shed abroad in our heart by the Holy Ghost, which is given unto us."[647]And the Lord Himself says:

"By this shall all men know that ye are my disciples, if ye have love one to another."[648]The law, then, is fulfilled both by the observance of its precepts and by the accomplishment of its prophecies.

For "the law was given by Moses, but grace and truth came by Jesus Christ." [649]The law itself, by being fulfilled, becomes grace and truth. Grace is the fulfillment of love, and truth is the accomplishment of the prophecies.

And as both grace and truth are by Christ, it follows that He came not to destroy the law, but to fulfill it; not by supplying any defects in the law, but by obedience to what is written in the law.

Christ's own words declare this.

For He does not say, One jot or one tittle shall in no wise pass from the law till its defects are supplied, but "till all be fulfilled."

Book XVIII - The relation of Christ to prophecy, continued

1.

Faustus said:

"I came not to destroy the law, but to fulfill it." If these are Christ's words, unless they have some other meaning, they are as much against you as against me.

Your Christianity as well as mine is based on the belief that Christ came to destroy the law and the prophets.

Your actions prove this, even though in words you deny it. It is on this ground that you disregard the precepts of the law and the prophets.

It is on this ground that we both acknowledge Jesus as the founder of the New Testament, in which is implied the acknowledgment that the Old Testament is destroyed.

How, then, can we believe that Christ said these words without first confessing that hitherto we have been wholly in error, and without showing our repentance by entering on a course of obedience to the law and the prophets, and of careful observance of their requirements, whatever they may be?

This done, we may honestly believe that Jesus said that he came not to destroy the law, but to fulfill it.

As it is, you accuse me of not believing what you do not believe yourself, and what therefore is false.

2.

But grant that we have been in the wrong hitherto.

What is to be done now?

Shall we come under the law, since Christ has not destroyed, but fulfilled it?

Shall we by circumcision add shame to shame, and believe that God is pleased with such sacraments?

Shall we observe the rest of the Sabbath, and bind ourselves in the fetters of Saturn? Shall we glut the demon of the Jews, for he is not God, with the slaughter of bulls, rams, and goats, not to say of men; and adopt, only with greater cruelty, in obedience to the law and the prophets, the practices on account of which we abandoned idolatry?

Shall we, in fine, call the flesh of some animals clean, and that of others unclean, among which, according to the law and the prophets, swine's flesh has a particular defilement?

Of course you will allow that as Christians we must not do any of these things, for you remember that Christ says that a man when circumcised becomes twofold a child of hell. [650]It is plain also that Christ neither observed the Sabbath himself, nor commanded it to be observed.

And regarding foods, he says expressly that man is not defiled by anything that goes into his mouth, but rather by the things which come out of it. [651]Regarding sacrifices, too, he often says that God desires mercy, and not sacrifice. [652]What becomes, then, of the statement that he came not to destroy the law, but to fulfill it?

If Christ said this, he must have meant something else, or, what is not to be thought of, he told a lie, or he never said it.

No Christian will allow that Jesus spoke falsely; therefore he must either not have said this, or said it with another meaning.

3.

For my part, as a Manichæan, this verse has little difficulty for me, for at the outset I am taught to believe that many things which pass in Scripture under the name of the Saviour are spurious, and that they must therefore be tested to find whether they are true, and sound, and genuine; for the enemy who comes by night has corrupted almost every passage by sowing tares among the wheat.

So I am not alarmed by these words, notwithstanding the sacred name affixed to them; for I still claim the liberty to examine whether this comes from the hand of the good sower, who sows in the day-time, or of the evil one, who sows in the night.

But what escape from this difficulty can there be for you, who receive everything without examination, condemning the use of reason, which is the prerogative of human nature, and thinking it impiety to distinguish between truth and falsehood, and as much afraid of separating between what is good and what is not as children are of ghosts?

For suppose a Jew or any one acquainted with these words should ask you why you do not keep the precepts of the law and the prophets, since Christ says that he came not to destroy but to fulfill them:

you will be obliged either to join in the superstitious follies of the Jews, or to declare this verse false, or to deny that you are a follower of Christ.

4.

Augustin replied:

Since you continue repeating what has been so often exposed and refuted, we must be content to repeat the refutation.

The things in the law and the prophets which Christians do not observe, are only the types of what they do observe.

These types were figures of things to come, and are necessarily removed when the things themselves are fully revealed by Christ, that in this very removal the law and the prophets may be fulfilled.

So it is written in the prophets that God would give a new covenant, "not as I gave to their fathers." [653] Such was the hardness of heart of the people under the Old Testament, that many precepts were given to them, not so much because they were good, as because they suited the people.

Still, in all these things the future was foretold and prefigured, although the people did not understand the meaning of their own observances. After the manifest appearance of the things thus signified, we are not required to observe the types; but we read them to see their meaning. So, again, it is foretold in the prophets, "I will take away their stony heart, and will give them a heart of flesh," [654] --that is, a sensible heart, instead of an insensible one.

To this the apostle alludes in the words:

"Not in tables of stone, but in the fleshy tables of the heart." [655] The fleshy tables of the heart are the same as the heart of flesh.

Since, then, the removal of these observances is foretold, the law and the prophets could not have been fulfilled but by this removal.

Now, however, the prediction is accomplished, and the fulfillment of the law and the prophets is found in what at first sight seems the very opposite.

5.

We are not afraid to meet your scoff at the Sabbath, when you call it the fetters of Saturn.

It is a silly and unmeaning expression, which occurred to you only because you are in the habit of worshipping the sun on what you call Sunday.

What you call Sunday we call the Lord's day, and on it we do not worship the sun, but the Lord's resurrection.

And in the same way, the fathers observed the rest of the Sabbath, not because they worshipped Saturn, but because it was incumbent at that time, for it was a shadow of things to come, as the apostle testifies. [656] The Gentiles, of whom the apostle says that they "worshipped and served the creature rather than the Creator," [657] gave the names of their gods to the days of the week.

And so far you do the same, except that you worship only the two brightest luminaries, and not the rest of the stars, as the Gentiles did. Besides, the Gentiles gave the names of their gods to the months.

In honor of Romulus, whom they believed to be the son of Mars, they dedicated the first month to Mars, and called it March.

The next month, April, is named not from any god, but from the word for opening, because the buds generally open in this month.

The third month is called May, in honor of Maia the mother of Mercury.

The fourth is called June, from Juno.

The rest to December used to be named according to their number.

The fifth and sixth, however, got the names of July and August from men to whom divine honors were decreed; while the others, from September to December, continued to be named from their number.

January, again, is named from Janus, and February from the rites of the Luperci called Februæ.

Must we say that you worship the god Mars in the month of March?

But that is the month in which you hold the feast you call Bema with great pomp.

But if you think it allowable to observe the month of March without thinking of Mars, why do you try to bring in the name of Saturn in connection with the rest of the seventh day enjoined in Scripture, merely because the Gentiles call the day Saturday?

The Scripture name for the day is Sabbath, which means rest.

Your scoff is as unreasonable as it is profane.

6.

As regards animal sacrifices, every Christian knows that they were enjoined as suitable to a perverse people, and not because God had any pleasure in them.

Still, even in these sacrifices there were types of what we enjoy; for we cannot obtain purification or the propitiation of God without blood.

The fulfillment of these types is in Christ, by whose blood we are purified and redeemed.

In these figures of the divine oracles, the bull represents Christ, because with the horns of His cross He scatters the wicked; the lamb, from His matchless innocence; the goat, from His being made in the likeness of sinful flesh, that by sin He might condemn sin. [658] Whatever kind of sacrifice you choose to specify, I will show you a prophecy of Christ in it.

Thus we have shown regarding circumcision, and the Sabbath, and the distinction of food, and the sacrifice of animals, that all these things were our examples, and our prophecies, which Christ came not to destroy, but to fulfill, by fulfilling what was thus foretold.

Your opponent is the apostle, whose opinion I give in his own words:
"All these things were our examples." [659]

7.

If you have learned from Manichæus the willful impiety of admitting only those parts of the Gospel which do not contradict your errors, while you reject the rest, we have learned from the apostle the pious caution of looking on every one as accursed that preaches to us another gospel than that which we have received.

Hence Catholic Christians look upon you as among the tares; for, in the Lord's exposition of the meaning of the tares, they are not falsehood mixed with truth in the Scriptures, but children of the wicked one--that is, people who imitate the deceitfulness of the devil.

It is not true that Catholic Christians believe everything; for they do not believe Manichæus or any of the heretics.

Nor do they condemn the use of human reason; but what you call reasoning they prove to be fallacious.

Nor do they think it profane to distinguish truth from falsehood; for they distinguish between the truth of the Catholic faith and the falsehood of your doctrines.

Nor do they fear to separate good from evil; but they contend that evil, instead of being natural, is unnatural.

They know nothing of your race of darkness, which, you say, is produced from a principle of its own, and fights against the kingdom of God, and of which your god seems really to be more frightened than children are of ghosts; for, according to you, he covered himself with a veil, that he might not see his own members taken and plundered by the assault of the enemy.

To conclude, Catholic Christians are in no difficulty regarding the words of Christ, though in one sense they may be said not to observe the law and the prophets; for by the grace of Christ they keep the law by their love to God and man; and on these two commandments hang all the law and the prophets. [660] Besides, they see in Christ and the Church the fulfillment of all the prophecies of the Old Testament, whether in the form of actions, or of symbolic rites, or of figurative language.

So we neither join in superstitious follies, nor declare this verse false; nor deny that we are followers of Christ; for on those principles which I have set forth to the best of my power, the law and the prophets which Christ came not to destroy, but to fulfill, are no other than those recognized by the Church.

Book XIX - Faustus is willing to admit that Christ may have said that He came not to destroy the law and the prophets, but to fulfill them; but if He did, it was to pacify the Jews and in a modified sense

Augustin replies, and still further elaborates the Catholic view of prophecy and its fulfillment.

1.

Faustus said:
I will grant that Christ said that he came not to destroy the law and the prophets, but to fulfill them.

But why did Jesus say this?

Was it to pacify the Jews, who were enraged at seeing their sacred institutions trampled upon by Christ, and regarded him as a wild blasphemer, not to be listened to, much less to be followed?

Or was it for our instruction as Gentile believers, that we might learn meekly and patiently to bear the yoke of commandment laid on our necks by the law and the prophets of the Jews?

You yourself can hardly suppose that Christ's words were intended to bring us under the authority of the law and the prophets of the Hebrews.

So that the other explanation which I have given of the words must be the true one.

Every one knows that the Jews were always ready to attack Christ, both with words and with actual violence.

Naturally, then, they would be enraged at the idea that Christ was destroying their law and their prophets; and, to appease them, Christ might very well tell them not to think that he came to destroy the law, but that he came to fulfill it. There was no falsehood or deceit in this, for he used the word law in a general sense, not of any particular law.

2.

There are three laws.

One is that of the Hebrews, which the apostle calls the law of sin and death. [661] The second is that of the Gentiles, which he calls the law of nature.

"For the Gentiles," he says, "do by nature the things contained in the law; and, not having the law, they are a law into themselves; who show the work of the law written on their hearts."[662] The third law is the truth of which the apostle speaks when he says, "The law of the spirit of life in Christ Jesus hath made me free from the law of sin and death." [663] Since, then, there are three laws, we must carefully inquire which of the three Christ spoke of when He said that He came not to destroy the law, but to fulfill it.

In the same way, there are prophets of the Jews, and prophets of the Gentiles, and prophets of truth.

With the prophets of the Jews, of course, every one is acquainted.

If any one is in doubt about the prophets of the Gentiles, let him hear what Paul says when writing of the Cretans to Titus:

"A prophet of their own has said, The Cretans are always liars, evil beasts, slow bellies."[664] This proves that the Gentiles also had their prophets.

The truth also has its prophets, as we learn from Jesus as well as from Paul.

Jesus says: "Behold, I send unto you wise men and prophets, and some of them ye shall kill in divers places." [665] And Paul says:

"The Lord Himself appointed first apostles, and then prophets." [666]

3.

As "the law and the prophets" may have three different meanings, it is uncertain in what sense the words are used by Jesus, though we may form a conjecture from what follows.

For if Jesus had gone on to speak of circumcision, and Sabbaths, and sacrifices, and the observances of the Hebrews, and had added something as a fulfillment, there could have been no doubt that it was the law and the prophets of the Jews of which He said that He came not to destroy, but to fulfill them.

But Christ, without any allusion to these, speaks only of commandments which date from the earliest times:

"Thou shall not kill; Thou shalt not commit adultery; Thou shalt not bear false witness."

These, it can be proved, were of old promulgated in the world by Enoch and Seth, and the other righteous men, to whom the precepts were delivered by angels of lofty rank, in order to tame the savage nature of men.

From this it appears that Jesus spoke of the law and the prophets of truth.

And so we find him giving a fulfillment of those precepts already quoted.

"Ye have heard," He says, "that it was said by them of old time, Thou shalt not kill; but I say unto you, Be not even angry."

This is the fulfillment.

Again:

"Ye have heard that it was said, Thou shalt not commit adultery; but I say unto you, Do not lust even."

This is the fulfillment.

Again:

"It has been said, Thou shalt not bear false witness; but I say unto you, Swear not."

This too is the fulfillment. He thus both confirms the old precepts and supplies their defects. Where He seems to speak of some Jewish precepts, instead of fulfilling them, He substitutes for them precepts of an opposite tendency.

He proceeds thus:

"Ye have heard that it has been said, An eye for an eye, and a tooth for a tooth; but I say unto you, Whosoever shall smite thee on thy right cheek, turn to him the other also."

This is not fulfillment, but destruction.

Again:

"It has been said, Thou shall love thy friend, and hate thine enemy; but I say unto you, Love your enemies, and pray for your persecutors."

This too is destruction. Again:

"It has been said, Whosoever shall put away his wife, let him give her a writing of divorcement; but I say unto you, That whosoever shall put away his wife, saving for the cause of fornication, causeth her to commit adultery, and is himself an adulterer if he afterwards marries another woman." [667] These precepts are evidently destroyed because they are the precepts of Moses; while the others are fulfilled because they are the precepts of the righteous men of antiquity.

If you agree to this explanation, we may allow that Jesus said that he came not to destroy the law, but to fulfill it.

If you disapprove of this explanation, give one of your own.

Only beware of making Jesus a liar, and of making yourself a Jew, by binding yourself to fulfill the law because Christ did not destroy it.

4.

If one of the Nazareans, or Symmachians, as they are sometimes called, were arguing with me from these words of Jesus that he came not to destroy the law, I should find some difficulty in answering him. For it is undeniable that, at his coming, Jesus was both in body and mind subject to the influence of the law and the prophets.

Those people, moreover, whom I allude to, practise circumcision, and keep the Sabbath, and abstain from swine's flesh and such like things, according to the law, although they profess to be Christians.

They are evidently misled as well as you, by this verse in which Christ says that he came not to destroy the law, but to fulfill it.

It would not be easy to reply to such opponents without first getting rid of this troublesome verse.

But with you I have no difficulty, for you have nothing to go upon; and instead of using arguments, you seem disposed, in mere mischief, to induce me to believe that Christ said what you evidently do not yourself believe him to have said.

On the strength of this verse you accuse me of dullness and evasiveness, without yourself giving any indication of keeping the law instead of destroying it.

Do you too, like a Jew or a Nazarean, glory in the obscene distinction of being circumcised?

Do you pride yourself in the observance of the Sabbath?

Can you congratulate yourself on being innocent of swine's flesh?

Or can you boast of having gratified the appetite of the Deity by the blood of sacrifices and the incense of Jewish offerings?

If not, why do you contend that Christ came not to destroy the law, but to fulfill it?

5.

I give unceasing thanks to my teacher, who prevented me from falling into this error, so that I am still a Christian.

For I, like you, from reading this verse without sufficient consideration, had almost resolved to become a Jew.

And with reason; for if Christ came not to destroy the law, but to fulfill it, and as a vessel in order to be filled full must not be empty, but partly filled already, I concluded that no one could become a Christian but an Israelite, nearly filled already with the law and the prophets, and coming to Christ to be filled to the full extent of his capacity.

I concluded, too, that in thus coming he must not destroy what he already possesses; otherwise it would be a case, not of fulfilling, but of emptying.

Then it appeared that I, as a Gentile, could get nothing by coming to Christ, for I brought nothing that he could fill up by his additions.

This preparatory supply is found, on inquiry, to consist of Sabbaths, circumcision, sacrifices, new moons, baptisms, feasts of unleavened bread, distinctions of foods, drink, and clothes, and other things, too many to specify.

This, then, it appeared, was what Christ came not to destroy, but to fulfill.

Naturally it must appear so:

for what is a law without precepts, or prophets without predictions?

Besides, there is that terrible curse pronounced upon those who abide not in all things that are written in the book of the law to do them. [668] With the fear of this curse appearing to come from God on the one side, and with Christ on the other side, seeming, as the Son of God, to say that he came not to destroy these things, but to fulfill them, what was to prevent me from becoming a Jew?

The wise instruction of Manichæus saved me from this danger.

6.

But how can you venture to quote this verse against me?
Or why should it be against me only, when it is as much against yourself?
If Christ does not destroy the law and the prophets, neither must Christians do so.
Why then do you destroy them?
Do you begin to perceive that you are no Christian?

How can you profane with all kinds of work the day pronounced sacred in the law and in all the prophets, on which they say that God, the maker of the world, himself rested, without dreading the penalty of death pronounced against Sabbath-breakers, or the curse on the transgressor?

How can you refuse to receive in your person the unseemly mark of circumcision, which the law and all the prophets declare to be honorable, especially in the case of Abraham, after what was thought to be his faith; for does not the God of the Jews proclaim that whosoever is without this mark of infamy shall perish from his people?

How can you neglect the appointed sacrifices, which were made so much of both by Moses and the prophets under the law, and by Abraham in his faith?

And how can you defile your souls by making no distinction in foods, if you believe that Christ came not to destroy these things, but to fulfill them?

Why do you discard the annual feast of unleavened bread, and the appointed sacrifice of the lamb, which, according to the law and the prophets, is to be observed for ever?

Why, in a word, do you treat so lightly the new moons, the baptisms, and the feast of tabernacles, and all the other carnal ordinances of the law and the prophets, if Christ did not destroy them?

I have therefore good reason for saying that, in order to justify your neglect of these things, you must either abandon your profession of being Christ's disciple, or acknowledge that Christ himself has already destroyed them; and from this acknowledgment it must follow, either that this text is spurious in which Christ is made to say that he came not to destroy the law, but to fulfill it, or that the words have an entirely different meaning from what you suppose.

7.

Augustin replied:

If you allow, in consideration of the authority of the Gospel, that Christ said that He came not to destroy the law and the prophets, but to fulfill them, you should show the same consideration to the authority of the apostle, when he says, "All these things were our examples;" and again of Christ, "He was not yea and nay, but in Him was yea; for all the promises of God are in Him yea;"[669] that is, they are set forth and fulfilled in Him.

In this way you will see in the clearest light both what law Christ fulfilled, and how He fulfilled it.

It is a vain attempt that you make to escape by your three kinds of law and your three kinds of prophets.

It is quite plain, and the New Testament leaves no doubt on the matter, what law and what prophets Christ came not to destroy, but to fulfill.

The law given by Moses is that which by Jesus Christ became grace and truth. [670]The law given by Moses is that of which Christ says, "He wrote of me." [671]For undoubtedly this is the law which entered that the offence might abound; [672] words which you often ignorantly quote as a reproach to the law.

Read what is there said of this law:
"The law is holy, and the commandment holy, and just, and good.
Was then that which is good made death unto me?
God forbid.
But sin, that it might appear sin, wrought death in me by that which is good." [673]The entrance of the law made the offense abound, not because the law required what was wrong, but because the proud and self-confident incurred additional guilt as transgressors after their acquaintance with the holy, and just, and good commandments of the law; so that, being thus humbled, they might learn that only by grace through faith could they be freed from subjection to the law as transgressors, and be reconciled to the law as righteous.

So the same apostle says:
"For before faith came, we were kept under the law, shut up unto the faith which was afterwards revealed.

Therefore the law was our schoolmaster in Christ Jesus; but after faith came, we are no longer under a schoolmaster." [674]That is, we are no longer subject to the penalty of the law, because we are set free by grace.

Before we received in humility the grace of the Spirit, the letter was only death to us, for it required obedience which we could not render.

Thus Paul also says: "The letter killeth, but the spirit giveth life." [675] Again, he says:

"For if a law had been given which could have given life, verily righteousness should have been by the law; but the Scripture hath concluded all under sin, that the promise by faith of Jesus Christ might be given to them that believe." [676] And once more:

"What the law could not do, in that it was weak through the flesh, God sent His Son in the likeness of sinful flesh, that by sin He might condemn sin in the flesh, that the righteousness of the law might be fulfilled in us, who walk not after the flesh, but after the Spirit." [677] Here we see Christ coming not to destroy the law, but to fulfill it.

As the law brought the proud under the guilt of transgression, increasing their sin by commandments which they could not obey, so the righteousness of the same law is fulfilled by the grace of the Spirit in those who learn from Christ to be meek and lowly in heart; for Christ came not to destroy the law, but to fulfill it.

Moreover, because even for those who are under grace it is difficult in this mortal life perfectly to keep what is written in the law, Thou shall not covet, Christ, by the sacrifice of His flesh, as our Priest obtains pardon for us.

And in this also He fulfills the law; for what we fail in through weakness is supplied by His perfection, who is the Head, while we are His members.

Thus John says:

"My little children, these things write I unto you, that ye sin not; and if any man sin, we have an Advocate with the Father, Jesus Christ the righteous:

He is the propitiation for our sins." [678]

8.

Christ also fulfilled the prophecies, because the promises of God were made good in Him.
As the apostle says in the verse quoted above, "The promises of God are in Him yea."
Again, he says:

"Now I say that Jesus Christ was a minister of the circumcision for the truth of God, to confirm the promises made unto the fathers." [679] Whatever, then, was promised in the prophets, whether expressly or in figure, whether by words or by actions, was fulfilled in Him who came not to destroy the law and the prophets, but to fulfill them.

You do not perceive that if Christians were to continue in the use of acts and observances by which things to come were prefigured, the only meaning would be that the things prefigured had not yet come.

Either the thing prefigured has not come, or if it has, the figure becomes superfluous or misleading.

Therefore, if Christians do not practise some things enjoined in the Hebrews by the prophets, this, so far from showing, as you think, that Christ did not fulfill the prophets, rather shows that He did.

So completely did Christ fulfill what these types prefigured, that it is no longer prefigured.
So the Lord Himself says:

"The law and the prophets were until John." [680] For the law which shut up transgressors in increased guilt, and to the faith which was afterwards revealed, became grace through Jesus Christ, by whom grace superabounded.

Thus the law, which was not fulfilled in the requirement of the letter, was fulfilled in the liberty of grace.

In the same way, everything in the law that was prophetic of the Saviour's advent, whether in words or in typical actions, became truth in Jesus Christ.

For "the law was given by Moses, but grace and truth came by Jesus Christ." [681] At Christ's advent the kingdom of God began to be preached; for the law and the prophets were until John:

the law, that its transgressors might desire salvation; the prophets, that they might foretell the Saviour.

No doubt there have been prophets in the Church since the ascension of Christ.

Of these prophets Paul says: "God hath set some in the Church, first apostles, secondarily prophets, thirdly teachers," and so on. [682] It is not of these prophets that it was said, "The law and the prophets were until John," but of those who prophesied the first coming of Christ, which evidently cannot be prophesied now that it has taken place.

9.

Accordingly, when you ask why a Christian is not circumcised if Christ came not to destroy the law, but to fulfill it, my reply is, that a Christian is not circumcised precisely for this reason, that what was prefigured by circumcision is fulfilled in Christ. Circumcision was the type of the removal of our fleshly nature, which was fulfilled in the resurrection of Christ, and which the sacrament of baptism teaches us to look forward to in our own resurrection.

The sacrament of the new life is not wholly discontinued, for our resurrection from the dead is still to come; but this sacrament has been improved by the substitution of baptism for circumcision, because now a pattern of the eternal life which is to come is afforded us in the resurrection of Christ, whereas formerly there was nothing of the kind.

So, when you ask why a Christian does not keep the Sabbath, if Christ came not to destroy the law, but to fulfill it, my reply is, that a Christian does not keep the Sabbath precisely because what was prefigured in the Sabbath is fulfilled in Christ.

For we have our Sabbath in Him who said, "Come unto me, all ye that labor and are heavy laden, and I will give you rest.

Take my yoke upon you, and learn of me; for I am meek and lowly in heart, and ye shall find rest unto your souls." [683]

10.

When you ask why a Christian does not observe the distinction in food as enjoined in the law, if Christ came not to destroy the law, but to fulfill it, I reply, that a Christian does not observe this distinction precisely because what was thus prefigured is now fulfilled in Christ, who admits into His body, which in His saints He has predestined to eternal life, nothing which in human conduct corresponds to the characteristics of the forbidden animals.

When you ask, again, why a Christian does not offer sacrifices to God of the flesh and blood of slain animals, if Christ came not to destroy the law, but to fulfill it, I reply, that it would be improper for a Christian to offer such sacrifices, now that what was thus prefigured has been fulfilled in Christ's offering of His own body and blood.

When you ask why a Christian does not keep the feast of unleavened bread as the Jews did, if Christ came not to destroy the law, but to fulfill it, I reply, that a Christian does not keep this feast precisely because what was thus prefigured is fulfilled in Christ, who leads us to a new life by purging out the leaven of the old life. [684]When you ask why a Christian does not keep the feast of the paschal lamb, if Christ came not to destroy the law, but to fulfill it, my reply is, that he does not keep it precisely because what was thus prefigured has been fulfilled in the sufferings of Christ, the Lamb without spot.

When you ask why a Christian does not keep the feasts of the new moon appointed in the law, if Christ came not to destroy the law, but to fulfill it, I reply, that he does not keep them precisely because what was thus prefigured is fulfilled in Christ.

For the feast of the new moon prefigured the new creature, of which the apostle says: "If therefore there is any new creature in Christ Jesus, the old things have passed away; behold, all things are become new." [685]When you ask why a Christian does not observe the baptisms for various kinds of uncleanness according to the law, if Christ came not to destroy the law, but to fulfill it, I reply, that he does not observe them precisely because they were figures of things to come, which Christ has fulfilled.

For He came to bury us with Himself by baptism into death, that as Christ rose again from the dead, so we also should walk in newness of life. [686]When you ask why Christians do not keep the feast of tabernacles, if the law is not destroyed, but fulfilled by Christ, I reply that believers are God's tabernacle, in whom, as they are united and built together in love, God condescends to dwell, so that Christians do not keep this feast precisely because what was thus prefigured is now fulfilled by Christ in His Church.

11.

I touch upon these things merely in passing with the utmost brevity, rather than omit them altogether.

The subjects, taken separately, have filled many large volumes, written to prove that these observances were typical of Christ.

So it appears that all the things in the Old Testament which you think are not observed by Christians because Christ destroyed the law, are in fact not observed because Christ fulfilled the law.

The very intention of the observances was to prefigure Christ.

Now that Christ has come, instead of its being strange or absurd that what was done to prefigure His advent should not be done any more, it is perfectly right and reasonable.

The typical observances intended to prefigure the coming of Christ would be observed still, had they not been fulfilled by the coming of Christ; so far is it from being the case that our not observing them now is any proof of their not being fulfilled by Christ's coming.

There can be no religious society, whether the religion be true or false, without some sacrament or visible symbol to serve as a bond of union.

The importance of these sacraments cannot be overstated, and only scoffers will treat them lightly.

For if piety requires them, it must be impiety to neglect them.

12.

It is true, the ungodly may partake in the visible sacraments of godliness, as we read that Simon Magus received holy baptism.

Such are they of whom the apostle says that "they have the form of godliness, but deny the power of it." [687] The power of godliness is the end of the commandment, that is, love out of a pure heart, and of a good conscience, and of faith unfeigned. [688] So the Apostle Peter, speaking of the sacrament of the ark, in which the family of Noah was saved from the deluge, says, "So by a similar figure baptism also saves you."

And lest they should rest content with the visible sacrament, by which they had the form of godliness, and should deny its power in their lives by profligate conduct, he immediately adds, "Not the putting away of the filth of the flesh, but the answer of a good conscience." [689]

13.

Thus the sacraments of the Old Testament, which were celebrated in obedience to the law, were types of Christ who was to come; and when Christ fulfilled them by His advent they were done away, and were done away because they were fulfilled.

For Christ came not to destroy, but to fulfill. And now that the righteousness of faith is revealed, and the children of God are called into liberty, and the yoke of bondage which was required for a carnal and stiffnecked people is taken away, other sacraments are instituted, greater in efficacy, more beneficial in their use, easier in performance, and fewer in number.

14.

And if the righteous men of old, who saw in the sacraments of their time the promise of a future revelation of faith, which even then their piety enabled them to discern in the dim light of prophecy, and by which they lived, for the just can live only by faith; [690] if, then, these righteous men of old were ready to suffer, as many actually did suffer, all trials and tortures for the sake of those typical sacraments which prefigured things in the future; if we praise the three children and Daniel, because they refused to be defiled by meat from the king's table, from their regard for the sacrament of their day; if we feel the strongest admiration for the Maccabees, who refused to touch food which Christians lawfully use; [691] how much more should a Christian in our day be ready to suffer all things for Christ's baptism, for Christ's Eucharist, for Christ's sacred sign, since these are proofs of the accomplishment of what the former sacraments only pointed forward to in the future!

For what is still promised to the Church, the body of Christ, is both clearly made known, and in the Saviour Himself, the Head of the body, the Mediator between God and men, the man Christ Jesus, has already been accomplished.

Is not the promise of eternal life by resurrection from the dead?

This we see fulfilled in the flesh of Him of whom it is said, that the Word became flesh and dwelt among us. [692] In former days faith was dim, for the saints and righteous men of those times all believed and hoped for the same things, and all these sacraments and ceremonies pointed to the future; but now we have the revelation of the faith to which the people were shut up under the law;[693] and what is now promised to believers in the judgment is already accomplished in the example of Him who came not to destroy the law and the prophets, but to fulfill them.

15.

It is a question among the students of the sacred Scriptures, whether the faith in Christ before His passion and resurrection, which the righteous men of old learned by revelation or gathered from prophecy, had the same efficacy as faith has now that Christ has suffered and risen; or whether the actual shedding of the blood of the Lamb of God, which was, as He Himself says, for many for the remission of sins, [694] conferred any benefit in the way of purifying or adding to the purity of those who looked forward in faith to the death of Christ, but left the world before it took place; whether, in fact, Christ's death reached to the dead, so as to effect their liberation. To discuss this question here, or to prove what has been ascertained on the subject, would take too long, besides being foreign from our present purpose.

16.
Meanwhile it is sufficient to prove, in opposition to Faustus' ignorant cavils, how greatly they mistake who conclude, from the change in signs and sacraments, that there must be a difference in the things which were prefigured in the rites of a prophetic dispensation, and which are declared to be accomplished in the rites of the gospel; or those, on the other hand, who think that as the things are the same, the sacraments which announce their accomplishment should not differ from the sacraments which foretold that accomplishment.

For if in language the form of the verb changes in the number of letters and syllables according to the tense, as done signifies the past, and to be done the future, why should not the symbols which declare Christ's death and resurrection to be accomplished, differ from those which predicted their accomplishment, as we see a difference in the form and sound of the words, past and future, suffered and to suffer, risen and to rise?

For material symbols are nothing else than visible speech, which, though sacred, is changeable and transitory.

For while God is eternal, the water of baptism, and all that is material in the sacrament, is transitory:

the very word "God," which must be pronounced in the consecration, is a sound which passes in a moment. The actions and sounds pass away, but their efficacy remains the same, and the spiritual gift thus communicated is eternal.

To say, therefore, that if Christ had not destroyed the law and the prophets, the sacraments of the law and the prophets would continue to be observed in the congregations of the Christian Church, is the same as to say that if Christ had not destroyed the law and the prophets, He would still be predicted as about to be born, to suffer, and to rise again; whereas, in fact, it is proved that He did not destroy, but fulfill those things, because the prophecies of His birth, and passion, and resurrection, which were represented in these ancient sacraments, have ceased, and the sacraments now observed by Christians contain the announcement that He has been born, has suffered, has risen.

He who came not to destroy the law and the prophets, but to fulfill them, by this fulfillment did away with those things which foretold the accomplishment of what is thus shown to be now accomplished.

Precisely in the same way, he might substitute for the expressions, "He is to be born, is to suffer, is to rise," which were in these times appropriate, the expressions, "He has been born, has suffered, has risen," which are appropriate now that the others are accomplished, and so done away.

17.
Corresponding to this change in words is the change which naturally took place in the substitution of new sacraments instead of those of the Old Testament.

In the case of the first Christians, who came to the faith as Jews, it was by degrees that they were brought to change their customs, and to have a clear perception of the truth; and permission was given them by the apostle to preserve their hereditary worship and belief, in which they had been born and brought up; and those who had to do with them were required to make allowance for this reluctance to accept new customs.

So the apostle circumcised Timothy, the son of a Jewish mother and a Greek father, when they went among people of this kind; and he himself accommodated his practice to theirs, not hypocritically, but for a wise purpose.

For these practices were harmless in the case of those born and brought up in them, though they were no longer required to prefigure things to come. It would have done more harm to condemn them as hurtful in the case of those to whose time it was intended that they should continue.

Christ, who came to fulfill all these prophecies, found those people trained in their own religion.

But in the case of those who had no such training, but were brought to Christ, the cornerstone, from the opposite wall of circumcision, there was no obligation to adopt Jewish customs.

If, indeed, like Timothy, they chose to accommodate themselves to the views of those of the circumcision who were still wedded to their old sacraments, they were free to do so.

But if they supposed that their hope and salvation depended on these works of the law, they were warned against them as a fatal danger.

So the apostle says:

"Behold, I Paul say unto you, that if ye be circumcised, Christ shall profit you nothing;" [695] that is, if they were circumcised, as they were intending to be, in compliance with some corrupt teachers, who told them that without these works of the law they could not be saved.

For when, chiefly through the preaching of the Apostle Paul, the Gentiles were coming to the faith of Christ, as it was proper that they should come, without being burdened with Jewish observances--for those who were grown up were deterred from the faith by fear of ceremonies to which they were not accustomed, especially of circumcision; and if they who had not been trained from their birth to such observances had been made proselytes in the usual way, it would have implied that the coming of Christ still required to be predicted as a future event;--when, then, the Gentiles were admitted without these ceremonies, those of the circumcision who believed, not understanding why the Gentiles were not required to adopt their customs, nor why they themselves were still allowed to retain them, began to disturb the Church with carnal contentions, because the Gentiles were admitted into the people of God without being made proselytes in the usual way by circumcision and the other legal observances.

Some also of the converted Gentiles were bent on these ceremonies, from fear of the Jews among whom they lived. Against these Gentiles the Apostle Paul often wrote, and when Peter was carried away by their hypocrisy, he corrected him with a brotherly rebuke. [696]Afterwards, when the apostles met in council, decreed that these works of the law were not obligatory in the case of the Gentiles, [697] some Christians of the circumcision were displeased, because they failed to understand that these observances were permissible only in those who had been trained in them before the revelation of faith, to bring to a close the prophetic life in those who were engaged in it before the prophecy was fulfilled, lest by a compulsory abandonment it should seem to be condemned rather than closed; while to lay these things on the Gentiles would imply either that they were not instituted to prefigure Christ, or that Christ was still to be prefigured.

The ancient people of God, before Christ came to fulfill the law and the prophets, were required to observe all these things by which Christ was prefigured.

It was freedom to those who understood the meaning of the observance, but it was bondage to those who did not.

But the people in those latter times who come to believe in Christ as having already come, and suffered, and risen, in the case of those whom this faith found trained to those sacraments, are neither required to observe them, nor prohibited from doing so; while there is a prohibition in the case of those who were not bound by the ties of custom, or by any necessity, to accommodate themselves to the practice of others, so that it might become manifest that these things were instituted to prefigure Christ, and that after His coming they were to cease, because the promises had been fulfilled.

Some believers of the circumcision who did not understand this were displeased with this tolerant arrangement which the Holy Spirit effected through the apostles, and stubbornly insisted on the Gentiles becoming Jews.

These are the people of whom Faustus speaks under the name of Symmachians or Nazareans. Their number is now very small, but the sect still continues.

18.

The Manichæans, therefore have no ground for saying, in disparagement of the law and the prophets, that Christ came to destroy rather than to fulfill them, because Christians do not observe what is there enjoined:

for the only things which they do not observe are those that prefigured Christ, and these are not observed because their fulfillment is in Christ, and what is fulfilled is no longer prefigured; the typical observances having properly come to a close in the time of those who, after being trained in such things, had come to believe in Christ as their fulfillment.

Do not Christians observe the precept of Scripture "Hear, O Israel; the Lord thy God is one God;" "Thou shalt not make unto thee an image," and so on?

Do make Christians not observe the precept, "Thou shalt not take the name of the Lord thy God in vain?"

Do Christians not observe the Sabbath, even in the sense of a true rest?

Do Christians not honor their parents, according to the commandment?

Do Christians not abstain from fornication, and murder, and theft, and false witness, from coveting their neighbor's wife, and from coveting his property,--all of which things are written in the law?

These moral precepts are distinct from typical sacraments:

the former are fulfilled by the aid of divine grace, the latter by the accomplishment of what they promise.

Both are fulfilled in Christ, who has ever been the bestower of this grace, which is also now revealed in Him, and who now makes manifest the accomplishment of what He in former times promised; for "the law was given by Moses, but grace and truth came by Jesus Christ." [698] Again, these things which concern the keeping of a good conscience are fulfilled in the faith which worketh by love; [699] while types of the future pass away when they are accomplished.

But even the types are not destroyed, but fulfilled; for Christ, in bringing to light what the types signified, does not prove them vain or illusory.

19.

Faustus, therefore, is wrong in supposing that the Lord Jesus fulfilled some precepts of righteous men who lived before the law of Moses, such as, "Thou shall not kill," which Christ did not oppose, but rather confirmed by His prohibition of anger and abuse; and that He destroyed some things apparently peculiar to the Hebrew law, such as, "An eye for an eye, and a tooth for a tooth," which Christ seems rather to abolish than to confirm, when He says, "But I say unto you, that ye resist not evil; but if any one smite thee on thy right cheek, turn to him the other also," [700] and so on.

But we say that even these things which Faustus thinks Christ destroyed by enjoining the opposite, were suitable to the times of the Old Testament, and were not destroyed, but fulfilled by Christ.

20.

In the first place let me ask our opponents if these ancient righteous men, Enoch and Seth, whom Faustus mentions particularly, and any others who lived before Moses, or even, if you choose, before Abraham, were angry with their brother without a cause, or said to their brother, Thou fool.

If not, why may they not have taught these things as well as preached them?

And if they taught these things, how can Christ be said to have fulfilled their righteousness or their teaching, any more than that of Moses, by adding, "But I say unto you, if any man is angry with his brother, or if he says Racha, or if he says, Thou fool, he shall be in danger of the judgment, or of the council, or of hell-fire," since these men did these very things themselves, and enjoined them upon others?

Will it be said that they were ignorant of its being the duty of a righteous man to restrain his passion, and not to provoke his brother with angry abuse; or that, knowing this, they were unable to act accordingly?

In that case, they deserved the punishment of hell, and could not have been righteous. But no one will venture to say that in their righteousness there was such ignorance of duty, and such a want of self-control, as to make them liable to the punishment of hell.

How, then, can Christ be said to have fulfilled the law, by which these men lived by means of adding things without which they could have had no righteousness at all?

Will it be said that a hasty temper and bad language are sinful only since the time of Christ, while formerly such qualities of the heart and speech were allowable; as we find some institutions vary according to the times, so that what is proper at one time is improper at another, and vice versa?

You will not be so foolish as to make this assertion. But even were you to do so, the reply will be that, according to this idea, Christ came not to fulfill what was defective in the old law, but to institute a law which did not previously exist; if it is true that with the righteous men of old it was not a sin to say to their brother, Thou fool, which Christ pronounces so sinful, that whoever does so is in danger of hell.

So, then, you have not succeeded in finding any law of which it can be said that Christ supplied its defect by these additions.

21.

Will it be said that the law in these early times was incomplete as regards not committing adultery, till it was completed by the Lord, who added that no one should look on a woman to lust after her?

This is what you imply in the way you quote the words, "Ye have heard that it has been said, Thou shalt not commit adultery:

but I say unto you, Do not lust even."

"Here," you say, "is the fulfillment."

But let us take the words as they stand in the Gospel, without any of your modifications, and see what character you give to those righteous men of antiquity.

The words are:

"Ye have heard that it has been said, thou shall not commit adultery; but I say unto you, that whosoever looketh on a woman to lust after her, hath committed adultery with her already in his heart." [701] In your opinion, then, Enoch and Seth, and the rest, committed adultery in their hearts; and either their heart was not the temple of God, or they committed adultery in the temple of God.

But if you dare not say this, how can you say that Christ, when He came, fulfilled the law,

The Writings Against the Manichaeans and Against the Donatists: Part I - The Manichaeans
which was already in the time of those men complete?

22.

As regards not swearing, in which also you say that Christ completed the law given to these righteous men of antiquity, I cannot be certain that they did not swear, for we find that Paul the apostle swore.

With you, swearing is still a common practice, for you swear by the light, which you love as flies do; for the light of the mind which lighteth every man that cometh into the world, as distinct from mere natural light, you know nothing of.

You swear, too, by your master Manichæus, whose name in his own tongue was Manes.

As the name Manes seemed to be connected with the Greek word for madness, you have changed it by adding a suffix, which only makes matters worse, by giving the new meaning of pouring forth madness.

One of your own sect told me that the name Manichæus was intended to be derived from the Greek words for pouring forth manna; for χέειν means to pour.

But, as it is, you only express the idea of madness with greater emphasis.

For by adding the two syllables, while you have forgotten to insert another letter in the beginning of the word, you make it not Mannichæus, but Manichæus; which must mean that he pours forth madness in his long unprofitable discourses.

Again, you often swear by the Paraclete,--not the Paraclete promised and sent by Christ to His disciples, but this same madness-pourer himself.

Since, then, you are constantly swearing, I should like to know in what sense you make Christ to have fulfilled this part of the law, which is one you mention as belonging to the earliest times.

And what do you make of the oaths of the apostle?

For as to your authority, it cannot weigh much with yourselves, not to speak of me or any other person.

It is therefore evident that Christ's words, "I am come not to destroy the law, but to fulfill it," have not the meaning which you give them.

Christ makes no reference in these words to His comments on the ancient sayings which He quotes, and of which His discourse was an explanation, but not a fulfillment.

23.

Thus, as regards murder, which was understood to mean merely the destruction of the body, by which a man is deprived of life, the Lord explained that every unjust disposition to injure our brother is a kind of murder.

So John also says, "He that hateth his brother is a murderer." [702] And as it was thought that adultery meant only the act of unlawful intercourse with a woman, the Master showed that the lust He describes is also adultery.

Again, because perjury is a heinous sin, while there is no sin either in not swearing at all or in swearing truly, the Lord wished to secure us from departing from the truth by not swearing at all, rather than that we should be in danger of perjury by being in the habit of swearing truly.

For one who never swears is less in danger of swearing falsely than one who is in the habit of swearing truly.

So, in the discourses of the apostle which are recorded, he never used an oath, lest he should ever fall unawares into perjury from being in the habit of swearing.

In his writings, on the other hand, where he had more leisure and opportunity for caution, we find him using oaths in several places, [703] to teach us that there is no sin in swearing truly, but that, on account of the infirmity of human nature, we are best preserved from perjury by not swearing at all.

These considerations will also make it evident that the things which Faustus supposes to be peculiar to Moses were not destroyed by Christ, as he says they were.

24.

To take, for instance, this saying of the ancients, "Thou shalt love thy neighbor, and hate thine enemy," how does Faustus make out that this is peculiar to Moses?

Does not the Apostle Paul speak of some men as hateful to God? [704] And, indeed, in connection with this saying, the Lord enjoins on us that we should imitate God.

His words are:

"That ye may be the children of your Father in heaven, who maketh the sun to rise upon the evil and the good, and sendeth rain on the just and the unjust." [705] In one sense we must hate our enemies, after the example of God, to whom Paul says some men are hateful; while, at the same time, we must also love our enemies after the example of God, who makes the sun to rise on the evil and the good, and sendeth rain on the just and the unjust.

If we understand this, we shall find that the Lord, in explaining to those who did not rightly understand the saying, Thou shalt hate thine enemy, made use of it to show that they should love their enemy, which was a new idea to them. It would take too long to show the consistency of the two things here. But when the Manichæans condemn without exception the precept, Thou shall hate thine enemy, they may easily be met with the question whether their god loves the race of darkness.

Or, if we should love our enemies now, because they have a part of good, should we not also hate them as having a part of evil?

So even in this way it would appear that there is no opposition between the saying of ancient times, Thou shall hate thine enemy, and that of the Gospel, Love your enemies.

For every wicked man should be hated as far as he is wicked; while he should be loved as a man.

The vice which we rightly hate in him is to be condemned, that by its removal the human nature which we rightly love in him may be amended.

This is precisely the principle we maintain, that we should hate our enemy for what is evil in him, that is, for his wickedness; while we also love our enemy for that which is good in him, that is, for his nature as a social and rational being. The difference between us and the Manichæans is, that we prove the man to be wicked, not by nature, either his own or any other, but by his own will; whereas they think that a man is evil on account of the nature of the race of darkness, which, according to them, was an object of dread to God when he existed entire, and by which also he was partly conquered, so that he cannot be entirely set free.

The intention of the Lord, then, is to correct those who, from knowing without understanding what was said by them of old time, Thou shalt hate thine enemy, hated their fellow-men instead of only hating their wickedness; and for this purpose He says, Love your enemies.

Instead of destroying what is written about hatred of enemies in the law, of which He said, "I am come not to destroy the law, but to fulfill it," He would have us learn, from the duty of loving our enemies, how it is possible in the case of one and the same person, both to hate him for his sin, and to love him for his nature.

It is too much to expect our perverse opponents to understand this.

But we can silence them, by showing that by their irrational objection they condemn their own god, of whom they cannot say that he loves the race of darkness; so that in enjoining on every one to love his enemy, they cannot quote his example.

There would appear to be more love of their enemy in the race of darkness than in the god of the Manichæans.

The story is, that the race of darkness coveted the domain of light bordering on their territory, and, from a desire to possess it, formed the plan of invading it.

Nor is there any sin in desiring true goodness and blessedness.

For the Lord says, "The kingdom of heaven suffereth violence, and the violent take it by force." [706]This fabulous race of darkness, then, wished to take by force the good they desired, for its beautiful and attractive appearance.

But God, instead of returning the love of those who wished to possess Him, hated it so as to endeavor to annihilate them.

If, therefore, the evil love the good in the desire to possess it, while the good hate the evil in fear of being defiled, I ask the Manichæans, which of these obeys the precept of the Lord, "Love your enemies"?

If you insist on making these precepts opposed to one another, it will follow that your god obeyed what is written in the law of Moses, "Thou shall hate thine enemy"; while the race of darkness obeyed what is written in the Gospel, "Love your enemies."

However, you have never succeeded in explaining the difference between the flies that fly in the day-time and the moths that fly at night; for both, according to you, belong to the race of darkness.

How is it that one kind love the light, contrary to their nature; while the other kind avoid it, and prefer the darkness from which they sprung?

Strange, that filthy sewers should breed a cleaner sort than dark closets!

25.

Nor, again, is there any opposition between that which was said by them of old time, "An eye for an eye, a tooth for a tooth," and what the Lord says, "But I say unto you, that ye resist not evil; but if any one smiteth thee on thy right cheek, turn to him the other also," and so on. [707]The old precept as well as the new is intended to check the vehemence of hatred, and to curb the impetuosity of angry passion. For who will of his own accord be satisfied with a revenge equal to the injury?

Do we not see men, only slightly hurt, eager for slaughter, thirsting for blood, as if they could never make their enemy suffer enough?

If a man receives a blow, does he not summon his assailant, that he may be condemned in the court of law?

Or if he prefers to return the blow, does he not fall upon the man with hand and heel, or perhaps with a weapon, if he can get hold of one?

To put a restraint upon a revenge so unjust from its excess, the law established the principle of compensation, that the penalty should correspond to the injury inflicted.

So the precept, "an eye for an eye, a tooth for a tooth," instead of being a brand to kindle a fire that was quenched, was rather a covering to prevent the fire already kindled from spreading.

For there is a just revenge due to the injured person from his assailant; so that when we pardon, we give up what we might justly claim.

Thus, in the Lord's prayer, we are taught to forgive others their debts that God may forgive us our debts.

There is no injustice in asking back a debt, though there is kindness in forgiving it.

But as, in swearing, one who swears, even though truly, is in danger of perjury, of which one is in no danger who never swears; and while swearing truly is not a sin, we are further from sin by not swearing; so that the command not to swear is a guard against perjury:

in the same way since it is sinful to wish to be revenged with an unjust excess, though there is no sin in wishing for revenge within the limits of justice, the man who wishes for no revenge at all is further from the sin of an unjust revenge.

It is sin to demand more than is due, though it is no sin to demand a debt.

And the best security against the sin of making an unjust demand is to demand nothing, especially considering the danger of being compelled to pay the debt to Him who is indebted to none.

Thus, I would explain the passage as follows:

It has been said by them of old time, Thou shall not take unjust revenge; but I say, Take no revenge at all:

here is the fulfillment.

It is thus that Faustus, after quoting, "It has been said, Thou shall not swear falsely; but I say unto you, swear not at all," adds:

here is the fulfillment.

I might use the same expression if I thought that by the addition of these words Christ supplied a defect in the law, and not rather that the intention of the law to prevent unjust revenge is best secured by not taking revenge at all, in the same way as the intention to prevent perjury is best secured by not swearing at all. For if "an eye for an eye" is opposed to "If any one smite thee on the cheek, turn to him the other also," is there not as much opposition between "Thou shalt perform unto the Lord thine oath," and "Swear not at all?" [708]If Faustus thinks that there is not destruction, but fulfillment, in the one case, he ought to think the same of the other. For if "Swear not" is the fulfillment of "Swear truly," why should not "Take no revenge" be the fulfillment of "Take revenge justly"?

So, according to my interpretation, there is in both cases a guard against sin, either of false swearing or of unjust revenge; though, as regards giving up the right to revenge, there is the additional consideration that, by forgiving such debts, we shall obtain the forgiveness of our debts.

The old precept was required in the case of a self-willed people, to teach them not to be extravagant in their demands.

Thus, when the rage eager for unrestrained vengeance, was subdued, there would be leisure for any one so disposed to consider the desirableness of having his own debt cancelled by the Lord, and so to be led by this consideration to forgive the debt of his fellow-servant.

26.

Again, we shall find on examination, that there is no opposition between the precept of the Lord about not putting away a wife, and what was said by them of old time:

"Whosoever putteth away his wife, let him give her a writing of divorcement." [709]The Lord explains the intention of the law, which required a bill of divorce in every case where a wife was put away.

The precept not to put away a wife is the opposite of saying that a man may put away his wife if he pleases; which is not what the law says.

On the contrary, to prevent the wife from being put away, the law required this intermediate step, that the eagerness for separation might be checked by the writing of the bill, and the man might have time to think of the evil of putting away his wife; especially since, as it is said, among the Hebrews it was unlawful for any but the scribes to write Hebrew:

for the scribes claimed the possession of superior wisdom; and if they were men of upright and pious character, their pursuits might justly entitle them to make this claim.

In requiring, therefore, that in putting away his wife, a man should give her a writing of divorcement, the design was that he should be obliged to have recourse to those from whom he might expect to receive a cautious interpretation of the law, and suitable advice against separation.

Having no other way of getting the bill written, the man should be obliged to submit to their direction, and to allow of their endeavors to restore peace and harmony between him and his wife.

In a case where the hatred could not be overcome or checked, the bill would of course be written.

A wife might with reason be put away when wise counsel failed to restore the proper feeling and affection in the mind of her husband.

If the wife is not loved, she is to be put away.

And that she may not be put away, it is the husband's duty to love her.

Now, while a man cannot be forced to love against his will, he may be influenced by advice and persuasion.

This was the duty of the scribe, as a wise and upright man; and the law gave him the opportunity, by requiring the husband in all cases of quarrel to go to him, to get the bill of divorcement written.

No good or prudent man would write the bill unless it were a case of such obstinate aversion as to make reconciliation impossible.

But according to your impious notions, there can be nothing in putting away a wife; for matrimony, according to you, is a criminal indulgence.

The word "matrimony" shows that a man takes a wife in order that she may become a mother, which would be an evil in your estimation.

According to you, this would imply that part of your god is overcome and captured by the race of darkness, and bound in the fetters of flesh.

27.

But, to explain the point in hand:

If Christ, in adding the words, "But I say unto you," to the quotations He makes of ancient sayings, neither fulfilled the law of primitive times by His additions, nor destroyed the law given to Moses by opposite precepts, but rather paid such deference to the Hebrew law in all the quotations He made from it, as to make His own remarks chiefly explanatory of what the law stated less distinctly, or a means of securing the design intended by the law, it follows that from the words, "I came not to destroy the law, but to fulfill it" we are not to understand that Christ by His precepts filled up what was wanting in the law; but that what the literal command failed in doing from the pride and disobedience of men, is accomplished by grace in those who are brought to repentance and humility.

The fulfillment is not in additional words, but in acts of obedience.

So the apostle says "Faith worketh by love;" [710] and again, He that loveth another hath fulfilled the law." [711] This love, by which also the righteousness of the law can be fulfilled was bestowed in its significance by Christ in His coming, through the spirit which He sent according to His promise; and therefore He said, "I came not to destroy the law, but to fulfill it."

This is the New Testament in which the promise of the kingdom of heaven is made to this love; which was typified in the Old Testament, suitably to the times of that dispensation.

So Christ says again; "A new commandment I give unto you, that ye love one another." [712]

28.

So we find in the Old Testament all or nearly all the counsels and precepts which Christ introduces with the words "But I say unto you." Against anger it is written, "Mine eyes troubled because of anger;" [713] and again, "Better is he that conquers his anger, than he that taketh a city."[714] Against hard words, "The stroke of a whip maketh a wound; but the stroke of the tongue breaketh the bones." [715]

Against adultery in the heart, "Thou shall not covet thy neighbor's wife." [716]It is not, "Thou shall not commit adultery;" but, "Thou shall not covet."

The apostle, in quoting this, says:

"I had not known lust, unless the law had said, Thou shalt not covet." [717] Regarding patience in not offering resistance, a man is praised who "giveth his cheek to him that smiteth him, and who is filled full with reproach." [718]Of love to enemies it is said:

"If thine enemy hunger, feed him; if he thirst, give him drink." [719]This also is quoted by the apostle. [720]In the Psalm, too, it is said, "I was a peace maker among them that hated peace;"[721] and in many similar passages.

The Writings Against the Manichaeans and Against the Donatists: Part I - The Manichaeans

In connection also with our imitating God in refraining from taking revenge, and in loving even the wicked, there is a passage containing a full description of God in this character; for it is written:

"To Thee alone ever belongeth great strength, and who can withstand the power of Thine arm?

For the whole world before Thee is as a little grain of the balance; yea, as a drop of the morning dew that falleth down upon the earth.

But Thou hast mercy upon all, for Thou canst do all things, and winkest at the sins of men, because of repentance.

For Thou lovest all things that are, and abhorrest nothing which Thou hast made; for never wouldest Thou have made anything if Thou hadst hated it.

And how could anything have endured, if it had not been Thy will? or been preserved, if not called by Thee?

But Thou sparest all; for they are Thine, O Lord, Thou lover of souls.

For Thy good Spirit is in all things; therefore chastenest Thou them by little and little that offend, and warnest them by putting them in remembrance wherein they have offended, that learning their wickedness, they may believe in Thee, O Lord." [722]Christ exhorts us to imitate this long-suffering goodness of God, who maketh the sun to rise upon the evil and the good, and sendeth rain on the just and on the unjust; that we may not be careful to revenge, but may do good to them that hate us, and so may be perfect, even as our Father in heaven is perfect. [723] From another passage in these ancient books we learn that, by not exacting the vengeance due to us, we obtain the remission of our own sins; and that by not forgiving the debts of others, we incur the danger of being refused forgiveness when we pray for the remission of our own debts:

"He that revengeth shall find vengeance from the Lord, and He will surely keep his sin in remembrance.

Forgive thy neighbor the hurt that he hath done to thee; so shall thy sins also be forgiven when thou prayest.

One man beareth hatred against another, and doth he seek pardon of the Lord?

He showeth no mercy to a man who is like himself; and doth he ask forgiveness of his own sins?

If he that is but flesh nourishes hatred, and asks for favor from the Lord, who will entreat for the pardon of his sins?" [724]

29.

As regards not putting away a wife, there is no need to quote any other passage of the Old Testament than that referred to most appropriately in the Lord's reply to the Jews when they questioned Him on this subject.

For when they asked whether it is lawful for a man to put away his wife for any reason, the Lord answered:

"Have ye not read, that He that made them at the beginning made them male and female, and said, For this cause shall a man leave his father and mother, and shall cleave to his wife, and they two shall be one flesh? Therefore they are no longer twain, but one flesh.

What therefore God hath joined, let no man put asunder." [725]Here the Jews, who thought that they acted according to the intention of the law of Moses in putting away their wives, are made to see from the book of Moses that a wife should not be put away.

And, by the way, we learn here, from Christ's own declaration, that God made and joined male and female; so that by denying this, the Manichæans are guilty of opposing the gospel of Christ as well as the writings of Moses.

And supposing their doctrine to be true, that the devil made and joined male and female, we see the diabolical cunning of Faustus in finding fault with Moses for dissolving marriages by granting a bill of divorce, and praising Christ for strengthening the union by the precept in the Gospel.

Instead of this, Faustus, consistently with his own foolish and impious notions, should have praised Moses for separating what was made and joined by the devil, and should have blamed Christ for ratifying a bond of the devil's workmanship.

To return, let us hear the good Master explain how Moses, who wrote of the conjugal chastity in the first union of male and female as so holy and inviolable, afterwards allowed the people to put away their wives.

For when the Jews replied, "Why did Moses then command to give a writing of divorcement, and to put her away?"

Christ said unto them, "Moses, because of the hardness of your heart, suffered you to put away your wives." [726]This passage we have already explained. [727]The hardness must have been great indeed which could not be induced to admit the restoration of wedded love, even though by means of the writing an opportunity was afforded for advice to be given to this effect by wise and upright men.

Then the Lord quoted the same law, to show both what was enjoined on the good and what was permitted to the hard; for, from what is written of the union of male and female, He proved that a wife must not be put away, and pointed out the divine authority for the union; and shows from the same Scriptures that a bill of divorcement was to be given because of the hardness of the heart, which might be subdued or might not.

30.

Since, then, all these excellent precepts of the Lord, which Faustus tries to prove to be contrary to the old books of the Hebrews, are found in these very books, the only sense in which the Lord came not to destroy the law, but to fulfill it, is this, that besides the fulfillment of the prophetic types, which are set aside by their actual accomplishment, the precepts also, in which the law is holy, and just, and good, are fulfilled in us, not by the oldness of the letter which commands, and increases the offence of the proud by the additional guilt of transgression, but by the newness of the Spirit, who aids us, and by the obedience of the humble, through the saving grace which sets us free.

For, while all these sublime precepts are found in the ancient books, still the end to which they point is not there revealed; although the holy men who foresaw the revelation lived in accordance with it, either veiling it in prophecy as suited the time, or themselves discovering the truth thus veiled.

31.

I am disposed, after careful examination, to doubt whether the expression so often used by the Lord, "the kingdom of heaven," can be found in these books.

It is said, indeed, "Love wisdom, that ye may reign for ever." [728] And if eternal life had not been clearly made known in the Old Testament, the Lord would not have said, as He did even to the unbelieving Jews:

"Search the Scriptures, for in them ye think that ye have eternal life, and they are they that testify of me." [729] And to the same effect are the words of the Psalmist:

"I shall not die, but live, and declare the works of the Lord." [730] And again:

"Enlighten mine eyes, lest I sleep the sleep of death." [731] Again, we read, "The souls of the righteous are in the hand of the Lord, and pain shall not touch them;" and immediately following:

"They are in peace; and if they have suffered torture from men, their hope is full of immortality; and after a few trouble, they shall enjoy many rewards." [732] Again, in another place:

"The righteous shall live for ever, and their reward is with the Lord, and their concern with the Highest; therefore shall they receive from the hand of the Lord a kingdom of glory and a crown of beauty." [733] These and many similar declarations of eternal life, in more or less explicit terms, are found in these writings.

Even the resurrection of the body is spoken of by the prophets.

The Pharisees, accordingly, were fierce opponents of the Sadducees, who disbelieved the resurrection.

This we learn not only from the canonical Acts of the Apostles, which the Manichæans reject, because it tells of the advent of the Paraclete promised by the Lord, but also from the Gospel, when the Sadducees question the Lord about the woman who married seven brothers, one dying after the other, whose wife she would be in the resurrection. [734] As regards, then, eternal life and the resurrection of the dead, numerous testimonies are to be found in these Scriptures.

But I do not find there the expression, "the kingdom of heaven."

This expression belongs properly to the revelation of the New Testament, because in the resurrection our earthly bodies shall, by that change which Paul fully describes, become spiritual bodies, and so heavenly, that thus we may possess the kingdom of heaven.

And this expression was reserved for Him whose advent as King to govern and Priest to sanctify His believing people, was ushered in by all the symbolism of the old covenant, in its genealogies, its typical acts and words, its sacrifices and ceremonies and feasts, and in all its prophetic utterances and events and figures.

He came full of grace and truth, in His grace helping us to obey the precepts, and in His truth securing the accomplishment of the promises.

He came not to destroy the law, but to fulfill it.

Book XX - Faustus repels the charge of sun-worship, and maintains that while the Manichæans believe that God's power dwells in the sun and his wisdom in the moon, they yet worship one deity, Father, Son, and Holy Spirit. They are not a schism of the Gentiles, nor a sect

Augustin emphasizes the charge of polytheism, and goes into an elaborate comparison of Manichæan and pagan mythology.

1.

Faustus said:
You ask why we worship the sun, if we are a sect or separate religion, and not Pagans, or merely a schism of the Gentiles. It may therefore be as well to inquire into the matter, that we may see whether the name of Gentiles is more applicable to you or to us. Perhaps, in giving you in a friendly way this simple account of my faith, I shall appear to be making an apology for it, as if I were ashamed, which God forbid, of doing homage to the divine luminaries. You may take it as you please; but I shall not regret what I have done if I succeed in conveying to some at least this much knowledge, that our religion has nothing in common with that of the Gentiles.

2.

We worship, then, one deity under the threefold appellation of the Almighty God the Father, and his son Christ, and the Holy Spirit. While these are one and the same, we believe also that the Father properly dwells in the highest or principal light, which Paul calls "light inaccessible," [735] and the Son in his second or visible light.

And as the Son is himself twofold, according to the apostle, who speaks of Christ as the power of God and the wisdom of God, [736] we believe that His power dwells in the sun, and His wisdom in the moon.

We also believe that the Holy Spirit, the third majesty, has His seat and His home in the whole circle of the atmosphere.

By His influence and spiritual infusion, the earth conceives and brings forth the mortal Jesus, who, as hanging from every tree, is the life and salvation of men. [737] Though you oppose these doctrines so violently, your religion resembles ours in attaching the same sacredness to the bread and wine that we do to everything.

This is our belief, which you will have an opportunity of hearing more of, if you wish to do so.

Meanwhile there is some force in the consideration that you or any one that is asked where his God dwells, will say that he dwells in light; so that the testimony in favor of my worship is almost universal.

3.

As to your calling us a schism of the Gentiles, and not a sect, I suppose the word schism applies to those who have the same doctrines and worship as other people, and only choose to meet separately.

The word sect, again, applies to those whose doctrine is quite unlike that of others, and who have made a form of divine worship peculiar to themselves.

If this is what the words mean, in the first place, in our doctrine and worship we have no resemblance to the Pagans.

We shall see presently whether you have.

The Pagan doctrine is, that all things good and evil, mean and glorious, fading and unfading, changeable and unchangeable, material and divine, have only one principle.

In opposition to this, my belief is that God is the principle of all good things, and Hyle [matters] of the opposite.

Hyle is the name given by our master in divinity to the principle or nature of evil.

The Pagans accordingly think it right to worship God with altars, and shrines, and images, and sacrifices, and incense.

Here also my practice differs entirely from theirs:

for I look upon myself as a reasonable temple of God, if I am worthy to be so; and I consider Christ his Son as the living image of his living majesty; and I hold a mind well cultivated to be the true altar, and pure and simple prayers to be the true way of paying divine honors and of offering sacrifices.

Is this being a schism of the Pagans?

4.

As regards the worship of the Almighty God, you might call us a schism of the Jews, for all Jews are bold enough to profess this worship, were it not for the difference in the form of our worship, though it may be questioned whether the Jews really worship the Almighty.

But the doctrine I have mentioned is common to the Pagans in their worship of the sun, and to the Jews in their worship of the Almighty.

Even in relation to you, we are not properly a schism, though we acknowledge Christ and worship Him; for our worship and doctrine are different from yours.

In a schism, little or no change is made from the original; as, for instance, you, in your schism from the Gentiles, have brought with you the doctrine of a single principle, for you believe that all things are of God.

The sacrifices you change into love-feasts, the idols into martyrs, to whom you pray as they do to their idols.

You appease the shades of the departed with wine and food.

You keep the same holidays as the Gentiles; for example, the calends and the solstices.

In your way of living you have made no change.

Plainly you are a mere schism; for the only difference from the original is that you meet separately.

In this you have followed the Jews, who separated from the Gentiles, but differed only in not having images.

For they used temples, and sacrifices, and altars, and a priesthood, and the whole round of ceremonies the same as those of the Gentiles, only more superstitious.

Like the Pagans, they believe in a single principle; so that both you and the Jews are schisms of the Gentiles, for you have the same faith, and nearly the same worship, and you call yourselves sects only because you meet separately.

The fact is, there are only two sects, the Gentiles and ourselves.

We and the Gentiles are as contrary in our belief as truth and falsehood, day and night, poverty and wealth, health and sickness.

You, again, are not a sect in relation either to truth or to error.

You are merely a schism and a schism not of truth, but of error.

5.

Augustin replied:

O hateful mixture of ignorance and cunning!

Why do you put arguments in the mouth of your opponent, which no one that knows you would use?

We do not call you Pagans, or a schism of Pagans; but we say that you resemble them in worshipping many gods.

But you are far worse than Pagans, for they worship things which exist, though they should not be worshipped:

for idols have an existence, though for salvation they are nought.

So, to worship a tree with prayers, instead of improving it by cultivation, is not to worship nothing, but to worship in a wrong way.

When the apostle says that "the things which the Gentiles sacrifice, they sacrifice to demons, and not to God,"[738] he means that these demons exist to whom the sacrifices are made, and with whom he wishes us not to be partakers.

So, too, heaven and earth, the sea and air, the sun and moon, and the other heavenly bodies, are all objects which have a sensible existence.

When the Pagans worship these as gods, or as parts of one great God (for some of them identify the universe with the Supreme Deity), they worship things which have an existence.

In arguing with Pagans, we do not deny the existence of these things, but we say that they should not be worshipped; and we recommend the worship of the invisible Creator of all these things, in whom alone man can find the happiness which all allow that he desires.

To those, again, who worship what is invisible and immaterial, but still is created, as the soul or mind of man, we say that happiness is not to be found in the creature even under this form, and that we must worship the true God, who is not only invisible, but unchangeable; for He alone is to be worshipped, in the enjoyment of whom the worshipper finds happiness, and without whom the soul must be wretched, whatever else it possesses.

You, on the other hand, who worship things which have no existence at all except in your fictitious legends, would be nearer true piety and religion if you were Pagans, or if you were worshippers of what has an existence, though not a proper object of worship.

In fact, you do not properly worship the sun, though he carries your prayers with him in his course round the heavens.

6.

Your statements about the sun himself are so false and absurd, that if he were to repay you for the injury done to him, he would scorch you to death.

First of all, you call the sun a ship, so that you are not only astray worlds off, as the saying is, but adrift.

Next, while every one sees that the sun is round, which is the form corresponding from its perfection to his position among the heavenly bodies, you maintain that he is triangular, that is, that his light shines on the earth through a triangular window in heaven.

Hence it is that you bend and bow your heads to the sun, while you worship not this visible sun, but some imaginary ship which you suppose to be shining through a triangular opening.

Assuredly this ship would never have been heard of, if the words required for the composition of heretical fictions had to be paid for, like the wood required for the beams of a ship.

All this is comparatively harmless, however ridiculous or pitiable.

Very different is your wicked fancy about youths of both sexes proceeding from this ship, whose beauty excites eager desire in the princes and princesses of darkness; and so the members of your god are released from this humiliating confinement in the members of the race of darkness, by means of sinful passion and sensual appetite.

And to these filthy rags of yours you would unite the mystery of the Trinity; for you say that the Father dwells in a secret light, the power of the Son in the sun, and His wisdom in the moon, and the Holy Spirit in the air.

7.

As for this threefold or rather fourfold fiction, what shall I say of the secret light of the Father, but that you can think of no light except what you have seen?

From your knowledge of visible light, with which beasts and insects as well as men are familiar, you form some vague idea in your mind, and call it the light in which God the Father dwells with His subjects.

How can you distinguish between the light by which we see, and that by which we understand, when, according to your ideas, to understand truth is nothing else than to form the conception of material forms, either finite or in some cases infinite; and you actually believe in these wild fancies?

It is manifest that the act of my mind in thinking of your region of light which has no existence, is entirely different from my conception of Alexandria, which exists, though I have not seen it.

And, again, the act of forming a conception of Alexandria, which I have never seen, is very different from thinking of Carthage, which I know.

But this difference is insignificant as compared with that between my thinking of material things which I know from seeing them, and my understanding justice, chastity, faith, truth, love, goodness, and things of this nature.

Can you describe this intellectual light, which gives us a clear perception of the distinction between itself and other things, as well as of the distinction between those things themselves?

And yet even this is not the sense in which it can be said that God is light, for this light is created, whereas God is the Creator; the light is made, and He is the Maker; the light is changeable.

For the intellect changes from dislike to desire, from ignorance to knowledge, from forgetfulness to recollection; whereas God remains the same in will, in truth, and in eternity.

From God we derive the beginning of existence, the principle of knowledge, the law of affection.

From God all animals, rational and irrational, derive the nature of their life, the capacity of sensation, the faculty of emotion.

From God all bodies derive their subsistence in extension, their beauty in number, and their order in weight.

This light is one divine being, in an inseparable triune existence; and yet, without supposing the assumption of any bodily form, you assign to separate places parts of the immaterial, spiritual, and unchangeable substance.

And instead of three places for the Trinity, you have four:

one, the light inaccessible, which you know nothing about, for the Father; two, the sun and moon, for the Son; and again one, the circle of the atmosphere, for the Holy Spirit.

Of the inaccessible light of the Father I shall say nothing further at present, for orthodox believers do not separate the Son and the Spirit from the Father in relation to this light.

8.

It is difficult to understand how you have been taken with the absurd idea of placing the power of the Son in the sun, and His wisdom in the moon.

For, as the Son remains inseparably in the Father, His wisdom and power cannot be separated from one another, so that one should be in the sun and the other in the moon.

Only material things can be thus assigned to separate places.

If you only understood this, it would have prevented you from taking the productions of a diseased fancy as the material for so many fictions.

But there is inconsistency and improbability as well as falsehood in your ideas.

For, according to you, the seat of wisdom is inferior in brightness to the seat of power.

Now energy and productiveness are the qualities of power, whereas light teaches and manifests; so that if the sun had the greater heat, and the moon the greater light, these absurdities might appear to have some likelihood to men of carnal minds, who know nothing except through material conceptions.

From the connection between great heat and motion, they might identify power with heat; while light from its brightness, and as making things discernible, they might represent wisdom.

But what folly as well as profanity, in placing power in the sun, which excels so much in light, and wisdom in the moon, which is so inferior in brightness!

And while you separate Christ from Himself, you do not distinguish between Christ and the Holy Spirit; whereas Christ is one, the power of God, and the wisdom of God, and the Spirit is a distinct person.

But according to you, the air, which you make the seat of the Spirit, fills and pervades the universe.

So the sun and moon in their course are always united to the air.

But the moon approaches the sun at one time, and recedes from it at another.

So that, if we may believe you, or rather, if we may allow ourselves to be imposed on by you, wisdom recedes from power by half the circumference of a circle, and again approaches it by the other half.

And when wisdom is full, it is at a distance from power.

For when the moon is full, the distance between the two bodies is so great, that the moon rises in the east while the sun is setting in the west.

But as the loss of power produces weakness, the fuller the moon is, the weaker must wisdom be.

If, as is certainly true, the wisdom of God is unchangeable in power, and the power of God unchangeable in wisdom, how can you separate them so as to assign them to different places?

And how can the place be different when the substance is the same?

Is this not the infatuation of subjection to material fancies; showing such a want of power and wisdom that your wisdom is as weak as your power is foolish?

This execrable absurdity would divide Christ between the sun and the moon,--His power in one, and His wisdom in the other; so that He would be incomplete in both, lacking wisdom in the sun, and power in the moon, while in both He supplies youths, male and female, to excite the affection of the princes and princesses of darkness.

Such are the tenets which you learn and profess.

Such is the faith which directs your conduct.

And can you wonder that you are regarded with abhorrence?

9.

But besides your errors regarding these conspicuous and familiar luminaries, which you worship not for what they are, but for what your wild fancy makes them to be, your other absurdities are still worse than this.

Your illustrious World-bearer, and Atlas who helps to hold him up, are unreal beings.

Like innumerable other creatures of your fancy, they have no existence, and yet you worship them.

For this reason we say that you are worse than Pagans, while you resemble them in worshipping many gods.

You are worse, because, while they worship things which exist though they are not gods, you worship things which are neither gods nor anything else, for they have no existence.

The Pagans, too, have fables, but they know them to be fables; and either look upon them as amusing poetical fancies, or try to explain them as representing the nature of things, or the life of man.

Thus they say that Vulcan is lame, because flame in common fire has an irregular motion:

that Fortune is blind, because of the uncertainty of what are called fortuitous occurrences:

that there are three Fates, with distaff, and spindle, and fingers spinning wool into thread, because there are three times,--the past, already spun and wound on the spindle; the present, which is passing through the fingers of the spinner; and the future, still in wool bound to the distaff, and soon to pass through the fingers to the spindle, that is, through the present into the future:

and that Venus is the wife of Vulcan, because pleasure has a natural connection with heat; and that she is the mistress of Mars, because pleasure is not properly the companion of warriors:

and that Cupid is a boy with wings and a bow, from the wounds inflicted by thoughtless, inconstant passion in the hearts of unhappy beings:

and so with many other fables.

The great absurdity is in their continuing to worship these beings, after giving such explanations; for the worship without the explanations, though criminal, would be a less heinous crime.

The very explanations prove that they do not worship that God, the enjoyment of whom can alone give happiness, but things which He has created.

And even in the creature they worship not only the virtues, as in Minerva, who sprang from the head of Jupiter, and who represents prudence,--a quality of reason which, according to Plato, has its seat in the head,--but their vices, too, as in Cupid.

Thus one of their dramatic poets says, "Sinful passion, in favor of vice, made Love a god."[739] Even bodily evils had temples in Rome, as in the case of pallor and fever.

Not to dwell on the sin of the worshippers of these idols, who are in a way affected by the bodily forms, so that they pay homage to them as deities, when they see them set up in some lofty place, and treated with great honor and reverence, there is greater sin in the very explanations which are intended as apologies for these dumb, and deaf, and blind, and lifeless objects.

Still, though, as I have said, these things are nothing in the way of salvation or of usefulness, both they and the things they are said to represent are real existences.

But your First Man, warring with the five elements; and your Mighty Spirit, who constructs the world from the captive bodies of the race of darkness, or rather from the members of your god in subjection and bondage; and your World-holder, who has in his hand the remains of these members, and who bewails the capture and bondage and pollution of the rest; and your giant Atlas, who keeps up the World-holder on his shoulders, lest he should from weariness throw away his burden, and so prevent the completion of the final imitation of the mass of darkness, which is to be the last scene in your drama;--these and countless other absurdities are not represented in painting or sculpture, or in any explanation; and yet you believe and worship things which have no existence, while you taunt the Christians with being credulous for believing in realities with a faith which pacifies the mind under its influence. The objects of your worship can be shown to have no existence by many proofs, which I do not bring forward here, because, though I could without difficulty discourse philosophically on the construction of the world, it would take too long to do so here.

One proof suffices.

If these things are real, God must be subject to change, and corruption, and contamination; a supposition as blasphemous as it is irrational. All these things, therefore, are vain, and false, and unreal.

Thus you are much worse than those Pagans, with whom all are familiar, and who still preserve traces of their old customs, of which they themselves are ashamed; for while they worship things which are not gods, you worship things which do not exist.

10.

If you think that your doctrines are true because they are unlike the errors of the Pagans, and that we are in error because we perhaps differ more from you than from them, you might as well say that a dead man is in good health because he is not sick; or that good health is undesirable, because it differs less from sickness than from death.

Or if the Pagans should be viewed in many cases as rather dead than sick, you might as well praise the ashes in the tomb because they have no longer the human shape, as compared with the living body, which does not differ so much from a corpse as from ashes.

It is thus we are reproached for having more resemblance to the dead body of Paganism than to the ashes of Manichæism.

But in division, it often happens that a thing is placed in different classes, according to the point of resemblance on which the division proceeds.

For instance, if animals are divided into those that fly and those that cannot fly, in this division men and beasts are classed together as distinct from birds, because they are both unable to fly.

But if they are divided into rational and irrational, beasts and birds are classed together as distinct from men, for they are both destitute of reason.

Faustus did not think of this when he said:

There are in fact only two sects, the Gentiles and ourselves, for we are directly opposed to them in our belief.

The opposition he means is this, that the Gentiles believe in a single principle, whereas the Manichæans believe also in the principle of the race of darkness.

Certainly, according to this division we agree in general with the Pagans.

But if we divide all who have a religion into those who worship one God and those who worship many gods, the Manichæans must be classed along with the Pagans, and we along with the Jews.

This is another distinction, which may be said to make only two sects.

Perhaps you will say that you hold all your gods to be of one substance, which the Pagans do not.

But you at least resemble them in assigning to your gods different powers, and functions, and employments.

One does battle with the race of darkness; another constructs the world from the part which is captured; another, standing above, has the world in his hand; another holds him up from below; another turns the wheels of the fires and winds and waters beneath; another, in his circuit of the heavens, gathers with his beams the members of your god from cesspools.

Indeed, your gods have innumerable occupations, according to your fabulous descriptions, which you neither explain nor represent in a visible form.

But again, if men were divided into those who believe that God takes an interest in human affairs and those who do not, the Pagans and Jews, and you and all heretics that have anything of Christianity, will be classed together, as opposed to the Epicureans, and any others holding similar views.

As this is a principle of importance, here again we may say that there are only two sects, and you belong to the same sect as we do.

You will hardly venture to dissent from us in the opinion that God is concerned in human affairs, so that in this matter your opposition to the Epicureans makes you side with us.

Thus, according to the nature of the division, what is in one class at one time, is in another at another time:

things joined here are separated there:

in some things we are classed with others, and they with us; in other things we are classed separately, and stand alone.

If Faustus thought of this, he would not talk such eloquent nonsense.

11.

But what are we to make of these words of Faustus:

The Holy Spirit, by his influence and spiritual infusion, makes the earth conceive and bring forth the mortal Jesus, who, as hanging from every tree, is the life and salvation of men?

Letting pass for a moment the absurdity of this statement, we observe the folly of believing that the mortal Jesus can be conceived through the power of the Holy Spirit by the earth, but not by the Virgin Mary.

Dare you compare the holiness of that chaste virgin's womb with any piece of ground where trees and plants grow?

Do you pretend to look with abhorrence upon a pure virgin, while you do not shrink from believing that Jesus is produced in gardens watered by the filthy drains of a city?

For plants of all kinds spring up and are nourished in such moisture.

You will have Jesus to be born in this way, while you cry out against the idea of His being born of a virgin.

Do you think flesh more unclean than the excrements which its nature rejects?

Is the filth cleaner than the flesh which expels it?

Are you not aware how fields are manured in order to make them productive?

Your folly comes to this, that the Holy Spirit, who, according to you, despised the womb of Mary, makes the earth conceive more fruitfully in proportion as it is carefully enriched with animal off-scourings.

Do you reply that the Holy Spirit preserves His incorruptible purity everywhere?

I ask again, Why not also in the virgin's womb?

Passing from the conception, you maintain in regard to the mortal Jesus--who, as you say, is born from the earth, which has conceived by the power of the Holy Spirit--that He hangs in the shape of fruit from every tree:

so that, besides this pollution, He suffers additional defilement from the flesh of the countless animals that eat the fruit; except, indeed, the small amount that is purified by your eating it.

While we believe and confess Christ the Son of God, and the Word of God, to have become flesh without suffering defilement, because the divine substance is not defiled by flesh, as it is not defiled by anything, your fanciful notions would make Jesus to be defiled even as hanging on the tree, before entering the flesh of any animal; for if He were not defiled, there would be no need of His being purified by your eating Him.

And if all trees are the cross of Christ, as Faustus seems to imply when he says that Jesus hangs from every tree, why do you not pluck the fruit, and so take Jesus down from hanging on the tree to bury Him in your stomach, which would correspond to the good deed of Joseph of Arimathea, when he took down the true Jesus from the cross to bury Him? [740] Why should it be impious to take Christ from the tree, while it is pious to lay Him in the tomb? Perhaps you wish to apply to yourselves the words quoted from the prophet by Paul, "Their throat is an open sepulchre:"[741] and so you wait with open mouth till some one comes to use your throat as the best sepulchre for Christ.

Once more, how many Christs do you make? Is there one whom you call the mortal Christ, whom the earth conceives and brings forth by the power of the Holy Spirit; and another crucified by the Jews under Pontius Pilate; and a third whom you divide between the sun and the moon?

Or is it one and the same person, part of whom is confined in the trees, to be released by the help of the other part which is not confined?

If this is the case, and you allow that Christ suffered under Pontius Pilate, though it is difficult to see how he could have suffered without flesh, as you say he did, the great question is, with whom he left those ships you speak of, that he might come down and suffer these things, which he certainly could not have suffered without having a body of some kind.

A mere spiritual presence could not have made him liable to these sufferings, and in his bodily presence he could not be at the same time in the sun, in the moon, and on the cross.

So, then, if he had not a body, he was not crucified; and if he had a body, the question is, where he got it:

for, according to you, all bodies belong to the race of darkness, though you cannot think of the divine substance except as being material.

Thus you must say either that Christ was crucified without a body; which is utterly absurd; or that he was crucified in appearance and not in reality, which is blasphemy; or that all bodies do not belong to the race of darkness, but that the divine substance has also a body, and that not an immortal body, but liable to crucifixion and death, which, again, is altogether erroneous; or that Christ had a mortal body from the race of darkness, so that, while you will not allow that Christ's body came from the Virgin Mary, you derive it from the race of demons.

Finally, as in Faustus' statement, in which he alludes in the briefest manner possible to the lengthy stories of Manichæan invention, the earth by the power of the Holy Spirit conceives and brings forth the mortal Jesus, who, hanging from every tree, is the life and salvation of men, why should this Saviour be represented by whatever is hanging, because he hung on the tree, and not by whatever is born, because he was born? But if you mean that the Jesus on the trees, and the Jesus crucified under Pontius Pilate, and the Jesus divided between the sun and the moon, are all one and the same substance, why do you not give the name of Jesus to your whole host of deities?

Why should not your World-holder be Jesus too, and Atlas, and the King of Honour, and the Mighty Spirit, and the First Man, and all the rest, with their various names and occupations?

12.

So, with regard to the Holy Spirit, how can you say that he is the third person, when the persons you mention are innumerable?

Or why is he not Jesus himself?

And why does Faustus mislead people, in trying to make out an agreement between himself and true Christians, from whom he differs only too widely, by saying, We worship one God under the threefold appellation of the Almighty God the Father, Christ his Son, and the Holy Spirit?

Why is the appellation only threefold, instead of being manifold?

And why is the distinction in appellation only, and not in reality, if there are as many persons as there are names?

For it is not as if you gave three names to the same thing, as the same weapon may be called a short sword, a dagger, or a dirk; or as you give the name of moon, and the lesser ship, and the luminary of night, and so on, to the same thing.

For you cannot say that the First Man is the same as the Mighty Spirit, or as the World-Holder, or as the giant Atlas.

They are all distinct persons, and you do not call any of them Christ.

How can there be one Deity with opposite functions?

Or why should not Christ himself be the single person, if in one substance Christ hangs on the trees, and was persecuted by the Jews, and exists in the sun and moon?

The fact is, your fancies are all astray, and are no better than the dreams of insanity.

13.

How can Faustus think that we resemble the Manichæans in attaching sacredness to bread and wine, when they consider it sacrilege to taste wine?

They acknowledge their god in the grape, but not in the cup; perhaps they are shocked at his being trampled on and bottled.

It is not any bread and wine that we hold sacred as a natural production, as if Christ were confined in corn or in vines, as the Manichæans fancy, but what is truly consecrated as a symbol.

What is not consecrated, though it is bread and wine, is only nourishment or refreshment, with no sacredness about it; although we bless and thank God for every gift, bodily as well as spiritual.

According to your notion, Christ is confined in everything you eat, and is released by digestion from the additional confinement of your intestines.

So, when you eat, your god suffers; and when you digest, you suffer from his recovery.

When he fills you, your gain is his loss.

This might be considered kindness on his part, because he suffers in you for your benefit, were it not that he gains freedom by escaping and leaving you empty.

There is not the least resemblance between our reverence for the bread and wine, and your doctrines, which have no truth in them.

To compare the two is even more foolish than to say, as some do, that in the bread and wine we worship Ceres and Bacchus.

I refer to this now, to show where you got your silly idea that our fathers kept the Sabbath in honor of Saturn.

For as there is no connection with the worship of the Pagan deities Ceres and Bacchus in our observance of the sacrament of the bread and wine, which you approve so highly that you wish to resemble us in it, so there was no subjection to Saturn in the case of our fathers, who observed the rest of the Sabbath in a manner suitable to prophetic times.

14.

You might have found a resemblance in your religion to that of the Pagans as regards Hyle [matter], which the Pagans often speak of.

You, on the contrary, maintain that you are directly opposed to them in your belief in the evil principle which your teacher in theology calls Hyle.

But here you only show your ignorance, and, with an affectation of learning, use this word without knowing what it means.

The Greeks, when speaking of nature, give the name Hyle to the subject-matter of things, which has no form of its own, but admits of all bodily forms, and is known only through these changeable phenomena, not being itself an object of sensation or perception.

Some Gentiles, indeed, erroneously make this matter co-eternal with God, as not being derived from Him, though the bodily forms are.

In this manifest error you resemble the Pagans, for you hold that Hyle has a principle of its own, and does not come from God.

It is only ignorance that leads you to deny this resemblance.

In saying that Hyle has no form of its own, and can take its forms only from God, the Pagans come near to the truth which we believe in contradistinction from your errors.

Not knowing what Hyle or the subject-matter of things is, you make it the race of darkness, in which you place not only innumerable bodily forms of five different kinds, but also a formative mind.

Such, indeed, is your ignorance or insanity, that you call this mind Hyle, and make it give forms instead of taking them.

If there were such a formative mind as you speak of, and bodily elements capable of form, the word Hyle would properly be applicable to the bodily elements, which would be the matter to be formed by the mind, which you make the principle of evil. Even this would not be a quite accurate use of the word Hyle, which has no form of any kind; whereas these elements, although capable of new forms, have already the form of elements, and belong to different kinds.

Still this use of the word would not be so much amiss, notwithstanding your ignorance; for it would thus be applied, as it properly is, to that which takes form, and not to that which gives it. Even here, however, your folly and impiety would appear in tracing so much that is good to the evil principle, from your not knowing that all natures of every kind, all forms in their proportion, and all weights in their order, can come only from the Father, the Son, and the Holy Spirit.

As it is, you know neither what Hyle is, nor what evil is. Would that I could persuade you to refrain from misleading people still more ignorant than yourselves!

15.

Every one must see the folly of your boasting of superiority to the Pagans because they use altars and temples, images and sacrifices and incense, in the worship of God, which you do not.

As if it were not better to build an altar and offer sacrifice to a stone, which has some kind of existence, than to employ a heated imagination in worshipping things which have no existence at all.

And what do you mean by saying that you are a rational temple of God?

Can that be God's temple which is partly the construction of the devil?

And is this not true of you, as you say that all your members and your whole body were formed by the evil principle which you call Hyle, and that part of this formative mind dwells in the body along with part of your god?

And as this part of your god is bound and confined, you should be called the prison of God rather than his temple.

Perhaps it is your soul that is the temple of God, as you have it from the region of light.

But you generally call your soul not a temple, but a part or member of God.

So, when you say you are the temple of God, it must be in your body, which, you say, was formed by the devil.

Thus you blaspheme the temple of God, calling it not only the workmanship of Satan, but the prison-house of God.

The apostle, on the other hand, says:

"The temple of God is holy, which temple ye are."

And to show that this refers not merely to the soul, he says expressly:

"Know ye not that your bodies are the temple of the Holy Ghost, which is in you, which ye have of God?" [742] You call the workmanship of devils the temple of God, and there, to use Faustus' words, you place Christ, the Son of God, the living image of living majesty.

Your impiety may well contrive a fabulous temple for a fabulous Christ.

The image you speak of must be so called, because it is the creature of your imagination.

16.

If your mind is an altar, you see whose altar it is.

You may see from the very doctrines and duties in which you say you are trained. You are taught not to give food to a beggar; and so your altar smokes with the sacrifice of cruelty.

Such altars the Lord destroys; for in words quoted from the law He tells us what offering pleases God:

"I desire mercy, and not sacrifice."

Observe on what occasion the Lord uses these words.

It was when, in passing through a field, the disciples plucked the ears of corn because they were hungry.

Your doctrine would lead you to call this murder.

Your mind is an altar, not of God, but of lying devils, by whose doctrines the evil conscience is seared as with a hot iron, [743] calling murder what the truth calls innocence.

For in His words to the Jews, Christ by anticipation deals a fatal blow to you:

"If ye had known what this meaneth, I desire mercy, and not sacrifice, ye would not have condemned the guiltless." [744]

17.

Nor can you say that you honor God with sacrifices in the shape of pure and simple prayers: for, in your low, dishonoring notions about the divine nature and substance, you make your god to be the victim in the sacrifices of Pagans; so far are you from pleasing the true God with your sacrifices.

For you hold that God is confined not only in trees and plants, or in the human body, but also in the flesh of animals, which contaminates Him with its impurity.

And how can your soul give praise to God, when you actually reproach Him by calling your soul a particle of His substance taken captive by the race of darkness; as if God could not maintain the conflict except by this corruption of His members, and this dishonorable captivity?

Instead of honoring God in your prayers, you insult Him.

For what sin did you commit, when you belonged to Him, that you should be thus punished by the god you cry to, not because you left Him sinfully of your own choice; for he himself gave you to His enemies, to obtain peace for His kingdom?

You are not even given as hostages to be honorably guarded.

Nor is it as when a shepherd lays a snare to catch a wild beast: for he does not put one of his own members in the snare, but some animal from his flock; and generally, so that the wild beast is caught before the animal is hurt.

You, though you are the members of your god, are given to the enemy, whose ferocity you keep off from your god only by being contaminated with their impurity, infected with their corruptions, without any fault of your own.

You cannot in your prayers use the words:

"Free us, O Lord, for the glory of Thy name; and for Thy name's sake pardon our sins."[745] Your prayer is:

"Free us by Thy skill, for we suffer here oppression, and torture, and pollution, only that Thou mayest mourn unmolested in Thy kingdom."

These are words of reproach, not of entreaty.

Nor can you use the words taught us by the Master of truth:

"Forgive us our debts, as we forgive our debtors." [746] For who are the debtors who have sinned against you?

If it is the race of darkness, you do not forgive their debts, but make them be utterly cast out and shut up in eternal imprisonment.

And how can God forgive your debts, when He rather sinned against you by sending you into such a state, than you against Him, whom you obeyed by going?

If this was not a sin in Him, because He was compelled to do it, this excuse must apply you, now that you have been overthrown in the conflict, more than to Him before the conflict began.

You suffer now from the mixture of evil, which was not the case with Him when nevertheless He was compelled to send you.

So either He requires that you should forgive Him his debt; or, if He is not in debt to you, still less are you to Him.

It appears that your sacrifices and your pure and simple prayers are false and vile blasphemies.

18.

How is it, by the way, that you use the words temple, altar, sacrifice, for the purpose of commending your own practices?

If such things can be spoken of as properly belonging to true religion, they must constitute the true worship of the true God.

And if there is such a thing as true sacrifice to the true God, which is implied in the expression divine honors, there must be some one true sacrifice of which the rest are imitations.

On the one hand, we have the spurious imitations in the case of false and lying gods, that is, of devils, who proudly demand divine honors from their deluded votaries, as is or was the case in the temples and idols of the Gentiles.

On the other hand, we have the prophetic intimations of one most true sacrifice to be offered for the sins of all believers, as in the sacrifices enjoined by God on our fathers; along with which there was also the symbolical anointing typical of Christ, as the name Christ itself means anointed. The animal sacrifices, therefore, presumptuously claimed by devils, were an imitation of the true sacrifice which is due only to the one true God, and which Christ alone offered on His altar.

Thus the apostle says:

"The sacrifices which the Gentiles offer, they offer to devils, and not to God." [747] He does not find fault with sacrifices, but with offering to devils.

The Hebrews, again, in their animal sacrifices, which they offered to God in many varied forms, suitably to the significance of the institution, typified the sacrifice offered by Christ.

This sacrifice is also commemorated by Christians, in the sacred offering and participation of the body and blood of Christ.

The Manichæans understand neither the sinfulness of the Gentile sacrifices, nor the importance of the Hebrew sacrifices, nor the use of the ordinance of the Christian sacrifice.

Their own errors are the offering they present to the devil who has deceived them.

And thus they depart from the faith, giving heed to seducing spirits, and to doctrines of devils, speaking lies in hypocrisy.

19.

It may be well that Faustus, or at least that those who are charmed with Faustus' writings, should know that the doctrine of a single principle did not come to us from the Gentiles; for the belief in one true God, from whom every kind of nature is derived, is a part of the original truth retained among the Gentiles, notwithstanding their having fallen away to many false gods.

For the Gentile philosophers had the knowledge of God, because, as the apostle says, "the invisible things of Him, from the creation of the world, are clearly seen, being understood by the things that are made, even His eternal power and Godhead; so that they are without excuse."

But, as the apostle adds, "when they knew God, they glorified Him not as God, neither were thankful; but became vain in their imaginations, and their foolish heart was darkened.

Professing themselves to be wise, they became fools, and changed the glory of the incorruptible God into an image made like to corruptible man, and to birds, and four-footed beasts, and creeping things." [748] These are the idols of the Gentiles, which they cannot explain except by referring to the creatures made by God; so that this very explanation of their idolatry, on which the more enlightened Gentiles were wont to pride themselves as a proof of their superiority, shows the truth of the following words of the apostle:

"They worshipped and served the creature rather than the Creator, who is blessed forever."[749] Where you differ from the Gentiles, you are in error; where you resemble them, you are worse than they.

You do not believe, as they do, in a single principle; and so you fall into the impiety of believing the substance of the one true God to be liable to subjugation and corruption.

As regards the worship of a plurality of gods, the doctrine of lying devils has led the Gentiles to worship many idols, and you to worship many phantasms.

20.

We do not turn the sacrifices of the Gentiles into love-feasts, as Faustus says we do.

Our love-feasts are rather a substitute for the sacrifice spoken of by the Lord, in the words already quoted:

"I will have mercy, and not sacrifice."

At our love-feasts the poor obtain vegetable or animal food; and so the creature of God is used, as far as it is suitable, for the nourishment of man, who is also God's creature.

You have been led by lying devils, not in self-denial, but in blasphemous error, "to abstain from meats which God hath created to be received with thanksgiving of them which believe and know the truth.

For every creature of God is good, and nothing to be refused, if it be received with thanksgiving." [750] In return for the bounties of the Creator, you ungratefully insult Him with your impiety; and because in our love-feasts flesh is often given to the poor, you compare Christian charity to Pagan sacrifices.

This indeed, is another point in which you resemble some Pagans.

You consider it a crime to kill animals, because you think that the souls of men pass into them; which is an idea found in the writings of some Gentile philosophers, although their successors appear to have thought differently.

But here again you are most in error:

for they dreaded slaughtering a relative in the animal; but you dread the slaughter of your god, for you hold even the souls of animals to be his members.

21.

As to our paying honor to the memory of the martyrs, and the accusation of Faustus, that we worship them instead of idols, I should not care to answer such a charge, were it not for the sake of showing how Faustus, in his desire to cast reproach on us, has overstepped the Manichæan inventions, and has fallen heedlessly into a popular notion found in Pagan poetry, although he is so anxious to be distinguished from the Pagans.

For in saying that we have turned the idols into martyrs, he speaks of our worshipping them with similar rites, and appeasing the shades of the departed with wine and food.

Do you, then, believe in shades?

We never heard you speak of such things, nor have we read of them in your books.

In fact, you generally oppose such ideas:

for you tell us that the souls of the dead, if they are wicked, or not purified, are made to pass through various changes, or suffer punishment still more severe; while the good souls are placed in ships, and sail through heaven to that imaginary region of light which they died fighting for.

According to you, then, no souls remain near the burying-place of the body; and how can there be any shades of the departed?

What and where are they?

Faustus' love of evil-speaking has made him forget his own creed; or perhaps he spoke in his sleep about ghosts, and did not wake up even when he saw his words in writing.

It is true that Christians pay religious honor to the memory of the martyrs, both to excite us to imitate them and to obtain a share in their merits, and the assistance of their prayers.

But we build altars not to any martyr, but to the God of martyrs, although it is to the memory of the martyrs.

No one officiating at the altar in the saints' burying-place ever says, We bring an offering to thee, O Peter! or O Paul! or O Cyprian!

The offering is made to God, who gave the crown of martyrdom, while it is in memory of those thus crowned.

The emotion is increased by the associations of the place, and love is excited both towards those who are our examples, and towards Him by whose help we may follow such examples.

We regard the martyrs with the same affectionate intimacy that we feel towards holy men of God in this life, when we know that their hearts are prepared to endure the same suffering for the truth of the gospel.

There is more devotion in our feeling towards the martyrs, because we know that their conflict is over; and we can speak with greater confidence in praise of those already victors in heaven, than of those still combating here.

What is properly divine worship, which the Greeks call latria, and for which there is no word in Latin, both in doctrine and in practice, we give only to God.

To this worship belongs the offering of sacrifices; as we see in the word idolatry, which means the giving of this worship to idols.

Accordingly we never offer, or require any one to offer, sacrifice to a martyr, or to a holy soul, or to any angel.

Any one falling into this error is instructed by doctrine, either in the way of correction or of caution.

For holy beings themselves, whether saints or angels, refuse to accept what they know to be due to God alone.

We see this in Paul and Barnabas, when the men of Lycaonia wished to sacrifice to them as gods, on account of the miracles they performed. They rent their clothes, and restrained the people, crying out to them, and persuading them that they were not gods.

We see it also in the angels, as we read in the Apocalypse that an angel would not allow himself to be worshipped, and said to his worshipper, "I am thy fellow-servant, and of thy brethen."[751] Those who claim this worship are proud spirits, the devil and his angels, as we see in all the temples and rites of the Gentiles.

Some proud men, too, have copied their example; as is related of some kings of Babylon.

Thus the holy Daniel was accused and persecuted, because when the king made a decree that no petition should be made to any god, but only to the king, he was found worshipping and praying to his own God, that is, the one true God. [752] As for those who drink to excess at the feasts of the martyrs, we of course condemn their conduct; for to do so even in their own houses would be contrary to sound doctrine.

But we must try to amend what is bad as well as prescribe what is good, and must of necessity bear for a time with some things that are not according to our teaching.

The rules of Christian conduct are not to be taken from the indulgences of the intemperate or the infirmities of the weak. Still, even in this, the guilt of intemperance is much less than that of impiety.

To sacrifice to the martyrs, even fasting, is worse than to go home intoxicated from their feast:

to sacrifice to the martyrs, I say, which is a different thing from sacrificing to God in memory of the martyrs, as we do constantly, in the manner required since the revelation of the New Testament, for this belongs to the worship or latria which is due to God alone.

But it is vain to try to make these heretics understand the full meaning of these words of the

The Writings Against the Manichaeans and Against the Donatists: Part I - The Manichaeans
Psalmist: "He that offereth the sacrifice of praise glorifieth me, and in this way will I show him my salvation." [753]Before the coming of Christ, the flesh and blood of this sacrifice were foreshadowed in the animals slain; in the passion of Christ the types were fulfilled by the true sacrifice; after the ascension of Christ, this sacrifice is commemorated in the sacrament.

Between the sacrifices of the Pagans and of the Hebrews there is all the difference that there is between a false imitation and a typical anticipation.

We do not despise or denounce the virginity of holy women because there were vestal virgins.

And, in the same way, it is no reproach to the sacrifices of our fathers that the Gentiles also had sacrifices.

The difference between the Christian and vestal virginity is great, yet it consists wholly in the being to whom the vow is made and paid; and so the difference in the being to whom the sacrifices of the Pagans and Hebrews are made and offered makes a wide difference between them.

In the one case they are offered to devils, who presumptuously make this claim in order to be held as gods, because sacrifice is a divine honor.

In the other case they are offered to the one true God, as a type of the true sacrifice, which also was to be offered to Him in the passion of the body and blood of Christ.

22.

Faustus is wrong in saying that our Jewish forefathers, in their separation from the Gentiles, retained the temple, and sacrifices, and altars, and priesthood, and abandoned only graven images or idols, for they might have sacrificed, as some do, without any graven image, to trees and mountains, or even to the sun and moon and the stars.

If they had thus rendered to these objects the worship called latria, they would have served the creature instead of the Creator, and so would have fallen into the serious error of heathenish superstition; and even without idols, they would have found devils ready to take advantage of their error, and to accept their offerings.

For these proud and wicked spirits feed not, as some foolishly suppose, on the smell of the sacrifice, and the smoke, but on the errors of men.

They enjoy not bodily refreshment, but a malevolent gratification, when they in any way deceive people, or when, with a bold assumption of borrowed majesty, they boast of receiving divine honors.

It was not, therefore, only the idols of the Gentiles that our Jewish forefathers abandoned. They sacrificed neither to the earth nor to any earthly thing, nor to the sea, nor to heaven, nor to the hosts of heaven, but laid the victims on the altar of the one God, Creator of all, who required these offerings as a means of foreshadowing the true victim, by whom He has reconciled us to Himself in the remission of sins through our Lord Jesus Christ.

So Paul, addressing believers, who are made the body of which Christ is the Head, says:

"I beseech you, therefore, brethren, by the mercies of God, that ye present your bodies a living sacrifice, holy, acceptable to God." [754]The Manichæans, on the other hand, say that human bodies are the workmanship of the race of darkness, and the prison in which the captive deity is confined.

Thus Faustus' doctrine is very different from Paul's.

But since whosover preaches to you another gospel than that ye have received must be accursed, what Christ says in Paul is the truth, while Manichæus in Faustus is accursed.

23.

Faustus says also, without knowing what he says, that we have retained the manners of the Gentiles.

But seeing that the just lives by faith, and that the end of the commandment is love out of a pure heart, and a good conscience, and faith unfeigned, and that these three, faith, hope, and love, abide to form the life of believers, it is impossible that there should be similarity in the manners of those who differ in these three things.

Those who believe differently, and hope differently, and love differently, must also live differently. And if we resemble the Gentiles in our use of such things as food and drink, and houses and clothes and baths, and those of us who marry, in taking and keeping wives, and in begetting and bringing up children as our heirs, there is still a great difference between the man who uses these things for some end of his own, and the man who, in using them, gives thanks to God, having no unworthy or erroneous ideas about God. For as you, according to your own heresy, though you eat the same bread as other men, and live upon the produce of the same plants and the water of the same fountain, and are clothed like others in wool and linen, yet lead a different life, not because you eat or drink, or dress differently, but because you differ from others in your ideas and in your faith, and in all these things have in view an end of your own--the end, namely, set forth in your false doctrines; in the same way we, though we resemble the Gentiles in the use of this and other things, do not resemble them in our life; for while the things are the same, the end is different:

for the end we have in view is, according to the just commandment of God, love out of a pure heart, and a good conscience, and faith unfeigned; from which some having erred, are turned to vain jangling.

In this vain jangling you bear the palm, for you do not attend to the fact that so great is the difference of life produced by a different faith, even when the things in possession and use are the same, that though your followers have wives, and in spite of themselves get children, for whom they gather and store up wealth; though they eat flesh, drink wine, bathe, reap harvests, gather vintages, engage in trade, and occupy high official positions, you nevertheless reckon them as belonging to you, and not to the Gentiles, though in their actions they approach nearer to the Gentiles than to you.

And though some of the Gentiles in some things resemble you more than your own followers,--those, for instance, who in superstitious devotion abstain from flesh, and wine, and marriage,--you still count your own followers, even though they use all these things, and so are unlike you, as belonging to the flock of Manichæus rather than those who resemble you in their practices.

You consider as belonging to you a woman that believes in Manichæus, though she is a mother, rather than a Sibyl, though she never marries.

But you will say that many who are called Catholic Christians are adulterers, robbers, misers, drunkards, and whatever else is contrary to sound doctrine.

I ask if none such are to be found in your company, which is almost too small to be called a company.

And because there are some among the Pagans who are not of this character, do you consider them as better than yourselves?

And yet, in fact, your heresy is so blasphemous, that even your followers who are not of such a character are worse than the Pagans who are.

It is therefore no impeachment to sound doctrine, which alone is Catholic, that many wish to take its name, who will not yield to its beneficial influence.

We must bear in mind the true meaning of the contrast which the Lord makes between the little company and the mass of mankind, as spread over all the world; for the company of saints and believers is small, as the amount of grain is small when compared with the heap of chaff; and yet the good grain is quite sufficient far to outnumber you, good and bad together, for good and bad are both strangers to the truth.

In a word, we are not a schism of the Gentiles, for we differ from them greatly for the better; nor are you, for you differ from them greatly for the worse. [755]

Book XXI - Faustus denies that Manichæans believe in two gods

Hyle no god. Augustin discusses at large the doctrine of God and Hyle, and fixes the charge of dualism upon the Manichæans.

1.

Faustus said:
Do we believe in one God or in two?
In one, of course.
If we are accused of making two gods, I reply that it cannot be shown that we ever said anything of the kind.
Why do you suspect us of this?
Because, you say, you believe in two principles, good and evil.
It is true, we believe in two principles; but one we call God, and the other Hyle, or, to use common popular language, the devil.
If you think this means two gods, you may as well think that the health and sickness of which doctors speak are two kinds of health, or that good and evil are two kinds of good, or that wealth and poverty are two kinds of wealth.
If I were describing two things, one white and the other black, or one hot and the other cold, or one sweet and the other bitter, it would appear like idiocy or insanity in you to say that I was describing two white things, or two hot things, or two sweet things.
So, when I assert that there are two principles, God and Hyle, you have no reason for saying that I believe in two gods.

Do you think that we must call them both gods because we attribute, as is proper, all the power of evil to Hyle, and all the power of good to God?

If so, you may as well say that a poison and the antidote must both be called antidotes, because each has a power of its own, and certain effects follow from the action of both.

So also, you may say that a physician and a poisoner are both physicians; or that a just and an unjust man are both just, because both do something.

If this is absurd, it is still more absurd to say that God and Hyle must both be gods, because they both produce certain effects.

It is a very childish and impotent way of arguing, when you cannot refute my statements, to make a quarrel about names.

I grant that we, too, sometimes call the hostile nature God; not that we believe it to be God, but that this name is already adopted by the worshippers of this nature, who in their error suppose it to be God.

Thus the apostle says:

"The god of this world has blinded the minds of them that believe not." [756] He calls him God, because he would be so called by his worshippers; adding that he blinds their minds, to show that he is not the true God.

2.

Augustin replied:

You often speak in your discourses of two gods, as indeed you acknowledge, though at first you denied it.

And you give as a reason for thus speaking the words of the apostle:

"The god of this world has blinded the minds of them that believe not."

Most of us punctuate this sentence differently, and explain it as meaning that the true God has blinded the minds of unbelievers.

They put a stop after the word God, and read the following words together.

Or without this punctuation you may, for the sake of exposition, change the order of the words, and read, "In whom God has blinded the minds of unbelievers of this world," which gives the same sense.

The act of blinding the minds of unbelievers may in one sense be ascribed to God, as the effect not of malice, but of justice.

Thus Paul himself says elsewhere, "Is God unjust, who taketh vengeance?" [757] and again, "What shall we say then?

Is there unrighteousness with God?

God forbid.

For Moses saith, I will have mercy on whom I will have mercy, and will have compassion on whom I will have compassion."

Observe what he adds, after asserting the undeniable truth that there is no unrighteousness with God:

"But what if God, willing to show His wrath, and to make His power known, endured with much long-suffering the vessels of wrath fitted for destruction, and that He might manifest the riches of His grace towards the vessels of mercy, which He hath before prepared unto glory?" [758] etc.

Here it evidently cannot be said that it is one God who shows his wrath, and makes known his power in the vessels of wrath fitted for destruction, and another God who shows his riches in the vessels of mercy.

According to the apostle's doctrine, it is one and the same God who does both.

Hence he says again, "For this cause God gave them up to the lusts of their own heart, to uncleanness, to dishonor their own bodies between themselves;" and immediately after, "For this cause God gave them up unto vile affections;" and again, "And even as they did not like to retain God in their knowledge, God gave them over to a reprobate mind." [759] Here we see how the true and just God blinds the minds of unbelievers.

For in all these words quoted from the apostle no other God is understood than He whose Son, sent by Him, came saying, "For judgment am I come into this world, that they which see not might see, and that they which see might be made blind." [760] Here, again, it is plain to the minds of believers how God blinds the minds of unbelievers.

For among the secret things, which contain the righteous principles of God's judgment, there is a secret which determines that the minds of some shall be blinded, and the minds of some enlightened.

Regarding this, it is well said of God, "Thy judgments are a great deep." [761] The apostle, in admiration of the unfathomable depth of this abyss, exclaims:

"O the depth of the riches both of the wisdom and of the knowledge of God! How unsearchable are His judgments, and His ways past finding out!" [762]

3.

You cannot distinguish between what God does in mercy and what He does in judgment, because you can neither understand nor use the words of our Psalter:

"I will sing of mercy and judgment unto Thee, O Lord." [763] Accordingly, whatever in the feebleness of your frail humanity seems amiss to you, you separate entirely from the will and judgment of God:

for you are provided with another evil god, not by a discovery of truth, but by an invention of folly; and to this god you attribute not only what you do unjustly, but also what you suffer justly.

Thus you assign to God the bestowal of blessings, and take from Him the infliction of judgments, as if He of whom Christ says that He has prepared everlasting fire for the wicked were a different being from Him who makes His sun to rise upon the evil and the good, and sends rain on the just and on the unjust.

Why do you not understand that this great goodness and great severity belong to one God, but because you have not learned to sing of mercy and judgment?

Is not He who causes the sun to rise on the evil and the good, and sends rain on the just and on the unjust, the same who also breaks off the natural branches, and engrafts contrary to nature the wild olive tree?

Does not the apostle, in reference to this, say of this one God:

"Thou seest, then, the goodness and severity of God:

to them which were broken off, severity; but toward thee, goodness, if thou continue in His goodness?" [764] Here it is to be observed how the apostle takes away neither judicial severity from God, nor free-will from man.

It is a profound mystery, impenetrable by human thought, how God both condemns the ungodly and justifies the ungodly; for both these things are said of Him in the truth of the Holy Scriptures.

But is the mysteriousness of the divine judgments any reason for taking pleasure in cavilling against them?

How much more becoming, and more suitable to the limitation of our powers, to feel the same awe which the apostle felt, and to exclaim, "O the depth of the riches both of the wisdom and of the knowledge of God!

How unsearchable are His judgments, and His ways past finding out!"

How much better thus to admire what you cannot explain, than to try to make an evil god in addition to the true God, simply because you cannot understand the one good God!

For it is not a question of names, but of actions.

4.

Faustus glibly defends himself by saying, "We speak not of two gods, but of God and Hyle."

But when you ask for the meaning of Hyle, you find that it is in fact another god.

If the Manichæans gave the name of Hyle, as the ancients did, to the unformed matter which is susceptible of bodily forms, we should not accuse them of making two gods.

But it is pure folly and madness to give to matter the power of forming bodies, or to deny that what has this power is God.

When you give to some other being the power which belongs to the true God of making the qualities and forms, by which bodies, elements, and animals exist, according to their respective modes, whatever name you choose to give to this being, you are chargeable with making another god.

There are indeed two errors in this blasphemous doctrine.

In the first place, you ascribe the act of God to a being whom you are ashamed to call god; though you must call him god as long as you make him do things which only God can do.

In the second place, the good things done by a good God you call bad, and ascribe to an evil god, because you feel a childish horror of whatever shocks the frailty of fallen humanity, and a childish pleasure in the opposite.

So you think snakes are made by an evil being; while you consider the sun so great a good, that you believe it to be not the creature of God, but an emission from His substance.

You must know that the true God, in whom, alas, you have not yet come to believe, made both the snake along with the lower creatures, and the sun along with other exalted creatures.

Moreover, among still more exalted creatures, not heavenly bodies, but spiritual beings, He has made what far surpasses the light of the sun, and what no carnal man can perceive, much less you, who, in your condemnation of flesh, condemn the very principle by which you determine good and evil.

For your only idea of evil is from the disagreeableness of some things to the fleshly sense; and your only idea of good is from sensual gratification.

5.

When I consider the things lowest in the scale of nature, which are within our view, and which, though earthly, and feeble, and mortal, are still the works of God, I am lost in admiration of the Creator, who is so great, in the great works and no less great in the small.

For the divine skill seen in the formation of all creatures in heaven and earth is always like itself, even in those things that differ from one another; for it is everywhere perfect, in the perfection which it gives to everything in its own kind.

We see each creature made not as a whole by itself, but in relation to the rest of the creation; so that the whole divine skill is displayed in the formation of each, arranging each in its proper place and order, and providing what is suitable for all, both separately and unitedly.

See here, lowest in the scale, the animals which fly, and swim, and walk, and creep. These are mortal creatures, whose life, as it is written, "is as a vapor which appeareth for a little time." [765] Each of these, according to the capacity of its kind, contributes the measure appointed in the goodness of the Creator to the completeness of the whole, so that the lowest partake in the good which the highest possess in a greater degree.

Show me, if you can, any animal, however despicable, whose soul hates its own flesh, and does not rather nourish and cherish it, by its vital motion minister to its growth and direct its activity, and exercise a sort of management over a little universe of its own, which it makes subservient to its own preservation.

Even in the discipline of his own body by a rational being, who brings his body under, that earthly passion may not hinder his perception of wisdom, there is love for his own flesh, which he then reduces to obedience, which is its proper condition.

Indeed, you yourselves, although your heresy teaches you a fleshly abhorrence of the flesh, cannot help loving your own flesh, and caring for its safety and comfort, both by avoiding all injury from blows, and falls, and inclement weather, and by seeking for the means of keeping it in health.

Thus the law of nature is too strong for your false doctrine.

6.

Looking at the flesh itself, do we not see in the construction of its vital parts, in the symmetry of form, in the position and arrangement of the limbs of action and the organs of sensation, all acting in harmony; do we not see in the adjustment of measures, in the proportion of numbers, in the order of weights, the handiwork of the true God, of whom it is truly said, "Thou hast ordered all things in measure, and number, and weight"? [766] If your heart was not hardened and corrupted by falsehood, you would understand the invisible things of God from the things which He has made, even in these feeble creatures of flesh.

For who is the author of the things I have mentioned, but He whose unity is the standard of all measure, whose wisdom is the model of all beauty, and whose law is the rule of all order?

If you are blind to these things, hear at least the words of the apostle.

7.

For the apostle, in speaking of the love which husbands ought to have for their wives gives, as an example, the love of the soul for the body.

The words are:

"He that loveth his wife, loveth himself: for no man ever yet hated his own flesh, but nourisheth and cherisheth it, even as Christ the Church." [767] Look at the whole animal creation, and you find in the instinctive self-preservation of every animal this natural principle of love to its own flesh.

It is so not only with men, who, when they live aright, both provide for the safety of their flesh, and keep their carnal appetites in subjection to the use of reason; the brutes also avoid pain, and shrink from death, and escape as rapidly as they can from whatever might break up the construction of their bodies, or dissolve the connection of spirit and flesh; for the brutes, too, nourish and cherish their own flesh.

"For no one ever yet," says the apostle, "hated his own flesh, but nourisheth and cherisheth it, even as Christ the Church."

See where the apostle begins, and to what he ascends.

Consider, if you can, the greatness which creation derives from its Creator, embracing as it does the whole extent from the host of heaven down to flesh and blood, with the beauty of manifold form, and the order of successive gradations.

8.

The same apostle again, when speaking of spiritual gifts as diverse, and yet tending to harmonious action, to illustrate a matter so great, and divine, and mysterious, makes a comparison with the human body,--thus plainly intimating that this flesh is the handiwork of God.

The whole passage, as found in the Epistle to the Corinthians, is so much to the point, that though it is long, I think it not amiss to insert it all:

"Now concerning spiritual gifts, brethren, I would not have you ignorant.

Ye know that ye were Gentiles, carried away unto these dumb idols, even as ye were led.

Wherefore I give you to understand, that no man speaking by the Spirit of God calleth Jesus accursed; and that no man can say that Jesus is the Lord, but by the Holy Ghost.

Now there are diversities of gifts, but the same Spirit. And there are diversities of administrations, but the same Lord.

And there are diversities of operations, but it is the same God which worketh all in all.

But the manifestation of the Spirit is given to every man to profit withal.

For to one is given by the Spirit the word of wisdom; to another the word of knowledge by the same Spirit; to another faith by the same Spirit; to another the gifts of healing by the same Spirit; to another the working of miracles; to another prophecy; to another discerning of spirits; to another divers kinds of tongues; to another the interpretation of tongues:

but all these worketh that one and the self-same Spirit, dividing to every man severally as He will.

For as the body is one, and hath many members, and all the members of that one body, being many, are one body:

so also is Christ.

For by one Spirit are we all baptized into one body, whether we be Jews or Gentiles, whether we be bond or free; and have been all made to drink into one Spirit.

For the body is not one member, but many.

If the foot shall say, Because I am not the hand, I am not of the body; is it therefore not of the body?

And if the ear shall say, Because I am not the eye, I am not of the body; is it therefore not of the body?

If the whole body were an eye, where were the hearing?

If the whole were hearing, where were the smelling?

But now hath God set the members every one of them in the body, as it hath pleased Him.

And if they were all one member, where were the body? But now are they many members, yet but one body.

And the eye cannot say unto the hand, I have no need of thee; nor again the head to the feet, I have no need of you.

Nay, much more those members of the body, which seem to be more feeble, are necessary; and those members of the body which we think to be less honorable, upon these we bestow more abundant honor; and our uncomely parts have more abundant comeliness. For our comely parts have no need; but God hath tempered the body together, having given more abundant honor to that part which lacked: that there should be no schism in the body, but that the members should have the same care one for another.

And whether one member suffer, all the members suffer with it; or one member be honored, all the members rejoice with it." [768] Apart altogether from Christian faith, which would lead you to believe the apostle, if you have common sense to perceive what is self-evident, let each examine and see for himself the plain truth regarding those things of which the apostle speaks,--what greatness belongs to the least, and what goodness to the lowest; for these are the things which the apostle extols, in order to illustrate by means of these common and visible bodily objects, unseen spiritual realities of the most exalted nature.

9.

Whoever, then, denies that our body and its members, which the apostle so approves and extols, are the handiwork of God, you see whom he contradicts, preaching contrary to what you have received.

So, instead of refuting his opinions, I may leave him to be accursed of all Christians.

The apostle says, God tempered the body.

Faustus says, Not God, but Hyle.

Anathemas are more suitable than arguments to such contradictions.

You cannot say that God is here called the God of this world.

And if any one understands the passage where this expression does occur to mean that the devil blinds the minds of unbelievers, we grant that he does so by his evil suggestions, from yielding to which, men lose the light of righteousness in God's righteous retribution. This is all in accordance with sacred Scripture.

The apostle himself speaks of temptation from without:

"I fear lest, as the serpent beguiled Eve through his subtilty, so your minds should be corrupted from the simplicity and purity that is in Christ." [769] To the same purpose are the words, "Evil communications corrupt good manners;" [770] and when he speaks of a man deceiving himself, "Whoever thinketh himself to be anything, when he is nothing, deceiveth himself;" [771] or again, in the passage already quoted of the judgment of God, "God gave them over to a reprobate mind, to do those things which are not convenient." [772] Similarly, in the Old Testament, after the words, "God did not create death, nor hath He pleasure in the destruction of the living," we read, "By the envy of the devil death entered into the world." [773] And again of death, that men may not put the blame from themselves, "The wicked invite her with hands and voice; and thinking her a friend, they are drawn down." [774] Elsewhere, however, it is said, "Good and evil, life and death, riches and poverty, are from the Lord God." [775] This seems perplexing to people who do not understand that, apart from the manifest judgment to follow hereafter upon every evil work, there is an actual judgment at the time; so that in one action, besides the craft of the deceiver and the wickedness of the voluntary agent, there is also the just penalty of the judge:

for while the devil suggests, and man consents, God abandons.

So, if you join the words, God of this world, and understand that the devil blinds unbelievers by his mischievous delusions, the meaning is not a bad one.

For the word God is not used by itself, but with the qualification of this world, that is, of wicked men, who seek to prosper only in this age.

In this sense the world is also called evil, where it is written, "that He might deliver us from this present evil age." [776] In the same way, in the expression, "whose god is their belly," it is only in connection with the word whose that the belly is called god.

So also, in the Psalms, the devils would not be called gods without adding "of the nations." [777] But in the passage we are now considering it is not said, The god of this world, or, Whose god is their belly, or, The gods of the nations are devils; but simply, God has tempered the body, which can be understood only of the true God, the Creator of all.

There is no disparaging addition here, as in the other cases.

But perhaps Faustus will say that God tempered the body, not as the maker of it, in the arrangement of its members, but by mixing His light with it.

Thus Faustus would attribute to some other being than God the construction of the body, and the arrangement of its members, while God tempered the evil of the construction by the mixture of His goodness.

Such are the inventions with which the Manichæans cram feeble minds.

But God, in aid of the feeble, by the mouth of the sacred writers rebukes this opinion.

For we read a few verses before: "God has placed the members every one of them in the body, as it has pleased Him."

Evidently, God is said to have tempered the body, because He has constructed it of many members, which in their union preserve the variety of their respective functions.

10.

Do the Manichæans suppose that the animals which, according to their wild notions, were constructed by Hyle in the race of darkness, had not this harmonious action of their members, commended by the apostle, before God mixed His light with them; so that then the head did say to the feet, or the eye to the hand, I have no need of thee? This is not and cannot be the Manichæan doctrine, for they describe the animals as using all these members, and speak of them as creeping, walking, swimming, flying, each in its own kind.

They could all see, too, and hear, and use the other senses, and nourish and cherish their own bodies with appropriate means and appliances.

Hence, moreover, they had the power of reproduction, for they are spoken of as having offspring.

All these things, of which Faust speaks disparagingly as the works of Hyle, could not be done without that harmonious arrangement which the apostle praises and ascribes to God.

Is it not now plain who is to be followed, and who is to be pronounced accursed? Indeed, the Manichæans tell us of animals that could speak; and their speeches were heard and understood and approved of by all creatures, whether creeping things, or quadrupeds, or birds, or fish.

Amazing and supernatural eloquence!

Especially as they had no grammarian or elocutionist to teach them, and had not passed through the painful experience of the cane and the birch.

Why, Faustus himself began late in life to learn oratory, that he might discourse eloquently on these absurdities; and with all his cleverness, after ruining his health by study, his preaching has gained a mere handful of followers.

What a pity that he was born in the light, and not in that region of darkness!

If he had discoursed there against the light, the whole animal creation, from the biped to the centipede, from the dragon to the shell-fish, would have listened eagerly, and obeyed at once; whereas, when he discourses here against the race of darkness, he is oftener called eloquent than learned, and oftener still a false teacher of the worst kind.

And among the few Manichæans who extol him as a great teacher, he has none of the lower animals as his disciples; and not even his horse is any the wiser for his master's instructions, so that the mixture of a part of deity seems only to make the animals more stupid.

What absurdity is this!

When will these deluded beings have the sense to compare the description in the Manichæan fiction of what the animals were formerly in their own region, with what they are now in this world?

Then their bodies were strong, now they are feeble; then their power of vision was such that they were induced to invade the region of God on account of the beauty which they saw, now it is too weak to face the rays of the sun; then they had intelligence sufficient to understand a discourse addressed to them, now they have no ability of the kind; then this astonishing and effective eloquence was natural, now eloquence of the most meagre kind requires diligent study and preparation.

How many good things did the race of darkness lose by the mixture of good!

11.

Faustus has displayed his ingenuity, in the remarks to which I am now replying, by making for himself a long list of opposites--health and sickness, riches and poverty, white and black, cold and hot, sweet and bitter.

We need not say much about black and white.

Or, if there is a character for good or evil in colors, so that white must be ascribed to God and black to Hyle; if God threw a white color on the wings of birds, when Hyle, as the Manichæans say, created them, where had the crows gone to when the swans got whitened?

Nor need we discuss heat and cold, for both are good in moderation, and dangerous in excess.

With regard to the rest, Faustus probably intended that good and evil, which he might as well have put first, should be understood as including the rest, so that health, riches, white, hot, sweet, should belong to good; and sickness, poverty, black, cold, bitter, to evil.

The ignorance and folly of this is obvious.

It might look like reviling if I were to take up separately white and black, hot and cold, sweet and bitter, health and sickness.

For if white and sweet are both good, and black and bitter evil, how is it that most grapes and all olives become black as they become sweet, and so get good by getting evil?

And if heat and health are both good, and cold and sickness evil, why do bodies become sick when heated?

Is it healthy to have fever?

But I let these things pass, for they may have been put down hastily, or they may have been given as merely instances of opposition, and not as being good and bad, especially as it is nowhere stated that the fire among the race of darkness is cold, so that heat in this case must unquestionably be evil.

12.

We pass on, then, to health, riches, sweetness, which Faustus evidently accounts good in his contrasts.

Was there no health of body in the race of darkness where animals were born and grew up and brought forth, and had such vitality, that when some that were with child were taken, as the story is, and were put in bonds in heaven, even the abortive offspring of a premature birth, falling from heaven to earth, nevertheless lived, and grew, and produced the innumerable kinds of animals which now exist?

Or were there no riches where trees could grow not only in water and wind, but in smoke and fire, and could bear such a rich produce, that animals, according to their several kinds, sprang from the fruit, and were provided with the means of subsistence from those fertile trees, and showed how well fed they were by a numerous progeny?

And all this where there was no toil in cultivation, and no inclement change from summer to winter, for there was no sun to give variety to the seasons by his annual course.

There must have been perennial productiveness where the trees were not only born in their own element, but had a supply of appropriate nourishment to make them constantly fertile; as we see orange-trees bearing fruit all the year round if they are well watered.

The riches must have been abundant, and they must have been secure from harm; for there could be no fear of hailstorms when there were no light-gatherers who, in your fable, set the thunder in motion.

13.

Nor would the beings in this race of darkness have sought for food if it had not been sweet and pleasant, so that they would have died from want.

For we find that all bodies have their peculiar wants, according to which food is either agreeable or offensive.

If it is agreeable, it is said to be sweet or pleasant; if it is offensive, it is said to be bitter or sour, or in some way disagreeable.

In human beings we find that one desires food which another dislikes, from a difference in constitution or habit or state of health.

Still more, animals of quite different make can find pleasure in food which is disagreeable to us.

Why else should the goats feed so eagerly on the wild olives?

This food is sweet to them, as in some sicknesses honey tastes bitter to us.

To a thoughtful inquirer these things suggest the beauty of the arrangement in which each finds what suits it, and the greatness of the good which extends from the lowest to the highest, and from the material to the spiritual.

As for the race of darkness, if an animal sprung from any element fed on what was produced by that element, doubtless the food must have been sweet from its appropriateness.

Again, if this animal had found food of another element, the want of appropriateness would have appeared in its offensiveness to the taste.

Such offensiveness is called sourness, or bitterness, or disagreeableness, or something of the kind; or if its adverse nature is such as to destroy the harmony of the bodily constitution, and so take away life or reduce the strength, it is called poison, simply on account of this want of appropriateness, while it may nourish the kind of life to which it is appropriate.

So, if a hawk eat the bread which is our daily food, it dies; and we die if we eat hellebore, which cattle often feed on, and which may itself in a certain form be used as a medicine.

If Faustus had known or thought of this, he would not have given poison and antidote as an example of the two natures of good and evil, as if God were the antidote and Hyle the poison.

For the same thing, of one and the same nature, kills or cures, as it is used appropriately or inappropriately.

In the Manichæan legends, their god might be said to have been poison to the race of darkness; for he so injured their bodies, that from being strong, they became utterly feeble.

But then again, as the light was itself taken, and subjected to loss and injury, it may be said to have been poison to itself.

14.

Instead of one good and one evil principle, you seem to make both good or both evil, or rather two good and two evil; for they are good in themselves, and evil to one another.

We may see afterwards which is the better or the worse; but meanwhile we may think of them as both good in themselves.

Thus God reigned in one region, while Hyle reigned in the other.

There was health in both kingdoms, and rich produce in both; both had a numerous progeny, and both tasted the sweetness of pleasures suitable to their respective natures.

But the race of darkness, say the Manichæans, excepting the part which was evil to the light which it bordered on, was also evil to itself.

As, however, I have already pointed out many good things in it, if you can point out its evils, there will still be two good kingdoms, though the one where there are no evils will be the better of the two.

What, then, do you call its evils?

They plundered, and killed, and devoured one another, according to Faustus.

But if they did nothing else than this, how could such numerous hosts be born and grow up to maturity?

They must have enjoyed peace and tranquillity too.

But, allowing the kingdom where there is no discord to be the better of the two, still they should both be called good, rather than one good and the other bad. Thus the better kingdom will be that where they killed neither themselves nor one another; and the worse, or less good, where, though they fought with one another, each separate animal preserved its own nature in health and safety.

But we cannot make much difference between your god and the prince of darkness, whom no one opposed, whose reign was acknowledged by all, and whose proposals were unanimously agreed to.

All this implies great peace and harmony.

Those kingdoms are happy where all agree heartily in obedience to the king.

Moreover, the rule of this prince extended not only to his own species, or to bipeds whom you make the parents of mankind, but to all kinds of animals, who waited in his presence, obeying his commands, and believing his declarations.

Do you think people are so stupid as not to recognize the attributes of deity in your description of this prince, or to think it possible that you can have another?

If the authority of this prince rested on his resources, he must have been very powerful; if on his fame, he must have been renowned; if on love, the regard must have been universal; if on fear, he must have kept the strictest order.

If some evils, then, were mixed with so many good things, who that knows the meaning of words would call this the nature of evil?

Besides, if you call this the nature of evil, because it was not only evil to the other nature, but was also evil in itself, was there no evil, think you, in the dire necessity to which your god was subjected before the mixture with the opposite nature, so that he was compelled to fight with it, and to send his own members to be swallowed up so mercilessly as to be beyond the hope of complete recovery?

This was a great evil in that nature before its mixture with the only thing you allow to be evil.

Your god must either have had it in his power not to be injured and sullied by the race of darkness, in which case his own folly must have brought him into trouble; or if his substance was liable to corruption, the object of your worship is not the incorruptible God of whom the apostle speaks. [778]Does not, then this liability to corruption, even apart from the actual experience, seem to you to be an evil in your god?

15.

It is plain, moreover, that either he must have been destitute of prescience,--a great defect, surely, in the Deity, not to know what is coming; or if he had prescience, he can never have felt secure, but must have been in constant terror, which you must allow to be a serious evil.

There must have been the fear at every moment, that the time might be come for that conflict in which his members suffered such loss and contamination, that to liberate and purify them costs infinite labor, and, after all, can be done only partially.

If it is going too far to attribute this state of alarm to the Deity himself, his members at least must have dreaded the prospect of suffering all these evils. Then, again, if they were ignorant of what was to happen, the substance of your god must have been so far wanting in prescience.

How many evils do you reckon in your chief good?

Perhaps you will say that they had no fear, because they foresaw, along with the suffering, their liberation and triumph.

But still they must have feared for their companions, if they knew that they were to be cut off from their kingdom, and bound for ever in the mass of darkness.

16.

Had they not the charity to feel a kindly sympathy for those who were doomed to suffer eternal punishment, without having committed any sin?

These souls that were to be bound up with the mass, were not they too part of your god?

Were they not of the same origin, the same substance?

They at least must have felt grief or fear in the prospect of their own eternal bondage.

To say that they did not know what was to happen, while the others did, is to make one and the same substance partly acquainted with the future, and partly ignorant.

How can you call this substance the pure, and perfect, and supreme good, if there were such evils in it, even before its mixture with the evil principle?

You will have to confess your two principles either both good or both evil.

If you make two evils, you may make either of them the worse, as you please.

But if you make two goods, we shall have to inquire which you make the better.

Meanwhile there is an end to your doctrine of two principles, one good and the other evil, which are in fact two gods, one good and the other evil.

But if hurting another is evil, they both hurt one another.

Perhaps the greater evil was in the principle that first began the attack.

But if one began the injury, the other returned it; and not by the law of compensation, an eye for an eye, which you are foolish enough to find fault with, but with far greater severity.

You must choose which you will call the worse,--the one that began the injury, or the one that had the will and the power to do still greater injury.

The one tried to get a share in the enjoyment of light; the other effected the entire overthrow of its opponent.

If the one had got what it desired, it would certainly have done no harm to itself.

But the other, in the discomfiture of its adversary, did great mischief to part of itself; reminding us of the well-known passionate exclamation, which is on record as having been actually used, "Perish our friends, if that will rid us of our enemies." [779]For part of your god was sent to suffer hopeless contamination, that there might be a covering for the mass in which the enemy is to be buried for ever alive.

So much will he continue to be dreaded even when conquered and bound, that the security, such as it is, of one part of the deity must be purchased by the eternal misery of the other parts.

Such is the harmlessness of the good principle!

Your god, it appears, is guilty of the crime with which you charge the race of darkness--of injuring both friends and enemies.

The charge is proved in the case of your god, by that final mass in which his enemies are confined, while his own subjects are involved in it.

In fact, the principle that you call god is the more injurious of the two, both to friends and to enemies.

In the case of Hyle, there was no desire to destroy the opposite kingdom, but only to possess it; and though some of its subjects were put to death by the violence of others, they appeared again in other forms, so that in the alternation of life and death they had intervals of enjoyment in their history.

But your god, with all the omnipotence and perfect excellence that you ascribe to him, dooms his enemies to eternal destruction, and his friends to eternal punishment.

And the height of insanity is in believing that while internal contest occasions the injury of the members of Hyle, victory brings punishment to the members of God.

What means this folly?

To use Faustus' comparison of God and Hyle to the antidote and poison, the antidote seems to be more mischievous than the poison.

We do not hear of Hyle shutting up God for ever in a mass of darkness, or driving its own members into it; or, which is worst of all, slandering this unfortunate remnant, as an excuse for not effecting its purification.

For Manichæus, in his Fundamental Epistle, says that these souls deserved to be thus punished, because they allowed themselves to be led away from their original brightness, and became enemies of holy light; whereas it was God himself that sent them to lose themselves in the region of darkness, that light might be opposed to light:

which was unjust, if he forced them against their will; while, if they went willingly, he is ungrateful in punishing them. These souls can never have been happy, if they were tormented with fear before the conflict, from knowing that they were to become enemies to their original principle, and then in the conflict were hopelessly contaminated, and afterwards eternally condemned.

On the other hand, they can never have been divine, if before the conflict they were unaware of what was coming, from want of prescience, and then showed feebleness in the conflict, and suffered misery afterwards.

And what is true of them must be true of God, since they are of the same substance.

Is there any hope of your seeing the folly of these blasphemies?

You attempt, indeed, to vindicate the goodness of God, by asserting that Hyle when shut up is prevented from doing any more injury to itself.

Hyle, it seems, is to get some good, when it has no longer any good mixed with it.

Perhaps, as God before the conflict had the evil of necessity, when the good was unmixed with evil, so Hyle after the conflict is to have the good of rest, when the evil is unmixed with good.

Your principles are thus either two evils, one worse than the other; or two goods, both imperfect, but one better than the other.

The better, however, is the more miserable; for if the issue of this great conflict is that the enemy gets some good by the cessation of mutual injuries in Hyle, while God's own subjects suffer the serious evil of being driven into the mass of darkness, we may ask who has got the victory.

The poison, we are to understand, is Hyle, where, nevertheless, animal life found a plentiful supply of the means of growth and productiveness; while the antidote is God, who could condemn his own members, but could not restore them.

In reality, it is as absurd to call the one Hyle, as it is to call the other God. These are the follies of men who turn to fables because they cannot bear sound doctrine. [780]

Book XXII - Faustus states his objections to the morality of the law and the prophets, and Augustin seeks by the application of the type and the allegory to explain away the moral difficulties of the Old Testament

1.
Faustus said:
You ask why we blaspheme the law and the prophets. We are so far from professing or feeling any hostility to the law and the prophets, that we are ready, if you will allow us, to declare the falsehood of all the writings which make the law and the prophets appear objectionable.

But this you refuse to admit, and by maintaining the authority of your writers, you bring a perhaps unmerited reproach upon the prophets; you slander the patriarchs, and dishonor the law. You are so unreasonable as to deny that your writers are false, while you uphold the piety and sanctity of those who are described in these writings as guilty of the worst crimes, and as leading wicked lives. These opinions are inconsistent; for either these were bad characters, or the writers were untruthful.

2.
Supposing, then, that we agree in condemning the writers, we may succeed in vindicating the law and the prophets.

By the law must be understood not circumcision, or Sabbaths, or sacrifices, or the other Jewish observances, but the true law, viz., Thou shall not kill, Thou shalt not commit adultery, Thou shalt not bear false witness, and so on.

To this law, promulgated throughout the world, that is, at the commencement of the present constitution of the world, the Hebrew writers did violence, by infecting it with the pollution of their disgusting precepts about circumcision and sacrifice.

As a friend of the law, you should join with me in condemning the Jews for injuring the law by this mixture of unsuitable precepts.

Plainly, you must be aware that these precepts are not the law, or any part of the law, since you claim to be righteous, though you make no attempt to keep the precepts.

In seeking to lead a righteous life, you pay great regard to the commandments which forbid sinful actions, while you take no notice of the Jewish observances; which would be unjustifiable if they were one and the same law.

You resent as a foul reproach being called negligent of the precept, "Thou shalt not kill," or "Thou shall not commit adultery."

And if you showed the same resentment at being called uncircumcised, or negligent of the Sabbath, it would be evident that you considered both to be the law and the commandment of God.

In fact, however, you consider the honor and glory of keeping the one no way endangered by disregard of the other.

It is plain, as I have said, that these observances are not the law, but a disfigurement of the law.

If we condemn them, it is not as being genuine, but as spurious. In this condemnation there is no reproach of the law, or of God its author, but only of those who published their shocking superstitions under these names.

If we sometimes abuse the venerable name of law in attacking the Jewish precepts, the fault is yours, for refusing to distinguish between Hebrew observances and the law.

Only restore to the law its proper dignity, by removing these foul Israelitish blots; grant that these writers are guilty of disfiguring the law, and you will see at once that we are the enemies not of the law, but of Judaism.

You are misled by the word law; for you do not know to what that name properly belongs.

3.

The Writings Against the Manichaeans and Against the Donatists: Part I - The Manichaeans

For my part, I see no reason for your thinking that we blaspheme your prophets and patriarchs.

There would indeed be some ground for the charge, if we had been directly or remotely the authors of the account given of their actions.

But as this account is written either by themselves, in a criminal desire to be famous for their misdeeds, or by their companions and coevals, why should you blame us?

You condemn them in abhorrence of the wicked actions of which they have voluntarily declared themselves guilty, though there was no occasion for such a confession.

Or if the narrative is only a malicious fiction, let its authors be punished, let the books be condemned, let the prophetic name be cleared from this foul reproach, let the patriarchs recover the respect due to their simplicity and purity of managers.

4.

These books, moreover, contain shocking calumnies against God himself.

We are told that he existed from eternity in darkness, and admired the light when he saw it; that he was so ignorant of the future, that he gave Adam a command, not foreseeing that it would be broken; that his perception was so limited that he could not see Adam when, from the knowledge of his nakedness, he hid himself in a corner of Paradise; that envy made him afraid lest his creature man should taste of the tree of life, and live for ever; that afterwards he was greedy for blood, and fat from all kinds of sacrifices, and jealous if they were offered to any one but himself; that he was enraged sometimes against his enemies, sometimes against his friends; that he destroyed thousands of men for a slight offense, or for nothing; that he threatened to come with a sword and spare nobody, righteous or wicked. The authors of such bold libels against God might very well slander the men of God.

You must join with us in laying the blame on the writers if you wish to vindicate the prophets.

5.

Again, we are not responsible for what is said of Abraham, that in his irrational craving to have children, and not believing God, who promised that his wife Sara should have a son, he defiled himself with a mistress, with the knowledge of his wife, which only made it worse; [781] or that, in sacrilegious profanation of his marriage, he on different occasions, from avarice and greed, sold his wife Sara for the gratification of the kings Abimelech and Pharas, telling them that she was his sister, because she was very fair. [782] The narrative is not ours, which tells how Lot, Abraham's brother, after his escape from Sodom, lay with his two daughters on the mountain [783] (better for him to have perished in the conflagration of Sodom, than to have burned with incestuous passion); or how Isaac imitated his father's conduct, and called his wife Rebecca his sister, that he might gain a shameful livelihood by her; [784] or how his son Jacob, husband of four wives--two full sisters, Rachel and Leah, and their handmaids--led the life of a goat among them, so that there was a daily strife among his women should be the first to lay hold of him when he came from the field, ending sometimes in their hiring him from one another for the night; [785] or, again, how his son Judah slept with his daughter-in-law Tamar, after she had been married to two of his sons, deceived, we are told, by the harlot's dress which Tamar put on, knowing that her father-in-law was in the habit of associating with such characters; [786] or how David, after having a number of wives, seduced the wife of his soldier Uriah, and caused Uriah himself to be killed in the battle; [787] or how his son Solomon had three hundred wives, and seven hundred concubines, and princesses without number; [788] or how the first prophet Hosea got children from a prostitute, and, what is worse, it is said that this disgraceful conduct was enjoined by God; [789] or how Moses committed murder, [790] and plundered Egypt, [791] and waged wars, and commanded, or himself perpetrated, many cruelties. [792] And he too was not content with one wife.

We are neither directly nor remotely the authors of these and similar narratives, which are found in the books of the patriarchs and the prophets.

Either your writers forged these things, or the fathers are really guilty.

Choose which you please; the crime in either case is detestable, for vicious conduct and falsehood are equally hateful.

6.

Augustin replied:

You understand neither the symbols of the law nor the acts of the prophets, because you do not know what holiness or righteousness means.

We have repeatedly shown at great length, that the precepts and symbols of the Old Testament contained both what was to be fulfilled in obedience through the grace bestowed in the New Testament, and what was to be set aside as a proof of its having been fulfilled in the truth now made manifest.

For in the love of God and of our neighbor is secured the accomplishment of the precepts of the law, while the accomplishment of its promises is shown in the abolition of circumcision, and of other typical observances formerly practised. By the precept men were led, through a sense of guilt to desire salvation; by the promise they were led to find in the typical observances the assurance that the Saviour would come.

The salvation desired was to be obtained through the grace bestowed on the appearance of the New Testament; and the fulfillment of the expectation rendered the types no longer necessary.

The same law that was given by Moses became grace and truth in Jesus Christ.

By the grace in the pardon of sin, the precept is kept in force in the case of those supported by divine help.

By the truth the symbolic rites are set aside, that the promise might, in those who trust in the divine faithfulness, be brought to pass.

7.

Those, accordingly, who, finding fault with what they do not understand, call the typical institutions of the law disfigurements and excrescences, are like men displeased with things of which they do not know the use.

As if a deaf man, seeing others move their lips in speaking, were to find fault with the motion of the mouth as needless and unsightly; or as if a blind man, on hearing a house commended, were to test the truth of what he heard by passing his hand over the surface of the wall, and on coming to the windows were to cry out against them as flaws in the level, or were to suppose that the wall had fallen in.

8.

How shall I make those whose minds are full of vanity understand that the actions of the prophets were also mystical and prophetic?

The vanity of their minds is shown in their thinking that we believe God to have once existed in darkness, because it is written, "Darkness was over the deep."[793] As if we called the deep God, where there was darkness, because the light did not exist there before God made it by His word.

From their not distinguishing between the light which is God, and the light which God made, they imagine that God must have been in darkness before He made light, because darkness was over the deep before God said, "Let there be light, and there was light."

In the New Testament both these things are ascribed to God.

For we read, "God is light, and in Him is no darkness at all;"[794] and again, "God, who commanded the light to shine out of darkness, hath shined in our hearts."[795] So also, in the Old Testament, the name "Brightness of eternal light"[796] is given to the wisdom of God, which certainly was not created, for by it all things were made; and of the light which exists only as the production of this wisdom it is said, "Thou wilt light my candle, O Lord; my God, Thou wilt enlighten my darkness."[797] In the same way, in the beginning, when darkness was over the deep, God said, "Let there be light, and there was light," which only the light-giving light, which is God Himself, could have made.

9.

For as God is His own eternal happiness, and is besides the bestower of happiness, so He is His own eternal light, and is also the bestower of light.

He envies the good of none, for He is Himself the source of happiness to all good beings; He fears the evil of none, for the loss of all evil beings is in their being abandoned by Him.

He can neither be benefited by those on whom He Himself bestows happiness, nor is He afraid of those whose misery is the doom awarded by His own judgment.

Very different, O Manichæus, is the object of your worship. You have departed from God in the pursuit of your own fancies, which of all kinds have increased and multiplied in your foolish roving hearts, drinking in through the sense of sight the light of the heavenly bodies.

This light, though it too is made by God, is not to be compared to the light created in the minds of the pious, whom God brings out of darkness into light, as He brings them out of sinfulness into righteousness.

Still less can it be compared to that inaccessible light from which all kinds of light are derived.

Nor is this light inaccessible to all; for "blessed are the pure in heart, for they shall see God."[798] "God is light, and in Him is no darkness at all;" but the wicked shall not see light, as is said in Isaiah.[799] To them the light-giving light is inaccessible.

From the light comes not only the spiritual light in the minds of the pious, but also the material light, which is not denied to the wicked, but is made to rise on the evil and on the good.

10.

So, when darkness was over the deep, He who was light said, "Let there be light."
From what light this light came is clear; for the words are, "God said."
What light is that which was made, is not so clear.

For there has been a friendly discussion among students of the sacred Scriptures, whether God then made the light in the minds of the angels, or, in other words, these rational spirits themselves, or some material light which exists in the higher regions of the universe beyond our ken.

For on the fourth day He made the visible luminaries of heaven.

And it is also a question whether these bodies were made at the same time as their light, or were somehow kindled from the light made already.

But whoever reads the sacred writings in the pious spirit which is required to understand them, must be convinced that whatever the light was which was made when, at the time that darkness was over the deep, God said, "Let there be light," it was created light, and the creating Light was the maker of it.

11.

Nor does it follow that God, before He made light, abode in darkness, because it is said that darkness was over the deep, and then that the Spirit of God moved on the waters.

The deep is the unfathomable abyss of the waters.

And the carnal mind might suppose that the Spirit abode in the darkness which was over the deep, because it is said that He moved on the waters.

This is from not understanding how the light shineth in darkness, and the darkness comprehendeth it not, till by the word of God those who were darkness are made light, and it is said to them, "Ye were once darkness, but now are ye light in the Lord." [800]But if rational minds which are in darkness through a sinful will cannot comprehend the light of the wisdom of God, though it is present everywhere, because they are separated from it not in place, but in disposition:

why may not the Spirit of God have moved on the darkness of the waters, when He moved on the waters, though at an immeasurable distance from it, not in place, but in nature?

12.

In all this I know I am singing to deaf ears; but the Lord, from whom is the truth which we speak, can open some ears to catch the strain.

But what shall we say of those critics of the Holy Scriptures who object to God's being pleased with His own works, and find fault with the words, "God saw the light that it was good," as if this meant that God admired the light as something new?

God's seeing His works that they were good, means that the Creator approved of His own works as pleasing to Himself.

For God cannot be forced to do anything against His will, so that He should not be pleased with His own work; nor can He do anything by mistake, so that He should regret having done it.

Why should the Manichæans object to our God seeing His work that it was good, when their god placed a covering before himself when he mingled his own members with the darkness?

For instead of seeing his work that it is good, he refuses to look at it because it is evil.

13.

Faustus speaks of our God as astonished, which is not said in Scripture; nor does it follow that one must be astonished when he sees anything to be good.

There are many good things which we see without being astonished, as if they were better than we expected; we merely approve of them as being what they ought to be.

We can, however, give an instance of God being astonished, not from the Old Testament, which the Manichæans assail with undeserved reproach, but from the New Testament, which they profess to believe in order to entrap the unwary.

For they acknowledge Christ as God, and use this as a bait to entice Christ's followers into their snares.

God, then, was astonished when Christ was astonished.

For we read in the Gospel, that when Christ heard the faith of a certain centurion, He was astonished, and said to His disciples, "Verily I have not found so great faith, no, not in Israel." [801]We have already given our explanation of the words, "God saw that it was good."

Better men may give a better explanation. Meanwhile let the Manichæans explain Christ's being astonished at what He foresaw before it happened, and knew before He heard it.

For though seeing a thing to be good is quite different from being astonished at it, in this case there is some resemblance, for Jesus was astonished at the light of faith which He Himself had created in the heart of the centurion; for Jesus is the true light, which enlighteneth every man that cometh into the world.

14.

Thus an irreligious Pagan might bring the same reproaches against Christ in the Gospel, as Faustus brings against God in the Old Testament.

He might say that Christ lacked foresight, not only because He was astonished at the faith of the centurion, but because He chose Judas as a disciple who proved disobedient to His commands; as Faustus objects to the precept given in Paradise, which, as it turned out, was not obeyed.

He might also cavil at Christ's not knowing who touched Him, when the woman suffering from an issue of blood touched the hem of His garment; as Faustus blames God for not knowing where Adam had hid himself.

If this ignorance is implied in God's saying, "Where art thou, Adam?" [802] the same may be said of Christ's asking, "Who touched me?" [803] The Pagans also might call Christ timid and envious, in not wishing five of the ten virgins to gain eternal life by entering into His kingdom, and in shutting them out, so that they knocked in vain in their entreaty to have the door opened, as if forgetful of His own promise, "Knock, and it shall be opened unto you;" [804] as Faustus charges God with fear and envy in not admitting man after his sin to eternal life.

Again, he might call Christ greedy of the blood, not of beasts, but of men, because he said, "He that loseth his life for my sake, shall keep it unto life eternal;" [805] as Faustus reproaches God in reference to those animal sacrifices which prefigured the sacrifice of blood-shedding by which we are redeemed. He might also accuse Christ of jealousy, because in narrating His driving the buyers and sellers out of the temple, the evangelist quotes as applicable to Him the words, "The jealousy of Thine house hath eaten me up;" [806] as Faustus accuses God of jealousy in forbidding sacrifices to be offered to other gods.

He might say that Christ was angry with both His friends and His enemies: with His friends, because He said, "The servant that knows his lord's will, and doeth it not, shall be beaten with many stripes;" and with His enemies, because He said, "If any one shall not receive you, shake off against him the dust of your shoes; verily I say unto you, that it shall be more tolerable for Sodom in the day of judgment than for that city;" [807] as Faustus accuses God of being angry at one time with His friends, and at another with His enemies; both of whom are spoken of thus by the apostle: "They that have sinned without law shall perish without law, and they that have sinned in the law shall be judged by the law." [808] Or he might say that Christ shed the blood of many without mercy, for a slight offense or for nothing.

For to a Pagan there would appear to be little or no harm in not having a wedding garment at the marriage feast, for which our King in the Gospel commanded a man to be bound hand and foot, and cast into outer darkness; [809] or in not wishing to have Christ for a king, which is the sin of which Christ says, "Those that would not have me to reign over them, bring hither and slay before me;" [810] as Faustus blames God in the Old Testament for slaughtering thousands of human beings for slight offenses, as Faustus calls them, or for nothing.

Again, if Faustus finds fault with God's threatening to come with the sword, and to spare neither the righteous nor the wicked, might not the Pagan find as much fault with the words of the Apostle Paul, when he says of our God," He spared not His own Son, but gave Him up for us all;"[811] or of Peter, when, in exhorting the saints to be patient in the midst of persecution and slaughter, he says, "It is time that judgment begin from the house of God; and if it first begin at us, what shall the end be of them that believe not the gospel of the Lord?

And if the righteous scarcely be saved, where shall the ungodly and sinner appear?"[812] What can be more righteous than the Only-Begotten, whom nevertheless the Father did not spare?

And what can be plainer than that the righteous also are not spared, but chastised with manifold afflictions, as is clearly implied in the words, "If the righteous scarcely are saved"?

As it is said in the Old Testament, "Whom the Lord loveth He correcteth, and chastiseth every son whom He receiveth;" [813] and, "If we receive good at the hand of the Lord, shall we not also receive evil?" [814] So we read also in the New Testament, "Whom I love I rebuke and chasten;"[815] and, "If we judge ourselves, we shall not be judged of the Lord; but when we are judged, we are corrected of the Lord, that we may not be condemned with the world." [816] If a Pagan were to make such objections to the New Testament, would not the Manichæans try to answer them, though they themselves make similar objections to the Old Testament?

But supposing them able to answer the Pagan, how absurd it would be to defend in the one Testament what they find fault with in the other!

But if they could not answer the objections of the Pagan, why should they not allow in both Testaments, instead of in one only, that what appears wrong to unbelievers, from their ignorance, should be believed to be right by pious readers even when they also are ignorant?

15.

Perhaps our opponents will maintain that these parallel passages quoted from the New Testament are themselves neither authoritative nor true:

for they claim the impious liberty of holding and teaching, that whatever they deem favorable to their heresy was said by Christ and the apostles; while they have the profane boldness to say, that whatever in the same writings is unfavorable to them is a spurious interpolation. I have already at some length, as far as the intention of the present work required, exposed the unreasonableness of this assault upon the authority of the whole of Scripture.

16.

At present I would call attention to the fact, that when the Manichæans, although they disguise their blasphemous absurdities under the name of Christianity, bring such objections against the Christian Scriptures, we have to defend the authority of the divine record in both Testaments against the Manichæans as much as against the Pagans. A Pagan might find fault with passages in the New Testament in the same way as Faustus does with what he calls unworthy representations of God in the Old Testament; and the Pagan might be answered by the quotation of similar passages from his own authors, as in Paul's speech at Athens. [817]Even in Pagan writings we might find the doctrine that God created and constructed the world, and that He is the giver of light, which does not imply that before light was made He abode in darkness; and that when His work was finished He was elated with joy, which is more than saying that He saw that it was good; and that He made a law with rewards for obedience, and punishments for disobedience, by which they do not mean to say that God was ignorant of the future, because He gave a law to those by whom it was to be broken.

Nor could they make asking questions a proof of a want of foresight even in a human being; for in their books many questions are asked only for the purpose of using the answers for the conviction of the persons addressed:

for the questioner knows not only what answer he desires, but what will actually be given.

Again, if the Pagan tried to make out God to be envious of any one, because He will not give happiness to the wicked, he would find many passages in the writings of his own authors in support of this principle of the divine government.

17.

The only objection that a Pagan would make on the subject of sacrifice would refer to our reason for finding fault with Pagan sacrifices, when in the Old Testament God is described as requiring men to offer sacrifice to Him.

If I were to reply at length on this subject, I might prove to him that sacrifice is due only to the one true God, and that this sacrifice was offered by the one true Priest, the Mediator of God and man; and that it was proper that this sacrifice should be pre-figured by animal sacrifices, in order to foreshadow the flesh and blood of the one sacrifice for the remission of sins contracted by flesh and blood, which shall not inherit the kingdom of God:

for the natural body will be endowed with heavenly attributes, as the fire in the sacrifice typified the swallowing up of death in victory.

Those observances properly belonged to the people whose kingdom and priesthood were prophetic of the King and Priest who should come to govern and to consecrate believers in all nations, and to lead them into the kingdom of heaven, and the holy society of angels and eternal life.

And as this true sacrifice was piously set forth in the Hebrew observances, so it was impiously caricatured by the Pagans, because, as the apostle says, what they offer they offer to devils, and not to God. [818]The typical rite of blood-shedding in sacrifice dates from the earliest ages, pointing forward from the outset of human history to the passion of the Mediator.

For Abel is mentioned in the sacred Scripture as the first who offered such sacrifices.[819]We need not therefore wonder that fallen angels who occupy the air, and whose chief sins are pride and falsehood, should demand from their worshippers by whom they wished to be considered as gods what they knew to be due to God only.

This deception was favored by the folly of the human heart, especially when regret for the dead led to the making of likenesses, and so to the use of images. [820]By the increase of this homage, divine honors came to be paid to the dead as dwelling in heaven, while devils took their place on earth as the objects of worship, and required that their deluded and degraded votaries should present sacrifices to them.

Thus the nature of sacrifice as due only to God appears not only when God righteously claims it, but also when a false god proudly arrogates it.

If the Pagan was slow to believe these things, I should argue from the prophecies, and point out that, though uttered long ago, they are now fulfilled.

If he still remained in unbelief, this is rather to be expected than to be wondered at; for the prophecy itself intimates that all would not believe.

18.

If the Pagan, in the next place, were to find fault with both Testaments as attributing jealousy to God and Christ, he would only show his own ignorance of literature, or his forgetfulness.

For though their philosophers distinguish between desire and passion, joy and gratification, caution and fear, gentleness and tender-heartedness, prudence and cunning, boldness and daring, and so on, giving the first name in each pair to what is good, and the second to what is bad, their books are notwithstanding full of instances in which, by the abuse of these words, virtues are called by the names which properly belong to vices; as passion is used for desire, gratification for joy, fear for caution, tender-heartedness for gentleness, cunning for prudence, daring for boldness.

The cases are innumerable in which speech exhibits similar inaccuracies.

Moreover, each language has its own idioms.

For in religious writings I remember no instance of the word tender-heartedness being used in a bad sense.

And common usage affords examples of similar peculiarities in the use of words.

In Greek, one word stands for two distinct things, labor and pain; while we have a separate name for each.

Again, we use the word in two senses, as when we say of what is not dead, that it has life; and again, of any one that he is a man of good life, whereas in Greek each of these meanings has a word of its own.

So that, apart from the abuse of words which prevails in all languages, it may be an Hebrew idiom to use jealousy in two senses, as a man is called jealous when he suffers from a diseased state of mind caused by distress on account of the faithlessness of his wife, in which sense the word cannot be applied to God; or as when diligence is manifested in guarding conjugal chastity, in which sense it is profitable for us not only unhesitatingly to admit, but thankfully to assert, that God is jealous of His people when He calls them His wife, and warns them against committing adultery with a multitude of false gods.

The same may be said of the anger of God. For God does not suffer perturbation when He visits men in anger; but either by an abuse of the word, or by a peculiarity of idiom, anger is used in the sense of punishment.

19.

The slaughter of multitudes would not seem strange to the Pagan, unless he denied the judgment of God, which Pagans do not; for they allow that all things in the universe, from the highest to the lowest, are governed by God's providence.

But if he would not allow this, he would be convinced either by the authority of Pagan writers, or by the more tedious method of demonstration; and if still obstinate and perverse, he would be left to the judgment which he denies.

Then, if he were to give instances of the destruction of men for no offense, or for a very slight one, we should show that these were offenses, and that they were not slight.

For instance, to take the case already referred to of the wedding garment, we should prove that it was a great crime in a man to attend the sacred feast, seeking not the bridegroom's glory, but his own, or whatever the garment may be found on better interpretation to signify.

And in the case of the slaughter before the king of those who would not have him to reign over them, we might perhaps easily prove that, though it may be no sin in a man to refuse to obey his fellow-man, it is both a fault and a great one to reject the reign of Him in whose reign alone is there righteousness, and happiness, and continuance.

20.

Lastly, as regards Faustus' crafty insinuation, that the Old Testament misrepresents God as threatening to come with a sword which will spare neither the righteous nor the wicked, if the words were explained to the Pagan, he would perhaps disagree neither with the Old Testament nor with the New; and he might see the beauty of the parable in the Gospel, which people who pretend to be Christians either misunderstand from their blindness, or reject from their perversity. The great husbandman of the vine uses his pruning-hook differently in the fruitful and in the unfruitful branches; yet he spares neither good nor bad, pruning one and cutting off the other. [821]There is no man so just as not to require to be tried by affliction to advance, or to establish, or to prove his virtue.

Do the Manichæans not reckon Paul as righteous, who, while confessing humbly and honestly his past sins, still gives thanks for being justified by faith in Jesus Christ?

Was Paul then spared by Him whom fools misunderstand, when He says, "I will spare neither the righteous nor the sinner"?

Hear the apostle himself:

"Lest I should be exalted above measure by the abundance of the revelation, there was given me a thorn in the flesh, a messenger of Satan to buffet me.

For this I besought the Lord thrice, that He would remove it from me; and He said unto me, My grace is sufficient for thee:

for strength is perfected in weakness." [822]Here a just man is not spared that his strength might be perfected in weakness by Him who had given him an angel of Satan to buffet him.

If you say that the devil gave this angel, it follows that the devil sought to prevent Paul's being exalted above measure by the abundance of the revelation, and to perfect his strength.

This is impossible.

Therefore He who gave up this righteous man to be buffeted by the messenger of Satan, is the same as He who, through Paul, gave up to Satan himself the wicked persons of whom Paul says:

"I have delivered them to Satan, that they may learn not to blaspheme." [823]Do you see now how the Most High spares neither the righteous nor the wicked?

Or is it the sword that frightens you?

For to be buffeted is not so bad as to be put to death.

But did not the thousands of martyrs suffer death in various forms?

And could their persecutors have had this power against them except it had been given them by God, who thus spared neither the righteous nor the wicked?

For the Lord Himself, the chief martyr, says expressly to Pilate:

"Thou couldst have no power at all against me, except it were given thee from above."[824]Paul also, besides recording his own experience, says that the afflictions and persecutions of the righteous exhibit the judgment of God. [825]This truth is set forth at length by the Apostle Peter in the passage already quoted, where he says:

"It is time that judgment should begin at the house of the Lord.

And if it first begin at us, what shall the end be of those that believe not the gospel of God?

And if the righteous scarcely are saved, where shall the ungodly and the sinner appear?"[826]Peter also explains how the wicked are not spared, for they are branches broken off to be burnt; while the righteous are not spared, because their purification is to be brought to perfection.

He ascribes these things to the will of Him who says in the Old Testament, I will spare neither the righteous nor the wicked; for he says:

"It is better, if the will of the Spirit of God be so, that we suffer for well-doing than for evil-doing." [827]So, when by the will of the Spirit of God men suffer for well-doing, the righteous are not spared; when they suffer for evil-doing, the wicked are not spared.

In both cases it is according to the will of Him who says:

I will spare neither the righteous nor the wicked; correcting the one as a son, and punishing the other as a transgressor.

21.

I have thus shown, to the best of my power, that the God we worship did not abide from eternity in darkness, but is Himself light, and in Him is no darkness at all; and in Himself dwells in light inaccessible; and the brightness of this light is His coeternal wisdom.

From what we have said, it appears that God was not taken by surprise by the unexpected appearance of light, but that light owes its existence to Him as its Creator, as its owes its continued existence to His approval.

Neither was God ignorant of the future, but the author of the precept as well as the punisher of disobedience; that by showing His righteous anger against transgression, He might provide a restraint for the time, and a warning for the future.

Nor does He ask questions from ignorance, but by His very inquiry declares His judgment.

Nor is He curious or timid, but excludes the transgressor from eternal life, which is the just reward of obedience.

Nor is He greedy for blood and fat; but by requiring from a carnal people sacrifices, suited to their character, He by certain types prefigures the true sacrifice.

Nor is His jealousy an emotion of pale anxiety, but of quiet benevolence, in desire to keep the soul, which owes chastity to the one true God, from being defiled and prostituted by serving many false gods.

Nor is He enraged with a passion similar to human anger, but is angry, not in the sense of desiring vengeance, but in the peculiar sense of giving full effect to the sentence of a righteous retribution.

Nor does He destroy thousands of men for trifling offenses, or for nothing, but manifests to the world the benefit to be obtained from fearing Him, by the temporal death of those already mortal.

Nor does He punish the righteous and sinners indiscriminately, but chastises the righteous for their good, in order to perfect them, and gives to sinners the punishment justly due to them.

Thus, ye Manichæans, do your suspicions lead you astray, when, by misunderstanding our Scriptures, or by hearing bad interpreters, you form a mistaken judgment of Catholics. Hence you leave sound doctrine, and turn to impious fables; and in your perversity and estrangement from the society of saints, you reject the instruction of the New Testament, which, as we have shown, contains statements similar to those which you condemn in the Old Testament.

So we are obliged to defend both Testaments against you as well as against the Pagans.

22.

But supposing that there is some one so deluded by carnality as to worship not the God whom we worship, who is one and true, but the fiction of your suspicions or your slanders, whom you say we worship, is not even this god better than yours?

Observe, I beseech you, what must be plain to the feeblest understanding; for here there is no need of great perspicacity.

I address all, wise and unwise.

I appeal to the common sense and judgment of all alike.

Hear, consider, judge. Would it not have been better for your god to have remained in darkness from eternity, than to have plunged the light coeternal with him and cognate to him into darkness?

Would it not have been better to have expressed admiration in surprise at the appearance of a new light coming to scatter the darkness, than to have been unable to baffle the assault of darkness except by the concession of his own light?

Unhappy if he did this in alarm, and cruel if there was no need of it.

Surely it would have been better to see light, made by himself, and to admire it as good, than to make the light begotten by himself evil; better than that his own light should become hostile to himself in repelling the forces of darkness.

For this will be the accusation against those who will be condemned for ever to the mass of darkness, that they suffered themselves to lose their original brightness, and became the enemies of sacred light.

If they did not know from eternity that they would be thus condemned, they must have suffered the darkness of eternal ignorance; or if they did know, the darkness of eternal fear. Thus part of the substance of your god really did remain from eternity in its own darkness; and instead of admiring new light on its appearance, it only met with another and a hostile darkness, of which it had always been in fear.

Indeed, God himself must have been in the darkness of fear for this part of himself, if he was dreading the evil coming upon it.

If he did not foresee the evil, he must have been in the darkness of ignorance.

If he foresaw it, and was not in fear, the darkness of such cruelty is worse than the darkness either of ignorance or of fear.

Your god appears to be destitute of the quality which the apostle commends in the body, which you insanely believe to be made not by God, but by Hyle:

"If one member suffers, all the members suffer with it." [828]But suppose he did suffer; he foresaw, he feared, he suffered, but he could not help himself.

Thus he remained from eternity in the darkness of his own misery; and then, instead of admiring a new light which was to drive away the darkness, he came in contact, to the injury of his own light, with another darkness which he had always dreaded.

Again, would it not have been much better, I say, not to have given a commandment like God, but even to have received a commandment like Adam, which he would be rewarded for keeping and punished for breaking, acting either way by his own free-will, than to be forced by inevitable necessity to admit darkness into his light in spite of himself?

Surely it would have been better to have given a precept to human nature, not knowing that it would become sinful, than to have been driven by necessity to sin contrary to his own divine nature.

Think for a moment, and say how darkness could be conquered by one who was himself conquered by necessity.

Conquered already by this greater enemy, he fought under his conqueror's orders against a less formidable opponent.

Would it not have been better not to know where Adam had hid himself, than to have been himself destitute of any means of escape, first from a hard and hateful necessity, and then from a dissimilar and hostile race?

Would it not have been better to grudge eternal life to human nature, than to consign to misery the divine nature; to desire the blood and fat of sacrifices, than to be himself slaughtered in so many forms, on account of his mixture with the blood and fat of every victim; to be disturbed by jealousy at these sacrifices being offered to other gods as well as to himself, than to be himself offered on all altars to all devils, as mixed up not only with all fruits, but also with all animals?

Would it not have been much better to be affected even with human anger, so as to be enraged against both his friends and his enemies for their sins, than to be himself influenced by fear as well as by anger wherever these passions exist, or than to share in all the sin that is committed, and in all punishment that is suffered?

For this is the doom of that part of your god which is in confinement everywhere, condemned to this by himself, not as guilty, but in order to conquer his dreaded enemy.

Doomed himself to such a fatal necessity, the part of himself which he has given over to condemnation might pardon him, if he were as humble as he is miserable.

But how can you pretend to find fault with God for His anger against both friends and enemies when they sin, when the god of your fancies first under compulsion compels his own members to go to be devoured by sin, and then condemns them to remain in darkness?

Though he does this, you say that it will not be in anger.

But will he not be ashamed to punish, or to appear to punish, those from whom he should ask pardon in words such as these:

"Forgive me, I beseech you.

You are my members; could I treat you thus, except from necessity?

You know yourselves, that you were sent here because a formidable enemy had arisen; and now you must remain here to prevent his rising again"? Again, is it not better to slay thousands of men for trifling faults, or for nothing, than to cast into the abyss of sin, and to condemn to the punishment of eternal imprisonment, God's own members, his substance--in fact, God himself?

It cannot properly be said of the real substance of God that it has the choice of sinning or not sinning, for God's substance is absolutely unchangeable.

God cannot sin, as He cannot deny Himself.

Man, on the contrary, can sin and deny God, or he can choose not to do so.

But suppose the members of your god had, like a rational human soul, the choice of sinning or not sinning; they might perhaps be justly punished for heinous offenses by confinement in the mass of darkness.

But you cannot attribute to these parts a liberty which you deny to God himself.

For if God had not given them up to sin, he would have been forced to sin himself, by the prevalence of the race of darkness.

But if there was no danger of being thus forced, it was a sin to send these parts to a place where they incurred this danger.

To do so, indeed, from free choice is a crime deserving the torment which your god unnaturally inflicts upon his own parts, more than the conduct of these parts in going by his command to a place where they lost the power of living in righteousness.

But if God himself was in danger of being forced to sin by invasion and capture, unless he had secured himself first by the misconduct and then by the punishment of his own parts, there can have been no free-will either in your god or in his parts.

Let him not set himself up as judge, but confess himself a criminal.

For though he was forced against his own will, he professes to pass a righteous sentence in condemning those whom he knows to have suffered evil rather than done it; making this profession that he may not be thought of as having been conquered; as if it could do a beggar any good to be called prosperous and happy. Surely it would have been better for your god to have spared neither righteous nor wicked in indiscriminate punishment (which is Faustus' last charge against our God), than to have been so cruel to his own members,--first giving them up to incurable contamination, and then, as if that was not enough, accusing them falsely of misconduct.

Faustus declares that they justly suffer this severe and eternal punishment, because they allowed themselves to be led astray from their original brightness, and became hostile to sacred light.

But the reason of this, as Faustus says, was that they were so greedily devoured in the first assault of the princes of darkness, that they were unable to recover themselves, or to separate themselves from the hostile principle.

These souls, therefore, did no evil themselves, but in all this were innocent sufferers.

The real agent was he who sent them away from himself into this wretchedness.

They suffered more from their father than from their enemy.

Their father sent them into all this misery; while their enemy desired them as something good, wishing not to hurt them, but to enjoy them.

The one injured them knowingly, the other in ignorance.

This god was so weak and helpless that he could not otherwise secure himself first against an enemy threatening attack, and then against the same enemy in confinement.

Let him, then, not condemn those parts whose obedience defended him, and whose death secures his safety.

If he could not avoid the conflict, why slander his defenders?

When these parts allowed themselves to be led astray from their original brightness, and became hostile to sacred light, this must have been from the force of the enemy; and if they were forced against their will, they are innocent; while, if they could have resisted had they chosen, there is no need of the origin of evil in an imaginary evil nature, since it is to be found in free-will.

Their not resisting, when they could have done so, is plainly their own fault, and not owing to any force from without.

For, supposing them able to do a thing, to do which is right, while not to do it is great and heinous sin, their not doing it is their own choice.

So, then, if they choose not to do it, the fault is in their will not in necessity.

The origin of sin is in the will; therefore in the will is also the origin of evil, both in the sense of acting against a just precept, and in the sense of suffering under a just sentence.

There is thus no reason why, in your search for the origin of evil, you should fall into so great an evil as that of calling a nature so rich in good things the nature of evil, and of attributing the terrible evil of necessity to the nature of perfect good, before any commixture with evil.

The cause of this erroneous belief is your pride, which you need not have unless you choose; but in your wish to defend at all hazards the error into which you have fallen, you take away the origin of evil from free-will, and place it in a fabulous nature of evil.

And thus you come at last to say, that the souls which are to be doomed to eternal confinement in the mass of darkness became enemies to sacred light not from choice, but by necessity; and to make your god a judge with whom it is of no use to prove, in behalf of your clients. that they were under compulsion, and a king who will make no allowance for your brethren, his own sons and members, whose hostility against you and against himself you ascribe not to choice, but to necessity.

What shocking cruelty! unless you proceed in the next place to defend your god, as also acting not from choice, but by necessity.

So, if there could be found another judge free from necessity, who could decide the question on the principles of equity, he would sentence your god to be bound to this mass, not by being fastened on the outside, but by being shut up inside along with the formidable enemy.

The first in the guilt of necessity ought to be first in the sentence of condemnation.

Would it not be much better, then, in comparison with such a god as this, to choose the god whom we indeed do not worship, but whom you think or pretend to think we worship?

Though he spares not his servants, whether righteous or sinful, making no proper separation, and not distinguishing between punishment and discipline, is he not better than the god who spares not his own members though innocent, if necessity is no crime, or guilty from their obedience to him, if necessity itself is criminal; so that they are condemned eternally by him, along with whom they should have been released, if any liberty was recovered by the victory, while he should have been condemned along with them if the victory reduced the force of necessity even so far as to give this small amount of force to justice?

Thus the god whom you represent us as worshipping, though he is not the one true God whom we really worship, is far better than your god.

Neither, indeed, has any existence; but both are the creatures of your imaginations.

But, according to your own representations, the one whom you call ours, and find fault with, is better than the one whom you call your own, and whom you worship. [829]

23.

So also the patriarchs and prophets whom you cry out against are not the men whom we honor, but men whose characters are drawn from your fancy, prompted by ill-will.

And yet even thus as you paint them, I will not be content with showing them to be superior to your elect, who keep all the precepts of Manichæus, but will prove their superiority to your god himself.

Before proving this, however, I must, with the help of God, defend our holy fathers the patriarchs and prophets against your accusations, by a clear exposition of the truth as opposed to the carnality of your hearts.

As for you Manichæans, it would be enough to say that the faults you impute to our fathers are preferable to what you praise in your own, and to complete your shame by adding that your god can be proved far inferior to our fathers as you describe them. This would be a sufficient reply for you.

But as, even apart from your perversities, some minds are of themselves disturbed when comparing the life of the prophets in the Old Testament with that of the apostles in the New,--not discerning between the manner of the time when the promise was under a veil, and that of the time when the promise is revealed,--I must first of all reply to those who either have the boldness to pride themselves as superior in temperance to the prophets, or quote the prophets in defence of their own bad conduct.

24.

First of all, then, not only the speech of these men, but their life also, was prophetic; and the whole kingdom of the Hebrews was like a great prophet, corresponding to the greatness of the Person prophesied.

So, as regards those Hebrews who were made wise in heart by divine instruction, we may discover a prophecy of the coming of Christ and of the Church, both in what they said and in what they did; and the same is true as regards the divine procedure towards the whole nation as a body.

For, as the apostle says, "all these things were our examples."

25.

Those who find fault with the prophets, accusing them of adultery for instance, in actions which are above their comprehension, are like those Pagans who profanely charge Christ with folly or madness because He looked for fruit from a tree out of the season; [830] or with childishness, because He stooped down and wrote on the ground, and, after answering the people who were questioning Him, began writing again. [831] Such critics are incapable of understanding that certain virtues in great minds resemble closely the vices of little minds, not in reality, but in appearance.

Such criticism of the great is like that of boys at school, whose learning consists in the important rule, that if the nominative is in the singular, the verb must also be in the singular; and so they find fault with the best Latin author, because he says, Pars in frusta secant. [832] He should have written, say they, secat.

And again, knowing that religio is spelt with one l, they blame him for writing relligio, when he says, Relligione patrum. [833] Hence it may with reason be said, that as the poetical usage of words differs from the solecisms and barbarisms of the unlearned, so, in their own way, the figurative actions of the prophets differ from the impure actions of the vicious.

Accordingly, as a boy guilty of a barbarism would be whipped if he pled the usage of Virgil; so any one quoting the example of Abraham begetting a son from Hagar, in defence of his own sinful passion for his wife's handmaid, ought to be corrected not by caning only, but by severe scourging, that he may not suffer the doom of adulterers in eternal punishment.

This indeed is a comparison of great and important subjects with trifles; and it is not intended that a peculiar usage in speech should be put on a level with a sacrament, or a solecism with adultery.

Still, allowing for the difference in the character of the subjects, what is called learning or ignorance in the proprieties and improprieties of speech, resembles wisdom or the want of it in reference to the grand moral distinction between virtue and vice. [834]

26.

Instead of entering on the distinctions between the praiseworthy and the blameworthy, the criminal and the innocent, the dangerous and the harmless, the guilty and the guiltless, the desirable and the undesirable, which are all illustrations of the distinction between sin and righteousness, we must first consider what sin is, and then examine the actions of the saints as recorded in the holy books, that, if we find these saints described as sinning, we may if possible discover the true reason for keeping these sins in memory by putting them on record.

Again, if we find things recorded which, though they are not sins, appear so to the foolish and the malevolent, and in fact do not exhibit any virtues, here also we have to see why these things are put into the Scriptures which we believe to contain wholesome doctrine as a guide in the present life, and a title to the inheritance of the future.

As regards the examples of righteousness found among the acts of the saints, the propriety of recording these must be plain even to the ignorant.

The question is about those actions the mention of which may seem useless if they are neither righteous nor sinful, or even dangerous if the actions are really sinful, as leading people to imitate them, because they are not condemned in these books, and so may be supposed not to be sinful, or because, though they are condemned, men may copy them from the idea that they must be venial if saints did them.

27.
Sin, then, is any transgression in deed, or word, or desire, of the eternal law.
And the eternal law is the divine order or will of God, which requires the preservation of natural order, and forbids the breach of it.
But what is this natural order in man?
Man, we know, consists of soul and body; but so does a beast.
Again, it is plain that in the order of nature the soul is superior to the body. Moreover, in the soul of man there is reason, which is not in a beast. Therefore, as the soul is superior to the body, so in the soul itself the reason is superior by the law of nature to the other parts which are found also in beasts; and in reason itself, which is partly contemplation and partly action, contemplation is unquestionably the superior part.
The object of contemplation is the image of God, by which we are renewed through faith to sight.
Rational action ought therefore to be subject to the control of contemplation, which is exercised through faith while we are absent from the Lord, as it will be hereafter through sight, when we shall be like Him, for we shall see Him as He is. [835]Then in a spiritual body we shall by His grace be made equal to angels, when we put on the garment of immortality and incorruption, with which this mortal and corruptible shall be clothed, that death may be swallowed up of victory, when righteousness is perfected through grace.
For the holy and lofty angels have also their contemplation and action.
They require of themselves the performance of the commands of Him whom they contemplate, whose eternal government they freely because sweetly obey.
We, on the other hand, whose body is dead because of sin, till God quicken also our mortal bodies by His Spirit dwelling in us, live righteously in our feeble measure, according to the eternal law in which the law of nature is preserved, when we live by that faith unfeigned which works by love, having in a good conscience a hope of immortality and incorruption laid up in heaven, and of the perfecting of righteousness to the measure of an inexpressible satisfaction, for which in our pilgrimage we must hunger and thirst, while we walk by faith and not by sight.

28.
A man, therefore, who acts in obedience to the faith which obeys God, restrains all mortal affections, and keeps them within the natural limit, regulating his desires so as to put the higher before the lower.
If there was no pleasure in what is unlawful, no one would sin.
To sin is to indulge this pleasure instead of restraining it. And by unlawful is meant what is forbidden by the law in which the order of nature is preserved.
It is a great question whether there is any rational creature for which there is no pleasure in what is unlawful.
If there is such a class of creatures, it does not include man, nor that angelic nature which abode not in the truth.
These rational creatures were so made, that they had the potentiality of restraining their desires from the unlawful; and in not doing this they sinned.
Great, then, is the creature man, for he is restored by this potentiality, by which, if he had so chosen, he would not have fallen. And great is the Lord, and greatly to be praised, who created man.
For He created also inferior natures which cannot sin, and superior natures which will not sin.
Beasts do not sin, for their nature agrees with the eternal law from being subject to it, without being in possession of it.
And again, angels do not sin, because their heavenly nature is so in possession of the eternal law that God is the only object of its desire, and they obey His will without any experience of temptation. But man, whose life on this earth is a trial on account of sin, subdues to himself what he has in common with beasts, and subdues to God what he has in common with angels; till, when righteousness is perfected and immortality attained, he shall be raised from among beasts and ranked with angels.

29.

The exercise or indulgence of the bodily appetites is intended to secure the continued existence and the invigoration of the individual or of the species.

If the appetites go beyond this, and carry the man, no longer master of himself, beyond the limits of temperance, they become unlawful and shameful lusts, which severe discipline must subdue.

But if this unbridled course ends in plunging the man into such a depth of evil habits that he supposes that there will be no punishment of his sinful passions, and so refuses the wholesome discipline of confession and repentance by which he might be rescued; or, from a still worse insensibility, justifies his own indulgences in profane opposition to the eternal law of Providence; and if he dies in this state, that unerring law sentences him now not to correction, but to damnation.

30.

Referring, then, to the eternal law which enjoins the preservation of natural order and forbids the breach of it, let us see how our father Abraham sinned, that is, how he broke this law, in the things which Faustus has charged him with as highly criminal.

In his irrational craving to have children, says Faustus, and not believing God, who promised that his wife Sara should have a son, he defiled himself with a mistress.

But here Faustus, in his irrational desire to find fault, both discloses the impiety of his heresy, and in his error and ignorance praises Abraham's intercourse with the handmaid.

For as the eternal law--that is, the will of God the Creator of all--for the preservation of the natural order, permits the indulgence of the bodily appetite under the guidance of reason in sexual intercourse, not for the gratification of passion, but for the continuance of the race through the procreation of children; so, on the contrary, the unrighteous law of the Manichæans, in order to prevent their god, whom they bewail as confined in all seeds, from suffering still closer confinement in the womb, requires married people not on any account to have children, their great desire being to liberate their god. Instead, therefore, of an irrational craving in Abraham to have children, we find in Manichæus an irrational fancy against having children.

So the one preserved the natural order by seeking in marriage only the production of a child; while the other, influenced by his heretical notions, thought no evil could be greater than the confinement of his god.

31.

So, again, when Faustus says that the wife's being privy to her husband's conduct made the matter worse, while he is prompted only by the uncharitable wish to reproach Abraham and his wife, he really, without intending it, speaks in praise of both.

For Sara did not connive at any criminal action in her husband for the gratification of his unlawful passions; but from the same natural desire for children that he had, and knowing her own barrenness, she warrantably claimed as her own the fertility of her handmaid; not consenting with sinful desires in her husband, but requesting of him what it was proper in him to grant.

Nor was it the request of proud assumption; for every one knows that the duty of a wife is to obey her husband.

But in reference to the body, we are told by the apostle that the wife has power over her husband's body, as he has over hers; [836] so that, while in all other social matters the wife ought to obey her husband, in this one matter of their bodily connection as man and wife their power over one another is mutual,--the man over the woman, and the woman over the man.

So, when Sara could not have children of her own, she wished to have them by her handmaid, and of the same seed from which she herself would have had them, if that had been possible.

No woman would do this if her love for her husband were merely an animal passion; she would rather be jealous of a mistress than make her a mother.

So here the pious desire for the procreation of children was an indication of the absence of criminal indulgence.

32.

Abraham, indeed, cannot be defended, if, as Faustus says, he wished to get children by Hagar, because he had no faith in God, who promised that he should have children by Sara.

But this is an entire mistake:

this promise had not yet been made.

Any one who reads the preceding chapters will find that Abraham had already got the promise of the land with a countless number of inhabitants, [837] but that it had not yet been made known to him how the seed spoken of was to be produced, whether by generation from his own body, or from his choice in the adoption of a son, or, in the case of its being from his own body, whether it would be by Sara or another.

Whoever examines into this will find that Faustus has made either an imprudent mistake or an impudent misrepresentation.

Abraham, then, when he saw that he had no children, though the promise was to his seed, thought first of adoption.

This appears from his saying of his slave, when speaking to God, "This is mine heir;" as much as to say, As Thou hast not given me a seed of my own, fulfill Thy promise in this man.

For the word seed may be applied to what has not come out of a man's own body, else the apostle could not call us the seed of Abraham:

for we certainly are not his descendants in the flesh; but we are his seed in following his faith, by believing in Christ, whose flesh did spring from the flesh of Abraham.

Then Abraham was told by the Lord "This shall not be thine heir; but he that cometh out of thine own bowels shall be thine heir." [838] The thought of adoption was thus removed; but it still remained uncertain whether the seed which was to come from himself would be by Sara or another.

And this God was pleased to keep concealed, till a figure of the Old Testament had been supplied in the handmaid.

We may thus easily understand how Abraham, seeing that his wife was barren, and that she desired to obtain from her husband and her handmaid the offspring which she herself could not produce, acted not in compliance with carnal appetite, but in obedience to conjugal authority, believing that Sara had the sanction of God for her wish; because God had already promised him an heir from his own body, but had not foretold who was to be the mother.

Thus, when Faustus shows his own infidelity in accusing Abraham of unbelief, his groundless accusation only proves the madness of the assailant.

In other cases, Faustus' infidelity has prevented him from understanding; but here, in his love of slander, he has not even taken time to read.

33.

Again, when Faustus accuses a righteous and faithful man of a shameless profanation of his marriage from avarice and greed, by selling his wife Sara at different times to the two kings Abimelech and Pharaoh, telling them that she was his sister, because she was very fair, he does not distinguish justly between right and wrong, but unjustly condemns the whole transaction.

Those who think that Abraham sold his wife cannot discern in the light of the eternal law the difference between sin and righteousness; and so they call perseverance obstinacy, and confidence presumption, as in these and similar cases men of wrong judgment are wont to blame what they suppose to be wrong actions.

Abraham did not become partner in crime with his wife by selling her to others:

but as she gave her handmaid to her husband, not to gratify his passion, but for the sake of offspring, in the authority she had consistently with the order of nature, requiring the performance of a duty, not complying with a sinful desire; so in this case, the husband, in perfect assurance of the chaste attachment of his wife to himself, and knowing her mind to be the abode of modest and virtuous affection, called her his sister, without saying that she was his wife, lest he himself should be killed, and his wife fall into the hands of strangers and evil-doers;

for he was assured by his God that He would not allow her to suffer violence or disgrace.

Nor was he disappointed in his faith and hope; for Pharaoh, terrified by strange occurrences, and after enduring many evils on account of her, when he was informed by God that Sara was Abraham's wife, restored her with honor uninjured.

Abimelech also did the same, after learning the truth in a dream.

34.

Some people, not scoffers and evil-speakers like Faustus, but men who pay due honor to the Scriptures, which Faustus finds fault with because he does not understand them, or which he fails to understand because of his fault-finding, in commenting on this act of Abraham, are of opinion that he stumbled from weakness of faith, and denied his wife from fear of death, as Peter denied the Lord.

If this is the correct view, we must allow that Abraham sinned; but the sin should not cancel or obliterate all his merits, any more than in the case of the apostle.

Besides, to deny his wife is not the same as to deny the Saviour.

But when there is another explanation, why not abide by it, instead of giving blame without cause, since there is no proof that Abraham told a lie from fear?

He did not deny that Sara was his wife in answer to any question on the subject; but when asked who she was, he said she was his sister, without denying her to be his wife:

he concealed part of the truth, but said nothing false.

35.

It is waste of time to observe Faustus' remark, that Abraham falsely called Sara his sister; as if Faustus had discovered the family of Sara, though it is not mentioned in Scripture.

In a matter which Abraham knew, and we do not, it is surely better to believe the patriarch when he says what he knows, than to believe Manichæus when he finds fault with what he knows nothing about.

Since, then, Abraham lived at that period in human history, when, though marriage had become unlawful between children of the same parents, or of the same father or mother, no law or authority interfered with the custom of marriage between the children of brothers, or any less degree of consanguinity, why should he not have had as wife his sister, that is, a woman descended from his father?

For he himself told the king, when he restored Sara, that she was his sister by his father, and not by his mother.

And on this occasion he could not have been led to tell a falsehood from fear, for the king knew that she was his wife, and was restoring her with honor, because he had been warned by God.

We learn from Scripture that, among the ancients, it was customary to call cousins brothers and sisters.

Thus Tobias says in his prayer to God, before having intercourse with his wife, "And now, O Lord, Thou knowest that not in wantonness I take to wife my sister;" [839] though she was not sprung immediately from the same father or the same mother, but only belonged to the same family.

And Lot is called the brother of Abraham, though Abraham was his uncle. [840] And, by the same use of the word, those called in the Gospel the Lord's brothers are certainly not children of the Virgin Mary, but all the blood relations of the Lord. [841]

36.

Some may say, Why did not Abraham's confidence in God prevent his being afraid to confess his wife?

God could have warded off from him the death which he feared, and could have protected both him and his wife while among strangers, so that Sara, although very fair, should not have been desired by any one, nor Abraham killed on account of her.

Of course, God could have done this; it would be absurd to deny it.

But if, in reply to the people, Abraham had told them that Sara was his wife, his trust in God would have included both his own life and the chastity of Sara.

Now it is part of sound doctrine, that when a man has any means in his power, he should not tempt the Lord his God.

So it was not because the Saviour was unable to protect His disciples that He told them, "When ye are persecuted in one city, flee to another." [842]

And He Himself set the example.

For though He had the power of laying down His own life, and did not lay it down till He chose to do so, still when an infant He fled to Egypt, carried by His parents; [843] and when He went up to the feast, He went not openly, but secretly, though at other times He spoke openly to the Jews, who in spite of their rage and hostility could not lay hands on Him, because His hour was not come, [844] --not the hour when He would be obliged to die, but the hour when He would consider it seasonable to be put to death.

Thus He who displayed divine power by teaching and reproving openly, without allowing the rage of his enemies to hurt Him, did also, by escaping and concealing Himself, exhibit the conduct becoming the feebleness of men, that they should not tempt God when they have any means in their power of escaping threatened danger.

So also in the apostle, it was not from despair of divine assistance and protection, or from loss of faith, that he was let down over the wall in a basket, in order to escape being taken by his enemies: [845] not from want of faith in God did he thus escape, but because not to escape, when this escape was possible, would have been tempting God.

Accordingly, when Abraham was among strangers, and when, on account of the remarkable beauty of Sara, both his life and her chastity were in danger, since it was in his power to protect not both of these, but one only,--his life, namely,--to avoid tempting God he did what he could; and in what he could not do, he trusted to God.

Unable to conceal his being a man, he concealed his being a husband, lest he should be put to death; trusting to God to preserve his wife's purity.

37.

There might also be a difference of opinion on the nice point whether Sara's chastity would have been violated even if some one had intercourse with her, since she submitted to this to save her husband's life, both with his knowledge and by his authority.

In this there would be no desertion of conjugal fidelity or rebellion against her husband's authority; in the same way as Abraham was not an adulterer, when, in submission to the lawful authority of his wife, he consented to be made a father by his wife's handmaid.

But, from the nature of the relationship, for a wife to have two husbands, both in life, is not the same thing as for a man to have two wives:

so that we regard the explanation already given of Abraham's conduct as the most correct and unobjectionable; that our father Abraham avoided tempting God by taking what measures he could for the preservation of his own life, and that he showed his hope in God by entrusting to Him the chastity of his wife.

38.

But a pleasure which all must feel is obtained from this narrative so faithfully recorded in the Holy Scriptures, when we examine into the prophetic character of the action, and knock with pious faith and diligence at the door of the mystery, that the Lord may open, and show us who was prefigured in the ancient personage, and whose wife this is, who, while in a foreign land and among strangers, is not allowed to be stained or defiled, that she may be brought to her own husband without spot or wrinkle.

Thus we find that the righteous life of the Church is for the glory of Christ, that her beauty may bring honor to her husband, as Abraham was honored on account of the beauty of Sara among the inhabitants of that foreign land.

To the Church, to whom it is said in the Song of Songs, "O thou fairest among women," [846] kings offer gifts in acknowledgment of her beauty; as king Abimelech offered gifts to Sara, admiring the grace of her appearance; all the more that, while he loved, he was not allowed to profane it.

The holy Church, too is in secret the spouse of the Lord Jesus Christ.

For it is secretly, and in the hidden depths of the Spirit, that the soul of man is joined to the word of God, so that they two are one flesh; of which the apostle speaks as a great mystery in marriage, as referring to Christ and the Church. [847] Again, the earthly kingdom of this world, typified by the kings which were not allowed to defile Sara, had no knowledge or experience of the Church as the spouse of Christ, that is, of how faithfully she maintained her relation to her Husband, till it tried to violate her, and was compelled to yield to the divine testimony borne by the faith of the martyrs, and in the person of later monarchs was brought humbly to honor with gifts the Bride whom their predecessors had not been able to humble by subduing her to themselves.

What, in the type, happened in the reign of one and the same king, is fulfilled in the earlier monarchs of this era and their successors.

39.

Again, when it is said that the Church is the sister of Christ, not by the mother but by the father, we learn the excellence of the relation, which is not of the temporary nature of earthly descent, but of divine grace, which is everlasting.

By this grace we shall no longer be a race of mortals when we receive power to be called and to become sons of God.

This grace we obtain not from the synagogue, which is the mother of Christ after the flesh, but from God the Father.

And when Christ calls us into another life where there is no death, He teaches us, instead of acknowledging, to deny the earthly relationship, where death soon follows upon birth; for He says to His disciples, "Call no man your father upon earth; for you have one Father, who is in heaven."[848] And He set us an example of this when He said, "Who is my mother, and who are my brethren?

And stretching forth His hand to His disciples, He said, These are my brethren."

And lest any one should think that He referred to an earthly relationship, He added, "Whosoever shall do the will of my Father, the same is my brother, and sister, and mother;"[849] as much as to say, I derive this relationship from God my Father, not from the Synagogue my mother; I call you to eternal life, where I have an immortal birth, not to earthly life, for to call you away from this life I have taken mortality.

40.

As for the reason why, though it is concealed among strangers whose wife the Church is, it is not hidden whose sister she is, it is plainly because it is obscure and hard to understand how the human soul and the Word of God are united or mingled, or whatever word may be used to express this connection between God and the creature.

It is from this connection that Christ and the Church are called bridegroom and bride, or husband and wife.

The other relationship, in which Christ and all the saints are brethren by divine grace and not by earthly consanguinity, or by the father and not by the mother, is more easily expressed in words, and more easily understood.

For the same grace makes all the saints to be also brethren of one another; while in their society no one is the bridegroom of all the rest.

So also, notwithstanding the surpassing justice and wisdom of Christ, His manhood was much more plainly and readily recognized by strangers, who, indeed, were not wrong in believing Him to be man, but they did not understand His being God as well as man.

Hence Jeremiah says:

"He is both a man, and who shall know Him?" [850] He is a man, for it is made manifest that He is a brother.

And who shall know Him? for it is concealed that He is a husband.

This must suffice as a defense of our father Abraham against Faustus' impudence and ignorance and malice.

41.

Lot also, the brother of Abraham, was just and hospitable in Sodom, and was found worthy to escape the conflagration which prefigured the future judgment; for he was free from all participation in the corruption of the people of Sodom.

He was a type of the body of Christ, which in the person of all the saints both groans now among the ungodly and wicked, to whose evil deeds it does not consent, and will at the end of the world be rescued from their society, when they are doomed to the punishment of eternal fire.

Lot's wife was the type of a different class of men,--of those, namely, who, when called by the grace of God, look back, instead of, like Paul, forgetting the things that are behind, and looking forward to the things that are before. [851] The Lord Himself says:

"No man that putteth his hand to the plough, and looketh back, is fit for the kingdom of Heaven." [852] Nor did He omit to mention the case of Lot's wife; for she, for our warning, was turned into a pillar of salt, that being thus seasoned we might not trifle thoughtlessly with this danger, but be on our guard against it.

So, when the Lord was admonishing every one to get rid of the things that are behind by the most strenuous endeavor to reach the things that are before, He said, "Remember Lot's wife."[853] And, in addition to these, there is still a third type in Lot, when his daughters lay with him.

For here Lot seems to prefigure the future law; for those who spring from the law, and are placed under the law, by misunderstanding it, stupefy it, as it were, and bring forth the works of unbelief by an unlawful use of the law.

"The law is good" says the apostle, "if a man use it lawfully." [854]

42.

It is no excuse for this action of Lot or of his daughters that it represented the perversity which was afterwards in certain cases to be displayed.

The purpose of Lot's daughters is one thing, and the purpose of God is another, in allowing this to happen that He might make some truth manifest; for God both pronounces judgment on the actions of the people of those times, and arranges in His providence for the prefigurement of the future.

As a part of Scripture, this action is a prophecy; as part of the history of those concerned, it is a crime.

43.

At the same time there is in this transaction no reason for the torrent of abuse which Faustus' blind hostility discharges on it.

By the eternal law which requires the preservation of the order of nature and condemns its violation, the judgment in this case is not what it would have been if Lot had been prompted by a criminal passion to commit incest with his daughters, or if they had been inflamed with unnatural desires.

In justice, we must ask not only what was done, but with what motive, in order to obtain a fair view of the action as the effect of that motive.

The resolution of Lot's daughters to lie with their father was the effect of the natural desire for offspring in order to preserve the race; for they supposed that there were no other men to be found, thinking that the whole world had been consumed in that conflagration, which, for all they knew, had left no one alive but themselves.

It would have been better for them never to have been mothers, than to have become mothers by their own father.

But still, the fulfillment of a desire like this is very different from the accursed gratification of lust.

44.

Knowing that their father would condemn their design, Lot's daughters thought it necessary to fulfill it without his knowledge.

We are told that they made him drunk, so that he was unaware of what happened.

His guilt therefore is not that of incest, but of drunkenness.

This, too, is condemned by the eternal law, which allows meat and drink only as required by nature for the preservation of health.

There is, indeed, a great difference between a drunk man and an habitual drunkard; for the drunkard is not always drunk, and a man may be drunk on one occasion without being a drunkard.

However, in the case of a righteous man, we require to account for even one instance of drunkenness.

What can have made Lot consent to receive from his daughters all the cups of wine which they went on mixing for him, or perhaps giving him unmixed?

Did they feign excessive grief, and did he resort to this consolation in their loneliness, and in the loss of their mother, thinking that they were drinking too, while they only pretended to drink?

But this does not seem a proper method for a righteous man to take in consoling his friends when in trouble.

Had the daughters learned in Sodom some vile art which enabled them to intoxicate their father with a few cups, so that in his ignorance he might sin, or rather be sinned against?

But it is not likely that the Scripture would have omitted all notice of this, or that God would have allowed His servant to be thus abused without any fault of his own.

45.

But we are defending the sacred Scriptures, not man's sins.

Nor are we concerned to justify this action, as if our God had either commanded it or approved of it; or as if, when men are called just in Scripture, it meant that they could not sin if they chose.

And as, in the books which those critics find fault with, God nowhere expresses approval of this action, what thoughtless folly it is to bring a charge from this narrative against these writings, when in other places such actions are condemned by express prohibitions!

In the story of Lot's daughters the action is related, not commended.

And it is proper that the judgment of God should be declared in some cases, and concealed in others, that by its manifestation our ignorance may be enlightened, and that by its concealment our minds may be improved by the exercise of recalling what we already know, or our indolence stimulated to seek for an explanation.

Here, then, God, who can bring good out of evil, made nations arise from this origin, as He saw good, but did not bring upon His own Scriptures the guilt of man's sin.

It is God's writing, but not His doing; He does not propose these things for our imitation, but holds them up for our warning.

46.

Faustus' effrontery appears notably in his accusing Isaac also, the son of Abraham of pretending that his wife Rebecca was his sister. [855]For as regards the family of Rebecca Scripture is not silent, and it appears that she was his sister in the well-known sense of the word.

His concealing that she was his wife is not surprising, nor is it insignificant, if he did it in imitation of his father, so that he can be justified on the same grounds.

We need only refer to the answer already given to Faustus' charge against Abraham, as being equally applicable to Isaac.

Perhaps, however some inquirer will ask what typical significance there is in the foreign king discovering Rebecca to be the wife of Isaac by seeing him playing with her; for he would not have known, had he not seen Isaac playing with Rebecca as it would have been improper to do with a woman not his wife.

When holy men act thus as husbands, they do it not foolishly, but designedly:

for they accommodate themselves to the nature of the weaker sex in words and actions of gentle playfulness; not in effeminacy, but in subdued manliness.

But such behavior towards any woman except a wife would be disgraceful.

This is a question in good manners, which is referred to only in case some stern advocate of insensibility should find fault with the holy man even for playing with his wife.

For if these men without humanity see a sedate man chatting playfully with children that he may adapt himself to the childish understanding with kindly sympathy, they think that he is insane; forgetting that they themselves were once children, or unthankful for their maturity.

The typical meaning, as regards Christ and His Church, which is to be found in this great patriarch playing with his wife, and in the conjugal relation being thus discovered, will be seen by every one who, to avoid offending the Church by erroneous doctrine, carefully studies in Scripture the secret of the Church's Bridegroom.

He will find that the Husband of the Church concealed for a time in the form of a servant the majesty in which He was equal to the Father, as being in the form of God, that feeble humanity might be capable of union with Him, and that so He might accommodate Himself to His spouse.

So far from being absurd, it has a symbolic suitableness that the prophet of God should use a playfulness which is of the flesh to meet the affection of his wife, as the Word of God Himself became flesh that He might dwell among us.

47.

Again, Jacob the son of Isaac is charged with having committed a great crime because he had four wives.

But here there is no ground for a criminal accusation:

for a plurality of wives was no crime when it was the custom; and it is a crime now, because it is no longer the custom.

There are sins against nature, and sins against custom, and sins against the laws.

In which, then, of these senses did Jacob sin in having a plurality of wives?

As regards nature, he used the women not for sensual gratification, but for the procreation of children. For custom, this was the common practice at that time in those countries.

And for the laws, no prohibition existed.

The only reason of its being a crime now to do this, is because custom and the laws forbid it.

Whoever despises these restraints, even though he uses his wives only to get children, still commits sin, and does an injury to human society itself, for the sake of which it is that the procreation of children is required.

In the present altered state of customs and laws, men can have no pleasure in a plurality of wives, except from an excess of lust; and so the mistake arises of supposing that no one could ever have had many wives but from sensuality and the vehemence of sinful desires.

Unable to form an idea of men whose force of mind is beyond their conception, they compare themselves with themselves, as the apostle says, [856] and so make mistakes.

Conscious that, in their intercourse though with one wife only, they are often influenced by mere animal passion instead of an intelligent motive, they think it an obvious inference that, if the limits of moderation are not observed where there is only one wife, the infirmity must be aggravated where there are more than one.

48.

But those who have not the virtues of temperance must not be allowed to judge of the conduct of holy men, any more than those in fever of the sweetness and wholesomeness of food.

Nourishment must be provided not by the dictates of the sickly taste, but rather by the judgment and direction of health, so as to cure the sickness.

If our critics, then, wish to attain not a spurious and affected, but a genuine and sound moral health, let them find a cure in believing the Scripture record, that the honorable name of saint is given not without reason to men who had several wives; and that the reason is this, that the mind can exercise such control over the flesh as not to allow the appetite implanted in our nature by Providence to go beyond the limits of deliberate intention.

By a similar misunderstanding, this criticism, which consists rather in dishonest slander than in honest judgment, might accuse the holy apostles too of preaching the gospel to so many people, not from the desire of begetting children to eternal life, but from the love of human praise.

There was no lack of renown to these our fathers in the gospel, for their praise was spread in numerous tongues through the churches of Christ.

In fact, no greater honor and glory could have been paid by men to their fellow-creatures. It was the sinful desire for this glory in the Church which led the reprobate Simon in his blindness to wish to purchase for money what was freely bestowed on the apostles by divine grace. [857]There must have been this desire of glory in the man whom the Lord in the Gospel checks in his desire to follow Him, saying, "The foxes have holes, and the birds of the air have nests, but the Son of man hath not where to lay His Head." [858] The Lord saw that his mind was darkened by false appearances and elated by sudden emotion, and that there was no ground of faith to afford a lodging to the Teacher of humility; for in Christ's discipleship the man sought not Christ's grace, but his own glory.

By this love of glory those were led away whom the Apostle Paul characterizes as preaching Christ not sincerely, but of contention and envy; and yet the apostle rejoices in their preaching, knowing that it might happen that, while the preachers gratified their desire for human praise, believers might be born among their hearers,--not as the result of the envious feeling which made them wish to rival or surpass the fame of the apostles, but by means of the gospel which they preached, though not sincerely; so that God might bring good out of their evil. So a man may be induced to marry by sensual desire, and not to beget children; and yet a child may be born, a good work of God, due to the natural power, not to the misconduct of the parent.

As, therefore, the holy apostles were gratified when their doctrine met with acceptance from their hearers, not because they were greedy for praise, but because they desired to spread the truth; so the holy patriarchs in their conjugal intercourse were actuated not by the love of pleasure, but by the intelligent desire for the continuance of their family. Thus the number of their hearers did not make the apostles ambitious; nor did the number of their wives make the patriarchs licentious.

But why defend the husbands, to whose character the divine word bears the highest testimony, when it appears that the wives themselves looked upon their connection with their husbands only as a means of getting sons?

So, when they found themselves barren, they gave their handmaids to their husbands; so that while the handmaids had the fleshly motherhood, the wives were mothers in intention.

49.

Faustus makes a most groundless statement when he accuses the four women of quarreling like abandoned characters for the possession of their husband.

Where Faustus read this I know not, unless it was in his own heart, as in a book of impious delusions, in which Faustus himself is seduced by that serpent with regard to whom the apostle feared for the Church, which he desired to present as a chaste virgin to Christ; lest, as the serpent had deceived Eve by his subtlety, so he should also corrupt their minds by turning them away from the simplicity of Christ. [859] The Manichæans are so fond of this serpent, that they assert that he did more good than harm.

From him Faustus must have got his mind corrupted with the lies instilled into it, which he now reproduces in these infamous calumnies, and is even bold enough to put down in writing.

It is not true that one of the handmaids carried off Jacob from the other, or that they quarreled about possessing him.

There was arrangement, because there was no licentious passion; and the law of conjugal authority was all the stronger that there was none of the lawlessness of fleshly desire.

His being hired by one of his wives proves what is here said, in plain opposition to the libels of the Manichæans.

Why should one have hired him, unless by the arrangement he was to have gone in to the other?

It does not follow that he would never have gone in to Leah unless she had hired him.

He must have gone to her always in her turn, for he had many children by her; and in obedience to her he had children by her hand-maid, and afterwards, without any hiring, by herself.

On this occasion it was Rachel's turn, so that she had the power so expressly mentioned in the New Testament by the apostle, "The husband hath not power over his own body, but the wife."[860] Rachel had a bargain with her sister, and, being in her sister's debt, she referred her to Jacob, her own debtor.

For the apostle uses this figure when he says, "Let the husband render unto the wife what is due." [861] Rachel gave what was in her power as due from her husband, in return for what she had chosen to take from her sister.

50.

If Jacob had been of such a character as Faustus in his incurable blindness supposes, and not a servant of righteousness rather than of concupiscence, would he not have been looking forward eagerly all day to the pleasure of passing the night with the more beautiful of his wives, whom he certainly loved more than the other, and for whom he paid the price of twice seven years of gratuitous service?

How, then, at the close of the day, on his way to his beloved, could he have consented to be turned aside, if he had been such as the ignorant Manichæans represent him?

Would he not have disregarded the wish of the women, and insisted upon going to the fair Rachel, who belonged to him that night not only as his lawful wife, but also as coming in regular order?

He would thus have used his power as a husband, for the wife also has not power over her own body, but the husband; and having on this occasion the arrangement in their obedience in favor of the gratification of his love of beauty, he might have enforced his authority the more successfully.

In that case it would be to the credit of the women, that while he thought of his own pleasure they contended about having a son.

As it was, this virtuous man, in manly control of sensual appetite, thought more of what was due from him than to him, and instead of using his power for his own pleasure, consented to be only the debtor in this mutual obligation.

So he consented to pay the debt to the person to whom she to whom it was due wished him to pay it.

When, by this private bargain of his wives, Jacob was suddenly and unexpectedly forced to turn from the beautiful wife to the plain one, he did not give way either to anger or to disappointment, nor did he try to persuade his wives to let him have his own way; but, like a just husband and an intelligent parent, seeing his wives concerned about the production of children, which was all he himself desired in marriage, he thought it best to yield to their authority, in desiring that each should have a child:

for, since all the children were his, his own authority was not impaired.

As if he had said to them: Arrange as you please among yourselves which is to be the mother; it matters not to me, since in any case I am the father.

This control over the appetites, and simple desire to beget children, Faustus would have been clever enough to see and approve, unless his mind had been corrupted by the shocking tenets of his sect, which lead him to find fault with everything in the Scripture, and, moreover, teach him to condemn as the greatest crime the procreation of children, which is the proper design of marriage.

51.

Now, having defended the character of the patriarch, and refuted an accusation arising from these detestable errors, let us avail ourselves of the opportunity of searching out the symbolical meaning, and let us knock with the reverence of faith, that the Lord may open to us the typical significance of the four wives of Jacob, of whom two were free, and two slaves.

We see that, in the wife and bond-slaves of Abraham, the apostle understands the two Testaments. [862]But there, one represents each; here, the application does not suit so well, as there are two and two.

There, also, the son of the bond-slave is disinherited; but here the sons of the slaves receive the land of promise along with the sons of the free women:

so that this type must have a different meaning.

52.

Supposing that the two free wives point to the New Testament, by which we are called to liberty, what is the meaning of there being two?

Perhaps because in Scripture, as the attentive reader will find, we are said to have two lives in the body of Christ,--one temporal, in which we suffer pain, and one eternal, in which we shall behold the blessedness of God.

We see the one in the Lord's passion, and the other in His resurrection.

The names of the women point to this meaning:

It is said that Leah means Suffering, and Rachel the First Principle made visible, or the Word which makes the First Principle visible.

The action, then, of our mortal human life, in which we live by faith, doing many painful tasks without knowing what benefit may result from them to those in whom we are interested, is Leah, Jacob's first wife.

And thus she is said to have had weak eyes.

For the purposes of mortals are timid, and our plans uncertain.

Again, the hope of the eternal contemplation of God, accompanied with a sure and delightful perception of truth, is Rachel.

And on this account she is described as fair and well-formed.

This is the beloved of every pious student, and for this he serves the grace of God, by which our sins, though like scarlet, are made white as snow. [863]For Laban means making white; and we read that Jacob served Laban for Rachel. [864] No man turns to serve righteousness, in subjection to the grace of forgiveness, but that he may live in peace in the Word which makes visible the First Principle, or God; that is, he serves for Rachel, not for Leah.

For what a man loves in the works of righteousness is not the toil of doing and suffering.

No one desires this life for its own sake; as Jacob desired not Leah, who yet was brought to him, and became his wife, and the mother of children.

Though she could not be loved of herself, the Lord made her be borne with as a step to Rachel; and then she came to be approved of on account of her children.

Thus every useful servant of God, brought into His grace by which his sins are made white, has in his mind, and heart, and affection, when he thus turns to God, nothing but the knowledge of wisdom.

This we often expect to attain as a reward for practising the seven precepts of the law which concern the love of our neighbor, that we injure no one: namely, Honor thy father and mother; Thou shall not commit adultery; Thou shall not kill; Thou shalt not steal; Thou shall not bear false witness; Thou shalt not desire thy neighbor's wife; Thou shall not covet thy neighbor's property.

When a man has obeyed these to the best of his ability, and, instead of the bright joys of truth which he desired and hoped for, finds in the darkness of the manifold trials of this world that he is bound to painful endurance, or has embraced Leah instead of Rachel, if there is perseverance in his love, he bears with the one in order to attain the other; and as if it were said to him, Serve seven other years for Rachel, he hears seven new commands,--to be poor in spirit, to be meek, to be a mourner, to hunger and thirst after righteousness, to be merciful, pure, and a peacemaker. [865] A man would desire, if it were possible, to obtain at once the joys of lovely and perfect wisdom, without the endurance of toil in action and suffering; but this is impossible in mortal life.

This seems to be meant, when it is said to Jacob:

"It is not the custom in our country to marry the younger before the elder." [866] The elder may very well mean the first in order of time.

So, in the discipline of man, the toil of doing the work of righteousness precedes the delight of understanding the truth.

53.

To this purpose it is written:

"Thou hast desired wisdom; keep the commandments, and the Lord shall give it thee."[867] The commandments are those concerning righteousness, and the righteousness is that which is by faith, surrounded with the uncertainty of temptations; so that understanding is the reward of a pious belief of what is not yet understood.

The meaning I have given to these words, "Thou hast desired wisdom; keep the commandments, and the Lord shall give it thee," I find also in the passage, "Unless ye believe, ye shall not understand;" [868] showing that as righteousness is by faith, understanding comes by wisdom.

Accordingly, in the case of those who eagerly demand evident truth, we must not condemn the desire, but regulate it, so that beginning with faith it may proceed to the desired end through good works.

The life of virtue is one of toil; the end desired is unclouded wisdom.

Why should I believe, says one, what is not clearly proved?

Let me hear some word which will disclose the first principle of all things.

This is the one great craving of the rational soul in the pursuit of truth.

And the answer is, What you desire is excellent, and well worthy of your love; but Leah is to be married first, and then Rachel.

The proper effect of your eagerness is to lead you to submit to the right method, instead of rebelling against it; for without this method you cannot attain what you so eagerly long for.

And when it is attained, the possession of the lovely form of knowledge will be in this world accompanied with the toils of righteousness.

For however clear and true our perception in this life may be of the unchangeable good, the mortal body is still a weight on the mind and the earthly tabernacle is a clog on the intellect in its manifold activity.

The end then, is one, but many things must be gone through for the sake of it.

54.

Thus Jacob has two free wives; for both are daughters of the remission of sins, or of whitening, that is, of Laban.

One is loved, the other is borne.

But she that is borne is the most and the soonest fruitful, that she may be loved, if not for herself, at least for her children.

For the toil of the righteous is specially fruitful in those whom they beget for the kingdom of God, by preaching the gospel amid many trials and temptations; and they call those their joy and crown [869] for whom they are in labors more abundantly, in stripes above measure, in deaths often, [870] --for whom they have fightings without and fears within. [871] Such births result most easily and plentifully from the word of faith, the preaching of Christ crucified, which speaks also of His human nature as far as it can be easily understood, so as not to hurt the weak eyes of Leah.

Rachel, again, with clear eye, is beside herself to God, [872] and sees in the beginning the Word of God with God, and wishes to bring forth, but cannot; for who shall declare His generation?

So the life devoted to contemplation, in order to see with no feeble mental eye things invisible to flesh, but understood by the things that are made, and to discern the ineffable manifestation of the eternal power and divinity of God, seeks leisure from all occupation, and is therefore barren.

In this habit of retirement, where the fire of meditation burns bright, there is a want of sympathy with human weakness, and with the need men have of our help in their calamities.

This life also burns with the desire for children (for it wishes to teach what it knows, and not to go with the corruption of envy [873]), and sees its sister-life fully occupied with work and with bringing forth; and it grieves that men run after that virtue which cares for their wants and weaknesses, instead of that which has a divine imperishable lesson to impart.

This is what is meant when it is said, "Rachel envied her sister." [874] Moreover, as the pure intellectual perception of that which is not matter, and so is not the object of the bodliy sense, cannot be expressed in words which spring from the flesh, the doctrine of wisdom prefers to get some lodging for divine truth in the mind by whatever material figures and illustrations occur, rather than to give up teaching these things; and thus Rachel preferred that her husband should have children by her handmaid, rather than that she should be without any children.

Bilhah, the name of her handmaid, is said to mean old; and so, even when we speak of the spiritual and unchangeable nature of God, ideas are suggested relating to the old life of the bodily senses.

55.

Leah, too, got children by her handmaid, from the desire of having a numerous family.

Zilpah, her handmaid, is, interpreted, an open mouth.

So Leah's handmaid represents those who are spoken of in Scripture as engaging in the preaching of the gospel with open mouth, but not with open heart.

Thus it is written of some:

"This people honor me with their lips, but their heart is far from me." [875] To such the apostle says:

"Thou that preachest that a man should not steal, dost thou steal?

Thou that sayest a man should not commit adultery, dost thou commit adultery?" [876] But that even by this arrangement the free wife of Jacob, the type of labor or endurance, might obtain children to be heirs of the kingdom, the Lord says:

"What they say, do; but do not after their works." [877] And again, the apostolic life, when enduring imprisonment, says:

"Whether Christ is preached in pretence or in truth, I therein do rejoice, yea, and will rejoice." [878] It is the joy of the mother over her numerous family, though born of her handmaid.

56.

In one instance Leah owed her becoming a mother to Rachel, who, in return for some mandrakes, allowed her husband to give her night to her sister.

Some, I know, think that eating this fruit has the effect of making barren women productive, and that Rachel, from her desire for children, was thus bent on getting the fruit from her sister.

But I should not agree to this, even had Rachel conceived at the time.

As Leah then conceived, and, besides, had two other children before God opened Rachel's womb, there is no reason for supposing any such quality in the mandrake, without any experience to prove it.

I will give my explanation; those better able than I may give a better.

Though this fruit is not often met with, I had once, to my great satisfaction, on account of its connection with this passage of Scripture, an opportunity of seeing it.

I examined the fruit as carefully as I could, not with the help of any recondite knowledge of the nature of roots or the virtues of plants, but only as to what I or any one might learn from the sight, and smell, and taste.

I thought it a nice-looking fruit, and sweet-smelling, but insipid; and I confess it is hard to say why Rachel desired it so much, unless it was for its rarity and its sweet smell.

Why the incident should be narrated in Scripture, in which the fancies of women would not be mentioned as important unless it was intended that we should learn some important lesson from them, the only thing I can think of is the very simple idea that the fruit represents a good character; not the praise given a man by a few just and wise people, but popular report, which bestows greatness and renown on a man, and which is not desirable for its own sake, but is essential to the success of good men in their endeavors to benefit their fellow-men.

So the apostle says, that it is proper to have a good report of those that are without; [879] for though they are not infallible, the lustre of their praise and the odor of their good opinion are a great help to the efforts of those who seek to benefit them.

And this popular renown is not obtained by those that are highest in the Church, unless they expose themselves to the toils and hazards of an active life.

Thus the son of Leah found the mandrakes when he went out into the field, that is, when walking honestly towards those that are without.

The pursuit of wisdom, on the other hand, retired from the busy crowd, and lost in calm meditation, could never obtain a particle of this public approval, except through those who take the management of public business, not for the sake of being leaders, but in order to be useful.

These men of action and business exert themselves for the public benefit, and by a popular use of their influence gain the approval of the people even for the quiet life of the student and inquirer after truth; and thus through Leah the mandrakes come into the hands of Rachel.

Leah herself got them from her first-born son, that is, in honor of her fertility, which represents all the useful result of a laborious life exposed to the common vicissitudes; a life which many avoid on account of its troublesome engagements, because, although they might be able to take the lead, they are bent on study, and devote all their powers to the quiet pursuit of knowledge, in love with the beauty of Rachel.

57.

But as it is right that this studious life should gain public approval by letting itself be known, while it cannot rightly gain this approval if it keeps its follower in retirement, instead of using his powers for the management of ecclesiastical affairs, and so prevents his being generally useful; to this purpose Leah says to her sister, "Is it a small matter that thou hast taken my husband? and wouldest thou take away my son's mandrakes also?" [880] The husband represents all those who, though fit for active life, and able to govern the Church, in administering to believers the mystery of the faith, from their love of learning and of the pursuit of wisdom, desire to relinquish all troublesome occupations, and to bury themselves in the classroom.

Thus the words, "Is it a small matter that thou hast taken my husband? and wouldest thou take away my son's mandrakes also?" mean, "Is it a small matter that the life of study keeps in retirement men required for the toils of public life? and does it ask for popular renown as well?"

58.

To get this renown justly, Rachel gives her husband to her sister for the night; that is, those who, by a talent for business, are fitted for government, must for the public benefit consent to bear the burden and suffer the hardships of public life; lest the pursuit of wisdom, to which their leisure is devoted, should be evil spoken of, and should not gain from the multitude the good opinion, represented by the fruit, which is necessary for the encouragement of their pupils.

But the life of business must be forced upon them.

This is clearly shown by Leah's meeting Jacob when coming from the field, and laying hold of him, saying, "Thou shalt come in to me; for I have hired thee with my son's mandrakes." [881] As if she said, Dost thou wish the knowledge which thou lovest to be well thought of?

Do not shirk the toil of business. The same thing happens constantly in the Church.

What we read is explained by what we meet with in our own experience.

Do we not everywhere see men coming from secular employments, to seek leisure for the study and contemplation of truth, their beloved Rachel, and intercepted mid-way by ecclesiastical affairs, which require them to be set to work, as if Leah said to them, You must come in to me?

When such men minister in sincerity the mystery of God, so as in the night of this world to beget sons in the faith, popular approval is gained also for that life, in love for which they were led to abandon worldly pursuits, and from the adoption of which they were called away to undertake the benevolent task of government.

In all their labors they aim chiefly at this, that their chosen way of life may have greater and wider renown, as having supplied the people with such leaders; as Jacob consents to go with Leah, that Rachel may obtain the sweet-smelling and good-looking fruit.

Rachel, too, in course of time, by the mercy of God, brings forth a child herself, but not till after some time; for it seldom happens that there is a sound, though only partial, apprehension, without fleshly ideas, of such sacred lessons of wisdom as this:

"In the beginning was the Word, and the Word was with God, and the Word was God." [882]

59.

This must suffice as a reply to the false accusations brought by Faustus against the three fathers, Abraham, Isaac, and Jacob, from whom the God whom the Catholic Church worship was pleased to take His name. This is not the place to discourse on the merits and piety of these three men, or on the dignity of their prophetic character, which is beyond the comprehension of carnal minds.

It is enough in this treatise to defend them against the calumnious attacks of malevolence and falsehood, in case those who read the Scriptures in a carping and hostile spirit should fancy that they have proved anything against the sacredness and the profitableness of these books, by their attempts to blacken the character of men who are there mentioned so honorably.

60.

It should be added that Lot, the brother, that is the blood relation, of Abraham, is not to be ranked as equal to those of whom God says, "I am the God of Abraham, of Isaac, and of Jacob;" nor does he belong to those testified to in Scripture as having continued righteous to the end, although in Sodom he lived a pious and virtuous life, and showed a praiseworthy hospitality, so that he was rescued from the fire, and a land was given by God to his seed to dwell in, for the sake of his uncle Abraham.

On these accounts he is commended in Scripture--not for intemperance or incest.

But when we find bad and good actions recorded of the same person, we must take warning from the one, and example from the other.

As, then, the sin of Lot, of whom we are told that he was righteous previous to this sin, instead of bringing a stain on the character of God, or the truth of Scripture, rather calls on us to approve and admire the record in its resemblance to a faithful mirror, which reflects not only the beauties and perfections, but also the faults and deformities, of those who approach it; still more, in the case of Judah, who lay with his daughter-in-law, we may see how groundless are the reproaches cast on the narrative. The sacred record has an authority which raises it far above not merely the cavils of a handful of Manichæans, but the determined enmity of the whole Gentile world; for, in confirmation of its claims, we see that already it has brought nearly all people from their idolatrous superstitions to the worship of one God, according to the rule of Christianity.

It has conquered the world, not by violence and warfare, but by the resistless force of truth.

Where, then, is Judah praised in Scripture?

Where is anything good said of him, except that in the blessing pronounced by his father he is distinguished above the rest, because of the prophecy that Christ would come in the flesh from his tribe? [883]

61.

Judah, as Faustus says, committed fornication; and besides that, we can accuse him of selling his brother into Egypt.

Is it any disparagement to light, that in revealing all things it discloses what is unsightly?

So neither is the character of Scripture affected by the evil deeds of which we are informed by the record itself.

Undoubtedly, by the eternal law, which requires the preservation of natural order, and forbids the transgression of it, conjugal intercourse should take place only for the procreation of children, and after the celebration of marriage, so as to maintain the bond of peace.

Therefore, the prostitution of women, merely for the gratification of sinful passion, is condemned by the divine and eternal law.

To purchase the degradation of another, disgraces the purchaser; so that, though the sin would have been greater if Judah had knowingly lain with his daughter-in-law (for if, as the Lord says, man and wife are no more two, but one flesh, [884] a daughter-in-law is the same as a daughter); still, it is plain that, as regards his own intention, he was disgraced by his intercourse with an harlot.

The woman, on the other hand, who deceived her father-in-law, sinned not from wantonness, or because she loved the gains of iniquity, but from her desire to have children of this particular family.

So, being disappointed in two of the brothers, and not obtaining the third, she succeeded by craft in getting a child by their father; and the reward which she got was kept, not as an ornament, but as a pledge.

It would certainly have been better to have remained childless than to become a mother without marriage.

Still, her desire to have her father-in-law as the father of her children was very different from having a criminal affection for him.

And when, by his order, she was brought out to be killed, on her producing the staff and necklace and ring, saying that the father of the child was the man who had given her those pledges, Judah acknowledged them, and said, "She hath been more righteous than I"--not praising her, but condemning himself.

He blamed her desire to have children less than his own unlawful passion, which had led him to one whom he thought to be an harlot.

In a similar sense, it is said of some that they justified Sodom;[885] that is, their sin was so great, that Sodom seemed righteous in comparison.

And even allowing that this woman is not spoken of as comparatively less guilty, but is actually praised by her father-in-law, while, on account of her not observing the established rites of marriage, she is a criminal in the eye of the eternal law of right, which forbids the transgression of natural order, both as regards the body, and first and chiefly as regards the mind, what wonder though one sinner should praise another?

62.

The mistake of Faustus and of Manichæism generally, is in supposing that these objections prove anything against us, as if our reverence for Scripture, and our profession of regard for its authority, bound us to approve of all the evil actions mentioned in it; whereas the greater our homage for the Scripture, the more decided must be our condemnation of what the truth of Scripture itself teaches us to condemn.

In Scripture, all fornication and adultery are condemned by the divine law; accordingly, when actions of this kind are narrated, without being expressly condemned, it is intended not that we should praise them, but that we should pass judgment on them ourselves.

Every one execrates the cruelty of Herod in the Gospel, when, in his uneasiness on hearing of the birth of Christ, he commanded the slaughter of so many infants.[886] But this is merely narrated without being condemned.

Or if Manichæan absurdity is bold enough to deny the truth of this narrative, since they do not admit the birth of Christ, which was what troubled Herod, let them read the account of the blind fury of the Jews, which is related without any expression of reproach, although the feeling of abhorrence is the same in all.

63.

But, it is said, Judah, who lay with his daughter-in-law, is reckoned as one of the twelve patriarchs.

And was not Judas, who betrayed the Lord, reckoned among the twelve apostles?

And was not this one of them, who was a devil, sent along with them to preach the gospel?[887] In reply to this, it will be said that after his crime Judas hanged himself, and was removed from the number of the apostles; while Judah, after his evil conduct, was not only blessed along with his brethren, but got special honor and approval from his father, who is so highly spoken of in Scripture.

But the main lesson to be learned from this is, that this prophecy refers not to Judah, but to Christ, who was foretold as to come in the flesh from his tribe; and the very reason for the mention of this crime of Judah is to be found in the desirableness of teaching us to look for another meaning in the words of his father, which are seen not to be applicable to him in his misconduct, from the praise which they express.

64.

Doubtless, the intention of Faustus' calumnies is to damage this very assertion, that Christ was born of the tribe of Judah. Especially, as in the genealogy given by Matthew we find the name of Zara, whom this woman Tamar bore to Judah.

Had Faustus wished to reproach Jacob's family merely, and not Christ's birth, he might have taken the case of Reuben the first-born, who committed the unnatural crime of defiling his father's bed, of which fornication the apostle says, that it was not so much as named among the Gentiles.[888] Jacob also mentions this in his blessing, charging his son with the infamous deed.

Faustus might have brought up this, as Reuben seems to have been guilty of deliberate incest, and there was no harlot's disguise in this case, were it not that Tamar's conduct in desiring nothing but to have children is more odious to Faustus than if she had acted from criminal passion, and did he not wish to discredit the incarnation, by bringing reproach on Christ's progenitors.

Faustus unhappily is not aware that the most true and truthful Saviour is a teacher, not only in His words, but also in His birth.

In His fleshly origin there is this lesson for those who should believe on Him from all nations, that the sins of their fathers need be no hindrance to them.

Besides, the Bridegroom, who was to call good and bad to His marriage, [889] was pleased to assimilate Himself to His guests, in being born of good and bad.

He thus confirms as typical of Himself the symbol of the Passover, in which it was commanded that the lamb to be eaten should be taken from the sheep or from the goats--that is, from the righteous or the wicked. [890] Preserving throughout the indication of divinity and humanity, as man He consented to have both bad and good as His parents, while as God He chose the miraculous birth from a virgin.

65.

The impiety, therefore, of Faustus' attacks on Scripture can injure no one but himself; for what he thus assails is now deservedly the object of universal reverence.

As has been said already, the sacred record, like a faithful mirror, has no flattery in its portraits, and either itself passes sentence upon human actions as worthy of approval or disapproval, or leaves the reader to do so.

And not only does it distinguish men as blameworthy or praiseworthy, but it also takes notice of cases where the blameworthy deserve praise, and the praiseworthy blame.

Thus, although Saul was blameworthy, it was not the less praiseworthy in him to examine so carefully who had eaten food during the curse, and to pronounce the stern sentence in obedience to the commandment of God. [891] So, too, he was right in banishing those that had familiar spirits and wizards out of the land. [892] And although David was praiseworthy, we are not called on to approve or imitate his sins, which God rebukes by the prophet.

And so Pontius Pilate was not wrong in pronouncing the Lord innocent, in spite of the accusations of the Jews; [893] nor was it praiseworthy in Peter to deny the Lord thrice; nor, again, was he praiseworthy on that occasion when Christ called him Satan because, not understanding the things of God, he wished to withhold Christ from his passion, that is, from our salvation.

Here Peter, immediately after being called blessed, is called Satan. [894] Which character most truly belonged to him, we may see from his apostleship, and from his crown of martyrdom.

66.

In the case of David also, we read of both good and bad actions. But where David's strength lay, and what was the secret of his success, is sufficiently plain, not to the blind malevolence with which Faustus assails holy writings and holy men, but to pious discernment, which bows to the divine authority, and at the same time judges correctly of human conduct.

The Manichæans will find, if they read the Scriptures, that God rebukes David more than Faustus does. [895] But they will read also of the sacrifice of his penitence, of his surpassing gentleness to his merciless and bloodthirsty enemy, whom David, pious as he was brave, dismissed unhurt when now and again he fell into his hands. [896] They will read of his memorable humility under divine chastisement, when the kingly neck was so bowed under the Master's yoke, that he bore with perfect patience bitter taunts from his enemy, though he was armed, and had armed men with him.

And when his companion was enraged at such things being said to the king, and was on the point of requiting the insult on the head of the scoffer, he mildly restrained him, appealing to the fear of God in support of his own royal order, and saying that this bad happened to him as a punishment from God, who had sent the man to curse him. [897] They will read how, with the love of a shepherd for the flock entrusted to him, he was willing to die for them, when, after he had numbered the people, God saw good to punish his sinful pride by lessening the number he boasted of.

In this destruction, God, with whom there is no iniquity, in His secret judgment, both took away the lives of those whom He knew to be unworthy of life, and by this diminution cured the vainglory which had prided itself on the number of the people.

They will read of that scrupulous fear of God in his regard for the emblem of Christ in the sacred anointing, which made David's heart smite him with regret for having secretly cut off a small piece of Saul's garment, that he might prove to him that he had no wish to kill him, when he might have done it.

They will read of his judicious behavior as regards his children, and also of his tenderness toward them--how, when one was sick, he entreated the Lord for him with many tears and with much self-abasement, but when he died, an innocent child, he did not mourn for him; and again, how, when his youthful son was carried away with unnatural hostility to an infamous violation of his father's bed, and in a parricidal war, he wished him to live, and wept for him when he was killed; for he thought of the eternal doom of a soul guilty of such crimes, and desired that he should live to escape this doom by being brought to submission and repentance.

These, and many other praiseworthy and exemplary things, may be seen in this holy man by a candid examination of the Scripture narrative, especially if in humble piety and unfeigned faith we regard the judgment of God, who knew the secrets of David's heart, and who, in His infallible inspection, so approves of David as to commend him as a pattern to his sons.

67.

It must have been on account of this inspection of the depths of David's heart by the Spirit of God that, when on being reproved by the prophet, he said, I have sinned, he was considered worthy to be told, immediately after this brief confession, that he was pardoned--that is, that he was admitted to eternal salvation.

For he did not escape the correction of the fatherly rod, of which God spoke in His threatening, that, while by his confession he obtained eternal exemption, he might be tried by temporal chastisement.

And it is a remarkable evidence of the strength of David's faith, and of his meek and submissive spirit, that, when he had been told by the prophet that God had forgiven him, although the threatened consequences were still permitted to follow, he did not accuse the prophet of having deluded him, or murmur against God as having mocked him with a declaration of forgiveness.

This deeply holy man, whose soul was lifted up unto God, and not against God, knew that had not the Lord mercifully accepted his confession and repentance, his sins would have deserved eternal punishment.

So when, instead of this, he was made to smart under temporal correction, he saw that, while the pardon remained good, wholesome discipline was also provided.

Saul, too, when he was reproved by Samuel, said, I have sinned. [898]Why, then, was he not considered fit to be told, as David was, that the Lord had pardoned his sin?

Is there acceptance of persons with God?

Far from it.

While to the human ear the words were the same, the divine eye saw a difference in the heart.

The lesson for us to learn from these things is, that the kingdom of heaven is within us, [899] and that we must worship God from our inmost feelings, that out of the abundance of the heart the mouth may speak, instead of honoring Him with our lips, like the people of old, while our hearts are far from Him.

We may learn also to judge of men, whose hearts we cannot see, only as God judges, who sees what we cannot, and who cannot be biased or misled.

Having, on the high authority of sacred Scripture, the plainest announcement of God's opinion of David, we may regard as absurd or deplorable the rashness of men who hold a different opinion.

The authority of Scripture, as regards the character of these men of ancient times, is supported by the evidence from the prophecies which they contain, and which are now receiving their fulfillment.

68.

We see the same thing in the Gospel, where the devils confess that Christ is the Son of God in the words used by Peter, but with a very different heart.

So, though the words were the same, Peter is praised for his faith, while the impiety of the devils is checked.

For Christ, not by human sense, but by divine knowledge, could inspect and infallibly discriminate the sources from which the words came. Besides, there are multitudes who confess that Christ is the Son of the living God, without meriting the same approval as Peter--not only of those who shall say in that day, "Lord, Lord," and shall receive the sentence, "Depart from me," but also of those who shall be placed on the right hand.

They may probably never have denied Christ even once; they may never have opposed His suffering for our salvation; they may never have forced the Gentiles to do as the Jews; [900] and yet they shall not be honored equally with Peter, who, though he did all these things, will sit on one of the twelve thrones, and judge not only the twelve tribes, but the angels.

So, again, many who have never desired another man's wife, or procured the death of the husband, as David did, will never reach the place which David nevertheless held in the divine favor.

There is a vast difference between what is in itself so undesirable that it must be utterly rejected, and the rich and plenteous harvest which may afterwards appear.

For farmers are best pleased with the fields from which, after weeding them, it may be, of great thistles, they receive an hundred-fold; not with fields which have never had any thistles, and hardly bear thirty-fold.

69.

So Moses, too, who was so faithful a servant of God in all his house; the minister of the holy, just, and good law; of whose character the apostle speaks in the words here quoted; [901] the minister also of the symbols which, though not conferring salvation, promised the Saviour, as the Saviour Himself shows, when He says, "If ye believed Moses, ye would also believe me, for he wrote of me,"--from which passage we have already sufficiently answered the presumptuous cavils of the Manichæans;--this Moses, the servant of the living, the true, the most high God, that made heaven and earth, not of a foreign substance, but of nothing--not from the pressure of necessity, but from plenitude of goodness--not by the suffering of His members, but by the power of His word;--this Moses, who humbly put from him this high ministry, but obediently accepted it, and faithfully kept it, and diligently fulfilled it; who ruled the people with vigilance, reproved them with vehemence, loved them with fervor, and bore with them in patience, standing for his subjects before God to receive His counsel, and to appease His wrath;--this great and good man is not to be judged of from Faustus' malicious representations, but from what is said by God, whose word is a true expression of His true opinion of this man, whom He knew because He made him.

For the sins of men are also known to God, though He is not their author; but He takes notice of them as a judge in those who refuse to own them, and pardons them as a father in those who make confession.

His servant Moses, as thus described, we love and admire and to the best of our power imitate, coming indeed far short of his merits, though we have killed no Egyptian, nor plundered any one, nor carried on any war; which actions of Moses were in one case prompted by the zeal of the future champion of his people, and in the other cases commanded by God.

70.

It might be shown that, though Moses slew the Egyptian, without being commanded by God, the action was divinely permitted, as, from the prophetic character of Moses, it prefigured something in the future. Now however, I do not use this argument, but view the action as having no symbolical meaning.

In the light, then, of the eternal law, it was wrong for one who had no legal authority to kill the man, even though he was a bad character, besides being the aggressor.

But in minds where great virtue is to come, there is often an early crop of vices, in which we may still discern a disposition for some particular virtue, which will come when the mind is duly cultivated.

For as farmers, when they see land bringing forth huge crops, though of weeds, pronounce it good for corn; or when they see wild creepers, which have to be rooted out, still consider the land good for useful vines; and when they see a hill covered with wild olives, conclude that with culture it will produce good fruit:

so the disposition of mind which led Moses to take the law into his own hands, to prevent the wrong done to his brother, living among strangers, by a wicked citizen of the country from being unrequited, was not unfit for the production of virtue, but from want of culture gave signs of its productiveness in an unjustifiable manner.

He who afterwards, by His angel, called Moses on Mount Sinai, with the divine commission to liberate the people of Israel from Egypt, and who trained him to obedience by the miraculous appearance in the bush burning but not consumed, and by instructing him in his ministry, was the same who, by the call addressed from heaven to Saul when persecuting the Church, humbled him, raised him up, and animated him; or in figurative words, by this stroke He cut off the branch, grafted it, and made it fruitful.

For the fierce energy of Paul, when in his zeal for hereditary traditions he persecuted the Church, thinking that he was doing God service, was like a crop of weeds showing great signs of productiveness.

It was the same in Peter, when he took his sword out of its sheath to defend the Lord, and cut off the right ear of an assailant, when the Lord rebuked him with something like a threat, saying, "Put up thy sword into its sheath; for he that taketh the sword shall perish by the sword." [902] To take the sword is to use weapons against a man's life, without the sanction of the constituted authority.

The Lord, indeed, had told His disciples to carry a sword; but He did not tell them to use it.

But that after this sin Peter should become a pastor of the Church was no more improper than that Moses, after smiting the Egyptian, should become the leader of the congregation.

In both cases the trespass originated not in inveterate cruelty, but in a hasty zeal which admitted of correction.

In both cases there was resentment against injury, accompanied in one case by love for a brother, and in the other by love, though still carnal, of the Lord.

Here was evil to be subdued or rooted out; but the heart with such capacities needed only, like good soil, to be cultivated to make it fruitful in virtue.

71.

Then, as for Faustus' objection to the spoiling of the Egyptians, he knows not what he says. In this Moses not only did not sin, but it would have been sin not to do it.

It was by the command of God, [903] who, from His knowledge both of the actions and of the hearts of men, can decide on what every one should be made to suffer, and through whose agency.

The people at that time were still carnal, and engrossed with earthly affections; while the Egyptians were in open rebellion against God, for they used the gold, God's creature, in the service of idols, to the dishonor of the Creator, and they had grievously oppressed strangers by making them work without pay.

Thus the Egyptians deserved the punishment, and the Israelites were suitably employed in inflicting it.

Perhaps, indeed, it was not so much a command as a permission to the Hebrews to act in the matter according to their own inclinations; and God, in sending the message by Moses, only wished that they should thus be informed of His permission.

There may also have been mysterious reasons for what God said to the people on this matter.

At any rate, God's commands are to be submissively received, not to be argued against.

The apostle says, "Who hath known the mind of the Lord? or who hath been His counsellor?"[904] Whether, then, the reason was what I have said, or whether in the secret appointment of God, there was some unknown reason for His telling the people by Moses to borrow things from the Egyptians, and to take them away with them, this remains certain, that this was said for some good reason, and that Moses could not lawfully have done otherwise than God told him, leaving to God the reason of the command, while the servant's duty is to obey.

72.

But, says Faustus, it cannot be admitted that the true God, who is also good, ever gave such a command.

I answer, such a command can be rightly given by no other than the true and good God, who alone knows the suitable command in every case, and who alone is incapable of inflicting unmerited suffering on any one.

This ignorant and spurious goodness of the human heart may as well deny what Christ says, and object to the wicked being made to suffer by the good God, when He shall say to the angels, "Gather first the tares into bundles to burn them."

The servants, however, were stopped when they wished to do this prematurely:

"Lest by chance, when ye would gather the tares, ye root up the wheat also with them."[905] Thus the true and good God alone knows when, to whom, and by whom to order anything, or to permit anything.

In the same way, this human goodness, or folly rather, might object to the Lord's permitting the devils to enter the swine, which they asked to be allowed to do with a mischievous intent, [906] especially as the Manichæans believe that not only pigs, but the vilest insects, have human souls.

But setting aside these absurd notions, this is undeniable, that our Lord Jesus Christ, the only son of God, and therefore the true and good God, permitted the destruction of swine belonging to strangers, implying loss of life and of a great amount of property, at the request of devils.

No one can be so insane as to suppose that Christ could not have driven the devils out of the men without gratifying their malice by the destruction of the swine.

If, then, the Creator and Governor of all natures, in His superintendence, which, though mysterious, is ever just, indulged the violent and unjust inclination of those lost spirits already doomed to eternal fire, why should not the Egyptians, who were unrighteous oppressors, be spoiled by the Hebrews, a free people, who would claim payment for their enforced and painful toil, especially as the earthly possessions which they thus lost were used by the Egyptians in their impious rites, to the dishonor of the Creator?

Still, if Moses had originated this order, or if the people had done it spontaneously, undoubtedly it would have been sinful; and perhaps the people did sin, not in doing what God commanded or permitted, but in some desire of their own for what they took.

The permission given to this action by divine authority was in accordance with the just and good counsel of Him who uses punishments both to restrain the wicked and to educate His own people; who knows also how to give more advanced precepts to those able to bear them, while He begins on a lower scale in the treatment of the feeble.

As for Moses, he can be blamed neither for coveting the property, nor for disputing, in any instance, the divine authority.

73.

According to the eternal law, which requires the preservation of natural order, and forbids the transgression of it, some actions have an indifferent character, so that men are blamed for presumption if they do them without being called upon, while they are deservedly praised for doing them when required.

The act, the agent, and the authority for the action are all of great importance in the order of nature.

For Abraham to sacrifice his son of his own accord is shocking madness.

His doing so at the command of God proves him faithful and submissive.

This is so loudly proclaimed by the very voice of truth, that Faustus, eagerly rummaging for some fault, and reduced at last to slanderous charges, has not the boldness to attack this action.

It is scarcely possible that he can have forgotten a deed so famous, that it recurs to the mind of itself without any study or reflection, and is in fact repeated by so many tongues, and portrayed in so many places, that no one can pretend to shut his eyes or his ears to it.

If, therefore, while Abraham's killing his son of his own accord would have been unnatural, his doing it at the command of God shows not only guiltless but praiseworthy compliance, why does Faustus blame Moses for spoiling the Egyptians?

Your feeling of disapproval for the mere human action should be restrained by a regard for the divine sanction.

Will you venture to blame God Himself for desiring such actions?

Then "Get thee behind me, Satan, for thou understandest not the things which be of God, but those which be of men."

Would that this rebuke might accomplish in you what it did in Peter, and that you might hereafter preach the truth concerning God, which you now, judging by feeble sense, find fault with! as Peter became a zealous messenger to announce to the Gentiles what he objected to at first, when the Lord spoke of it as His intention.

74.

Now, if this explanation suffices to satisfy human obstinacy and perverse misinterpretation of right actions of the vast difference between the indulgence of passion and presumption on the part of men, and obedience to the command of God, who knows what to permit or to order, and also the time and the persons, and the due action or suffering in each case, the account of the wars of Moses will not excite surprise or abhorrence, for in wars carried on by divine command, he showed not ferocity but obedience; and God in giving the command, acted not in cruelty, but in righteous retribution, giving to all what they deserved, and warning those who needed warning.

What is the evil in war?

Is it the death of some who will soon die in any case, that others may live in peaceful subjection?

This is mere cowardly dislike, not any religious feeling.

The real evils in war are love of violence, revengeful cruelty, fierce and implacable enmity, wild resistance, and the lust of power, and such like; and it is generally to punish these things, when force is required to inflict the punishment, that, in obedience to God or some lawful authority, good men undertake wars, when they find themselves in such a position as regards the conduct of human affairs, that right conduct requires them to act, or to make others act in this way.

Otherwise John, when the soldiers who came to be baptized asked, What shall we do? would have replied, Throw away your arms; give up the service; never strike, or wound, or disable any one.

But knowing that such actions in battle were not murderous but authorized by law, and that the soldiers did not thus avenge themselves, but defend the public safety, he replied, "Do violence to no man, accuse no man falsely, and be content with your wages." [907] But as the Manichæans are in the habit of speaking evil of John, let them hear the Lord Jesus Christ Himself ordering this money to be given to Cæsar, which John tells the soldiers to be content with.

"Give," He says, "to Cæsar the things that are Cæsar's." [908] For tribute-money is given on purpose to pay the soldiers for war. Again, in the case of the centurion who said, "I am a man under authority, and have soldiers under me:

and I say to one, Go, and he goeth; and to another, Come, and he cometh; and to my servant, Do this, and he doeth it," Christ gave due praise to his faith; [909] He did not tell him to leave the service.

But there is no need here to enter on the long discussion of just and unjust ways.

75.

A great deal depends on the causes for which men undertake wars, and on the authority they have for doing so; for the natural order which seeks the peace of mankind, ordains that the monarch should have the power of undertaking war if he thinks it advisable, and that the soldiers should perform their military duties in behalf of the peace and safety of the community.

When war is undertaken in obedience to God, who would rebuke, or humble, or crush the pride of man, it must be allowed to be a righteous war; for even the wars which arise from human passion cannot harm the eternal well-being of God, nor even hurt His saints; for in the trial of their patience, and the chastening of their spirit, and in bearing fatherly correction, they are rather benefited than injured.

No one can have any power against them but what is given him from above.

For there is no power but of God, [910] who either orders or permits.

Since, therefore, a righteous man, serving it may be under an ungodly king, may do the duty belonging to his position in the State in fighting by the order of his sovereign,--for in some cases it is plainly the will of God that he should fight, and in others, where this is not so plain, it may be an unrighteous command on the part of the king, while the soldier is innocent, because his position makes obedience a duty,--how much more must the man be blameless who carries on war on the authority of God, of whom every one who serves Him knows that He can never require what is wrong?

76.

If it is supposed that God could not enjoin warfare, because in after times it was said by the Lord Jesus Christ, "I say unto you, That ye resist not evil:

but if any one strike thee on the right cheek, turn to him the left also," [911] the answer is, that what is here required is not a bodily action, but an inward disposition.

The sacred seat of virtue is the heart, and such were the hearts of our fathers, the righteous men of old.

But order required such a regulation of events, and such a distinction of times, as to show first of all that even earthly blessings (for so temporal kingdoms and victory over enemies are considered to be, and these are the things which the community of the ungodly all over the world are continually begging from idols and devils) are entirely under the control and at the disposal of the one true God.

Thus, under the Old Testament, the secret of the kingdom of heaven, which was to be disclosed in due time, was veiled, and so far obscured, in the disguise of earthly promises. But when the fullness of time came for the revelation of the New Testament, which was hidden under the types of the Old, clear testimony was to be borne to the truth, that there is another life for which this life ought to be disregarded, and another kingdom for which the opposition of all earthly kingdoms should be patiently borne.

Thus the name martyrs, which means witnesses, was given to those who, by the will of God, bore this testimony, by their confessions, their sufferings, and their death.

The number of such witnesses is so great, that if it pleased Christ--who called Saul by a voice from heaven, and having changed him from a wolf to a sheep, sent him into the midst of wolves--to unite them all in one army, and to give them success in battle, as He gave to the Hebrews, what nation could withstand them? what kingdom would remain unsubdued?

But as the doctrine of the New Testament is, that we must serve God not for temporal happiness in this life, but for eternal felicity hereafter, this truth was most strikingly confirmed by the patient endurance of what is commonly called adversity for the sake of that felicity.

So in fullness of time the Son of God, made of a woman, made under the law, that He might redeem them that were under the law, made of the seed of David according to the flesh sends His disciples as sheep into the midst of wolves, and bids them not fear those that can kill the body, but cannot kill the soul, and promises that even the body will be entirely restored, so that not a hair shall be lost. [912]Peter's sword He orders back into its sheath, restoring as it was before the ear of His enemy that had been cut off.

He says that He could obtain legions of angels to destroy His enemies, but that He must drink the cup which His Father's will had given Him. [913]He sets the example of drinking this cup, then hands it to His followers, manifesting thus, both in word and deed, the grace of patience.

Therefore God raised Him from the dead, and has given Him a name which is above every name; that in the name of Jesus every knee should bow, of things in heaven and of things in earth, and of things under the earth; and that every tongue should confess that Jesus is Lord, to the glory of God the Father. [914]The patriarchs and prophets, then, have a kingdom in this world, to show that these kingdoms, too, are given and taken away by God:

the apostles and martyrs had no kingdom here, to show the superior desirableness of the kingdom of heaven.

The prophets, however, could even in those times die for the truth, as the Lord Himself says, "From the blood of Abel to the blood of Zacharia; [915] and in these days, since the commencement of the fulfillment of what is prophesied in the psalm of Christ, under the figure of Solomon, which means the peacemaker, as Christ is our peace, [916] "All kings of the earth shall bow to Him, all nations shall serve Him," [917] we have seen Christian emperors, who have put all their confidence in Christ, gaining splendid victories over ungodly enemies, whose hope was in the rites of idolatry and devil-worship.

There are public and undeniable proofs of the fact, that on one side the prognostications of devils were found to be fallacious, and on the other, the predictions of saints were a means of support; and we have now writings in which those facts are recorded.

77.

If our foolish opponents are surprised at the difference between the precepts given by God to the ministers of the Old Testament, at a time when the grace of the New was still undisclosed, and those given to the preachers of the New Testament, now that the obscurity of the Old is removed, they will find Christ Himself saying one thing at one time, and another at another.

"When I sent you," He says, "without scrip, or purse, or shoes, did ye lack anything?

And they said, Nothing.

Then saith He to them, But now, he that hath a scrip, let him take it, and also a purse; and he that hath not a sword, let him sell his garment, and buy one."

If the Manichæans found passages in the Old and New Testaments differing in this way, they would proclaim it as a proof that the Testaments are opposed to each other.

But here the difference is in the utterances of one and the same person.

At one time He says, "I sent you without scrip, or purse, or shoes, and ye lacked nothing;" at another, "Now let him that hath a scrip take it, and also a purse; and he that hath a tunic, let him sell it and buy a sword."

Does not this show how, without any inconsistency, precepts and counsels and permissions may be changed, as different times require different arrangements?

If it is said that there was a symbolical meaning in the command to take a scrip and purse, and to buy a sword, why may there not be a symbolical meaning in the fact, that one and the same God commanded the prophets in old times to make war, and forbade the apostles?

And we find in the passage that we have quoted from the Gospel, that the words spoken by the Lord were carried into effect by His disciples.

For, besides going at first without scrip or purse, and yet lacking nothing, as from the Lord's question and their answer it is plain they did, now that He speaks of buying a sword, they say, "Lo, here are two swords;" and He replied, "It is enough."

Hence we find Peter with a weapon when he cut off the assailant's ear, on which occasion his spontaneous boldness was checked, because, although he had been told to take a sword, he had not been told to use it. [918] Doubtless, it was mysterious that the Lord should require them to carry weapons, and forbid the use of them.

But it was His part to give the suitable precepts, and it was their part to obey without reserve.

78.

It is therefore mere groundless calumny to charge Moses with making war, for there would have been less harm in making war of his own accord, than in not doing it when God commanded him.

And to dare to find fault with God Himself for giving such a command, or not to believe it possible that a just and good God did so, shows, to say the least, an inability to consider that in the view of divine providence, which pervades all things from the highest to the lowest, time can neither add anything nor take away; but all things go, or come, or remain according to the order of nature or desert in each separate case, while in men a right will is in union with the divine law, and ungoverned passion is restrained by the order of divine law; so that a good man wills only what is commanded, and a bad man can do only what is permitted, at the same time that he is punished for what he wills to do unjustly.

Thus, in all the things which appear shocking and terrible to human feebleness, the real evil is the injustice; the rest is only the result of natural properties or of moral demerit.

This injustice is seen in every case where a man loves for their own sake things which are desirable only as means to an end, and seeks for the sake of something else things which ought to be loved for themselves. For thus, as far as he can, he disturbs in himself the natural order which the eternal law requires us to observe.

Again, a man is just when he seeks to use things only for the end for which God appointed them, and to enjoy God as the end of all, while he enjoys himself and his friend in God and for God.

For to love in a friend the love of God is to love the friend for God.

Now both justice and injustice, to be acts at all, must be voluntary; otherwise, there can be no just rewards or punishments; which no man in his senses will assert.

The ignorance and infirmity which prevent a man from knowing his duty, or from doing all he wishes to do, belong to God's secret penal arrangement, and to His unfathomable judgments, for with Him there is no iniquity.

Thus we are informed by the sure word of God of Adam's sin; and Scripture truly declares that in him all die, and that by him sin entered into the world, and death by sin. [919] And our experience gives abundant evidence, that in punishment for this sin our body is corrupted, and weighs down the soul, and the clay tabernacle clogs the mind in its manifold activity; [920] and we know that we can be freed from this punishment only by gracious interposition.

So the apostle cries out in distress, "O wretched man that I am! who shall deliver me from the body of this death? The grace of God through Jesus Christ our Lord." [921]

So much we know; but the reasons for the distribution of divine judgment and mercy, why one is in this condition, and another in that, though just, are unknown.

Still, we are sure that all these things are due either to the mercy or the judgment of God, while the measures and numbers and weights by which the Creator of all natural productions arranges all things are concealed from our view.

For God is not the author, but He is the controller of sin; so that sinful actions, which are sinful because they are against nature, are judged and controlled, and assigned to their proper place and condition, in order that they may not bring discord and disgrace on universal nature.

This being the case, and as the judgments of God and the movements of man's will contain the hidden reason why the same prosperous circumstances which some make a right use of are the ruin of others, and the same afflictions under which some give way are profitable to others, and since the whole mortal life of man upon earth is a trial, [922] who can tell whether it may be good or bad in any particular case--in time of peace, to reign or to serve, or to be at ease or to die--or in time of war, to command or to fight, or to conquer or to be killed?

At the same time, it remains true, that whatever is good is so by the divine blessing, and whatever is bad is so by the divine judgment.

79.

Let no one, then, be so daring as to make rash charges against men, not to say against God.

If the service of the ministers of the Old Testament, who were also heralds of the New, consisted in putting sinners to death, and that of the ministers of the New Testament, who are also interpreters of the Old, in being put to death by sinners, the service in both cases is rendered to one God, who, varying the lesson to suit the times, teaches both that temporal blessings are to be sought from Him, and that they are to be forsaken for Him, and that temporal distress is both sent by Him and should be endured for Him. There was, therefore, no cruelty in the command, or in the action of Moses, when, in his holy jealousy for his people, whom he wished to be subject to the one true God, on learning that they had fallen away to the worship of an idol made by their own hands, he impressed their minds at the time with a wholesome fear, and gave them a warning for the future, by using the sword in the punishment of a few, whose just punishment God, against whom they had sinned, appointed in the depth of His secret judgment to be immediately inflicted.

That Moses acted as he did, not in cruelty, but in great love, may be seen from the words in which he prayed for the sins of the people:

"If Thou wilt forgive their sin, forgive it; and if not, blot me out of Thy book." [923] The pious inquirer who compares the slaughter with the prayer will find in this the clearest evidence of the awful nature of the injury done to the soul by prostitution to the images of devils, since such love is roused to such anger.

We see the same in the apostle, who, not in cruelty, but in love, delivered a man up to Satan for the destruction of the flesh, that the spirit might be saved in the day of the Lord Jesus.[924] Others, too, he delivered up, that they might learn not to blaspheme. [925] In the apocryphal books of the Manichæans there is a collection of fables, published by some unknown authors under the name of the apostles.

The books would no doubt have been sanctioned by the Church at the time of their publication, if holy and learned men then in life, and competent to determine the matter, had thought the contents to be true.

One of the stories is, that the Apostle Thomas was once at a marriage feast in a country where he was unknown, when one of the servants struck him, and that he forthwith by his curse brought a terrible punishment on this man.

For when he went out to the fountain to provide water for the guests, a lion fell on him and killed him, and the hand with which he had given a slight blow to the apostle was torn off, in fulfillment of the imprecation, and brought by a dog to the table at which the apostle was reclining.

What could be more cruel than this?

And yet, if I mistake not, the story goes on to say, that the apostle made up for the cruelty by obtaining for the man the blessing of pardon in the next world; so that, while the people of this strange country learned to fear the apostle as being so dear to God, the man's eternal welfare was secured in exchange for the loss of this mortal life.

It matters not whether the story is true or false.

At any rate, the Manichæans, who regard as genuine and authentic books which the canon of the Church rejects, must allow, as shown in the story, that the virtue of patience, which the Lord enjoins when He says, "If any one smite thee on the right cheek, turn to him thy left also," may be in the inward disposition, though it is not exhibited in bodily action or in words.

For when the apostle was struck, instead of turning his other side to the man, or telling him to repeat the blow, he prayed to God to pardon his assailant in the next world, but not to leave the injury unpunished at the time.

Inwardly he preserved a kindly feeling, while outwardly he wished the man to be punished as an example.

As the Manichæans believe this, rightly or wrongly, they may also believe that such was the intention of Moses, the servant of God, when he cut down with the sword the makers and worshippers of the idol; for his own words show that he so entreated for pardon for their sin of idolatry as to ask to be blotted out of God's book if his prayer was not heard.

There is no comparison between a stranger being struck with the hand, and the dishonor done to God by forsaking Him for an idol, when He had brought the people out of the bondage of Egypt, had led them through the sea, and had covered with the waters the enemy pursuing them.

Nor, as regards the punishment, is there any comparison between being killed with the sword and being torn in pieces by wild beasts.

For judges in administering the law condemn to exposure to wild beasts worse criminals than are condemned to be put to death by the sword.

80.

Another of Faustus' malicious and impious charges which has to be answered, is about the Lord's saying to the prophet Hosea, "Take unto thee a wife of whoredoms and children of whoredoms." [926] As regards this passage, the impure mind of our adversaries is so blinded that they do not understand the plain words of the Lord in His gospel, when He says to the Jews, "The publicans and harlots shall go into the kingdom of heaven before you." [927] There is nothing contrary to the mercifulness of truth, or inconsistent with Christian faith, in a harlot leaving fornication, and becoming a chaste wife.

Indeed, nothing could be more unbecoming in one professing to be a prophet than not to believe that all the sins of the fallen woman were pardoned when she changed for the better.

So when the prophet took the harlot as his wife, it was both good for the woman to have her life amended, and the action symbolized a truth of which we shall speak presently.

But it is plain what offends the Manichæans in this case; for their great anxiety is to prevent harlots from being with child.

It would have pleased them better that the woman should continue a prostitute, so as not to bring their god into confinement, than that she should become the wife of one man, and have children.

81.

As regards Solomon, it need only be said that the condemnation of his conduct in the faithful narrative of holy Scripture is much more serious than the childish vehemence of Faustus' attacks.

The Scripture tells us with faithful accuracy both the good that Solomon had at first, and the evil actions by which he lost the good he began with; while Faustus, in his attacks, like a man closing his eyes, or with no eyes at all, seeks no guidance from the light, but is prompted only by violent animosity.

To pious and discerning readers of the sacred Scriptures evidence of the chastity of the holy men who are said to have had several wives is found in this, that Solomon, who by his polygamy gratified his passions, instead of seeking for offspring, is expressly noted as chargeable with being a lover of women.

This, as we are informed by the truth which accepts no man's person, led him down into the abyss of idolatry.

82.
Having now gone over all the cases in which Faustus finds fault with the Old Testament, and having attended to the merit of each, either defending men of God against the calumnies of carnal heretics, or, where the men were at fault, showing the excellence and the majesty of Scripture, let us again take the cases in the order of Faustus' accusations, and see the meaning of the actions recorded, what they typify, and what they foretell.

This we have already done in the case of Abraham, Isaac, and Jacob, of whom God said that He was their God, as if the God of universal nature were the God of none besides them; not honoring them with an unmeaning title, but because He, who could alone have a full and perfect knowledge, knew the sincere and remarkable charity of these men; and because these three patriarchs united formed a notable type of the future people of God, in not only having free children by free women, as by Sarah, and Rebecca, and Leah, and Rachel, but also bond children, as of this same Rebecca was born Esau, to whom it was said, "Thou shalt serve thy brother;" [928] and in having by bond women not only bond children, as by Hagar, but also free children, as by Bilhah and Zilphah.

Thus also in the people of God, those spiritually free not only have children born into the enjoyment of liberty, like those to whom it is said, "Be ye followers of me, as I also am of Christ,"[929] but they have also children born into guilty bondage, as Simon was born of Philip.[930] Again, from carnal bondmen are born not only children of guilty bondage, who imitate them, but also children of happy liberty, to whom it is said, "What they say, do; but do not after their works."[931] Whoever rightly observes the fulfillment of this type in the people of God, keeps the unity of the Spirit in the bond of peace, by continuing to the end in union with some, and in patient endurance of others.

Of Lot, also, we have already spoken, and have shown what the Scripture mentions as praiseworthy in him, and what as blameworthy and the meaning of the whole narrative.

83.
We have next to consider the prophetic significance of the action of Judah in lying with his daughter-in-law.

But, for the sake of those whose understanding is feeble, we shall begin with observing, that in sacred Scripture evil actions are sometimes prophetic not of evil, but of good.

Divine providence preserves throughout its essential goodness, so that, as in the example given above, from adulterous intercourse a man-child is born, a good work of God from the evil of man, by the power of nature, and not due to the misconduct of the parents; so in the prophetic Scriptures, where both good and evil actions are recorded, the narrative being itself prophetic, foretells something good even by the record of what is evil, the credit being due not to the evil-doer, but to the writer.

Judah, when, to gratify his sinful passion, he went in to Tamar, had no intention by his licentious conduct to typify anything connected with the salvation of men, any more than Judas, who betrayed the Lord, intended to produce any result connected with the salvation of men.

So then if from the evil deed of Judas the Lord brought the good work of our redemption by His own passion, why should not His prophet, of whom He Himself says "He wrote of me," for the sake of instructing us make the evil action of Judah significant of something good?

Under the guidance and inspiration of the Holy Spirit, the prophet has compiled a narrative of actions so as to make a continuous prophecy of the things he designed to foretell. In foretelling good, it is of no consequence whether the typical actions are good or bad.

If it is written in red ink that the Ethiopians are black, or in black ink that the Gauls are white, this circumstance does not affect the information which the writing conveys.

No doubt, if it was a painting instead of a writing, the wrong color would be a fault; so when human actions are represented for example or for warning much depends on whether they are good or bad. But when actions are related or recorded as types, the merit or demerit of the agents is a matter of no importance, as long as there is a true typical relation between the action and the thing signified.

So in the case of Caiaphas in the Gospel as regards his iniquitous and mischievous intention, and even as regards his words in the sense in which he used them, that a just man should be put to death unjustly, assuredly they were bad; and yet there was a good meaning in his words which he did not know of when he said, "It is expedient that one man should die for the people and that the whole nation perish not."

So it is written of Him, "This he spake not of himself; but being the high priest, he prophesied that Jesus should die for the people." [932] In the same way the action of Judah was bad as regards his sinful passion, but it typified a great good he knew nothing of.

Of himself he did evil while it was not of himself that he typified good.

These introductory remarks apply not only to Judah, but also to all the other cases where in the narrative of bad actions is contained a prophecy of good.

84.

In Tamar, then, the daughter-in-law of Judah, we see the people of the kingdom of Judah, whose kings, answering to Tamar's husbands, were taken from this tribe.

Tamar means bitterness; and the meaning is suitable, for this people gave the cup of gall to the Lord. [933]The two sons of Judah represent two classes of kings who governed ill--those who did harm and those who did no good.

One of these sons was evil or cruel before the Lord; the other spilled the seed on the ground that Tamar might not become a mother.

There are only those two kinds of useless people in the world--the injurious and those who will not give the good they have but lose it or spill it on the ground.

And as injury is worse than not doing good, the evil-doer is called the elder and the other the younger.

Er, the name of the elder, means a preparer of skins, which were the coats given to our first parents when they were punished with expulsion from paradise. [934]Onan, the name of the younger, means, their grief; that is, the grief of those to whom he does no good, wasting the good he has on the earth.

The loss of life implied in the name of the elder is a greater evil than the want of help implied in the name of the younger.

Both being killed by God typifies the removal of the kingdom from men of this character.

The meaning of the third son of Judah not being joined to the woman, is that for a time the kings of Judah were not of that tribe.

So this third son did not become the husband of Tamar; as Tamar represents the tribe of Judah, which continued to exist, although the people received no king from it.

Hence the name of this son, Selom, means, his dismission.

None of those types apply to the holy and righteous men who, like David, though they lived in those times, belong properly to the New Testament, which they served by their enlightened predictions. Again, in the time when Judah ceased to have a king of its own tribe, the elder Herod does not count as one of the kings typified by the husbands of Tamar; for he was a foreigner, and his union with the people was never consecrated with the holy oil.

His was the power of a stranger, given him by the Romans and by Cæsar.

And it was the same with his sons, the tetrarchs, one of whom, called Herod, like his father, agreed with Pilate at the time of the Lord's passion. [935] So plainly were these foreigners considered as distinct from the sacred monarchy of Judah, that the Jews themselves, when raging against Christ, exclaimed openly, "We have no king but Cæsar." [936]Nor was Cæsar properly their king, except in the sense that all the world was subject to Rome.

The Jews thus condemned themselves, only to express their rejection of Christ, and to flatter Cæsar.

85.

The time when the kingdom was removed from the tribe of Judah was the time appointed for the coming of Christ our Lord, the true Saviour, who should come not for harm, but for great good.

Thus was it prophesied, "A prince shall not fail from Judah, nor a leader from his loins, till He come for whom it is reserved:

He is the desire of nations." [937]Not only the kingdom, but all government, of the Jews had ceased, and also, as prophesied by Daniel, the sacred anointing from which the name Christ or Anointed is derived.

Then came He for whom it was reserved, the desire of nations; and the holy of holies was anointed with the oil of gladness above His fellows. [938]Christ was born in the time of the elder Herod, and suffered in the time of Herod the tetrarch.

He who thus came to the lost sheep of the house of Israel was typified by Judah when he went to shear his sheep in Thamna, which means, failing.

For then the prince had failed from Judah, with all the government and anointing of the Jews, that He might come for whom it was reserved.

Judah, we are told, came with his Adullamite shepherd, whose name was Iras; and Adullamite means, a testimony in water.

So it was with this testimony that the Lord came, having indeed greater testimony than that of John; [939] but for the sake of his feeble sheep he made use of the testimony in water.

The name Iras, too, means, vision of my brother.

So John saw his brother, a brother in the family of Abraham, and from the relationship of

Mary and Elisabeth; and the same person he recognised as his Lord and his God, for, as he himself says, he received of His fullness. [940] On account of this vision, among those born of woman, there has arisen no greater than he; [941] because, of all who foretold Christ, he alone saw what many righteous men and prophets desired to see and saw not. He saluted Christ from the womb; [942] he knew Him more certainly from seeing the dove; and therefore, as the Adullamite, he gave testimony by water.

The Lord came to shear His sheep, in releasing them from painful burdens, as it is said in praise of the Church in the Song of Songs, that her teeth are like a flock of sheep after shearing. [943]

86.

Next, we have Tamar changing her dress; for Tamar also means changing.

Still, the name of bitterness must be retained--not that bitterness in which gall was given to the Lord, but that in which Peter wept bitterly. [944] For Judah means confession; and bitterness is mingled with confession as a type of true repentance.

It is this repentance which gives fruitfulness to the Church established among all nations.

For "it behoved Christ to suffer, and to rise from the dead, and that repentance and the remission of sins be preached among all nations in His name, beginning at Jerusalem." [945] In the dress Tamar put on there is a confession of sins; and Tamar sitting in this dress at the gate of Ænan or Ænaim, which means fountain, is a type of the Church called from among the nations.

She ran as a hart to the springs of water, to meet with the seed of Abraham; and there she is made fruitful by one who knows her not, as it is foretold, "A people whom I have not known shall serve me." [946] Tamar received under her disguise a ring, a bracelet, a staff; she is sealed in her calling, adorned in her justification, raised in her glorification.

For "whom He predestinated, them He also called: and whom He called, them He also justified:

and whom He justified, them He also glorified." [947] This was while she was still disguised, as I have said; and in the same state she conceives, and becomes fruitful in holiness.

Also the kid promised is sent to her as to a harlot.

The kid represents rebuke for sin, and it is sent by the Adullamite already mentioned, who, as it were, uses the reproachful words, "O generation of vipers!" [948] But this rebuke for sin does not reach her, for she has been changed by the bitterness of confession.

Afterwards, by exhibiting the pledges of the ring and bracelet and staff, she prevails over the Jews, in their hasty judgment of her, who are now represented by Judah himself; as at this day we hear the Jews saying that we are not the people of Christ, and have not the seed of Abraham.

But when we exhibit the sure tokens of our calling and justification and glorification, they will immediately be confounded, and will acknowledge that we are justified rather than they.

I should enter into this more particularly, taking, as it were, each limb and joint separately, as the Lord might enable me, were it not that such minute inquiry is prevented by the necessity of bringing this work to a close, for it is already longer than is desirable.

87.

As regards the prophetic significance of David's sin, a single word must suffice.

The names occurring in the narrative show what it typifies.

David means, strong of hand, or desirable; and what can be stronger than the Lion of the tribe of Judah, who has conquered the world, or more desirable than He of whom the prophet says, "The desire of all nations shall come?" [949] Bersabee means, well of satisfaction, or seventh well:

either of these interpretations will suit our purpose.

So, in the Song of Songs, the spouse, who is the Church, is called a well of living water; [950] or again, the number seven represents the Holy Spirit, as in the number of days in Pentecost, when the Holy Spirit came from heaven.

We learn also from the book of Tobit, that Pentecost was the feast of seven weeks. [951] To forty-nine, which is seven times seven, one is added to denote unity.

To this effect is the saying of the apostle:

"Bearing with one another in love, endeavoring to keep the unity of the Spirit in the bond of peace." [952] The Church becomes a well of satisfaction by this gift of the Spirit, the number seven denoting its spirituality; for it is in her a fountain of living water springing up unto everlasting life, and he who has it shall never thirst. [953] Uriah, Bersabee's husband, must, from the meaning of his name, be understood as representing the devil.

It is in union to the devil that all are bound whom the grace of God sets free, that the Church without spot or wrinkle may be married to her true Saviour.

Uriah means, my light of God; and Hittite means, cut off, referring either to his not abiding in the truth, when he was cut off on account of his pride from the celestial light which he had of God, or to his transforming himself into an angel of light, because after losing his real strength by his fall, he still dares to say, My light is of God.

The literal David, then, was guilty of a heinous crime, which God by the prophet condemned in the rebuke addressed to David, and which David atoned for by his repentance.

On the other hand, He who is the desire of all nations loved the Church when washing herself on the roof, that is, when cleansing herself from the pollution of the world, and in spiritual contemplation mounting above her house of clay, and trampling upon it; and after commencing an acquaintance, He puts to death the devil, whom He first entirely removes from her, and joins her to Himself in perpetual union.

While we hate the sin, we must not overlook the prophetical significance; and while we love, as is His due, that David who in His mercy has freed us from the devil, we may also love the David who by the humility of his repentance healed the wound made by his transgression.

88.
Little need be said of Solomon, who is spoken of in Holy Scripture in terms of the strongest disapproval and condemnation, while nothing is said of his repentance and restoration to the divine favor.

Nor can I find in his lamentable fall even a symbolical connection with anything good.

Perhaps the strange women he lusted after may be thought to represent the Churches chosen from among the Gentiles.

This idea might have been admissible, if the women had left their gods for Solomon's sake to worship his God.

But as he for their sakes offended his God and worshipped their gods, it seems impossible to think of any good meaning.

Doubtless, something is typified, but it is something bad, as in the case already explained of Lot's wife and daughters.

We see in Solomon a notable pre-eminence and a notable fall.

Now, this good and evil which we see in him at different periods, first good and then evil, are in our day found together in the Church.

What is good in Solomon represents, I think, the good members of the Church; and what was bad in him represents the bad members.

Both are in one man, as the bad and the good are in the chaff and grain of one floor, or in the tares and wheat of one field.

A closer inquiry into what is said of Solomon in Scripture might disclose, either to me or to others of greater learning and greater worth, some more probable interpretation. But as we are now engaged on a different subject, we must not allow this matter to break the connection of our discourse.

89.
As regards the prophet Hosea, it is unnecessary for me to explain the meaning of the command, or of the prophet's conduct, when God said to him, "Go and take unto thee a wife of whoredoms and produce children of whoredoms," for the Scripture itself informs us of the origin and purpose of this direction.

It proceeds thus:

"For the land hath committed great whoredom, departing from the Lord.

So he went and took Gomer the daughter of Diblaim; which conceived, and bare him a son. And the Lord said unto him, Call his name Jezreel; for yet a little while, and I will avenge the blood of Jezreel upon the house of Judah, and will cause to cease the kingdom of the house of Israel.

And it shall come to pass at that day, that I will break the bow of Israel in the valley of Jezreel.

And she conceived again, and bare a daughter. And God said unto him, Call her name No-mercy:

for I will no more have mercy upon the house of Israel; but I will utterly take them away.

But I will have mercy upon the house of Judah, and will save them by the Lord their God, and will not save them by bow, nor by sword, nor by battle, by horses, nor by horsemen.

Now when she had weaned No-mercy, she conceived, and bare a son.

Then said God, Call his name Not-my-people:

for ye are not my people, and I will not be your God. Yet the number of the children of Israel shall be as the sand of the sea, which cannot be measured for multitude; and it shall come to pass that in the place where it was said unto them, Ye are not my people, there it shall be said unto them, Ye are the sons of the living God. Then shall the children of Israel and the children of Judah be gathered together, and appoint themselves one head, and they shall come up out of the land:

for great shall be the day of Jezreel.

Say ye unto your brethren, My people; and to your sister, She hath found mercy." [954] Since the typical meaning of the command and of the prophet's conduct is thus explained in the same book by the Lord Himself, and since the writings of the apostles declare the fulfillment of this prophecy in the preaching of the New Testament, every one must accept the explanation thus given of the command and of the action of the prophet as the true explanation.

Thus it is said by the Apostle Paul, "That He might make known the riches of His glory on the vessels of mercy, which He had afore prepared unto glory, even us, whom He hath called, not of the Jews only, but also of the Gentiles.

As He saith also in Hosea, I will call them my people, which were not my people; and her beloved, which was not beloved.

And it shall come to pass, that in the place where it was said unto them, Ye are not my people, there shall they be called the children of the living God." [955] Here Paul applies the prophecy to the Gentiles.

So also Peter, writing to the Gentiles, without naming the prophet, borrows his expressions when he says, "But ye are a chosen generation, a royal priesthood, a holy nation, a peculiar people; that ye might show forth the praises of Him who has called you out of darkness into His marvellous light; which in time past were not a people, but are now the people of God:

which had not obtained mercy, but now have obtained mercy." [956] From this it is plain that the words of the prophet, "And the number of the children of Israel shall be as the sand of the sea, which cannot be measured for multitude," and the words immediately following, "And it shall be that in the place where it was said unto them, Ye are not my people, there they shall be called the children of the living God," do not apply to that Israel which is after the flesh, but to that of which the apostle says to the Gentiles, "Ye therefore are the seed of Abraham, and heirs according to the promise." [957] But, as many Jews who were of the Israel after the flesh have believed, and will yet believe; for of these were the apostles, and all the thousands in Jerusalem of the company of the apostles, as also the churches of which Paul speaks, when he says to the Galatians, "I was unknown by face to the churches of Judæa which were in Christ;" [958] and again, he explains the passage in the Psalms, where the Lord is called the cornerstone, [959] as referring to His uniting in Himself the two walls of circumcision and uncircumcision, "that He might make in Himself of twain one new man, so making peace; and that He might reconcile both unto God in one body by the cross, having slain the enmity thereby;

and that He might come and preach peace to them that are far off, and to them that are nigh," that is, to the Gentiles and to the Jews; "for He is our peace, who hath made of both one;" [960] to the same purpose we find the prophet speaking of the Jews as the children of Judah, and of the Gentiles as children of Israel, where he says, "The children of Judah and the children of Israel shall be gathered together, and shall make to themselves one head, and shall go up from the land."

Therefore, to speak against a prophecy thus confirmed by actual events, is to speak against the writings of the apostles as well as those of the prophets; and not only to speak against writings, but to impugn in the most reckless manner the evidence clear as noonday of established facts.

In the case of the narrative of Judah, it is perhaps not so easy to recognize, under the disguise of the woman called Tamar, the harlot representing the Church gathered from among the corruption of Gentile superstition; but here, where Scripture explains itself, and where the explanation is confirmed by the writings of the apostles, instead of dwelling longer on this, we may proceed at once to inquire into the meaning of the very things to which Faustus objects in Moses the servant of God.

90.

Moses killing the Egyptian in defending one of his brethren reminds us naturally of the destruction of the devil, our assailant in this land of strangers, by our defender the Lord Christ.

And as Moses hid the dead body in the sand, even so the devil, though slain, remains concealed in those who are not firmly settled.

The Lord, we know, builds the Church on a rock; and those who hear His word and do it, He compares to a wise man who builds his house upon a rock, and who does not yield or give way before temptation; and those who hear and do not, He compares to a foolish man who builds on the sand, and when his house is tried its ruin is great. [961]

91.

Of the prophetic significance of the spoiling of the Egyptians, which was done by Moses at the command of the Lord his God, who commands nothing but what is most just, I remember to have set down what occurred to me at the time in my book entitled On Christian Doctrine; [962] to the effect that the gold and silver and garments of the Egyptians typified certain branches of learning which may be profitably learned or taught among the Gentiles.

This may be the true explanation; or we may suppose that the vessels of gold and silver represent the precious souls, and the garments the bodies, of those from among the Gentiles who join themselves to the people of God, that along with them they may be freed from the Egypt of this world. Whatever the true interpretation may be, the pious student of the Scriptures will feel certain that in the command, in the action, and in the narrative there is a purpose and a symbolic meaning.

92.

It would take too long to go through all the wars of Moses.

It is enough to refer to what has already been said, as sufficient for the purpose in this reply to Faustus of the prophetic and symbolic character of the war with Amalek. [963] There is also the charge of cruelty made against Moses by the enemies of Scriptures, or by those who have never read anything.

Faustus does not make any specific charge, but speaks of Moses as commanding and doing many cruel things. But, knowing the things they are in the habit of bringing forward and of misrepresenting, I have already taken a particular case and have defended it, so that any Manichæans who are willing to be corrected, and all other ignorant and irreligious people, may see that there is no ground for their accusations.

We must now inquire into the prophetic significance of the command, that many of those who, while Moses was absent, made an idol for themselves should be slain without regard to relationship.

It is easy to see that the slaughter of these men represents the warfare against the evil principles which led the people into the same idolatry.

Against such evil we are commanded to wage war in the words of the psalm, "Be ye angry and sin not." [964] And a similar command is given by the apostle, when he says, "Mortify your members which are on earth fornication, uncleanness, luxury, evil concupiscence, and covetousness, which is idolatry." [965]

93.

It requires closer examination to see the meaning of the first action of Moses in burning the calf in fire, and grinding it to powder, and sprinkling it in the water for the people to drink.

The tables given to him, written with the finger of God, that is, by the agency of the Holy Spirit, he may have broken, because he judged the people unworthy of having them read to them; and he may have burned the calf, and ground it, and scattered it so as to be carried away by the water, in order to let nothing of it remain among the people.

But why should he have made them drink it?

Every one must feel anxious to discover the typical significance of this action.

Pursuing the inquiry, we may find that in the calf there was an embodiment of the devil, as there is in men of all nations who have the devil as their head or leader in their impious rites.

The calf is gold, because there is a semblance of wisdom in the institution of idolatrous worship.

Of this the apostle says, "Knowing God, they glorified Him not as God, nor were thankful; but they became vain in their imaginations, and their foolish heart was darkened.

Professing themselves to be wise they became foolish, and changed the glory of the incorruptible God into the likeness of corruptible man, and of birds, and of four-footed beasts, and of creeping things." [966] From this so-called wisdom came the golden calf, which was one of the forms of idolatry among the chief men and professed sages of Egypt.

The calf, then, represents every body or society of Gentile idolaters.

This impious society the Lord Christ burns with that fire of which He says in the Gospel, "I am come to send fire on the earth;" [967] for, as there is nothing hid from His heat, [968] when the Gentiles believe in Him they lose the form of the devil in the fire of divine influence.

Then all the body is ground, that is, after the dissolution of the combination in the membership of iniquity comes humiliation under the word of truth.

Then the dust is sprinkled in the water, that the Israelites, that is, the preachers of the gospel, may in baptism admit those formerly idolaters into their own body, that is, the body of Christ.

To Peter, who was one of those Israelites, it was said of the Gentiles, "Kill, and eat." [969] To kill and eat is much the same as to grind and drink.

So this calf, by the fire of zeal, and the keen penetration of the word, and the water of baptism, was swallowed up by the people, instead of their being swallowed up by it.

94.

Thus, when the very passages on which the heretics found their objections to the Scriptures are studied and examined, the more obscure they are the more wonderful are the secrets which we discover in reply to our questions; so that the mouths of blasphemers are completely stopped, and the evidence of the truth so stifles them that they cannot even utter a sound.

The unhappy men who will not receive into their hearts the sweetness of the truth must feel its force as a gag in their mouths.

All those passages speak of Christ.

The head now ascended into heaven along with the body still suffering on earth is the full development of the whole purpose of the authors of Scripture, which is well called Sacred Scripture.

Every part of the narrative in the prophetical books should be viewed as having a figurative meaning, except what serves merely as a framework for the literal or figurative predictions of this king and of his people.

For as in harps and other musical instruments the musical sound does not come from all parts of the instrument, but from the strings, and the rest is only for fastening and stretching the strings so as to tune them, that when they are struck by the musician they may give a pleasant sound; so in these prophetical narratives the circumstances selected by the prophetic spirit either predict some future event, or if they have no voice of their own, they serve to connect together other significant utterances.

95.

Should the heretics reject our exposition of those allegorical narratives, or even insist on understanding them only in a literal sense, to dispute about such a difference of understanding would be as useless as to dispute about a difference of taste.

Only, the fact that the divine precepts have either a moral and religious character or a prophetic meaning must be believed, whether intelligently or not. Moreover, the figurative interpretations must all be in the interest of morality and religion.

So, if the Manichæans or any others disagree with our interpretation, or differ from us in method or in any particular opinion, suffice it that the character of the fathers whom God commends for their conduct and obedience to His precepts is vindicated on a principle which all but those inveterate in their hostility will acknowledge to be true; and that the purity and dignity of the Scriptures are maintained in reference to those passages which the enemies of the truth find fault with, where certain actions are either praised or blamed, or merely narrated for us to form a judgment of them.

96.

In fact, nothing could have been devised more likely to instruct and benefit the pious reader of sacred Scripture than that, besides describing praiseworthy characters as examples, and blameworthy characters as warnings, it should also narrate cases where good men have gone back and fallen into evil, whether they are restored to the right path or continue irreclaimable; and also where bad men have changed, and have attained to goodness, whether they persevere in it or relapse into evil; in order that the righteous may be not lifted up in the pride of security, nor the wicked hardened in despair of cure.

And even those passages in Scripture which contain no examples or warnings are either required for connection, so as to pass on to essential matters, or, from their very appearance of superfluity, indicate the presence of some secret symbolical meaning.

For in the books we speak of, so far from there being a want or a scarcity of prophetical announcements, such announcements are numerous and distinct; and now that the fulfillment has actually taken place, the testimony thus borne to the divine authority of the books is irresistibly strong, so that it is mere madness to suppose that there can be any useless or unmeaning passages in books to which all classes of men and of minds do homage, and which themselves predict what we see thus actually coming to pass.

97.

If, then, any one reading of the action of David, of which he repented when the Lord rebuked and threatened him, find in the narrative an encouragement to sin, is Scripture to be blamed for this? Is not the man's own guilt in proportion to the abuse which he makes for his own injury or destruction of what was written for his recovery and release?

David is set forth as a great example of repentance, because men who fall into sin either proudly disregard the cure of repentance, or lose themselves in despair of obtaining salvation or of meriting pardon.

The example is for the benefit of the sick, not for the injury of those in health.

If madmen destroy themselves, or if evil-doers destroy others, with surgical instruments, it is not the fault of surgery.

98.

Even supposing that our fathers the patriarchs and prophets, of whose devout and religious habits so good a report is given in that Scripture which every one who knows it, and has not lost entirely the use of his reason, must admit to have been provided by God for the salvation of men, were as lustful and cruel as the Manichæans falsely and fanatically allege, they might still be shown to be superior not only to those whom the Manichæans call the Elect, but also to their god himself.

Is there in the licentious intercourse of man with woman anything so bad as the self-abasement of unclouded light by mixture with darkness?

Here, is a man prompted by avarice and greed to pass off his wife as his sister and sell her to her lover; but worse still and more shocking, that one should disguise his own nature to gratify criminal passion, and submit gratuitously to pollution and degradation.

Why, even one who knowingly lies with his own daughters is not equally criminal with one who lets his members share in the defilement of all sensuality as gross as this, or grosser.

And is not the Manichæan god a partaker in the contamination of the most atrocious acts of uncleanness?

Again, if it were true, as Faustus says, that Jacob went from one to another of his four wives, not desiring offspring, but resembling a he-goat in licentiousness, he would still not be sunk so low as your god, who must not only have shared in this degradation, from his being confined in the bodies of Jacob and his wives so as to be mixed up with all their movements, but also, in union with this very he-goat of Faustus' coarse comparison, must have endured all the pains of animal appetite, incurring fresh defilement at every step, as partaking in the passion of the male, the conception of the female, and the birth of the kid.

And, in the same way, supposing Judah to have been guilty not only of fornication, but of incest, a share in the heats and impurities of this incestuous passion would also belong to your god.

David repented of his sin in loving the wife of another, and in ordering the death of her husband; but when will your god repent of giving up his members to the wanton passion of the male and female chiefs of the race of darkness, and of putting to death not the husband of his mistress, but his own children, whom he confines in the members of the very demons who were his own lovers?

Even if David had not repented, nor been thus restored to righteousness, he would still have been better than your god.

David may have been defiled by this one act, or to the extent to which one man is capable of such defilement; but your god suffers the pollution of his members in all such actions by whomsoever committed.

The prophet Hosea, too, is accused by Faustus:

and, supposing him to have taken the harlot to wife because he had a criminal affection for her, if he is licentious and she a prostitute, their souls, according to your own assertion, are parts and members of your god and of his nature.

In plain language, the harlot herself must be your god.

You cannot pretend that your god is not confined in the contaminated body, or that he is only present, while preserving entire the purity of his own nature; and you acknowledge that the members of your god are so defiled as to require a special purification.

This harlot, then, for whom you venture to find fault with the man of God, even if she had not been changed for the better by becoming a chaste wife, would still have been your god; at least you must admit her soul to have been a part, however small, of your god.

But one single harlot is not so bad as your god, for he on account of his mixture with the race of darkness shares in every act of prostitution; and wherever such impurities are perpetrated, he goes through the corresponding experiences of abandonment, of release, and of confinement, and this from generation to generation, till this most corrupt part reaches its final state in the mass of darkness, like an irreclaimable harlot.

Such are the evils and such the shameful abominations which your god could not ward off from his members, and to which he was brought irresistibly by his merciless enemy; for only by the sacrifice of his own subjects, or rather his own parts, could he effect the destruction of his formidable assailant.

Surely, there was nothing so bad as this in killing an Egyptian so as to preserve uninjured a fellow-countryman.

Yet Faustus finds fault with this most absurdly, while with amazing infatuation he overlooks the case of his own god.

Would it not have been better for him to have carried off the gold and silver vessels of the Egyptians, than to let his members be carried off by the race of darkness?

And yet the worshippers of this unfortunate god find fault with the servant of our God for carrying on wars, in which he with his followers were always victorious, so that, under the leadership of Moses, the children of Israel carried captive their enemies, men and women, as your god would have done too, if he had been able.

You profess to accuse Moses of doing wrong, while in fact you envy his success.

There was no cruelty in punishing with the sword those who had sinned grievously against God.

Indeed, Moses entreated pardon for this sin, even offering to bear himself in their stead the divine anger.

But even had he been cruel instead of compassionate, he would still have been better than your god.

For if any of his followers had been sent to break the force of the enemy and had been taken captive, he would never, if victorious, have condemned him when he had done no wrong, but acted in obedience to orders.

And yet this is what your god is to do with the part of himself which is to be fastened in the mass of darkness, because it obeyed orders, and advanced at the risk of its own life in defence of his kingdom against the body of the enemy.

But, says the Manichæan, this part, after mixture and combination with evil during the course of ages, has not been obedient.

But why?

If the obedience was voluntary, the guilt is real, and the punishment just.

But from this it would follow that there is no nature opposed to sin; otherwise it would not sin voluntarily; and so the whole system of Manichæism falls at once.

If, again, this part suffers from the power of this enemy against whom it was sent, and is subdued by a force it was unable to resist, the punishment is unjust, and flagrantly cruel.

The god who is defended on the plea of necessity is a fit object of worship to those who refuse to worship the one true God.

Still, it must be allowed that, however debasing the worship of this god may be, the worshippers are so far better than their deity, that they have an existence, while he is nothing more than a fabulous invention.

Proceed we now to the rest of Faustus' vagaries. [970]

Book XXIII - Faustus recurs to the genealogical difficulty and insists that even according to Matthew Jesus was not Son of God until His baptism. Augustin sets forth the Catholic view of the relation of the divine and the human in the person of Christ

1.

Faustus said:

On one occasion, when addressing a large audience, I was asked by one of the crowd, Do you believe that Jesus was born of Mary?

I replied, Which Jesus do you mean? for in the Hebrew it is the name of several people.

One was the son of Nun, the follower of Moses; [971] another was the son of Josedech the high priest; [972] again, another is spoken of as the son of David; [973] and another is the Son of God. [974] Of which of these do you ask whether I believe him to have been born of Mary?

His answer was, The Son of God, of course.

On what evidence, said I, oral or written, am I to believe this?

He replied, On the authority of Matthew.

What, said I, did Matthew write?

He replied, "The book of the generation of Jesus Christ, the son of David, the son of Abraham" (Matt. i. 1).

Then said I, I was afraid you were going to say, The book of the generation of Jesus Christ, the Son of God; and I was prepared to correct you.

Now that you have quoted the verse accurately, you must nevertheless be advised to pay attention to the words.

Matthew does not profess to give an account of the generation of the Son of God, but of the son of David.

2.

I will, for the present, suppose that this person was right in saying that the son of David was born of Mary.

It still remains true, that in this whole passage of the generation no mention is made of the Son of God till we come to the baptism; so that it is an injurious misrepresentation on your part to speak of this writer as making the Son of God the inmate of a womb.

The writer, indeed, seems to cry out against such an idea, and in the very title of his book to clear himself of such blasphemy, asserting that the person whose birth he describes is the son of David, not the Son of God.

And if you attend to the writer's meaning and purpose, you will see that what he wishes us to believe of Jesus the Son of God is not so much that He was born of Mary, as that He became the Son of God by baptism at the river Jordan.

He tells us that the person of whom he spoke at the outset as the son of David was baptized by John, and became the Son of God on this particular occasion, when about thirty years old, according to Luke, when also the voice was heard saying to Him, "Thou art my Son; this day have I begotten Thee." [975]

It appears from this, that what was born, as is supposed, of Mary thirty years before, was not the Son of God, but what was afterwards made so by baptism at Jordan, that is, the new man, the same as in us when we were converted from Gentile error, and believe in God.

This doctrine may or may not agree with what you call the Catholic faith; at all events, it is what Matthew says, if Matthew is the real author.

The words, Thou art my Son, this day I have begotten Thee, or, This is my beloved Son, in whom I am well pleased, do not occur in connection with the story of Mary's motherhood, but with the putting away of sin at Jordan.

This is what is written; and if you believe this doctrine, you must be called a Matthæan, for you will no longer be a Catholic.

The Catholic doctrine is well known; and it is as unlike Matthew's representations as it is unlike the truth.

In the words of your creed, you declare that you believe in Jesus Christ, the Son of God, who was born of the Virgin Mary.

According to you, therefore, the Son of God comes from Mary; according to Matthew, from the Jordan; while we believe Him to come from God.

Thus the doctrine of Matthew, if we are right in assigning the authorship to him, is as different from yours as from ours; only we acknowledge that he is more cautious than you in ascribing the being born of a woman to the son of David, and not to the Son of God.

As for you, your only alternative is to deny that those statements were made, as they appear to be, by Matthew, or to allow that you have abandoned the faith of the apostles.

3.

For our part, while no one can alter our conviction that the Son of God comes from God, we might indulge a credulous disposition, to the extent of admitting the fiction, that Jesus became the Son of God at Jordan, but not that the Son of God was born of a woman.

Then, again, the son said to have been born of Mary cannot properly be called the son of David, unless it is ascertained that he was begotten by Joseph. You say he was not, and therefore you must allow him not to have been the son of David, even though he were the son of Mary.

The genealogy proceeds in the line of Hebrew fathers from Abraham to David, and from David to Joseph; and as we are told that Joseph was not the real father of Jesus, Jesus cannot be said to be the son of David.

To begin with calling Jesus the son of David, and then to go on to tell of his being born of Mary before the consummation of her marriage with Joseph, is pure madness.

And if the son of Mary cannot be called the son of David, on account of his not being the son of Joseph, still less can the name be given to the Son of God.

4.

Moreover, the Virgin herself appears to have belonged not to the tribe of Judah, to which the Jewish kings belonged, and which all agree was David's tribe, but to the priestly tribe of Levi.

This appears from the fact that the Virgin's father Joachim was a priest; and his name does not occur in the genealogy.

How, then, can Mary be brought within the pale of relationship to David, when she has neither father nor husband belonging to it?

Consequently, Mary's son cannot possibly be the son of David, unless you can bring the mother into some connection with Joseph, so as to be either his wife or his daughter.

5.

Augustin replied:

The Catholic, which is also the apostolic, doctrine, is, that our Lord and Saviour Jesus Christ is both the Son of God in His divine nature, and the Son of David after the flesh.

This we prove from the writings of the evangelists and apostles, so that no one can reject our proofs without also rejecting these writings. Faustus' plan is to represent some one as saying a few words, without bringing forward any evidence in answer to Faustus' fertile sophistry. But with all his ingenuity, the proofs I have to give will leave Faustus no reply, but that these passages are spurious interpolations in the sacred record,--a reply which serves as a means of escaping, or of trying to escape, the force of the plainest statements in Holy Scripture.

We have already in this treatise sufficiently exposed the irrational absurdity, as well as the daring profanity, of such criticism; and not to exceed all limits, we must avoid repetition.

It cannot be necessary that we should bring together all the passages scattered throughout Scripture, which show, in answer to Faustus, that in the books of the highest and most sacred authority He who is called the only-begotten Son of God, even God with God, is also called the Son of David, on account of His taking the form of a servant from the Virgin Mary, the wife of Joseph.

To instance only Matthew, since Faustus' argument refers to this Gospel, as the whole book cannot be quoted here, let whoever choose read it, and see how Matthew carries on to the passion and the resurrection the narrative of Him whom He calls the Son of David in the introduction to the genealogy.

Of this same Son of David he speaks as being conceived and born of the Virgin Mary by the Holy Ghost.

He also applies to this the declaration of the prophet, "Behold, a virgin shall conceive, and shall bear a son, and they shall call His name Emmanuel, which is being interpreted, God with us."[976] Again, He who was called, even from the Virgin's womb, God-with-us, is said to have heard, when He was baptized by John, a voice from heaven, saying, "This is my beloved Son, in whom I am well pleased." [977] Will Faustus say that to be called God is less than to be called the Son of God?

He seems to think so, for he tries to prove that because this voice came from heaven at the time of the baptism, therefore, according to Matthew, He must then have become the Son of God; whereas the same evangelist, in a previous passage, quotes the sacred announcement made by the prophet, in which the child born of the Virgin is called God-with-us.

6.

It is remarkable how, amid his wild irrelevancies, this wretched trifler loses no available opportunity of darkening the declarations of Scripture by the fabulous creations of his own fancy.

Thus he says of Abraham, that when he took his handmaid to wife he disbelieved God's promise that he should have a child by Sarah; whereas, in fact, this promise had not at that time been given.

Then he accuses Abraham of falsehood in calling Sarah his sister, not having read what may be learned on the authority of Scripture about the family of Sarah. Abraham's son Isaac also he accuses of falsely calling his wife his sister, though a distinct account is given of her family.

Then he accuses Jacob of there being a daily quarrel among his four wives, which should be the first to appropriate him on his return from the field, while nothing of this is said in Scripture.

And this is the man who pretends to hate the writers of the sacred books for their falsehood, and who has the effrontery so to misrepresent even the gospel record, though its authority is admitted by all as possessing the most abundant confirmation, as to try to make it appear, not indeed that Matthew himself,--for in that case he would have been forced to yield to apostolic authority,--but that some one under the name of Matthew, has written about Christ what he refuses to believe, and attempts to refute with a contumelious ingenuity!

7.

The voice from heaven at the Jordan should be compared with the voice heard on the Mount.[978] In neither case do the words, "This is my beloved Son, in whom I am well pleased," imply that He was not the Son of God before; for He who from the Virgin's womb took the form of a servant "was in the form of God, and thought it no robbery to be equal with God." [979] And the same Apostle Paul himself says distinctly elsewhere, "But in the fullness of time, God sent His Son, made of a woman, made under the law;" [980] that is, a woman in the Hebrew sense, not a wife, but one of the female sex.

The Son of God is both Lord of David in His divine nature, and Son of David as being of the seed of David after the flesh.

And if it were not profitable for us to believe this, the same apostle would not have made it so prominent as he does, when he says to Timothy, "Remember that Christ Jesus, of the seed of David, rose from the dead, according to my gospel." [981] And he carefully enjoins believers to regard as accursed whoever preaches another gospel contrary to this.

8.

This assailant of the holy Gospel need find no difficulty in the fact that Christ is called the Son of David, though He was born of a virgin, and though Joseph was not His real father; while the genealogy is brought down by the evangelist Matthew, not to Mary, but to Joseph. First of all, the husband, as the man, is the more honorable; and Joseph was Mary's husband, though she did not live with him, for Matthew himself mentions that she was called Joseph's wife by the angel; as it is also from Matthew that we learn that Mary conceived not by Joseph, but by the Holy Spirit.

But if this, instead of being a true narrative written by Matthew the apostle, was a false narrative written by some one else under his name, is it likely that he would have contradicted himself in such an apparent manner, and in passages so immediately connected, as to speak of the Son of David as born of Mary without conjugal intercourse, and then, in giving His genealogy, to bring it down to the very man with whom the Virgin is expressly said not to have had intercourse, unless he had some reason for doing so? Even supposing there were two writers, one calling Christ the Son of David, and giving an account of Christ's progenitors from David down to Joseph; while the other does not call Christ the Son of David, and says that He was born of the Virgin Mary without intercourse with any man; those statements are not irreconcilable, so as to prove that one or both writers must be false.

It will appear on reflection that both accounts might be true; for Joseph might be called the husband of Mary, though she was his wife only in affection, and in the intercourse of the mind, which is more intimate than that of the body.

In this way it might be proper that the husband of the virgin-mother of Christ should have a place in the list of Christ's ancestors.

It might also be the case that some of David's blood flowed in Mary herself, so that the flesh of Christ, although produced from a virgin, still owed its origin to David's seed.

But as, in fact, both statements are made by one and the same writer, who informs us both that Joseph was the husband of Mary and that the mother of Christ was a virgin, and that Christ was of the seed of David, and that Joseph is in the list of Christ's progenitors in the line of David, those who prefer the authority of the sacred Gospel to that of heretical fiction must conclude that Mary was not unconnected with the family of David, and that she was properly called the wife of Joseph, because being a woman she was in spiritual alliance with him, though there was no bodily connection.

Joseph, too, it is plain, could not be omitted in the genealogy; for, from the superiority of his sex, such an omission would be equivalent to a denial of his relation to the woman with whom he was inwardly united; and believers in Christ are taught not to think carnal connection the chief thing in marriage, as if without this they could not be man and wife, but to imitate in Christian wedlock as closely as possible the parents of Christ, that so they may have the more intimate union with the members of Christ.

9.

We believe that Mary, as well as Joseph, was of the family of David, because we believe the Scriptures, which assert both that Christ was of the seed of David after the flesh, and that His mother was the Virgin Mary, He having no human father.

Therefore, whoever denies the relationship of Mary to David, evidently opposes the pre-eminent authority of these passages of Scripture; and to maintain this opposition he must bring evidence in support of his statement from writings acknowledged by the Church as canonical and catholic, not from any writings he pleases.

In the matters of which we are now treating, only the canonical writings have any weight with us; for they only are received and acknowledged by the Church spread over all the world, which is itself a fulfillment of the prophecies regarding it contained in these writings.

Accordingly, I am not bound to admit the uncanonical account of Mary's birth which Faustus adopts, that her father was a priest of the tribe of Levi, of the name of Joachim.

But even were I to admit this account, I should still contend that Joachim must have in some way belonged to the family of David, and had somehow been adopted from the tribe of Judah into that of Levi; or if not he, one of his ancestors; or, at least, that while born in the tribe of Levi, he had still some relation to the line of David; as Faustus himself acknowledges that Mary, though belonging to the tribe of Levi, could be given to a husband of the tribe of Judah; and he expressly says that if Mary were Joseph's daughter, the name Son of David would be applicable to Christ.

In this way, by the marriage of Joseph's daughter in the tribe of Levi, her son, though born in the tribe of Levi, might not improperly be called the Son of David.

And so, if the mother of that Joachim, who in the passage quoted by Faustus is called the father of Mary, married in the tribe of Levi while she belonged to the tribe of Judah and to the family of David, there would thus be a sufficient reason for speaking of Joachim and Mary and Mary's son as belonging to the seed of David.

If I felt obliged to pay any regard to the apocryphal scripture in which Joachim is called the father of Mary, I should adopt some such explanation as the above, rather than admit any falsehood in the Gospel, where it is written both that Jesus Christ, the Son of God, and our Saviour, was of the seed of David after the flesh, and that He was born of the Virgin Mary.

It is enough for us that the enemies of these Scriptures, which record these truths and which we believe, cannot prove against them any charge of falsehood.

10.

Faustus cannot pretend then I am unable to prove that Mary was of the family of David, as I have shown him unable to prove that she was not.

I produce the strongest evidence from Scriptures of established authority, which declare that Christ was of the seed of David, and that He was born without a father of the Virgin Mary.

Faustus expresses what he considers a most becoming indignation against impropriety when he says, It is an injurious misrepresentation of the writer to make him speak of the Son of God as the inmate of a womb.

Of course, the Catholic doctrine which teaches that Christ the Son of God was born in the flesh of a virgin, does not make the Son of God the inmate of her womb in the sense of having no existence beyond it, as if He had abandoned the government of heaven and earth, or as if He had left the presence of the Father.

The mistake is with the Manichæans, whose understanding is so incapable of forming a conception of anything except what is material, that they cannot comprehend how the Word of God, who is the virtue and wisdom of God, while remaining in Himself and with the Father, and while governing the universe, reaches from end to end in strength, and sweetly orders all things. [982]In the faultless procedure of this adorable providence, He appointed for Himself an earthly mother; and to free His servants from the bondage of corruption He took in this mother the form of a servant, that is, a mortal body; and this body which He took He showed openly, and when it had been exposed, even to suffering and death, He raised it again from the dead, and built again the temple which had been destroyed.

You who shrink from this doctrine as blasphemous, make the members of your god to be confined not in a virgin's womb, but in the wombs of all female animals, from elephants down to flies.

Perhaps you think the less of the true Christ, because the Word is said so to have become incarnate in the Virgin's womb as to provide a temple for Himself in human nature, while His own nature continued unaltered in its integrity; and, on the other hand, you think the more of your god, because in the bonds and pollution of his confinement in flesh, in the part which is to be made fast to the mass of darkness, he seeks for help to no purpose, or is even rendered powerless to ask for help.

Book XXIV - Faustus explains the Manichæan denial that man was made by God as applying to the fleshly man not to the spiritual

Augustin elucidates the Apostle Paul's contrasts between flesh and spirit so as to exclude the Manichæan view.

1.

Faustus said:
We are asked the reason for our denial that man is made by God.
But we do not assert that man is in no sense made by God; we only ask in what sense, and when, and how.
For, according to the apostle, there are two men, one of whom he calls sometimes the outer man, generally the earthy, sometimes, too, the old man:
the other he calls the inner or heavenly or new man. [983] The question is, Which of these is made by God?
For there are likewise two times of our nativity; one when nature brought us forth into this light, binding us in the bonds of flesh; and the other, when the truth regenerated us on our conversion from error and our entrance into the faith.
It is this second birth of which Jesus speaks in the Gospel, when He says, "Except a man be born again, he cannot see the kingdom of God." [984] Nicodemus, not knowing what Christ meant, was at a loss, and inquired how this could be, for an old man could not enter into his mother's womb and be born a second time.
Jesus said in reply, "Except a man be born of water and of the Holy Spirit, he cannot see the kingdom of God."
Then He adds, "That which is born of the flesh is flesh; and that which is born of the Spirit is spirit."
Hence, as the birth in which our bodies originate is not the only birth, but there is another in which we are born again in spirit, an important question arises from this distinction as to which of those births it is in which God makes us.
The manner of birth also is twofold.
In the humiliating process of ordinary generation, we spring from the heat of animal passion; but when we are brought into the faith, we are formed under good instruction in honor and purity in Jesus Christ, by the Holy Spirit. For this reason, in all religion, and especially in the Christian religion, young children are invited to membership.
This is hinted at in the words of His apostle:
"My little children, of whom I travail in birth again until Christ be formed in you." [985] The question, then, is not whether God makes man, but what man He makes, and when, and how.
For if it is when we are fashioned in the womb that God forms us after His own image, which is the common belief of Gentiles and Jews, and which is also your belief, then God makes the old man, and produces us by means of sensual passion, which does not seem suitable to His divine nature.
But if it is when we are converted and brought to a better life that we are formed by God, which is the general doctrine of Christ and His apostles, and which is also our doctrine, in this case God makes us new men, and produces us in honor and purity, which would agree perfectly with His sacred and adorable majesty.
If you do not reject Paul's authority, we will prove to you from him what man God makes, and when, and how.
He says to the Ephesians, "That ye put off according to your former conversation the old man, which is corrupt through deceitful lusts; and be renewed in the spirit of your mind; and put on the new man, which after God is created in righteousness and holiness of truth." [986] This shows that in the creation of man after the image of God, it is another man that is spoken of, and another birth, and another manner of birth.
The putting off and putting on of which he speaks, point to the time of the reception of the truth; and the assertion that the new man is created by God implies that the old man is created neither by God nor after God.
And when he adds, that this new man is made in holiness and righteousness and truth, he thus points to another manner of birth of which this is the character, and which, as I have said, differs widely from the manner in which bodily generation is effected.

And as he declares that only the former is of God, it follows that the latter is not.

Again, writing to the Colossians, he uses words to the same effect:

"Put off the old man with his deeds, and put on the new man, which is renewed in the knowledge of God according to the image of Him who created Him in you."

Here he not only shows that it is the new man that God makes, but he declares the time and manner of the formation, for the words in the knowledge of God point to the time of believing.

Then he adds, according to the image of Him who created him, to make it clear that the old man is not the image of God, nor formed by God.

Moreover, the following words, "Where there is neither male nor female, Jew nor Greek, Barbarian nor Scythian," [987] show more plainly still that the birth by which we are made male and female, Greeks and Jews, Scythians and Barbarians, is not the birth in which God effects the formation of man; but that the birth with which God has to do is that in which we lose the difference of nation and sex and condition, and become one like Him who is one, that is, Christ.

So the same apostle says again, "As many as have been baptized in Christ have put on Christ: there is neither Jew nor Greek, there is neither male nor female, there is neither bond nor free; but all are one in Christ." [988] Man, then, is made by God, not when from one he is divided into many, but when from many he becomes one.

The division is in the first birth, or that of the body; union comes by the second, which is immaterial and divine.

This affords sufficient ground for our opinion, that the birth of the body should be ascribed to nature, and the second birth to the Supernal Majesty.

So the same apostle says again to the Corinthians, "I have begotten you in Christ Jesus by the gospel;" [989] and, speaking of himself, to the Galatians, "When it pleased Him, who separated me from my mother's womb, to reveal His Son in me, that I might preach Him among the Gentiles, immediately I conferred not with flesh and blood." [990]

It is plain that everywhere he speaks of the second or spiritual birth as that in which we are made by God, as distinct from the indecency of the first birth, in which we are on a level with other animals as regards dignity and purity, as we are conceived in the maternal womb, and are formed, and brought forth.

You may observe that in this matter the dispute between us is not so much about a question of doctrine as of interpretation.

For you think that it is the old or outer or earthy man that is said to have been made by God; while we apply this to the heavenly man, giving the superiority to the inner or new man.

And our opinion is not rash or groundless, for we have learned it from Christ and His apostles, who are proved to have been the first in the world who thus taught.

2.

Augustin replied:

The Apostle Paul certainly uses the expression the inner man for the spirit of the mind, and the outer man for the body and for this mortal life; but we nowhere find him making these two different men, but one, which is all made by God, both the inner and the outer.

However, it is made in the image of God only as regards the inner, which, besides being immaterial, is rational, and is not possessed by the lower animals.

God, then, did not make one man after His own image, and another man not after that image; but the one man, which includes both the inner and the outer, He made after His own image, not as regards the possession of a body and of mortal life, but as regards the rational mind with the power of knowing God, and with the superiority as compared with all irrational creatures which the possession of reason implies.

Faustus allows that the inner man is made by God, when, as he says, it is renewed in the knowledge of God after the image of Him that created him.

I readily admit this on the apostle's authority.

Why does not Faustus admit on the same authority that "God has placed the members every one in the body, as it has pleased Him"? [991] Here we learn from the same apostle that God is the framer of the outer man too.

Why does Faustus take only what he thinks to be in his own favor, while he leaves out or rejects what upsets the follies of the Manichæans?

Moreover, in treating of the earthy and the heavenly man, and making the distinction between the mortal and the immortal, between that which we are in Adam and that which we shall be in Christ, the apostle quotes the declaration of the law regarding the earthy or natural body, referring to the very book and the very passage where it is written that God made the earthy man too.

Speaking of the manner in which the dead shall rise again, and of the body with which they shall come, after using the similitude of the seeds of corn, that they are sown bare grain, and that

God gives them a body as it pleases Him, and to every seed his own body,--thus, by the way, overthrowing the error of the Manichæans, who say that grains and plants, and all roots and shoots, are created by the race of darkness, and not by God, who, according to them, instead of exerting power in the production of these objects, is Himself subject to confinement in them,--he goes on, after this refutation of Manichæan impieties, to describe the different kinds of flesh.

"All flesh," he says, "is not the same flesh."

Then he speaks of celestial and terrestrial bodies, and then of the change of our body by which it will become spiritual and heavenly.

"It is sown," he says, "in dishonor, it shall rise in glory; it is sown in weakness, it shall rise in power; it is sown a natural body, it shall rise a spiritual body."

Then, in order to show the origin of the animal body, he says, "There is a natural body, and there is a spiritual body; as it is written, The first man, Adam, was made a living soul." [992]Now this is written in Genesis, [993] where it is related how God made man, and animated the body which He had formed of the earth.

By the old man the apostle simply means the old life, which is a life in sin, and is after the manner of Adam, of whom it is said, "By one man sin entered into the world, and death by sin; and so death passed upon all men, in that all have sinned." [994]

Thus the whole of this man, both the inner and the outer part, has become old because of sin, and liable to the punishment of mortality. There is, however, a restoration of the inner man, when it is renewed after the image of its Creator, in the putting off of unrighteousness--that is, the old man, and putting on righteousness--that is, the new man.

But when that which is sown a natural body shall rise a spiritual body, the outer man too shall attain the dignity of a celestial character; so that all that has been created may be created anew, and all that has been made may be remade by the Creator and Maker Himself.

This is briefly explained in the words:

"The body is dead because of sin; but the spirit is life because of righteousness.

But if the Spirit of Him who raised up Jesus from the dead dwell in you, He that raised up Christ from the dead will also quicken your mortal bodies by His Spirit dwelling in you." [995] No one instructed in the Catholic doctrine but knows that it is in the body that some are male and some female, not in the spirit of the mind, in which we are renewed after the image of God.

But elsewhere the apostle teaches that God is the Maker of both; for he says, "Neither is the woman without the man, nor the man without the woman, in the Lord; for as the woman is of the man, so is the man by the woman; but all things are of God." [996]The only reply given to this, by the perverse stupidity of those who are alienated from the life of God by the ignorance which is in them, on account of the blindness of their heart, is, that whatever pleases them in the apostolic writings is true, and whatever displeases them is false.

This is the insanity of the Manichæans, who will be wise if they cease to be Manichæans.

As it is, if they are asked whether it is He that remakes and renews the inner man (which they acknowledge to be renewed after the image of God, and they themselves quote the passage in support of this; and, according to Faustus, God makes man when the inner man is renewed in the image of God), they will answer, yes.

And if we then go on to ask when God made what He now renews, they must devise some subterfuge to prevent the exposure of their absurdities.

For, according to them, the inner man is not formed or created or originated by God, but is part of His own substance sent against His enemies; and instead of becoming old by sin, it is through necessity captured and damaged by the enemy.

Not to repeat all the nonsense they talk, the first man they speak of is not the man of the earth earthy that the apostle speaks of, [997] but an invention proceeding from their own magazine of untruths.

Faustus, though he chooses man as a subject for discussion, says not a word of this first man; for he is afraid that his opponents in the discussion might come to know something about him.

Philip Schaff, D.D., LL.D.

Book XXV - Faustus seeks to bring into ridicule the orthodox claim to believe in the infinity of God by caricaturing the anthropomorphic representations of the Old Testament

Augustin expresses his despair of being able to induce the Manichæans to adopt right views of the infinitude of God so long as they continue to regard the soul and God as extended in space.

1.

Faustus said:

Is God finite or infinite?

He must be finite unless you are mistaken in addressing Him as the God of Abraham and Isaac and Jacob; unless, indeed, the being thus addressed is different from the God you call infinite.

In the case of the God of Abraham and Isaac and Jacob, the mark of circumcision, which separated these men from fellowship with other people, marked also the limit of God's power as extending only to them.

And a being whose power is finite cannot himself be infinite.

Moreover, in this address, you do not mention even the ancients before Abraham, such as Enoch, Noah, and Shem, and others like them, whom you allow to have been righteous though in uncircumcision; but because they lacked this distinguishing mark, you will not call God their God, but only of Abraham and his seed.

Now, if God is one and infinite, what need of such careful particularity in addressing Him, as if it was not enough to name God, without adding whose God He is--Abraham's, namely, and Isaac's and Jacob's; as if Abraham were a landmark to steer by in your invocation, to escape shipwreck among a shoal of deities?

The Jews, who are circumcised, may very properly address this deity, as having a reason for it, because they call God the God of circumcision, in contrast to the gods of uncircumcision.

But why you should do the same, it is difficult to understand; for you do not pretend to have Abraham's sign, though you invoke his God.

If we understand the matter rightly, the Jews and their God seem to have set marks upon one another for the purpose of recognition, that they might not lose each other.

So God gave them the disgusting mark of circumcision, that, in whatever land or among whatever people they might be, they might by being circumcised be known to be His.

They again marked God by calling Him the God of their fathers, that, wherever He might be, though among a crowd of gods, He might, on hearing the name God of Abraham, God of Isaac, God of Jacob, know at once that He was addressed.

So we often see, in a number of people of the same name, that no one answers till called by his surname.

In the same way the shepherd or herdsman makes use of a brand to prevent his property being taken by others.

In thus marking God by calling Him the God of Abraham and Isaac and Jacob, you show not only that He is finite, but also that you have no connection with Him, because you have not the mark of circumcision by which He recognizes His own.

Therefore, if this is the God you worship, there can be no doubt of His being finite.

But if you say that God is infinite, you must first of all give up this finite deity, and by altering your invocation, show your penitence for your past errors.

We have thus proved God to be finite, taking you on your own ground.

But to determine whether the supreme and true God is infinite or not, we need only refer to the opposition between good and evil.

If evil does not exist, then certainly God is infinite; otherwise He must be finite. Evil, however, undoubtedly exists; therefore God is not infinite.

It is where good stops that evil begins.

2.

Augustin replied:
No one that knows you would dream of asking you about the infinitude of God, or of discussing the matter with you. For, before there can be any degree of spirituality in any of your conceptions, you must first have your minds cleared by simple faith, and by some elementary knowledge, from the illusions of carnal and material ideas.

This your heresy prevents you from doing, for it invariably represents the body and the soul and God as extended in space, either finite or infinite, while the idea of space is applicable only to the body.

As long as this is the case, it will be better for you to leave this matter alone; for you can teach no truth regarding it, any more than in other matters; and in this you are unfit for learning, as you might do in other things, if you were not proud and quarrelsome.

For in such questions as how God can be finite, when no space can contain Him; how He can be infinite, when the Son knows Him perfectly; how He can be finite, and yet unbounded; how He can be infinite, and yet perfect; how He can be finite, who is without measure; how He can be infinite, who is the measure of all things--all carnal ideas go for nothing; and if the carnality is to be removed, it must first become ashamed of itself.

Accordingly, your best way of ending the matter you have brought forward of God as finite or infinite, is to say no more about it till you cease going so far astray from Christ, who is the end of the law.

Of the God of Abraham and Isaac and Jacob we have already said enough to show why He who is the true God of all creatures wished to be familiarly known by His people under this name.

On circumcision, too, we have already spoken in several places in answer to ignorant reproaches.

The Manichæans would find nothing to ridicule in this sign if they would view it as appointed by God, to be an appropriate symbol of the putting off of the flesh.

They ought thus to consider the rite with a Christian instead of a heretical mind; as it is written, "To the pure all things are pure."

But, considering the truth of the following words, "To the unclean and unbelieving nothing is pure, but even their mind and conscience are defiled," [998] we must remind our witty opponents, that if circumcision is indecent, as they say it is, they should rather weep than laugh at it; for their god is exposed to restraint and contamination in conjunction both with the skin which is cut and with the blood which is shed.

Book XXVI - Faustus insists that Jesus might have died though not born, by the exercise of divine power, yet he rejects birth and death alike. Augustin maintains that there are some things that even God cannot do, one of which is to die

He refutes the docetism of the Manichæans.

1.

Faustus said:
You ask, If Jesus was not born, how did He die? Well this is a probability, such as one makes use of in want of proofs.

We will, however, answer the question by examples taken from what you generally believe.

If they are true, they will prove our case; if they are false, they will help you no more than they will us. You say then, How could Jesus die, if He were not man?

In return, I ask you, How did Elias not die, though he was a man?

Could a mortal encroach upon the limits of immortality, and could not Christ add to His immortality whatever experience of death was required?

If Elias, contrary to nature, lives for ever, why not allow that Jesus, with no greater contrariety to nature, could remain in death for three days? Besides that, it is not only Elias, but Moses and Enoch you believe to be immortal, and to have been taken up with their bodies to heaven.

Accordingly, if it is a good argument that Jesus was a man because He died, it is an equally good argument that Elias was not a man because he did not die.

But as it is false that Elias was not a man, notwithstanding his supposed immortality, so it is false that Jesus was a man, though He is considered to have died.

The truth is, if you will believe it, that the Hebrews were in a mistake regarding both the death of Jesus and the immortality of Elias.

For it is equally untrue that Jesus died and that Elias did not die.

But you believe whatever you please; and for the rest, you appeal to nature.

And, allowing this appeal, nature is against both the death of the immortal and the immortality of the mortal.

And if we refer to the power of effecting their purpose as possessed by God and by man, it seems more possible for Jesus to die than for Elias not to die; for the power of Jesus is greater than that of Elias.

But if you exalt the weaker to heaven, though nature is against it, and, forgetting his condition as a mortal, endow him with eternal felicity, why should I not admit that Jesus could die if He pleased, even though I were to grant His death to have been real, and not a mere semblance?

For, as from the outset of His taking the likeness of man He underwent in appearance all the experiences of humanity, it was quite consistent that He should complete the system by appearing to die.

2.

Moreover, it is to be remembered that this reference to what nature grants as possible, should be made in connection with all the history of Jesus, and not only with His death.

According to nature, it is impossible that a man blind from his birth should see the light; and yet Jesus appears to have performed a miracle of this kind, so that the Jews themselves exclaimed that from the beginning of the world it was not seen that one opened the eyes of a man born blind.[999] So also healing a withered hand, giving the power of utterance and expression to those born dumb, restoring animation to the dead, with the recovery of their bodily frame after dissolution had begun, produce a feeling of amazement, and must seem utterly incredible in view of what is naturally possible and impossible.

And yet, as Christians, we believe all the things to have been done by the same person; for we regard not the law of nature, but the powerful operation of God.

There is a story, too, of Jesus having been cast from the brow of a hill, and having escaped unhurt.

If, then, when thrown down from a height He did not die, simply because He chose not to die, why should He not have had the power to die when He pleased?

We take this way of answering you because you have a fancy for discussion, and affect to use logical weapons not properly belonging to you.

As regards our own belief, it is no more true that Jesus died than that Elias is immortal.

3.

Augustin replied:

As to Enoch and Elias and Moses, our belief is determined not by Faustus' suppositions, but by the declarations of Scripture, resting as they do on foundations of the strongest and surest evidence.

People in error, as you are, are unfit to decide what is natural, and what contrary to nature.

We admit that what is contrary to the ordinary course of human experience is commonly spoken of as contrary to nature.

Thus the apostle uses the words, "If thou art cut out of the wild olive, and engrafted contrary to nature in the good olive."[1000] Contrary to nature is here used in the sense of contrary to human experience of the course of nature; as that a wild olive engrafted in a good olive should bring forth the fatness of the olive instead of wild berries.

But God, the Author and Creator of all natures, does nothing contrary to nature; for whatever is done by Him who appoints all natural order and measure and proportion must be natural in every case.

And man himself acts contrary to nature only when he sins; and then by punishment he is brought back to nature again.

The natural order of justice requires either that sin should not be committed or that it should not go unpunished.

In either case, the natural order is preserved, if not by the soul, at least by God. For sin pains the conscience, and brings grief on the mind of the sinner, by the loss of the light of justice, even should no physical sufferings follow, which are inflicted for correction, or are reserved for the incorrigible.

There is, however, no impropriety in saying that God does a thing contrary to nature, when it is contrary to what we know of nature.

For we give the name nature to the usual common course of nature; and whatever God does contrary to this, we call a prodigy, or a miracle.

But against the supreme law of nature, which is beyond the knowledge both of the ungodly and of weak believers, God never acts, any more than He acts against Himself.

As regards spiritual and rational beings, to which class the human soul belongs, the more they partake of this unchangeable law and light, the more clearly they see what is possible, and what impossible; and again, the greater their distance from it, the less their perception of the future, and the more frequent their surprise at strange occurrences.

4.

Thus of what happened to Elias we are ignorant; but still we believe the truthful declarations of Scripture regarding him.

Of one thing we are certain, that what God willed happened, and that except by God's will nothing can happen to any one.

So, if I am told that it is possible that the flesh of a certain man shall be changed into a celestial body, I allow the possibility, but I cannot tell whether it will be done; and the reason of my ignorance is, that I am not acquainted with the will of God in the matter.

That it will be done if it is God's will, is perfectly clear and indubitable.

Again, if I am told that something would happen if God did not prevent it from happening, I reply confidently that what is to happen is the action of God, not the event which might otherwise have happened.

For God knows His own future action, and therefore He knows also the effect of that action in preventing the happening of what would otherwise have happened; and, beyond all question, what God knows is more certain than what man thinks.

Hence it is as impossible for what is future not to happen, as for what is past not to have happened; for it can never be God's will that anything should, in the same sense, be both true and false.

Therefore all that is properly future cannot but happen; what does not happen never was future; even as all things which are properly in the past did indubitably take place.

5.

Accordingly, to say, if God is almighty, let Him make what has been done to be undone, is in fact to say, if God is almighty, let Him make a thing to be in the same sense both true and false.

God can put an end to the existence of anything, when the thing to be put an end to has a present existence; as when He puts an end by death to the existence of any one who has been brought into existence in birth; for in this case there is an actual existence which may be put a stop to. But when a thing does not exist, the existence cannot be put a stop to.

Now, what is past no longer exists and whatever has an existence which can be put an end to cannot be past.

What is truly past is no longer present; and the truth of its past existence is in our judgment, not in the thing itself which no longer exists.

The proposition asserting anything to be past is true when the thing no longer exists. God cannot make such a proposition false, because He cannot contradict the truth.

The truth in this case, or the true judgment, is first of all in our own mind, when we know and give expression to it.

But should it disappear from our minds by our forgetting it, it would still remain as truth.

It will always be true that the past thing which is no longer present had an existence; and the truth of its past existence after it has stopped is the same as the truth of its future existence before it began to be.

This truth cannot be contradicted by God, in whom abides the supreme and unchangeable truth, and whose illumination is the source of all the truth to be found in any mind or understanding.

Now God is not omnipotent in the sense of being able to die; nor does this inability prevent His being omnipotent.

True omnipotence belongs to Him who truly exists, and who alone is the source of all existence, both spiritual and corporeal.

The Creator makes what use He pleases of all His creatures; and His pleasure is in harmony with true and unchangeable justice, by which, as by His own nature, He, Himself unchangeable, brings to pass the changes of all changeable things according to the desert of their natures or of their actions.

No one, therefore, would be so foolish as to deny that Elias being a creature of God could be changed either for the worse or for the better; or that by the will of the omnipotent God he could be changed in a manner unusual among men.

So we can have no reason for doubting what on the high authority of Scripture is related of him, unless we limit the power of God to things which we are familiar with.

6.

Faustus' argument is, If Elias who was a man could escape death, why might not Christ have the power of dying, since He was more than man?

This is the same as to say, If human nature can be changed for the better, why should not the divine nature be changed for the worse?--a weak argument, seeing that human nature is changeable, while the divine nature is not.

Such a method of inference would lead to the glaring absurdity, that if God can bestow eternal glory on man, He must also have the power of consigning Himself to eternal misery.

Faustus will reply that his argument refers only to three days of death for God, as compared with eternal life for man.

Well, if you understood the three days of death in the sense of the death of the flesh which God took as a part of our mortal nature, you would be quite correct; for the truth of the gospel makes known that the death of Christ for three days was for the eternal life of men.

But in arguing that there is no impropriety in asserting a death of three days of the divine nature itself, without any assumption of mortality, because human nature can be endowed with immortality, you display the folly of one who knows neither God nor the gifts of God.

And indeed, since you make part of your god to be fastened to the mass of darkness for ever, how can you escape the absurd conclusion already mentioned, that God consigns Himself to eternal misery?

You will then require to prove that part of light is light, while part of God is not God.

To give you in a word, without argument, the true reason of our faith, as regards Elias having been caught up to heaven from the earth, though only a man, and as regards Christ being truly born of a virgin, and truly dying on the cross, our belief in both cases is grounded on the declaration of Holy Scripture, [1001] which it is piety to believe, and impiety to disbelieve.

What is said of Elias you pretend to deny, for you will pretend anything.

Regarding Christ, although even you do not go the length of saying that He could not die, though He could be born, still you deny His birth from a virgin, and assert His death on the cross to have been feigned, which is equivalent to denying it too, except as a mockery for the delusion of men; and you allow so much merely to obtain indulgence for your own falsehoods from the believers in these fictions.

7.

The question which Faustus makes it appear that he is asked by a Catholic, If Jesus was not born, how could He die? could be asked only by one who overlooked the fact that Adam died, though he was not born. Who will venture to say that the Son of God could not, if He had pleased, have made for Himself a true human body in the same way as He did for Adam; for all things were made by Him? [1002] or who will deny that He who is the Almighty Son of the Almighty could, if He had chosen, have taken a body from a heavenly substance, or from air or vapor, and have so changed it into the precise character of a human body, as that He might have lived as a man, and have died in it?

Or, once more, if He had chosen to take a body of none of the material substances which He had made, but to create for Himself from nothing real flesh, as all things were created by Him from nothing, none of us will oppose this by saying that He could not have done it.

The reason of our believing Him to have been born of the Virgin Mary, is not that He could not otherwise have appeared among men in a true body, but because it is so written in the Scripture, which we must believe in order to be Christians, or to be saved.

We believe, then, that Christ was born of the Virgin Mary, because it is so written in the Gospel; we believe that He died on the cross, because it is so written in the Gospel; we believe that both His birth and death were real, because the Gospel is no fiction.

Why He chose to suffer all these things in a body taken from a woman is a matter known only to Himself.

Perhaps He took this way of giving importance and honor to both the sexes which He had created, taking the form of a man, and being born of a woman; or there may have been some other reason, we cannot tell.

But this may be confidently affirmed, that what took place was exactly as we are told in the Gospel narrative, and that what the wisdom of God determined upon was exactly what ought to

The Writings Against the Manichaeans and Against the Donatists: Part I - The Manichaeans have happened.

We place the authority of the Gospel above all heretical discussions; and we admire the counsel of divine wisdom more than any counsel of any creature.

8.

Faustus calls upon us to believe him, and says, The truth is, if you will believe it, that the Hebrews were in a mistake regarding both the death of Jesus and the immortality of Elias.

And a little after he adds, As from the outset of His taking the likeness of man He underwent in appearance all the experiences of humanity, it was quite consistent that He should seal the dispensation by appearing to die.

How can this infamous liar, who declares that Christ feigned death, expect to be believed?

Did Christ utter falsehood when He said, "It behoves the Son of man to be killed, and to rise the third day?" [1003] And do you tell us to believe what you say, as if you utter no falsehoods?

In that case, Peter was more truthful than Christ when he said to Him, "Be it far from Thee, Lord; this shall not be unto Thee;" for which it was said to him, "Get thee behind me, Satan."[1004] This rebuke was not lost upon Peter, for, after his correction and full preparation, he preached even to his own death the truth of the death of Christ.

But if Peter deserved to be called Satan for thinking that Christ would not die, what should you be called, when you not only deny that Christ died, but assert that He feigned death?

You give, as a reason for Christ's appearing to die, that He underwent in appearance all the experiences of humanity.

But that He feigned all the experiences of humanity is only your opinion in opposition to the Gospel.

In reality, when the evangelist says that Jesus slept, [1005] that He was hungry, [1006] that He was thirsty, [1007] that He was sorrowful, [1008] or glad, and so on,--these things are all true in the sense of not being feigned, but actual experiences; only that they were undergone, not from a mere natural necessity, but in the exercise of a controlling will, and of divine power.

In the case of a man, anger, sorrow, sleeping, being hungry and thirsty, are often involuntary; in Christ they were acts of His own will.

So also men are born without any act of their own will, and suffer against their will; while Christ was born and suffered by His own will.

Still, the things are true; and the accurate narrative of them is intended to instruct whoever believes in Christ's gospel in the truth, not to delude him with falsehoods.

Book XXVII - Faustus warns against pressing too far the argument, that if Jesus was not born He cannot have suffered

Augustin accepts the birth and death alike on the testimony of the Gospel narrative, which is higher authority than the falsehood of Manichæus.

1.

Faustus said:

If Jesus was not born, He cannot have suffered; but since He did suffer, He must have been born.

I advise you not to have recourse to logical inference in these matters, or else your whole faith will be shaken.

For, even according to you, Jesus was born miraculously of a virgin; which the argument from consequents to antecedents shows to be false.

For your argument might thus be turned against you:

If Jesus was born of a woman, He must have been begotten by a man; but He was not begotten by a man, therefore He was not born of a woman.

If, as you believe, He could be born without being begotten, why could He not also suffer without being brought forth?

2.
Augustin replied:
The argument which you here reply to is one which could be used only by such ignorant people as you succeed in misleading, not by those who know enough to refute you.

Jesus could both be born without being begotten and suffer without being brought forth.

His being one and not the other was the effect of His own will.

He chose to be born without being begotten, and not to suffer without being brought forth.

And if you ask how I know that He was brought forth, and that He suffered, I read this in the faithful Gospel narrative.

If I ask how you know what you state, you bring forward the authority of Manichæus, and charge the Gospel with falsehood.

Even if Manichæus did not set forth falsehood as an excellence in Christ, I should not believe his statements.

His praise of falsehood comes from nothing that he found in Christ, but from his own moral character.

Book XXVIII - Faustus recurs to the genealogy and insists upon examining it as regards its consistency with itself

Augustin takes his stand on Scripture authority and maintains that Matthew's statements as to the birth of Christ must be accepted as final.

1.
Faustus said:
Christ, you say, could not have died, had He not been born.

I reply, If He was born, He cannot have been God; or if He could both be God and be born, why could He not both be born and die? Plainly, arguments and necessary consequences are not applicable to those matters, where the question is of the account to be given of Jesus.

The answer must be obtained from His own statements, or from the statements of His apostles regarding Him.

The genealogy must be examined as regards its consistency with itself, instead of arguing from the supposition of Christ's death to the fact of His birth; for He might have suffered without having been born, or He might have been born, and yet never have suffered; for you yourselves acknowledge that with God nothing is impossible, which is inconsistent with the denial that Christ could have suffered without having been born.

2.
Augustin replied:
You are always answering arguments which no one uses, instead of our real arguments, which you cannot answer.

No one says that Christ could not die if He had not been born; for Adam died though he had not been born.

What we say is, Christ was born, because this is said not by this or that heretic, but in the holy Gospel; and He died, for this too is written, not in some heretical production, but in the holy Gospel.

You set aside argument on the question of the true account to be given of Jesus, and refer to what He says of Himself, and what His apostles say of Him; and yet, when I begin to quote the Gospel of His apostle Matthew, where we have the whole narrative of Christ's birth, you forthwith deny that Matthew wrote the narrative, though this is affirmed by the continuous testimony of the whole Church, from the days of apostolic presidency to the bishops of our own time.

What authority will you quote against this?

Perhaps some book of Manichæus, where it is denied that Jesus was born of a virgin.

As, then, I believe your book to be the production of Manichæus, since it has been kept and handed down among the disciples of Manichæus, from the time when he lived to the present time, by a regular succession of your presidents, so I ask you to believe the book which I quote to have been written by Matthew, since it has been handed down from the days of Matthew in the Church, without any break in the connection between that time and the present.

The question then is, whether we are to believe the statements of an apostle who was in the

The Writings Against the Manichaeans and Against the Donatists: Part I - The Manichaeans
company of Christ while He was on earth, or of a man away in Persia, born long after Christ.

But perhaps you will quote some other book bearing the name of an apostle known to have been chosen by Christ; and you will find there that Christ was not born of Mary.

Since, then, one of the books must be false, the question in this case is, whether we are to yield our belief to a book acknowledged and approved as handed down from the beginning in the Church founded by Christ Himself, and maintained through the apostles and their successors in an unbroken connection all over the world to the present day; or to a book which this Church condemns as unknown, and which, moreover, is brought forward by men who prove their veracity by praising Christ for falsehood.

3.

Here you will say, Examine the genealogy as given in the two Gospels, and see if it is consistent with itself.

The answer to this has been given already. [1009] Your difficulty is how Joseph could have two fathers.

But even if you could not have thought of the explanation, that one was his own father, and the other adopted, you should not have been so ready to put yourself in opposition to such high authority.

Now that this explanation has been given you, I call upon you to acknowledge the truth of the Gospel, and above all to cease your mischievous and unreasonable attacks upon the truth.

4.

Faustus most plausibly refers to what Jesus said of Himself.

But how is this to be known except from the narratives of His disciples? And if we do not believe them when they tell us that Christ was born of a virgin, how shall we believe what they record as said by Christ of Himself?

For, as regards any writing professing to come immediately from Christ Himself, if it were really His, how is it not read and acknowledged and regarded as of supreme authority in the Church, which, beginning with Christ Himself, and continued by His apostles, who were succeeded by the bishops, has been maintained and extended to our own day, and in which is found the fulfillment of many former predictions, while those concerning the last days are sure to be accomplished in the future?

In regard to the appearance of such a writing, it would require to be considered from what quarter it issued.

Supposing it to have issued from Christ Himself, those in immediate connection with Him might very well have received it, and have transmitted it to others. In this case, the authority of the writing would be fully established by the traditions of various communities, and of their presidents, as I have already said.

Who, then, is so infatuated as in our day to believe that the Epistle of Christ issued by Manichæus is genuine, or to disbelieve Matthew's narrative of Christ's words and actions?

Or, if the question is of Matthew being the real author, who would not, in this also, believe what he finds in the Church, which has a distinct history in unbroken connection from the days of Matthew to the present time, rather than a Persian interloper, who comes more than two hundred years after, and wishes us to believe his account of Christ's words and actions rather than that of Matthew; whereas, even in the case of the Apostle Paul, who was called from heaven after the Lord's ascension, the Church would not have believed him, had there not been apostles in life with whom he might communicate, and compare his gospel with theirs, so as to be recognized as belonging to the same society?

When it was ascertained that Paul preached what the apostles preached, and that he lived in fellowship and harmony with them, and when God's testimony was added by Paul's working miracles like those done by the apostles, his authority became so great, that his words are now received in the Church, as if, to use his own appropriate words, Christ were speaking in him. [1010] Manichæus, on the other hand, thinks that the Church of Christ should believe what he says in opposition to the Scriptures, which are supported by such strong and continuous evidence, and in which the Church finds an emphatic injunction, that whoever preaches to her differently from what she has received must be anathema. [1011]

5.

Faustus tells us that he has good grounds for concluding that these Scriptures are unworthy of credit.

And yet he speaks of not using arguments.

But the argument too shall be refuted.

The end of the whole argument is to bring the soul to believe that the reason of its misery in this world is, that it is the means of preventing God from being deprived of His kingdom, and that God's substance and nature is so exposed to change, corruption, injury, and contamination, that part of it is incurably defiled, and is consigned by Himself to eternal punishment in the mass of darkness, though, when it was in harmless union with Himself, and guilty of no crime, He knowingly sent it where it was to suffer defilement.

This is the end of all your arguments and fictions; and would that there were an end of them as regards your heart and your lips, that you might sometime desist from believing and uttering those execrable blasphemies!

But, says Faustus, I prove from the writings themselves that they cannot be in all points trustworthy, for they contradict one another.

Why not say, then, that they are wholly untrustworthy, if their testimony is inconsistent and self-contradictory?

But, says Faustus, I say what I think to be in accordance with truth.

With what truth?

The truth is only your own fiction, which begins with God's battle, goes on to His contamination, and ends with His damnation.

No one, says Faustus, believes writings which contradict themselves.

But if you think they do this, it is because you do not understand them; for your ignorance has been manifested in regard to the passages you have quoted in support of your opinion, and the same will appear in regard to any quotations you may still make.

So there is no reason for our not believing these writings, supported as they are by such weighty testimony; and this is itself the best reason for pronouncing accursed those whose preaching differs from what is there written.

Book XXIX - Faustus seeks to justify the docetism of the Manichæans

Augustin insists that there is nothing disgraceful in being born.

1.

Faustus said:

If Christ was visible, and suffered without having been born, this was sorcery.

This argument of yours may be turned against you, by replying that it was sorcery if He was conceived or brought forth without being begotten.

It is not in accordance with the law of nature that a virgin should bring forth, and still less that she should still be a virgin after bringing forth.

Why, then, do you refuse to admit that Christ, in a preternatural manner, suffered without submitting to the condition of birth?

Believe me:

in substance, both our beliefs are contrary to nature; but our belief is decent, and yours is not.

We give an explanation of Christ's passion which is at least probable, while the only explanation you give of His birth is false.

In fine, we hold that He suffered in appearance, and did not really die; you believe in an actual birth, and conception in the womb.

If it is not so, you have only to acknowledge that the birth too was a delusion, and our whole dispute will be at an end.

As to what you frequently allege, that Christ could not have appeared or spoken to men without having been born, it is absurd; for, as our teachers have shown, angels have often appeared and spoken to men.

2.

Augustin replied:

We do not say that to die without having been born is sorcery; for, as we have said already, this happened in the case of Adam.

But, though it had never happened, who will venture to say that Christ could not, if He had so pleased, have come without taking His body from a virgin, and yet appearing in a true body to redeem us by a true death?

However, it was better that He should be, as He actually was, born of a virgin, and, by His condescension, do honor to both sexes, for whose deliverance He was to die, by taking a man's body born of a woman.

In this He testifies emphatically against you, and refutes your doctrine, which makes the sexes the work of the devil.

What we call sorcery in your doctrine is your making Christ's passion and death to have been only in appearance, so that, by a spectral illusion, He seemed to die when He did not.

Hence you must also make His resurrection spectral and illusory and false; for if there was no true death, there could not be a real resurrection.

Hence also the marks which He showed to His doubting disciples must have been false; and Thomas was not assured by truth, but cheated by a lie, when he exclaimed, "My Lord, and my God." [1012] And yet you would have us believe that your tongue utters truth, though Christ's whole body was a falsehood.

Our argument against you is, that the Christ you make is such that you cannot be His true disciples unless you too practise deceit.

The fact that Christ's body was the only one born of a virgin does not prove that there was sorcery in His birth, any more than there is sorcery in its being the only body to rise again on the third day, never to die any more.

Will you say that there was sorcery in all the Lord's miracles because they were unusual?

They really happened, and their appearance, as seen by men, was true, and not an illusion; and when they are said to be contrary to nature, it is not that they oppose nature, but that they transcend the method of nature to which we are accustomed.

May God keep the minds of His people who are still babes in Christ from being influenced by Faustus, when he recommends as a duty that we should acknowledge Christ's birth to have been illusory and not real, that so we may end our dispute!

Nay, verily, rather let us continue to contend for the truth against them, than agree with them in falsehood.

3.

But if we are to end the controversy by saying this, why do not our opponents themselves say it?

While they assert the death of Christ to have been not real but feigned, why do they make out that He had no birth at all, not even of the same kind as His death?

If they had so much regard for the authority of the evangelist as to oblige them to admit that Christ suffered, at least in appearance, it is the same authority which testifies to His birth.

Two evangelists, indeed, give the story of the birth; [1013] but in all we read of Jesus having a mother. [1014] Perhaps Faustus was unwilling to make the birth an illusion, because the difference of the genealogies given in Matthew and Luke causes an apparent discrepancy.

But, supposing a man ignorant, there are many things also relating to the passion of Christ in which he will think the evangelists disagree; suppose him instructed, he finds entire agreement.

Can it be right to feign death, and wrong to feign birth?

And yet Faustus will have us acknowledge the birth to be feigned, in order to put an end to the dispute.

It will appear presently in our reply to another objection what we think to be the reason why Faustus will not admit of any birth, even a feigned one.

4.

We deny that there is anything disgraceful in the bodies of saints.

Some members, indeed, are called uncomely, because they have not so pleasing an appearance as those constantly in view. [1015] But attend to what the apostle says, when from the unity and harmony of the body he enjoins charity on the Church:

"Much more those members of the body, which seem to be feeble, are necessary:

and those members of the body, which we think to be less honorable, upon these we bestow more abundant honor; and our uncomely parts have more abundant comeliness. For our comely parts have no need:

but God hath tempered the body together, having given more abundant honor to that part which lacked: that there should be no schism in the body." [1016]The licentious and intemperate use of those members is disgraceful, but not the members themselves; for they are preserved in purity not only by the unmarried, but also by wedded fathers and mothers of holy life, in whose case the natural appetite, as serving not lust, but an intelligent purpose in the production of children, is in no way disgraceful.

Still more, in the holy Virgin Mary, who by faith conceived the body of Christ, there was nothing disgraceful in the members which served not for a common natural conception, but for a miraculous birth.

In order that we might conceive Christ in sincere hearts, and, as it were, produce Him in confession, it was meet that His body should come from the substance of His mother without injury to her bodily purity.

We cannot suppose that the mother of Christ suffered loss by His birth, or that the gift of productiveness displaced the grace of virginity.

If these occurrences, which were real and no illusion, are new and strange, and contrary to the common course of nature, the reason is, that they are great, and amazing, and divine; and all the more on this account are they true, and firm, and sure.

Angels, says Faustus, appeared and spoke without having been born.

As if we held that Christ could not have appeared or spoken without having been born of a woman!

He could, but He chose not; and what He chose was best.

And that He chose to do what He did is plain, because He acted, not like your god, from necessity, but voluntarily. That He was born we know, because we put faith not in a heretic, but in Christ's gospel.

Book XXX - Faustus repels the insinuation that the prophecy of Paul with reference to those that should forbid to marry, abstain from meats, etc., applies to the Manichæans more than to the Catholic ascetics, who are held in the highest esteem in the Church

Augustin justifies this application of the prophecy, and shows the difference between Manichæan and Christian asceticism.

1.

Faustus said:

You apply to us the words of Paul:

"Some shall depart from the faith, giving heed to lying spirits, and doctrines of devils; speaking lies in hypocrisy; having their consciences seared as with a hot iron; forbidding to marry, abstaining from meats, which God has created to be received with thanksgiving by believers."[1017] I refuse to admit that the apostle said this, unless you first acknowledge that Moses and the prophets taught doctrines of devils, and were the interpreters of a lying and malignant spirit; since they enjoin with great emphasis abstinence from swine's flesh and other meats, which they call unclean.

This case must first be settled; and you must consider long and carefully how their teaching is to be viewed;

whether they said these things from God, or from the devil. As regards these matters, either Moses and the prophets must be condemned along with us; or we must be acquitted along with them.

You are unjust in condemning us, as you do now, as followers of the doctrine of devils, because we require the priestly class to abstain from animal food; for we limit the prohibition to the priesthood, while you hold that your prophets, and Moses himself, who forbade all classes of men to eat the flesh of swine, and hares, and conies, besides all varieties of cuttle-fish, and all fish wanting scales, said this not in a lying spirit, nor in the doctrine of devils, but from God, and in the Holy Spirit.

Even supposing, then, that Paul said these words, you can convince me only by condemning

Moses and the prophets; and so, though you will not do it for reason or truth, you will contradict Moses for the sake of your belly.

2.

Besides, you have in your Book of Daniel the account of the three youths, which you will find it difficult to reconcile with the opinion that to abstain from meats is the doctrine of devils.

For we are told that they abstained not only from what the law forbade, but even from what it allowed; [1018] and you are wont to praise them, and count them as martyrs; though they too followed the doctrine of devils, if this is to be taken as the apostle's opinion.

And Daniel himself declares that he fasted for three weeks, not eating flesh or drinking wine, while he prayed for his people. [1019] How is it that he boasts of this doctrine of devils, and glories in the falsehood of a lying spirit?

3.

Again, what are we to think of you, or of the better class of Christians among you, some of whom abstain from swine's flesh, some from the flesh of quadrupeds, and some from all animal food, while all the Church admires them for it, and regards them with profound veneration, as only not gods?

You obstinately refuse to consider that if the words quoted from the apostle are true and genuine, these people too are misled by doctrines of devils.

And there is another observance which no one will venture to explain away or to deny, for it is known to all, and is practised yearly with particular attention in the congregation of Catholics all over the world--I mean the fast of forty days, in the due observance of which a man must abstain from all the things which, according to this verse, were created by God that we might receive them, while at the same time he calls this abstinence a doctrine of devils.

So, my dear friends, shall we say that you too, during this fast, while celebrating the mysteries of Christ's passion, live after the manner of devils, and are deluded by a seducing spirit, and speak lies in hypocrisy, and have your conscience seared with a hot iron?

If this does not apply to you, neither does it apply to us. What is to be thought of this verse, or its author; or to whom does it apply, since it agrees neither with the traditions of the Old Testament, nor with the institutions of the New?

As regards the New Testament, the proof is from your own practice; and though the Old requires abstinence only from certain things, still it requires abstinence.

On the other hand, this opinion of yours makes all abstinence from animal food a doctrine of devils.

If this is your belief, once more I say it, you must condemn Moses, and reject the prophets, and pass the same sentence on yourselves; for, as they always abstained from certain kinds of food, so you sometimes abstain from all food.

4.

But if you think that in making a distinction in food, Moses and the prophets established a divine ordinance, and not a doctrine of devils; if Daniel in the Holy Spirit observed a fast of three weeks; if the youths Ananias, Azarias, and Mishael, under divine guidance, chose to live on cabbage or pulse; if, again, those among you who abstain, do it not at the instigation of devils; if your abstinence from wine and flesh for forty days is not superstitious, but by divine command,--consider, I beseech you, if it is not perfect madness to suppose these words to be Paul's that abstinence from food and forbidding to marry are doctrines of devils.

Paul cannot have said that to dedicate virgins to Christ is a doctrine of devils.

But you read the words, and inconsiderately, as usual, apply them to us, without seeing that this stamps your virgins too as led away by the doctrine of devils, and that you are the functionaries of the devils in your constant endeavors to induce virgins to make this profession, so that in all your churches the virgins nearly outnumber the married women.

Why do you still adhere to such practises?

Why do you ensnare wretched young women, if it is the will of devils, and not of Christ, that they fulfill?

But, first of all, I wish to know if making virgins is, in all cases, the doctrine of devils, or only the prohibition of marriage.

If it is the prohibition, it does not apply to us, for we too hold it equally foolish to prevent one who wishes, as it is criminal and impious to force one who has some reluctance.

But if you say that to encourage the proposal, and not to resist such a desire, is all the doctrine of devils, to say nothing of the consequence as regards you, the apostle himself will be thus brought into danger, if he must be considered as having introduced the doctrines of devils into Iconium, when Thecla, after having been betrothed, was by his discourse inflamed with the desire of perpetual virginity. [1020]And what shall we say of Jesus, the Master Himself, and the source of all sanctity, who is the unwedded spouse of the virgins who make this profession, and who, when specifying in the Gospel three kinds of eunuchs, natural, artificial, and voluntary, gives the palm to those who have "made themselves eunuchs for the kingdom of heaven," [1021] meaning the youths of both sexes who have extirpated from their hearts the desire of marriage, and who in the Church act as eunuchs of the King's palace?

Is this also the doctrine of devils?

Are those words, too, spoken in a seducing spirit?

And if Paul and Christ are proved to be priests of devils, is not their spirit the same that speaks in God? I do not mention the other apostles of our Lord, Peter, Andrew, Thomas, and the example of celibacy, the blessed John, who in various ways commended to young men and maidens the excellence of this profession, leaving to us, and to you too, the form for making virgins.

I do not mention them, because you do not admit them into the canon, and so you will not scruple impiously to impute to them doctrines of devils.

But will you say the same of Christ, or of the Apostle Paul, who, we know, everywhere expressed the same preference for unmarried women to the married, and gave an example of it in the case of the saintly Thecla? But if the doctrine preached by Paul to Thecla, and which the other apostles also preached, was not the doctrine of devils, how can we believe that Paul left on record his opinion, that the very exhortation to sanctity is the injunction and the doctrine of devils?

To make virgins simply by exhortation, without forbidding to marry, is not peculiar to you.

That is our principle too; and he must be not only a fool, but a madman, who thinks that a private law can forbid what the public law allows.

As regards marriage, therefore, we too encourage virgins to remain as they are when they are willing to do so; we do not make them virgins against their will.

For we know the force of will and of natural appetite when opposed by public law; much more when the law is only private, and every one is at liberty to disobey it.

If, then, it is no crime to make virgins in this manner, we are guiltless as well as you.

If it is wrong to make virgins in any way, you are guilty as well as we.

So that what you mean, or intend, by quoting this verse against us, it is impossible to say.

5.

Augustin replied:

Listen, and you shall hear what we mean and intend by quoting this verse against you, since you say that you do not know.

It is not that you abstain from animal food; for, as you observe, our ancient fathers abstained from some kinds of food, not, however, as condemning them, but with a typical meaning, which you do not understand, and of which I have said already in this work all that appeared necessary.

Besides, Christians, not heretics, but Catholics, in order to subdue the body, that the soul may be more humbled in prayer, abstain not only from animal food, but also from some vegetable productions, without, however, believing them to be unclean.

A few do this always; and at certain seasons or days, as in Lent, almost all, more or less, according to the choice or ability of individuals.

You, on the other hand, deny that the creature is good, and call it unclean, saying that animals are made by the devil of the worst impurities in the substance of evil and so you reject them with horror, as being the most cruel and loathsome places of confinement of your god.

You, as a concession, allow your followers, as distinct from the priests, to eat animal food; as the apostle allows, in certain cases, not marriage in the general sense, but the indulgence of passion in marriage. [1022] It is only sin which is thus made allowance for.

This is the feeling you have toward all animal food; you have learned it from your heresy, and you teach it to your followers.

You make allowance for your followers, because, as I said before, they supply you with necessaries; but you grant them indulgence without saying that it is not sinful. For yourselves, you shun contact with this evil and impurity; and hence our reason for quoting this verse against you is found in the words of the apostle which follow those with which you end the quotation. Perhaps it was for this reason that you left out the words, and then say that you do not know what we mean or intend by the quotation; for it suited you better to omit the account of our intention than to express it.

For, after speaking of abstaining from meats, which God has created to be received with thanksgiving by believers, the apostle goes on, "And by them who know the truth; for every creature of God is good, and nothing to be refused, if it be received with thanksgiving: for it is sanctified by the word of God and prayer." [1023]This you deny; for your idea, and motive, and belief in abstaining from such food is, that they are not typically, but naturally, evil and impure. In this assuredly you blaspheme the Creator; and in this is the doctrine of devils.

You need not be surprised that, so long before the event, this prediction regarding you was made by the Holy Spirit.

6.

So, again, if your exhortations to virginity resembled the teaching of the apostle, "He who giveth in marriage doeth well, and he who giveth not in marriage doeth better;" [1024] if you taught that marriage is good, and virginity better, as the Church teaches which is truly Christ's Church, you would not have been described in the Spirit's prediction as forbidding to marry.

What a man forbids he makes evil; but a good thing may be placed second to a better thing without being forbidden.

Moreover, the only honorable kind of marriage, or marriage entered into for its proper and legitimate purpose, is precisely that you hate most.

So, though you may not forbid sexual intercourse, you forbid marriage; for the peculiarity of marriage is, that it is not merely for the gratification of passion, but, as is written in the contract, for the procreation of children. And, though you allow many of your followers to retain their connection with you in spite of their refusal, or their inability, to obey you, you cannot deny that you make the prohibition.

The prohibition is part of your false doctrine, while the toleration is only for the interests of the society.

And here we see the reason, which I have delayed till now to mention, for your making not the birth but only the death of Christ feigned and illusory.

Death being the separation of the soul, that is, of the nature of your god, from the body which belongs to his enemies, for it is the work of the devil, you uphold and approve of it; and thus, according to your creed, it was meet that Christ, though He did not die, should commend death by appearing to die.

In birth, again, you believe your god to be bound instead of released; and so you will not allow that Christ was born even in this illusory fashion.

You would have thought better of Mary had she ceased to be a virgin without being a mother, than as being a mother without ceasing to be a virgin. You see, then, that there is a great difference between exhorting to virginity as the better of two good things, and forbidding to marry by denouncing the true purpose of marriage; between abstaining from food as a symbolic observance, or for the mortification of the body, and abstaining from food which God has created for the reason that God did not create it.

In one case, we have the doctrine of the prophets and apostles; in the other, the doctrine of lying devils.

Book XXXI - The scripture passage

"To the pure all things are pure, but to the impure and defiled is nothing pure; but even their mind and conscience are defiled," is discussed from both the Manichæan and the Catholic points of view, Faustus objecting to its application to his party and Augustin insisting on its application.

1.

Faustus said:
"To the pure all things are pure.
But to the impure and defiled is nothing pure; but even their mind and conscience are defiled."

As regards this verse, too, it is very doubtful whether, for your own sake, you should believe it to have been written by Paul.

For it would follow that Moses and the prophets were not only influenced by devils in making so much in their laws of the distinctions in food, but also that they themselves were impure and defiled in their mind and conscience, so that the following words also might properly be applied to them:

"They profess to know God, but in works deny Him." [1025] This is applicable to no one more than to Moses and the prophets, who are known to have lived very differently from what was becoming in men knowing God.

Up to this time I have thought only of adulteries and frauds and murders as defiling the conscience of Moses and the prophets; but now, from what this verse says, it is plain that they were also defiled, because they looked upon something as defiled.

How, then, can you persist in thinking that the vision of the divine majesty can have been bestowed on such men, when it is written that only the pure in heart can see God?

Even supposing that they had been pure from unlawful crimes, this superstitious abstinence from certain kinds of food, if it defiles the mind, is enough to debar them from the sight of deity.

Gone for ever, too, is the boast of Daniel, and of the three youths, who, till now that we are told that nothing is unclean, have been regarded among the Jews as persons of great purity and excellence of character, because, in observance of hereditary customs, they carefully avoided defiling themselves with Gentile food, especially that of sacrifices. [1026]Now it appears that they were defiled in mind and conscience most of all when they were closing their mouth against blood and idol-feasts.

2.

But perhaps their ignorance may excuse them; for, as this Christian doctrine of all things being pure to the pure had not then appeared, they may have thought some things impure.

But there can be no excuse for you in the face of Paul's announcement, that there is nothing which is not pure, and that abstinence from certain food is the doctrine of devils, and that those who think anything defiled are polluted in their mind, if you not only abstain, as we have said, but make a merit of it, and believe that you become more acceptable to Christ in proportion as you are more abstemious, or, according to this new doctrine, as your minds are defiled and your conscience polluted.

It should also be observed that, while there are three religions in the world which, though in a very different manner, appoint chastity and abstinence as the means of purification of the mind, the religions, namely, of the Jews, the Gentiles, and the Christians, the opinion that everything is pure cannot have come from any one of the three.

It is certainly not from Judaism, nor from Paganism, which also makes a distinction of food; the only difference being, that the Hebrew classification of animals does not harmonize with the Pagan.

Then as to the Christian faith, if you think it peculiar to Christianity to consider nothing defiled, you must first of all confess that there are no Christians among you.

For things offered to idols, and what dies of itself, to mention nothing else, are regarded by you all as great defilement.

If, again, this is a Christian practice, on your part, the doctrine which is opposed to all abstinence from impurities cannot be traced to Christianity either.

How, then, could Paul have said what is not in keeping with any religion?

In fact, when the apostle from a Jew became a Christian, it was a change of customs more than of religion.

As for the writer of this verse, there seems to be no religion which favors his opinion.

3.

Be sure, then, whenever you discover anything else in Scripture to assail our faith with, to see, in the first place, that it is not against you, before you commence your attack on us.

For instance, there is the passage you continually quote about Peter, that he once saw a vessel let down from heaven in which were all kinds of animals and serpents, and that, when he was surprised and astonished, a voice was heard, saying to him, Peter, kill and eat whatsoever thou seest in the vessel, and that he replied, Lord I will not touch what is common or unclean.

On this the voice spoke again, What I have cleansed, call not unclean. [1027]This, indeed, seems to have an allegorical meaning, and not to refer to the absence of distinction in food.

But as you choose to give it this meaning, you are bound to feed upon all wild animals, and scorpions, and snakes, and reptiles in general, in compliance with this vision of Peter's.

In this way, you will show that you are really obedient to the voice which Peter is said to have heard.

But you must never forget that you at the same time condemn Moses and the prophets, who considered many things polluted which, according to this utterance, God has sanctified.

4.

Augustin replied:

When the apostle says, "To the pure all things are pure," he refers to the natures which God had created,--as it is written by Moses in Genesis, "And God made all things; and behold they were very good," [1028] --not to the typical meanings, according to which God, by the same Moses, distinguished the clean from the unclean.

Of this we have already spoken at length more than once, and need not dwell on it here.

It is clear that the apostle called those impure who, after the revelation of the New Testament, still advocated the observance of the shadows of things to come, as if without them the Gentiles could not obtain the salvation which is in Christ, because in this they were carnally minded; and he called them unbelieving, because they did not distinguish between the time of the law and the time of grace.

To them, he says, nothing is pure, because they made an erroneous and sinful use both of what they received and of what they rejected; which is true of all unbelievers, but especially of you Manichæans, for to you nothing whatever is pure.

For, although you take great care to keep the food which you use separate from the contamination of flesh, still it is not pure to you, for the only creator of it you allow is the devil.

And you hold, that, by eating it, you release your god, who suffers confinement and pollution in it. One would think you might consider yourselves pure, since your stomach is the proper place for purifying your god.

But even your own bodies, in your opinion, are of the nature and handiwork of the race of darkness; while your souls are still affected by the pollution of your bodies.

What, then, is pure to you?

Not the things you eat; not the receptacle of your food; not yourselves, by whom it is purified.

Thus you see against whom the words of the apostle are directed; he expresses himself so as to include all who are impure and unbelieving, but first and chiefly to condemn you.

To the pure, therefore, all things are pure, in the nature in which they were created; but to the ancient Jewish people all things were not pure in their typical significance; and, as regards bodily health, or the customs of society, all things are not suitable to us.

But when things are in their proper places, and the order of nature is preserved, to the pure all things are pure; but to the impure and unbelieving, among whom you stand first, nothing is pure.

You might make a wholesome application to yourselves of the following words of the apostle, if you desired a cure for your seared consciences.

The words are:

"Their very mind and conscience are defiled."

Book XXXII - Faustus fails to understand why he should be required either to accept or reject the New Testament as a whole, while the Catholics accept or reject the various parts of the Old Testament at pleasure

Augustin denies that the Catholics treat the Old Testament arbitrarily, and explains their attitude towards it.

1.

Faustus said:

You say, that if we believe the Gospel, we must believe everything that is written in it.

Why, then, since you believe the Old Testament, do you not believe all that is found in any part of it?

Instead of that, you cull out only the prophecies telling of a future King of the Jews, for you suppose this to be Jesus, along with a few precepts of common morality, such as, Thou shalt not kill, Thou shalt not commit adultery; and all the rest you pass over, thinking of the other things as Paul thought of the things which he held to be dung. [1029]Why, then, should it seem strange or singular in me that I select from the New Testament whatever is purest, and helpful for my salvation, while I set aside the interpolations of your predecessors, which impair its dignity and grace?

2.

If there are parts of the Testament of the Father which we are not bound to observe (for you attribute the Jewish law to the Father, and it is well known that many things in it shock you, and make you ashamed, so that in heart you no longer regard it as free from corruption, though, as you believe, the Father Himself partly wrote it for you with His own finger while part was written by Moses, who was faithful and trustworthy), the Testament of the Son must be equally liable to corruption, and may equally well contain objectionable things; especially as it is allowed not to have been written by the Son Himself, nor by His apostles, but long after, by some unknown men, who, lest they should be suspected of writing of things they knew nothing of, gave to their books the names of the apostles, or of those who were thought to have followed the apostles, declaring the contents to be according to these originals.

In this, I think, they do grievous wrong to the disciples of Christ, by quoting their authority for the discordant and contradictory statements in these writings, saying that it was according to them that they wrote the Gospels, which are so full of errors and discrepancies, both in facts and in opinions, that they can be harmonized neither with themselves nor with one another.

This is nothing else than to slander good men, and to bring the charge of dissension on the brotherhood of the disciples.

In reading the Gospels, the clear intention of our heart perceives the errors, and, to avoid all injustice, we accept whatever is useful, in the way of building up our faith, and promoting the glory of the Lord Christ, and of the Almighty God, His Father, while we reject the rest as unbecoming the majesty of God and Christ, and inconsistent with our belief.

3.

To return to what I said of your not accepting everything in the Old Testament.

You do not admit carnal circumcision, though that is what is written; [1030] nor resting from all occupation on the Sabbath, though that is enjoined; [1031] and instead of propitiating God, as Moses recommends, by offerings and sacrifices, you cast these things aside as utterly out of keeping with Christian worship, and as having nothing at all to recommend them.

In some cases, however, you make a division, and while you accept one part, you reject the other.

Thus, in the Passover, which is also the annual feast of the Old Testament, while it is written that in this observance you must slay a lamb to be eaten in the evening, and that you must abstain from leaven for seven days, and be content with unleavened bread and bitter herbs, [1032] you accept the feast, but pay no attention to the rules for its observance.

It is the same with the feast of Pentecost, or seven weeks, and the accompaniment of a certain kind and number of sacrifices which Moses enjoins: [1033] you observe the feast, but you condemn the propitiatory rites, which are part of it, because they are not in harmony with Christianity.

As regards the command to abstain from Gentile food, you are zealous believers in the uncleanness of things offered to idols, and of what has died of itself; but you are not so ready to believe the prohibition of swine's flesh, and hares, and conies, and mullets, and cuttle-fish, and all the fish that you have a relish for, although Moses pronounces them all unclean.

4.

I do not suppose that you will consent, or even listen, to such things as that a father-in-law should lie with his daughter-in-law, as Judah did; or a father with his daughters, like Lot; or prophets with harlots, like Hosea; or that a husband should sell his wife for a night to her lover, like Abraham; or that a man should marry two sisters, like Jacob; or that the rulers of the people and the men you consider as most inspired should keep their mistresses by hundreds and thousands; or, according to the provision made in Deuteronomy about wives, that the wife of one brother, if he dies without children, should marry the surviving brother, and that he should raise up seed from her instead of his brother; and that if the man refuses to do this, the fair plaintiff should bring her case before the elders, that the brother may be called and admonished to perform this religious duty; and that, if he persists in his refusal, he must not go unpunished, but the woman must loose his shoe from his right foot, and strike him in the face, and send him away, spat upon and accursed, to perpetuate the reproach in his family. [1034] These, and such as these, are the examples and precepts of the Old Testament.

If they are good, why do you not practise them?

If they are bad, why do you not condemn the Old Testament, in which they are found?

But if you think that these are spurious interpolations, that is precisely what we think of the New Testament.

You have no right to claim from us an acknowledgment for the New Testament which you yourselves do not make for the Old.

5.
Since you hold to the divine authorship of the Old as well as of the New Testament, it would surely be more consistent and more becoming, as you do not obey its precepts, to confess that it has been corrupted by improper additions, than to treat it so contemptuously, if it is genuine and uncorrupted.

Accordingly, my explanation of your neglect of the requirements of the Old Testament has always been, and still is, that you are either wise enough to reject them as spurious, or that you have the boldness and irreverence to disregard them if they are true.

At any rate, when you would oblige me to believe everything contained in the documents of the New Testament because I receive the Testament itself, you should consider that, though you profess to receive the Old Testament, you in your heart disbelieve many things in it.

Thus, you do not admit as true or authoritative the declaration of the Old Testament, that every one that hangeth on a tree is accursed, [1035] for this would apply to Jesus; or that every man is accursed who does not raise up seed in Israel, [1036] for that would include all of both sexes devoted to God; or that whoever is not circumcised in the flesh of his foreskin will be cut off from among his people, [1037] for that would apply to all Christians; or that whoever breaks the Sabbath must be stoned to death; [1038] or that no mercy should be shown to the man who breaks a single precept of the Old Testament.

If you really believe these things as certainly enjoined by God, you would, in the time of Christ, have been the first to assail Him, and you would now have no quarrel with the Jews, who, in persecuting Christ with heart and soul, acted in obedience to their own God.

6.
I am aware that instead of boldly pronouncing these passages spurious, you make out that these things were required of the Jews till the coming of Jesus; and that now that He is come, according, as you say, to the predictions of this Old Testament, He Himself teaches what we should receive, and what we should set aside as obsolete.

Whether the prophets predicted the coming of Jesus we shall see presently. Meanwhile, I need say no more than that if Jesus, after being predicted in the Old Testament, now subjects it to this sweeping criticism, and teaches us to receive a few things and to throw over many things, in the same way the Paraclete who is promised in the New Testament teaches us what part of it to receive, and what to reject; as Jesus Himself says in the Gospel, when promising the Paraclete, "He shall guide you into all truth, and shall teach you all things, and bring all things to your remembrance."[1039] So then, with the help of the Paraclete, we may take the same liberties with the New Testament as Jesus enables you to take with the Old, unless you suppose that the Testament of the Son is of greater value than that of the Father, if it is really the Father's; so that while many parts of the one are to be condemned, the other must be exempted from all disapproval; and that, too, when we know, as I said before, that it was not written by Christ or by His apostles.

7.
Hence, as you receive nothing in the Old Testament except the prophecies and the common precepts of practical morality, which we quoted above, while you set aside circumcision, and sacrifices, and the Sabbath and its observance, and the feast of unleavened bread, why should not we receive nothing in the New Testament but what we find said in honor and praise of the majesty of the Son, either by Himself or by His apostles, with the proviso, in the case of the apostles, that it was said by them after reaching perfection, and when no longer in unbelief; while we take no notice of the rest, which, if said at the time, was the utterance of ignorance or inexperience, or, if not, was added by crafty opponents with a malicious intention, or was stated by the writers without due consideration, and so handed down as authentic?

Take as examples, the shameful birth of Jesus from a woman, His being circumcised like the Jews, His offering sacrifice like the Gentiles, His being baptized in a humiliating manner, His being led about by the devil in the wilderness, and His being tempted by him in the most distressing way.

With these exceptions, besides whatever has been inserted under the pretence of being a quotation from the Old Testament, we believe the whole, especially the mystic nailing to the cross, emblematic of the wounds of the soul in its passion; as also the sound moral precepts of Jesus, and His parables, and the whole of His immortal discourse, which sets forth especially the distinction of the two natures, and therefore must undoubtedly be His.

There is, then, no reason for your thinking it obligatory in me to believe all the contents of the Gospels; for you, as has been proved, take so dainty a sip from the Old Testament, that you hardly, so to speak, wet your lips with it.

8.

Augustin replied:

We give to the whole Old Testament Scriptures their due praise as true and divine; you impugn the Scriptures of the New Testament as having been tampered with and corrupted.

Those things in the Old Testament which we do not observe we hold to have been suitable appointments for the time and the people of that dispensation, besides being symbolical to us of truths in which they have still a spiritual use, though the outward observance is abolished; and this opinion is proved to be the doctrine of the apostolic writings.

You, on the other hand, find fault with everything in the New Testament which you do not receive, and assert that these passages were not spoken or written by Christ or His apostles.

In these respects there is a manifest difference between us.

When, therefore, you are asked why you do not receive all the contents of the New Testament, but, while you approve of some things, reject a great many in the very same books as false and spurious interpolations, you must not pretend to imitate us in the distinction which we make, reverently and in faith, but must give account of your own presumption.

9.

If we are asked why we do not worship God as the Hebrew fathers of the Old Testament worshipped Him, we reply that God has taught us differently by the New Testament fathers, and yet in no opposition to the Old Testament, but as that Testament itself predicted.

For it is thus foretold by the prophet:

"Behold, the days come, saith the Lord, when I will make a new covenant with the house of Israel, and with the house of Judah; not according to the covenant which I made with their fathers when I took them by the hand to bring them out of the land of Egypt." [1040]Thus it was foretold that that covenant would not continue, but that there would be a new one.

And to the objection that we do not belong to the house of Israel or to the house of Judah, we answer according to the teaching of the apostle, who calls Christ the seed of Abraham, and says to us, as belonging to Christ's body, "Therefore ye are Abraham's seed." [1041]Again, if we are asked why we regard that Testament as authoritative when we do not observe its ordinances, we find the answer to this also in the apostolic writings; for the apostle says, "Let no man judge you in meat or drink, or in respect of a holiday, or a new moon, or of Sabbaths, which are a shadow of things to come." [1042]Here we learn both that we ought to read of these observances, and acknowledge them to be of divine institution, in order to preserve the memory of the prophecy, for they were shadows of things to come; and also that we need pay no regard to those who would judge us for not continuing the outward observance; as the apostle says elsewhere to the same purpose, "These things happened to them for an example; and they are written for our admonition, on whom the end of the ages are come." [1043]So, when we read anything in the books of the Old Testament which we are not required to observe in the New Testament, or which is even forbidden, instead of finding fault with it, we should ask what it means; for the very discontinuance of the observance proves it to be, not condemned, but fulfilled.

On this head we have already spoken repeatedly.

10.

To take, for example, this requirement on which Faustus ignorantly grounds his charge against the Old Testament, that a man should take his brother's wife to raise up seed for his brother, to be called by his name; what does this prefigure, but that every preacher of the gospel should so labor in the Church as to raise up seed to his deceased brother, that is, Christ, who died for us, and that this seed should bear His name?

Moreover, the apostle fulfills this requirement not now in the typical observance, but in the spiritual reality, when he reproves those of whom he says that he had begotten them in Christ Jesus by the gospel, [1044] and points out to them their error in wishing to be of Paul.

"Was Paul," he says, "crucified for you?

Or were ye baptized in the name of Paul?" [1045]As if he should say, I have begotten you for my deceased brother; your name is Christian, not Paulian.

Then, too, whoever refuses the ministry of the gospel when chosen by the Church, justly deserves the contempt of the Church.

So we see that the spitting in the face is accompanied with a sign of reproach in loosing a shoe from one foot, to exclude the man from the company of those to whom the apostle says, "Let your feet be shod with the preparation of the gospel of peace;" [1046] and of whom the prophet thus speaks, "How beautiful are the feet of them who publish peace, who bring good tidings of good!"[1047]The man who holds the faith of the gospel so as both to profit himself and to be ready when called to serve the Church, is properly represented as shod on both feet.

But the man who thinks it enough to secure his own safety by believing, and shirks the duty of benefiting others, has the reproach of being unshod, not in type, but in reality.

11.

Faustus needlessly objects to our observance of the passover, taunting us with differing from the Jewish observance:

for in the gospel we have the true Lamb, not in shadow, but in substance; and instead of prefiguring the death, we commemorate it daily, and especially in the yearly festival.

Thus also the day of our paschal feast does not correspond with the Jewish observance, for we take in the Lord's day, on which Christ rose.

And as to the feast of unleavened bread, all Christians sound in the faith keep it, not in the leaven of the old life, that is, of wickedness, but in the truth and sincerity of the faith; [1048] not for seven days, but always, as was typified by the number seven, for days are always counted by sevens. And if this observance is somewhat difficult in this world since the way which leads to life is strait and narrow, [1049] the future reward is sure; and this difficulty is typified in the bitter herbs, which are a little distasteful.

12.

The Pentecost, too, we observe, that is, the fiftieth day from the passion and resurrection of the Lord, for on that day He sent to us the Holy Paraclete whom He had promised; as was prefigured in the Jewish passover, for on the fiftieth day after the slaying of the lamb, Moses on the mount received the law written with the finger of God. [1050] If you read the Gospel, you will see that the Spirit is there called the finger of God. [1051] Remarkable events which happened on certain days are annually commemorated in the Church, that the recurrence of this festival may preserve the recollection of things so important and salutary.

If you ask, then, why we keep the passover, it is because Christ was then sacrificed for us.

If you ask why we do not retain the Jewish ceremonies, it is because they prefigured future realities which we commemorate as past; and the difference between the future and the past is seen in the different words we use for them.

Of this we have already said enough.

13.

Again, if you ask why, of all the kinds of food prohibited in the former typical dispensation, we abstain only from food offered to idols and from what dies of itself, you shall hear, if for once you will prefer the truth to idle calumnies.

The reason why it is not expedient for a Christian to eat food offered to idols is given by the apostle: "I would not," he says, "that ye should have fellowship with demons." Not that he finds fault with sacrifice itself, as offered by the fathers to typify the blood of the sacrifice with which Christ has redeemed us.

For he first says, "The things which the Gentiles offer, they offer to demons, and not to God;" and then adds these words:

"I would not that ye should have fellowship with demons." [1052] If the uncleanness were in the nature of sacrificial flesh, it would necessarily pollute even when eaten in ignorance.

But the reason for not partaking knowingly is not in the nature of the food, but, for conscience sake, not to seem to have fellowship with demons.

As regards what dies of itself, I suppose the reason why such food was prohibited was that the flesh of animals which have died of themselves is diseased, and is not likely to be wholesome, which is the chief thing in food.

The observance of pouring out the blood which was enjoined in ancient times upon Noah himself after the deluge, [1053] the meaning of which we have already explained, is thought by many to be what is meant in the Acts of the Apostles, where we read that the Gentiles were required to abstain from fornication, and from things sacrificed, and from blood, [1054] that is, from flesh of which the blood has not been poured out.

Others give a different meaning to the words, and think that to abstain from blood means not to be polluted with the crime of murder.

It would take too long to settle this question, and it is not necessary.

For, allowing that the apostles did on that occasion require Christians to abstain from the blood of animals, and not to eat of things strangled, they seem to me to have consulted the time in choosing an easy observance that could not be burdensome to any one, and which the Gentiles might have in common with the Israelites, for the sake of the Corner-stone, who makes both one in Himself; [1055] while at the same time they would be reminded how the Church of all nations was prefigured by the ark of Noah, when God gave this command,--a type which began to be fulfilled in the time of the apostles by the accession of the Gentiles to the faith.

But since the close of that period during which the two walls of the circumcision and the uncircumcision, although united in the Corner-stone, still retained some distinctive peculiarities, and now that the Church has become so entirely Gentile that none who are outwardly Israelites are to be found in it, no Christian feels bound to abstain from thrushes or small birds because their blood has not been poured out, or from hares because they are killed by a stroke on the neck without shedding their blood.

Any who still are afraid to touch these things are laughed at by the rest:

so general is the conviction of the truth, that "not what entereth into the mouth defileth you, but what cometh out of it;" [1056] that evil lies in the commission of sin, and not in the nature of any food in ordinary use.

14.

As regards the deeds of the ancients, both those which seem sinful to foolish and ignorant people, when they are not so, and those which really are sinful, we have already explained why they have been written, and how this rather adds to than impairs the dignity of Scripture.

So, too, about the curse on him who hangeth on a tree, and on him who raises not up seed in Israel, our reply has already been given in the proper place, when meeting Faustus' objections.[1057] And in reply to all objections whatsoever, whether we have already answered them separately, or whether they are contained in the remarks of Faustus which we are now considering, we appeal to our established principles, on which we maintain the authority of sacred Scripture. The principle is this, that all things written in the books of the Old Testament are to be received with approval and admiration, as most true and most profitable to eternal life; and that those precepts which are no longer observed outwardly are to be understood as having been most suitable in those times, and are to be viewed as having been shadows of things to come, of which we may now perceive the fulfillments. Accordingly, whoever in those times neglected the observance of these symbolical precepts was righteously condemned to suffer the punishment required by the divine statute, as any one would be now if he were impiously to profane the sacraments of the New Testament, which differ from the old observances only as this time differs from that.

For as praise is due to the righteous men of old who refused not to die for the Old Testament sacraments, so it is due to the martyrs of the New Testament.

And as a sick man should not find fault with the medical treatment, because one thing is prescribed to-day and another to-morrow, and what was at first required is afterwards forbidden, since the method of cure depends on this; so the human race, sick and sore as it is from Adam to the end of the world, as long as the corrupted body weighs down the mind, [1058] should not find fault with the divine prescriptions, if sometimes the same observances are enjoined, and sometimes an old observance is exchanged for one of a different kind; especially as there was a promise of a change in the appointments.

15.

Hence there is no force in the analogy which Faustus institutes between Christ's pointing out to us what to believe and what to reject in the Old Testament, in which He Himself is predicted, and the Paraclete's doing the same to you as regards the New Testament, where there is a similar prediction of Him.

There might have been some plausibility in this, had there been anything in the Old Testament which we denounced as a mistake, or as not of divine authority, or as untrue.

We do nothing of the kind; we receive everything, both what we observe as rules of conduct, and what we no longer observe, but still recognize as having been prophetical observances, once enjoined and now fulfilled.

And besides, the promise of the Paraclete is found in those books, all the contents of which you do not accept; and His mission is recorded in the book which you shrink from even naming.

For, as is stated above, and has been said repeatedly, there is a distinct narrative in the Acts of the Apostles of the mission of the Spirit on the day of Pentecost, and the effect produced showed who it was.

For all who first received Him spoke with tongues; [1059] and in this sign there was a promise that in all tongues, or in all nations, the Church of after times would faithfully proclaim the doctrine of the Spirit as well as of the Father and of the Son.

16.

Why, then, do you not accept everything in the New Testament?

Is it because the books have not the authority of Christ's apostles, or because the apostles taught what was wrong?

You reply that the books have not the authority of the apostles.

That the apostles were wrong in their teaching is what Pagans say.

But what can you say to prove that the publication of these books cannot be traced to the apostles? You reply that in many things they contradict themselves and one another.

Nothing could be more untrue; the fact is, you do not understand.

In every case where Faustus has brought forward what you think a discrepancy, we have shown that there was none; and we will do the same in every other case.

It is intolerable that the reader or learner should dare to lay the blame on Scriptures of such high authority, instead of confessing his own stupidity.

Did the Paraclete teach you that these writings are not of the apostles' authorship, but written by others under their names?

But where is the proof that it was the Paraclete from whom you learned this?

If you say that the Paraclete was promised and sent by Christ, we reply that your Paraclete was neither promised nor sent by Christ; and we also show you when He sent the Paraclete whom He promised.

What proof have you that Christ sent your Paraclete?

Where do you get the evidence in support of your informant, or rather misinformant?

You reply that you find the proof in the Gospel.

In what Gospel?

You do not accept all the Gospel, and you say that it has been tampered with.

Will you first accuse your witness of corruption, and then call for his evidence?

To believe him when you wish it, and then disbelieve him when you wish it, is to believe nobody but yourself.

If we were prepared to believe you, there would be no need of a witness at all.

Moreover, in the promise of the Holy Spirit as the Paraclete, it is said, "He shall lead you into all truth;" [1060] but how can you be led into all truth by one who teaches you that Christ was a deceiver?

And again, if you were to prove that all that is said in the Gospel of the promise of the Paraclete could apply to no one but Manichæus, as the predictions of the prophets are applicable to Christ; and if you quoted passages from those manuscripts which you say are genuine, we might say that on this very point, as proving Manichæus to be the only person intended, the passages have been altered in the interest of your sect.

Your only answer to this would be, that you could not possibly alter documents already in the possession of all Christians; for at the very outset of such an attempt, it would be met by an appeal to older copies.

But if this proves that the books could not be corrupted by you, it also proves that they could not be corrupted by any one.

The first person who ventured to do such a thing would be convicted by a comparison of older manuscripts; especially as the Scripture is to be found not in one language only, but in many.

As it is, false readings are sometimes corrected by comparing older copies or the original language.

Hence you must either acknowledge these documents as genuine, and then your heresy cannot stand a moment; or if they are spurious, you cannot use their authority in support of your doctrine of the Paraclete, and so you refute yourselves.

17.

Further, what is said in the promise of the Paraclete shows that it cannot possibly refer to Manichæus, who came so many years after. For it is distinctly said by John, that the Holy Spirit was to come immediately after the resurrection and ascension of the Lord:

"For the Spirit was not yet given, because that Jesus was not yet glorified." [1061] Now, if the reason why the Spirit was not given was, that Jesus was not glorified, He would necessarily be given immediately on the glorification of Jesus.

In the same way, the Cataphrygians [1062] said that they had received the promised Paraclete; and so they fell away from the Catholic faith, forbidding what Paul allowed, and condemning second marriages, which he made lawful.

They turned to their own use the words spoken of the Spirit, "He shall lead you into all truth," as if, forsooth, Paul and the other apostles had not taught all the truth, but had left room for the Paraclete of the Cataphrygians.

The same meaning they forced from the words of Paul: "We know in part, and we prophesy in part; but when that which is perfect is come, then that which is in part shall be done away;" [1063] making out that the apostle knew and prophesied in part, when he said, "Let him do what he will; if he marries, he sinneth not," [1064] and that this is done away by the perfection of the Phrygian

Paraclete. [1065] And if they are told that they are condemned by the authority of the Church, which is the subject of such ancient promises, and is spread all over the world, they reply that this is in exact fulfillment of what is said of the Paraclete, that the world cannot receive Him. [1066] And are not those passages, "He shall lead you into all truth," and, "When that which is perfect is come, that which is in part shall be done away," and, "The world cannot receive Him," precisely those in which you find a prediction of Manichæus?

And so every heresy arising under the name of the Paraclete will have the boldness to make an equally plausible application to itself of such texts.

For there is no heresy but will call itself the truth; and the prouder it is, the more likely it will be to call itself perfect truth:

and so it will profess to lead into all truth; and since that which is perfect has come by it, it will try to do away with the doctrine of the apostles, to which its own errors are opposed.

And as the Church holds by the earnest admonition of the apostle, that "whoever preaches another gospel to you than that which ye have received, let him be accursed;" [1067] when the heretical preacher begins to be pronounced accursed by all the world, will he not forthwith exclaim, This is what is written, "The world cannot receive Him"?

18.

Where, then, will you find the proof required to show that it is from the Paraclete that you have learned that the Gospels were not written by the apostles?

On the other hand, we have proof that the Holy Spirit, the Paraclete, came immediately after the glorification of Jesus.

For "He was not yet given, because that Jesus was not yet glorified."

We have proof also that He leads into all truth, for the only way to truth is by love, and "the love of God," says the apostle, "is shed abroad in our hearts by the Holy Ghost who is given unto us." [1068] We show, too, that in the words, "when that which is perfect is come," Paul spoke of the perfection in the enjoyment of eternal life.

For in the same place he says:

"Now we see through a glass darkly, but then face to face." [1069] You cannot reasonably maintain that we see God face to face here.

Therefore that which is perfect has not come to you.

It is thus clear what the apostle thought on this subject.

This perfection will not come to the saints till the accomplishment of what John speaks of:

"Now we are the sons of God, and it doth not yet appear what we shall be; but we know that when it shall appear we shall be like Him, for we shall see Him as He is." [1070] Then we shall be led into all truth by the Holy Spirit, of which we have now received the pledge.

Again, the words, "The world cannot receive Him," plainly point to those who are usually called the world in Scripture--the lovers of the world, the wicked, or carnal; of whom the apostle says:

"The natural man perceiveth not the things which are of the Spirit of God." [1071] Those are said to be of this world who can understand nothing beyond material things, which are the objects of sense in this world; as is the case with you, when, in your admiration of the sun and moon, you suppose all divine things to resemble them.

Deceivers, and being deceived, you call the author of this silly theory the Paraclete.

But as you have no proof of his being the Paraclete, you have no reliable ground for the statement that the Gospel writings, which you receive only in part, are not of apostolic authorship.

Thus your only remaining argument is, that these writings contain things disparaging to the glory of Christ; such as, that He was born of a virgin, that He was circumcised, that the customary sacrifice was offered for Him, that He was baptized, that He was tempted of the devil.

19.

With those exceptions, including also the testimonies quoted from the Old Testament, you profess, to use the words of Faustus, to receive all the rest, especially the mystic nailing to the cross, emblematic of the wounds of the soul in its passion; as also the sound moral precepts of Jesus, and the whole of His immortal discourse, which sets forth especially the distinction of the two natures, and therefore must undoubtedly be His.

Your design clearly is to deprive Scripture of all authority, and to make every man's mind the judge what passage of Scripture he is to approve of, and what to disapprove of.

This is not to be subject to Scripture in matters of faith, but to make Scripture subject to you.

Instead of making the high authority of Scripture the reason of approval, every man makes his approval the reason for thinking a passage correct.

If, then, you discard authority, to what, poor feeble soul, darkened by the mists of carnality, to what, I beseech you, will you betake yourself?

Set aside authority, and let us hear the reason of your beliefs.

Is it by a logical process that your long story about the nature of God concludes necessarily with this startling announcement, that this nature is subject to injury and corruption?

And how do you know that there are eight continents and ten heavens, and that Atlas bears up the world, and that it hangs from the great world-holder, and innumerable things of the same kind?

Who is your authority?

Manichæus, of course, you will say.

But, unhappy being, this is not sight, but faith.

If, then, you submit to receive a load of endless fictions at the bidding of an obscure and irrational authority, so that you believe all those things because they are written in the books which your misguided judgment pronounces trustworthy, though there is no evidence of their truth, why not rather submit to the authority of the Gospel, which is so well founded, so confirmed, so generally acknowledged and admired, and which has an unbroken series of testimonies from the apostles down to our own day, that so you may have an intelligent belief, and may come to know that all your objections are the fruit of folly and perversity; and that there is more truth in the opinion that the unchangeable nature of God should take part of mortality, so as, without injury to itself from this union, to do and to suffer not feignedly, but really, whatever it behoved the mortal nature to do and to suffer for the salvation of the human race from which it was taken, than in the belief that the nature of God is subject to injury and corruption, and that, after suffering pollution and captivity, it cannot be wholly freed and purified, but is condemned by a supreme divine necessity to eternal punishment in the mass of darkness?

20.

You say, in reply, that you believe in what Manichæus has not proved, because he has so clearly proved the existence of two natures, good and evil, in this world.

But here is the very source of your unhappy delusion; for as in the Gospels, so in the world, your idea of what is evil is derived entirely from the effect on your senses of such disagreeable things as serpents, fire, poison, and so on; and the only good you know of is what has an agreeable effect on your senses, as pleasant flavors, and sweet smells, and sunlight, and whatever else recommends itself strongly to your eyes, or your nostrils, or your palate, or any other organ of sensation.

But had you begun with looking on the book of nature as the production of the Creator of all, and had you believed that your own finite understanding might be at fault wherever anything seemed to be amiss, instead of venturing to find fault with the works of God, you would not have been led into these impious follies and blasphemous fancies with which, in your ignorance of what evil really is, you heap all evils upon God.

21.

We can now answer the question, how we know that these books were written by the apostles.

In a word, we know this in the same way that you know that the books whose authority you are so deluded as to prefer were written by Manichæus.

For, suppose some one should raise a question on this point, and should contend, in arguing with you, that the books which you attribute to Manichæus are not of his authorship; your only reply would be, to ridicule the absurdity of thus gratuitously calling in question a matter confirmed by successive testimonies of such wide extent.

As, then, it is certain that these books are the production of Manichæus, and as it is ridiculous in one born so many years after to start objections of his own, and so raise a discussion on the point; with equal certainty may we pronounce it absurd, or rather pitiable, in Manichæus or his followers to bring such objections against writings originally well authenticated, and carefully handed down from the times of the apostles to our own day through a constant succession of custodians.

22.

We have now only to compare the authority of Manichæus with that of the apostles.

The genuineness of the writings is equally certain in both cases.

But no one will compare Manichæus to the apostles, unless he ceases to be a follower of Christ, who sent the apostles.

Who that did not misunderstand Christ's words ever found in them the doctrine of two natures opposed to one another, and having each its own principle? Again, the apostles, as becomes the disciples of truth, declare the birth and passion of Christ to have been real events; while Manichæus, who boasts that he leads into all truth, would lead us to a Christ whose very passion he declares to have been an illusion.

The apostles say that Christ was circumcised in the flesh which He took of the seed of Abraham; Manichæus says that God, in his own nature, was cut in pieces by the race of darkness.

The apostles say that a sacrifice was offered for Christ as an infant in our nature, according to the institutions of the time; Manichæus, that a member, not of humanity, but of the divine substance itself, must be sacrificed to the whole host of demons by being introduced into the nature of the hostile race.

The apostles say that Christ, to set us an example, was baptized in the Jordan; Manichæus, that God immersed himself in the pollution of darkness, and that he will never wholly emerge, but that the part which cannot be purified will be condemned to eternal punishment.

The apostles say that Christ, in our nature, was tempted by the chief of the demons; Manichæus, that part of God was taken captive by the race of demons.

And in the temptation of Christ He resists the tempter; while in the captivity of God, the part taken captive cannot be restored to its origin even after victory.

To conclude, Manichæus, under the guise of an improvement, preaches another gospel, which is the doctrine of devils; and the apostles, after the doctrine of Christ, enjoin that whoever preaches another gospel shall be accursed. [1072]

Book XXXIII - Faustus does not think it would be a great honor to sit down with Abraham, Isaac and Jacob, whose moral characters as set forth in the Old Testament he detests

He justifies his subjective criticism of Scripture.

Augustin sums up the argument, claims the victory, and exhorts the Manichæans to abandon their opposition to the Old Testament notwithstanding the difficulties that it presents, and to recognize the authority of the Catholic Church.

1.

Faustus said:

You quote from the Gospel the words, "Many shall come from the east and the west, and shall sit down with Abraham, and Isaac, and Jacob, in the kingdom of heaven," [1073] and ask why we do not acknowledge the patriarchs.

Now, we should be the last to grudge to any human being that God should have compassion on him, and bring him out of perdition to salvation.

At the same time, we should acknowledge in such a case the clemency shown in this act of compassion, and not the merit of the person whose life is undeniably blameworthy.

Thus, in the case of the Jewish fathers, Abraham, and Isaac, and Jacob, who are mentioned by Christ in this verse, supposing it to be genuine, although they led wicked lives, as we may learn from their descendant Moses, or whoever was the author of the history called Genesis, which describes their conduct as having been most shocking and detestable; we are ready to allow that they may, after all, be in the kingdom of heaven, in the place which they neither believed in, nor hoped for, as is plain enough from their books.

But then it must be kept in mind that, as you yourselves confess, if they did attain to what is spoken of in this verse, it was something very different from the nether dungeons of woe to which their own deserts consigned them, and that their deliverance was the work of our Lord Christ, and the result of His mystic passion.

Who would grudge to the thief on the cross that deliverance was granted to him by the same Lord, and that Christ said that on that very day he should be with Him in the paradise of His Father? [1074] Who is so hard-hearted as to disapprove of this act of benevolence?

Still, it does not follow that, because Jesus pardoned a thief, we must approve of the habits and practices of thieves; any more than of the publicans and harlots, whose faults Jesus pardoned, declaring that they would go into the kingdom of heaven before those who behaved proudly.[1075] For, when He acquitted the woman accused by the Jews as sinful, and as having been caught in adultery, He told her to sin no more. [1076] If, then, He has done something of the same kind in the case of Abraham, and Isaac, and Jacob, all the praise is His; for such actions towards souls are becoming in Him who maketh His sun to rise upon the evil and upon the good, and sendeth rain on the just and on the unjust. [1077] One thing perplexes me in your doctrine:

why you limit your statements to the fathers of the Jews, and are not of opinion that the Gentile patriarchs had also a share in this grace of our Redeemer; especially as the Christian Church consists of their children more than of the seed of Abraham, Isaac, and Jacob.

You will say that the Gentiles worshipped idols, and the Jews the Almighty God, and that therefore Jesus had regard only to the Jews.

It would seem from this that the worship of the Almighty God is the sure way to hell, and that the Son must come to the aid of the worshipper of the Father.

That is as you please.

For my part, I am ready to join you in the belief that the fathers reached heaven, not by any merit of their own, but by that divine mercy which is stronger than sin.

2.

However, there is a difficulty in deciding as regards this verse too, whether the words were really spoken to Christ, for there is a discrepancy in the narratives.

For while two evangelists, Matthew and Luke, both alike tell of the centurion whose servant was sick, and to whom these words of Jesus are supposed to have applied, that He had not seen so great faith, no, not in Israel, as in this man, though a Gentile and a Pagan, because he said that he was not worthy that Jesus should come under his roof, but wished Him only to speak the word, and his servant should be healed; Matthew alone adds that Jesus went on to say, "Verily I say unto you, that many shall come from the east and from the west, and shall sit down with Abraham, and Isaac, and Jacob, in the kingdom of heaven; but the children of the kingdom shall be cast into outer darkness."

By the many who should come are meant the Pagans, on account of the centurion, in whom, although he was a Gentile, so great faith was found; and the children of the kingdom are the Jews, in whom there was no faith found.

Luke, again, though he too mentions the occurrence in his Gospel as part of the narrative of the miracles of Christ, says nothing of Abraham, Isaac, and Jacob.

If it is said that he omitted it because it had been already said by Matthew, why does he tell the story at all of the centurion and his servant, since that, too, has the advantage of being recorded at length in Matthew's ingenious narrative?

But the passage is corrupt.

For, in describing the centurion's application to Jesus, Matthew says that he came himself to ask for a cure; while Luke says he did not, but sent elders of the Jews, and that they, in case Jesus should despise the centurion as a Gentile (for they will have Jesus to be a thorough Jew), set about persuading Him, by saying that he was worthy for whom He should do this, because he loved their nation, and had built them a synagogue; [1078] here again taking for granted that the Son of God was concerned in a pagan centurion having thought it proper to build a synagogue for the Jews.

The words in question are, indeed, found in Luke also, perhaps because on reflection he thought they might be genuine; but they are found in another place, and in a connection altogether different.

The passage is where Jesus says to His disciples, "Strive to enter in at the strait gate; for many shall come seeking to enter in, and shall not be able.

When once the Master of the house has entered in, and has shut to the door, ye shall begin to stand without, and to knock, saying Lord, open to us.

And He shall answer and say, I know you not.

Then ye shall begin to say, We have eaten and drunk in Thy presence, and Thou hast taught in our streets and synagogues; but He shall say unto you, I know not whence ye are; depart from me, all ye workers of iniquity.

There shall be weeping and gnashing of teeth, when ye shall see Abraham, and Isaac, and Jacob, and all the prophets, entering into the kingdom of God, and you yourselves cast out.

And they shall come from the east, and from the west, and from the north, and from the south, and shall sit down in the kingdom of God." [1079]The part where it is said that many shall be shut out of the kingdom of God, who have only borne the name of Christ, without doing His works, is not left out by Matthew; but he makes no mention here of Abraham, and Isaac, and Jacob.

In the same way, Luke mentions the centurion and his servant, without alluding in that connection to Abraham, and Isaac, and Jacob.

Since it is uncertain when the words were spoken, we are at liberty to doubt whether they were spoken at all.

3.

It is not without reason that we bring a critical judgment to the study of Scriptures where there are such discrepancies and contradictions.

By thus examining everything, and comparing one passage with another, we determine which contains Christ's actual words, and what may or may not be genuine.

For your predecessors have made many interpolations in the words of our Lord, which thus appear under His name, while they disagree with His doctrine.

Besides, as we have proved again and again, the writings are not the production of Christ or of His apostles, but a compilation of rumors and beliefs, made, long after their departure, by some obscure semi-Jews, not in harmony even with one another, and published by them under the name of the apostles, or of those considered the followers of the apostles, so as to give the appearance of apostolic authority to all these blunders and falsehoods.

But whatever you make of that, as regards this verse, I repeat that I do not insist on rejecting it.

It is enough for my position, that, as I said before, and as you are obliged to confess, before the coming of our Lord all the patriarchs and prophets of Israel lay in infernal darkness for their sins.

Even though they may have been restored to light and liberty by Christ, that has nothing to do with the hateful character of their lives.

We hate and eschew not their persons, but their characters; not as they are now, when they are purified, but as they were, when impure.

So, whatever you think of this verse, it does not affect us:

for if it is genuine, it only illustrates Christ's goodness and compassion; and if it is spurious, those who wrote it are to blame.

Our cause is as safe as it always is.

4.

Augustin replied:

Poor safety, indeed! when you contradict yourself by hating the patriarchs as impure, at the same time that you grieve for your impure god.

You allow that, since the advent of the Saviour, the patriarchs have had purity restored, and have enjoyed the rest of the blessed; while your god, even after the Saviour's advent, still lies in darkness, is still sunk in the ocean of iniquity, still wallows in the mire of all uncleanness.

These men, therefore, were not only better than your god in their lives, but also happier in their death.

Where was the abode of the just who departed from this life before Christ's coming in the flesh, and whether their condition also was improved by the passion of Christ, in whom they had believed as to come, and to suffer, and to rise again, and had, moreover, foretold this in suitable language under the guidance of the Spirit of prophecy, is to be discovered from the Holy Scriptures, if any clear discovery in this matter is possible; we are not called on to adopt the crude notions of all and sundry, still less the heretical opinions of men who have gone astray into such egregious error.

There is a vain attempt here on the part of Faustus to introduce by a side-door the idea that we may obtain something after this life besides the due reward of our conduct in this life.

It will be better for you to abandon your error while you are still alive, and to embrace and hold the truths of the Catholic faith.

Otherwise the expectations of the unrighteous will be sadly disappointed when God begins to fulfill His threatenings to the unrighteous.

5.

I have already given what I considered a sufficient answer to Faustus' calumnies of the lives of the patriarchs.

That they were punished at their death, or that they were justified after the Lord's passion, is not what we learn from His commendation of them, when He admonished the Jews that, if they were Abraham's children, they should do the works of Abraham, and said that Abraham desired to see His day, and was glad when he saw it; [1080] and that it was into his bosom, that is, some deep recess of blissful repose, that the angels carried the poor sufferer who was despised by the proud rich man. [1081] And what are we to make of the Apostle Paul?

Is there any idea of justification after death in his praise of Abraham, when he says that before he was circumcised he believed God, and that it was counted to him for righteousness? [1082] And so much importance does he attach to this, that the single ground which he specifies for our becoming Abraham's children, though not descended from him in the flesh, is, that we follow the footsteps of his faith.

6.

You are so hardened in your errors against the testimonies of Scripture, that nothing can be made of you; for whenever anything is quoted against you, you have the boldness to say that it is written not by the apostle, but by some pretender under his name.

The doctrine of demons which you preach is so opposed to Christian doctrine, that you could not continue, as professing Christians, to maintain it, unless you denied the truth of the apostolic writings.

How can you thus do injury to your own souls?

Where will you find any authority, if not in the Gospel and apostolic writings?

How can we be sure of the authorship of any book, if we doubt the apostolic origin of those books which are attributed to the apostles by the Church which the apostles themselves founded, and which occupies so conspicuous a place in all lands, and if at the same time we acknowledge as the undoubted production of the apostles what is brought forward by heretics in opposition to the Church, whose authors, from whom they derive their name, lived long after the apostles?

And do we not see in profane literature that there are well-known authors under whose names many things have been published after their time which have been rejected, either from inconsistency with their ascertained writings, or from their not having been known in the lifetime of the authors, so as to be banded down with the confirmatory statement of the authors themselves, or of their friends?

To give a single example, were not some books published lately under the name of the distinguished physician Hippocrates, which were not received as authoritative by physicians? And this decision remained unaltered in spite of some similarity in style and matter:

for, when compared to the genuine writings of Hippocrates, these books were found to be inferior; besides that they were not recognized as his at the time when his authorship of his genuine productions was ascertained.

Those books, again, from a comparison with which the productions of questionable origin were rejected, are with certainty attributed to Hippocrates; and any one who denies their authorship is answered only by ridicule, simply because there is a succession of testimonies to the books from the time of Hippocrates to the present day, which makes it unreasonable either now or hereafter to have any doubt on the subject.

How do we know the authorship of the works of Plato, Aristotle, Cicero, Varro, and other similar writers, but by the unbroken chain of evidence?

So also with the numerous commentaries on the ecclesiastical books, which have no canonical authority, and yet show a desire of usefulness and a spirit of inquiry.

How is the authorship ascertained in each case, except by the author's having brought his work into public notice as much as possible in his own lifetime, and, by the transmission of the information from one to another in continuous order, the belief becoming more certain as it becomes more general, up to our own day; so that, when we are questioned as to the authorship of any book, we have no difficulty in answering?

But why speak of old books?

Take the books now before us:

should any one, after some years, deny that this book was written by me, or that Faustus' was written by him, where is evidence for the fact to be found but in the information possessed by some at the present time, and transmitted by them through successive generations even to distant times?

From all this it follows, that no one who has not yielded to the malicious and deceitful suggestions of lying devils, can be so blinded by passion as to deny the ability of the Church of the apostles--a community of brethren as numerous as they were faithful--to transmit their writings unaltered to posterity, as the original seats of the apostles have been occupied by a continuous succession of bishops to the present day, especially when we are accustomed to see this happen in the case of ordinary writings both in the Church and out of it.

7.

But Faustus finds contradictions in the Gospels.

Say, rather, that Faustus reads the Gospels in a wrong spirit, that he is too foolish to understand, and too blind to see.

If you were animated with piety instead of being misled by party spirit, you might easily, by examining these passages, discover a wonderful and most instructive harmony among the writers.

Who, in reading two narratives of the same event, would think of charging one or both of the authors with error or falsehood, because one omits what the other mentions, or one tells concisely, but with substantial agreement, what the other relates in detail, so as to indicate not only what was done, but also how it was done?

This is what Faustus does in his attempt to impeach the truth of the Gospels; as if Luke's omitting some saying of Christ recorded in Matthew implied a denial on the part of Luke of Matthew's statement.

There is no real difficulty in the case; and to make a difficulty shows want of thought, or of the ability to think.

There is, indeed, a point in the narrative of the centurion which is discussed among believers, and on which objections are raised by unbelievers of no great learning, who prove their quarrelsomeness, when, after being instructed, they do not give up their errors.

The point is, that Matthew says that the centurion came to Jesus "beseeching Him, and saying;" while Luke says that he sent to Jesus the elders of the Jews with this same request, that He would heal his servant who was sick; and that when He came near the house he sent others, through whom he said that he was not worthy that Jesus should come into his house, and that he was not worthy to come himself to Jesus.

How, then, do we read in Matthew, "He came to Him, beseeching Him, and saying, My servant lieth at home sick of the palsy, and grievously tormented?" [1083] The explanation is, that Matthew's narrative is correct, but brief, mentioning the centurion's coming to Jesus, without saying whether he came himself or by others, or whether the words about his servant were spoken by himself or through others. But is it not common to speak of a person as coming near to a thing, although he may not reach it?

And even the word reach, which is the strongest form of expression, is frequently used in cases where the person spoken of acts through others, as when we say he took his case to court, he reached the presence of the judge; or, again, he reached the presence of some man in power, although it may probably have been through his friends, and the person may not have seen him whose presence he is said to have reached.

And from the word for to reach we give the name of Perventors to those who by ambitious arts gain access, either personally or through friends, to the, so to speak, inaccessible minds of the great.

Are we, then, in reading to forget the common usage of speech?

Or must the sacred Scripture have a language of its own?

The cavils of forward critics are thus met by a reference to the usual forms of speech.

8.

Those who examine this matter not in a disputatious but in a calm believing spirit are invited to come to Jesus, not outwardly but in heart, not in bodily presence but in the power of faith, as the centurion did, and then they will better understand Matthew's narrative.

To such it is said in the Psalm "Come unto Him, and be enlightened; and your faces shall not be ashamed." [1084] Hence we learn that the centurion, whose faith was so highly spoken of, came to Christ more truly than the people who carried his message.

We find an analogous case in the woman with the issue of blood, who was healed by touching the hem of Christ's garment, when Christ said, "Some one hath touched me."

The disciples wondered what Christ meant by saying, "Who hath touched me?" "Some one hath touched me," when the crowd was thronging Him.

In fact, they made this reply:

"The crowd throngeth Thee, and sayest Thou, Who hath touched me?" [1085] Now, as the people thronged Christ while the woman touched Him, so the messengers were sent to Christ, but the centurion really came to Him.

In Matthew we have a not infrequent form of expression, and at the same time a symbolical import; while in Luke there is a simple narrative of the whole event, such as to draw our attention to the manner in which Matthew has recorded it.

I wish one of those people who found their silly objections to the Gospels on such trifling difficulties would himself tell a story twice over, honestly giving a true account of what happened, and that his words were written down and read over to him. We should then see whether he would not say more or less at one time than at another; and whether the order would not be changed, not only of words, but of things; and whether he would not put some opinion of his own into the mouth of another, because, though he never heard him say it, he knew it perfectly well to be in his mind; and whether he would not sometimes put in a few words what he had before related at length.

In these and other ways, which might perhaps be reduced to rule, the narratives of the same thing by two persons, or two narratives by the same person, might differ in many things without being opposed, might be unlike without being contradictory.

Thus are undone all the bandages with which poor Manichæans stifle themselves to keep in the spirit of error, and to keep out all that might lead to their salvation.

9.

Now that all Faustus' calumnies have been refuted, those at least on the subjects here treated of at large and explained fully as the Lord has enabled me, I close with a word of counsel to you who are implicated in those shocking and damnable errors, that, if you acknowledge the supreme authority of Scripture, you should recognise that authority which from the time of Christ Himself, through the ministry of His apostles, and through a regular succession of bishops in the seats of the apostles, has been preserved to our own day throughout the whole world, with a reputation known to all.

There the Old Testament too has its difficulties solved, and its predictions fulfilled.

If you ask for demonstration, consider first what you are, how unfit for comprehending the nature of your own soul, not to speak of God; I mean an intelligent comprehension, such as you profess to desire, or to have once desired, and not the notions of a credulous fancy.

Admitting this incompetency, which must continue while you remain as you are, you may at least be referred to the natural conviction of every human mind, unless it is corrupted by error, of the perfect unchangeableness and incorruptibility of the nature and substance of God.

Admit this, or believe it, and you will no longer be Manichæans, so that in course of time you may become Catholics.

Footnotes:

296. Confessions, v. 3, 6.
297. Ps. xxxvii. 23.
298. Col. ii. 5; cf. 1 Thess. iii. 10.
299. 1 Cor. iii. 9.
300. Matt. i. 1.
301. 2 Tim. ii. 8.
302. 1 Cor. xv. 11.
303. Gal. i. 8, 9.
304. 1 Cor. xv. 47-49.
305. 2 Tim. iv. 4.
306. [This mixture of the substance of Primordial Man, with the kingdom of darkness, and the formation of stars out of portions thereof, was probably a part of primitive Manichæan teaching.--A.H.N.]
307. [Compare Book xx. 2, where Faustus states the Manichæan doctrine of the Jesus patabilis.

Beausobre, Mosheim and Baur agree in thinking that Augustin has not distinguished accurately in these two passages between names Christ and Jesus, as used by the Manichæans.

See Baur: Das Manichäische Religionssystem, p. 72.--A.H.N.]
308. Rom. ix. 4, 5.
309. Rom. viii. 23.
310. Gal. iv. 4, 5.
311. Phil. ii. 6.
312. John i. 12.
313. [It cannot be said that Augustin adequately meets the difficulty that Faustus finds in the genealogies of our Lord.

Cf. Hervey:

The Genealogies of Our Lord, and the recent commentaries, such as Meyer's, Lange's, The International Revision, and especially Broadus on Matthew.--A.H.N.]
314. 1 Cor. x. 6, 11.
315. Luke xxiv. 44.
316. Isa. vii. 9.
317. Matt. xiii. 52.
318. 2 Tim. ii. 16-18.
319. [A good argumentum ad hominem, a species of argument which Augustin is fond of using.--A.H.N.]
320. Matt. xix. 29.
321. Matt. v. 3-11.
322. Matt. xi. 2-6.
323. [This is a good description of ideal Manichæan religious life. Whether Faustus lived up to the claims here set forth is another question.--A.H.N.]
324. Matt. vii. 21.
325. Matt. xxviii. 19, 20.
326. John xv. 14.
327. John xv. 10.
328. Matt v. 3-10.
329. Matt. xxv. 35.
330. Matt. xix. 21.
331. Matt. xvi. 7.
332. 1 Cor. xv. 47.
333. Gal. i. 8, 9.
334. 2 Tim. ii. 8.
335. Rom. iv. 25.
336. John v. 25-27.
337. Acts. i. 14.
338. John iii. 14, 15.
339. 1 John v. 20, iv. 3.
340. 1 Cor. xiii. 3.
341. 1 Tim. i. 5.
342. [Augustin confounds saving faith with orthodox doctrine, as has been too commonly done since.--A.H.N.]
343. 1 Cor. vii. 5, 6.
344. 1 Cor. vi. 7, 4.
345. Matt. x. 38-42.
346] Book iv.
347. 1 Cor. x. 6.
348. Col. ii. 16, 17.
349. Tit. i. 15.
350. Wisd. vii. 24, 25.
351. [In bringing to notice the absurdities of the Manichæan moral system,

Augustin may seem to be trifling, but he is in reality striking at the root of the heresy.--A.H.N.]
352. 1 Cor. x. 11.
353. Matt. viii. 32.
354. Luke v. 14.
355. Phil. iii. 19.
356. Tit. i. 15.
357. Matt. xvi. 11.
358. Tit. i. 15.
359. Prov. xxi. 20.
360. [Compare the Introduction, where an abstract is given of the Fihrist's account of the creation.--A.H.N.]
361. [These biological blunders belong to the age, and are not Augustin's peculiar fancies. Of course, the argumentative value of them depends on their general acceptance.--A.H.N.]
362. 1 Cor. x. 11.
363. Rom. xv. 4.
364. [It will be seen in subsequent portions of this treatise that Augustin carries the typological idea to an absurd extreme.--A.H.N.]
365. 1 Cor. ix. 9, 10.
366. Cf. Lev. xxi. 18.
367. Matt. xii. 48.
368. Matt. xxiii. 9.
369. John i. 1-5.
370. Matt. ix. 16.
371. Gal. iv. 9.
372. 1 Cor. x. 11.
373. Matt. xiii. 52.
374. Matt. xvi. 23.
375. Rom. xi. 16-26.
376. Book vi. 2.
377. Rom. i. 3.
378. 2 Cor. v. 16.
379. 1 Cor. xiii. 11.
380. [The extremely subjective method of dealing with Scripture which Augustin ascribes to Faustus, was characteristic of Manichæism in general.--A.H.N.]
381. Gal. iv. 4, 5.
382. 2 Tim. ii. 8.
383. 1 Cor. xv. 3, 4, 12.
384. Gen. ii. 22.
385. 1 Cor. xi. 5.
386. Vulg.
387. 1 Cor. xv. 35-53.
388. 1 Tim. i. 17.
389. Natus.
390. Factus.
391. Phil. iii. 15.
392. [This is an excellent statement of the doctrine of Scriptural authority, that has been held to by Protestants with far more consistency than by Catholics.--A.H.N.]
393. Luke xxiv. 39.
394. 1 Cor. xv. 50-53.
395. Rom. vi. 9.
396. Col. iii. 1, 2.
397. Tit. iii. 5.
398. Rom. viii. 23-25.
399. 2 Cor. v. 14-18.
400. Eph. ii. 4-7.
401. Rom. vii. 5.
402. Rom. viii. 8, 9.
403. 1 Cor. xiii. 11.
404. Matt. iii. 17.
405. John xvi. 28.
406. John viii. 13-18.
407. John x. 38.
408. Rom. i. 21.
409. Lib. xi.
410. Rom. i. 1-3.
411. Rom. ix. 1-5.
412. Gal. iv. 4, 5.
413. Rom. iii. 1, 2.
414. John v. 46.
415. Luke xxiv. 44.
416. 2 Cor. iii. 15, 16.
417. Luke xvi. 27-31.
418. Rom. iii. 21.
419. 2 Cor. i. 20.
420. Rom. ix. 6-8.
421. Gal. iii. 16.
422. Col. iii. 10.
423. John vi. 53.
424. Rom. v. 14.
425. Eph. v. 31, 32.
426. Phil. ii. 6, 7.
427. Vulg.
428. Matt. ix. 12, 13.
429. John viii. 34, 36.
430. Ps. xli. 4.
431. John ix. 31.
432. Gal. iii. 10.
433. 2 Cor. xiii. 4.
434. Ps. lxvi. 9.
435. Ps. xxxvi. 11.
436. Ps. xiii. 4.
437. Ps. xvi. 8.
438. Ps. xxx. 6, 7.
439. 2 Cor. vi. 11.
440. Rom. v. 5.
441. Isa. xi. 2, 3.
442. Eph. iv. 3.
443. Matt. xii. 30.
444. 1 Cor. i. 23-25.
445. Eph. ii. 12, 19, 20.
446. 1 Cor. xi. 19.
447. John i. 47-51.
448. Gen. xxviii. 11-18.
449. 1 Cor. iii. 1-3.
450. 2 Cor. v. 13-15.
451. Ps. cxix. 83.
452. 1 Cor. x. 1-4.
453. John iii. 14.
454. John i. 29.
455. John xix. 36.

456. Luke xi. 20.
457. John xvi. 33.
458. Rom. xi. 5.
459. 2 Cor. ix. 7.
460. Matt. iii. 10.
461. 1 Tim. ii. 1-4.
462. Ps. xxx. 11, 12.
463. 1 Cor. x. 10, 6.
464. 2 Cor. iii. 16.
465. Gen. xxii. 18.
466. Gen. xxvi. 4.
467. Gen. xxviii. 14.
468. Ex. iii. 6.
469. Gen. xxiv. 2.
470. Gen. xlix. 1, 2, 8-12.
471. Prov. xxx. 30.
472. Isa. i. 18.
473. Isa. liii.
474. Ps. xxii.
475. Ps. lvii. 4. (Vulg.).
476. Ps. lvii. 4.
477. Ps. ii. 8, 9.
478. Baruch iii. 37, 38.
479. Dan. vii. 13, 14.
480. Matt. xxiv. 15.
481. Dan. ix. 24-27.
482. Wisd. ii. 18-21.
483. Rom. x. 14, 15.
484. Isa. vii. 9 (Vulg.).
485. Gal. iii. 6, 8.
486. Rom. iv. 11, 12.
487. Isa. vi. 3.

488. [It is unnecessary to point out in detail the vicious elements in Augustin's allegorizing and typologizing.

It should be said that his exegetical fancies were not original, but were derived from Philo, Origen, and their followers.--A.H.N.]

489. [On the Sibylline books, see article by G. H. Schodde in the Schaff-Hertzog Encyclopædia of Religious Knowledge, and the works there referred to.

The Christian writers of the first three centuries seem not to have suspected the real character of these pseudo-prophetical writings, and to have regarded them as remarkable testimonies from the heathen world to the Truth of the Christian religion.--A.H.N.]

490. ["The Mercurius or Hermes Trismegistus of legend was a personage, an Egyptian sage or succession of sages, who, since the time of Plato, has been identified with the Thoth (the name of the month September), of that people.... He was considered to be the impersonation of the religion, art, learning and sacerdotal discipline of the Egyptian priesthood.

He was by several of the Fathers, and, in modern times, by three of his earliest editors, supposed to have existed before the time of Moses, and to have obtained the appellation of Thrice greatest', from his threefold learning and rank of Philosopher, Priest and King, and that of Hermes,' or Mercurius, as messenger and authoritative interpreter of divine things."

The author of the books that go under the name of Hermes Trismegistus is thought to have lived about the beginning of the second century, and was a Christian Neo-Platonist. See J. C. Chambers:

The Theological and Philosophical Works of Hermes Trismegistus, translated from the original Greek, with Preface, Notes and Index, Edinburh, 1882.--A.H.N.]

491. Rom. i. 2, 3.
492. Isa. xi. 10.
493. Isa. vii. 14.
494. Matt. xxii. 42-44.
495. Matt. xxiv. 24, 25.
496. Ps. ii. 7, 8.
497. Ps. lxxii. 10.
498. Ps. xlv. 7.
499. Jer. x. 11.
500. Jer. xvi. 19-21.
501. Jer. xvii. 5-8.
502. Jer. xvii. 9.
503. Phil. ii. 6.
504. John i. 1.
505. John xiv. 9.
506. Isa. ii. 17-20.
507. Isa. i. 3.
508. Isa. lxv. 2; cf. Rom. x. 21.
509. Isa. vi. 10; cf. Rom. xi.
510. Rom. i. 28.
511. 1 Cor. ii. 8.
512. 2 Tim. iii. 8.
513. Jer. xvii. 12.
514. 1 Cor. iii. 17.
515. Matt. v. 14.
516. Dan. ii. 34, 35.
517. John vi. 54.
518. Cant. ii. 2.
519. Ps. cxx. 7.
520. Ezek. ix. 1.
521. Matt. xiii. 30.
522. 1 Cor. iii. 21.
523. Jer. xvii. 14.
524. Rom. xv. 4.
525. Gal. i. 9.
526. Deut. xxi. 23.
527. Deut. xxv. 5-10.
528. Gal. iii. 10.
529. Rom. vi. 6.
530. Rom. viii. 3.
531. 2 Cor. v. 21.
532. 1 Tim. iv. 1, 2.
533. Rom. i. 25.
534. 1 Tim. iv. 4.
535. 1 Cor. xv. 40.
536. Matt. x. 28.
537. Rom. vi. 6.

538. Rom. viii. 3.
539. 2 Cor. v. 21.
540. Isa. lvi. 4, 5.
541. [In scarcely any other Manichæan record do we find the Manichæan hostility to Judaism expressed with so much ardor and with so much precision as in the blasphemous statements of Faustus in this treatise.--A.H.N.]
542. 2 Cor. iii. 5, 6.
543. Rom. vii. 2, 3.
544. Rom. i. 1-3.
545. 1 Cor. xi. 19.
546. Lib. viii.
547. Matt. xiii. 52.
548. Matt. vi. 24.
549. 2 Cor. xi. 2, 3.
550. Ps. xxxi. 19.
551. 2 Cor. iii. 2, 3.
552. Ezek. xi. 19.
553. 1 Pet. ii. 4-8.
554. Rom. xiii. 9, 10.
555. Matt. xxii. 37-40.
556. 2 Tim. iv. 4.
557. Deut. vi. 4.
558. 1 Cor. xiii. 9.
559. Gal. iii. 19.
560. Rom. v. 20.
561. Rom. iv. 15.
562. Rom. vii. 7-13.
563. 1 Cor. viii. 1.
564. 2 Cor. xi. 2, 3.
565. 1 Tim. iv. 1-4.
566. Ps. lxxxiv. 4.
567. Ps. cxlviii. 1.
568. Ps. xlv. 10-17.
569. John viii. 13, 17, 18.
570. Deut. xviii. 15.
571. Deut. xxviii. 66.
572. Deut. xiii. 5.
573. John v. 17.
574. Gen. xvii. 9-14.
575. Matt. xxiii. 15.
576. Matt. x. 25.
577. John ii. 19.
578. Matt. v. 24.
579. Matt. viii. 4.
580. 1 Cor. iii. 17.
581. Rom. xii. 1.
582. John v. 46.
583. John viii. 17, 18.
584. Deut. xix. 15.
585. Deut. xviii. 15.
586. John i. 29.
587. 1 Cor. x. 4.
588. Rom. ix. 5.
589. 1 Tim. ii. 5.
590. Rom. viii. 3.
591. Luke i. 35.
592. 1 Tim. i. 15.
593. Num. ix. 10-12.
594. Matt. xiv. 30.
595. 1 Cor. x. 4.
596. Matt. v. 14.
597. 1 Cor. i. 23, 24.
598. Matt. xvi. 22, 23.
599. Gal. ii. 20.
600. Matt. xiii. 57.
601. Num. xiii. 9, xiv. 6.
602. John xiv. 3.
603. Ex. xxiii. 20, 21.
604. Matt. v. 4.
605. Deut. xxviii. 16.
606. John xiv. 6.
607. Rom. xii. 14.
608. 2 Tim. iv. 14.
609. Gal. v. 12.
610. Matt. xix. 12.
611. John xi. 49-51.
612. Matt. xxii. 31, 32, and Luke xx. 37, 38.
613. Matt. viii. 10-12.
614. Gal. iii. 8.
615. Matt. xv. 3-6.
616. Rom. i. 14.
617. 1 Cor. x. 6.
618. Col. ii. 16, 17.
619. Matt. xii. 7.
620. Col. ii. 15.
621. 1 Cor. xv. 50-59.
622. Hab. ii. 4, and Rom. i. 17.
623. Rom. x. 9.
624. Rom. iv. 25.
625. Rom. iv. 11.
626. Matt. xxiii. 15.
627. Matt. xxiii. 2, 3.
628. Rom. ii. 26.
629. Matt. xi. 18, 19.
630. Matt. iii. 4.
631. Tit. i. 15.
632. Matt. xv. 16-20.
633. Matt. xxiii. 23, 24.
634. Matt. ix. 9.
635. Deut. xii. 32.
636. Gal. i. 9.
637. John xxi. 25.
638. John xii. 41.
639. John v. 46.
640. John xxi. 20-24.
641. Luke xviii. 8.
642. Matt. xi. 19.
643. John v. 25.
644. Matt. xxiii. 3.
645. Matt. v. 17-20.
646. Rom. xiii. 10.
647. Rom. v. 5.
648. John xiii. 35.
649. John i. 7.
650. Matt. xxiii. 15.
651. Matt. xv. 11.
652. Matt. ix. 13.
653. Jer. xxxi. 32.
654. Ezek. xi. 19.
655. 2 Cor. ii. 3.

656. Col. ii. 17.
657. Rom. i. 25.
658. Rom. viii. 3.
659. 1 Cor. x. 6.
660. Matt. xxii. 40.
661. Rom. viii. 2.
662. Rom. ii. 14, 15.
663. Rom. viii. 2.
664. Tit. i. 12.
665. Matt. xxiii. 34.
666. Eph. iv. 11.
667. Matt. v. 21-44.
668. Deut. xxvii. 15.
669. 2 Cor. i. 19, 20.
670. John i. 17.
671. John v. 46.
672. Rom. v. 20.
673. Rom. vii. 12, 13.
674. Gal. iii. 23, 25.
675. 2 Cor. iii. 6.
676. Gal. iii. 21, 22.
677. Rom. viii. 3, 4.
678. 1 John ii. 1, 2.
679. Rom. xv. 8.
680. Luke xvi. 16.
681. John i. 17.
682. 1 Cor. xii. 28.
683. Matt. xi. 28, 29.
684. 1 Cor. v. 7.
685. 2 Cor. v. 17.
686. Rom. vi. 4.
687. 2 Tim. iii. 5.
688. 1 Tim. i. 5.
689. 1 Pet. iii. 21.
690. Rom. i. 17.
691. 2 Macc. vii.
692. John i. 14.
693. Gal. iii. 23.
694. Matt. xxvi. 28.
695. Gal. v. 2.
696. Gal. ii. 14.
697. Acts. xv. 6-11.
698. John i. 17.
699. Gal. v. 6.
700. Matt. v. 38, 39.
701. Matt. v. 27, 28.
702. 1 John iii. 15.
703. Rom. i. 9; Phil. i. 8, and 2 Cor. i. 23.
704. Rom. i. 30.
705. Matt. v. 45.
706. Matt. xi. 12.
707. Ex. xxi. 24, and Matt. v. 39.
708. Matt. v. 33, 34.
709. Deut. xxiv. i, and Matt. v. 31, 32.
710. Gal. v. 6.
711. Rom. xiii. 8.
712. John xiii. 34.
713. Ps. vi. 7.
714. Prov. xvi. 32.
715. Ecclus. xxviii. 21.
[Augustin makes no distinction between the Old Testament Apocrypha and the canonical books.
Indeed, the Platonizing Apocryphal writings, such as Ecclesiasticus and Wisdom, seem to have been his favorites.--A.H.N.]
716. Ex. xx. 17.
717. Rom. vii. 7.
718. Lam. iii. 30.
719. Prov. xxv. 21.
720. Rom. xii. 20.
721. Ps. cxx. 6.
722. Wisd. xi. 21, xii. 2.
723. Matt. v. 44, 48.
724. Ecclus. xxviii. 1-5.
725. Matt. xix. 4-6.
726. Matt. xix. 7, 8.
727. Sec. 26.
728. Wisd. vi. 22.
729. John v. 39.
730. Ps. cxviii. 16.
731. Ps. xii. 3.
732. Wisd. iii. 1-5.
733. Wisd. v. 16, 17.
734. Matt. xxii. 23-28.
735. 1 Tim. vi. 16.
736. 1 Cor. i. 24.
737. [The Manichæan doctrine of the Jesus patabilis is more fully expounded in this book than elsewhere.
Of course, this is only a way of expressing the familiar Manichæan notion that the divine life which is imprisoned in the world and which is trying to escape through the growth of plants, etc., suffers from any sort of injury done to plants.
Compare Baur:
Das Manichäische Religionssystem, pp. 72-77.--A.H.N.]
738. 1 Cor. x. 20.
739. Sen. Hipp. vv. 194, 195.
740. John xix. 38.
741. Rom. iii. 13.
742. 1 Cor. iii. 17, and vi. 19.
743. 1 Tim. iv. 2.
744. Matt. xii. 7.
745. Ps. lxxix. 9.
746. Matt. vi. 12.
747. 1 Cor. x. 30.
748. Rom. i. 20-23.
749. Rom. i. 25.
750. 1 Tim. iv. 3, 4.
751. Rev. xix. 10.
752. Dan. vi.
753. Ps. l. 23.
754. Rom. xii. 1.
755. [Augustin's exposure of the paganism of Manichæism is an admirable and effective piece of argumentum ad hominem.
That the Christianity of Augustin's time was becoming paganized is undoubted,

but Manichæism was pure paganism.--A.H.N.]
756. 2 Cor. iv. 4.
757. Rom. iii. 5.
758. Rom. ix. 14, 15, 22, 23.
759. Rom. i. 24, 25, 28.
760. John ix. 39.
761. Ps. xxxvi. 6.
762. Rom. xi. 33.
763. Ps. ci. 1.
764. Rom. xi. 17-24.
765. Jas. iv. 15.
766. Wisd. xi. 21.
767. Eph. v. 28, 29.
768. 1 Cor. xii. 1-26.
769. 2 Cor. xi. 3.
770. 1 Cor. xv. 33.
771. Gal. vi. 3.
772. Rom. i. 28.
773. Wisd. i. 13, and ii. 24.
774. Wisd. i. 16.
775. Ecclus. xi. 14.
776. Gal. i. 4.
777. Ps. xcvi. 5.
778. 1 Tim. i. 17.
779. Quoted Cic. pro Dejor. § 9.
780. [This is one of Augustin's most effective refutations of Manichæan dualism.--A.H.N.]
781. Gen. xvi. 2-4.
782. Gen. xii. 13, and xx. 2.
783. Gen. xix. 33, 35.
784. Gen. xxvi. 7.
785. Gen. xxix. and xxx.
786. Gen. xxxviii.
787. 2 Sam. xi. 4, 15.
788. 1 Kings xi. 1-3.
789. Hos. i. 2, 3.
790. Ex. ii. 12.
791. Ex. xii. 35, 36.
792. Ex. xvii. 9.
793. Gen. i. 2.
794. 1 John i. 5.
795. 2 Cor. iv. 6.
796. Wisd. vii. 26.
797. Ps. xviii. 28.
798. Matt. v. 8.
799. Isa. viii. 20.
800. Eph. v. 8.
801. Matt. viii. 10.
802. Gen. iii. 9.
803. Luke viii. 44, 45.
804. Matt. vii. 7.
805. Matt. x. 39.
806. John ii. 17.
807. Matt. x. 14, 15.
808. Rom. ii. 12.
809. Matt. xxii. 11, 15.
810. Luke xix. 27.
811. Rom. viii. 32.
812. 1 Pet. iv. 17, 18.
813. Prov. iii. 12.
814. Job ii. 10.
815. Rev. iii. 19.
816. 1 Cor. xi. 31, 32.
817. Acts xvii. 28.
818. 1 Cor. x. 20.
819. Gen. iv. 4.
820. Wisd. xiv. 15.
821. John xv. 1-3.
822. 2 Cor. xii. 7-9.
823. 1 Tim. i. 20.
824. John xix. 11.
825. 2 Thess. i. 5.
826. 1 Pet. iv. 17, 18.
827. 1 Pet. iii. 17.
828. 1 Cor. xii. 26.
829. [Augustin certainly makes it appear that the God in the Old Testament is not so bad as the God of the Manichæans, yet he cannot be said to reach a complete theodicy.--A.H.N.]
830. Matt. xxi. 19.
831. John viii. 6-8.
832. Æn. i. 212.
833. Æn. ii. 715.
834. [This comparison of the objectors to the Old Testament to blundering school-boys is very fine.--A.H.N.]
835] 1 John iii. 2.
836. 1 Cor. vii. 4.
837. Gen. xii. 3.
838. Gen. xv. 3, 4.
839. Tob. viii. 9.
840. Gen. xiii. 8, and xi. 31.
841. Matt. xii. 46.
842. Matt. x. 23.
843. Matt. ii. 14.
844. John vii. 10, 30.
845. Acts ix. 25.
846. Cant. i. 7.
847. Eph. v. 31, 32.
848. Matt. xxiii. 9.
849. Matt. xii. 48-50.
850. Jer. xvii. 9.
851. Phil. iii. 13.
852. Luke ix. 62.
853. Luke xvii. 32.
854. 1 Tim. i. 8.
855. Gen. xxvi. 7.
856. 2 Cor. x. 12.
857. Acts viii. 18-20.
858. Matt. viii. 20.
859. 2 Cor. xi. 2, 3.
860. 1 Cor. vii. 4.
861. 1 Cor. vii. 3.
862. Gal. iv. 22-24.
863. Isa. i. 18.
864. Gen. xxix. 17.
865. Matt. v. 3-9.
866. Gen. xxix. 26.
867. Ecclus. i. 33.
868. Isa. vii. 9, Vulg.
869. Phil. iv. 1.

870. 2 Cor. xi. 23.
871. 2 Cor. vii. 5.
872. 2 Cor. v. 13.
873. Wisd. vi. 23.
874. Gen. xxx. 1.
875. Isa. xxix. 13.
876. Rom. ii. 21, 22.
877. Matt. xxiii. 3.
878. Phil. i. 18.
879. 1 Tim. iii. 7.
880. Gen. xxx. 15.
881. Gen. xxx. 16.
882. John i. 1.
883. Gen. xlix. 8-12.
884. Matt. xix. 6.
885. Ezek. xvi. 52.
886. Matt. ii. 16.
887. John vi. 70, 71.
888. 1 Cor. v. 1.
889. Matt. xxii. 10.
890. Ex. xii. 3-5.
891. 1 Sam. xiv.
892. 1 Sam. xxviii. 3.
893. John xix. 4, 6.
894. Matt. xvi. 17, 22, 23.
895. 2 Sam. xii.
896. 1 Sam. xxiv. and xxvi.
897. 2 Sam. xvi.
898. 1 Sam. xv. 24.
899. Luke xvii. 28.
900. Gal. ii. 14.
901. Heb. iii. 5.
902. Matt. xxvi. 51, 52.
903. Ex. iii. 21, 22; xi. 2; xii. 35, 36.
904. Rom. xi. 34.
905. Matt. xiii. 29, 30.
906. Matt. viii. 31, 32.
907. Luke iii. 14.
908. Matt. xxii. 21.
909. Matt. viii. 9, 10.
910. Rom. xiii. 1.
911. Matt. v. 39.
912. Matt. x. 16, 28, 30.
913. Matt. xxvi. 52, 53; Luke xxii. 42, 51; John xviii. 11.
914. Phil. ii. 9-11.
915. Matt. xxiii. 35.
916. Eph. ii. 14.
917. Ps. lxxii. 11.
918. Luke xxii. 35-38, 50, 51.
919. Rom. v. 12, 19.
920. Wisd. ix. 15.
921. Rom. vii. 24, 25.
922. Job vii. 4.
923. Ex. xxxii. 32.
924. 1 Cor. v. 5.
925. 1 Tim. i. 20.
926. Hos. i. 2.
927. Matt. xxi. 31.
928. Gen. xxvii. 40.
929. 1 Cor. iv. 16.
930. Acts viii. 13.
931. Matt. xxiii. 3.
932. John xi. 50, 51.
933. Matt. xxvii. 34.
934. Gen. iii. 21.
935. Luke xxiii. 12.
936. John xix. 15.
937. Gen. xlix. 10.
938. Dan. ix. 24, and Ps. xlv. 7.
939. John v. 36.
940. John i. 6.
941. Matt. xi. 11.
942. Luke i. 44.
943. Cant. iv. 2.
944. Matt. xxvi. 75.
945. Luke xxiv. 46, 47.
946. Ps. xviii. 43.
947. Rom. viii. 30.
948. Matt. iii. 7.
949. Hag. ii. 8.
950. Cant. iv. 15.
951. Tob. ii. 1.
952. Eph. iv. 2, 3.
953. John iv. 13, 14.
954. Hos. i. 2-ii. 1.
955. Rom. ix. 23-26.
956. 1 Pet. ii. 9, 10.
957. Gal. iii. 29.
958. Gal. i. 22.
959. Ps. cxviii. 22.
960. Eph. ii. 11-22.
961. Matt. vii. 24-27.
962. ii. sec. 40.
963. L. xii. sec. 30.
964. Ps. iv. 4.
965. Col. iii. 5.
966. Rom. i. 21-23.
967. Luke xii. 49.
968. Ps. xix. 6.
969. Acts x. 13.
970. [This book is one of the most unsatisfactory parts of the entire treatise. We have here some of the worst specimens of perverse Scripture interpretation.--A.H.N.]
971. Ex. xxiii. 11.
972. Hag. i. 1.
973. Rom. i. 1-3.
974. Mark i. 1.
975. Luke iii. 22, 23.
976. Isa. viii. 14, and Matt. i. 23.
977. Matt. iii. 17.
978. Matt. xvii. 5.
979. Phil. ii. 6.
980. Gal. iv. 4.
981. 2 Tim. ii. 8.
982. Wisd. viii. 1.
983. Rom. vi., vii.; 1 Cor. xv.; 2 Cor. iv.; Eph. iii., iv.; and Col. iii.
984. John iii. 3.
985. Gal. iv. 19.
986. Eph. iv. 22-24.
987. Col. iii. 9-11.

988. Gal. iii. 27, 28.
989. 1 Cor. iv. 15.
990. Gal. i. 15, 16.
991. 1 Cor. xii. 18.
992. 1 Cor. xv. 33-45.
993. Gen. ii. 7.
994. Rom. v. 12.
995. Rom. viii. 10, 11.
996. 1 Cor. xi. 11, 12.
997. 1 Cor. xv. 47.
998. Tit. i. 15.
999. John ix.
1000. Rom. xi. 24.
1001. 2 Kings ii. 11; Matt. i. 25, xvii. 50.
1002. John i. 3.
1003. Luke xxiv. 7.
1004. Matt. xvi. 22, 23.
1005. Matt. viii. 24.
1006. Matt. iv. 2.
1007. John xix. 28.
1008. Matt. xxvi. 37.
1009. III. 3.
1010. 2 Cor. xiii. 3.
1011. Gal. i. 8, 9.
1012. John xx. 28.
1013. Matt. i. 25; Luke ii. 7.
1014. Matt. ii. 11; Mark iii. 32; Luke ii. 33; John ii. 1.
1015. In the Retractations, ii. sec 7, Augustin refers in correction of this remark to his Reply to the Second Answer of Julian, iv. sec. 36, where he makes uncomeliness the effect of sin.
1016. 1 Cor. xii. 22-25.
1017. 1 Tim. iv. 1-3.
1018. Dan. i. 12.
1019. Dan. x. 2, 3.
1020. See the apocryphal book, Paul and Thecla.
1021. Matt. xix. 12.
1022. 1 Cor. vii. 5, 6.
1023. 1 Tim. iv. 3-5.
1024. 1 Cor. vii. 38.
1025. Tit. i. 16.
1026. Dan. i. 12.
1027. Acts x. 11-15.
1028. Gen. i. 31.
1029. Phil. iii. 8.
1030. Gen. xvii. 9-14.
1031. Ex. xxxi. 13.
1032. Ex. xii.
1033. Lev. xxiii.
1034. Deut. xxv. 5-10.
1035. Deut. xxi. 23.
1036. Deut. xxv. 5-10.
1037. Gen. xvii. 14.
1038. Num. xv. 35.
1039. John xvi. 13, xiv. 26.
1040. Jer. xxxi. 31, 32.
1041. Gal. iii. 29.
1042. Col. ii. 16, 17.
1043. 1 Cor. x. 11.
1044. 1 Cor. iv. 15.
1045. 1 Cor. ii. 13.
1046. Eph. vi. 15.
1047. Isa. lii. 7.
1048. 1 Cor. v. 8.
1049. Matt. vii. 13.
1050. Ex. xix.-xxxi.
1051. Luke xi. 8.
1052. 1 Cor. x. 20.
1053. Gen. ix. 6.
1054. Acts xv. 29.
1055. Eph. ii. 11-22.
1056. Matt. xv. 11.
1057. Book XXII.
1058. Wisd. ix. 15.
1059. Acts ii.
1060. John xvi. 13.
1061. John vii. 39.
1062. [Another name for the Montanists, who arose in Phrygia shortly after the middle of the second century.--A.H.N.]
1063. 1 Cor. xiii. 9, 10.
1064. 1 Cor. vii. 36.
1065. Montanus.
1066. John xiv. 17.
1067. Gal. i. 9.
1068. Rom. v. 5.
1069. 1 Cor. xiii. 12.
1070. 1 John iii. 2.
1071. 1 Cor. ii. 14.
1072. Gal. i. 8.
1073. Matt. viii. 11.
1074. Luke xxiii. 43.
1075. Matt. xxi. 31.
1076. John viii. 3-11.
1077. Matt. v. 45.
1078. Matt. viii. 5-13; Luke vii. 2-10.
1079. Luke xiii. 24-29.
1080. John viii. 39, 56.
1081. Luke xvi. 23.
1082. Rom. iv. 3.
1083. Matt. viii. 5-13; Luke vii. 2-10.
1084. Ps. xxxiv. 5.
1085. Luke viii. 43, 46.

Concerning the Nature of Good, Against the Manichæans

[de natura boni contra manichæos].
In One Book.
circa A.D. 405.
translated by albert h. newman, d.d., ll.d.,
professor of church history and comparative religion, in toronto baptist (theological) college, toronto, canada.

It is put in the Retractations immediately after the De Actis cum Felice Manichæo, which was written about the end of the year 404.
It is one of the most argumentative of the Anti-Manichæan treatises, and so one of the most abstruse and difficult.
The lines of argument here pursued have already been employed in part in the earlier treatises.
The most interesting portions of the contents of the treatise, and the most damaging to the Manichæans, are the long extracts from Mani's Thesaurus, and his Fundamental Epistle.--A.H.N.

Chapter 1 - God the Highest and Unchangeable Good, from Whom are All Other Good Things, Spiritual and Corporeal

The highest good, than which there is no higher, is God, and consequently He is unchangeable good, hence truly eternal and truly immortal.

All other good things are only from Him, not of Him.

For what is of Him, is Himself.

And consequently if He alone is unchangeable, all things that He has made, because He has made them out of nothing, are changeable.

For He is so omnipotent, that even out of nothing, that is out of what is absolutely non-existent, He is able to make good things both great and small, both celestial and terrestrial, both spiritual and corporeal.

But because He is also just, He has not put those things that He has made out of nothing on an equality with that which He begat out of Himself.

Because, therefore, no good things whether great or small, through whatever gradations of things, can exist except from God; but since every nature, so far as it is nature, is good, it follows that no nature can exist save from the most high and true God:

because all things even not in the highest degree good, but related to the highest good, and again, because all good things, even those of most recent origin, which are far from the highest good, can have their existence only from the highest good.

Therefore every spirit, though subject to change, and every corporeal entity, is from God, and all this, having been made, is nature.

For every nature is either spirit or body.

Unchangeable spirit is God, changeable spirit, having been made, is nature, but is better than body; but body is not spirit, unless when the wind, because it is invisible to us and yet its power is felt as something not inconsiderable, is in a certain sense called spirit.

Chapter 2 - How This May Suffice for Correcting the Manichæans

But for the sake of those who, not being able to understand that all nature, that is, every spirit and every body, is naturally good, are moved by the iniquity of spirit and the mortality of body, and on this account endeavor to bring in another nature of wicked spirit and mortal body, which God did not make, we determine thus to bring to their understanding what we say can be brought.

For they acknowledge that no good thing can exist save from the highest and true God, which also is true and suffices for correcting them, if they are willing to give heed.

Chapter 3 - Measure, Form, and Order, Generic Goods in Things Made by God

For we Catholic Christians worship God, from whom are all good things whether great or small; from whom is all measure great or small; from whom is all form great or small; from whom is all order great or small.

For all things in proportion as they are better measured, formed, and ordered, are assuredly good in a higher degree; but in proportion as they are measured, formed, and ordered in an inferior degree, are they the less good.

These three things, therefore, measure, form, and order,--not to speak of innumerable other things that are shown to pertain to these three,--these three things, therefore, measure, form, order, are as it were generic goods in things made by God, whether in spirit or in body.

God is, therefore, above every measure of the creature, above every form, above every order, nor is He above by local spaces, but by ineffable and singular potency, from whom is every measure, every form, every order.

These three things, where they are great, are great goods, where they are small, are small goods; where they are absent, there is no good.

And again where these things are great, there are great natures, where they are small, there are small natures, where they are absent, there is no nature.

Therefore all nature is good.

Chapter 4 - Evil is Corruption of Measure, Form, or Order

When accordingly it is inquired, whence is evil, it must first be inquired, what is evil, which is nothing else than corruption, either of the measure, or the form, or the order, that belong to nature. Nature therefore which has been corrupted, is called evil, for assuredly when incorrupt it is good; but even when corrupt, so far as it is nature it is good, so far as it is corrupted it is evil.

Chapter 5 - The Corrupted Nature of a More Excellent Order Sometimes Better Than an Inferior Nature Even Uncorrupted

But it may happen, that a certain nature which has been ranked as more excellent by reason of natural measure and form, though corrupt, is even yet better than another incorrupt which has been ranked lower by reason of an inferior natural measure and form:

as in the estimation of men, according to the quality which presents itself to view, corrupt gold is assuredly better than incorrupt silver, and corrupt silver than incorrupt lead; so also in more powerful spiritual natures a rational spirit even corrupted through an evil will is better than an irrational though incorrupt, and better is any spirit whatever even corrupt than any body whatever though incorrupt.

For better is a nature which, when it is present in a body, furnishes it with life, than that to which life is furnished.

But however corrupt may be the spirit of life that has been made, it can furnish life to a body, and hence, though corrupt, it is better than the body though incorrupt.

Chapter 6 - Nature Which Cannot Be Corrupted is the Highest Good; That Which Can, is Some Good

But if corruption take away all measure, all form, all order from corruptible things, no nature will remain.

And consequently every nature which cannot be corrupted is the highest good, as is God.

But every nature that can be corrupted is also itself some good; for corruption cannot injure it, except by taking away from or diminishing that which is good.

Chapter 7 - The Corruption of Rational Spirits is on the One Hand Voluntary, on the Other Penal

But to the most excellent creatures, that is, to rational spirits, God has offered this, that if they will not they cannot be corrupted; that is, if they should maintain obedience under the Lord their God, so should they adhere to his incorruptible beauty; but if they do not will to maintain obedience, since willingly they are corrupted in sins, unwillingly they shall be corrupted in punishment, since God is such a good that it is well for no one who deserts Him, and among the things made by God the rational nature is so great a good, that there is no good by which it may be blessed except God.

Sinners, therefore, are ordained to punishment; which ordination is punishment for the reason that it is not conformable to their nature, but it is justice because it is conformable to their fault.

Chapter 8 - From the Corruption and Destruction of Inferior Things is the Beauty of the Universe

But the rest of things that are made of nothing, which are assuredly inferior to the rational soul, can be neither blessed nor miserable. But because in proportion to their fashion and appearance are things themselves good, nor could there be good things in a less or the least degree except from God, they are so ordered that the more infirm yield to the firmer, the weaker to the stronger, the more impotent to the more powerful; and so earthly things harmonize with celestial, as being subject to the things that are pre-eminent.

But to things falling away, and succeeding, a certain temporal beauty in its kind belongs, so that neither those things that die, or cease to be what they were, degrade or disturb the fashion and appearance and order of the universal creation; as a speech well composed is assuredly beautiful, although in it syllables and all sounds rush past as it were in being born and in dying.

Chapter 9 - Punishment is Constituted for the Sinning Nature that It May Be Rightly Ordered

What sort of punishment, and how great, is due to each fault, belongs to Divine judgment, not to human; which punishment assuredly when it is remitted in the case of the converted, there is great goodness on the part of God, and when it is deservedly inflicted, there is no injustice on the part of God; because nature is better ordered by justly smarting under punishment than by rejoicing with impunity in sin; which nature nevertheless, even thus having some measure, form, and order, in whatever extremity there is as yet some good, which things, if they were absolutely taken away, and utterly consumed, there will be accordingly no good, because no nature will remain.

Chapter 10 - Natures Corruptible, Because Made of Nothing

All corruptible natures therefore are natures at all only so far as they are from God, nor would they be corruptible if they were of Him; because they would be what He himself is.

Therefore of whatever measure, of whatever form, of whatever order, they are, they are so because it is God by whom they were made; but they are not immutable, because it is nothing of which they were made.

For it is sacrilegious audacity to make nothing and God equal, as when we wish to make what has been born of God such as what has been made by Him out of nothing.

Chapter 11 - God Cannot Suffer Harm, Nor Can Any Other Nature Except by His Permission

Wherefore neither can God's nature suffer harm, nor can any nature under God suffer harm unjustly:

for when by sinning unjustly some do harm, an unjust will is imputed to them; but the power by which they are permitted to do harm is from God alone, who knows, while they themselves are ignorant, what they ought to suffer, whom He permits them to harm.

Chapter 12 - All Good Things are from God Alone

All these things are so perspicuous, so assured, that if they who introduce another nature which God did not make, were willing to give attention, they would not be filled with so great blasphemies, as that they should place so great good things in supreme evil, and so great evil things in God.

For what the truth compels them to acknowledge, namely, that all good things are from God alone, suffices for their correction, if they were willing to give heed, as I said above.

Not, therefore, are great good things from one, and small good things from another; but good things great and small are from the supremely good alone, which is God.

Chapter 13 - Individual Good Things, Whether Small or Great, are from God

Let us, therefore, bring before our minds good things however great, which it is fitting that we attribute to God as their author, and these having been eliminated let us see whether any nature will remain.

All life both great and small, all power great and small, all safety great and small, all memory great and small, all virtue great and small, all intellect great and small, all tranquillity great and small, all plenty great and small, all sensation great and small, all light great and small, all suavity[1086] great and small, all measure great and small, all beauty great and small, all peace great and small, and whatever other like things may occur, especially such as are found throughout all things, whether spiritual or corporeal, every measure, every form, every order both great and small, are from the Lord God.

All which good things whoever should wish to abuse, pays the penalty by divine judgment; but where none of these things shall have been present at all, no nature will remain.

Chapter 14 - Small Good Things in Comparison with Greater are Called by Contrary Names

But in all these things, whatever are small are called by contrary names in comparison with greater things; as in the form of a man because the beauty is greater, the beauty of the ape in comparison with it is called deformity.

And the imprudent are deceived, as if the former is good, and the latter evil, nor do they regard in the body of the ape its own fashion, the equality of members on both sides, the agreement of parts, the protection of safety, and other things which it would be tedious to enumerate.

Chapter 15 - In the Body of the Ape the Good of Beauty is Present, Though in a Less Degree

But that what we have said may be understood, and may satisfy those too slow of comprehension, or that even the pertinacious and those repugnant to the most manifest truth may be compelled to confess what is true, let them be asked, whether corruption can harm the body of an ape?

But if it can, so that it may become more hideous, what diminishes but the good of beauty? Whence as long as the nature of the body subsists, so long something will remain.

If, accordingly, good having been consumed, nature is consumed, the nature is therefore good. So also we say that slow is contrary to swift, but yet he who does not move at all cannot even be called slow.

So we say that a heavy voice is contrary to a sharp voice, or a harsh to a musical; but if you completely remove any kind of voice, there is silence where there is no voice, which silence, nevertheless, for the simple reason that there is no voice, is usually opposed to voice as something contrary thereto.

So also lucid and obscure are called as it were two contrary things, yet even obscure things have something of light, which being absolutely wanting, darkness is the absence of light in the same way in which silence is the absence of voice.

Chapter 16 - Privations in Things are Fittingly Ordered by God

Yet even these privations of things are so ordered in the universe of nature, that to those wisely considering they not unfittingly have their vicissitudes.

For by not illuminating certain places and times, God has also made the darkness as fittingly as the day.

For if we by restraining the voice fittingly interpose silence in speaking, how much more does He, as the perfect framer of all things, fittingly make privations of things?

Whence also in the hymn of the three children, light and darkness alike praise God, [1087] that is, bring forth praise in the hearts of those who well consider.

Chapter 17 - Nature, in as Far as It is Nature, No Evil

No nature, therefore, as far as it is nature, is evil; but to each nature there is no evil except to be diminished in respect of good. But if by being diminished it should be consumed so that there is no good, no nature would be left; not only such as the Manichæans introduce, where so great good things are found that their exceeding blindness is wonderful, but such as any one can introduce.

Chapter 18 - Hyle, Which Was Called by the Ancients the Formless Material of Things, is Not an Evil

For neither is that material, which the ancients called Hyle, to be called an evil.

I do not say that which Manichæus with most senseless vanity, not knowing what he says, denominates Hyle, namely, the former of corporeal beings; whence it is rightly said to him, that he introduces another god.

For nobody can form and create corporeal beings but God alone; for neither are they created unless there subsist with them measure, form, and order, which I think that now even they themselves confess to be good things, and things that cannot be except from God.

But by Hyle I mean a certain material absolutely formless and without quality, whence those qualities that we perceive are formed, as the ancients said.

For hence also wood is called in Greek ὕλη, because it is adapted to workmen, not that itself may make anything, but that it is the material of which something may be made. Nor is that Hyle, therefore, to be called an evil which cannot be perceived through any appearance, but can scarcely be thought of through any sort of privation of appearance.

For this has also a capacity of forms; for if it cannot receive the form imposed by the workman, neither assuredly may it be called material.

Hence if form is some good, whence those who excel in it are called beautiful, [1088] as from appearance they are called handsome, [1089] even the capacity of form is undoubtedly something good.

As because wisdom is a good, no one doubts that to be capable of wisdom is a good.

And because every good is from God, no one ought to doubt that even matter, if there is any, has its existence from God alone.

Chapter 19 - To Have True Existence is an Exclusive Prerogative of God

Magnificently and divinely, therefore, our God said to his servant: "I am that I am," and "Thou shalt say to the children of Israel, He who is sent me to you."[1090] For He truly is because He is unchangeable. For every change makes what was not, to be: therefore He truly is, who is unchangeable; but all other things that were made by Him have received being from Him each in its own measure.

To Him who is highest, therefore nothing can be contrary, save what is not; and consequently as from Him everything that is good has its being, so from Him is everything that by nature exists; since everything that exists by nature is good.

Thus every nature is good, and everything good is from God; therefore every nature is from God.

Chapter 20 - Pain Only in Good Natures

But pain which some suppose to be in an especial manner an evil, whether it be in mind or in body, cannot exist except in good natures. For the very fact of resistance in any being leading to pain, involves a refusal not to be what it was, because it was something good; but when a being is compelled to something better, the pain is useful, when to something worse, it is useless.

Therefore in the case of the mind, the will resisting a greater power causes pain; in the case of the body, sensation resisting a more powerful body causes pain.

But evils without pain are worse:

for it is worse to rejoice iniquity than to bewail corruption; yet even such rejoicing cannot exist save from the attainment of inferior good things.

But iniquity is the desertion of better things.

Likewise in a body, a wound with pain is better than painless putrescence, which is especially called the corruption which the dead flesh of the Lord did not see, that is, did not suffer, as was predicted in prophecy:

"Thou shall not suffer Thy Holy one to see corruption." [1091] For who denies that He was wounded by the piercing of the nails, and that He was stabbed with the lance? [1092] But even what is properly called by men corporeal corruption, that is, putrescence itself, if as yet there is anything left to consume, increases by the diminution of the good.

But if corruption shall have absolutely consumed it, so that there is no good, no nature will remain, for there will be nothing that corruption may corrupt; and so there will not even be putrescence, for there will be nowhere at all for it to be.

Chapter 21 - From Measure Things are Said to Be Moderate-Sized [1093]

Therefore now by common usage things small and mean are said to have measure, because some measure remains in them, without which they would no longer be moderate-sized, but would not exist at all.

But those things that by reason of too much progress are called immoderate, are blamed for very excessiveness; but yet it is necessary that those things themselves be restrained in some manner under God who has disposed all things in extension, number, and weight. [1094]

Chapter 22 - Measure in Some Sense is Suitable to God Himself

But God cannot be said to have measure, lest He should seem to be spoken of as limited.

Yet He is not immoderate by whom measure is bestowed upon all things, so that they may in any measure exist.

Nor again ought God to be called measured, as if He received measure from any one.

But if we say that He is the highest measure, by chance we say something; if indeed in speaking of the highest measure we mean the highest good.

For every measure in so far as it is a measure is good; whence nothing can be called measured, modest, modified, without praise, although in another sense we use measure for limit, and speak of no measure where there is no limit, which is sometimes said with praise as when it is said:

"And of His kingdom there shall be no limit." [1095] For it might also be said, "There shall be no measure," so that measure might be used in the sense of limit; for He who reigns in no measure, assuredly does not reign at all.

Chapter 23 - Whence a Bad Measure, a Bad Form, a Bad Order May Sometimes Be Spoken of

Therefore a bad measure, a bad form, a bad order, are either so called because they are less than they should be, or because they are not adapted to those things to which they should be adapted; so that they may be called bad as being alien and incongruous; as if any one should be said not to have done in a good measure because he has done less than he ought, or because he has done in such a thing as he ought not to have done, or more than was fitting, or not conveniently; so that the very fact of that being reprehended which is done in a bad measure, is justly reprehended for no other cause than that the measure is not there maintained.

Likewise a form is called bad either in comparison with something more handsome or more beautiful, this form being less, that greater, not in size but in comeliness; or because it is out of harmony with the thing to which it is applied, so that it seems alien and unsuitable.

As if a man should walk forth into a public place naked, which nakedness does not offend if seen in a bath.

Likewise also order is called bad when order itself is maintained in an inferior degree.

Hence not order, but rather disorder, is bad; since either the ordering is less than it should be, or not as it should be.

Yet where there is any measure, any form, any order, there is some good and some nature; but where there is no measure, no form, no order, there is no good, no nature.

Chapter 24 - It is Proved by the Testimonies of Scripture that God is Unchangeable

The Son of God Begotten, Not Made.

Those things which our faith holds and which reason in whatever way has traced out, are fortified by the testimonies of the divine Scriptures, so that those who by reason of feebler intellect are not able to comprehend these things, may believe the divine authority, and so may deserve to know.

But let not those who understand, but are less instructed in ecclesiastical literature, suppose that we set forth these things from our own intellect rather than what are in those Books.

Accordingly, that God is unchangeable is written in the Psalms:

"Thou shalt change them and they shall be changed; but Thou thyself art the same." [1096] And in the book of Wisdom, concerning wisdom:

"Remaining in herself, she renews all things." [1097] Whence also the Apostle Paul:

"To the invisible, incorruptible, only God." [1098] And the Apostle James:

"Every best giving and every perfect gift is from above, descending from the Father of light, with whom there is no changeableness, neither obscuring of influence." [1099] Likewise because what He begat of Himself is what He Himself is, it is said in brief by the Son Himself:

"I and the Father are one." [1100] But because the Son was not made, since through Him were all things made, thus it is written:

"In the beginning was the Word, and the Word was with God, and God was the Word; this was in the beginning with God.

All things were made through Him, and without Him was made nothing;" [1101] that is, without Him was not anything made.

Chapter 25 - This Last Expression Misunderstood by Some

For no attention should be paid to the ravings of men who think that nothing should be understood to mean something, and moreover think to compel any one to vanity of this kind on the ground that nothing is placed at the end of the sentence.

Therefore, they say, it was made, and because it was made, nothing is itself something.

They have lost their senses by zeal in contradicting, and do not understand that it makes no

difference whether it be said:
"Without Him was made nothing," or "without Him nothing was made."
For even if the order were the last mentioned, they could nevertheless say, that nothing is itself something because it was made.
For in the case of what is in truth something, what difference does it make if it be said "Without him a house was made," so long as it is understood that something was made without him, which something is a house?
So also because it is said:
"Without Him was made nothing," since nothing is assuredly not anything, when it is truly and properly spoken, it makes no difference whether it be said:
"Without Him was made nothing or Without Him nothing was made," or "nothing was made."
But who cares to speak with men who can say of this very expression of mine "It makes no difference," "Therefore it makes some difference, for nothing itself is something?"
But those whose brains are not addled, see it as a thing most manifest that this something is to be understood when it says "It makes no difference," as when I say "It matters in no respect."
But these, if they should say to any one, "What hast thou done?" and he should reply that he has done nothing, would, according to this mode of disputation, falsely accuse him saying, "Thou hast done something, therefore, because thou hast done nothing; for nothing is itself something."
But they have also the Lord Himself placing this word at the end of a sentence, when He says: "And in secret have I spoken nothing." [1102] Let them read, therefore, and be silent. [1103]

Chapter 26 - That Creatures are Made of Nothing

Because therefore God made all things which He did not beget of Himself, not of those things that already existed, but of those things that did not exist at all, that is, of nothing," the Apostle Paul says:
"Who calls the things that are not as if they are." [1104] But still more plainly it is written in the book of Maccabees:
"I pray thee, son, look at the heaven and the earth and all the things that are in them; see and know that it was not these of which the Lord God made us." [1105] And from this that is written in the Psalm:
"He spake, and they were made." [1106] It is manifest, that not of Himself He begat these things, but that He made them by word and command.
But what is not of Himself is assuredly of nothing.
For there was not anything of which he should make them, concerning which the apostle says most openly:
"For from Him, and through Him, and in Him are all things." [1107]

Chapter 27 - "From Him" And "Of Him" Do Not Mean The Same Thing

But "from Him" does not mean the same as "of Him." [1108] For what is of Him may be said to be from Him; but not everything that is from Him is rightly said to be of Him.
For from Him are heaven and earth, because He made them; but not of Him because they are not of His substance.
As in the case of a man who begets a son and makes a house, from himself is the son, from himself is the house, but the son is of him, the house is of earth and wood.
But this is so, because as a man he cannot make something even of nothing; but God of whom are all things, through whom are all things, in whom are all things, had no need of any material which He had not made to assist His omnipotence.

Chapter 28 - Sin Not From God, But From The Will of Those Sinning

But when we hear:
"All things are from Him, and through Him, and in Him," we ought assuredly to understand all natures which naturally exist.
For sins, which do not preserve but vitiate nature, are not from Him; which sins, Holy Scripture in many ways testifies, are from the will of those sinning, especially in the passage where

the apostle says:

"But dost thou suppose this, O man, that judgest those who do such things, and doest them, that thou shall escape the judgment of God?

Or dost thou despise the riches of His goodness, and patience, and long-suffering, not knowing that the patience of God leadeth thee to repentance?

But according to the hardness of thy heart and thy impenitent heart, thou treasurest up for thyself wrath against the day of wrath and of the revelation of the just judgment of God, who will render unto every one according to his works." [1109]

Chapter 29 - That God is Not Defiled by Our Sins

And yet, though all things that He established are in Him, those who sin do not defile Him, of whose wisdom it is said:

"She touches all things by reason of her purity, and nothing defiled assails her." [1110] For it behooves us to believe that as God is incorruptible and unchangeable, so also is He consequently undefilable.

Chapter 30 - That Good Things, Even the Least, and Those that are Earthly, are by God

But that God made even the least things, that is, earthly and mortal things, must undoubtedly be understood from that passage of the apostle, where, speaking of the members of our flesh:

"For if one member is glorified, all the members rejoice with it, and if one member suffers, all the members suffer with it;" also this he then says:

"God has placed the members each one of them in the body as he willed;" and "God has tempered the body, giving to that to which it was wanting greater honor, that there should be no schism in the body, but that the members should have the same care one for another." [1111] But what the apostle thus praises in the measure and form and order of the members of the flesh, you find in the flesh of all animals, alike the greatest and the least; for all flesh is among earthly goods, and consequently is esteemed among the least.

Chapter 31 - To Punish and to Forgive Sins Belong Equally to God

Likewise because it belongs to divine judgment, not human, what sort of punishment and how great is due to every fault, it is thus written:

"O the height of the riches of the wisdom and the knowledge of God! how inscrutable are His judgments and his ways past finding out!" [1112] Likewise because by the goodness of God sins are forgiven to the converted, the very fact that Christ was sent sufficiently shows, who not in His own nature as God, but in our nature, which He assumed from a woman, died for us; which goodness of God with reference to us, and which love of God, the apostle thus sets forth:

"But God commendeth His love toward us, in that while we were yet sinners Christ died for us; much more now being justified in His blood we shall be saved from wrath through Him.

For if when we were enemies we were reconciled to God through the death of His Son, much more being reconciled we shall be saved in His life." [1113] But because even when due punishment is rendered to sinners, there is no unrighteousness on God's part, he thus says:

"What shall we say?

Is God unrighteous who visiteth with wrath?" [1114] But in one place he has briefly admonished that goodness and severity are alike from Him, saying:

"Thou seest then the goodness and severity of God; toward them that have fallen, severity, but towards thee goodness, if thou shouldst continue in goodness." [1115]

Chapter 32 - From God Also is the Very Power to Be Hurtful

Likewise because the power even of those that are hurtful is from God alone, thus it stands written, Wisdom speaking:

"Through me kings reign and tyrants hold the land through me." [1116] The apostle also says:

"For there is no power but of God." [1117] But that it is worthily done is written in the book of Job:

"Who maketh to reign a man that is a hypocrite, on account of the perversity of the people."[1118] And concerning the people of Israel God says:

"I gave them a king in my wrath." [1119] For it is not unrighteous, that the wicked receiving the power of being hurtful, both the patience of the good should be proved and the iniquity of the evil punished.

For through power given to the Devil both Job was proved so that he might appear righteous,[1120] and Peter was tempted lest he should be presumptuous, [1121] and Paul was buffeted lest he should be exalted, [1122] and Judas was damned so that he should hang himself. [1123] When, therefore, through the power which He has given the Devil, God Himself shall have done all things righteously, nevertheless punishment shall at last be rendered to the Devil not for these things justly done, but for the unrighteous willing to be hurtful, which belonged to himself, when it shall be said to the impious who persevered in consenting to his wickedness, "Go ye into everlasting fire which my God has prepared for the Devil and his angels." [1124]

Chapter 33 - That Evil Angels Have Been Made Evil, Not by God, But by Sinning

But because evil angels also were not constituted evil by God, but were made evil by sinning, Peter in his epistle says:

"For if God spared not angels when they sinned, but casting them down into the dungeons of smoky hell, He delivered them to be reserved for punishment in judgment." [1125] Hence Peter shows that there is still due to them the penalty of the last judgment, concerning which the Lord says:

"Go ye into everlasting fire, which has been prepared for the Devil and his angels."

+ Although they have already penally received this hell, that is, an inferior smoky air as a prison, which nevertheless since it is also called heaven, is not that heaven in which there are stars, but this lower heaven by the smoke of which the clouds are conglobulated, and where the birds fly; for both a cloudy heaven is spoken of, and flying things are called heavenly.

As when the Apostle Paul calls those evil angels, against whom as enemies by living piously we contend, "spiritual things of wickedness in heavenly places." [1126] That this may not be understood of the upper heavens, he plainly says elsewhere:

"According to the presence of the prince of this air, who now worketh in the sons of disobedience." [1127]

Chapter 34 - That Sin is Not the Striving for an Evil Nature, But the Desertion of a Better

Likewise because sin, or unrighteousness, is not the striving after evil nature but the desertion of better, it is thus found written in the Scriptures:

"Every creature of God is good." [1128] And accordingly every tree also which God planted in Paradise is assuredly good.

Man did not therefore strive after an evil nature when he touched the forbidden tree; but by deserting what was better, he committed an evil deed.

Since the Creator is better than any creature which He has made, His command should not have been deserted, that the thing forbidden, however good, might be touched; since the better having been deserted, the good of the creature was striven for, which was touched contrary to the command of the Creator.

God did not plant an evil tree in Paradise; but He Himself was better who prohibited its being touched.

Chapter 35 - The Tree Was Forbidden to Adam Not Because It Was Evil, But Because It Was Good for Man to Be Subject to God

For besides, He had made the prohibition, in order to show that the nature of the rational soul ought not to be in its own power, but in subjection to God, and that it guards the order of its salvation through obedience, corrupting it through disobedience.

Hence also He called the tree, the touching of which He forbade, the tree "of the knowledge of good and evil;" [1129] because when man should have touched it in the face of the prohibition, he would experience the penalty of sin, and so would know the difference between the good of obedience, and the evil of disobedience.

Chapter 36 - No Creature of God is Evil, But to Abuse a Creature of God is Evil

For who is so foolish as to think a creature of God, especially one planted in Paradise, blameworthy; when indeed not even thorns and thistles, which the earth brought forth, according to the judiciary judgment of God, for wearing out the sinner in labor, should be blamed?

For even such herbs have their measure and form and order, which whoever considers soberly will find praiseworthy; but they are evil to that nature which ought thus to be restrained as a recompense for sin.

Therefore, as I have said, sin is not the striving after an evil nature, but the desertion of a better, and so the deed itself is evil, not the nature which the sinner uses amiss.

For it is evil to use amiss that which is good.

Whence the apostle reproves certain ones as condemned by divine judgment, "Who have worshipped and served the creature more than the Creator." [1130] He does not reprove the creature, which he who should do would act injuriously towards the Creator, but those who, deserting the better, have used amiss the good.

Chapter 37 - God Makes Good Use of the Evil Deeds of Sinners

Accordingly, if all natures should guard their own proper measure and form and order, there would be no evil:

but if any one should wish to misuse these good things, not even thus does he vanquish the will of God, who knows how to order righteously even the unrighteous; so that if they themselves through the iniquity of their will should misuse His good things, He through the righteousness of His power may use their evil deeds, rightly ordaining to punishment those who have perversely ordained themselves to sins.

Chapter 38 - Eternal Fire Torturing the Wicked, Not Evil

For neither is eternal fire itself, which is to torture the impious, an evil nature, since it has its measure, its form and its order depraved by no iniquity; but it is an evil torture for the damned, to whose sins it is due.

For neither is yonder light, because it tortures the blear-eyed, an evil nature.

Chapter 39 - Fire is Called Eternal, Not as God Is, But Because Without End

But fire is eternal, not as God is eternal, because, though without end, yet is not without beginning; but God is also without beginning. Then, although it may be employed perpetually for the punishment of sinners, yet it is mutable nature.

But that is true eternity which is true immortality, that is that highest immutability, which cannot be changed at all.

For it is one thing not to suffer change, when change is possible, and another thing to be absolutely incapable of change. Therefore, just as man is called good, yet not as God, of whom it was said, "There is none good save God alone;" [1131] and just as the soul is called immortal, yet not as God, of whom it was said, "Who alone hath immortality;" [1132] and just as a man is called wise, yet not as God, of whom it was said, "To God the only wise;" [1133] so fire is called eternal, yet not as God, whose alone is immortality itself and true eternity.

Chapter 40 - Neither Can God Suffer Hurt, Nor Any Other, Save by the Just Ordination of God

Since these things are so, according to the Catholic faith, and wholesome doctrine, and truth perspicuous to those of good understanding, neither can any one hurt the nature of God, nor can the nature of God unrighteously hurt any one, or suffer any one to do hurt with impunity.

"For he that doeth hurt shall receive," says the apostle, "according to the hurt that he has done; and there is no accepting of persons with God." [1134]

Chapter 41 - How Great Good Things the Manichæans Put in the Nature of Evil, and How Great Evil Things in the Nature of Good

But if the Manichæans were willing, without pernicious zeal for defending their error, and with the fear of God, to think, they would not most criminally blaspheme by supposing two natures, the one good, which they call God, the other evil, which God did not make:

so erring, so delirious, nay so insane, are they that they do not see, that even in what they call the nature of supreme evil they place so great good things:

life, power, safety, memory, intellect, temperance, virtue, plenty, sense, light, suavity, extensions, numbers, peace, measure, form, order; but in what they call supreme good, so many evil things:

death, sickness, forgetfulness, foolishness, confusion, impotence, need, stolidity, blindness, pain, unrighteousness, disgrace, war, intemperance, deformity, perversity.

For they say that the princes of darkness also have been alive in their own nature, and in their own kingdom were safe, and remembered and understood.

For they say that the Prince of Darkness harangued in such a manner, that neither could he have said such things, nor could he have been heard by those by whom he was said to have been heard, without memory and understanding; and to have had a temper suitable to his mind and body, and to have ruled by virtue of power, and to have had abundance and fruitfulness with respect to his elements, and they are said to have perceived themselves mutually and the light as near at hand, and to have had eyes by which they could see the light afar off; which eyes assuredly could not have seen the light without some light (whence also they are rightly called light); and they are said to have enjoyed exceedingly the sweetness of their pleasures, and to have been determined by measured members and dwelling-places.

But unless there had been some sort of beauty there, they would not have loved their wives, nor would their bodies have been steady by adaptation of parts; without which, those things could not have been done there which the Manichæans insanely say were done.

And unless some peace had been there, they would not have obeyed their Prince.

Unless measure had been there, they would have done nothing else than eat or drink, or rage, or whatever they might have done, without any society:

although not even those that did these things would have had determinate forms, unless measure had been there.

But now the Manichæans say that they did such things that they cannot be denied to have had in all their actions measures suitable to themselves.

But if form had not been there, no natural quality would have there subsisted.

But if there had been no order there, some would not have ruled, others been ruled; they would not have lived harmoniously in their element; in fine, they would not have had their members adapted to their places, so that they could not do all those things that the Manichæans vainly fable.

But if they say that God's nature does not die, what according to their vanity does Christ raise from the dead?

If they say that it does not grow sick, what does He cure?

If they say that it is not subject to forgetfulness, what does He remind?

If they say that it is not deficient in wisdom, what does He teach?

If they say that it is not confused, what does He restore?

If they say that it was not vanquished and taken captive, what does He liberate?

If they say that it was not in need, to what does He minister aid?

If they say that it did not lose feeling, what does He animate?

If they say that it has not been blinded, what does He illuminate?

If it is not in pain, to what does He give relief?

If it is not unrighteous, what does He correct through precepts?

If it is not in disgrace, what does He cleanse?

If it is not in war, to what does He promise peace?

If it is not deficient in moderation, upon what does He impose the measure of law?

If it is not deformed, what does He reform?

If it is not perverse, what does He emend?

For all these things done by Christ, they say, are to be attributed not to that thing which was made by God, and which has become depraved by its own free choice in sinning, but to the very nature, yea to the very substance of God, which is what God Himself is.

Chapter 42 - Manichæan Blasphemies Concerning the Nature of God

What can be compared to those blasphemies?

Absolutely nothing, unless the errors of other sectaries be considered; but if that error be compared with itself in another aspect, of which we have not yet spoken, it will be convicted of far worse and more execrable blasphemy.

For they say that some souls, which they will have to be of the substance of God and of absolutely the same nature, which have not sinned of their own accord, but have been overcome and oppressed by the race of darkness, which they call evil, for combating which they descended not of their own accord, but at the command of the Father, are fettered forever in the horrible sphere of darkness.

So according to their sacrilegious vaporings, God liberated Himself in a certain part from a great evil, but again condemned Himself in another part, which He could not liberate, and triumphed over the enemy itself as if it had been vanquished from above.

O criminal, incredible audacity, to believe, to speak, to proclaim such things about God!

Which when they endeavor to defend, that with their eyes shut they may rush headlong into yet worse things, they say that the commingling of the evil nature does these things, in order that the good nature of God may suffer so great evils:

for that this good nature in its own sphere could or can suffer no one of these things.

As if a nature were lauded as incorruptible, because it does not hurt itself, and not because it cannot suffer hurt from another.

Then if the nature of God hurt the nature of darkness, and the nature of darkness hurt the nature of God, there are therefore two evil things which hurt each other in turn, and the race of darkness was the better disposed, because if it committed hurt it did it unwillingly; for it did not wish to commit hurt, but to enjoy the good which belonged to God.

But God wished to extinguish it, as Manichæus most openly raves forth in his epistle of the ruinous Foundation.

For forgetting that he had shortly before said:

"But His most resplendent realms were so founded upon the shining and happy land, that they could never be either moved or shaken by any one;" he afterwards said:

"But the Father of the most blessed light, knowing that great ruin and desolation which would arise from the darkness, threaten his holy worlds, unless he should send in opposition a deity excellent and renowned, mighty in strength, by whom he might at the same time overcome and destroy the race of darkness, which having been extinguished, the inhabitants of light would enjoy perpetual rest." Behold, he feared ruin and desolation that threatened his worlds! Assuredly they were so founded upon the shining and happy land that they never could be either moved or shaken by any one?

Behold, from fear he wished to hurt the neighboring race, which he endeavored to destroy and extinguish, in order that the inhabitants of light might enjoy perpetual rest.

Why did he not add, and perpetual bondage?

Were not these souls that he fettered forever in the sphere of darkness, the inhabitants of light, of whom he says plainly, that "they have suffered themselves to err from their former bright nature?" when against his will he is compelled to say, that they sinned by free will, while he wishes to ascribe sin only to the necessity of the contrary nature: everywhere ignorant what to say, and as if he were himself already in the sphere of darkness which he invented, seeking, and not finding, how he may escape.

But let him say what he will to the seduced and miserable men by whom he is honored far more highly than Christ, that at this price he may sell to them such long and sacrilegious fables. Let him say what he will, let him shut up, as it were, in a sphere, as in a prison, the race of darkness, and let him fasten outside the nature of light, to which he promised perpetual rest on the extinction of the enemy:

behold, the penalty of light is worse than that of darkness; the penalty of the divine nature is worse than that of the adverse race.

But since although the latter is in the midst of darkness it pertains to its nature to dwell in darkness; but souls which are the very same thing that God is, cannot be received, he says, into those peaceful realms, and are alienated from the life and liberty of the holy light, and are fettered in the aforesaid horrible sphere: whence he says, "Those souls shall adhere to the things that they have loved, having been left in the same sphere of darkness, bringing this upon themselves by their own deserts."

Is not this assuredly free voluntary choice?

See how insanely he ignores what he says, and by making self-contradictory statements wages a worse war against himself than against the God of the race of darkness itself.

Accordingly, if the souls of light are damned, because they loved darkness, the race of darkness, which loved light, is unjustly damned.

And the race of darkness indeed loved light from the beginning, violently, it may be, but yet so as to wish for its possession, not its extinction:

but the nature of light wished to extinguish in war the darkness; therefore when vanquished it loved darkness.

Choose which you will:

whether it was compelled by necessity to love darkness, or seduced by free will. If by necessity, wherefore is it damned? if by free will, wherefore is the nature of God involved in so great iniquity?

If the nature of God was compelled by necessity to love darkness, it did not vanquish, but was vanquished:

if by free will, why do the wretches hesitate any longer to attribute the will to sin to the nature which God made out of nothing, lest they should thereby attribute it to the light which He begat?

Chapter 43 - Many Evils Before His Commingling with Evil are Attributed to the Nature of God by the Manichæans

What if we should also show that before the commingling of evil, which stupid fable they have most madly believed, great evils were in what they call the nature of light? what will it seem possible to add to these blasphemies?

For before the conflict, there was the hard and inevitable necessity of fighting:

here is truly a great evil, before evil is commingled with good.

Let them say whence this is, when as yet no commingling had taken place?

But if there was no necessity, there was therefore free will:

whence also this so great evil, that God himself should wish to hurt his own nature, which could not be hurt by the enemy, by sending it to be cruelly commingled, to be basely purged, to be unjustly damned?

Behold, the great evil of a pernicious, noxious, and savage will, before any evil from the contrary nature was mingled with it!

Or perchance he did not know that this would happen to his members, that they should love darkness and become hostile to holy light, as Manichæus says, that is, not only to their own God, but also to the Father from whom they had their being?

Whence therefore this so great evil of ignorance, before any evil from the nature of darkness was mingled with it?

But if he knew that this would happen, either there was in him everlasting cruelty, if he did not grieve over the contamination and damnation of his own nature that was to take place, or everlasting misery, if he did so grieve:

whence also this so great evil of your supreme good before any commingling with your supreme evil?

Assuredly that part of the nature itself which was fettered in the eternal chain of that sphere, if it knew not that this fate awaited it, even so was there everlasting ignorance in the nature of God, but if it knew, then everlasting misery:

whence this so great evil before any evil from the contrary nature was commingled?

Or perchance did it, in the greatness of its love (charity), rejoice that through its punishment perpetual rest was prepared for the residue of the inhabitants of light?

Let him who sees how abominable it is to say this, pronounce an anathema.

But if this should be done so that at least the good nature itself should not become hostile to the light, it might be possible, perchance, not for the nature of God indeed, but for some man, as it were, to be regarded as praiseworthy, who for the sake of his country should be willing to suffer something of evil, which evil indeed could be only for a time, and not forever:

but now also they speak of that fettering in the sphere of darkness as eternal, and not indeed of a certain thing but of the nature of God; and assuredly it were a most unrighteous, and execrable, and ineffably sacrilegious joy, if the nature of God rejoiced that it should love darkness, and should become hostile to holy light.

Whence this so monstrous and abominable evil before any evil from the contrary nature was commingled?

Who can endure insanity so perverse and so impious, as to attribute so great good things to supreme evil, and so great evils to supreme good, which is God?

Chapter 44 - Incredible Turpitudes in God Imagined by Manichæus

But now when they speak of that part of the nature of God as everywhere mixed up in heaven, in earth, in all bodies dry and moist, in all sorts of flesh, in all seeds of trees, herbs, men, and animals:

not as present by the power of divinity, for administering and ruling all things, undefilably, inviolably, incorruptibly, without any connection with them, which we say of God; but fettered, oppressed, polluted, to be loosed and liberated, as they say, not only through the running to and fro of the sun and the moon, and through the powers of light, but also through their Elect:

what sacrilegious and incredible turpitudes this kind of error recommends to them even if it does not induce them to accept, it is horrible to speak of.

For they say that the powers of light are transformed into beautiful males and are set over against the women of the race of darkness; and that the same powers again are transformed into beautiful females and are set over against the males of the race of darkness; that through their beauty they enkindle the foulest lust of the princes of darkness, and in this manner vital substance, that is, the nature of God, which they say is held fettered in their bodies, having been loosed from their members relaxed through lust, flies away, and when it has been taken up or cleansed, is liberated.

This the wretches read, this they say, this they hear, this they believe, this they put as follows, in the seventh book of their Thesaurus (for so they call a certain writing of Manichæus, in which these blasphemies stand written):

"Then the blessed Father, who has bright ships, little apartments, dwelling-places, or magnitudes, according to his indwelling clemency, brings the help by which he is drawn out and liberated from the impious bonds, straits, and torments of his vital substance.

And so by his own invisible nod he transforms those powers of his, which are held in this most brilliant ship, and makes them to bring forth adverse powers, which have been arranged in the various tracts of the heavens.

Since these consist of both sexes, male and female, he orders the aforesaid powers to bring forth partly in the form of beardless youths, for the adverse race of females, partly in the form of bright maidens, for the contrary race of males: knowing that all these hostile powers on account of the deadly and most foul lust innate in them, are very easily taken captive, delivered up to these most beautiful forms which appear, and in this manner they are dissolved.

But you may know that this same blessed Father of ours is identical with his powers, which for a necessary reason he transforms into the undefiled likeness of youths and maidens.

But these he uses as his own arms, and through them he accomplishes his will.

But there are bright ships full of these divine powers, which are stationed after the likeness of marriage over against the infernal races, and who with alacrity and ease effect at the very moment what they have planned. Therefore, when reason demands that these same holy powers should appear to males, straightway also they show by their dress the likeness of most beautiful maidens.

Again when females are to be dealt with, putting aside the forms of maidens, they show the forms of beardless youths.

But by this handsome appearance of theirs, ardor and lust increase, and in this way the chain of their worst thoughts is loosed, and the living soul which was held by their members, relaxed by this occasion escapes, and is mingled with its own most pure air; when the souls thoroughly cleansed ascend to the bright ships, which have been prepared for conveying them and for ferrying them over to their own country.

But that which still bears the stains of the adverse race, descends little by little through billows and fires, and is mingled with trees and other plants and with all seeds, and is plunged into divers fires.

And in what manner the figures of youths and maidens from that great and most glorious ship appear to the contrary powers which live in the heavens and have a fiery nature; and from that handsome appearance, part of the life which is held in their members having been released is conducted away through fires into the earth: in the same manner also, that most high power, which dwells in the ship of vital waters appears in the likeness of youths and holy maidens to those powers whose nature is cold and moist, and which are arranged in the heavens.

And indeed to those that are females, among these the form of youths appears, but to the males, the form of maidens.

By his changing and diversity of divine and most beautiful persons, the princes male and female of the moist and cold race are loosed, and what is vital in them escapes; but whatever should remain, having been relaxed, is conducted into the earth through cold, and is mingled with all the races of darkness"

Who can endure this?

Who can believe, not indeed that it is true, but that it could even be said?

Behold those who fear to anathematize Manichæus teaching these things, and do not fear to believe in a God doing them and suffering them!

Chapter 45 - Certain Unspeakable Turpitudes Believed, Not Without Reason, Concerning the Manichæans Themselves

But they say, that through their own Elect that same commingled part and nature of God is purged, by eating and drinking forsooth, (because they say that it is held fettered in all foods); that when they are taken up by the Elect for the nourishment of the body in eating and drinking, it is loosed, sealed, and liberated through their sanctity. Nor do the wretches pay heed to the fact that this is believed about them not without good reason, and they deny it in vain, so long as they do not anathematize the books of Manichæus and cease to be Manichæans. For if, as they say, a part of God is fettered in all seeds, and is purged by eating on the part of the Elect; who may not properly believe, that they do what they read in the Thesaurus was done among the powers of heaven and the princes of darkness; since indeed they say that their flesh is also from the race of darkness, and since they do not hesitate to believe and to affirm that the vital substance fettered in them is a part of God?

Which assuredly if it is to be loosed, and purged by eating, as their lamentable error compels them to acknowledge; who does not see, who does not shudder at the greatness and the unspeakableness of what follows?

Chapter 46 - The Unspeakable Doctrine of the Fundamental Epistle

For they even say that Adam, the first man, was created by certain princes of darkness so that the light might be held by them lest it should escape.

For in the epistle which they call Fundamental, Manichæus wrote as follows respecting the way in which the Prince of Darkness, whom they represent as the father of the first man, spoke to the rest of his allied princes of darkness, and how he acted: "Therefore with wicked inventions he said to those present:

What does this huge light that is rising seem to you to be?

See how the pole moves, how it shakes most of the powers.

Wherefore it is right for me rather to ask you beforehand for whatever light you have in your powers:

since thus I will form an image of that great one who has appeared in his glory, through which we may be able to rule, freed in some measure from the conversation of darkness.

Hearing these things, and deliberating for a long time among themselves, they thought it most just to furnish what was demanded of them.

For they did not have confidence in being able to retain the light that they had forever; hence they thought it better to offer it to their Prince, by no means without hope that in this way they would rule.

It must be considered therefore how they furnished the light that they had.

For this also is scattered throughout all the divine scriptures and the heavenly secrets; but to the wise it is easy enough to know how it was given: for it is known immediately and openly by him who should truly and faithfully wish to consider.

Since there was a promiscuous throng of those who had come together, females and males of course, he impelled them to copulate among themselves:

in which copulation the males emitted seed, the females were made pregnant.

But the offspring were like those who had begotten them, the first obtaining as it were the largest portion of the parents' strength.

Taking these as a special gift their Prince rejoiced.

And just as even now we see take place, that the nature of evil taking thence strength forms the fashioner of bodies, so also the aforesaid Prince, taking the offspring of his companions, which had the senses of their parents, sagacity, light, procreated at the same time with themselves in the process of generation, devoured them; and very many powers having been taken from food of this kind, in which there was present not only fortitude, but much more astuteness and depraved sensibilities from the ferocious race of the progenitors, he called his own spouse to himself, springing from the same stock as himself, emitted, like the rest the abundance of evils that he had devoured, himself also adding something from his own thought and power, so that his disposition became the former and arranger of all the things that he had poured forth; whose consort received these things as soil cultivated in the best way is accustomed to receive seed.

For in her were constructed and woven together the images of all heavenly and earthly powers, so that what was formed obtained the likeness, so to speak, of a full orb."

Chapter 47 - He Compels to the Perpetration of Horrible Turpitudes

O abominable monster!
O execrable perdition and ruin of deluded souls!
I am not speaking of the blasphemy of saying these things about the nature of God which is thus fettered.

Let the wretches deluded and hunted by deadly error give heed to this at least, that if a part of their God is fettered by the copulation of males and females which they profess to loose and purge by eating it, the necessity of this unspeakable error compels them not only to loose and purge the part of God from bread and vegetables and fruits, which alone they are seen publicly to partake of, but also from that which might be fettered through copulation, if conception should take place.

That they do this some are said to have confessed before a public tribunal, not only in Paphlagonia, but also in Gaul, as I heard in Rome from a certain Catholic Christian; and when they were asked by the authority of what writing they did these things, they betrayed this fact concerning the Thesaurus that I have just mentioned.

But when this is cast in their teeth, they are in the habit of replying, that some enemy or other has withdrawn from their number, that is from the number of their Elect, and has made a schism, and has founded a most foul heresy of this kind.

Whence it is manifest that even if they do not themselves practise this thing, some who do practise it do it on the basis of their books.

Therefore let them reject the books, if they abhor the crime, which they are compelled to commit, if they hold to the books; or if they do not commit them, they endeavor in opposition to the books to live more purely.

But what do they do when it is said to them, either purge the light from whatever seeds you can, so that you cannot refuse to do that which you assert that you do not do; or else anathematize Manichæus, when he says that a part of God is in all seeds, and that it is fettered by copulation, but that whatever of light, that is, of the aforesaid part of God, should become the food of the Elect, is purged by being eaten.

Do you see what he compels you to believe, and do you still hesitate to anathematize him?
What do they do, I say, when this is said to them?

To what subterfuges do they betake themselves, when either so nefarious a doctrine is to be anathematized, or so nefarious a turpitude committed, in comparison with which all those intolerable evils to which I have already called attention, seem tolerable, namely, that they say of the nature of God that it was pressed by necessity to wage war, that it was either secure by everlasting ignorance, or was disturbed by everlasting grief and fear, when the corruption of commingling and the chain of everlasting damnation should come upon it, that finally as a result of the conflict it should be taken captive, oppressed, polluted, that after a false victory it should be fettered forever in a horrible sphere and separated from its original blessedness, while if considered in themselves they cannot be endured?

Chapter 48 - Augustin Prays that the Manichæans May Be Restored to Their Senses

O great is Thy patience, Lord, full of compassion and gracious, slow to anger, and plenteous in mercy, and true; [1135] who makest Thy sun to rise upon the good and the evil, and who sendest rain upon the just and the unjust; [1136] who willest not the death of the sinner, so much as that he return and live; [1137] who reproving in parts, dost give place to repentance, that wickedness having been abandoned, they may believe on Thee, O Lord; [1138] who by Thy patience dost lead to repentance, although many according to the hardness of their heart and their impenitent heart treasure up for themselves wrath against the day of wrath and of the revelation of Thy righteous judgment, who wilt render to every man according to his works; [1139] who in the day when a man shall have turned from his iniquity to Thy mercy and truth, wilt forget all his iniquities: [1140] stand before us, grant unto us that through our ministry, by which Thou hast been pleased to refute this execrable and too horrible error, as many have already been liberated, many also may be liberated, and whether through the sacrament of Thy holy baptism, or through the sacrifice of a broken spirit and a contrite and humbled heart, [1141] in the sorrow of repentance, they may deserve to receive the remission of their sins and blasphemies, by which through ignorance they have offended Thee.

For nothing is of any avail, save Thy surpassing mercy and power, and the truth of Thy baptism, and the keys of the kingdom of heaven in Thy holy Church; so that we must not despair of men as long as by Thy patience they live on this earth, who even knowing how great an evil it is to think or to say such things about Thee, are detained in that malign profession on account of the use or the attainment of temporal or earthly convenience, if rebuked by Thy reproaches they in any way flee to Thy ineffable goodness, and prefer to all the enticements of the carnal life, the heavenly and eternal life.

Footnotes:

1086. Or sanity, according to another reading.--A.H.N.
1087. Dan. iii. 72.
1088. Forma--formosus.
1089. Species--speciosus.
1090. Ex. iii. 14.
1091. Ps. xvi. 10.
1092. John xix. 18, 34.
1093. Modus, modica.
1094. Wisd. xi. 21.
1095. Luke i. 33.
1096. Ps. cii. 27.
1097. Wisd. vii. 27.
1098. 1 Tim. i. 17.
1099. James i. 17.
1100. John x. 30.
1101. John i. 1-3.
1102. John xviii. 20.
1103. It is difficult for us to understand why Augustin should have thought it worth while to refute so elaborately an argument so puerile. But it is his way to be prolix in such matters.--A.H.N.
1104. Rom. iv. 17.
1105. 2 Mac. vii. 28.
1106. Ps. cxlviii. 5.
1107. Rom. xi. 36.
1108. Ex ipso and de ipso.
1109. Rom. ii. 3-6.
1110. Wisd. vii. 24, 25.
1111. 1 Cor. xii. 26, 18, 24, 25.
1112. Rom. xi. 33.
1113. Rom. v. 8-10.
1114. Ibid. iii. 5.
1115. Ibid. xi. 22.
1116. Prov. viii. 15.
1117. Rom. xiii. 1.
1118. Job xxxiv. 30. Compare the Revised English Version. The sense seems to be completely missed in Augustin's text.--A.H.N.
1119. Hos. xiii. 11.
1120. Job i. and ii.
1121. Matt. xxvi. 31-35, 69-75.
1122. 2 Cor. xii. 7.
1123. Matt. xxvii. 5.
1124. Matt. xxv. 41.
1125. 2 Pet. ii. 4.
1126. Eph. vi. 12.
1127. Ibid. ii. 2.
1128. 1 Tim. iv. 4.
1129. Gen. ii. 9.
1130. Rom. i. 25.
1131. Mark. x. 18.
1132. 1 Tim. vi. 16.
1133. Rom. xvi. 27.
1134. Col. iii. 25.
1135. Ps. ciii. 8.
1136. Matt. v. 45.
1137. Ezek. xxxiii. 11.
1138. Wisd. xii. 2.
1139. Rom. ii. 4-6.
1140. Ezek. xviii. 21.
1141. Ps. li. 17.

www.ingramcontent.com/pod-product-compliance
Lightning Source LLC
Chambersburg PA
CBHW020940230426
43666CB00005B/103